GLOBAL E-BUSINESS LAW & TAXATION

GLOBAL E-BUSINESS LAW & TAXATION

Editor in Chief

Ana D. Penn, BA, JD, LLM

Senior Editor

Martha L. Arias, LLB, JD, LLM

iBLS
Internet Business Law Services

OXFORD
UNIVERSITY PRESS

OXFORD
UNIVERSITY PRESS

Oxford University Press, Inc., publishes works that further Oxford University's objective of excellence in research, scholarship, and education.

Oxford New York
Auckland Cape Town Dar es Salaam Hong Kong Karachi Kuala Lumpur Madrid Melbourne
Mexico City Nairobi New Delhi Shanghai Taipei Toronto

With offices in
Argentina Austria Brazil Chile Czech Republic France Greece Guatemala Hungary Italy
Japan Poland Portugal Singapore South Korea Switzerland Thailand Turkey Ukraine
Vietnam

Published by Oxford University Press, Inc.
198 Madison Avenue, New York, New York 10016

Library of Congress Cataloging-in-Publication Data

Global e-Business law & taxation / edited by Internet Business Law Services (ibls) / editor-in-chief, Ana Penn, senior editor, Martha L. Arias.
p. cm.
Includes bibliographical references and index.
ISBN 978-0-19-536721-8 ((hardback) : alk. paper)
1. Electronic commerce--Law and legislation. 2. Corporations--Taxation--Law and legislation. I. Penn, Ana. II. Arias, Martha L.
III. Title: Global e-Business law and taxation.
K1005.G56 2009
343.05'267--dc22

2009000575

Note to Readers

This publication is designed to provide accurate and authoritative information in regard to the subject matter covered. It is based upon sources believed to be accurate and reliable and is intended to be current as of the time it was written. It is sold with the understanding that the publisher is not engaged in rendering legal, accounting, or other professional services. If legal advice or other expert assistance is required, the services of a competent professional person should be sought. Also, to confirm that the information has not been affected or changed by recent developments, traditional legal research techniques should be used, including checking primary sources where appropriate.

(Based on the Declaration of Principles jointly adopted by a Committee of the American Bar Association and a Committee of Publishers and Associations.)

About IBLS

Internet Business Law Services (IBLS) (www.ibls.com) is an online legal publisher and the world's leading source of legal information on internet and e-commerce law. Products and services offered by IBLS include a Global Legal Network, an Internet Law Digital Library, Internet law e-books, Internet law news portals, its Internet Law Blog, E-Commerce University online diploma programs (www.ECUniversity.com), and the Global E-Commerce Council (www.ecommercecouncil.org). IBLS headquarters are in Irvine, California, with offices in Miami, Florida, and Barcelona, Spain.

Contents

Introduction

Among the numerous topics related to e-commerce, taxation is the one that still has not established homogeneity among different countries' legislation and still represents a critical issue to be addressed from both a business and legal perspective. This book intends to provide an overview of the e-commerce and e-commerce taxation laws and principles applied by diverse countries.

With the advent of e-commerce, countries on every continent were prompt to adopt, some faster than others, the same or similar version of the UNCITRAL E-Commerce Model Code. At the same time, electronic and digital signatures and electronic contracts obtained international and domestic legislative recognition. Hence, the electronic contractual era began, and with it, numerous and novel business models. For instance, along with the sale of traditional physical goods from remote distances, e-commerce allows transacting in digital goods and services. Yet, even though the legality of e-contracts is no longer an issue under the laws of most countries, taxation of specific e-commerce models is still a developing subject. In this book, the reader will learn how countries have dealt with various e-commerce taxation questions.

In addition to the fundamental e-commerce taxation principles applied in developed and developing countries around the world, this book offers examples of the latest approaches to taxation of digital products and voice-over Internet protocol services (VoIP). These two topics are the most sophisticated and highly controversial in the e-commerce/tax environment.

Regarding e-commerce taxation in developed countries, readers may expect to see two major approaches: the European Union (EU) approach and the United States (U.S.) approach. Both the European Union and United States have incorporated some of the Organization for Economic Cooperation and Development (OECD) suggested principles on e-commerce taxation. Likewise, some of the newer EU member states apply a mixture of OECD principles and domestic tax interpretations to e-transactions. In the developing countries, taxation of e-commerce transactions is usually accomplished through traditional taxation principles that have found new interpretations in the digital environment. Intriguingly, some of these interpretations differ from the OECD's suggested principles. Finally, this book will discuss some of the EU E-Commerce Tax Directives to be implemented in the member states, and their corollary, the approach of individual U.S. states to taxing e-commerce transactions.

The e-commerce tax topics covered in this book were researched and prepared by expert attorneys from countries such as Canada, Colombia, Germany, Israel, Italy, Mexico, Netherlands, Nigeria, South Africa, Spain, Turkey, Ukraine, the United Kingdom, and the United States, among others.

This book is presented by Internet Business Law Services (IBLS, www.ibls.com) in partnership with Oxford University Press. IBLS and its global legal network of experts bring you a representative masterpiece of global e-commerce and tax legislation.

ANA PENN

CEO, INTERNET BUSINESS LAW SERVICES

PART I

Africa

Chapter 1

Nigeria: The Challenge of E-Commerce to Tax Laws and Administration in Nigeria

Rudolf Ezeani
Adejumo Ekisola and Ezeani

I. INTRODUCTION

In 2007, Nigeria made a substantial and long-overdue review of some of its tax laws. The specific areas reviewed were the administration mechanism and system, the company income tax law, and the value-added tax regime. A lot more, however, still needs to be done.

Taxation has become a hot topic for government in Nigeria because of the dwindling fortunes in oil exploration, production, and sales. Oil still accounts for about 40 percent of gross domestic product (GDP), 90 percent of exports, and 80 percent of government revenue.[1] The Niger Delta area of the country, which is the source of most of the oil, has become notorious for disruptions in oil exploration and production. Other reasons for taxation's rising profile include the current view of small- and medium-scale enterprises as the engine of growth in the economy and the attempt government's attempts to attract much-needed foreign investment.

At the recently concluded First Stakeholders Conference on Taxation, organized by the Lagos state government and held on December 3, 2007, the governor of the state, his excellency, Mr. Babatunde Raji Fashola SAN, captured the urgency and need for a fair and efficient tax regime when he said,

> In Lagos, our only tool for survival growth [*sic*] is an efficient, fair and equitable income tax regime. . . . At the beginning of this year, the total population of London was 7.5 million; Washington 6.4 million and Johannesburg 9 million. With about 18 million people in Lagos, we are struggling with at least double the average

1 2008 Budget Speech of the President of the Federal Republic of Nigeria at the Joint Session of the national Assembly, available at http://www.nigeria.gov.ng/NR/exeres/B30C7654-36D9-4C57-837C-1EAB4A103091.htm?id=1927#NewsSection.

population of these renowned cities. Yet the situation here is made worse by a higher population growth rate, much poorer infrastructure, higher poverty rate and less refined culture of refuse handling, driving, tax compliance, law enforcement and many other spheres of social life . . . Given the enormity of these problems, there can be no doubt that Lagos state has to optimize its tax potentials by achieving a very substantial, if not total, coverage of its taxpayer base. In simple terms, it has become imperative for us to bring all taxable persons into the tax net.[2]

The federal government is also focused on expanding the tax base. Under the 2008 budget proposal, non-oil revenue, made up of company income tax, value-added tax, and customs and excise duties, is estimated to contribute 20 percent to the federal government's account and to grow by 10 percent in the fiscal year.[3] Thus, taxation of commercial enterprises will continue to be a key source of revenue for government at all levels in Nigeria.

As the standard of living improves[4] and Internet penetration and telecommunication density deepen, commercial enterprise will change from the brick-and-mortar kind to a Web-based, Internet-driven form. An indicator of this shift and the government's awareness of its revenue potentials is afforded by the travel, tourism, and leisure industries. Without a doubt, the tourism and leisure industries lend themselves to e-commerce. Worldwide, the e-ticket is now the preferred evidence of a contract of carriage while booking online for hotels and tours. Policy makers in Nigeria seem aware of these trends and desire to harness them to increase government revenue. For instance, the Lagos state government has now established a full-fledged Ministry of Tourism and has another ministry dedicated to waterfront infrastructure development. The Lagos state government intends to make Lagos the preferred tourist destination in Africa and plans to rely especially on hotels and restaurants, the primary beneficiaries of tourism, to assist in collecting sales and other applicable taxes. To this end, the governor plans to introduce a bill to the State House of Assembly with the intent of creating a separate regime of consumption tax for the tourism and leisure industry while exempting them from the Lagos state sales tax. According to the governor of the state, "The opportunity to make Lagos excel in this area is too good to be missed."[5]

---

2 Address of Governor Babatunde Fashola SAN at the stakeholders Conference on Taxation, Dec. 3, 2007, at 4, 8–9, available at http://www.lagosstate.gov.ng/c/portal/layout?p_l_id=PUB.1001.173&p_p_id=20&p_p_action=0&p_p_state=maximized&p_p_mode=view&p_p_col_id=&p_p_col_pos=0&p_p_col_count=0&_20_struts_action=%2Fdocument_library%2Fview&_20_folderId=5.

3 2008 Budget Speech of the President of the Federal republic of Nigeria at the Joint session of the National Assembly, available at http://www.nigeria.gov.ng/NR/exeres/B30C7654-36D9-4C57-837C-1EAB4A103091.htm?id=1927#NewsSection.

4 GDP per capita improved from stagnation levels to $400 at the turn of the twenty-first century and then to $1000 per capita at the end of 2007 from the president's budget speech, available at http://www.nigeria.gov.ng/NR/exeres/B30C7654-36D9-4C57-837C-1EAB4A103091.htm?id=1927#NewsSection.

5 Address of Governor Babatunde Fashola SAN at the stakeholders Conference on Taxation, Dec. 3, 2007.

With plans such as these, taxation of e-commerce will increase significantly over the next few years. It is therefore prudent to examine carefully the issues and questions involved in taxation of e-commerce in Nigeria. In addition to providing an overview of Nigerian tax law and administration, this chapter will discuss (1) e-commerce in Nigeria and among its neighbors; (2) e-commerce taxation standards; and (3) how e-commerce is taxed in Nigeria and among its neighbors. Finally, it will offer some conclusions and recommendations.

II. OVERVIEW OF NIGERIAN TAX LAW AND ADMINISTRATION

A. Overview of the Nigerian Tax System

1. Taxation in the Nigerian Federation Nigeria runs a federal system of government. One principal effect of this form of government is that the legislative powers over taxation and other matters are shared between the federal and state governments. Their respective powers are listed in the legislative lists contained in the constitution.[6] The federal government has exclusive legislative competence over all matters contained in the exclusive legislative list, while the state governments have exclusive competence on matters in the residual list. Both governments have power to legislate over matters in the concurrent list subject to the limits imposed or stated therein. Matters contained in the exclusive list include accounts of the government of the federation; arms, ammunition, and explosives; bankruptcy and insolvency; banks, banking, bills of exchange, and promissory notes; citizenship, naturalization, and aliens; copyright; defense; evidence; export duties; insurance; taxation of incomes, profits, and capital gains; and trade and commerce. Among the matters in the concurrent list are allocation of revenue among the various levels of government and collection of taxes. With respect to the latter, although the federal legislature may make law providing for the collection of certain taxes by the government of a state or other authority, a state government may make provisions for the collection of any tax, fee, or rate or for the administration of the law by its local government authority.

The division of powers between the strata of government- federal and -state has led to controversy over which of these two governments has power to impose or collect certain taxes, such as the sales tax. The controversy still rages, but the Supreme Court of Nigeria has had opportunity to pronounce on it and establish broad guidelines. One such opportunity presented itself in *Attorney General of Ogun State v. Alhaja Ayinke Aberuagba.*[7] In that case, the court held that either of the two levels of government may impose sales tax. The state government, however, does not have power to do any of the following:

1. Make sales tax law affecting any of the matters in the exclusive legislative list;
2. Make any sales tax law affecting any matter in the concurrent list that would be inconsistent with any law validly made by the federation; or

---

6 Nigerian Constitution, S.4 (1999).

7 1984 SC 20.

3. Make any sales tax law affecting matter in the concurrent legislative list where any law validly made by the federation has covered the field.

2. Taxation Is Statutory Another feature of the Nigerian tax system is that it is purely statutory. This has two main implications. The first is that there can be no tax unless a statute imposes one. Consequently, if there is no valid statute imposing tax on a person or a particular transaction or type of transaction, that person or transaction cannot be taxed. This point came up for decision recently in *Eti Osa Local Government v. Jegede.*[8] The local government made a bylaw by which it sought to impose a corporate trade permit levy on the respondents, who took out an originating summons at the high court to challenge the bylaw and imposition of the levy. The challenge was based on the grounds that the levy was not among the approved taxes contained in the Local Government Taxes and Levies (Approved List for Collection) Act No. 21 of 1998. The high court granted the respondents' prayers for relief against the levy, holding that the powers to impose taxes must be derived from statute. The court of appeal affirmed.

The second implication is that there are many statutes that impose tax on persons, groups, transactions, or operations in Nigeria, such as the Personal Income Tax Act, the Companies Income Tax Act, the Petroleum Profits Tax Act, the Value-Added Tax Act, and the Stamp Duties Act.[9] One may therefore have to examine several statutes carefully before one can determine one's tax liability with certainty.

3. Approved Taxes and Levies While the power to impose tax is generally reserved to the federal government unless otherwise proscribed by the Nigerian Constitution,[10] the state governments may collect some of these taxes (state governments may not, however, collect taxes relating to companies).[11] Due to the frequent confusion about which taxes are approved and the relevant authority to collect them, the national legislature enacted the Taxes and Levies (Approved List for Collection) Act.[12] The act clearly states which taxes are to be collected by the various tiers of government. For instance the federal government collects the following taxes:[13]

- Companies tax
- Withholding tax
- Petroleum profit tax
- Value-added tax
- Stamp duties on instruments executed by bodies corporate and residents of the Federal Capital Territory
- Personal income tax from

---

8 10 NWLR, part 1043, CA 537 (2007).

9 All discussed in this chapter.

10 Nigerian Constitution S.4 (1999) and item 59 of the exclusive legislative list.

11 Item 7 of the concurrent legislative list contained in the Second Schedule to the 1999 constitution.

12 Now CAP T2, Laws of the Federation of Nigeria (2004).

13 *Id.* at part 1 of the schedule.

- Residents of the Federal Capital Territory
- Members of the police
- Members of the armed forces of the federation
- Staff of the Ministry of Foreign Affairs and non-resident individuals

Examples of tax collected by the state governments include[14]

- Withholding tax (individuals only)
- Personal income tax in respect of
  - Pay-as-you-earn
  - Direct taxation (self-assessment)
- Pools betting and lotteries, gaming, and casino taxes
- Stamp duties on instruments executed by individuals

The local governments collect the following taxes, among others:

- Shops and kiosks rates
- Market taxes and levies excluding any market where state finance is involved
- Cattle tax payable by cattle farmers only
- Signboard and advertisement permit fees
- Tenement rates

4. Two Basic Principles The Nigerian tax regime is based on the two principles of residence and source. Therefore, residents of Nigeria are liable to pay tax on their worldwide income, whether arising from a trade, business, profession, or vocation carried on in or outside Nigeria. On the other hand, persons who are not resident in the country are also liable for Nigerian tax if they have income arising from or attributable to a source in Nigeria. Taxation of individuals is governed by the Personal Income Tax Act,[15] and for companies by the Companies Act[16] and the Education Tax Act.[17]

5. Reliefs, Tax Holidays, and Exemptions The tax system offers some tax holidays, reliefs, and exemptions. When the income of any person can be taxed simultaneously in Nigeria and in another country, the taxpayer may get relief against double taxation if the foreign country is one with which Nigeria has entered into a double taxation treaty. Among the nations with which Nigeria has entered into double taxation arrangements are the United Kingdom, France, and Canada.

Tax holidays are available for companies operating in "Pioneer" industries, that is, industries that the president determines are not being carried on in Nigeria either at all on a scale suitable to the country's economic requirements, or for which there are

14 *Id.* at part II of the schedule.
15 CAP P8, Laws of the Federation of Nigeria (LFN) (2004).
16 CAP C21, LFN (2004).
17 CAP E4, LFN (2004).

favorable prospects of further development.[18] The president may also accord Pioneer status to companies operating in industries in which it is in the public interest to encourage development. Examples of industries already accorded Pioneer status are cultivation and processing of food crops, manufacture of cement, manufacture of surgical dressings, and manufacture of pharmaceuticals.

Finally, a few of the income-related exemptions from tax include (1) the profits of any company formed for the purpose of promoting sporting activities, where such profits are wholly expendable for such purpose, subject to certain conditions; (2) dividends, interest, rent, or royalty derived by a foreign company and brought into Nigeria through government-approved channels; and (3) dividends received from investments in wholly export-oriented businesses.[19] One of the latest exemptions, granted in 2007, relates to the profits of a company established within an export processing zone or free-trade zone, provided that 100 percent of such company's production is for export; otherwise tax shall accrue proportionately on the profits of the company.

6. Mechanisms for Assessing and Collecting Tax The mechanisms for assessing and collecting tax may broadly be categorized as the payee system[20] and the nonpayee system. The payee system applies to employees, is forward-looking, and depends on the employer to remit the taxes deducted at the end of each month. Here, at the beginning of the year, the employee fills in returns on his or her expected annual income. The employer deducts the tax from the employee's monthly income including allowances or benefits in kind. The nonpayee system, meanwhile, taxes income received from a trade, business, or vocation. It is backward-looking in that the basis of the assessment is the previous year's income adjusted by adding back disallowed expenses, if any, and subtracting nontaxable income or profits. It is worth noting that special rules apply for new businesses, businesses that have ceased operation, and changes of accounting dates. Persons coming under the nonpayee system may voluntary subject themselves to self-assessment or may have a best-of-judgment (BOJ) assessment imposed on them. People are generally encouraged to adopt the self-assessment mode, since it saves the tax authorities' resources.

7. Challenging the Assessment Avenues exist for challenging imposed tax assessments.[21] Appeals from assessments of the relevant tax authorities are initially to the body of appeal commissioners,[22] and thereafter to the high court of a state, or in the case of company income tax, the Federal High Court.[23]

The new Federal Inland Revenue Service (Establishment) Act No. 13 of 2007 (FIRS Act) sets up an appeals tribunal charged with handling appeals arising from the act's operations or from any dispute about assessment arising under any of the tax laws

18 S.1 Industrial Development (Income Tax Relief) Act CAP I7, LFN (2004).
19 S.23 Companies Income Tax Act (*supra*).
20 S.81 Personal Income Tax Act CAP P8.
21 S.58 Personal Income Tax Act CAP P8; S. 69 Companies Income Tax Act CAP C21 LFN (2004).
22 *Id.* at S.61; S72 Companies Income Tax Act CAP C21, LFN (2004).
23 *Id.* at S.65; S.75 Companies Income Tax Act CAP C21 LFN (2004).

in force.[24] But the FIRS Act does not repeal the provisions of any of the extant tax legislation relating to appeals and challenge of assessments. It follows that they may therefore be seen as existing side by side, leading to difficult questions about jurisdiction.[25] The situation is compounded by the fact that the FIRS Act's transitional provisions[26] provide for continuation of proceedings and causes of action under FIRS without stipulating whether it should continue at the new appeals tribunals established by the FIRS Act or at the old tribunals. Other questions as to jurisdiction of the appeals tribunal under the FIRS Act arise from the apparent inconsistency between S.59 and the Fifth Schedule to the Act. S.59(2) provides that the appeals tribunals shall have power to settle disputes arising from the operations of the FIRS Act ". . . and under the First Schedule." The First Schedule contains a list of the sections of the act that FIRS will administer; it is the Fifth Schedule to the act, however, that deals with appeals tribunal jurisdiction. Furthermore, appeals from the appeals tribunal under the FIRS Act are to the Federal High Court. We hope that these drafting errors will be amended at the earliest opportunity to avoid controversy and establish the correct procedure for challenging assessments.

The above broad sketch provides a fair overview of Nigerian tax law, the topical issues it raises, and the controversies surrounding it. Armed with this sketch, we can then begin to put in context the machinery for the administration of the tax laws and resulting issues raised in order to appreciate its state of development.

B. Tax Administration in Nigeria

The tax laws are administered through five main channels.

1. Federal Inland Revenue Service The year 2007 saw various amendments to the tax administration system, particularly at the federal level. By Act No. 13 of 2007, the National Assembly established the Federal Inland Revenue Service (FIRS). The act vests the FIRS with the powers of assessment, collection of, and accounting for the revenues accruable to the federation's government. The aim was to establish an independent and professional body, which will be properly motivated and result oriented, to handle tax administration in Nigeria. The FIRS was, therefore, established as an autonomous corporate body with perpetual succession and Common Seal.

The FIRS is managed and supervised by the Federal Inland Revenue Service Board, made up of an executive chairman, who is appointed by the president subject to Senate ratification, and fourteen other members. Apart from the chairman, all other members

---

24 S.59 Federal Inland Revenue Service (Establishment) Act no. 13 (2007).

25 S.18 of the Companies Income Tax (Amendment) Act, no. 11 (2007), rectifies this anomaly with respect to appeals arising under the Companies Income Tax Act by deleting all the provisions in the principal legislation relating to appeals to the Body of Appeal Commissioners. The same is true for appeals under the Value-Added Tax (Amendment) Act, no. 12 (2007). *See* S.10 & 14 of the amendment to the act.

26 *Id.* at S.64(5).

serve part-time on the board.[27] The FIRS administers the following tax laws, and all regulations, rules, notices, or proclamations made under any them: the Companies Income Tax Act, Petroleum Profits Tax Act, Personal Income Tax Act, Capital Gains Tax Act, Value-Added Tax Act, Stamp Duty Act, Tax and Levies (Approved List for Collection) Act.[28]

2. *State Boards of Internal Revenue* Each state has a board of internal revenue, which, among other functions, oversees the assessment and collection of tax for the state. The state boards were established by the Personal Income Tax Act.[29]

3. *Joint Tax Board* S.86 of the Personal Income Tax Act[30]established the Joint Tax Board. This body is made up of representatives of each state government and the FIRS. The board's main object is to ensure harmony in the interpretation and enforcement of the tax laws throughout the federation. Before the board was established, there was disparity in the way the states interpreted and enforced the tax laws, leading to multiplicity of taxes and double taxation of persons.

4. *Local Government Revenue Committee* The Local Government Revenue Committee is to the local government what the State Board of Internal Revenue is to the state. It is also established by the Personal Income Tax Act[31] to assess and collect all taxes, fines, and rates under its jurisdiction and account for them to the chairman of the local government.[32]

5. *Joint State Revenue Committee* This body, which is also established by the Personal Income Tax Act, interprets and implements decisions by the Joint Tax Board.[33]

C. The State of Tax Administration in Nigeria

The story of tax administration in Nigeria has not been one of great success or efficiency. From 1929—when women in Aba, a commercial town in the east of the country, rioted when the colonial power attempted to impose taxes on them—until the present, tax administration has faced huge challenges and recorded little success. The main causes of this have been the popular view that tax is an unjustified expropriation of limited resources by governments and the lack of adequate, educated, well-equipped, and professional manpower. Confusing and numerous tax statutes, their failure to address local circumstances and conditions, multiple types of taxes, and the failure of government to provide

27 S.3 FIRS Act.

28 *Id.* at S.25 and First Schedule.

29 S.87. CAP P8, LFN.

30 CAP P8, LFN (2004).

31 *Id.* at S.90.

32 *Id.* at S.91.

33 *Id.* at S.93.

adequate infrastructure and security of life and property strengthen the public's lack of faith in the system. Other factors, such as illiteracy and a poor record-keeping culture, worsen the situation. Mr. Babatunde Raji Fashola, governor of Lagos State, highlighted these problems recently when he said, "One must admit that this default is aided by the outdated and outmoded provisions of our tax laws. To the average trader or artisan, the tax provisions are Greek. The assumed distinction between personal and business expense is a fiction and the essential records for tax assessment are mostly non-existent. In this regard, we are somewhat handicapped, when as in the case of Personal Income Tax, Capital Gains Tax and Stamp Duty, the laws are Acts of the National Assembly."[34]

Recently there has been a move to address some of these problems by modifying and updating the country's tax laws. In 2007, three tax laws were amended[35] under this plan, while others are awaiting debate at the National Assembly. Other indications of a likely change in the state of tax administration include the establishment of professional tax administrative bodies such as the FIRS and the similar bodies in the states. Lagos State, for example, has followed the federal government in establishing an autonomous state internal revenue service, which can recruit and train its own staff independent of the civil service. This new body, the Lagos State Internal Revenue Service (LSIRS), has a guaranteed income stream and is designed to operate with optimal efficiency and professionalism. LSIRS already has introduced electronic tax clearance certificates and aims to achieve lower costs in tax collection and establish taxpayer-friendly processes.

III. E-COMMERCE IN NIGERIA AND AMONG ITS NEIGHBORS

Before delving into the issues involved in e-commerce taxation in Nigeria, one must understand the nature and status of e-commerce in the country. E-Commerce is still in its infancy. Internet penetration is shallow but has improved at a relatively great speed over the last few years. Its deepening has been driven largely by the telecommunications explosion and liberalization of the communications sector. In September 2007, there were 10 million Internet users (about 7.2 percent of the population), 500 broadband Internet subscribers, and about 400 licensed Internet service providers.[36] By contrast, in 2004 the Economist Intelligence Unit estimated the number of Internet users per 100 persons at 1.25, and in 2005 it stood at 1.82.[37] Most recent figures[38] show the volume and value of Web-enabled transactions at ₦222,210 and ₦3 billion, respectively.

---

34 Address delivered at the first Lagos State stakeholders conference on taxation held on Dec. 3, 2007.

35 Companies Income Tax (Amendment) Act no. 11 (2007); Value-Added Tax (Amendment) Act no. 12 (2007); and Federal Inland Revenue Service (Establishment) Act no. 13 (2007).

36 Per the ITU (International Telecommunication Union, available at http://www.internetworldstats.com/africa.htm.

37 *See* http://globaltechforum.eiu.com/index.asp?categoryid=&channelid=&doc_id=8403&layout=rich_story&search=Nigerian.

38 CBN annual reports 2006.

Volume of Electronic Card Transactions in 2006

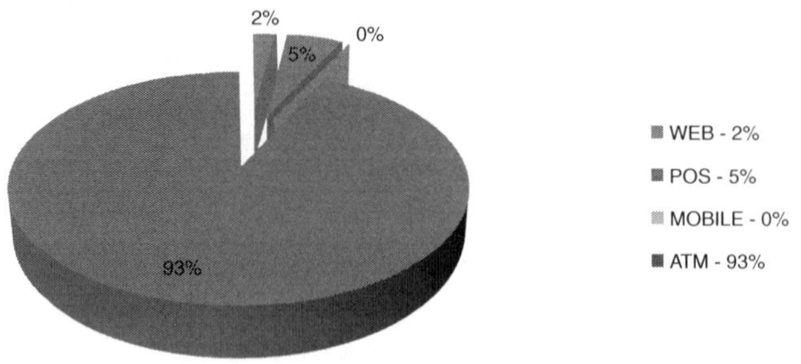

Value of Electronic Card Transactions in 2006

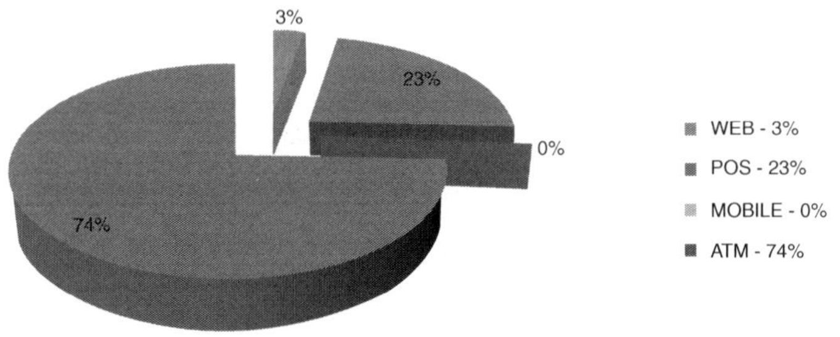

The most significant evidence of the potential for growth in Internet penetration is the number of telephone lines (connected and active) in use in the country. According to the Nigerian Communication Commission,[39] there were over 39 million active subscribers and over 51 million connected subscribers on the network as at October 2007. Compare this to 2001, shortly after the deregulation of the telecom sector, when there were fewer than 900,000 connected telephone lines, and to before 2001, when the total number of connected telephone lines was about 600,000. With Internet-ready mobile phones increasing in number and the prices continuing to fall, one can envisage a rapid spread in Internet penetration within a very short time. Figures from the Central Bank of Nigeria show the volume and value of mobile banking transactions through the GSM (Global System for Mobile Communications) standing at 40,733 transactions and ₦97.5 million, respectively.

Another factor that encourages e-commerce in Nigeria is the introduction of online payment systems. Several e-payment companies, including such recognized international brands as Visa and MasterCard, are already issuing Internet-enabled credit and debit cards. Governments now encourage online payment of some services, and travel tickets, hotels, music, and videos can be purchased with one or more of these e-cash methods. According to the Central Bank of Nigeria, there were 13 million payment cards in issue as of December 31, 2006.[40]

---

39 NCC Web site http://www.ncc.gov.ng/index5_e.htm.

40 Annual reports for 2006.

The industries currently taking advantage of e-commerce are travel (especially with the worldwide shift from paper tickets to e-ticketing), banking,[41] hotels, and leisure and entertainment.[42] Most banks in Nigeria now offer online, real-time banking services through which customers can view their accounts, make transfers or payments, and engage in various other transactions. Banks are encouraging online banking through their promotion of e-banking days and the increasing number of e-payment cards. One of the larger banks claims to have already issued five million cards, with 800 ATMs at various places in the country.[43]

The primary reasons for poor Internet penetration and e-commerce include low density and poor telecommunications services. The Economist Intelligence Unit estimates that the stock of personal computers grew from 10.66 per 1,000 persons to 11.09 in 2005.[44] The government and private partners are making great efforts to improve on these numbers. Programs include the Computers for All Nigerians Initiative (CANI),[45] under which public- and private- sector employees are encouraged not only to become computer literate, but also to purchase computers at significantly discounted rates. The program provides bank financing for the purchases up to 24 months. Other signs of the coming explosion in e-commerce include the ongoing laying of fiber-optic cables by a second national carrier licensed by the Nigerian Communications Commission and the massive roll-out of ATMs, with some banks coming together to set up a company for that specific purpose.

Other causes of poor e-commerce growth in Nigeria are unstable or nonexistent power supply in many areas, low income, illiteracy, poor business practices, and a totally cash-dependent economy. Like the computer density issue, these factors are slowly being addressed. For example, although the last government spent a whopping 1.2 trillion (about $10 billion) on the power sector between 2001 and 2007 without achieving any result, the incumbent government is determined to improve power supply up to at least 6000 megawatts by 2009.

The situation amongst Nigeria's neighbors is similar. They are beset by the same problems of lack of network capacity, low telecommunications and computer density, low income, and the absence of an e-payment infrastructure, among others. Consequently, the state of e-commerce in these countries is equally abysmal. ECOWAS[46] member states rely on the automated system for customs data (ASYCUDA) for a comprehensive database covering customs posts, agents, traders, transport modes, regimes, products, countries, taxes, measurements, and other data. Also, member states have available an automated goods clearing, forwarding, and payments system and an automatic

41 Most banks in Nigeria now offer online banking, e.g., First Inland Bank Plc, Zenith International Bank Plc, Diamond Bank Plc, Guaranty TrustBank Plc, IBTC-Chartered Bank Plc, Standard Chartered Bank Plc.

42 Funafric Limited, (http://www.funafric.com).

43 *See* http://www.ubagroup.com/news/pressnews_112207.asp.

44 *See* http://globaltechforum.eiu.com/index.asp?categoryid=&channelid=&doc_id=8403&layout=rich_story&search=nigerian.

45 *See* http://www.cani-nigeria.org/scheme_design.htm.

46 The Economic Community of West African States.

manifest control system to monitor cargo movement in transit. Otherwise, nothing much exists in the form of e-commerce within the region.

IV. STANDARDS IN E-COMMERCE TAXATION

Actions by international organizations and many other countries and regions of the world have produced some standards for taxation of e-commerce. Most notable among these are the Organization for Economic Cooperation and Development Principles for Taxation of Electronic Commerce.[47] According to these principles,[48] the rules that guide governments when taxing conventional commerce apply equally to the taxation of e-commerce and can be implemented even with the present stage of technological and commercial development. The OECD includes these other important measures:

- The current state of technology and electronic commerce can be utilized and applied to improve service to taxpayers.
- New administrative or legislative measures or modifications to existing measures can be introduced, provided that these are intended to assist in the application of existing tax principles and do not discriminate in the taxation or treatment of e-commerce.
- Only the jurisdiction in which consumption occurs should apply consumption tax.
- Supply of digitized products should not be treated as a supply of goods for consumption tax purposes.
- Tax collection procedures and information requirements should be fair and neutral to ensure a comparable standard with what is obtainable in the collection of tax in cases of conventional commerce.

One African country that has made an effort to comply with these principles is South Africa. It has amended the South African Income Tax Act of 1962 to change the basis of taxation from source-based to residence-based.

V. TAXATION OF E-COMMERCE IN NIGERIA

Nigeria does not have a tax statute that specifically applies to e-commerce. Tax liability depends on whether one's operations or income is governed by any of the approved taxes and levies. For individuals, tax liability therefore depends on residence in Nigeria. For companies, liability to Nigerian tax is source-based, that is, it depends on whether the tax accrues in, is derived from, is brought into, or is received in Nigeria. Other

---

47 Agreed at the 1998 OECD Ministerial Conference in Ottawa, Canada.

48 *See* http://www.oecd.org/dataoecd/46/3/1923256.pdf.

Nigerian tax statutes directly affecting e-commerce include the Petroleum Profits Tax Act (PPTA)[49] and the Value-Added Tax Act (VAT).[50] These statutes are discussed below.

A. Taxation of Individuals

In any given years, tax is imposed on an individual only by the state[51] in which the individual is deemed to be resident for that year.[52] For an individual whose source of income is derived from a trade, business profession, or vocation but not from an employment or pension, his or her residence is the territory in which he or she has a place of residence or principal place of residence on the first day of January of the year of assessment.[53] "Place of residence" means a place available for an individual's domestic use in Nigeria on January 1, and cannot be a hotel, rest house or other place of temporary lodging, unless no permanent place is available for his or her use on that day.[54] Meanwhile, "principal place of residence," in relation to an individual with two or more places of residence in different territories, refers to the place that is nearest to his or her usual place of work on January 1 of the year in question.

B. Taxation of Companies

The Company Income Tax Act distinguishes between companies incorporated in Nigeria and those incorporated outside Nigeria. The profits of a Nigerian company are deemed to accrue in Nigeria no matter where they have arisen, regardless of whether those profit have been brought into or received in Nigeria.[55] The profits of a company incorporated outside Nigeria shall be deemed to be derived in Nigeria in any of the following circumstances:[56]

- If that company has a fixed base of business in Nigeria, profits are considered to be derived from Nigeria to the extent that the profits are attributable to the fixed base.
- If the company has no fixed base in Nigeria but habitually operates a trade or business through a person in Nigeria authorized to act on its behalf or on behalf of some other company controlled by it, or which has a controlling interest in it or habitually maintains a stock of goods or merchandise in Nigeria from which deliveries are regularly made by a person on its behalf, profits are deemed to be derived in Nigeria to the extent that the profit is attributable to the business, trade, or activity carried on through that person.

---

49 CAP P13, LFN (2004).
50 CAP V1, LFN (2004).
51 Nigeria is made up of 36 states.
52 S.2(2) Personal Income Tax Act (PITA) Cap P8, LFN (2004).
53 Paragraph 6 to Schedule 1, PITA CAP P8, LFN (2004).
54 Paragraph 1 to Schedule 1, PITA CAP P8, LFN (2004).
55 S.11(1) Companies Income Tax Act CAP C21, LFN (2004).
56 *Id.* at S.13.

- If that trade, business, or activity involves a single contract for surveys, deliveries, installations, or construction, the profit from that contract; is considered to be derived from Nigeria.
- Where the trade, business, or activity is between the company and another person controlled by it or that has a controlling interest in it, and the FIRS deems that their commercial or financial relations are artificial or fictitious, the amount of the profit adjusted to reflect an arm's-length transaction will be deemed to be derived from Nigeria.

These definitions of deemed profits raise a number of questions in their application, even in cases of conventional commerce. It is therefore expected that the issues will be more complicated when the definitions are applied to e-commerce. Most of these issues concern the definitions of "fixed base;" "operate a business or trade;" "authorized to act;" "maintain a stock of goods or merchandise;" and "make deliveries."

1. "Fixed Base" For purposes of determining what constitutes a fixed base of business in Nigeria, facilities solely used to store or display goods or merchandise and facilities solely used to collect information are not considered.[57] A key question is whether facilities such as a computer or bank of computers, a data bank, or a server are exempted from the meaning of "fixed base."

While there is no statutory guide to the term "fixed base," the Court of Appeal has given some guidance on what would qualify.[58] In *Shell B.V.*, the court held that in the absence of clear statutory definitions of the term, it is wrong to equate "fixed base" with "residence" or "ordinary residence." Shell B.V. was incorporated in the Netherlands but since 1958 had been rendering technical and management services to Shell Petroleum Development Company Limited (SPDC), its local Nigerian sister. Each year, officers of Shell B.V. come into Nigeria to collect information and impart expert knowledge or advice. Whenever those officers came, they made use of any available space at SPDC offices. SPDC paid Shell B.V. for these services; Shell B.V. paid income tax on similar payments from companies like SPDC in the Netherlands. Shell B.V. never paid taxes in Nigeria until 1989, when the Tax Board requested its tax returns. Subsequently, the parties agreed that 7.5 percent of payments received from SPDC would be deemed as profit, and the appellant paid tax on this basis from 1983 till 1992. In 1993, the Tax Board increased Shell B.V.'s yearly assessment to 10 percent of the payments from SPDC. Shell B.V. challenged the assessment, claiming among other things that it was not liable to tax in Nigeria. Its challenge was turned down by the Tax Appeal Commissioners, and its further appeals to the Federal High Court and the Court of Appeal were dismissed. For Shell B.V., SPDC was a "fixed base."

2. "Operate a Business or Trade" Will an ISP based in Nigeria that hosts a server for several people from all over the world be deemed to be operating a business or trade on

57 *Id.* at S.13(3).

58 Shell International Petroleum Maatschappij B.V. v. Federal Board of Inland Revenue, 3 NWLR (pt 859) 46 (2004) (hereinafter *Shell B.V.*).

behalf of those companies? What is the level of responsibility or authority, if any, that a person must shoulder or wield before he or she can be held to operate a business or trade? *In Edicomsa International Inc. & Associates v. Citec International Estates Ltd.,*[59] the Court of Appeal considered the meaning of the phrase "carry on business."[60] Under *Edicomsa*, this means to conduct, prosecute, or continue a particular vocation or business as a continuous operation or permanent occupation; according to the court, "the repetition of acts may be sufficient."[61] Edicomsa, an American company, was not registered in Nigeria. It entered into an agreement with the respondent, Citec, to provide architectural designs, drawings, civil infrastructure, and construction of 5000 housing units for Citec and the federal government of Nigeria. When disputes arose between the parties concerning payments, Edicomsa sued Citec. Citec objected on the ground that the contract between them was illegal and void since Edicomsa, by virtue of the contract, was carrying on business in Nigeria without being registered in the country. On appeal, the court agreed with Citec and held that Edicomsa was indeed carrying on business in Nigeria. The phrase, "to operate a business or trade," must likely carry the same meaning.

3. "Authorize" the Conduct of a Business or Trade When is something "authorized" in the context of e-commerce? Nigeria's company law[62] provides, in effect, that a company may make contracts or sign in the same way as an individual—orally or in writing. Where writing or writing under seal is required by law of a contract made by individuals, a company will also be required to contract in writing or by writing and fixing its common seal. Will electronic communications qualify as writing in Nigeria? The authors believe it does,[63] but what about seals? How will the requirement for sealing be met? Will digital signatures be acceptable?

4. "Maintain a Stock of Goods and Merchandise" What will qualify as a stock of goods and merchandise? For instance, will digital books or music qualify? Or will they be held not to be goods, as advised by the OECD framework of principles? Nigeria is not a member of the OECD.

5. "Make Deliveries" Similar questions apply here: when can one be held to make a delivery? Is it when the goods or merchandise are sent to the recipient, or when he downloads it? When the music or video file is streamed online, has a delivery been made?

These questions are still unanswered here in Nigeria and cannot be finally dealt with except by judicial interpretation or, preferably, legislation. The Electronic Commerce Bill is pending the National Assembly and attempts to address these questions. It is patterned after the United Nations Commission on International Trade Law (UNCITRAL) Model Law on Electronic Commerce but has been pending since 2004.

---

59 4 NWLR (Pt 969) CA 114 (2006) (hereafter "*Edicomsa*").

60 As used in S.54 Companies and Allied Matters Act CAP C20, LFN (2004).

61 Page 125G.

62 Companies and Allied Matters Act CAP C20, LFN (2004), S.71.

63 S.18 Interpretation Act CAP I23 defines ""writing" in a statute thus: "writing" and expressions referring to writing include printing, lithography, photography, typewriting and other modes of representing or reproducing words or figures in a visible form."

C. Taxation of Petroleum Profits

1. Ambit of the Tax Companies that engage in petroleum operations are taxed under the Petroleum Profits Tax Act.[64] This act is relevant to e-commerce because petroleum operations are defined as

> the winning or obtaining and transportation of petroleum or chargeable oil[65] in Nigeria by or on behalf of a company for its own account by any drilling, mining, extracting or other like operations or process, not including refining at a refinery, in the course of a business carried on by the company engaged in such operations, and all operations incidental thereto and any sale of or any disposal of chargeable oil by or on behalf of the company.[66]

The emphasis is on the phrase, "all operations incidental thereto," which is broad enough to encompass a range of activities. In the *Shell B.V case*[67] already cited, Shell B.V. was engaged in rendering technical and managerial services. Although it was based in the Netherlands and did not have offices in Nigeria, the Inland Revenue saw it as engaging in petroleum operations. This view is potentially applicable to e-commerce transactions. Furthermore, the phrase "all operations incidental thereto" does not apply to the sale or disposal of chargeable oil by or on behalf of a company. Commercial transactions with companies engaged only in selling or disposal of chargeable oil are therefore not subject to tax under the Petroleum Profits Tax Act. It is to be noted that in the case of chargeable oil owned by a company engaged in petroleum operations, the act defines "disposal" to mean delivery, without sale, to a refinery or adjacent storage tank for refining by the company.[68]

2. Persons Chargeable Only companies or partnerships (joint ventures) formed by companies are chargeable to the tax.[69] According to the Petroleum Profits Tax Act, it is an offense for any person (other than a company) to engage in petroleum operations, either of his or her own account or jointly with any other person or in partnership with any other person, with a view to sharing the profits arising from those operations.

In view of the great simplifications and improvements brought by technology, and the broad definition the act gives to the term "petroleum operations," one can question why petroleum operations are reserved only for companies. Indeed, one of the main conclusions of the OECD in its framework principles for electronic commerce is that the technologies that underlie electronic commerce offer significant new opportunities to improve taxpayer service.

---

64 CAP P13. LFN (2004).

65 The act does not define "chargeable oil."

66 *Id.* at S.2.

67 Shell International Petroleum Maatschappi B.V. v. Federal Board of Inland Revenue, 3 NWLR (pt 859) 46 (2004).

68 CAP P13, LFN (2004) S.2.

69 *Id.* at S.8.

D. Companies Not Resident in Nigeria

A company not resident in Nigeria that is or has been engaged in petroleum operations is taxable either directly or in the name of its manager or other person resident in Nigeria who manages the petroleum operations. It is easy in light of technological advances and e-commerce for a company not resident in Nigeria nevertheless to be engaged in petroleum operations there. This is one of the areas where the FIRS will have to depend on technological advances to improve tax administration. Otherwise, many companies will slip through the tax net by operating remotely outside Nigeria.

E. Withholding Tax on E-Commerce

Withholding is one of the mechanisms for tax collection provided under the Nigeria's tax statutes. It is one way through which collection difficulties, such as collection of tax from nonresident companies, can be avoided or at least reduced.

Withholding tax is deductible by any person paying or crediting another in respect of any of the following:

1. Rent[70]
2. Interest, royalty, and similar payments[71]
3. Dividends or similar distribution[72]
4. Director's fees[73]
5. Any other withholding payment must be authorized by the relevant tax authority[74]

Regulations[75] made under the Companies Income Tax Act give directions as to withholding tax under item (5) above with respect to payments made or credits given by companies. Consequently a company is obliged to deduct tax when making payments relating to

1. All aspects of building, construction, and related activities[76]
2. All types of contracts and agency arrangements, other than sales in the ordinary course of business[77]
3. Consultancy and professional services[78]

---

70 S.69 Personal Income Tax Act CAP P8; S.79 Companies Income Tax Act CAP C21.

71 S.70, Personal Income Tax Act CAP P8; S.78 Companies Income Tax Act CAP C21. In the case of companies, withholding tax is not due on interest on interbank deposits.

72 S.71 Personal income Tax Act CAP P8; S.80 Companies Income Tax Act CAP C21.

73 S.72 Personal Income Tax Act CAP P8.

74 S.73 Personal Income Tax Act CAP P8; S.81 Companies Income Tax Act CAP C21.

75 Companies Income Tax (Rates, etc. of tax deducted at source (withholding tax)) Regulation 1997 as amended.

76 Current rates are 5% of total payments.

77 Same rate applies.

78 Current rate is 10%.

4. Management services[79]
5. Technical services[80]
6. Commissions[81]

One thing to note about these provisions is that liability under them is not dependent on the subject matter of the contract or transaction, but rather on the nature of payment. Consequently, they appear to sidestep the controversy raised by the digitized nature of most goods or subject of electronic commerce. This is, however, not clear cut. For example, is "rent" as used in the tax statutes, a technical term referring only to physical accommodations, or can it, for example, be applied to rent of cyberspace or rent of space on a server?

F. Value-Added Tax and E-Commerce

This tax is imposed on the supply of all goods and services,[82] except those exempted. It is to be collected by every "taxable person" who carries out an economic activity, who exploits tangible or intangible property to obtain income therefrom by way of trade or business, or a person or agency of government acting in the latter capacity. The definition of "taxable person"[83] is broad enough to bind persons engaged in e-commerce if such person is either carrying on an economic activity in a place or is exploiting tangible or intangible property (e.g., digitized books, music, videos, etc.) to obtain income therefrom.

All taxable persons are required to register with the FIRS for purposes of this tax.[84] A nonresident company that carries on business in Nigeria shall also register for the tax, using the address of the person with whom it has an existing contract as its address for tax-related correspondence.[85]

G. Stamp Duties

Because the stamp duty is a tax on instruments,[86] it is the most directly relevant to e-commerce. Consequently, it is the tax most threatened by modern technology and

79 Current rate is 10%.
80 Current rate is 10%.
81 Current rate is 10%.
82 SS.1 & 2 Value-Added Tax Act CAP V1, LFN (2004). Exempted goods and services include all medical and pharmaceutical products, basic food items, books and educational materials, baby products, fertilizer, locally produced agricultural products and veterinary medicine, farming machinery and farming transportation equipment, all exports, medical services, and plays and performances conducted by educational institutions as part of learning and all exported services. *See* Schedule 1 to the act.
83 S.12 Value-Added Tax (Amendment) Act (2007).
84 S.8 Value-Added Tax CAP V1, LFN (2004).
85 *Id.* at S.10.
86 S.23 Stamp Duty Act CAP S8, LFN (2004).

advances in business communications. Within the Stamp Duty Act, an instrument is defined to include every written document.[87] As already indicated,[88] the definition of "writing," under Nigerian law is broad enough to cover business communication by electronic means.

The challenge posed for taxation here is in its enforcement and administration as it applies to electronic communications. Nigerian tax administrators are mostly not Internet savvy, nor are their offices Internet ready. Evasion by businesses engaged in e-commerce is therefore likely to be high. When one adds to these the fact that most Internet applications are used by private businesses, one can begin to see the enormity of the problem. But Nigeria is not alone. Even tax administrators in well-advanced countries realize that modern technology and ways of conducting business are capable of eroding the stamp duty base, and are determining ways to collect these duties electronically.[89] The United Kingdom has begun online administration of stamp duties and has registered about 46 percent of solicitors and conveyancers who now use the system.[90]

VI. TAXATION OF E-COMMERCE AMONG NIGERIA'S NEIGHBORS

Most African countries have not seriously had to consider taxation of e-commerce because of the low, and in some cases nonexistent, level and number of e-commerce transactions. This is due in part to the poor level of infrastructure, poor Internet penetration, and lack of e-payment facilities. However, a few countries have set the tone by adopting legislation designed to accommodate e-commerce.[91]

Among the countries of the ECOWAS region, e-commerce is also still in its fetal stage, and even then it is not evenly spread. Each country has its own tax policy, which is focused on brick-and-mortar businesses. But the ECOWAS secretariat, realizing the importance of the world trend and the opportunity it presents, has begun to think about jump-starting the move to e-commerce. It took a significant step by commissioning a consultancy under the auspices of the Economic Commission for Africa on how to develop a harmonized legal framework for electronic commerce in the region. The report was submitted in May 2005.[92]

As already mentioned, ECOWAS countries currently have a common platform under the ASYCUDA system for charging and collecting duties. The authors believe that with the steps ECOWAS has already taken to develop and harmonize a framework for

---

87 *Id.* at S.2.

88 S.18 Interpretation Act CAP I23, LFN (2004).

89 For instance the Inland Revenue Service in the UK held such consultations in 2002. *See* http://www.hmrc.gov.uk/consult_new/mod_stamp_duty.pdf.

90 *See* http://www.publictechnology.net/modules.php?op=modload&name=News&file=article&sid=13725.

91 See, e.g., Mauritius, Tunisia, Cape Verde and South Africa.

92 *See* http://www.uneca.org/disd/events/2006/ecowas-uemoa/content/The%20Development%20of%20an%20E-Commerce%20Legal%20Framework%20for%20ECOWAS%20-%20EN.pdf.

e-commerce, it will not be long before the countries of the region develop a common policy on taxation of income from this source.

VII. CONCLUSION

E-Commerce is new but growing in Nigeria. As the charts and data given in this book show, the volume and value of electronic business is growing. This presents challenges for taxation law and policy. This is the best time to introduce policies, both at the national and regional level, to harness the Internet's potential and address some of the issues of interpretation and application of the tax laws to this new way of doing business. Nigeria began amending its tax laws in 2007. It is also working on improving tax administration by trying to give the FIRS and its state equivalents autonomy and a professional staff. It should maintain this momentum and seek to address the taxation issues raised by e-commerce.

To do so, the authors recommend the following steps be taken, not necessarily seriatim:

1. In keeping with global trends, and based on other countries' experiences, Nigeria should formally adopt the OECD framework principles on e-commerce to guide its tax policy for source of income.
2. To this end, it is best to seize the opportunity offered by the current low level of e-commerce and Internet penetration to anticipate and correct anomalies that occur due to the nature of electronic communications or because of technological advancement. For instance, although the authors are of the firm view that "writing," as defined in Nigeria, incorporates communication by electronic means, matters such as the requirement of sealing of documents (as in the case of a deed) need to provide for electronic signatures. Furthermore, other terms contained in the statutes that were designed for use in brick-and-mortar situations are vague or at best are stretched if applied to electronic commerce. To this end the authors commend the National Assembly for its work on the electronic commerce bill and the cybercrime bills but urge them to speed up the process. These bills have been pending since 2004.
3. In legislating or making the policy changes, however, we should always consider local circumstances and conditions. Matters such as regulatory issues and law enforcement have to be considered and strengthened to ensure that genuine Nigerian businesses are encouraged while protecting privacy and the integrity of the financial systems.
4. Our tax administration requires being Internet savvy in approach, and administrators need to be trained to appreciate the nature, customs, and circumstances of electronic communications and commerce.

Chapter 2

South Africa: The Basis for Imposing Corporate Income Tax in South Africa's E-Commerce Environment

Kyle Eric Mandy
Werksmans Tax & Advisory Services (PTY) Ltd.

I. INTRODUCTION

The imposition of corporate tax in South Africa is regulated by the Income Tax Act 58 of 1962, as amended (the Income Tax Act). It contains no provisions aimed specifically at e-commerce or digital environments, and very few special provisions find application in these environments. It is therefore, largely, the general provisions of the Income Tax Act and the principles established in respect thereof that need to be interpreted and applied in the e-commerce context.

As illustrated in this chapter, this can result in difficulties and uncertainty as to whether or not such transactions are subject to tax in South Africa and, if so, the extent to which they should be taxed. This chapter discusses the relevant provisions of the Income Tax Act that provide for taxation of corporate entities in South Africa and the principles applicable thereto, and considers the application of those provisions and principles in the e-commerce environment.

II. BASIS OF TAXATION IN SOUTH AFRICA

South Africa adopted a residence minus system of taxation in 2001, whereby it taxes residents on their worldwide income, with certain income derived outside South Africa being exempt from taxation. Before 2001, the tax system was primarily based on a source-plus system, whereby only income sourced in South Africa or deemed to be sourced in South Africa was subject to tax. Nonresidents of South Africa continue to be subject to tax on the source-plus basis.

One of the main reasons for changing to a residence basis of taxation was to cater more effectively for the taxation of e-commerce due to the difficulties associated with taxing such activities on a source basis.

Allowing for certain exemptions and deductions, a company is subject to income tax in South Africa on any amount that constitutes gross income as defined in the Income Tax Act. Gross income is, essentially, any amount not of a capital nature received by or accrued to a person from any source, in the case of a South African tax resident, or from a source in or deemed to be in South Africa, in the case of a non-South African tax resident.

Amounts of a capital nature, meanwhile, are subject to capital gains tax to the extent that they arise from the disposal of any assets by residents of South Africa or, in the case of nonresidents, immovable property or an interest in immovable property situated in South Africa or any asset attributable to a permanent establishment of that person in South Africa. The definition of permanent establishment for purposes of the Income Tax Act follows that of Article 5 of the Organization of Economic Cooperation and Development (OECD) Model Tax Convention on Income and Capital.

III. RESIDENTS OF SOUTH AFRICA

Companies that are tax residents of South Africa are, as a general rule, currently subject to income tax at a rate of 29 percent on revenue profits and at an effective rate on capital gains of 14.5 percent. In addition, South African tax resident companies are liable for secondary tax on companies on the net amount of any dividend declared at a rate of 10 percent. Secondary tax on companies is not a tax on dividends at the shareholder level but rather an additional tax on income of the company payable on the declaration of a dividend. The effective rate of tax for South African tax resident companies declaring all their profits as dividends is therefore 35.45 percent on revenue profits and 22.27 percent on capital gains.

It was announced in the 2007 budget review that the secondary tax on companies is to be replaced by a dividend withholding tax at the same rate of 10 percent. However, the timing of this is uncertain because it depends on South Africa renegotiating a number of double taxation agreements to provide for a minimum withholding tax rate on dividends of 5 percent.

A company is regarded as a tax resident of South Africa if it is incorporated in South Africa or has its place of effective management in South Africa. Specifically excluded, however, is any company that is deemed to be exclusively a resident of another country for purposes of any double taxation agreement entered into between South Africa and that other country.

The Income Tax Act contains no definition of the term "place of effective management." A detailed discussion as to what constitutes the place of effective management of a company goes beyond the scope of this chapter. It should be noted, however, that there is no South African legal precedent on the meaning of the term. The South African Revenue Service has issued an interpretation note on the meaning of "effective management" in the context of the definition of a resident to the effect that they regard it as the implementation of policy and strategy decisions, made by the board of directors, by the directors or senior managers of the company on a regular or day-to-day basis, irrespective of where the overriding control is exercised, or where the board of directors meets.[1] In other words, the South African Revenue Service regards the place of effective management of a company, as a general rule, as being the place where the executive management of the company is located. Interpretation notes released by the South African Revenue Service are, however, not law and are therefore not binding on taxpayers or the courts. This aspect of the definition of a resident therefore remains a significant area of uncertainty.

IV. SOURCE-BASED TAXATION

As noted earlier, nonresidents of South Africa are subject to tax on income derived from a source in or deemed to be in South Africa. Such companies are subject to tax on income at a rate of 34 percent and on capital gains at an effective rate of 17 percent. Nonresident-companies are not subject to the secondary tax on companies, nor are they likely to be subject to the dividend withholding tax when this replaces the secondary tax on companies. South Africa also does not levy a branch profits tax on the repatriation of branch profits.

A. Meaning of Source

The Income Tax Act contains no definition of the word "source." However, because South Africa has a long history of source-based taxation, the general principles are well established for identifying income as source in the context of the gross income definition, There is a substantial amount of legal precedent in this regard.

South African courts have held that the word "source" in the context of the definition of gross income means the originating cause of the receipt of the money; this originating cause is the work that is done to earn it or the quid pro quo that is given in return therefor.[2] Ascertaining whether an amount is from a South African source therefore involves an inquiry as to the originating cause of that amount and the location of that originating cause. Where there is more than one possible originating cause, the dominant or main cause of the income and the location thereof determines that income's source.[3]

The problem that arises concerning the source of income is that it is sometimes difficult to establish its originating cause. Each case needs to be decided on its own facts and circumstances. In *CIR v. Lever Brothers*, the court held that "[s]ource means not a legal concept but something which the practical man would regard as a real source of income. The ascertaining of the actual source is a practical hard matter of fact."[4]

---

1 Interpretation Note no. 6 (March 26, 2002).

2 CIR v. Lever Bros & Unilever Ltd, 1946 AD 441, 14 SATC 1.

3 CIR v. Black, 1957 (3) SA 536 (A), 21 SATC 226.

4 *Id.* at 13.

Nevertheless, the courts have recognized that the originating cause of income may be located in South Africa and one or more other countries. In the *Lever Brothers case*, the court commented in dicta that locating the originating cause may present considerable difficulties and it may be necessary to conclude that the source of a particular receipt is located partly in one country and partly in another, and that such a state of affairs may lead to the conclusion that the whole of a receipt, or part of it, or none of it, is taxable as income from a source in South Africa.[5]

Naturally, the source of income in the e-commerce environment needs to be considered with due regard to the principles laid down by the courts. The example of a company that sells goods over the Internet illustrates the problem with a source test in this environment. The source of that income may well be very different depending on whether it sources those goods in South Africa or elsewhere. Where the company's buying activities are considered to be the dominant originating cause of the income and are carried out in South Africa, the income may be regarded as being from a South African source. Where the buying activities are not the dominant originating cause of the income, however, this may result in the source of the income's source being located in a country other than South Africa. The circumstances in which the buying activities could be considered the dominant originating cause of the income could obviously vary. However, this is more likely to be the case where the goods are, for example, of a specialist nature or difficult to source.

Similar considerations could arise where sales activities are regarded as the dominant originating cause of the income. Insofar as e-commerce transactions are concerned, this situation is the most probable. For example, where a retailer of goods, such as a book dealer, acquires goods that are readily available and of a general nature and sells these over the Internet, the place where the sale is made has historically been regarded as the source of that income.

However, this interpretation was developed before the advent of the Internet, and the question now is whether it is appropriate for transactions occurring in cyberspace. If a book dealer has a store located in South Africa and a customer enters that store to conclude the sales transaction, it is fairly obvious that the sale took place in South Africa and that South Africa is the source of the income. The problem with an Internet transaction is that the purchaser may be located in South Africa, but the seller could be located anywhere in the world. Where then does the sale take place? A contract of sale, in simple terms, consists of two actions: an offer and the acceptance of the offer. When the offer and acceptance take place at different locations, determining where the sale occurs becomes a more complex problem.

If the sale's location is not an appropriate test of the source of income, should one then consider the place where the offer is made or where acceptance occurs? These are both possibilities, but not without their own difficulties. Take, for example, the case of a South African individual who decides to order goods online for his personal use in South Africa. In one instance he orders those goods while sitting at home, and in another he orders them while travelling in Europe. Why should the source of the income be

5 *Id.* at 10.

different simply because in one case he happened to be at home in South Africa and in the other he was out of the country? Clearly the different outcomes are irreconcilable.

Perhaps then one should look to where the offer was made to determine the source of the income. However, this will also not necessarily provide the appropriate source of the income.

Courts therefore have to consider the facts and circumstances applicable to the e-commerce environment, as well as those of the underlying case, when ascertaining the source of income. The case would need to identify the e-tailer's actions rather than the purchaser's actions to determine the source of income. Depending on the situation, the source of the income may be where the Website is located, where the goods are located, where the company effects the transaction, or some other place.

In summary, the question of the source of income has always been one of the most contentious and litigious aspects of South African tax law. In the modern world, where the Internet and communications span national boundaries and continents, this is not likely to be any less the case, and any attempt by the South African Revenue Service to levy tax on nonresident companies in this environment could well end up in litigation.

Fortunately, a company can sometimes avoid the question of the source of income when it is resident in a country with which South Africa has a double-taxation agreement, particularly when it has no permanent establishment in South Africa. This of course can present its own difficulties in the e-commerce environment, which are considered later in this chapter. For those companies domiciled in jurisdictions with which South Africa has no double-taxation agreement, this aspect of South African tax law remains a minefield. Any such nonresident companies transacting over the Internet potentially face tax liability in South Africa, depending on the circumstances of their particular case. Of course, the difficulty facing the South African Revenue Service and tax authorities in other jurisdictions around the world is identifying these transactions and enforcing their respective tax laws.

B. Deemed Source

The Income Tax Act deems certain types of income to accrue from a source in South Africa. In the context of e-commerce only one of these is of any great significance, namely, the use or right of use in South Africa of, inter alia, any design, copyright, formula, or any property or right of a similar nature as is contemplated in section 35 of the Income Tax Act, which relates to the royalty withholding tax discussed later in this chapter.

V. THE EFFECT OF DOUBLE-TAXATION AGREEMENTS

As indicated earlier, where South Africa has entered into a double-taxation agreement with another country and income is either derived from a South African source by a person who is a resident in that other country or derived by a South African resident person from a source in that other country, the double-taxation agreement will regulate

South Africa's right to tax income. While a comprehensive discussion regarding the difficulties of interpreting double-taxation agreements in the e-commerce environment goes beyond the scope of this chapter, it is worth noting that South Africa's double-taxation agreements are not immune to such difficulties. Most of South Africa's double-taxation agreements are based on the OECD Model Tax Convention, and the issues set forth in the commentary regarding Article 7 and permanent establishments in the e-commerce environment are therefore applicable to South Africa's double-taxation agreements. Key in this regard is the comment that a Website does not in itself constitute a permanent establishment, although the server on which the Website is stored may. Another issue raised in the commentary is whether the business of an enterprise that is wholly or partly carried on through such a server needs to be examined on a case-by-case basis. Even where a person is regarded as carrying on business through a server that constitutes a permanent establishment, the attribution of profits to that permanent establishment is a complex and uncertain exercise, as raised by the OECD Business Profits Technical Advisory Group in a discussion paper released in February 2001.

VI. ROYALTIES

A. Introduction

Section 35 of the Income Tax Act provides for a final withholding tax, known as the withholding tax on royalties, at a rate of 12 percent for certain amounts received by or accruing to any person who is not a tax resident of South Africa or a controlled foreign company.[6] The withholding tax does not, however, apply when the amount is received by or accrues to any company that is not a tax resident of South Africa if it is derived by that company from a trade carried on through a branch or agency in South Africa and is subject to tax in South Africa. Because any amounts contemplated in section 35 of the Income Tax Act are deemed to be from a South African source, if they are derived through a branch or agency in South Africa, they will be subject to income tax in South Africa and will therefore not be subject to the withholding tax.

Anyone who incurs a liability to pay an amount subject to the withholding tax to a person who is not a resident is obliged to pay the tax on behalf of the nonresident. The payor is entitled to deduct or withhold the amount of the tax from the amount payable to the nonresident or to recover the amount of tax from that person. Any amount that is subject to the withholding tax is exempt from the normal tax in terms of section 10(1)(l) of the Income Tax Act.

B. Applicability in the E-Commerce Environment

The withholding tax applies, inter alia, to the use or right of use, or the grant of permission to use in South Africa, any patent, design, trademark, copyright, model,

---

6 For a description of a controlled foreign company refer to the discussion later in this chapter.

pattern, plan, formula, process or any property or right of a similar nature (hereinafter collectively referred to as intellectual property). It applies regardless of where that intellectual property is produced, the right of use is granted, or payment is made.

Copyrights or property of a similar nature are the intellectual property most relevant to the e-commerce environment. The copyright referred to in section 35 of the Income Tax Act is that as defined in the Copyright Act 98 of 1978 (the Copyright Act). The Copyright Act is applicable to certain works whose creator is, in the case of a company, incorporated in South Africa or that are made in South Africa. Eligible works include, inter alia, literary, musical, or artistic works, cinematograph films, sound recordings, and computer programs. Works that do not qualify for copyright under the Copyright Act, because the author is not a South African registered company or the works were not made in South Africa, would be regarded as property of a similar nature for purposes of section 35 of the Income Tax Act. (Both types of works are hereinafter referred to collectively as copyrights.) The result is that when a nonresident (licensor) receives payment for the use of a copyright in South Africa, it is liable for the 12 percent withholding tax in respect, and the licensee must pay this tax to the South African Revenue Service on the licensor's behalf.

It has become commonplace for computer programs, music, videos, photographs, mobile phone ringtones and wallpapers, films, books, and many other copyrighted materials to be downloaded from the Internet and duplicated in return for payment of a fee. This amount grants permission to reproduce the material in other words, it authorizes the use of the copyright. When the download occurs in South Africa, any payment for the use of the copyright is deemed to be from a South African source and is subject to the withholding tax on royalties if accruing to a nonresident that does not carry on a trade through a branch or agency in South Africa or is not a foreign-controlled company.

C. Issues Arising in the E-Commerce Environment

A major issue that arises in the e-commerce environment is whether a payment made for a transaction that permits a customer to download a copyrighted work amounts to payment for the use of the copyright or for something else. Only if the payment is received by virtue of the use of the copyright will it be deemed to be from a South African source and subject to the withholding tax on royalties.

This issue was addressed, in the context of double-taxation agreements, by the OECD Technical Advisory Group on Treaty Characterisation of Electronic Commerce Payments in a report issued on February 1, 2001. The report concluded that when the essential consideration is for something other than the use of the copyright, and the use of the copyright is limited to such rights as are required to enable downloading, storage, and operation by the customer, the use of the copyright should be disregarded in analyzing the payment's character for treaty purposes. The report discusses an example where payment is made for the downloading and operation of a copy of a computer program as illustrating a situation in which the payment is not essentially made for the use of any copyright in that program. In this situation, the report states that the payment is made to acquire data transmitted in the form of a digital signal for the purchaser's own use or enjoyment and, to the extent that the act of copying the digital signal onto storage media constitutes the use of a copyright, this is merely an incidental part of the process of capturing and storing the digital signal.

Although the report's approach is entirely sensible, a few matters must be noted in this regard. First, the report concerns itself only with the characterisation of payments under double-taxation agreements, and then only those based on the OECD Model Tax Convention. Second, although the report resulted in changes to the commentary on Article 12 of the OECD Model Tax Convention on January 28, 2003, the commentary does not have the status of law in South Africa, but instead may be of persuasive authority to courts interpreting South African double-taxation agreements based on the OECD Model Tax Convention. Third, when it comes to interpreting the provisions of section 35 of the Income Tax Act as opposed to a double-taxation agreement, the report and the commentary would be of little persuasive value.

Having said that, in the context of the South African domestic legislation, the courts would likely follow a similar approach to that adopted in the report. However, the facts and circumstances of each particular case would be key in determining whether the payment was for the use of the copyright or for the acquisition of the data in question. While in the vast majority of circumstances payment would most likely be for something other than the use of the copyright, this may not always be the case.

In addition to the issues around characterization of the income, other questions arise regarding enforcement of the withholding tax on royalties in the e-commerce environment, assuming that the amounts in question are paid for use of a copyright. The first problem that arises is the difficulty that the licensee faces in identifying whether the licensor is a South African tax resident or nonresident or, if a nonresident, whether the licensor is a controlled-foreign company. Unfortunately, section 35 of the Income Tax Act provides little assistance to the licensee in this regard and has not kept pace with the development of such online transactions. Section 35 simply makes, in circumstances largely unhelpful, the proviso that a person having an address outside South Africa will be deemed not to be a resident until the contrary is proven. Although any decent Website usually contains the details and location of the company supplying the download service, this is not always the case. Licensees can therefore be left in the dark as to the licensor's location and therefore uncertain as to the other party's tax residence.

The second problem facing licensees is that when the licensor is a nonresident of South Africa for tax purposes and the withholding tax on royalties is payable, there is usually no mechanism for the licensee to deduct the withholding tax from the payment to the licensor. Payment is usually made online by way of credit card or some other mechanism with no means of deducting the amount of the withholding tax. Even when payment is made offline by way of, for example, a bank deposit or electronic funds transfer, the licensor is unlikely to provide the licence until the licensee pays in full.

The problem here is that section 35 of the Income Tax Act holds the licensee personally liable for paying the withholding tax to the South African Revenue Service. The amount is deemed to be a tax due by that person and may be recovered from him or her pursuant to the Income Tax Act's tax recovery provision, which would potentially include the obtaining of a civil judgment, the attachment of assets, and the sequestration of his or her estate. The problem is further compounded because holding the licensee responsible for the withholding tax results in thirty-year applicable period of prescription. Section 35 provides the licensee with the right to recover from the licensor any amount of withholding tax that the licensee paid but did not deduct from the payment to the licensor. However, from a practical perspective, this is a rather useless toothless right afforded to the licensee given that the licensor may not have a presence or any assets in South Africa. In most cases relating to e-commerce transactions, the cost of enforcing this right in any other jurisdiction (and for that matter in South Africa) is likely to be prohibitive.

The effect of the above-mentioned issue is that the South African licensee is likely to be left carrying the liability for the withholding tax, even if contractually he or she is not obliged to do so. Compounding this issue is that the withholding tax on royalties that would have to be paid to the South African Revenue Service in such circumstances is not simply 12 percent of the amount paid to the licensor. In determining the amount of the withholding tax, the payment to the licensor is required to be grossed up on the basis that the payment to the licensor represents only 88 percent of the total liability. The result is that the cost of the licence to the licensee is actually 13.6 percent higher than the payment made to the licensor.

The third problem that arises relates to the enforcement of the withholding tax provisions in practice. Two considerations arise in this regard. First, the licensees are usually relatively unsophisticated end-users who, in most instances, are probably not even aware of the existence of the withholding tax on royalties or, even if they were aware of it, would have no idea that it was applicable to the transactions that they are entering into or what the requirements are. Second, the very nature of e-commerce is usually one of high-volume/low-value transactions. Although the transactions in aggregate may be of an extremely high value, the need to collect relatively small amounts of withholding tax from thousands of licensees makes enforcement extremely difficult, administratively burdensome, and cost-prohibitive. The result is that the withholding taxes usually go uncollected, and the licensors, particularly those located in offshore financial centers with little or no corporate income taxes, benefit from the difficulties of enforcing taxes in e-commerce transactions.

D. Application of Double-Taxation Agreements

As noted earlier, South Africa has numerous double-taxation agreements, many of which are based on the OECD Model Tax Convention on Income and Capital, Article 12, which grants the sole taxing rights in respect of royalties to the country of residence unless they are effectively connected with a permanent establishment of the licensor in the source country. A comprehensive analysis of the various double-taxation agreements to which South Africa is a party is beyond the scope of this chapter. However, there are a few issues that require consideration.

First, not all of the double-taxation agreements to which South Africa is a party grant sole taxing rights in respect of royalties to the country of residence. Many of these double-taxation agreements grant taxing rights to the country of source ranging from 5 percent to 10 percent of the gross amount of the royalties. Double-taxation agreements where the country of source has no taxing rights in respect of royalties, the permanent establishment exception aside, include, inter alia, those with France, Germany, Ireland, Luxembourg, Mauritius, the Netherlands, Switzerland, the United Kingdom, and the United States of America. Other countries with which South Africa has a double-taxation agreement (and their respective withholding tax rates on royalties) include, inter alia, Singapore (5%), Canada (6%), Australia, China, India, and Japan (all 10%).

Second, the definition of royalties in the double-taxation agreements does not always correspond with those amounts that are subject to the withholding tax on royalties in terms of the Income Tax Act. For example, many of the double-taxation agreements do not include the consideration for the use of software as a royalty. The result of this is that any consideration for the use of such copyrights would be dealt with as business profits rather than royalties, often with a very different outcome in terms of the allocation of taxing rights between the country of source and the country of residence.

VII. FOREIGN-CONTROLLED COMPANIES

The income of certain non resident companies in which South African tax residents own the majority of the participation rights or voting rights (foreign-controlled companies) is taxable in the hands of the South African tax residents. The provisions of section 9D of the Income Tax Act, which regulate the taxation of income of foreign-controlled companies, and the issues typical in the e-commerce environment, are discussed in the section that follows.

A. Introduction

A foreign-controlled company is a company that is not a South African tax resident in which South African tax residents, in aggregate, directly or indirectly, hold more than 50 percent of the total participation rights or voting rights. For example, if South African resident A holds 20 percent of the participation rights in a nonresident company and South African resident B holds 40 percent of such participation rights, the company will be a foreign-controlled company for South African tax purposes. Participation rights are the right to participate directly in the company's share capital, share premium, current or accumulated profits, or reserves or, where no person has such rights or such rights cannot be determined, the right to exercise any voting rights in the company.

Subject to the exclusions discussed what follows, any South African tax resident holding 10 percent or more of the participation or voting rights in a foreign-controlled company is required to include the proportional amount of the net income of that foreign-controlled company in its income for South African income tax purposes. The proportional amount is determined by the ratio of the South African tax resident's participation rights of the South African to the foreign-controlled company's total participation rights. The net income of the foreign-controlled company is usually an amount equal to the taxable income of the company determined as if it was a South African taxpayer. In other words, the net income is calculated taking into account all amounts comprising income and deductions or allowances under the Income Tax Act.

B. Exclusions

In determining the net income of a foreign-controlled company, certain amounts are excluded. Several exclusions are relevant to the context of this article.

The first, and most important, exclusion is the so-called foreign business establishment exclusion. Section 9D of the Income Tax Act defines the term "foreign business establishment" and includes, inter alia and in so far as is relevant, what can be paraphrased as a place of business with a structure that the foreign-controlled company use or will continue to use for a period of at least a year whereby the business of the company is carried on. To qualify as a foreign business establishment, that place of business must be suitably staffed with the foreign-controlled company's on-site, full-time managerial and operational employees who conduct the business' primary operations; the place of business must be suitably equipped for such purposes; and it must be located in a country other than South Africa for bona fide business purposes other than the avoidance of South African tax.

As a general rule, any amount that is attributable to such a foreign business establishment is excluded from the net income of the foreign-controlled company. However, certain amounts do not qualify for exclusion from net income under this provision. In addition to certain transactions involving connected persons in relation to the foreign-controlled company that are not relevant for purposes of this chapter and not discussed, certain types of passive income do not qualify for the exclusion from net income. The types most relevant to this article are royalties or capital gains determined in relation to the disposal or deemed disposal of any asset from which such amounts are or could be earned.

However, some relief is provided in relation to such passive income. First, when the foreign-controlled company has active income, passive income of up to 10 percent of the active income may qualify for the foreign business establishment exclusion. Second, the passive income rule does not apply in relation to amounts arising from the disposal or deemed disposal of certain intangible assets (other than those created, devised, or developed in South Africa) that formed an integral part of any business conducted by the foreign-controlled company. The intangible assets include copyrights. Third, the commissioner of the South African Revenue Service is empowered to rule that the passive income rule will be disregarded in cases where he is satisfied that such income will be subject to tax in any country other than South Africa, such that the tax thereon will be equal to at least two-thirds of the South African tax that would otherwise arise in that regard, after taking into account any double-taxation agreement and credit or tax rebate from any other country and after disregarding any assessed tax losses.

Other exclusions from net income that are potentially applicable include those in which the amount is included in the taxable income of the foreign-controlled company and has not been or will not be exempt or taxed at a reduced rate in South Africa under a double-taxation agreement. This situation arises when the income is derived from a source in or deemed to be in South Africa.

C. Issues Arising in the E-Commerce Environment

A number of issues can arise in the e-commerce environment that affects the application of the foreign-controlled company provisions. Most of these issues relate to the foreign business establishment exclusion of amounts from net income. The first involves the requirement that a foreign business establishment must be suitably staffed with on-site, full-time managerial and operational employees of the foreign-controlled company who conduct the business's primary operations. Very often in the e-commerce environment it would not be necessary for the foreign-controlled company employees to be located at its place of business for purposes of conducting the primary operations. For example, a company whose only operations relate to an Internet Website from which music can be downloaded for a fee would require few or no activities that would necessarily have to be carried out at the site at which the company's infrastructure is located. In fact, that infrastructure could consist of little more than a room containing a server that hosts the Website. Any maintenance of the Website could be done remotely from another location anywhere in the world, as could the company's other day-to-day operations. Assuming that any hardware maintenance is outsourced to a third party, such a company would not necessarily need to have any employees employed at the site at which the server is located and may therefore fail to meet this requirement for the existence of a foreign business establishment.

There is, in any event, an element of uncertainty regarding this "suitably staffed" requirement of the foreign business establishment definition. Would a company that outsources all or most of its functions relating to this place of business be suitably staffed? Given the reference to primary operations, any outsourcing of secondary or ancillary operations, such as administration or accounting, would not prevent this requirement from being met. Rather, the company must be suitably staffed with employees located at the place of business for the performance of its core operations. The test of whether or not the requirement is met is therefore largely a subjective one, with inherent uncertainty. The extent to which a company has full-time, on-site employees at such a place of business could vary from one extreme of having no employees to the other extreme of having a full-scale operation with few or no functions of the company being outsourced. At a minimum, a company would need to have one such employee located at its place of business whose function it is to perform the core operations of that place of business. However, the question of whether that place of business is suitably staffed would depend on the facts and circumstances of each case and particularly what he business's primary operations comprise. Using the example of a Website that allows users to download music for a fee, if the staffing requirement were met, at the very least the persons responsible for maintaining the Website and sourcing content may be required to be located at that place of business, unless its primary operation is to host the Website.

Another consideration in applying of the foreign business establishment definition is the requirement that there must be a place of business used by the company whereby the business of the company is carried on. When a Website is hosted by a service provider, it is doubtful that the South African Revenue Service would consider this to constitute a place of business of the foreign-controlled company. Support for this contention is to be found in the changes to the commentary on the OECD Model Tax Convention adopted by the Committee on Fiscal Affairs on December 22, 2000, concerning the application of the permanent establishment definition in e-commerce. The commentary makes it clear that a Website is merely a combination of software and electronic data and does not have a location that, in itself, constitutes a place of business. In this regard, there is a distinction between the Website and its host server. If the server is owned or leased by the foreign-controlled company, the place at which the server is located might constitute a foreign business establishment, provided that the other requirements are met.

Of course, there is no requirement that the place at which the Website is hosted must constitute a foreign business establishment, and the company may have a foreign business establishment located elsewhere. In such a situation, the question of whether the company's income is attributable to the Website or the foreign business establishment is likely to become an issue. This, of course, is a question of fact and would turn on the merits of each case. For example, if the Website's purpose is for downloading music, it may be arguable that the income should be regarded as attributable to that Website, rather than to the other relatively minor functions performed elsewhere. However, if the Website simply acts as a sales interface, the goods being sold over the Internet require physical delivery, and the company has a significant infrastructure for buying, warehousing, or delivering those goods, the outcome may be very different. For example, it would be inconceivable that a food retailer who allows customers to select and purchase its products online for delivery, but has its Website hosted in another jurisdiction, would have its income attributed to its Website rather than to its other infrastructure.

Another consideration is that the place of business must be located outside South Africa for a bona fide business purpose other than to avoid South African taxes. This is an often overlooked requirement of the definition of a foreign business establishment, but a very important one, particularly when the place of business is located in an offshore financial center offering lower tax rates than South Africa. Often, particularly in the case of groups of companies, the only purpose behind the establishment of a nonresident company and its place of business in a foreign jurisdiction is tax avoidance, and no consideration is given to the commercial rationale for such a decision. This is particularly pertinent in the e-commerce environment, given the relative ease with which such operations can be run from foreign jurisdictions.

PART II

Asia

Chapter 3

China: Taxation of E-Commerce in China

Horace King (Chaowu Jin)
Thomas Jefferson School of Law

Although China boasts the largest number of Internet users in the world, it does not yet have any specific law or regulation devoted to the taxation of e-commerce. To have a better idea of how such taxation is handled, a basic knowledge of China's tax structure and e-commerce regulation is necessary. Although e-commerce in China is hardly different in any way from that of other countries, the tax structure is considerably different; this makes the issue of taxation on e-commerce more complicated.

I. TYPES OF E-COMMERCE IN CHINA

E-Commerce has become popular in the business world, yet a precise definition of e-commerce seems to be impossible given its constant evolution. The wide use of e-mails has virtually replaced traditional means of communication such as telegraph, telex, and letters, which makes it possible for people to do their business transactions online. Generally speaking, e-commerce could be divided into the following types:

1. B2B Both the buyer and seller are business entities that take advantage of the Internet to realize the sale or purchase or provision of labor services, exchange of information, delivery of instruments, to make payments, or to complete other transactions.
2. B2C- A business sells or buys goods or services to consumers through the Internet. Typical B2C e-commerce includes online purchases made by consumers, such as the sale of music or movies for consumers to download or enjoy online.
3. C2C- Transactions occur between two independent individual consumers through the Internet not for the purpose of profit making.
4. B2G Transactions occur between enterprises and government organs.
5. C2G- An individual purchases government services.

II. THE TAX CONSEQUENCES OF E-COMMERCE

China imposes variety of taxes on the taxpayer during different points in the chain of business operations, that is, on the conduct itself, on the subject matter, or the proceedings arising from the transaction. The tax consequences for each of the above-described business models vary.

With respect to taxation, there is little difference whether an enterprise conducts business through the Internet or by traditional means, as long as it operates legally and does not evade taxes. Like in other countries, China requires all enterprises to register with the respective government authority, and enterprises have to make and receive payments through their own bank accounts rather than the bank account of an investor or manager. Enterprises are required by law to keep records of their transactions.[1] Under Chinese law on accounting and taxation, taxpayers and withholders should keep their account books according to the relevant rules. Such account books and vouchers include general ledgers, subsidiary ledgers, journal accounts, and other supplementary account books.[2] Generally speaking, the account books, vouchers, financial statements, tax payment certificates, and other relevant materials must be kept by taxpayers and withholders of taxes for no less than ten years.[3]

Because the government is generally exempted from any taxation for its ordinary exercise of administrative power, e-commerce will have very little impact on the government organs' purchases of goods or services or issuances of licenses.

III. CHALLENGES IMPOSED BY E-COMMERCE ON TAXATION

Due to the complexity of transactions resulting from the use of the Internet, some tax issues have become complex, accordingly. Such complexity arises only when a transaction has gone beyond a country's tax jurisdiction, usually, its territory. In other words, these tax problems are largely "international" problems.

A. Determining Tax Jurisdiction

In the context of international transactions, the state, which is the collector of taxes, exercises sovereignty of taxation over taxpayers. Generally speaking, there are two

1 Under the Interim Guiding Opinions of the Ministry of Commerce on Online Transactions (*shangwubu guanyu wangshang jiaoyi de zhidao yijian (zanxing)*, 商务部关于网上交易的指导意见（暂行） (Announcement no. 19 [2007]), the Ministry of Commerce also requires the parties who complete an online transaction to keep records of the transaction to serve as proof in case any dispute arises in the future.

2 Chaowu Jin, William S. Hein, The Regulatory Environment of Chinese Taxation, 44 (2006).

3 Art. 29, The Detailed Rules for the Implementation of the Law of the People's Republic of China on the Administration of Tax Collection (*zhonghua renmin gongheguo shuishou zhengshou guanli fa shishi xize*, 《中华人民共和国税收征收管理法实施细则》), promulgated by the State Council on Sept. 7, 2002.

types of tax jurisdictions: (1) personal jurisdiction and (2) territorial jurisdiction. Personal jurisdiction is exercised based on the status of the taxpayer: whether the taxpayer is a citizen or resident of the country for purposes of taxation. China taxes its citizens on their worldwide income. The resident status of a natural person could be determined by that individual's place of residence, place of abode, duration of stay, or nationality, whereas the residency of a corporate person could be determined by the place of incorporation, the place of actual management, the place of control, and the location of the corporation's headquarters. For one who is not a citizen, if that person has stayed in China for a period of time long enough so that he is treated as a resident for purposes of taxation, he may be subject to taxation on his worldwide income or his China-source income only.

Territorial jurisdiction is based on the geographical source of the taxable income, which must be reflected in some nexus between the taxpayer and the source income. For example, the nexus for income from real estate is the geographical location of the real estate; that for income from business operations is the place where the business is registered or situated; that for income from labor services is the place where the services are provided; and that for income from a stock dividend, bank deposit interest, rent, or other such income, is generally the place where that income is paid.

Whether a country taxes a sale of goods or services provided through the Internet largely depends on the type of tax jurisdiction. Most countries believe in the priority of the source-of-income jurisdiction. However, the emergence of e-commerce has made it difficult to determine the source of income. For example, in international taxation, the determination of source income is usually based on the location of an entity's permanent establishment (PE, which could be the place of management, a branch organization, office, worksite, factory, or other location. If a nonresident taxpayer has a PE in China, China would be entitled to tax the income of the PE. However, if the nonresident taxpayer only hires an agent in China to represent it in the conclusion of contracts, collection of orders, and so forth, then such agent is not treated as a PE for taxation purposes, and China will not be able to exercise tax jurisdiction over the nonresident taxpayer's income. The Internet makes it possible for nonresident taxpayers to sell their goods and services without having to establish a PE in China. This makes it hard for China to exercise tax jurisdiction over such transactions, because under the traditional standards for determining PE, the sale of goods and provision of labor services online could hardly be regarded as having established a PE in the country of sale or provision of services,[4] and thus the foreign enterprise is not subject to taxation on its sale or provision of services.

Further, the principle of personal jurisdiction also makes it difficult to determine the country with tax jurisdiction over cross-border transactions carried out through the Internet. For example, if an American software company sells its software to a Chinese user through the Internet by creating an ID and password to allow the buyer to download directly from its server in Canada, it would be impossible for the Chinese

4 Neither Article 5 of the United Nations Model Tax Convention nor Article 5 of the Organization of Economic Cooperation and Development (OECD) Model Tax Convention has expanded the definition of permanent establishment to include online sales or provision of labor services through the Internet.

government to tax the American software company.[5] According to the place-of-incorporation test, the software company is an American resident, and the U.S. government has jurisdiction over the sale; however, according to the actual-management-and-control test, the Canadian government would have jurisdiction.[6]

B. Determining Taxpayer Identity

A taxpayer could be a citizen, corporation, or any other organization. Tax laws have to specify who shall pay a defined tax to ensure their implementation. Yet, the use of the Internet has made it more complex to determine who the appropriate taxpayer is. As discussed earlier, an enterprise may find it unnecessary to create a PE in a foreign country to sell its products there if it is able to do so through the Internet. In order to solve this problem, it has been suggested that a server be treated as a resident for tax purposes. In a case involving a German corporation with a server in Switzerland, the Tax Court of Schleswig-Holstein held in 2001 that a server was a PE to which apparently substantial amounts of income should be attributed. The Federal Fiscal Court took the matter on appeal and reversed the lower court's judgment finding a tax obligation in Germany. The court, however, did not decide the question of whether the server constituted a PE. The court did not consider it necessary to address the question of PE, because the server was a passive business activity, the income from which could give rise to a possible double-taxation treaty issue, which would then result in a settlement of the Swiss and German taxes under the treaty.[7]

These government challenges to taxing sellers even exist where the foreign seller is established or where the server is located if the foreign seller collects payments through a bank account in a third country, which leaves virtually no trace for the tax authority of either the country of its incorporation or the country where the server is located.

C. Determining the Object of Taxation

The taxation object may be commodities, income, proceeds, resources, property, or conduct, among others. A specific type of tax must have its own specific taxation object.

---

5 However, if the software company delivers a CD containing the software to the Chinese buyer, it may pay a Chinese tariff, although the tax burden is ultimately assumed by the Chinese buyer.

6 There is sharp dispute with regard to whether a server would constitute a "resident." In the opinion of the author, the idea of treating a server as a resident is a bit far-fetched, because, according to *Black's Law Dictionary*, a resident is "a person who lives in a particular place" or "a person who has a home in a particular place." *See* Bryan A. Garner, Black's Law Dictionary (8th ed), Thomson, 2004). Even though the meaning of "resident" has been broadened to include business entities, it must be one that has "a mind" that can make decisions. A server is like a home; only the home owner will be treated as a resident, not the home itself. For example, if one buys a vacation home in a different country for a short holiday of ten days each year and does not rent it to other people during his or her absence, few governments would believe that the home owner is resident in that country. Similarly, a server should not be treated as a resident. It is the operator or owner of the server that should have this treatment.

7 *See* Klaus Resing, *The German Tax Treatment of Income Received from Foreign Related Entities*, available at http://www.worldlink-law.com/pdf/DP_Presentation%20Florence%202003.pdf.

For example, a property tax takes property as its object, while a conduct tax takes a certain kind of conduct as its object. Generally speaking, it is not difficult to determine the object of taxation in traditional business activities because traces are easily found, such as customs declarations or records of bank payments, based on which the value and volume of the transactions can be determined. However, business carried out in the virtual world is easily transformed into "digitized information," which makes it more difficult for the tax authority to say whether the object of the transaction is a commodity, provision of services, or a license. Accordingly, it is hard to determine the nature of the income arising therefrom; is it income from sales, income from the provision of services, or royalties from the transfer of franchises?

Additionally, it is challenging for the tax authority to determine the sales volume and revenue. For example, an enterprise may transfer its patents, know-how, software, or network services through the Internet. In this situation, there is no physical carrier for the product, and this invisibility makes it hard for the tax authority to decide whether value-added tax (VAT) should be levied on the sale of goods or business tax be levied on the transfer of intangible assets. The invisibility also makes it difficult to determine the sales volume as well. For example, if a book is sold in hard copy, it is not difficult to determine the sales volume based on the copies that have been printed. However, if the book is sold in digital form by allowing buyers to read it online or download it, it is almost impossible for the tax authority to find out the exact sales volume and sales revenue. The *PanAmSat* case may illustrate such difficulty, even though it is not an e-commerce case in the strict sense.

In April 1996, PanAmSat entered into an agreement with CCTV to provide signal transmission services to CCTV via PanAmSat's satellite. According to the agreement, CCTV had to pay service and equipment charges. In January 1999, the Beijing Municipal Administration of State Taxation, No. 2 Office of the Foreign Taxation Branch instructed CCTV to withhold income taxes on the charges it paid to PanAmSat for renting its satellite. PanAmSat complained to the Foreign Taxation Branch for administrative review of the questionable decision of the No. 2 Office. When the Foreign Taxation Branch sustained the decision of the No. 2 Office, PanAmSat lodged an action with the Beijing No. 2 Intermediate People's Court.

In the course of litigation, the No. 2 Office revoked the notice it issued to CCTV, so PanAmSat pleaded with the court for *nolle prosequi*. Four days later, however, the No. 2 Office issued a new notice, requiring CCTV to withhold taxes on the grounds that the charges it paid to PanAmSat were royalties as defined in (1) Article 11 of the U.S.-China Tax Convention,[8] (2) the Notice of the State Administration of Taxation on the Issue of Taxation of the Income Obtained by Foreign Enterprises from Leasing Their Satellite Communications Lines,[9] (3) Official Reply of the State Administration of Taxation on

---

8 *See* Art. 11, The Agreement between the Government of the United States of America and the Government of the People's Republic of China for the Avoidance of Double Taxation and the Prevention of Tax Evasion with Respect to Taxes on Income.

9 *See Notice* of the State Administration of Taxation on the Issue of Taxation of the Income Obtained by Foreign Enterprises from Leasing Their Satellite Communications Lines (*guojia shuiwu zongju guanyu waiguo qiye chuzu weixing tongxun xianlu suo qude de shouru zhengshui wenti de tongzhi*, 国家税务总局关于外国企业出租卫星通讯线路所取得的收入征税问题的通知), (no. 201 [1998]) issued Nov. 12, 1998.

the Collection of Income Tax on the Rent that PanAmSat Obtains from CCTV for Using Its Satellite Communications Line,[10] and (4) Article 6 of the Detailed Rules for the Implementation of the Law on the Income Tax of Foreign-funded Enterprises and Foreign Enterprises.[11] PanAmSat again filed an administrative reconsideration application with the Foreign Taxation Branch, which again sustained the No. 2 Office's position. On November 29, 2000, PanAmSat lodged an action with the No. 1 Intermediate People's Court against the No. 2 Office, taking CCTV as a third party. When the No. 1 Intermediate Court ruled in favor of the defendant, PanAmSat appealed the case before the Higher People's Court of Beijing Municipality, which made the final ruling to sustain the decision of the No. 1 Intermediate People's Court. This action, which lasted for almost three years and aroused international attention, also reveals the difficulty in determining the object of taxation with the emergence of new technology.

IV. THE IMPACT OF E-COMMERCE ON TAX COLLECTION AND ADMINISTRATION IN CHINA

If effective government measures are taken, it is quite possible to prevent the loss of tax revenue from e-commerce transactions. An effective suggestion seems to be to tax e-commerce at the source.[12] In e-commerce, the buyer and seller may not have met each other and may have to pay through their online bank accounts or physical bank accounts to perform the transaction. If the tax authority is able to check the bank accounts of the enterprises involved, it will be able to find traces of the online transactions and levy taxes on them. In view of the existing legal provisions, to effectively prevent the evasion of taxes, it is the author's suggestion that enterprises be taxed at the source when the online transactions are made and that the following measures be taken:

- Under the Interim Guiding Opinions of the Ministry of Commerce on Online Transactions, online business service providers should keep the various records and materials relating to online transactions and should adopt corresponding technical means to ensure their integrity, precision, and security.
- All enterprises that plan to open a bank account, whether an online bank account or not, should file an application with the competent tax authority for approval, without which banks must not open the online bank account. The enterprises' tax registration numbers must be labeled on the online bank account so as to make it easy for the tax authority to track down the transactions the enterprises make through the Internet.

---

10 Official Reply of the State Administration of Taxation on the Collection of Income Tax on the Rent That PanAmSat Obtains from CCTV for Using Its Satellite Communications Line (*guojia shuiwu zongju guanyu fanmei weixing gongsi cong zhongyang dianshitai qude weixing tongxun xianlu zujin zhengshou suodeshui wenti de pifu,* 国家税务总局关于泛美卫星公司从中央电视台取得卫星通讯线路租金征收所得税问题的批复), no. 566 [1999], issued Aug. 19, 1999.

11 *See* Art. 6, Detailed Rules for the Implementation of the Law of the People's Republic of China on Foreign-Funded Enterprises and Foreign Enterprises.

12 GUO WEIHUA, JIN CHAOWU & WANG JIN, et. al. (郭卫华、金朝武、王静等), APPROACHING THE INTERNET: LEGAL PROBLEMS AND SOLUTIONS 329 (*wangluo zhongde falv wenti jiqi duice*, 网络中的法律问题及其对策) (Beijing, Law Press, 2001).

- A tax item should be created in the settlement of accounts and the purpose of payment be specified so that each time an account is settled, the corresponding taxes are calculated, and a tax return is printed with the payment statement.[13]
- A special encrypted electronic invoice should be designed to suit the special needs of e-commerce. Whenever an online transaction is made, the seller must issue an invoice to the buyer, and send it concurrently by e-mail to the bank, without which the bank must refuse to settle the accounts for them.
- To preserve these records for future reference, the parties to an online transaction should send all the transactional records to the competent tax authority in either electronic or hard copy for purposes of tax inspection.[14]

V. THE IMPACT OF E-COMMERCE ON TAX INSPECTION

Tax inspection, a Chinese term for the Western concept "tax auditing," is a system whereby the tax authority inspects taxpayers and withholders with respect to their performance of the liability to pay or withhold taxes under the laws, regulations, and accounting rules.[15] A tax inspection may involve the following actions,

1. Inspecting the taxpayers' and withholding agents' accounting books, vouchers, statements, and other relevant information;
    - Inspecting the taxpayers' taxable commodities, goods, or other properties at the taxpayers's places where production or business operations are conducted and where goods are stored;
    - Inspecting withholding agents's operational conditions in respect of the withholding, collection, and remittance of taxes;
    - Ordering taxpayers or withholding agents to provide the documents, evidentiary materials, and other information relating to the payment of taxes or the amount of taxes withheld;
2. Making inquiries of taxpayers or withholding agents regarding questions concerning the payment of taxes or the amount of taxes withheld;
3. Inspecting the documents, vouchers, and information relating to taxable commodities, goods, or other items transported by consignment or sent by post by taxpayers at railway stations, docks, airports, postal services, and the branches thereof;
4. Inquiring, upon approval of the commissioner of a tax bureau (or a sub-bureau thereof) at the county level or above, about the deposit accounts that the taxpayers and withholding agents have opened with a bank or other financial institution.

When investigating a tax law violation, a tax authority may inquire about the savings and deposits of the defendants upon approval of the commissioner of a tax bureau

---

13 *See* Interim Guiding Opinions of the Ministry of Commerce on Online Transactions, art. III, subsection 1, item 8 on the keeping of records of online business transactions.

14 Approaching the Internet, *supra* 329–330.

15 *Id.* at 349.

(or a sub-bureau thereof) of a city divided into districts or an autonomous prefecture or a level above. The information obtained by tax authorities through inquiry must not be used for any purpose other than taxation.[16]

The provisions in the law on the collection and administration of taxes were written for traditional business operations. In e-commerce, however, the scenario would be substantially different, because the transactions are generally intangible, the contracts between the parties may exist only electronically, and the deals may be accomplished through an anonymous bank account. All these paperless operations complicate the traditional tax inspection. According to the Working Rules for Tax Inspection, as compiled by the State Administration of Taxation, there are three primary methods of tax inspection: making inquiries, reviewing accounting books and other written materials, and conducting field audits.[17] However, these three methods become difficult in the context of e-commerce. First, the audit's subject may not be easily identifiable because in e-commerce both the seller and buyer may appear pseudonymously and hide behind the platform of the ISP (i.e., Internet service provider). Even though it is advised that both parties to an online transaction make more efforts to know as much of its counterpart as possible,[18] there is no law, nor is it feasible, to provide that the parties to an online transaction must use their real names.[19] Second, an enterprise's residence, place of contract conclusion, place of contract performance, banks involved, and so forth, may be situated in different locations, making it hard for tax authorities to conduct field audits. Third, the electronic form of transactional records makes it possible for the parties concerned to alter or erase them, even if they are required by the tax authority to submit such materials for tax audit. Fortunately, this risk has been considerably reduced by the fact that enterprises are required to adopt the accounting software designated by the tax authority and file monthly statements electronically, which makes it very difficult for the enterprises to make changes unless they do so through, and upon the approval of, the tax authority.

VI. THE IMPACT OF E-COMMERCE ON SPECIFIC TAXES

China's tax system is not based on income taxes. Tax exists in all areas of business life. The following is a discussion of the effects of e-commerce on some of the major types of taxes in China.

---

16 Law of the People's Republic of China on the Collection and Administration of Taxes, art. 54.

17 *See* Art. 22, Working Rules for Tax Inspection (*shuiwu jicha gongzuo guicheng*, 税务稽查工作规程), issued by the State Administration of Taxation by Notice no. 266 on Dec. 1, 1995.

18 *See* Art. III, subsection 1, item 2, Interim Guiding Opinions of the Ministry of Commerce on Online Transactions (*shangwubu guanyu wangshang jiaoyi de zhidao yijian (zanxing)*,《商务部关于网上交易的指导意见（暂行）), (Announcement no. 19 [2007]).

19 Due to the recent suicide of Choi Jin-sil, a famous Korean movie star, who killed herself because she could not tolerate a rumor that was widely spread on the Internet, the Korean ruling party lawmakers decide d, as is reported, to amend the cyber law so as to ensure that all Web sites with 100,000 clicks or more must have the real identity of the visitors. This act is nicknamed the "Choi Jin-sil Act." *See* http://www.individual.com/story.php?story=89577008 (last visited 10/06/2008) and http://ent.sina.com.cn/s/j/2008-10-06/02012193066.shtml (last visited 10/06/2008).

A. The Impact of E-Commerce on VAT

VAT is a tax imposed on the entities and individuals engaged in the sale of goods, provision of processing, repair and replacement services, and the importation of goods within the territory of the People's Republic of China.[20] All payers of VAT must apply to the competent authority for industry and commerce for the status of a qualified ordinary taxpayer of VAT or a small-scale taxpayer of VAT.[21] Because the balance between the output taxes and input taxes is the real amount that a taxpayer has to pay to the tax office, and all VAT must be supported by special VAT invoices,[22] all taxpayers have the incentive to obtain special invoices when they make a purchase. E-Commerce should have very little impact on the VAT itself as long as the enterprise does not try to evade taxes. The claim that paperless transactions make it impossible to levy the VAT is fatuous because tax evasion does not depend on the paperlessness of transactions.[23] Overloaded paperwork may not help if the taxpayer intends to evade the taxes; it could resort to other illegal means such as fabricating invoices and purchasing invoices from illegal channels. On the other hand, if the enterprise operates lawfully, even if it sells all its products through the Internet, it is difficult to avoid paying VAT.

However, sometimes the offline sale of traditional products may cause a problem when they are sold online. For example, computer software, music CDs, books, pictures, and similar media are tangible when they are sold offline, but they can also be sold online by allowing buyers to download directly from the server. In the case of offline sale, the seller is subject to VAT of 17 percent of the sales revenue, while in the case of online sale, it could be treated as a transfer of intangible assets which is subject to 5 percent business tax. How can this conflict be solved? It is suggested that VAT be levied on the offline sale of tangible goods (CDs, books, etc.), and business tax be levied on the online sale in the form of downloads rather than concluding electronic contracts online for the sale and deliver the tangible goods (CDs and books, pictures, etc.) to the buyer offline.[24]

---

20 Interim Regulation on the VAT, art. 1.

21 *See* Art. 3 & 4, Measures for the Small-Scale Taxpayers of VAT (*zengzhishui xiaoguimo nashuiren zhengshou guanli banfa*, 增值税小规模纳税人征收管理办法), issued by the State Administration of Taxation no. 116 on April 23, 1994; and Art. 1, Measures for the Determination of Ordinary Taxpayers of VAT (*zengzhishui yiban nashuiren shenqing rending banfa*, 增值税一般纳税人申请认定办法), issued by the State Administration of Taxation no. 59 on March 15, 1994.

22 It is important to note that invoices play a significant role in tax administration in China. Unlike in many Western countries, which allow taxpayers to print and issue invoices by themselves, invoices are exclusively designed and printed by the tax authorities, and no one except qualified taxpayers may purchase blank invoices from the tax offices. The administration of blank special VAT invoices is even more rigid. For more information about the special role of the invoices in the tax administration, please *see* CHAOWU JIN, WILLIAM S. HEIN, THE REGULATORY ENVIRONMENT OF CHINESE TAXATION 49–52 (2001).

23 For this claim, see Ma Liying (马丽颖), *Tax-Related Legal Disputes of E-Commerce and Their Possible Solutions* (*dianzi shangwu sheshui falv chongtu jiqi jiejue fang'an tantao,* 电子商务涉税法律冲突及其解决方案探讨), 3 JOURNAL OF THE CENTRAL UNIVERSITY FOR NATIONALITIES (Philosophy and Social Sciences Edition) 19 (2004).

24 Lei Chao (雷超), THE CHALLENGES AND IMPACTS OF E-COMMERCE ON CHINA'S VAT LAW AND THEIR SOLUTIONS (*dianzi shangwu dui woguo zengzhi shuifa de chongji, yingxiang he duice,*

B. The Impact of E-Commerce on Business Tax

The business tax is levied on those enterprises that provide labor services in certain areas not subject to VAT, assign intangible assets, or sell real property inside the People's Republic of China.[25] In the context of e-commerce carried out through the Internet, it is very likely that individuals will not pay the business tax because those transactions may not be noticed by the tax authorities.[26] However, if enterprises provide taxable labor services or transfer intangible assets, for example, patent, copyright, or know-how, the likelihood of taxation increases considerably because businesses are required by law to withhold business tax when payments for these services are made.[27] Nonetheless, even individuals will find it difficult to avoid the business tax when they assign real property,[28] because the assignment is not effective until the title has been transferred to the buyer at the relevant government authority, which generally requires that they have paid the business and individual income taxes before transferring the title in order to complete the assignment.

C. The Impact of E-Commerce on Consumption Tax

The consumption tax is an indirect tax levied on some consumer goods and consumption activities. The consumer goods and consumption activities are those listed in the Table of Consumption Tax Items and Rates as appended to the Detailed Rules for the Implementation of the Consumption Tax.[29] The following consumer goods and consumption activities subject to consumption tax:

- Cigarettes
- Alcohol and alcoholic drinks
- Cosmetics
- Skin-care and hair-care products
- Valuable jewels, gems, and jade
- Firecrackers and fireworks
- Gasoline

电子商务对我国增值税法的冲击、影响和对策), INTERNATIONAL TAXATION IN CHINA (*shewai shuiwu*, 涉外税务) 50 no. 6, 2000).

25 *Interim Regulation on the Business Tax*, art. 1.

26 It is difficult for an enterprise to avoid business tax unless it chooses to evade it by creating a pseudonymous bank account and has buyers or transferees pay the pseudonymous bank account or pay in cash, which it then puts in the pseudonymous bank account. *See* discussion hereafter.

27 *Interim Regulation on the Business Tax*, art. 11.

28 The assignment of real property is not exactly the same concept as the sale of real property in Western countries, because real property consists of both land and the buildings on the land. According to Chinese law, land is owned by the state or the villagers' committees, and anyone else can only have the right to use the land for a certain period of time. Such land-use rights can only be assigned rather than "sold," even though it is by nature a "sale."

29 Detailed Rules for the Implementation of the Interim Regulation on the Consumption Taxation, art. 2.

- Diesel oil
- Vehicle tires
- Motorcycles
- Mini-cars

From this list we could see that consumption tax is hardly affected by e-commerce because none of these consumer goods can be produced electronically on a server. The online conclusion of electronic contracts for the purchase of raw materials or sale of finished products would not help the maker or manufacturer to avoid the consumption tax.

D. The Impact of E-Commerce on Individual Income Tax

The impact of e-commerce on taxation of individuals is obvious. The Internet enables individuals to work online and provide their labor services in exchange for money. Unless there is an employment relationship between such individual and an enterprise so that the enterprise pays the individual a salary, or if the enterprise pays the individual out of its bank account, there may be no way for the tax offices to find out who has been paid, and for what. Unlike the United States, individual income tax is not paid annually on all of the individual's income; instead, it is levied on the different categories of income at different tax rates with different legal requirements. Under Chinese tax law, the incomes of individuals subject to individual income tax are classified into the following categories:

Category of Income	*Rates*	*Remarks*
Wages & salaries	5%–45%	Divided into 9 brackets
Income of individual industrial and commercial households (IICHs)	5%–35%	Divided into 5 brackets
Income from contracting or leasing operations	5%–35%	Divided into 5 brackets
Authorship remunerations (royalties)	20%	Actual rate of 14% after 30% off the taxes payable
Royalties from franchises, deposit interest, stock interest, dividends, bonuses, lease of property, assignment of property, fortuitous income, and other income	20%	
Income from provision of labor services	20%–40%	Divided into 3 brackets

From the preceding table one can see that, with the help of the Internet, an individual may be able to obtain income from authorship remunerations for his publications overseas, license his franchises to licensees overseas, obtain dividends from overseas investment, lease or sell his property located overseas, or even provide labor services to people overseas and, thus leave no evidence inside China for the tax office to find to tax him.

E. The Impact of E-Commerce on the Stamp Tax

The impact of e-commerce on the stamp tax could be the most conspicuous one of all. The stamp tax is a kind of tax levied on entities and individuals that create, use, or obtain instruments of legal validity in their business activities and exchanges.[30] Under the Chinese stamp tax law, the following categories of documents are taxable documents:

1. Contracts or documents in the nature of a contract with regard to purchase or sale, the undertaking of processing, contracting for construction projects, property leasing, commodity transport, warehousing loans, property insurance, and technology contracts
2. Documents transferring property rights
3. Business account books
4. Certificates proving rights or licenses
5. Other documents that the Ministry of Finance determines to be taxable[31]

To pay stamp tax, a taxpayer has to buy stamps from the tax authority and put them on the taxable documents. Normally, stamps are pasted to a document's cover page or signature page. Once the stamps or receipts are affixed, they can be invalidated by either chopping a seal on the stamps or writing horizontal pen strokes across the face of the stamps. However, in the context of e-commerce, the stamp tax is generally avoided when the contract exists only electronically. Of course, the stamp tax on other documents, for example, accounting books, certificates providing rights or licenses, documents on transferring property rights cannot be avoided because they are invariably required to exist in hard copy.

VII. CONCLUSION

The rise of the Internet has made it possible for people to do business online. This new technology has imposed challenges to taxation. Such challenges mostly exist in international transactions, although they also affect taxation of domestic transactions. E-Commerce has made it difficult for the tax authority to determine, sometimes, which government has jurisdiction over a transaction, particularly with respect to determining whether a PE has been established in the country of the sale of goods or provision of services. E-Commerce also makes it difficult to determine the nature of an income to which to attribute different types of taxes, and the appropriate taxpayers. The paperless nature of e-commerce has increased the difficulty of collecting and administering taxes as well as tax auditing. The specific major types of taxes in China that are affected by e-commerce include the VAT, business tax, individual income tax, and stamp tax.

---

30 Chaowu Jin, William S. Hein, The Regulatory Environment of Chinese Taxation 349 (2006).

31 Interim Regulation on the Stamp Tax, art. 2.

Chapter 4

India: India E-Commerce Taxation

Professor William H. Byrnes, IV & Christopher M. Sove
Thomas Jefferson School of Law

I. INTRODUCTION

Indian tax law does not include particular provisions governing the taxation of e-commerce transactions. E-Commerce transactions are taxed under the same law as traditional transactions. However, the application of the Income Tax Act to e-commerce transactions is often challenging, requiring Indian courts and the Authority for Advance Rulings to reframe e-commerce transactions as traditional transactions and stretch the language of the Income Tax Act to apply to transactions in the new media.

II. DOMESTIC TAX LAW

A. Introduction

The Central Indian Government levies an income tax, service tax, customs duties, and a central excise tax. The states and territories levy a value-added tax (VAT) or sales tax and other taxes. The Indian Income Tax Act (ITA), Central Board of Revenue rules, rulings from the Authority for Advance Rulings, international treaties, and case law govern taxation in India.

B. Income Tax

1. In General India assesses an income tax against the "total income" of resident and nonresident persons.[1]

---

1 Income Tax Act § 4(1) (1961).

Every item of income is classified under a "head of income." The heads of income include salaries, income from house property, profits and gains of business or profession, capital gains, and income from other sources.[2] The calculation of total income includes deductions against gross income, which reduce total income.[3] Aggregate deductions may not exceed gross income.[4] Deductions are different for income generated under each head of income. Generally, the greatest range of deductions applies against income classified as "profits and gains of business or profession."[5]

2. *Residency*

A. DEFINITIONS A person is an Indian resident for a particular tax year if that person (1) is in India for an aggregate period of 182 days or more in the tax year, or (2) is in India for an aggregate period of at least 60 days in the tax year and was present in India for at least 365 days in the four years preceding the tax year.[6]

A person is "not ordinarily resident" in India for a particular tax year if the person has been a nonresident for nine of the past ten years preceding the tax year or has been present in India for 729 days or fewer in the seven years preceding the tax year.[7]

A company is a resident of India for a tax year if (1) the company is an Indian company, or (2) the company's control and management was situated wholly in India for the tax year.[8]

B. TAXATION BASED ON RESIDENCY STATUS An Indian resident's total income includes their worldwide income "from whatever source derived." Thus, a resident's income need not be received in India to be subject to the income tax. An Indian resident's total income includes income received in India, income "accruing or arising in India," and income "accruing or arising outside India."[9]

The total income of a person who is not ordinarily resident in India does not include foreign source income unless the income is derived from an Indian company.[10] A non-resident's total income includes income received in India and income "accruing or arising" in India.[11] India's domestic tax law applies to nonresidents when the domestic tax law is more beneficial to the taxpayer.[12] Income is deemed to accrue or arise in India when it comes directly or indirectly from any business connection in India. Additionally, the ITA enumerates categories of income that are deemed to accrue or arise in India. Of particular relevance to e-commerce transactions is income from

---

2 Income Tax Act §§ 14-59. Some types of income are excluded from the calculation of total income. Income Tax Act, § 10-13A.

3 Income Tax Act § 80A-80VV.

4 Income Tax Act § 80A(2).

5 Income Tax Act §§ 28-44DB.

6 Income Tax Act § 6(1).

7 Income Tax Act § 5(6).

8 Income Tax Act § 3.

9 Income Tax Act § 5(1).

10 Income Tax Act § 5(1) (flush language).

11 Income Tax Act § 5(2).

12 Income Tax Act § 90(2).

royalties, "income by way of fees paid for technical services," and income accruing or arising from a business connection in India.[13]

3. *Source Rules*

A. INTRODUCTION The Indian government taxes some types of income based on the source of the income. Of particular importance to e-commerce is the source-based taxation of fees for royalties, fees for technical services, and income from a business connection in India.

B. FEES FOR ROYALTIES

i. In General Nonresident companies will be taxed in India, and tax must be withheld at the source, if payments to the nonresident are classified as royalties. Indian taxation authorities have interpreted the term "royalties" very broadly. Of particular relevance in e-commerce is the fact that, in some cases, companies without a presence in India may be subject to income tax in India when their income is classified as fees for royalties. "Income by way of royalty payable by" the government or a resident person is deemed to accrue or arise in India, and is thus included in the recipient's total income. An exception is made for royalties payable to a resident for a "right, property, or information used or services" used for carrying on business or a profession outside of India or for making money outside of India. Such royalty payments to a resident person will not be deemed to arise or accrue in India.[14] Royalty payments payable by a nonresident are deemed to arise or accrue in India when the "right, property, or information used or services" associated with the payment will be used by the payor to carry on a business or profession in India or for the purpose of earning income in India.

The ITA provides that the following types of payments will be classified as royalties:[15]

(i) [T]he transfer of rights in respect of a patent, invention, model, design, secret formula or process or trade mark or similar property;
(ii) [T]he imparting of any information concerning the working of, or the use of, a patent, invention, model, design, secret formula or process or trade mark or similar property;
(iii) [T]he use of any patent, invention, model, design, secret formula or process or trade mark or similar property;
(iv) [T]he imparting of any information concerning technical, industrial, commercial or scientific knowledge, experience or skill;
(iva) [T]he use or right to use any industrial, commercial or scientific equipment;
(v) [T]he transfer of all or any rights (including the granting of a license) in respect of any copyright, literary, artistic or scientific work including films or video tapes for use in connection with television or tapes for use in connection with radio broadcasting, but not including consideration for the sale, distribution or exhibition of cinematographic films; or
(vi) [T]he rendering of any services in connection with the activities referred to in sub-clauses (i) to (iv), (iva) and (v).

---

13 Income Tax Act § 9(1)(i).
14 Income Tax Act § 9(3)(b).
15 Income Tax Act § 8(1).

Subsections (iv) and (iva) are particularly relevant to e-commerce transactions. The Indian courts and the Authority for Advance Rulings have interpreted these provisions in an extraordinarily broad manner.

ii. Payments for Use of Satellites and Web Portals The Indian authorities do not view Web portals and satellites as mere conduits through which information passes. Rather they classify satellites and Web portals as scientific equipment or a process, or may classify the payments as payments for services associated with the process or equipment. As a result, when a resident of India makes a payment to a nonresident for access to or use of a satellite or Web portal, the payment will often be classified as a royalty under the ITA section 9(1)(iva). Thus, the nonresident may be liable for income tax in India, even when the nonresident has no direct contact with India.

Two of these decisions are examined here in detail. Fees for accessing a Web portal and fees for access to a satellite transponder have been held to be royalties, even when the company receiving the fees has no direct connection with India. Based on these decisions, it is likely that many Web portals and e-commerce sites will be taxed on fees they receive for access to their servers and for the provision of services in connection with their Web portals.

iii. Taxation of Fees for Satellite Access under Domestic Law The Indian Income Tax Appellate Tribunal has held that satellite operators who receive fees for broadcasting television programs into India are subject to the income tax, even if the satellite operator is a nonresident and payments are made by a nonresident.[16]

Asia Satellite Telecommunications Co. Ltd. (AST), a Hong Kong resident, owned satellites orbiting in a United States orbital slot. AST leased some of its transponder capacity to television channels that produced television content intended to be disseminated into India. India was included in the geographical area that could receive a signal from AST's satellite. AST did not have any control over the signals and had no rights to the signals. AST did not operate in India and had no agents or establishments in India. Hong Kong does not have a double-taxation avoidance agreement (DTAA) with India. The television channels leasing transponder capacity from AST received most of their advertising revenue from advertisements originating in India, but the channels were not Indian residents. However, most of the television programs carried by the television stations were filmed in India using Indian actors. The court held the following:

1. AST did not have a business connection in India and could not be taxed by virtue of having a business connection in India. A business connection must involve "an intimate relationship between trading activity carried on outside India and trading activity within India." The court found that AST did not have such a relationship.
2. The fees paid to AST by the television companies for use of AST's satellites constituted royalty payments taxable in India. The TV channels were using the process

16 Asia Satellite Telecommunication Co. Ltd v. Dy. CIT, 85 ITD 478 Delhi (2003) (hereinafter Asia Satellite Telecomm.

provided by AST. Under the ITA, "royalty" includes consideration for the use of any process.[17] They held that whether the TV channels used the process provided by AST, or services in connection with the process, either fell within the definition of "royalty."

3. The TV channels used AST's process for the purpose of carrying on their business in India. Royalty payments include payments by a nonresident where "the royalty is payable in respect of any . . . services utilized for the purposes of a business or profession carried on by such person in India or earning any income from any source in India."[18]
4. The statutory test for determining the place of accrual is not the place where the services for which the payments are being made are rendered, but rather the place where the services are utilized. The nonresident TV channels utilized the services of AST for earning income from advertisers and cable operators being the source in India by ultimately relaying the programs in the Indian territories.

iii. Web-Portal Access Fees Taxable as Royalties The Indian Authority for Advance Ruling (AAR) issued a 2007 decision that subjected a foreign-based, nonresident Web portal to the Indian income tax. The AAR held that payments made by Indian persons for the use of a foreign Web portal enabling them to book cargo space on commercial flights are royalties. The payments are taxable in India and thus subject to deduction at the source.

The applicant, Ezycargo, provided a Web portal called Ezycargo, which enabled customers to access airline schedules and available cargo space. Subscribers to the Ezycargo Web portal are charged a subscription fee, connection fees, and support fees. Ezycargo's portal translates English requests into "Cargo IMP"[19] and also translates information provided by airlines from Cargo IMP to English. Agents are able to book flights though the portal. The portal also provides agents with status reports.

Ezycargo opened a liaison office in India that acts as a communication channel between India and the head office. The liaison office does not conduct any commercial activities or provide consultancy or other services. The expenses of the liaison office are met directly by the Singapore head office, although the liaison office does maintain a bank account in India. The two employees stationed in India receive messages between Indian subscribers and the Singapore head office. Agents make subscription payments directly to the Singapore head office. Agents are given a password to the portal. Software is not installed on the agents' computers. The company provides an Indian help desk, and also provides training on the use of the system.

In reaching their decision, the AAR emphasized the technical means by which the Ezycargo portal functioned and the services it provided to customers. They focused on what they perceived as sophisticated services that were offered to subscribers by the server. They characterized the Singapore-based server as scientific equipment,

17 Income Tax Act § 9(1)(vi) expln. 2.

18 Income Tax Act § 9(1)(vi)(c).

19 Cargo-IMP is a messaging protocol that facilitates electronic transmission of information between trading partners.

and considered the fees Indian agents paid for access to the server as royalties under the ITA.

India's DTAA with Singapore and the ITA include identical language defining royalties and fees for technical services. Royalties include "the use or right to use any industrial, commercial or scientific equipment." Fees for technical services" include payments made in consideration for "services of a managerial, technical, or consultancy nature."[20] The AAR classified the server as "scientific equipment, authorized to be used for commercial purposes," thus bringing fees paid for access to the server squarely within the definition of "royalties" found in the ITA.[21]

Note that Advance Rulings may only be relied on (1) by the applicant who sought the ruling with respect to the transaction for which the applicant sought the ruling, and (2) by the commissioner with respect to the taxpayer and the transaction for which the ruling is sought.[22] Although Advance Rulings may not be relied on by third parties, they provide a useful guide for deciphering how the Indian authorities classify and tax particular types of transactions.

C. FEES FOR TECHNICAL SERVICES Income from fees for technical services is deemed to arise in India when paid by any of the following:[23]

1. The Indian Government
2. An Indian resident, except when the fees are paid for the purpose of running a business or earning income outside of India
3. A nonresident, when the fees are paid for the purpose of running a business or earning income within India

"Fees for technical services" mean "any consideration . . . for the rendering of any managerial, technical or consultancy services . . . but does not include consideration for any construction, assembly, and mining or like project undertaken by the recipient or consideration which would be income of the recipient chargeable under the head Salaries."[24]

D. BUSINESS CONNECTION Income accruing or arising, directly or indirectly, from any business connection in India is deemed to accrue or arise in India.[25] But when some of a business's operations are carried on outside of India, only income reasonably attributable to operations in India is deemed to accrue or arise in India.[26] A nonresident is

---

20 Agreement for Avoidance of Double Taxation and Prevention of Fiscal Evasion with Singapore, India-Singapore, Aug. 8, 1994, India Income Tax Department § 41 (1961).

21 *See* A.A.R. no. 670 of 2006 (Nov. 6, 2006), available at http://www.bcasonline.org/ContentType/Contentin.asp?1538.

22 Income Tax Act § 245S(1).

23 Income Tax Act § 1(vii).

24 Income Tax Act § 9(i)(vii), expln. 2.

25 Income Tax Act § 9(1)(i).

26 Income Tax Act § 9(1)(i)(a).

deemed to have a business connection with India where that person carries on business through another person who acts on behalf of the nonresident and[27]

1. Regularly concludes contracts on behalf of the nonresident (except when those contracts are exclusively for the purchase of goods);
2. Does not have such authority, but maintains a stock of goods in India for the nonresident and consistently delivers those good on behalf of the nonresident; or
3. Regularly secures orders for the nonresident, or secures orders for the nonresident and other nonresidents controlled by, controlling, or subject to the same common control as the nonresident.

4. Income Tax Rates Fees for royalties and technical services paid to the Indian government are taxed at 10 percent, without any allowance for deductions.[28] Fees for royalties or technical services received from a nonresident are not taxed at the rate for royalties when the activities giving rise to such fees qualify as "business." The fees are taxed at the same rate as business profits, with an allowance for deductions.[29] The Indian taxation authorities have not considered the rate of tax for fees paid to a non-resident, when the activity giving rise to the fees does not qualify as business. Presumably, the fees will be taxed as "income from other sources."

Fees for technical services are taxed as business profits when the applicable DTAA does not have a separate provisions covering fees for technical services.[30] After May 31, 2007, fees for royalties and technical services are taxed at 10 percent, without any allowance for deductions.[31] The income tax rate for companies is 30 percent, plus a 10 percent surcharge on income in excess of ten million rupees, and an education cess of 3 percent, chargeable on the tax payable.[32]

C. Service Tax

1. Introduction The service tax applies to anyone who renders, in India, any of the over 100 services enumerated in clause 105 of the Finance Act of 1994. Anyone liable to pay the service tax must register as a taxable service provider with the jurisdictional Central Excise Office. The service tax rate is 12 percent[33] plus a 3 percent education cess (levied on the amount of the 12% tax), for an effective tax rate of 12.36 percent.[34] The person providing services is responsible for paying the service tax. There is a 10 lakh rupees exemption from the service tax. The exemption does not apply to

27 Income Tax Act § (1)(i)(expln.2).
28 Income Tax Act § 115(A).
29 Asia Satellite Telecomm, 85 ITD 478 Delhi, at 24–25.
30 A.A.R. no. 750 (2007).
31 Income Tax Act § 115(A).
32 The education cess (tax) is used to fund education projects.
33 Finance Act (1994), as amended by the Finance Bill (2008), § 66.
34 Finance Bill (2008) §§ 11, 12.

"services provided by a person under a brand name or trade name of another person."[35] Exported services are exempt from the service tax. Services will be treated as exported services if the services are provided from India and used outside India, and payment for the services is received in convertible foreign exchange. If service tax is paid on exported services, the tax may be refunded.[36] Some of the taxable services relevant to e-commerce are services rendered

1. To a customer, by a commercial concern, in relation to online information and database access or retrieval or both in electronic form through computer network, in any manner;[37]
2. To any person, by any other person in relation to information technology software for use in the course, or furtherance, of business or commerce;[38]
3. To any person, by any other person, in relation to Internet telecommunication service;[39]
4. To any person, by any other person in relation to sale of space or time for advertisement, in any manner.[40]

2. Service Tax on Information Technology Software Services One of the enumerated classes of services subject to the service tax is service provided "to any person in relation to information technology software for use in the course, or furtherance, of business or commerce."[41]

"Information technology software" is defined by the Finance Act as "any representation of instructions, data, sound or image, including source code and object code, recorded in a machine readable form, and capable of being manipulated or providing interactivity to a user, by means of a computer or an automatic data processing machine or any other device or equipment."[42] The types of services relating to "information technology software" that will be taxed under the act include a wide range of activities that are essential to e-commerce. The act states that taxable services include services provided[43]

> to any person, by any other person in relation to information technology software for use in the course, or furtherance, of business or commerce, including,
>
> (i) development of information technology software,
> (ii) study, analysis, design and programming of information technology software,
> (iii) adaptation, up-gradation, enhancement, implementation and other similar services related to information technology software,

35 Finance Act § 93; no. 8 (2008-Service Tax).
36 Finance Act, Export of Service Rules § 3(2) (2005).
37 Export of Service Rules § 65(105) (zh).
38 Export of Service Rules § 65(105)(zzzze).
39 Export of Service Rules § 65(105) (zzzu).
40 Export of Service Rules § 65(105)(zzzm).
41 Export of Service Rules § 65(105)(zzzze).
42 *Id.*
43 *Id.*

(iv) providing advice, consultancy and assistance on matters related to information technology software, including conducting feasibility studies on implementation of a system, specifications for a database design, guidance and assistance during the start-up phase of a new system, specifications to secure a database, advice on proprietary information technology software,

(v) acquiring the right to use information technology software for commercial exploitation including right to reproduce, distribute and sell information technology software and right to use software components for the creation of and inclusion in other information technology software products, and

(vi) acquiring the right to use information technology software supplied electronically.

3. Service Tax on Internet Telecommunication Services Internet Telecommunication services are subject to the service tax, and they include[44] "(i) internet backbone services, including carrier services of internet traffic by one Internet Service Provider to another Internet Service Provider; (ii) internet access services, including provision of a direct connection to the internet and space for the customer's web page; (iii) provision of telecommunication services, including fax, telephony, audio conferencing and video conferencing, over the internet."

4. Service Tax on the Sale of Advertising Space The sale of space or time for non-print advertising, including Web advertising, is taxed as the provision of services. "Sale of space or time" includes "providing space or time, as the case may be, for display, advertising, showcasing of any product or service in video programmes, television programmes or motion pictures or music albums, or on billboards, public places, buildings, conveyances, cell phones, automated teller machines, and internet."[45]

Companies selling Web advertising space to other businesses have taxable service income under the foregoing provision. In a 2005 ruling, the AAR held that the service tax applies to Google on the sale of advertising space to Indian residents through its Ad Sense program. "Sale of space for advertisement" includes "providing space or time, as the case may be, for display, advertising, showcasing of any product or service . . . on the Internet."[46]

Under the 2006 amendments to the Finance Act, companies like Google are clearly liable for revenue generated through the sale of space on their Web site for advertising. It is not so clear whether Indian resident subscribers to programs such as Google AdSense, Yahoo Publisher Network, and Microsoft ContentAds are liable for the service tax on revenue generated by Google ads placed on their Web sites. Because the subscriber is providing Google with space for advertisement, it is likely that Indian taxation authorities will view subscribers as being subject to the service tax.

---

44 Finance Act § 57(a).

45 Export of Service Rules § 65(105)(zzzm).

46 Finance Act (1994), as amended by Finance Act (2006) § 105(zzzm)(expln.1).

III. TREATY LAW

A. Introduction

The Income Tax Act gives the Indian government the power to enter into DTAAs with foreign governments.[47] The Indian government has entered into DTAAs with a number of foreign governments, including the United States, Russia, the United Kingdom, Singapore, Australia, and others. India's DTAAs are generally based on the U.N. Model Double Taxation Convention.

B. Permanent Establishments and E-Commerce

1. In General Business income is taxable in India if the income is attributable to a permanent establishment in India. A nonresident person may be taxed in India even if the nonresident does not have a physical presence in India. For instance, the Income Tax Appellate Tribunal has held that nonresident companies operating reservation systems servicing Indian residents are subject to the income tax under Indian treaty law (and domestic law).

Under India's (DTAAs), the business profits of a nonresident may only be taxed in India if the profits are attributable to a permanent establishment in India. The definition of "permanent establishment" (PE) under India's DTAAs is generally consistent with the definition found in the UN Model Convention. Included in the definition of PE is a person, other than an independent agent, who has the authority to, and does habitually, conclude contracts in the name of the nonresident person. Also included is a person authorized to, and who habitually does, keep a stock of goods for the nonresident and regularly delivers the goods on behalf of the nonresident.[48]

2. Motorola/Ericsson/Nokia In a combined ruling, the Special Bench of the Delhi Tribunal answered the question of whether income from the sale of software and equipment to Indian cellular operators was taxable as business income attributable to a PE in India.[49]

A. ERICSSON Ericsson entered into a contract with ten Indian cellular operators to supply telecommunication equipment and software (the system). The cellular operators also entered into short-term contracts with an Indian Ericsson subsidiary to install the system. Ericsson and the Indian subsidiary had a marketing agreement. Ericsson employees entered India to negotiate contracts, determine placement of the network, and collect payments from the cellular operators. Ericsson employees were also assigned to the subsidiary to assist with the installation of the system. Ericsson, its

47 Income Tax Act § 90.

48 *See* Convention for the Avoidance of Double Taxation and the Prevention of Fiscal Evasion with Respect to Taxes on Income, India-Austria, Nov. 8, 1999, art. 5.

49 Motorola, Nokia, Ericson v. CIT, 2005-TIOL-103-ITAT-DEL-SB (2005).

Indian subsidiary, a branch of an Ericsson group company, and the cellular operators entered into contracts to coordinate the supply of the system and its installation. The contract between Ericsson and the cellular operators specified that the system would be supplied outside of India (with title and risk passing outside India), the supply contract was negotiated in India by Ericsson employees, and the acceptance test was to be conducted by Ericsson's Indian subsidiary. The test was to be binding on Ericsson.

The court held that Ericsson, its Indian subsidiary, and branch were conducting business independently, as independent entities, and that the branch and subsidiary were not PEs of Ericsson. The supply, installation, and overall contracts were held to be three separate agreements. Ericsson was found not to have a fixed place of business or PE in India. Although Ericsson had an overall responsibility to ensure that the system was installed properly, the subsidiary and branch entered into separate installation contracts with the cellular operators. Thus, Ericsson was held not to have an installment PE in India,[50] because the subsidiary and branch facilities were not available for Ericsson employees in India.[51] Also, the court held that since the branch and subsidiary were independent, they were not agents of Ericsson, and thus Ericsson did not have an agency PE in India. Additionally, all contracts were completed by Ericsson, and the Indian subsidiary and branch were not authorized to conclude contracts on Ericsson's behalf.[52] The Indian subsidiary and branch did not maintain a stock of goods and did not secure orders for Ericsson.[53]

B. MOTOROLA The facts in the Motorola case were similar, except that the contract risk was deemed to pass inside India. Also, Motorola's employees used the subsidiary's offices while in India. Motorola's Indian subsidiary entered into a service contract with Motorola. The contract was to be performed for the year prior to the start of business in India.

In contrast to Ericsson, the court held that the fact that risk passed in India did not necessarily mean that the sale occurred in India. The court held that the service contract was of a preparatory or auxiliary character and thus did not constitute a PE under the India-U.S. DTAA. The court did hold, however, that the offices of the subsidiary were a fixed place of business in India for Motorola since Motorola employees were able to use the subsidiary's offices while in India. Thus, Motorola had a fixed place of business in India.

C. NOKIA Here, Nokia assigned installation contracts to its Indian liaison office. The subsidiary in this case was a 100 percent subsidiary of Nokia that supported Nokia in fulfilling the terms of its agreements. Nokia, its subsidiary, and the liaison office had a common employee. The supply contract was signed by the common employee, who thereafter became the managing director of the subsidiary. Also, the installation

---

50 Agreement for Avoidance of Double Taxation and Prevention of Fiscal Evasion, India-Sweden, Dec. 17, 1997, art. 5(3).

51 *Id.* Art. 5(4).

52 *Id.* Art. 5(6)(a).

53 *Id.* Art. 5(6)(b), (c).

contracts were transferred to the subsidiary, which had no experience with installation. Otherwise, the facts are similar to those in Ericsson. The liaison office was held not to be a PE for Motorola since the work it completed was preliminary and preparatory. In contrast, the subsidiary was held to be a PE of Nokia since, as a 100 percent subsidiary that entered into contracts with Motorola that were not at arm's length, the subsidiary operated as an extension of Nokia in India.

3. Computer Reservation System as Permanent Establishment The Income Tax Appellate Tribunal (ITAT) has held that operation of a computer reservation system servicing India constitutes a PE under the India-U.S. DTAA. Galileo International operated an electronic reservation system allowing travel agents to book flights, hotel rooms, ground transportation, and tours. The network through which the system operated was provided by a third party, and Galileo contracted with another party to market and distribute the reservation system to Indian travel agents. Hardware used for accessing the system was installed on travel agents' computers.[54]

Galileo claimed that information was merely displayed on the agents' computers in India. The ITAT disagreed, holding that the company had a direct business connection with India that gave rise to income tax liability under the ITA. The ITAT also held that Galileo was taxable under the U.S.-Indian DTAA. In their view, Galileo's reservation system partially existed on the agents' computers in India. In some cases, Galileo had the computers installed at the agents' offices, and the agents were not free to move the systems from one office to another or even within an office. Thus, the ITAT held that Galileo had a fixed place of business in India since Galileo exercised complete control over the reservation system's components installed in the agents'offices.

Galileo was also found to have an agency PE in India by virtue of the fact that the marketing and distribution company with whom Galileo worked had the authority to enter into contracts on behalf of Galileo and also provided training and other services in India on behalf of Galileo.[55] Note that, under the DTAA, only the income attributable to Galileo's business connection with India can be taxed.[56]

4. Permanent Establishment Established by Location of Server in India India has concluded that the presence of a company's server in India is enough to find that the company has a PE in India. In 2003, the United States and India mutually agreed that Visa has a PE in India and is liable to pay taxes in India under the India-U.S. DTAA. The parties agreed that the company's server located in India is a fixed place of business and, as a result, constitutes a PE of Visa in India.[57] While this agreement is only binding on Visa, it demonstrates India's perspective on the status companies operating servers located in India.

---

54 Galileo International Inc. v. DCIT, ITA No. 1733/Del/2001; 2473 to 2475/Del/2000; 820 to 823/Del of 2005 (Nov. 30, 2007).

55 *Id.*

56 *See* e.g. DTAA India-U.S., art. 7(2).

57 Johnathan Rickman, *Server Constitutes PE; Visa Liable to Tax in India*, Tax Analysts World Tax Daily (Oct. 3, 2003).

C. Royalties and Fees for Technical Services under India's DTAAs

1. In General The definitions of "royalties" and "fees for technical services" (FTSs) in India's DTAAs have been held to mirror the definitions found in the ITA.[58] In most of India's DTAAs, Article 12(1) states that "Royalties and fees for technical services arising in a contracting state and paid to a resident of the other contracting state may be taxed in that other state."[59] Generally, a person's country of residence has the right to tax royalties and FTSs arising in the other contracting state. Some of India's treaties provide for exclusive taxation of royalties and FTSs in the source state.[60]

Under most of India's DTAAs, royalties sourced to a contracting state may be taxed in the source state in accordance with the source state's domestic law. If the beneficial owner of the royalties is a resident of the nonsource state, the tax on royalties will be limited. For instance, the U.S. treaty with India limits source-state taxation to 20 percent of the gross amount of royalties and associated services when the beneficial owner of the royalty is a resident of the nonsource country.[61]

2. Payments for Use of Satellite Capacity under the India-U.S. DTAA A recent decision by the Delhi Branch of the ITAT stands in contrast to the ruling in the Asian Satellite Telecomm. case.[62] The ITAT held that under the India-U.S. DTAA, payments by a nonresident for use of a satellite's transponder capacity are not taxable as royalties.

Under the India-U.S. DTAA, "royalties" are defined as "payments of any kind received as a consideration for the use of, or the right to use, any. . . . patent, . . . secret formula or process, . . . including gains derived from the alienation of any such right or property which are contingent on the productivity, use, or disposition thereof."[63]

The facts in *PanAmSat International Systems LLC, USA* are identical to the facts in Asian Satellite Telecomm. except that AST is a Hong Kong resident and PanAmSat is a resident of the United States. Hong Kong does not have a DTAA with India, but the United States does have an agreement. The court in Asian Satellite Telecomm. held that the definition of "royalty" in India's DTAAs and the definition in the ITA are equivalent. In *PanAmSat*, the ITAT agreed with the court in Asian Satellite Telecomm. that the processing and dispersal of signals by the satellite constituted a process under section 9 of the ITA. But the tribunal held that the India-U.S. DTAA's definition of "royalty" varies in a slight, but important way from the definition in the ITA. In Asian Satellite Telecomm., the court found that under the ITA, the word "secret" modified only the word "formula" and not the word "process." In contrast, in *PanAmSat*, the Commissioner of Income Tax Appeals (CITA) held that under the DTAA, a process will fall under the

---

58 Income Tax Act § 44(D).

59 *See, e.g.*, DTAA India-U.S., art. 12(1).

60 *See, e.g.*, DTAA India-Egypt, art. 13(1).

61 *See id.*, art. 13(2).

62 Asia Satellite Telecomm, 85 ITD 478 Delhi.

63 DTAA India-U.S., art. 12(3)(a).

definition of "royalty" only if the process is secret. They found that satellite technology is not secret, and thus does not fall under the DTAA's definition of royalty.

Additionally, since the patent for the satellite technology was not transferred to PanAmSat, it could not be transferred to the TV stations. Thus, the ITAT held that the payment for use of transponder capacity did not qualify as "gains derived form the alienation of any . . . right or property that are contingent on . . . productivity." At least one commentator has expressed disagreement with the holding in *PanAmSat*. He points out that the lease agreement entered into by PanAmSat and the TV stations was for ten years. This ten–year lease can be considered an "alienation of a right or property." And the fees may be considered contingent on productivity, since the fee is contingent on the number of transmission hours used.[64] If the holding is indeed in error, it is possible for the ITAT to reverse its own order since the CITA has the authority, on its own motion, to amend its ruling within four years of the date of the order.[65]

3. Payments for Use of a CPU as Royalty Payment The Authority for Advance Rulings has held that payments by an Indian resident to an Indian nonresident for use of a CPU (central processing unit) located outside of India are taxable as royalties. The AAR emphasized the fact that the CPU operator designed the software used on its CPU and that the software was secret. They viewed the Indian resident's payments as "consideration for the right to use . . . a secret formula or process," thus qualifying as royalties under the India-U.S. DTAA.[66]

The AAR considered whether the payments were for use of scientific equipment or use of a secret process. The distinction was relevant because, at the time, a different withholding rate applied to each type of royalty payment. The AAR held that the nonresident CPU operator did more than just provide access to equipment, since the processing of data on the CPU required the use of secret processes. As a result, even if a nonresident receives payment from an Indian resident for use of a CPU that does not utilize "secret" software or processes, the Indian taxation authorities are still likely to tax the payments for the "right to use, any industrial, commercial, or scientific equipment."[67]

IV. WITHHOLDING TAX

Under Indian domestic tax law, some payments to nonresidents are subject to a nonfinal withholding tax. Royalties and FTS are subject to 10 PERCENT withholding when paid to a nonresident.[68] Income from other sources is subject to withholding at the current rates in force.[69] When the applicable DTAA does not have a separate provisions

64 Surendra Bhargava, *Indian Tax Tribunal's Judgment on Space Taxation May Not Fly* (Feb. 19, 2007), available at http://findarticles.com/p/articles/mi_hb4692/is_200702/ai_n19247293.

65 Income Tax Act § 254(2).

66 Abc, In re Authority for Advance Rulings, Case P. no. 30 of 1999; *see also* India-U.S. DTAA art. 12(3)(a).

67 *Id.* at Art. 12(3)(b).

68 Income Tax Act § 194(J).

69 Income Tax Act § 195(1).

covering fees for technical services, FTS are taxed as business profits.[70] Any person in India who has a business connection with a nonresident or from whom the nonresident receives income directly or indirectly is considered to be an agent of the nonresident.[71] An agent is treated as a "representative assessee" of the nonresident and must deduct the tax at the source and pay that amount to the government.[72] India's DTAAs generally include a maximum withholding rate for royalty payments to nonresidents and, in some treaties, FTS. Otherwise, domestic rates apply (see the following table).

Withholding Rates for Royalties (and Fees for Technical Services)

Domestic Rates			
Entity	*%*		
Companies	10		
Individuals	10		
	Treaty Rates		
Country	*%*	*Country*	*%*
Armenia	10	Namibia	10
Australia	10/15[1]	Nepal	15
Austria	10	Netherlands	20
Azerbaijan	15/20[2]	New Zealand	10
Bangladesh	10	Norway	20
Belarus	15	Oman	15
Belgium	20	Philippines	15
Botswana	10	Poland	22.5
Brazil	15/25[3]	Portugal	10
Bulgaria	15/20[2]	Qatar	10
Canada	10/15[4]	Romania	22.5
China	10	Russia	10
Cyprus	15	Saudi Arabia	10
Czech Republic	10	Singapore	10/15[5]
Denmark	20	Slovak Republic	30
Egypt	*	Slovenia	10
Faroe Islands	20	South Africa	10
Finland	10/15[4]	Spain	10/20[6]
France	20	Sri Lanka	10
Germany	10	Sudan	10
Greece	*	Sweden	10
Hungary	10	Switzerland	10
Indonesia	15	Syria	10

70 A.A.R. no. 750 of 2007.

71 Income Tax Act § 163(1)(b), (c).

72 Income Tax Act §§ 161, 190.

Treaty Rates			
Country	*%*	*Country*	*%*
Ireland	10	Tajikistan	15/20[2]
Israel	10	Tanzania	20
Italy	20	Thailand	15
Japan	10	Trinidad and Tobago	10
Jordan	20	Turkey	15
Kazakhstan	10	Turkmenistan	10
Kenya	20	Uganda	10
Korea	15	Ukraine	10
Kyrgyzstan	15	United Arab Emirates	10
Libya	*	United Kingdom	10/15[4]
Malaysia	10	United States	10/15[4]
Malta	15	Uzbekistan	15
Mauritius	15	Vietnam	10
Mongolia	15	Zambia	10
Morocco	10		

* The domestic rate applies.

[1] The lower rate applies to

a. The use of, or the right to use, any industrial, commercial or scientific equipment;

b. Payments or credits for the rendering of any technical or consultancy services that are ancillary and subsidiary to the application or enjoyment of any property or right relating to the use of, or the right to use, any industrial, commercial, or scientific equipment;

c. Total or partial forbearance in respect of the use or supply of the use of, or the right to use, any industrial, commercial or scientific equipment.

[2] The lower rate applies to royalties relating to "copyrights of literary, artistic or scientific works, other than cinematograph films or films or tapes used for radio or television broadcasting."

[3] The higher rate applies to royalties for the right to use trademarks.

[4] The lower rate applies to payments for "the use of, or the right to use, any industrial, commercial, or scientific equipment" and related services.

[5] The 15% rate applies to "any copyright of a literary, artistic or scientific work, including cinematograph films or films or tapes used for radio or television broadcasting, any patent, trademark, design or model, plan, secret formula or process, or for information concerning industrial, commercial or scientific experience, including gains derived from the alienation of any such right, property or information." The 10% rate applies to "any industrial, commercial or scientific equipment, other than payments derived by an enterprise from . . . the incidental lease of ships or aircraft used in such transportation . . . [or] the use, maintenance or rental of containers (including trailers and related equipment for the transport of containers) in connection with such transportation."

[6] The lower rate applies "in the case of royalties relating to the payments for the use of, or the right to use, industrial, commercial or scientific equipment."

V. ISSUES IN E-COMMERCE

A. Privacy and Internet Security

1. In General India was among the first countries to adopt an e-commerce law. The Information Technology Act (2000) was groundbreaking legislation for India that addresses many of the issues raised by e-commerce. The act supports e-commerce by allowing it to operate efficiently, and protects computers and servers from hackers and other e-criminals. Unfortunately, the act did not go far enough to protect the privacy of data flowing through the channels of e-commerce. At present, anyone with access to customer records is free to sell the data, or use it for direct marketing. Pending legislation, the Personal Data Protection Bill (2006), will, if passed in the Indian Parliament, protect data provided to the government and private entities from being sold or used for direct marketing.

2. *Information Technology Act (2000)*

A. INTRODUCTION The Information Technology Act (2000) attempts to bridge the gap between e-commerce and traditional commerce by recognizing the validity of digital records and digital signatures. The act (and its amendments) also provides penalties for contravention of the act and criminal offenses involving computer systems.[73]

B. DIGITAL RECORDS Any law with a writing requirement may be satisfied by an electronic or digital signature. The Indian government is authorized to utilize electronic systems when the law provides for the filing of forms; issuance of licenses, permits, sanction or approvals; and the receipt or payment of money. Also, the government is authorized to use electronic storage in place of physical storage when the law provides for the retention of documents, records, or information.[74] But the law specifies that the foregoing provisions do not confer on the government the authority to force anyone to use electronic means in place of their traditional counterparts.

C. DIGITAL SIGNATURE CERTIFICATES The act creates Certifying Authorities, who are authorized to issue digital signature certificates (DSCs). A DSC acts as a secure replacement for a physical signature. Each DSC consists of a public key and a corresponding private key. Taken together, these keys are used to verify a person's identity in the same way a signature verifies identity on paper documents.[75] The Controller of Certifying Authorities (CCA), created by the act, acts as a repository for all DSCs and issues licenses that allow the holder to issue DSCs.[76] The CCA has broad power to direct government agencies to "intercept any information transmitted through any computer resource."[77] Subscribers or others in charge of a computer system are charged with the responsibility of assisting such agencies to decrypt information on the system.[78] A person who fails to assist an agency to access a system can be punished by up to seven years of imprisonment. Anyone attempting to obtain a license or DSC who makes

---

73 Information Technology Act (2000), no. 21, Acts of Parliament (2000).
74 Information Technology Act § 3(1).
75 Information Technology Act § 35.
76 Information Technology Act § 36.
77 Information Technology Act § 69(1).
78 Information Technology Act § 69(2).

a misrepresentation to the CCA or a Certifying Authority may be subject to a fine, imprisonment, or both.

D. PENALTIES AND ADJUDICATION The IT Act provides penalties for hacking and unauthorized use of computer systems. A person will be liable for civil damages if, without permission of the owner, that person participates in any of the following activities:[79]

1. Accesses a computer or network
2. Downloads or copies data from a system or removable storage device
3. Introduces a virus or "other contaminant" into a system
4. Damages a computer or network
5. Disrupts a system's operation
6. Denies an authorized user access to a system
7. Assists another person to access a computer system
8. Charges services used by one person to another person by manipulating or tampering with a system

E. CRIMINAL OFFENSES

i. Introduction The IT Act also provides for criminal punishment for a number of activities. Offenses under the act apply to any person regardless of the person's nationality and whether the offense was committed outside India, as long as the offense or contravention involved a computer system or network located in India.[80] Ranking police officers are given the authority to enter any public place, including "any public conveyance, hotel, shop, or other place accessible to the public and search and arrest any person who is reasonably suspected of committing any offense under the Act."[81] The act contains broad language that strictly prohibits a wide range of activities that interfere with and destroy computer systems, data, and networks:

> Whoever knowingly or intentionally conceals, destroys or alters or intentionally or knowingly causes another to conceal, destroy or alter any computer source code used for a computer, computer programme, computer system or computer network, when the computer source code is required to be kept or maintained by law for the time being in force, shall be punishable with imprisonment up to three years, or with fine which may extend up to two lakh rupees, or with both. [82]

In addition, the act prohibits the publication of obscenity in electronic form. Publication of obscenity is punishable by imprisonment of up to five years and imposition of a substantial fine.[83]

---

79 Information Technology Act § 66.
80 Information Technology Act § 75.
81 Information Technology Act § 80.
82 Information Technology Act § 65.
83 *See* "Adult Entertainment," *infra*.

ii. Network Service Provider Liability Indian law subjects network service providers (NSP) to liability for some third-party contravention of the IT Act. This provision of the law is of particular interest to e-commerce businesses since the definition of NSP under Indian law is very broad and encompasses many e-commerce portals that would not ordinarily be classified as NSPs. For the purposes of the act, NSP means intermediary, and "third-party information" means "any information dealt with by a network service provider in his capacity as an intermediary."[84] An NSP can be held responsible for a violation or contravention of the IT Act by any third-party information made available by the NSP. The burden of proof is with the NSP to show that the offense or contravention of the act, rules, or regulations was committed without the NSP knowledge, or the NSP exercised due diligence to prevent offense or contravention.[85] In addition to the NSP, executives of the NSP can be held responsible for violations of the act by the NSP. [86]

f. Offenses by Companies If a company contravenes any provision of the act, every person who was in charge of and responsible to the company for the conduct of business of the company, and the company itself, are liable to be proceeded against and punished. But no one can be punished who proves that the contravention occurred without his or her knowledge or that he or she exercised due diligence to prevent the contravention.

An executive at eBay India has been charged with violating the obscenity prohibitions of the IT Act even though he did not have personal knowledge of a third-party auction of material deemed obscene by the Indian authorities on his company's site.[87]

3. The Personal Data Protection Bill (2006) The Indian legislature has introduced a bill that fills some of the gaps left in the IT Act by prohibiting the unauthorized use of data collected from individuals for a specific purpose (such as customer data associated with an e-commerce transaction). The bill applies to both government agencies and private industry. Under the bill, data collected for a particular purpose cannot be processed without the consent of the person from whom the data was collected, unless the data has been made public.[88] Specifically, data collected from individuals cannot be used for direct marketing or for other commercial gain.[89] The bill provides that anyone who has their information used without their consent is entitled to damages from the offending party.[90] The bill provides exceptions for the following purposes: (1) prevention or detection of a crime, (2) prosecution of offenders, and (3) assessment or collection of tax or duty.[91] Data Controllers—a post created by the act—will oversee the administration of the bill and investigate complaints about improper use of data.[92]

---

84 Information Technology Act § 79.

85 *Id.*

86 *See* "Offenses by Companies,"*infra*.

87 *See* "Adult Entertainment,"*infra*.

88 Personal Data Protection Bill (2006), no. 91, Acts of Parliament (2006) § 3.

89 Personal Data Protection Act § 4.

90 Personal Data Protection Act § 5.

91 Personal Data Protection Act § 3

92 Personal Data Protection Act § 6.

Every organization, both public and private, has the following obligations with respect to private data: (1) inform the Data Controller of the type of personal information collected and the purpose for which it is being collected; (2) take "adequate measures to maintain confidentiality and security in the handling of personal data and information; (3) limit the collection of personal data to data essential to the transactions they are engaged in with the individual.[93]

The bill provides that anyone who violates the act may be subject to incarceration and fines.[94] When a company violates the provisions of the bill, "every person who, at the time the contravention was committed, was in charge of, and was responsible to, the company for the conduct of business of the company as well as the company, shall be guilty of the contravention" and may be prosecuted and punished for the violation.[95] Such person will not be liable for a violation of the provisions of the bill if the person proves that "the contravention took place without his knowledge or that he exercised all due diligence to prevent such contravention."[96]

B. Online Gambling

Gambling, other than wagering on horse racing and lotteries, is largely illegal in India. Under the Indian Contract Act of 1874 (ICA), wagering contracts are void and cannot be enforced in the courts.[97] States are given the authority to organize or prohibit lotteries.[98] Several states run Internet lotteries. Anyone running an unauthorized lottery may be subject to criminal prosecution.[99]

C. Adult Entertainment

1. Introduction India's commitment to strict enforcement of the obscenity provisions of the IT Act is readily apparent. In a 2008 case, a doctor who filmed his patients naked was convicted of publishing those photographs. The court sentenced the doctor to the maximum penalty possible, five years imprisonment and a fine of 1 lakh rupees. For all his crimes, the doctor received a sentence amounting to life in prison, so the court may have been influenced by the severity of the doctor's other offenses when sentencing him under the IT Act.[100]

93 Personal Data Protection Act § 7.
94 Personal Data Protection Act § 9.
95 Personal Data Protection Act § 10.
96 *Id.*
97 Personal Data Protection Act § 30.
98 The Lotteries (Regulation) Act (1998), no. 17, Acts of Parliament (1998) §§ 4–5.
99 India Pen. Code (1860), § 294(a).
100 *Dr. Porn Gets Life for Selling Patient Photos on Net*, TELEGRAPH (Feb. 8, 2008), available at http://www.telegraphindia.com/1080208/jsp/nation/story_8877571.jsp.

2. NSP and Intermediary Liability for Publication of Obscenity The Information Technology Act (2000) provides criminal penalties for "publishing information which is obscene in electronic form." Section 67 of the act provides as follows:

> Whoever publishes or transmits or causes to be published in the electronic form, any material which is lascivious or appeals to the prurient interest or if its effect is such as to tend to deprave and corrupt persons who are likely, having regard to all relevant circumstances, to read, see or hear the matter contained or embodied in it, shall be punished on first conviction with imprisonment . . . and with fine.

An individual may be subject to up to five years of imprisonment and up to a 1 lakh rupees fine on first conviction and up to ten years imprisonment and up to a 2 lakh rupees fine for subsequent convictions.[101]

In a high-profile case, video of illicit activity between two 17-year-olds was auctioned on Baazee.com (now eBay India). The Manager and CEO of eBay India were arrested when the auction came to the attention of the Indian authorities. Although the current version of the IT Act protects some (NSPs) from liability for the criminal acts of people using the NSP's system,[102] that provision of the act was not added until 2006. It is unclear whether the court will apply the NSP protections retroactively.

---

101 Information Technology Act § 67.

102 *See* "NSP Liability,"*supra*.

Chapter 5

Japan: E-Commerce and Taxation in Japan

Maji Christine Rhee
Portland State University &
Thomas Jefferson School of Law

I. INTRODUCTION TO E-COMMERCE AND TAXATION IN JAPAN

This chapter introduces Japan's current business laws and their relationship to e-commerce, and analyzes Japan's effort to craft tax laws—specifically, a definition of permanent establishment (PE) that will accommodate the distinguishing characteristics of e-commerce. A question central to this discussion will be whether an Internet server qualifies as a PE, because double taxation and direct income tax law are based on the concept of a PE.

The importance of the concept of PE in Japan has been modified by recent changes to Japan's tax laws. Under these changes, a company's independent agent in Japan no longer constitutes a PE. E-Commerce and taxation in Japan has been modeled largely on the Organization for Economic Cooperation and Development (OECD) Model Tax Convention and the Ottawa Taxation Framework Conditions. Japan's domestic tax treatment of e-commerce resulted from and developed in response to OECD's e-commerce report, which concluded that (1) e-commerce technologies offer taxation authorities new means of improving taxpayer service; and (2) governments should tax e-commerce activities based on the taxation model used for conventional business. Government agencies have also considered the differences between the U.S. protective policy against discriminatory taxes imposed on e-commerce activities and the European Union practice of applying a Value-added tax (VAT).

E-Commerce has become prevalent in Japan, and the country's legal infrastructure has been updated to keep pace with the development of international taxation. There are some 77 million Internet users in Japan, 50 percent of households have a broadband connection to the Internet, and the business-to-consumer e-commerce market size is estimated at over US$30 billion.[1] But there is growing concern that the expansion of e-commerce may lead to the spread of tax shelters and tax avoidance that may reduce tax revenues in the public finance sector.

II. E-JAPAN

A. Tax Principles

The growth of e-commerce in Japan has been due, in part, to the E-Japan project. E-Japan is a government initiative intended to promote the tax principles of "efficiency, neutrality, brevity, and certainty." The objective of E-Japan was to implement these tax principles in the following manner:[2]

1. *Efficiency principle*—Accommodate changes in the business environment and (1) review of tax treaties, (2) review of the unified (consolidated) taxation, (3) transfer pricing to be applied to companies, (4) add the transaction net margin method (TNMM) as a method of transfer pricing, and (5) exclude international trading deriving from thin capitalization.
2. *Brevity and certainty principle*—Confirmation and active use of procedures including (1) effective use of information exchange with treaty nations, (2) taxation of foreign association agents, (3) simplification of procedures, and (4) expansion of transfer pricing taxation.

B. Implementation of E-Japan

The E-Japan program has three major goals:[3] (1) integrate the broadband network throughout Japan, (2) increase e-commerce activities, and (3) replace personal seals (*inkan*) with digitized certificates. Although the E-Japan project has been implemented, there is no specific tax law focusing solely on e-commerce in Japan, and Japan has no equivalent of the U.S. Internet Tax Freedom Act (ITF), which imposes no tax on e-commerce activities. Japan is still at the stage of reviewing the OECD Model Convention on Tax, the United States' ITF, and the European model on VAT. The process of revising Japan's tax law to encompass e-commerce taxation will not only require revision of Japan's domestic tax law but also the cooperation of nations with whom Japan has double-taxation agreements (DTAAs).

---

1 Ministry of Economy, Trade, and Industry, White Paper on International Economy and Trade 2006, available at http://www.meti.go.jp/english/report/data/gIT2006maine.html (last visited Aug. 26, 2008).

2 Yoshike Takeuchi, Kokusai Kazei no Saimondai, *Problems Related to International Taxation*, Financial Review 5–21, 13–14 (2006). (Jp.)

3 Articles 14, 30, and 84 of the Japanese Constitution state the principles of legitimacy of taxation and legal equity. Nihonkoku Kenpo [Constitution] (Jp.).

III. THE NATIONAL TAX AGENCY (*KOKUZEICHO*)

Unlike the United States—where a legislative committee prepares proposed legislative changes, which are then approved or denied by Congress—in Japan, the National Tax Agency (NTA), or Kokuzeicho, has the power to draft tax law changes directly. The Japanese legislature makes the final decision on any tax law changes based on drafts by the government tax investigation agency, *Jiminto*-led (majority party) tax investigation agency, and the Advisory Council on Economic and Fiscal Planning Agency under the Cabinet Office (*Naikakufu*).

The E-Tax project directed by the NTA was a prominent step toward putting an emphasis on the unique attributes of "Japanese style e-commerce." In business-to-consumer (B2C) transactions, customers do not usually rely on Japanese credit cards. Instead, Japan uses non-PC Internet connections via a personal cellular phone system, of which NTT Mobile Communications network dominates. E-Money, such as PASCO and SUIKA, are often used in both convenience and online stores, including 7-Eleven Japan Co. and Softbank.

Global trading by Japanese banks highlights some of the unique features of business-to-business (B2B) e-commerce. Since Japanese yen are frequently purchased and sold via branch hub offices located in London and New York, the 24-hour exchange rate and prospective profits from effective exchange rates have been studied. A possible implementation of a "Tobin tax" a sales tax on currency trades across borders has been discussed.[4]

The NTA (*Kokuzeicho*) has recognized the growing number of cybercrimes, including international tax avoidance. Domestic measures to facilitate tax payment have included the expansion of documents exempt from submission in e-filing, and the creation of a tracking information reporting system for foreign exchange margin trading.

The NTA established the Professional Team for E-Commerce Taxation (PROJECT), with a location at each regional taxation bureau, to (1) collect information on e-commerce and promote the "self-assessment system," and (2) to develop and accumulate investigation methods to detect "tax evaders."[5]

The IT Strategy Headquarters, housed in the Cabinet in 2000, conducted initial research into Japan's efforts in the global IT revolution. The research done resulted in the headquarters stating several goals, including (1) safety in the usage of the Internet; (2) promoting reliability of e-commerce, including the free usage of software; and (3) providing public access to the original code to prevent tortious acts.[6]

---

4 Kenji Miki & Yoshikazu Maeda, Kokusaizeimu Jinmon, Easy to Comprehend Introduction to International Taxation, 242 (2008).

5 Tax evasion methods include "intentional concealment of sales and recording of costs at unreasonably high figures" in the domestic market and in overseas corporations. In 2004, 171 cases were resolved by sentencing. The average fine was about ¥27 million per case, and the average prison sentence was 15.3 months. Prison sentences without probation have been handed down every year since 1980. NTA "professional teams" have investigated the network auction of over ¥200,000 (US$2,100). One of the agencies, the Osaka National Tax Agency, collected some ¥1,250 billion taxable money in 2004. Kokuzeichō, *Kokuzeichō Repōto* [National Tax Agency, *National Agency Tax Report 2005*,], available at http://www.nta.go.jp/kohyo/katsudou/report/2005/04_3.htm#g.

6 Fuhō akusesu gōi [Tortuous acts] (1999, art. 128).

IV. JAPANESE DOMESTIC TAXATION OF E-COMMERCE

A. PEs under Domestic Tax Law

1. Introduction Of central importance to the taxation of e-commerce are the notion of (PE) and the application of Japanese domestic income tax law to e-commerce transactions. Since the income tax and withholding rates are based on the presence or absence of a PE in Japan, the two concepts are intertwined. Problems of taxation deriving from the inherent structure of business in e-commerce prompt the question of whether Japan's existing taxation paradigm is sufficient to address the nature and extent of Internet-based commerce,[7] or whether tax law must be reformulated to accommodate e-commerce's intricacies.[8]

The Japanese definition of PE is more expansive than the OECD definition, since the existence of a PE under Japanese law depends on the nature of business activities rather than physical presence. Under this line of reasoning, when e-commerce is not confined to manufacturing and sales, a server engaged in the sale of intangible goods or services will be classified as a PE of the company selling goods through the server.

See Figure 1, supra, for a summary of Japan's tax treatment of nonresident businesses.

2. Definition of PE The Japanese domestic definition of PE is based on the "consolidated approach."[9] The treaty-based definition of PE and the Attributable Income Rule focus on whether business profits are attributed to a PE; if business income is not attributable to a PE, the income will be treated as if it does not belong to a PE.[10] The Japanese definition of PE applies to nonresident customers and foreign corporations. The type of PE will be further categorized based on the type of foreign corporation operating it. According to the Corporate Tax Law, Article 141, there are four types of PE:

- Type 1 Branch offices, factories, warehouses, and other places of business. One of the exemptions includes a fixed place of business that a foreign corporation uses for the maintenance of a stock of goods.

---

7 Characteristics of doing e-commerce:
   (1) Producer and consumers are in direct dealing. There is no need for intermediaries when products such as music or software are digitalized in the cross-border trading. The source-based taxation becomes difficult because the business activities can occur without having a PE.
   (2) Domain names cannot identify tax payers.
   (3) The issuance of digital identification may have limitations since a taxing authority would have difficulty in tracking the taxing point.
   (5) Difficulty in identifying the content of sales since tangible goods can be transformed to intangible goods.
   (6) Digital receipts may not be tracked effectively.

8 A BT (binary digit tax) was proposed by Arthur Cordell and Thomas Ide in 1994. BT is taxation based on the quantity of digital bits of information included in voice and images.

9 Hōjinzei [Corporate Income Tax], art. 141.

10 *See* Convention for the Avoidance of Double Taxation and the Prevention of Fiscal Evasion with Respect to Taxes on Income, arts. 7(1) & 9, U.S.-Japan, Nov. 6, 2003 (focusing on the use of PE rather than an existence of PE).

Figure 1 Withholding Tax (WT) and Corporations Tax (CT)

	Branch PE	*Construction PE/ Agent PE*	*No PE*
Business income	CT	CT	No Tax
Income from management, ownership, transference	CT	CT	CT applied only to certain business profit designated by the policy regulation.
Income from transference of real estate property, services, or rent	WT + CT	WH + CT	WH + CT
Interest from bonds, dividends, user fee, awards from advertisement, pension annuity, and interest allocated from anonymous associations	WH+CT	If the business is affiliated with a domestic company, WH+CT. If not affiliated with a domestic company, WH only.	WH

- Type 2 PE Construction, installation, or other construction project sites present in Japan for more than one year.
- Type 3 PE Agency PEs including
  (1) Agents exercising authority to conclude contracts in Japan;
  (2) Agents who maintain or deliver goods to meet the customers' need; and
  (3) Agents who exclusively secure orders, negotiate, or perform other acts leading to the conclusion of contracts.
- Type 4 Foreign companies other than Type 3 PEs.

3. Agency PEs The 2008 Tax Reform defines the scope of agents deemed to be a PE with respect to e-commerce. An independent agent has a more limited authorization to conduct business than an agent under the definition of PE. This change conforms to the OECD Model Treaty, Article 5, which does not give an independent agent a PE status.[11]

4. Servers as PEs A primary question is whether Internet servers constitute a PE in Japan. Under the OECD Model, a Web site is not a PE because it is not a "fixed place of business." However, a server—a physical computer—can be a PE under Japanese

11 Zaimushō, Heisei nijūnendo kaisei kankei sankō shiryō kokusai kazeikankei [Ministry of Finance, Materials Related to International Taxation,]1-9, 3 (2008) available at http://www.mof.go.jp/jouhou/syuzei/siryou/h20kaiseikokusai.pdf.

law since software can be stored in "a combination of software and electronic data." The server on which a company's Web site is stored can be a PE, but only if the server is "at the disposal" of the company that owns the Web site.

B. Income Tax

1. Classifications of Income The international aspects of income tax in Japan are based on a withholding tax applied to payments to nonresidents and foreign corporations.[12] Income paid to nonresidents and foreign corporations is subject to the Japanese withholding tax. Below is a list of types of income on which foreign corporations must pay tax (Article 138):[13]

Item 1. Income tax from profits made by sales in Japan
Item 2. Income from property ownership
Item 3. Income from transference of property
Item 4. All other income from Japan
Item 5. Income from remuneration for professional or technical services
Item 6. Income from renting real estate property
Item 7. Income from interest
Item 8. Income from dividends
Item 9. Capital gain from interest from real estate property rent
Item 10. User fees, including copyright fees: (1) royalty (patent) payments, and (2) copyright fees.

2. Classification of Nonresident Corporations for Tax Purposes The above income categories are selectively taxed depending on the type of foreign corporation. The classification of income with respect to the domestic income tax will be according to the type of business it belongs to. There are four types of foreign businesses: (1) businesses with branch offices in Japan, (2) businesses manufacturing goods in Japan and pursuing sales in Japan, (3) businesses manufacturing goods overseas and pursuing sales both in Japan and overseas, and (4) businesses selling Japanese goods in Japan and overseas. All foreign business income will be withheld except where a foreign business entity is engaged in the sales of Japanese goods in Japan and abroad.

---

12 The income tax withholding rates are as follows:
Article 138(3), human resources 20%
Article 138(4), profit from interest 15%
Article 138(5), profits from dividends 20%
Article 138(7), user fee 20%
Article 138(9), life insurance 20%
Article 138(11), profits from anonymous association 20%

13 Hōjinzei [Corporate Tax Law], art. 138.

- For type one foreign corporations renting real property for a branch office, Item 6 applies. The withholding rate is 20 percent, and the corporate income tax from the branch office must be filed for retroactive deduction.
- In the case of a foreign construction company present in Japan for more than a year through an agent's office, Items 2 and 10 are applied. Upon filing, the withheld user fees will be deducted.
- When a foreign corporation without a PE earns capital gain from stocks and dividends, Items 3 and 8 apply. Because it lacks a PE, the corporation need not file a corporate income tax return, but 20 percent of income gain will be withheld.
- When a foreign corporation without a PE purchases a piece of property in Japan and transfers ownership, Item 3 applies. At the time of the transfer, 20 percent of income is withheld.

The corporate income tax in Articles 212(1) and 213(1) also states the PE requirements. If the PE requirements are not met and there is no PE, all business income under Article 138 (see *supra*) is exempted. However, there are situations in which a company without a PE will be subject to source-based taxation.

3. Source-Based Taxation Article 164 of the Japanese Income Tax Law states that a source-based income tax is imposed on any interest, dividend, or user fee generated by a PE in Japan. When a business transaction is not based on the existence of a PE, then Article 162 of the Japanese Income Tax Law will apply. Under Article 162 interest, dividends, and user fees are all separately taxed.

For the taxation of royalties, Japan has adopted the OECD Model, which taxes (assesses) royalties on the recipient side. So, for example, between an American licensor and Japanese licensee, the American licensor will receive royalty payments and will be taxed on the payments. However, if an American company has a PE with a resident staff (agent) in Japan, the "user fee" will not be classified as income from royalties but rather as business corporate income. In a situation where a foreign company without a PE purchases Japanese software on the Internet, downloads the software, and distributes it to its branch offices, the foreign corporation income tax applies.[14] If a foreign company without a PE intends to duplicate Japanese software programs for sale, and transfers copyright to the company, under Item 10 of Article 138, the user fee will be taxed.

C. Consumption Tax

The PE concept also relates to the Japanese consumption tax. If a Japanese person purchases a piece of digitized music on the Internet and makes a payment to a company without a PE, the company's profit from the Japanese person's purchase of the music will not be subject to Japanese taxation. The following hypothetical relates to

---

14 Sato Masakatsu, Kokyuteki Shisetsu No Gainen, *Notion of Permanent Establishment*, 35(1) Asia University Law Review, 35–69 (2000).

the Japanese Consumption Tax Law, Article 4, which states that a business entity is responsible for a taxable capital transfer. In these types of transactions, proxies are generally used.[15]

Example 1 When the product's import value is 100, the customs rate is at 5 percent, resulting in a tax of 5 on the import. If the imported product is sold to a customer at 120, the tax to be paid to the authority becomes 120 × 0.05–5 (buyer tax exemption) = 1. Thus, the total tax amount becomes 6 percent (5% + 1%) of the product's import value.

Example 2 When digitalized goods are sold in e-commerce, there will not be an import custom tax. Thus, there will be no tax on the value of the import, 100. In the B2C transaction, when a Japanese person purchases and downloads a music album from an overseas company, no custom duties are levied. The final consumer will not have to pay the consumption tax.

V. E-SIGNATURES

A. Introduction

E-Signatures were introduced in Japan in 2000 by the Electronic Signatures and Certification Services Law (ESCSL). An e-signature is a secure electronic measure, attached to an e-document, used to verify the identity of the sender and ensure the integrity of an electronic document. Under Japanese law, an e-document is presumed to be authentic if a principle's e-signature is attached to the document.[16]

B. E-Notarization

E-Notarization, which facilitates the authentication of electronic documents, was introduced in Japan in 2002.[17] The Japan National Notaries Association facilitates e-notarization in Japan. E-Notarization in Japan is based on the public-key infrastructure (PKI) model used throughout the world for digital authentication. E-Notarization services are performed through the E-Notarization Center, owned by the Japan National Notaries Association, and technical maintenance of the center are outsourced to Hitachi Corp. The process of authenticating a document through an e-notary is as follows:[18] (1) the client creates a PDF document with a digital signature attached;

---

15 Tetsuya Fujimoto, Kokusai sozeiho [International Taxation Law] 265 (2005).

16 Electronic Signatures and Certification Services Law, ch. 2 (2001). The law recognizes an electronic document as a substitute for a physical document if the party receiving the document agrees to accept the e-document.

17 Japan's Notary Law was amended in 2000 to supplement traditional notarization with e-notarization.

18 Hidetsugu Kato, *E-Notarization in Japan* 3–4, available at http://www.nationalnotary.org/intlforum/pdf/enotarization_kato.pdf (2008).

(2) a request is made for e-notarization services online; (3) the notary downloads the documents to be notarized; (4) the notary determines whether the documents are appropriate for e-notarization; and (5) if the document is appropriate for notarization, the e-notary will digitally sign a certificate acknowledging the authenticity of the document. The notary's e-signature is equivalent to the seal used by a traditional notary.

C. Certification Providers

The ESCSL provides for accreditation of private e-signature service providers.[19] Foreign certification providers (providers) are competent to register under the law. If a provider is accredited by a foreign agency with standards similar to the Japanese agency's standards, and the foreign country to which the accrediting agency belongs has a treaty with Japan allowing reciprocal certification of providers, the foreign provider may be accredited in Japan through a simplified written application process.[20]

D. Penalties

The ESCSL includes severe penalties for causing an accredited certification provider to falsely certify an e-document. The penalty includes imprisonment of up to three years and a fine of up to 2 million (about US$18,500).

VI. ELECTRONIC CONTRACTS

The Law on Special Provisions to the Civil Code Concerning Electronic Consumer Contracts and Electronic Notice of 2003 provides rules for electronic consumer contracts. The law allows a consumer engaged in an electronic transaction to nullify the contract when the consumer entered into the contract under a mistake. A contract may not be nullified by the customer if the business has taken "appropriate measures to confirm the consumer's intention of entering into the contract." In addition, the law provides that a contract is formed when the notice of acceptance is received by the offeror in electronic form. This stands in contrast to the traditional rule for absentee contracts (contracts with parties that do not meet face to face). Such traditional contracts are formed when the notice of acceptance is sent by the offeree.[21]

---

19 Electronic Signatures and Certification Services Law, ch. 3, § 1.

20 *Id.* at ch. 3, § 2.

21 *See* Act on Special Provisions to the Civil Code Concerning Electronic Consumer Contracts and Electronic Acceptance Notice, no. 95, art. 4 (2001), available at http://www.cas.go.jp/jp/seisaku/hourei/data/ASP.pdf; United Nations Public Assistance Network, Consumer Policies in Japan, Fiscal Year 2001, Annual Report 5 (2001), available at http://unpan1.un.org/intradoc/groups/public/documents/APCITY/UNPAN019942.pdf.

VII. PROTECTION OF PERSONAL DATA

A. Introduction

The Act on the Protection of Personal Information (APPL) of 2003 protects the privacy rights of individuals by restricting the use of personal data obtained by businesses and government entities. The APPL came into force, in part, on March 30, 2003, but enforcement of restrictions on the use of personal data by private entities came into force later, on April 1, 2005. The APPL only provides a framework for the protection of personal data privacy and a foundation for further privacy laws.[22] The APPL charges the Japanese state and local public bodies with responsibility for "comprehensively formulating and implementing measures necessary for ensuring the proper handling of personal information . . . in conformity with the purport of this Act."[23]

There are more specific privacy rules for particular businesses. Depending on the type of business, a particular government minister may promulgate personal data privacy rules and require businesses to make a report on their handling of personal information.[24] For instance, the Minister of Health, Labor, and Welfare is empowered to advise businesses as to the proper procedures for protecting personal data privacy when the data is collected for "employment management" purposes.[25] Protection of personal data collected for purposes other than "employment management" is the responsibility of the minister "with jurisdiction over the business of the entity handling personal information."[26]

B. Definition of "Personal Data"

"Personal data" is defined by the APPL as "information about a living individual which can identify the specific individual by name, date of birth or other description contained in such information (including such information as will allow easy reference to other information and will thereby enable the identification of the specific individual)."[27]

C. Business's Obligations When Handling Personal Data

Businesses collecting personal data are subject to the following requirements:

1. The purpose for which the data is collected must "be specified as clearly as possible;"[28]

---

22 Personal Data Protection Act, art. 1 (2003); Electronic Commerce Promotion Council of Japan, Recent Trend in Personal Data Protection in Japan, Legislation of Bill to Protect Personal Data, available at http://www.ecom.jp/ecom_e/home/research_file/20011119recenttrend.pdf.

23 *Id.* at Arts. 4,5, and 6.

24 *Id.* at Arts. 32 & 33.

25 *Id.* at Art. 36(1)(1).

26 *Id.* at Art. 36(1)(2).

27 *Id.* at Art. 2(1).

28 *Id.* at Art. 15.

2. Personal data must be used only for the purpose for which it was collected.[29]
3. Personal data must not be provided to a third party without the consent of the subject.[30]

A subject's consent is not required for the release of personal data in limited circumstances. The subject need not consent to the disclosure if[31] (a) the subject is notified prior to the disclosure; (b) the disclosure is required by law; (c) the disclosure must be made to "protect life, body, or property of an individual," when it will be difficult to secure consent from the principal; (d) disclosure is necessary for public health; and (e) the disclosure is made to the government, and securing permission from the principal will harm the government's purpose.

In addition to the foregoing situations, consent of the principle is not required when the business using personal information agrees to suspend use of identifying personal information at the request of the principle, and informs the principle of the following:[32] (a) the purpose for which the personal information is obtained is to distribute the information to third parties; (b) the specific types of personal data that will be disclosed to third parties; (c) the means by which the personal information will be disclosed to third parties; and (d) the fact that the distribution of personal information to third parties will be suspended at the request of the principle.

4. Personal data must not be obtained by fraud or dishonesty.[33]
5. Personal data must be updated as necessary to maintain its accuracy. [34]
6. The security of the data must be maintained through any appropriate means.[35]
7. Employees and subcontractors who are given access to personal information must be properly supervised.[36]
8. Information on personal data usage must be released to the public.[37]
9. Information on personal data usage must be "made available to the subject."[38]
10. Personal data must be disclosed to the subject of the data if requested.[39]
11. Erroneous personal data must be corrected if requested by the principal.[40]
12. Use of personal data must be suspended on the request of the principal.[41]
13. All complaints with respect to the use of personal data must be "handled appropriately and promptly."[42]

---

29 *Id.* at Art. 16.
30 *Id.* at Art. 23.
31 *Id*, at Art. 23(1).
32 *Id.* at Art. 23(2).
33 *Id.* at Art. 17.
34 *Id.* at Art. 19.
35 *Id.* at Art. 20.
36 *Id.* at Arts. 21, 22.
37 *Id.* at Art. 24.
38 *Id.* at Art. 18.
39 *Id.* at Art. 25.
40 *Id.* at Art. 26.
41 *Id.* at Art. 27.
42 *Id.* at Art. 31.

D. The Privacy Mark System

The Japan Information Processing Development Corporation[43] (JIPDEC) created the Privacy Mark System (PMS).[44] JIPDEC grants businesses the right to use the PMS logo when they have instituted a personal information compliance program. Use of the PMS logo is intended to develop customers' trust that a business ensures the privacy of its customers' personal data. As of June 30, 2008, there have been 10,694 companiesaccredited by Privacy Mark. A majority of accredited institutions are in the service industry.[45] Accreditation by Japan's Privacy Mark program implies mutual recognition by the China Dalian Software Industry Association's Privacy Information Protection Assessment (PIPA) program and the Korea Association of Information and Telecommunications' E-Privacy program.[46]

VIII. ANTI-SPAM LAWS[47]

A. Rules for Sending Commercial E-Mail

In Japan, commercial e-mail may only be sent to the following categories of recipients:[48] (1) individuals who agree, in advance, to receive commercial e-mail from the sender; (2) individuals who have provided their e-mail address to the sender; (3) individuals with whom the sender has a prior business relationship; (4) individuals engaged in business activities and organizations that publicly broadcast their e-mail addresses.

Additionally, commercial e-mail may not be sent to anyone requesting not to receive such e-mail. Commercial e-mail must not be sent once such a request is received by the sender.[49]

Anyone sending commercial e-mail must maintain records showing that recipients fit into one of the categories enumerated above.[50] Commercial e-mail must include the sender's name, title, e-mail address, and an opt-out message.[51] E-Mail messages may not be sent using a program that automatically generates e-mail addresses, and valid e-mail

43 JIPDEC's Web site is found at http://www.jipdec.or.jp/eng/.

44 *See* Privacy Mark's Web site at www.privacymark.org; *see also* Privacy Mark System, http://privacymark.org/news/2008/0801/ThePrivacyMarkSystem_June_30_2008.pdf (last updated June 30, 2008), for a summary of the Privacy Mark System.

45 *See* Japan Information Processing Development Corporation, Rules for the Establishment and Operation of the Privacy Mark System, http://privacymark.org/reference/pdf/pmark_guide070323.pdf.

46 *See id.* at 17.

47 The Japanese government has not yet released an official English translation of the 2008 amendments to the Anti-Spam Law. The following discussion is based on the summary of the law found at Morrison & Foerster, Japanese New Anti-Spam Law, http://www.mofo.com/news/updates/bulletins/14219.html#_ftnref8 (2008).

48 New Anti-Spam Law, art. 3.1 (2008).

49 *Id.*

50 *Id.* at Art 3.2.

51 *Id.* at Art. 4.

addresses may not be obtained by sending blank messages to putative e-mail addresses. Also, no one sending commercial e-mail may disguise their true e-mail address.[52]

B. Penalties

The Ministry of Internal Affairs and Communication (MIC) may order anyone sending commercial e-mail in violation of the statute to bring itself into compliance with the law.[53] If a sender violates an order from the ministry or disguises its e-mail address when sending commercial e-mail, the sender may be subject to a fine of up to ¥1,000,000 (about US$9,300) or a year of imprisonment.[54]

The MIC may also require anyone sending commercial e-mail to supply MIC with a report detailing the sender's commercial e-mailing activity.[55] The ministry may inspect the sender's books and other documentation to ensure compliance with the law.[56] Anyone sending commercial e-mail may be subject to a fine of up to ¥30,000,000 (about US$278,000) if the sender's agent violates a MIC order. In addition, a sender may be subject to a fine of up to ¥1,000,000 (aboutUS$9,300) if the sender's agent refuses to cooperate with an investigation by MIC.[57]

IX. CONCLUSION

E-Commerce law in Japan is in an ongoing review stage, and there is no clear demarcation that sets apart e-commerce and Japanese income tax or consumer tax laws. Recognizing that the notion of a PE can be applied to Japanese domestic taxation, government agencies are reviewing issues as to how the consumption tax will evolve relating to e-commerce, whether the Internet server truly can be equivalent to a traditional business entity, and whether residence-based taxation can replace source-based income tax.

---

52 *Id.* at Art. 7.

53 *Id.* at Art. 34.

54 *Id.*

55 *Id.* at Art. 28.

56 *Id.* at Art. 35.

57 *Id.* at Art. 37.

Chapter 6

Singapore: E-Commerce Taxation in Singapore

Professor William H. Byrnes, IV & Christopher M. Sove
Thomas Jefferson School of Law

I. INTRODUCTION

Singapore's user-friendly tax system, competitive tax rates,[1] and source-based domestic taxation make it a preferred international business center and, in particular, an ideal home for e-commerce businesses. In addition to an income tax, Singapore levies a goods and services tax (GST), stamp duty, estate duty, lottery and other gambling-related duties, and other taxes. Singapore's tax law does not include particular provisions governing the taxation of e-commerce transactions. Generally, e-commerce transactions are taxed under the same law as traditional transactions. However, the Internal Revenue Authority of Singapore (IRAS) has released two publications that provide guidance on the treatment of e-commerce under the GST and income.[2]

II. INCOME TAX

A. Introduction

Singapore's income tax is levied on "income accruing in or derived from Singapore or received in Singapore from outside Singapore."[3] An operations test is applied to determine whether income is accrued or derived from Singapore. Under the operations

1 Singapore boasts a top corporate income tax rate of 18% and individual rates ranging from 3.5% and 20%. Capital gains are not taxed in Singapore.

2 *See* Internal Revenue Authority of Singapore, Income Tax Guide on E-Commerce (2001), available at http://www.iras.gov.sg/irasHome/uploadedFiles/Quick_Links/e-Tax_Guides/2001ec1.pdf, and Internal Revenue Authority of Singapore, Goods and Services Tax Guide on E-Commerce (2004), available at http://www.iras.gov.sg/irasHome/uploadedFiles/GST/GST_for_specific_industries/ecommercenov2004revisedformat22nov2007.pdf, discussed *supra*.

3 Income Tax Act, Cap. 134, § 10(1). (Sing.)

test, "income from business operations carried out in Singapore will generally be sourced to Singapore."[4] Whether business operations are "carried out in Singapore" is a question of facts and degree. In many cases, it will be more difficult to determine whether a company's business operations are carried out in Singapore when the company is engaged in e-commerce rather than traditional transactions.[5] The IRAS's Income Tax Guide on E-Commerce provides guidance by analyzing whether companies fitting five profiles will be subject to the income tax when they engage in e-commerce.

B. Income Tax as Applied to E-Commerce Business Operations

1. In General The IRAS has issued guidance for determining whether a company's business operations are carried out in Singapore when the company engages in e-commerce transactions. The publication examines the income tax status of companies fitting five general e-business models.[6] The income tax liability of businesses that do not fit squarely within one of the five models discussed in the IRAS guidance will depend on the facts and circumstances in that particular case. If, overall, the facts indicate that the company's business operations are carried out in Singapore, the operations will be subject to Singapore's income tax. Otherwise, the company will not be subject to the income tax in Singapore. The tax treatment of e-commerce businesses is summarized in the following table.

Business Operations	*Web Site Hosted In*	*Branch*	*Liable for Income Tax in Singapore?*
Singapore	Singapore	No	Yes
Singapore	Foreign	No	Yes
Singapore	Foreign	Foreign	Yes/No • Income attributable to Singapore business operations will be subject to the income tax. • Income attributable to the foreign branch will not be subject to the income tax
Foreign	Singapore	No	No
Foreign	Singapore	Singapore	Yes/No • Income attributable to Singapore business operations will be subject to the income tax. • Income attributable to the foreign branch will not be subject to the income tax.

2. Business Operations in Singapore That Generate Income from a Web Site Hosted on a Server in Singapore When all of a company's business operations are carried out in Singapore, all of its income will be sourced to Singapore and thus taxed in Singapore.[7]

4 *See* Income Tax Guide on E-Commerce, *supra* note 2, at 1.

5 *Id.*

6 *Id.* at 3–8.

7 *Id.* at 3.

3. *Business Operations in Singapore That Generate Income from a Web Site Hosted on a Server Located Outside Singapore, with No Foreign Branch*

A. IN GENERAL The tax treatment of income generated by a company with its business operations in Singapore, through a site hosted outside Singapore, is best analyzed using two examples: a company manufacturing, in Singapore, the goods sold through its portal, and a company supplying intangible products (e.g., e-books and software). While the result is likely the same in both cases—the income of both will be taxed in Singapore—the analysis is nuanced depending on whether a company produces tangible or intangible goods.[8]

B. COMPANY MANUFACTURING TANGIBLE GOODS IN SINGAPORE A company manufacturing goods in Singapore and selling them through a Web portal located outside Singapore is generating its business income through Singapore, even if the sales are technically occurring on the foreign server. The company is manufacturing its products, providing product information for its Web portal, receiving payment, and handling customer inquiries and service issues in Singapore. Thus, overall, the business's operations are carried out in Singapore, and its income will be sourced to Singapore and subject to the income tax.[9]

C. COMPANY SUPPLYING INTANGIBLE PRODUCTS A company supplying intangible products over the Internet probably does not have the same level of connection with Singapore as a company manufacturing its products in Singapore. But the company will still be taxed on its income in Singapore since the operations supporting the sale of the intangible products are carried out there. These operations include supplying the intangible products, advertising, site maintenance, customer support, and receipt of payments. When the bulk of a business's operations is thus carried out in Singapore, its income is considered sourced to Singapore and will be subject to the income tax.[10]

4. *Business Operations in Singapore That Generate Income from a Web Site Hosted on a Server Located Outside Singapore, with a Foreign Branch*

Income attributable to a company's operations in Singapore is sourced to Singapore and will be subject to the income tax. The branch's income, however, will not be sourced to or taxed in Singapore since the branch's operations are carried on outside the country. If the branch remits income back to its Singapore operations, that income will be taxed in Singapore.[11]

Whether income generated by the Web site will be considered profits of the branch depends on the branch's level of involvement with the activities leading to the generation of income through the site. If the branch markets and sells the company's products and completes the sales originated on the Web site, the income generated by the site is likely to be sourced to the branch and will not be subject to tax in Singapore. If the

8 *Id.* at 3–4.
9 *Id.*
10 *Id.*
11 *Id.* at 4–5.

branch only incidentally participates in the company's sales, income will be sourced to the company's Singapore operations and will be taxed in Singapore.[12]

5. *Business Operations Outside Singapore That Generate Income through a Web Site Hosted in Singapore*

A. IN GENERAL In this case, the company is not likely to be subject to income tax in Singapore. The result will be the same whether the company supplies intangible products or manufactures, in a foreign country, the products it sells through its Web portal. Although the result will be the same with respect to the income tax, there may be withholding consequences for a company supplying intangible goods.[13]

B. COMPANY MANUFACTURES TANGIBLE GOODS OUTSIDE SINGAPORE FOR SALE ON ITS SINGAPORE SITE The result in this case contrasts with the case in which a company bases its business operations in Singapore and makes sales through a portal operated outside Singapore. In that case, the operations supporting the sale of products through its Web site occurred almost entirely in Singapore, with only incidental support from its foreign site. Here, the company's operations are carried out almost entirely outside Singapore with only incidental support from its Singapore Web portal. As a result, the company's income will not be sourced to or taxed in Singapore.[14]

C. COMPANY SUPPLIES INTANGIBLE GOODS A company supplying intangible goods is not likely to have the extensive physical infrastructure of a manufacturer. But when what operations the company does have are situated outside Singapore, with only incidental support from its Web portal located in Singapore, the company's income will not be sourced to or taxed in Singapore.[15]

Although a foreign company supplying intangible goods through a Singapore site is not subject to the income tax, payments to the company may still be subject to the withholding tax. Tax must be withheld from payments made by a Singapore resident or permanent establishment in Singapore for the "use or right to use" digitized products. The customer making the payment will be responsible for withholding the tax and paying the tax to the comptroller.[16]

6. *Business Operations Outside Singapore with Web site Hosted in Singapore, Singapore Branch*

A. COMPANY MANUFACTURES AND SELLS TANGIBLE GOODS The company will not be subject to income tax on its business operations carried on outside Singapore, but since the branch's business operations are carried out in Singapore the branch's income will be taxed there.[17] Whether income from the Web site will be sourced to the branch or its foreign head office depends on the nature and extent of the branch's activities. If the

12 *Id.*
13 *Id.* at 5–6.
14 *Id.*
15 *Id.*
16 *Id.*
17 *Id.* at 7–8.

branch markets and sells the company's products and completes the sales originated on the Web site, the income generated by the site is likely to be sourced to the branch and will be subject to the income tax in Singapore. If the branch provides only incidental support for the company's sales and the foreign head office (or a foreign branch) has primary responsibility for the sales, the income will be sourced outside Singapore and will not be subject to the income tax in Singapore.[18]

B. COMPANY SUPPLIES INTANGIBLE GOODS As above, the company supplying intangible goods will have fewer physical connections to Singapore. But if the Singapore branch plays a substantial part in completing transactions in Singapore, the branch will be considered to be carrying on a business in Singapore.[19] Whether a company's activities are carried out in Singapore in a particular case is a question of facts and degree. Activities substantiating the branch's role in completing transactions in Singapore may include marketing, customer service, and electronic delivery.[20]

D. Royalty and Other Payments

In addition to income from business operations in Singapore, the income tax is also levied on other payments that are deemed sourced to Singapore. Some royalty payments and profits from nonresidents in the business of transmitting messages via cable or wirelessly are deemed to be sourced to Singapore and will thus be subject to the income tax. Royalty payments and payments for the right to use "scientific, technical, industrial or commercial knowledge," or services in connection with that knowledge, are deemed to be sourced to Singapore when they are paid by a Singapore resident or permanent establishment.[21] The profits of nonresidents in the business of transmitting messages via cable or any wireless means are deemed sourced to Singapore to the extent the payments are received for transmitting messages into Singapore.[22]

III. GOODS AND SERVICES TAX (GST)

A. Introduction

The GST is a value-added tax on direct consumption in Singapore, levied on GST-taxable persons.[23] GST-taxable persons must collect the GST from customers, and the tax must be paid at the time goods or services are purchased.[24] E-Commerce merchants have the same responsibility for collecting and paying the GST as traditional merchants.[25]

---

18 *Id.*
19 *Id.*
20 *Id.*
21 Income Tax Act, Cap. 134, § 12(7) (Sing.).
22 Income Tax Act, Cap. 134, § 12(3) (Sing.).
23 Goods and Services Tax Act, Cap. 117A, § 8 (Sing.).
24 Goods and Services Tax Act, Cap. 117A, § 8(1) (Sing.).
25 GOODS AND SERVICES TAX GUIDE ON E-COMMERCE, *supra* note 2, at 3.

B. GST-Registered Persons

A person is GST taxable if[26] (1) that person's taxable supplies exceed S$1 million for a quarter and the 3 preceding quarters, or (2) at any time the person's taxable supplies are expected to exceed S$1 million for the next 12 months. GST-taxable persons must register for the GST.[27] Anyone who is GST taxable and does not register for the GST may be subject to a fine.[28] Only GST-registered persons may charge and collect the GST from customers.

C. GST Rates

Goods and services subject to the GST will be either standard-rated or zero-rated. The GST was introduced in 1994 with a standard rate of 3 percent; the rate was increased to 5 percent in 2004; and the current rate of 7 percent was effective from July 1, 2007.[29] Some goods and services are zero-rated. When goods or services are zero-rated, they attract the GST at a 0 percent rate, and the GST need not be collected from customers. A supply of exported goods or international services can be zero-rated.[30]

D. Physical Goods

The destination of physical goods sold in e-commerce determines whether the transaction may be zero- or standard-rated. The GST will apply to the sale of goods over the Internet if the supply is made in Singapore. Thus, a GST-registered person who sells physical goods over the Internet must charge customers for the GST on purchases that will be delivered locally. And a GST-registered person selling physical goods over the Internet may zero-rate any goods delivered outside Singapore.[31]

E. Services (Including Digitized Goods)

1. Introduction A GST-registered person must charge customers "belonging in Singapore" for the GST on the sale of services. Sale of services includes the sale of digitized goods—including music, software, and e-books—over the Internet. The sale may only be zero-rated if the purchaser does not "belong in Singapore."[32] Whether a person belongs in Singapore will be determined based on the customer's IP address, domain name, and business address.[33]

---

26 Goods and Services Tax Act, Cap. 117A, First Schedule, § 1. (Sing.).
27 Goods and Services Tax Act, Cap. 117A, § 8(2). (Sing.).
28 Goods and Services Tax Act, Cap. 117A, § 61 (Sing.).
29 Goods and Services Tax Act, Cap. 117A, § 16 (Sing.).
30 Goods and Services Tax Act, Cap. 117A, § 21(3) (Sing.).
31 GOODS AND SERVICES TAX GUIDE ON E-COMMERCE, *supra* note 2, at 2.
32 *Id.* at 3.
33 *Id.* at 4.

2. "Belonging" Defined A supplier of goods or services will be treated as belonging in a country if the supplier has

1. A business establishment or other fixed establishment in that country and no establishment anywhere else;
2. Its usual place of residence is in that country, but no establishment; or
3. Multiple establishments, but the establishment most directly connected with the supply is in that country.[34]

According to the IRAS's guidance, with respect to e-commerce, a person has a fixed establishment in Singapore if that person has

1. A Singapore address;
2. A Singapore domain name; or
3. A Singapore IP address.[35]

Otherwise, a person has a fixed establishment in a country outside Singapore if

1. The person's address is outside Singapore;
2. The person's domain name or IP address indicates that the business is a foreign establishment;
3. The person gives a declaration, at the time of transaction, that the company is located outside Singapore; and
4. There is other information indicating the person belongs outside Singapore.[36]

3. Zero-Rated Goods and Services

A. EXPORTED GOODS Exported goods will be zero-rated, and customers need not be charged for the GST, if the supplier can prove the goods are being exported.[37] To prove that goods are being exported, necessary export documents must be maintained.[38] Necessary export documents include a bill of lading, an invoice to the customer, purchase orders, packing lists and delivery notes, insurance documents, and evidence of payment.[39] GST-registered exporters should ensure that the necessary export documents are available at the point of supply, but they have up to sixty days from the date of supply to gather the documents.[40]

---

34 Goods and Services Tax Act, Cap. 117A, § 15(3) (Sing.).

35 GOODS AND SERVICES TAX GUIDE ON E-COMMERCE, *supra* note 2, at 4.

36 *Id.*

37 Goods and Services Tax Act, Cap. 117A, § 21(1) (Sing.).

38 Goods and Services Tax Act, Cap. 117A, § 22(6) (Sing.); Goods and Services Tax (General) Regulations § 105 (Sing.).

39 GOODS AND SERVICES TAX GUIDE ON E-COMMERCE, *supra* note 2, at 8.

40 INTERNAL REVENUE AUTHORITY OF SINGAPORE, GOODS AND SERVICES TAX: A GUIDE ON EXPORTS, Preamble, paragraph 2 (2005), available at http://www.iras.gov.sg/irasHome/uploadedFiles/Quick_Links/e-Tax_Guides/GST/gstguideonexports(1).pdf.

B. INTERNATIONAL SERVICES A supply of services will be zero-rated only if the services are international services. A list of zero-rated services that will be deemed international is found in the Goods and Services Tax Act.[41] International services include (1) the supply of international transport (e.g., sale of airline tickets); (2) services related to the supply of goods situated outside Singapore, or entertainment services performed wholly outside Singapore; and (3) services under a contract with a person belonging outside Singapore benefiting a person belonging outside Singapore who is outside Singapore at the time the services are rendered.[42]

F. Imported Goods and Services

GST-registered persons importing goods with a value exceeding S$400.00 must pay the GST to Singapore Customs on the value of the goods. However, the GST need not be paid on downloaded, digitized goods when they are downloaded. When services are imported, the GST need not be paid if the person performing the services does not "belong in Singapore."[43]

IV. TREATY LAW

Singapore's double-taxation avoidance agreements (DTAAs) generally follow the Organization for Economic Cooperation and Development (OECD) Model Convention.

V. RETENTION OF ELECTRONIC RECORDS

A. Electronic Records in General

The Income Tax Act and GST Act require businesses to maintain business records for at least five years. While compliance with this requirement is relatively simple in the case of traditional businesses, e-commerce businesses are less likely to produce paper records than traditional businesses, and electronic records can take an infinite variety of forms. The IRAS has issued guidance approving electronic record-keeping and clarifying requirements for businesses that choose to retain electronic rather than paper records.[44] Taxpayers do not need approval from the IRAS to keep electronic records, but they

41 Goods and Services Tax Act, Cap. 117A, § 21(3) (Sing.).

42 Goods and Services Tax Act, Cap. 117A, § 21(3) (Sing.).

43 GOODS AND SERVICES TAX GUIDE ON E-COMMERCE, *supra* note 2, at 3.

44 INTERNAL REVENUE AUTHORITY OF SINGAPORE, GOODS AND SERVICES TAX: KEEPING MACHINE-SENSIBLE RECORDS AND ELECTRONIC INVOICING 1 (2007), available at http://www.iras.gov.sg/irasHome/uploadedFiles/Businesses/For_sole-proprietors_self-employed/Before_filing/machine_sensible.pdf. The guidance was issued under the title "Goods and Services Tax." However, the publication does discuss both the GST and the income tax and states that taxpayers, in general, must comply with the guide.

must follow the guidelines laid out by the IRAS in the publication.[45] Generally, businesses that keep electronic records must "ensure the integrity, completeness, accuracy and availability of the retained records." While records may be kept by a third party, responsibility for the records always falls on the business for which the records are kept.[46] The IRAS lists 12 requirements for businesses that keep records in electronic form:[47]

1. The records must accurately "capture all transactions completely."
2. The records must contain sufficient details to verify the transactions.
3. Records must be kept in their original format, or if the format is changed, documentation on the conversion process must be maintained.
4. Passwords and computer-generated records such as digital signatures and decryption keys must be maintained.
5. Records must be capable of being retrieved and printed as a hard copy.
6. Internal controls must be adequate to ensure that every transaction is recorded and retained.
7. Internal controls must be "adequate to ensure the reliability of the electronic storage system."
8. Internal controls must be adequate to ensure the "integrity, completeness, accuracy and availability" of the electronic records.
9. Security precautions must be adequate to ensure the records will not be damaged.
10. There must be "backup and recovery procedures" in place to ensure that the records will be available in the event that they are damaged or lost.
11. The business must provide the resources necessary to allow the IRAS to "locate, retrieve, read and reproduce" the records.
12. When the IRAS requires access to records, the business must be able to produce the records in hard- and soft-copy formats.

B. Electronic Tax Invoices

Businesses that issue electronic tax invoices must comply with the following requirements:[48]

1. Internal controls must be established to ensure that the tax invoices that are transmitted to customers are "complete and accurate."
2. The business must ensure that the invoices cannot be manipulated at any time.
3. Internal controls must be established to "ensure that all output GST will be fully accounted for."
4. Tax invoices must contain the information required by the GST regulations.

---

45 *Id.* at 1.

46 *Id.* at 2.

47 *Id.* at 3–5.

48 *Id.* at 5–6.

5. Tax invoices may not be issued in both paper and electronic form for the same transaction unless the business takes the steps necessary to prevent the customer from "double claiming" the input tax.
6. If the business does not intend to keep the invoices in electronic form, the invoices must be printed in hard copy and retained.

C. Penalties for Noncompliance

Failure to comply with the IRAS publication's guidance on electronic record keeping is an offense under the GST and Income Tax Acts. Under the Income Tax Act, the fine is up to S$1,000 or imprisonment for up to six months if the fine payment is not made. Under the GST Act, the penalty is a fine of up to S$5,000 or six months imprisonment, or both.[49]

VI. PROHIBITED ACTIVITY ON THE INTERNET

A. Introduction

Two of the most significant sources of e-commerce revenue, adult entertainment and gambling, are illegal in Singapore. The country takes a hard stance against both these popular market segments, imposing significant penalties on consumers, producers, operators, and distributors of these products and services.

B. Media Development Authority

Singapore's Media Development Authority (MDA) is responsible for, inter alia, licensing and regulating media services in Singapore.[50] The MDA "has the power to impose sanctions, including fines, on licensees who contravene this Code of Practice."[51] The Internet Code of Practice, published by the MDA, provides guidance for Internet broadcasting licensees about prohibited content. Internet service providers (ISPs) and Internet content providers (ICPs) are charged with ensuring that their services are not used for the promotion or creation of pornography, gambling, fortune telling, licensable professional services, or prostitution.[52] In addition to licensing and regulating Internet providers, the MDA blocks sites it deems to be "high impact illegal websites." Although the MDA has considerable power to regulate the Internet,the agency recognizes that regulation of the Internet is an impossible task and encourages self-regulation by providers.[53]

---

49 *Id.* at 6.

50 Media Development Authority of Singapore Act, Cap. 172, § 11(1)(a) (Sing.).

51 Media Development Authority of Singapore, Internet Code of Practice § 1(2) (1997) (Sing.).

52 Broadcasting (Class Licence) Notification § 15 (1996) (Sing.).

53 Media Development Authority of Singapore, 1001 Questions: Frequently Asked Questions Answered, http://www.mda.gov.sg/wms.www/1001qns.aspx?sid=165&fid=62&qid=1152#Html Anchor_Anchor (last visited Aug. 26, 2008).

C. Licensees Regulated by the MDA

ISPs and ICPs are automatically deemed licensees under the Broadcasting Act, whether they register as licensees or not.[54] ICPs include any individual providing content through the Internet for "business, political, or religious purposes." Also included are corporations or groups of individuals providing content through the Internet, whether or not the content is for "business, political, or religious purposes." Web publishers and Web server administrators are deemed ICPs.[55] Thus, individuals who post content on the Internet are not regulated by the MDA unless they post content for "business, political, or religious purposes."

The Internet Code of Practice, published by the MDA, provides guidance for licensees, defining, and at least marginally elucidating, broad categories of material the MDA considers to be "prohibited material."

D. Online Gambling

1. Introduction Singapore strictly prohibits unauthorized gambling and advertising or promotion of gambling. The primary laws governing gambling in Singapore are the Betting Act and the Common Gaming Houses Act, both of which reach particular businesses and online gambling activities.

2. The Betting Act

A. INTRODUCTION The Betting Act (BA) focuses primarily on wagering on horseracing and other sports. Whether the BA prohibits Internet sports wagering is a matter of interpretation, because the BA does not refer specifically to Internet forms of gambling. It is an offense under the BA to manage or assist in the management of a common betting house or betting information center.[56] While not specifically including Web-based gambling establishments, both terms are likely to catch some Internet gambling establishments.

B. COMMON BETTING HOUSES Under the act, "common betting house" means[57]

(a) Any place kept or used for betting or wagering on any event or contingency of or relating to any horse-race or other sporting event to which the public or any class of the public has or may have access;

(b) Any place kept or used for habitual betting or wagering on any such event or contingency as aforesaid, whether the public has, or may have, access thereto or not; and

---

54 Broadcasting (Class Licence) Notification § 3 & Schedule § 1 (1996) (Sing.).

55 Broadcasting (Class Licence) Notification § 2 (1996) (Sing.).

56 Betting Act, Cap. 21, § 3(1) (Sing.).

57 Betting Act, Cap. 21, § 2(1) (Sing.).

(c) Any place used by a bookmaker for the purpose of receiving or negotiating bets or wagers on any such event or contingency as aforesaid whether or not the bets or wagers reach the bookmaker by the hand of the person placing the bet or his agent or the bookmaker's agent or through the telephone or by post or by telegram or by any other means.

Subsections (a) and (b) above likely apply to unauthorized Internet gambling sites run from Singapore, and subsection (c) reaches Singapore residents hosting gambling sites anywhere in the world. Thus, it is an offense for any Singapore resident to operate an Internet gambling site regardless of where the site's servers are located. It is also an offense for a nonresident to operate an Internet gambling site from servers within Singapore. However, it is unlikely the Singapore government will attempt to reach foreign sites operating from outside Singapore.

C. BETTING INFORMATION CENTERS "Betting information center" is defined by the BA as "any place kept or used for receiving or transmitting by telephone or other means any information relating to any horserace or other sporting event for the purpose of betting or wagering in contravention of this Act." Because of the broad definition in the BA, "betting information center" likely includes Internet sites operated in Singapore. Thus, operating a site providing only information that is intended to be used for gambling on sports or horse racing is an offense under the BA.

3. The Common Gaming Houses Act The Common Gaming Houses Act (CGHA) criminalizes activities associated with gaming and unauthorized lotteries. The CGHA prohibits any person from operating a common gaming house or gambling therein. "Common gaming house" includes any place used for gaming, to which the public has access, and any place used for habitual gaming, whether the public has access or not.[58] Presumably, Internet gambling sites are "common gambling houses" under the definition.

Gaming in a common gaming house is an offense under the CGHA.[59] Additionally, it is an offense under the CGHA for an individual to gamble in a public place, like a cyber-café.[60] It is also an offense under the CGHA to deposit money (or money's worth), as a stake or for purchasing a lottery ticket, with any person running a common gaming house.[61] Any lottery ticket brought into the country must be forfeited to the government.[62]

4. Advertising of Gambling Sites The BA and CGHA prohibit the advertisement of common betting houses, common gaming houses, and betting information centers.[63] Such advertisement is prohibited regardless of the location of the gambling house. Thus Internet advertising for any type of gambling is strictly prohibited. While Singapore is

58 Common Gaming Houses Act, Cap. 49, § 2(1) (Sing.).
59 Common Gaming Houses Act, Cap. 49, § 7 (Sing.).
60 Common Gaming Houses Act, Cap. 49, § 8 (Sing.).
61 Common Gaming Houses Act, Cap. 49, § 9(1) (Sing.).
62 Common Gaming Houses Act, Cap. 49, § 9(3) (Sing.).
63 Betting Act, Cap. 21, § 3(1)(e) (Sing.); Common Gaming Houses Act, Cap. 49, § 4(1)(d) (Sing.).

not likely to pursue offshore gambling sites, companies with a connection to Singapore should avoid advertising gambling sites.

D. Responsibility of ISP and ICP

Under the Broadcast (Class License) Notification (BCLN), "A licensee who provides any licensable broadcasting service … shall: (a) ensure that its service is not used for, or in furtherance of, games and lotteries, the conduct of which is an offence under the Common Gaming Houses Act (Cap. 49) unless the licensee is exempted from the provisions of that Act; (b) avoid the broadcast of horse-racing analyses, commentaries or tips, other than horse-racing results, for the purpose of gambling."[64]

Thus service providers in Singapore (like payment gateway providers or Internet access providers) who knowingly provide services that would "assist" an Internet gambling Web site could be prosecuted for an offence under section 5(a) of the CGHA. There does not appear to be any similar provision in the notification applying to "sports-type betting" offenses under the BA.

E. Pornography

1. Prohibited Material under the Internet Code of Practice The Internet Code of Practice provides that a licensee "shall use his best efforts to ensure that prohibited material is not broadcast via the Internet to users in Singapore."[65] The MDA's Internet Code of Practice provides a general definition of "prohibited material" and an enumerated list of factors that should be taken into account when determining whether material is prohibited. "Prohibited material is material that is objectionable on the grounds of public interest, public morality, public order, public security, national harmony, or is otherwise prohibited by applicable Singapore laws."[66]The Internet Code of Practice provides a list of factors that should be taken into account when making the determination of whether material should be deemed prohibited:[67]

(a) whether the material depicts nudity or genitalia in a manner calculated to titillate;
(b) whether the material promotes sexual violence or sexual activity involving coercion or non-consent of any kind;
(c) whether the material depicts a person or persons clearly engaged in explicit sexual activity;
(d) whether the material depicts a person who is, or appears to be, under 16 years of age in sexual activity, in a sexually provocative manner or in any other offensive manner;
(e) whether the material advocates homosexuality or lesbianism, or depicts or promotes incest, pedophilia, bestiality and necrophilia;

64 Broadcasting (Class License) Notification, Schedule, ¶ 15(a), (b).
65 Media Development Authority of Singapore, Internet Code of Practice § 2 (1997) (Sing.).
66 Media Development Authority of Singapore, Internet Code of Practice § 2 (1997) (Sing.).
67 Media Development Authority of Singapore, Internet Code of Practice § 4(1) (1997) (Sing.).

(f) whether the material depicts detailed or relished acts of extreme violence or cruelty; and
(g) whether the material glorifies, incites or endorses ethnic, racial or religious hatred, strife or intolerance.

The FAQ on the MDA's Web site provides guidance with respect to whether the MDA polices individuals accessing prohibited material on the Internet. Responding to the question of whether "accessing pornography on the Internet is illegal," the MDA site states that "the MDA does not monitor or track users' access to any sites on the Internet and does not interfere with what an individual accesses in the privacy of their homes. We are primarily concerned with the purveyors and distributors of pornography. Unless you engage in such activities, the mere act of visiting such sites is not an offence."[68]

The MDA analysis of the legality of viewing pornography in Singapore is potentially misleading since the Internet Code of Practice applies only to licensees, not consumers. While the MDA will not pursue individuals who view pornography on their computers, Singapore's criminal law strictly prohibits the production, sale, or possession of most adult material.

2. Criminal Sale and Possession of Obscene Material Pornography is illegal in Singapore, and the prohibition is explicitly extended to include adult material transmitted over the Internet. The Penal Code prohibits a broad range of activities associated with pornography, including the possession, sale, transmission by electronic means, or exhibition of any obscene object (hereafter collectively referred to as "the offenses under this section").[69] Under the Penal Code, "obscene" means "any thing or matter the effect of which is, if taken as a whole, such as to tend to deprave and corrupt persons who are likely, having regard to all relevant circumstances, to read, see or hear the matter contained or embodied in it."[70] "Objects" include data stored or transmitted electronically.[71] The Penal Code also prohibits the following acts:[72]

- Exporting or importing obscene objects for the purpose of committing any of the offenses under this section
- Profiting from or participating in a business that the person knows, or should know, engages in any of the offenses under this section
- Offering to or attempting to commit any of the offenses under this section
- Advertising any of the offenses under this section

Violation of the aforementioned section may result in imprisonment of up to three months, or a fine, or both.[73]

68 Media Development Authority of Singapore, 1001 Questions, Frequently Asked Questions Answered, http://www.mda.gov.sg/wms.www/1001qns.aspx?sid=-1&fid=1&qid=1160#HtmlAnchor_Anchor (last visited Aug. 26, 2008).
69 Penal Code, Cap. 224, § 292(a) (Sing.).
70 Penal Code, Cap. 224, § 42 (Sing.).
71 Penal Code, Cap. 224, § 292(2) (Sing.).
72 Penal Code, Cap. 224, § 292(b)–(e). (Sing.).
73 Penal Code, Cap. 224, § 292(1), (Sing.)

PART III

Australia

Chapter 7

Taxation and E-Commerce in Australia

Peter Norman
Deacons

I. INTRODUCTION

A. E-Commerce in Australia

As has been the case with most developed economies throughout the world, e-commerce activity in Australia has burgeoned in recent years as evidenced by the following data published by the Australian Bureau of Statistics regarding the business use of information technology and Internet commerce:[1]

	2002–2003	*2005–2006*
Proportion of businesses which reported		
Internet use (%)	71.4	81.3
Web presence (%)	23.0	29.8
Proportion of businesses which		
Placed orders via the Internet or Web (%)	27.8	37.3
Received orders via the Internet or Web (%)	13.3	20.9
Internet income (A$ billion)	24.3	56.7
Proportion of businesses with Internet access via broadband connections	N/A[2]	82.5

1 Business Use of Information Technology, Ref. 8129.0, AUSTRALIAN BUREAU OF STATISTICS (2005–2006).

2 In 2003–2004 the proportion was reported to be 41.5%. *Id.*

The wholesale trade sector had the highest number of orders received via the Internet (39%), followed by the manufacturing sector, which received 35 percent of orders via the Internet.

B. Approach of the Australian Legislature and Australian Taxation Office to E-Commerce

1. Electronic Transactions Legislation Each state and territory of Australia, as well as the Commonwealth of Australia, has electronic transactions legislation based on the UNCITRAL 1996 Model Law on Electronic Commerce.[3] This legislation is intended to be uniform and to facilitate e-commerce. For example, section 3 of the Electronic Transactions Act of 2000 (NSW) specifies the objects of the act as being to provide a regulatory framework that

> recognizes the importance of the information economy to the future economic and social prosperity of Australia; and facilitates the use of electronic transactions; and promotes business and community confidence in the use of electronic transactions; and enables business and the community to use electronic communications in their dealings with government.

The legislation in each Australian jurisdiction generally provides that, "for the purposes of the law of the jurisdiction, a transaction is not invalid because it took place by means of one or more electronic communications." The following requirements imposed under the law of a relevant jurisdiction can generally be met in electronic form: (1) a requirement to give information in writing; (2) a requirement to provide a signature; (3) a requirement to produce a document; (4) a requirement to record information; and (5) a requirement to retain a document. This legislation also provides rules for determining the time and place of the dispatch and receipt of an electronic communication, and the purported originator of an electronic communication is bound by it for the purposes of a law of the relevant jurisdiction only if the communication was sent by the purported originator or with his authority.[4]

Under the legislation, an "electronic communication" is defined as "a communication of information in the form of data, text or images by means of guided and/or unguided electromagnetic energy; or a communication of information in the form of speech by means of guided and/or misguided electronic energy, where the speech is processed at its destination by an automated voice recognition system."[5]

---

3 Electronic Transactions Act 1999 (Cth); Electronic Transactions Act 2001 (ACT); Electronic Transactions Act 2000 (NSW); Electronic Transactions (Northern Territory) Act 2000 (NT); Electronic Transactions (Queensland) Act 2001 (Qld); Electronic Transactions Act 2000 (Tas); Electronic Transactions (Victoria) Act 2000 (Vic); Electronic Transactions Act 2003 (WA).

4 *See*, e.g., simplified outlines of the legislation provided in Electronic Transactions Act 2000 (NSW), § 4; *See also*, Electronic Transactions Act 1999 (Cth), § 4.

5 *See, e.g.,* Electronic Transactions Act 2000 (NSW), § 5; *See also*, Electronic Transactions Act 1999 (Cth), § 6.

2. Australian Taxation Office The legislature in Australia cannot be said to have been active in addressing various issues concerning the taxation of e-commerce transactions. Accordingly, the provisions of Australian taxation law applicable to transactions in general need to be applied as best they can to e-commerce transactions. Section II below discusses the application of Australian tax rules concerning direct taxation (the Australian income tax), and section III discusses the rules concerning indirect taxation.

Similarly, the Australian Taxation Office (ATO) has also not been active recently in dealing with taxation of e-commerce transactions. In 1996, when the commercial application of the Internet was starting to be appreciated, the ATO created the Electronic Commerce Project to examine and report on the tax implications of e-commerce. It published the resulting "Tax and the Internet" discussion report in August 1997. This was followed in December 1999 with "Tax and the Internet: Second Report" which was published following consultation by the ATO with business, academics, and government agencies on various issues raised in the first report. That consultation process led the ATO to conclude that

> . . . while electronic commerce does not prove any significant threat to revenue at this time, there are some immediate actions that can and should be taken to address electronic commerce issues in the current environment to ensure that the ATO is well positioned to take advantage of the opportunities offered by the new technology and meet the challenges as and when they emerge.[6]

The ATO emphasized that tax neutrality should determine the legal and administrative framework for the taxation of e-commerce:

> The overriding principle is that there should be broad neutrality between the treatment of businesses engaged in traditional physical commerce and those engaged in electronic commerce. Practically this means that, wherever possible and subject to the differences in the environments, business engaged in electronic commerce should be subject to equivalent arrangements as businesses engaged in physical commerce.[7]

Part of the action plan that the ATO proposed in the Electronic Commerce Project's second report was to establish an Australian consultative forum with business-sector representatives to facilitate open and inclusive discussions on e-commerce taxation issues.[8] This forum, the Electronic Commerce Industry Partnership, dealt mainly with goods and services tax (GST) issues that had been identified in the e-commerce context and led to the publication of the ATO's "Issue Register."[9] The ATO has also issued a number of taxation rulings, practice statements, and interpretative decisions relevant to e-commerce transactions, which are discussed below.

---

6 ATO, *Tax and the Internet: Second Report*, Australian Government Publishing Service, Canberra, 4, (Dec. 1999).

7 ATO, *Tax and the Internet: Discussion Report*, Australian Government Publishing Service, Canberra, p.96., (Aug. 1997).

8 *Id.* at p.12.

9 http://www.ato.gov.au/print.asp?doc=/content/18428.htm

Finally, the ATO has been very successful in developing and encouraging the electronic filing of tax returns—referred to as e-tax. The ATO reported that 1.9 million filed their 2007 tax returns online using e-tax.[10]

II. DIRECT TAXATION ISSUES

A. Introduction

The ATO's Electronic Commerce Project indicated that "one of the fundamental issues that will need to be resolved is when and to what extent an entity involved in electronic commerce comes within the tax jurisdiction of a country."[11] These issues are examined in the paragraphs following.

B. Residence of Entities Involved in E-Commerce Transactions

1. Jurisdictional Operation of Australian Income Taxation Section 6-5 of the Income Tax Assessment Act 1997 (Cth) (ITAA97) sets forth the jurisdictional operation of Australia's income tax laws:

- An Australian resident's assessable income includes ordinary income derived from all sources during the income year, whether in or out of Australia (ITAA97, § 6-5(2)).
- A foreign resident's assessable income includes ordinary income derived directly or indirectly during the income year from all Australian sources, as well as ordinary income that a provision includes in their assessable income on some basis other than having an Australian source (ITAA97, § 6-6(3)).

"Ordinary income" is defined as income according to ordinary concepts (ITAA97, § 6-6(3)). There is also "statutory income," which comprises amounts that are not ordinary income included in a taxpayer's assessable income (ITAA97, § 6-10). There are similar source rules for statutory income although, in the case of nonresidents, assessable income will also include statutory income that a provision in the tax law includes in their assessable income on some basis other than having an Australian source (ITAA97,§ 6-10(5)).

For nonresidents, Australian capital gains tax applies to "taxable Australian property," which includes taxable Australian real property and assets used by a nonresident in carrying on business through a permanent establishment in Australia (ITAA97, § 855-15). Attention has been paid to issues relating to the source of income and the potential for foreign residents participating in e-commerce transactions with Australian parties to arrange the transaction so that income derived under that transaction is not treated as having an Australian source. E-Commerce can, however, also give rise to some questions concerning whether a party to that transaction is treated as an Australian resident.

---

10 ATO Media Release 2008/04, (Jan. 18, 2008).

11 *Id.* at p.76.

2. Residence of Individuals An individual will, under the definition of "resident" in section 6(1) of the Income Tax Assessment Act of 1936 (Cth) (ITAA36) be treated as a resident of Australia if, amongst other things

- That person has their domicile in Australia, unless the commissioner of taxation is satisfied that the person has a permanent place of abode outside Australia; or
- That person has actually been in Australia, continuously or intermittently, for more than one-half of the year of income, unless the commissioner is satisfied that the person's usual place of abode is outside Australia and the person does not intend to take up residence in Australia.

Generally, the test of residence for individuals requires some degree of physical connection with Australia. Accordingly, even if a person is able to conduct a transaction via e-commerce from a location outside Australia, if that person has the requisite physical connection with Australia, that person will be treated as an Australian resident. The challenges that e-commerce presents to the jurisdictional ability of Australia to extract tax from Internet transactions relate mainly to the ability of an individual resident in Australia to structure the transaction, via e-commerce, from a location outside Australia using an entity not resident in Australia.

The question of whether a company can be organized in such a manner to not be treated as an Australian resident is dealt with in paragraph II.B.3 below. Otherwise Australia does have controlled foreign company (CFC) rules that can operate, in certain circumstances, to attribute to an Australian resident taxpayer certain types of income derived by a foreign company controlled by the Australian resident taxpayer or a group of Australian resident taxpayers. Such attributed income would then be subject to tax in Australia. "Tainted income" derived by the foreign company would typically be subject to attribution under the CFC rules.[12] There is, however, an active income test so that if less than 5 percent of the gross turnover of the CFC is tainted income, then generally there will be no attribution to Australian resident shareholders. The CFC rules are extremely complex, and it is beyond the scope of this chapter to deal with them in any detail in the context of e-commerce. However, if the CFC is engaged in trading activities with unrelated third parties, it is unlikely that income from those trading activities will be treated as tainted income and, accordingly, unlikely to be subject to attribution to Australian resident shareholders. It would be possible for a CFC, therefore, to engage in e-commerce trading activities and earn income from those activities with a low risk of that income being attributed to Australian resident shareholders under the CFC rules. In order to successfully achieve this result, however, it is necessary that the CFC, notwithstanding that it is established in a foreign jurisdiction, not be treated as a resident of Australia under Australia's tax residence rules (as to which see paragraph II. B. 3 below).

The issues that the CFC legislation presented for e-commerce and the active income test had been identified in 1999 as an area for the ATO to examine and determine whether income from e-commerce should be treated as tainted income for the purposes

12 ITAA36, § 435. This includes passive income (e.g., dividends, interest, certain royalties and certain rentals), tainted sales income, and tainted services income.

of the CFC rules. This was due to what the ATO perceived as "the highly mobile nature of electronic commerce and its potential sensitivity to effective tax rates."[13] However, this issue appears to have now lapsed. The Board of Taxation was charged in 2007 with undertaking a review of Australia's foreign-source income antideferral regimes. While this review would examine the types of income that should be treated as active and as tainted, there was no specific mention in the board's discussion paper of any issues posed by CFCs engaged in e-commerce transactions.[14]

3. Residence of Companies A company will be treated as a resident of Australia under ITAA 36, § 6(1) under the following conditions:

- It is incorporated in Australia.
- If not incorporated in Australia, it carries on business in Australia and has either
  - Its central management and control in Australia; or
  - Australian resident shareholders control their voting powers.

The first test of residence of a corporation—namely, incorporation in Australia—does not present e-commerce issues. There would seem to be few good reasons why a nonresident engaged in e-commerce transactions that are predominantly with other nonresidents would choose to incorporate a company in Australia as the business vehicle for those activities.

The second test of residence does, however, potentially pose a number of issues. The first is whether a company incorporated outside Australia and engaged in e-commerce transactions involving parties in Australia can arrange its activities so that it does not appear to carry on business in Australia for purposes of the test. In the decision of the High Court of Australia in *Malayan Shipping Co Ltd v FCT*, 71 CLR 156 (1946), Williams J. explained the relationship between a company carrying on business in Australia and having its central management and control in Australia:

> The purpose of requiring that, in addition to carrying on business in Australia, the central management and control of the business . . . be . . . in Australia is, in my opinion, to make it clear that the mere trading in Australia by a company not incorporated in Australia will not of itself be sufficient to cause a company to become resident of Australia. But if the business of the company carried on in Australia consists of or includes its central management and control, then the company is carrying on business in Australia and its central management and control is in Australia.[15]

The second test of residence has generally been interpreted so that, if a company is found to have its central management and control in Australia, then that company is deemed to carry on business in Australia. On this basis, it was generally considered

13 ATO, *Tax and the Internet: Second Report*, Australian Government Publishing Service, Canberra, 16 (Dec. 1999).

14 Board of Taxation, *Review of Foreign Source Income Anti-Tax-Deferral Regimes*, Chapter 4, *Types of Income*, pp 35–53 (2007).

15 *Malayan Shipping*, 71 CLR 156 (1946).

sufficient that a company be found to have its central management and control in Australia without separately considering whether that company carried on business in Australia.

In Taxation Ruling TR 2004/15 the ATO set forth its views as to the interpretation of this test:

> If no business is carried on in Australia, the company cannot meet the requirements of the second statutory test and, in these circumstances it is not a resident of Australia under the second statutory test. In these situations there is no need to determine the location of the company's CM&C [central management and control], separate from its consideration of whether the company carries on business in Australia. If the company carries on business in Australia it also has to have its CM&C in Australia to meet the second statutory test.
>
> However, there are situations where the nature of the business or the level of control over the business requires the exercise of CM&C at the place where the business is carried on. Where a company's business is management of its investment assets and it undertakes only minor operational activities, the factors determining where a company is carrying on a business may be similar to those determining where it is exercising CM&C. In these situations the location of CM&C is indicative of where the company carries on business and vice versa. (at ¶¶ 6 and 7).

The ruling indicates that, in determining where a company's business is carried on, the ATO draws a distinction between a company with operational activities (e.g., trading, service provision, manufacturing, or mining activities) and a company that has a more investment-oriented business. A company that has major operational activities relative to the whole of its business carries on business where those activities take place and not necessarily where its CM&C is located. On the other hand, a company whose income-earning outcomes are largely dependent on the investment decisions made regarding its assets carries on its business where these decisions are made. This is often where CM&C is located.

The ruling also indicates (at ¶ 13) that the level of management and control necessary to satisfy the CM&C test involves high-level decision-making processes, including activities as general policy and strategic directions, major agreements, and significant financial matters. It also includes activities such as the monitoring of the company's overall corporate performance and the review of strategic recommendations made in light thereof. While location of CM&C is a question of fact, the ATO, to reduce uncertainty, will accept as a matter of practical compliance that a company will be resident if its CM&C is exercised by a board of directors that holds a majority of its meetings in Australia. The ATO will not accept this position, however, if the outcome concerning CM&C is artificial or contrived—such as "where the decisions are made by someone other than the Board."

Notwithstanding the laudable objectives of the ATO in TR 2004/15 in seeking to clarify the CM&C test to confine its operation, it has been commented that the commissioner's arguments in the ruling "struggle in light of the overwhelming weight of precedent endorsing the statements of *Williams J.* in *Malayan Shipping*."[16]

---

16 M. Dirkis, *Selected Aspects of Source and Residency in the New Millennium*, Taxation Institute of Australia, 12 (22nd National Convention, March 2007).

The potential width of the current tests for when a company will be treated as a resident were a motivation for the Australian Treasury to issue the Review of International Tax Arrangements Consultation Paper, which canvassed alternatives to the current tests of residence for companies.[17] The Board of Taxation had recommended that the only test of residence should be whether a company was incorporated in Australia.[18] The government deferred consideration of any changes pending release by the ATO of a ruling that clarified the operation of the CM&C test of corporate residence.[19] Although Taxation Ruling TR 2004/15 was issued in 2004, there has been no indication from the government whether the test of corporate residence would be changed in line with the Board of Taxation's recommendation.

Accordingly, it is possible that a company incorporated outside Australia may be treated as an Australian company if it has its CM&C in Australia. While, following the ATO's release of Ruling TR 2004/15, the risk of the ATO asserting that a company is an Australian resident in circumstances where it carries on significant operational activities outside Australia would appear to be low, it nevertheless remains an issue for companies in the business, for example, of managing investment assets. Care needs to be taken to ensure that such companies are not treated as having CM&C in Australia. This can require some amount of careful planning and, importantly, ensuring that such plans that are devised are in fact adhered to.

In an e-commerce environment, the potential uncertainty posed by the CM&C test becomes acute. For example, while ascertaining the place where a majority of board meetings are held may not be difficult when the directors hold meetings in person, it is becoming more common for directors to meet using electronic conference facilities.[20] When directors convene a meeting electronically from a number of countries, it may be difficult to determine whether the meeting took place in a particular jurisdiction. It would appear a somewhat capricious result if, because there were coincidentally a larger number of directors in Australia than in any other country at the time of a directors' meeting, that circumstance would result in the company being treated as an Australian resident and thereby subject to tax on its worldwide income.

There are also issues in determining the location of significant operational activities conducted in an e-commerce environment. Accordingly, on the basis of the ATO's views in TR 2004/15, when a company conducting significant operational activities clearly has its CM&C in Australia, it will only be treated as an Australian resident for tax purposes if those operational activities are conducted in Australia. The issues discussed in paragraph II.C, later in this chapter, regarding the potential difficulties in determining the location of an e-commerce company's operational activities to identify the source of income arising from e-commerce transactions are relevant in this regard.

---

17 Treasury, Commonwealth of Australia, *Review of International Taxation Arrangements—Consultation Paper,* 2002.

18 Board of Taxation, Commonwealth of Australia, *International Taxation: A Report to the Treasurer*, *Recommendation* 3.12 (Feb. 28, 2003).

19 Treasurer, Press Release, no. 32 (May 13, 2003).

20 Corporation Act (Cth) § 248D provides, "A directors' meeting may be called or held using any technology consented to by all the directors. The consent may be a standing one. A director may only withdraw their consent within a reasonable period before the meeting."

C. SOURCE OF INCOME DERIVED IN E-COMMERCE TRANSACTIONS

1. Introduction As indicated in paragraph II.B.1 above, under Australian tax law an Australian resident is subject to tax on assessable income derived from all sources during the income year. A foreign resident is generally subject to tax on assessable income that has an Australian source.[21] Accordingly, the question of source of income is important as far as nonresidents are concerned because it bears directly on Australian taxing jurisdiction.

ITAA97, § 995-1(1) rather unhelpfully defines "Australian source" in the following terms:

> [O]rdinary income or statutory income has an Australian source if, and only if, it is derived from a source in Australia for the purposes of the Income Tax Assessment Act 1936.

The search for some sort of clarity in Australian source rules can be a daunting task—particularly when e-commerce transactions are concerned. Much of the law relating to Australian source rules was developed at a time when taxpayers' activities could be more readily identified with a particular physical location. E-Commerce transactions are not so confined and largely take place across borders often without a clear connection to a particular physical location.

2. Statutory Source Rules The Review of Business Taxation in 1999 recommended that Australia's existing source rules be consolidated in Australia's tax law.[22] While there are some statutory source rules, common-law principles are more relevant to determining source of income in most cases—particularly when e-commerce transactions are concerned (as indicated in paragraph II.C.3 below).

Interestingly, since the Review of Business Taxation's recommendation, some of the statutory source rules have been removed rather than been consolidated.[23] Australia does, somewhat by default, have an extensive body of statutory source rules in the numerous double-taxation agreements (DTAAs) to which it is a party. Australia has DTAAs with 44 countries, which largely comprise Australia's main trading partners. These DTAAs are incorporated into Australian tax legislation and have effect, notwithstanding anything inconsistent with the provisions contained in that legislation.[24] The DTAAs typically deem certain income, profits, or gains, which under the relevant agreement may be taxed in a certain state, to have a source in that state.

The issues relating to e-commerce transactions in relation to DTAAs are dealt with in paragraph II. D. below. Other than the source rules under the DTAAs, there is a disparate sprinkling of source rules for various types of income. These rules

---

21 ITAA 97 § 6-5(3).

22 Review of Business Taxation, *A Tax System Redesigned, Recommendation 23.2(c),* 684 (1999).

23 § 25(2), ITAA36, which deemed certain interest payments to have an Australian source, and §§ 38–43, ITAA36, which dealt with the source of profit when goods purchased or manufactured outside Australia were imported into Australia and when goods purchased or manufactured in Australia were exported and sold outside Australia, were repealed with effect from Sept. 14, 2006, by the Tax Laws Amendment (Repeal of Inoperative Provisions) Act of 2006.

24 International Tax Agreements Act 1953 (Cth) § 4.

1. Determine when royalties paid or credited to a nonresident are treated as being derived from sources in Australia (ITAA36, § 6C);
2. Deem natural resource income to be attributable to sources in Australia (ITAA36, § 6CA);
3. Subject a nonresident to tax on dividends paid by a company to the extent paid out of profits derived from Australian sources (ITAA36, § 44(1)(b));
4. Relate to the source of income of a ship-owner or charterer (ITAA36, § 129,); and
5. Concern the source of premiums derived by a nonresident insurer (ITAA36, § 142).

The most relevant of these statutory source rules to e-commerce transactions is possibly section 6C, which deals with royalties paid or credited to a non resident. The application of common-law principles for determining the source of income (discussed below) occasioned some difficulty in the context of royalties, although as indicated below, those rules can also be troublesome for other types of income. Section 6C deems the following royalties to have an Australian source, thereby seeking to simplify the jurisdictional basis on which Australia can tax those royalties:

- Royalties paid or credited to a nonresident by an Australian resident, except when the royalty is an expense incurred by the resident in a business carried outside Australia.
- Royalties paid or credited by a nonresident to another nonresident when the royalties are expenses incurred by the first nonresident in carrying on business in Australia through a permanent establishment.

Although these source rules are relevant for purposes of taxing nonresidents on Australian source income under section 6-5(3) (for ordinary income) and section 6-10(5) (for statutory income), the source of royalties is less relevant since the introduction of the royalty withholding tax in 1992. ITAA36, section 128B(2B) imposes royalty withholding tax in the respect of royalties paid in the same circumstances as that referred to above in the context of section 6C. The rate of the royalty withholding tax is 30 percent unless reduced under a DTAA (typically to 10%).[25] Royalties paid in the context of e-commerce transactions pose the question of whether the payments may constitute royalties or have another character with attendant different tax consequences.

3. Common-Law Source Rules As mentioned above, the common-law rules are the most relevant to determining the source of income, including income derived in the context of e-commerce transactions. The ATO's Electronic Commerce project indicated in its second report that the ATO's action plan included

1. An examination of how existing common-law source rules apply to electronic commerce. Options for statutory source rules would be considered "if it appears that

25 Five percent in the case of the DTAAs with the United States, the United Kingdom and, more recently, Japan.

such rules are necessary to overcome uncertainties in the application of common-law source rules and difficulties in their application and administration;"[26] and

2. "[M]onitoring the application of existing source rules to determine whether these are manipulated in the electronic commerce environment for tax planning purposes."[27]

The principal difficulty in applying common-law source rules in the context of e-commerce transactions is that the law in this area was developed well before the advent of the Internet and, in many cases, the use of computer technology in business.

The oft-cited starting point for determining source is the statement by Isaacs J. in *Nathan v. FCT*[28]

> The legislature in using the word "source" meant, not a legal concept, but something which a practical man would regard as the real source of income. Legal concepts must, of course, enter into the question when we have to consider to whom a given source belongs. But the ascertainment of the actual source of a given income is a practical, hard matter of fact.

The challenges of determining whether a specific location is the source of income are obvious. This is particularly the case with e-commerce transactions, which frequently occur across borders and where the relevant business deriving income from the transaction often cannot readily be identified as having a particular location. In the early 1900s, businesses generally had a particular location from which they operated. In today's commercial environment, the business may, for example, be located in one jurisdiction, have a server through which it conducts its e-commerce activities in another jurisdiction, and direct that payment by its customers be made to yet in another jurisdiction.

Courts seeking to determine the source of income have given attention to various factors, including (1) where any relevant contracts are negotiated or concluded; (2) where contracts are performed; (3) the governing law of the contracts; (4) the currency in which the transaction is carried out; and (5) the place where payment is made.[29]

In the case of a simple sale of goods, the factor that has been seen as important is the contract of sale.[30] This factor has also been seen as important in other business contexts.[31] The place where the contract is made will usually, in such cases, be important in determining the source of the relevant income in question.

Under Australian law, a contract of sale is generally made when the last act necessary to create a binding obligation takes place. This is generally at the place where acceptance of the offer is communicated. Rules dealing with contracts formed electronically are very similar to those governing traditional contracts.[32]

---

26 *Id.* at 16.

27 *Id.*

28 *Nathan v. FCT*, 25 CLR 183 at 189, (1918).

29 ATO, *Tax and the Internet: Second Report, supra note* 13 at 79.

30 *C of T (WA) v. D & W Murray Limited*, 43 CLR 332 (1929).

31 Such as in reinsurance—*Tariff Reinsurance Limited v C of T (Vic)*, 1 AITR 281 (1938).

32 *See* Geoff Masel, [Ed.], Thomson, The Laws of Australia, *Electronic Contracts* at 8.9.1. (2002) ||

Rules as to formation of contracts, when postal communication was the predominant form, established that acceptance of an offer could complete a contract on the proper posting of a letter of acceptance, as long as it could be inferred that the offeror contemplated and intended that the offer could be accepted in this manner.[33] The postal acceptance rule has not, however, generally been extended to modern methods of communication such as facsimile and e-mail. In *Entores Ltd v. Miles Far Eastern Corporation*,[34] Denning L.J. stated that where the communication between the offeror and offeree is by some instantaneous method of communication rather than by post, the acceptance will only be effective when it is received, not when it is transmitted. The contract is made at the place where acceptance is received.

The application of the *Entores* rule to e-commerce transaction can lend itself to arranging the transaction so that a contract is deemed formed in a particular location. Where the seller of goods operates through a Web site, the location of the Web site may be determinative of the place of formation of the contract rather than the country of residence of the seller or the place where the stock of goods from which orders are filled is kept.

While it may be easy enough for a seller of products to be able to arrange its business methods so that a Web site is maintained in a particular location, the other issue that presents itself in an e-commerce transaction involving the sale of goods is the point at which there has been a valid offer to sell goods and effective acceptance of that offer. This can be a matter of Web site design and the seller's intentions:

- If the seller is merely making an "invitation to treat," that is, requesting potential buyers to make offers to purchase or enter into negotiations with the seller to purchase the goods, the contractual structure of the transaction may be that the purchaser responds to the seller's invitation to treat by transmitting an offer to purchase goods to the seller. The location of the purchaser (or purchaser's Web site, if that is the medium used) when the seller communicates its acceptance of the offer would then be the location of the contract.
- If the seller is making an offer to sell, the seller's Web site will generally offer products in a clear and definite manner with nothing left for negotiation. In this case, the *Entores* rule has clear application, and the place of acceptance of the offer, the seller's Web site, will generally be the location of the contract.

Businesses are frequently more complex than a simple sale transaction, and, in the context of a trading business, other factors will be considered apart from where the relevant contracts are formed because the income will be derived from a number of operations, not just the entry into a contract. In such cases, courts will consider the whole series of operations carried on by the business to generate income.[35] The analysis involves a

33 *Id.* at 7.1.700.

34 *Entores Ltd. V. Miles Far Eastern Corporation*, 2 QB 327 at 332–4 (1955), followed by the NSW Supreme Court in *Mendelson-Zeller Co. Inc. v T&C Providores Ltd*, 1 NSWLR 366, (1981).

35 *Thorpe Nominees Pty Limited v. FCT*, 19 ATR 1834 (1988).

determination of what transactions produced the profits earned by the business and where those transactions took place.[36] In the context of a business engaged in e-commerce, this can be challenging.

Businesses sales activities have been seen as important by Australian courts. This prompted the following comment by the ATO:

> Where the functions and activities of the trader that give rise to the sales profit are effectively conducted through a website, it would seem that the relevant activity of the enterprise is the operation of the software which constitutes the website.
>
> Since these operations are conducted by the enterprise on the server where the software is located, and in the absence of any value-adding activity performed by the trader in the jurisdiction of the customer, a court may well find that the trading activities are conducted at the location of the server where the website is situated. On this view, an enterprise would not be considered to be trading in Australia simply because it operates a website that is accessible by Australian residents, from which those residents can purchase goods.[37]

The maintenance, however, by a nonresident of a Web site located on a server in Australia through which goods are sold and the maintenance of a store of goods in Australia were seen by the ATO as giving rise to an Australian source.[38]

It may be expected that an analysis of the various operations in an e-commerce business may point to the profit having both an Australian source and a foreign source. Somewhat perversely, the provisions in ITAA36, §§ 38–41, which were repealed in 2006, did contain rules for apportioning profits in the context of the purchase and manufacture of goods. With the repeal of these provisions, although they did not necessarily cover all possible cases, one needs to turn to common-law principles to determine an appropriate apportionment. However, the Australian cases dealing with apportionment do not readily present easily applicable rules.[39]

Common-law principles also determine of the source of services income. In the case of remuneration received by an employee, or earnings for personal services earned otherwise as an employee, the factors that the courts have considered relevant are (1) the place where the employment contract or service contract is made; (2) the place of receipt of the remuneration or fees; and (3) the place of performance of the services.[40]

As in the case of determination of the source of income from a business engaged in e-commerce, where services are provided via the Internet, identifying a particular location using any of these factors can be difficult. The factors noted above for determining the place of formation of electronic contracts would also be relevant for contracts of employment/services that are formed electronically. For a foreign provider of services to

---

36 *CIR(HK) v. Hang Seng Bank Ltd*, 1 AC 306 (1991); *CIR(HK) v. HK-TVB*, STC 723 (1992). *See generally* T. Magney, *Some Aspects of Source of Income*, TAXATION INSTITUTE OF AUSTRALIA, 5th National Tax Retreat (1997).

37 ATO, *Tax and the Internet: Second Report, supra note* 13 at 81.

38 *Id.*

39 *For example, C of T (NSW) v. Kirk, AC 588 (1900); see also Mt. Morgan Gold Mining Co. Ltd v. C of T (Qld),* 33 CLR 76 (1922–23).

40 *See* T.W. Magney, *Source of Income*, TAXATION INSTITUTE OF AUSTRALIA, NSW State Convention, 26–32.

an Australian resident that performs the services offshore, it would generally be possible to use these factors to find that the remuneration or fees has a foreign source.

Where the result of the performance of the services is more important than the location at which they are actually performed, such as when the services involve a substantial creative endeavour or the use of specialized knowledge, the ATO's view is that factors such as the place of contract, the place of payment, or the place of utilization of the services are important in determining source.[41] The ATO provided an example where an Australian resident entered into a contract for the provision of accounting services over the Internet. In that case, the place or places where the services are actually performed may be of less relevance than the place of contract and where payments are made.

Despite the enormous increase in services being provided to Australian residents from foreign locations, particularly through outsourcing (the movement of internal business processes to an organization contracted to carry out the business processes) and offshoring (the transfer of an organisational function to a foreign location, regardless of whether the work is outsourced or stays within the same corporation), the ATO has paid little attention to issues concerning source of income in this context.

D. DOUBLE-TAXATION AGREEMENTS

1. Introduction As mentioned above, Australia has 44 DTAAs with major trading partners. The allocation of taxing rights between Australia and those partners under the DTAAs will, in most cases, be more important than Australia's statutory and common-law source rules. Insofar as the DTAAs, in allocating taxing rights between the contracting states, deem certain income, profits, and gains to also have a source in one of these states, those agreements could be considered to be a type of statutory source rule—albeit confined to the particular countries to which the relevant DTAA relates.

2. Permanent Establishment Concept DTAAs to which Australia is a party follow the Organization for Economic Cooperation and Development (OECD) Model Tax Convention. Accordingly, the ability of a contracting state to tax the business profits of an enterprise of the other contracting state will depend upon whether the enterprise carries on business in the source country through a permanent establishment situated therein. The definition of "permanent establishment" for these purposes generally follows the definition in Article 5 of the OECD Model. In this regard, in Australia the OECD Commentary on the OECD Model can be referred when interpreting Australia's DTAAs.[42]

The application of the permanent establishment definition in DTAAs to enterprises engaged in e-commerce activities presents a number of issues. If a relevant enterprise maintains a physical presence, such as a branch, that will clearly constitute a permanent establishment. However, enterprises often do not need a definite physical presence and, in some cases, no physical presence at all, to engage in e-commerce. In such a business an electronic presence, such as a web site, could typically replace a physical presence.

The usual starting point for determining whether a permanent establishment exists is the first part of the definition in the DTAAs, where it is defined as "a fixed place of

41 ATO, *Tax and the Internet: Second Report*, *supra* note 13 at 91.

42 *Thiel v. FCT*, 171 CLR 338 (1990).

business through which the business of an enterprise is wholly or partly carried on."[43] A Web site itself does not involve any tangible property and so cannot itself constitute a "place of business." If, however, the Web site is maintained on a server in Australia, then, arguably, that could constitute a "fixed place of business," particularly if the server is maintained in that location for a period of time. On the other hand, if the Web site is regularly moved from server to server, it may not be "fixed," because the definition of permanent establishment typically requires some connection between the place of business and a specific location which has a certain degree of permanency.[44] The OECD Model Commentary suggests that ". . . a server will need to be located at a certain place for a sufficient period of time so as to become fixed within the meaning of paragraph 1."[45]

Unlike the OECD Model, many of the DTAAs include provisions similar to that which appears in Article 4(3)(b) of the Australia-Singapore DTAA:

> (3) An enterprise of a Contracting State shall be deemed to have a permanent establishment and to carry on trade or business through that permanent establishment in the other Contracting State if—
>
> (b) substantial equipment is being used in that other State by, for or under contract with the enterprise.

The Full Federal Court of Australia considered the Singapore provision in *McDermott Industries (Aust) Pty Ltd v. FCT*[46] in relation to the bare boat charter of barges. The court stated,

> . . . it is clear that the article is concerned with equipment that is not, either in a relative, or in an absolute sense, insubstantial. Floating oil rigs are a good example of equipment which would properly be treated as substantial.[47]

Applying *McDermott* to the treatment of ship and aircraft leasing profits in the context of the United States (U.S.) and United Kingdom (UK) DTAAs in Taxation Ruling TR 2007/10, the ATO stated,

> . . . the Commissioner considers that whether the equipment in question is substantial is a question of fact and degree to be determined:
>
> - on balance, according to the facts and circumstances of each particular case; and
> - in an absolute sense, that is, when viewed independently, not in comparison with something else; or
> - in a relative sense, that is, by comparing it to something else.[48]

---

43 *For example*, Australia-U.S. DTAA, art. 5(1).

44 Commentary on Article 5, OECD Model Tax Convention on Income and Capital, OECD Committee on Fiscal Affairs, ¶¶ 5 and 6.

45 *Id.* at ¶ 42.4.

46 ATC 4398 (2005).

47 *Id.* at 4408.

48 TR 2007/10 at ¶ 110 (2007).

The ATO had little difficulty concluding in that the ships and the types of aircraft that were the subject of the cross-border leases to which the ruling applied were "substantial equipment" for the purposes of the double-taxation agreements. Ships, barges, and aircraft may be more readily identified as "substantial equipment," however, than a computer server used in an e-commerce business.

In ATO Interpretative Decision 2006/337, the meaning of the term "substantial equipment" was considered in relation to a computer system used to trade securities. This case did not concern a DTAA but rather the definition of "permanent establishment" in ITAA36, § 6(1). The ATO thought that this would not affect the meaning of the term. The computer system was used to conduct electronic and manual trading, with each type constituting 50 percent of the use. The system comprised ten pieces of hardware, including servers, routers, and software for market access and trading algorithms. The collective dimensions of the system were 260 centimeters × 298 centimeters × 470 centimeters. It weighed approximately 164 kilograms and had a value of A$200,000. The ATO considered that size, quantity (where part of a unified process), value, and importance (in terms of whether the equipment played a core role in income production) were relevant factors in determining whether equipment was "substantial." In this decision, the ATO did not consider that the computer system size, value, or its role in income production were substantial, because only 50 percent of the business activities involved electronic trading through the computer system.

In the DTAAs to which Australia is a party, there is typically a provision that a permanent establishment will not be found where facilities, a stock of goods, or a fixed place of business, is maintained solely for carrying on activities of a preparatory or auxiliary character.[49] This can raise issues in relation to e-commerce, "where many automated functions can be disaggregated and spread between a number of websites or locations."[50] The ATO gave the example of a warehouse maintained by an e-commerce business in the source country for the delivery of goods. The maintenance of the warehouse for delivery of goods may be argued to be an activity of a preparatory or auxiliary character. If the delivery of goods in the source country were a substantial part of the activity of the business, however, the ATO thought appropriate to conclude that the "preparatory or auxiliary" exception would not apply because the activities carried on through the warehouse were an essential part of the business.[51] This view is consistent with the OECD commentary.[52]

3. Services Income Professional personal services that give rise to income would, under an applicable DTAA, typically be dealt with under the "Independent Personal Services" article of that agreement. Such income would be taxable only in the country of residence unless the individual or firm had a fixed base regularly available in the source country for the purpose of performing the individual's or firm's activities, in which case so much of the income as is attributable to activities exercised from the

49 Such as UK DTAA, art. 5(5).

50 ATO, *Tax and the Internet: Second Report, supra note* 13 at 101.

51 *Id.*

52 Commentary on Article 5, *supra* note 44 at ¶ 42.8.

fixed based may be taxed in the source country. Source country taxation will also be permitted where the individual or firm stays in the source country for a period or periods of 183 days or more.[53] Accordingly, the ATO appears to accept that many services of a professional nature can be provided remotely without the need for a physical presence in the source country and, therefore, without source country taxation.

Services that do not fall within the definition of "professional services,"[54] such as a call center located in a foreign jurisdiction, would be dealt with under the business profits article. As long as no permanent establishment is maintained in the source country, there would be no source country taxation.

Individuals deriving income from services rendered in the course of employment would generally be dealt with under the dependent personal services article of a relevant DTAA. Such individuals would be subject to resident country taxation unless employment was exercised in the source country, in which case such income may be taxed in the source country unless the employee was present for not more than 183 days, the employer was not resident in the source country, and the remuneration was not deductible in determining the taxable profits of the employer's permanent establishment in the source country.[55]

With e-commerce it is quite possible for an employee to provide services without needing to be physically present in a particular country. The ATO considered this situation in Interpretative Decision 2003/1076 regarding the UK DTAA, where an Australian resident was employed by a UK company. The employee performed his work by accessing the employer's databases and systems through the internet. The employer used the results of this work in the United Kingdom. It was clear that the employee, as an Australian resident, was subject to Australian taxation. Under the UK DTAA, the ATO considered whether the United Kingdom may also tax the employee's income on the basis that the employment was exercised in the United Kingdom. The ATO decided that, because the employee was physically present in Australia when performing his employment duties, the employment was exercised in Australia, even though the employer exploited the results of the employee's work in the United Kingdom.

E. CHARACTERIZATION OF INCOME DERIVED IN E-COMMERCE TRANSACTIONS Accurately identifying the nature of the payments received in an e-commerce transaction can have significant Australian tax ramifications. For example, the payment could be, for (1) the acquisition of a product, (2) the acquisition of services, (3) the use of or right to use intellectual property, (4) the transfer of intellectual property, or (5) the disposal of a capital asset.

How a transaction is characterized for tax purposes can result in very different taxation consequences. The characterization issue that frequently arises in e-commerce is the distinction between a royalty and business or services income. A payment that is made to a

53 *See*, e.g., Indian DTAA, art. 14(1).

54 "Professional services" are defined in the Indian DTAA to include "services performed in the exercise of independent scientific, literary, artistic, educational or teaching activities as well as in the exercise of the independent activities of physicians, surgeons, lawyers, engineers, architects, dentists and accountants."

55 *See*, e.g., UK DTAA, art. 14; *see also* U.S. DTAA, art. 15.

nonresident and is treated as a "royalty" will be subject to the royalty withholding tax provisions, in the case where that payment is not otherwise derived by the nonresident in carrying on business through an Australian permanent establishment.[56] Such a payment would be subject to 30 percent royalty withholding tax unless a lower rate under a DTAA applied.[57] However, business profits or services income derived by a nonresident would only be subject to Australian tax by assessment if derived from a source in Australia—in the case of a non-DTAA jurisdiction (see paragraph II.C above) or if attributable to a permanent establishment (business profits) or a fixed base or presence (services income) in the source country in the case of a DTAA jurisdiction (see paragraph II.D above).

The term "royalty" is defined in ITAA36, § 6(1) to include, for example,

> any amount paid or credited, however described or computed, and whether the payment or credit is periodical or not, to the extent to which it is paid or credited, as the case may be, as consideration for:
>
> (a) the use of, or the right to use, any copyright, . . . secret formula or process, trademark, or other like property or right;
> (b) the use of, or the right to use, any industrial, commercial or scientific equipment;
> (c) the supply of scientific, technical, industrial or commercial knowledge or information;
> (d) the supply of any assistance that is ancillary and subsidiary to, and is furnished as a means of enabling the application or enjoyment of, any such property or right as is mentioned in paragraph (a), any such equipment as is mentioned in paragraph (b) or any such knowledge or information as is mentioned in paragraph (c);
> (da) the reception of, or the right to receive, visual images or sounds, or both transmitted to the public by:
> *(i) satellite; or*
> *(ii) cable, optic fibre, or similar technology;*
> (e) the use of, or the right to use:
> (i) motion picture films;
> (ii) films or video tapes for use in connection with television;
> (iii) tapes for use in connection with radio broadcasting.

Each of Australia's DTAAs also contains definitions of the term "royalties" that encompass payments similar to those dealt with in the above definition.

The conversion of products and services into digital form in e-commerce can affect the characterization of a payment. For example, purchasing a newspaper or magazine from a shop clearly gives rise to business income. In an e-commerce environment, however, the nature of the payment for an electronic newspaper or magazine may not be so readily apparent. The newspaper may be viewed on the consumer's computer screen, it may be downloaded to the hard drive of the consumer's computer, or it might be printed out by the consumer.

---

56 ITAA36 §§ 128B(2B), 128B(3).

57 Typically reduced to 10% other than in the United Kingdom, United States, and Japan DTAAs, where it is reduced to 5%.

Some guidance to the ATO's approach to characterising payments made in such an e-commerce transaction may be found in ruling TR 93/12, which considered the income tax implications arising from the development and marketing of computer software.

The ATO's view was that the characterization of payments in respect of computer software depended upon the terms of the partie's agreement. The payment would be considered to be a royalty where

1. It was consideration for the granting of a licence to reproduce or modify the computer program in a manner that would, without such a licence, constitute an infringement of copyright (such as payments for the right to manufacture copies of a program from a master copy for distribution); or
2. It was consideration for the supplying of know-how (such as payments for the supply of source code or program algorithms).[58]

Payments of the following type would not generally be royalties:

1. Payments for the transfer of all rights relating to copyright in the program;
2. Payments for the granting of a license that allows only simple use of the software (e.g. allowing the running of the software on a computer or network);
3. Proceeds from a sale of goods, such as where hardware and software are sold in unbundled form, or where property in tangible goods (such as a disk or magnetic tape) is transferred to the consumer; and
4. Payments for the provision of services in the modification or creation of software[59]

Some similarities of analysis exist in relation to the acquisition of digital products in an e-commerce transaction:

> . . . when consumers enter into an arrangement that enables them to download digitized information, the principal purpose of the transaction is to transfer rights to use the resulting digital product. . . . In such arrangements, the rights to use copyright are generally limited to the making of a single copy of the digitized information. In these circumstances, it may be appropriate to treat the transaction as principally concerning the granting of rights to use the digital product, and then to characterize the payments as income as business profits. Any consideration attributable to the granting of rights to use the copyright would be insignificant.[60]

The ATO did recognize that there were differences between software licenses and transactions in other digital products and that characterization issues would require further consideration.

---

58 TR 93/12 at ¶ 3.

59 TR 93/12 at ¶ 4.

60 ATO, *Tax and the Internet: Second Report, supra* note 13 at 125.

III. INDIRECT TAXATION ISSUES

A. Introduction

The most important Australian indirect tax is the goods and services tax (GST). The GST is fairly recent, having been introduced in July 2000 as a broad-based consumption tax on "taxable supplies" and "taxable importations." It is imposed at the rate of 10 percent. The main legislation imposing GST is the New Tax System (Goods and Services Tax) Act 1999 (Cth) (GST Act).

The ATO's December 1999 "Tax and the Internet: Second Report," was released approximately at the same time as the GST Act was passed, which perhaps explains why there was little consideration in that report of the issues that e-commerce poses to the imposition of GST. Notwithstanding that, there have been a number of ATO interpretative decisions dealing with e-commerce issues as well as the formation of an Electronic Commerce Industry Partnership, a consultative group comprising the ATO and representatives of the e-commerce sector, which identified specific GST issues arising in the context of e-commerce. GST is generally payable on taxable importations and taxable supplies.

B. Taxable Importations

A "taxable importation" is made if goods are imported and those goods are intended for home consumption (within the meaning of the Customs Act 1901 (Cth)) (§ 13-5, GST Act). "Goods" is defined in the GST Act as "any form of tangible personal property."

The importer of the goods pays the GST on a taxable importation. E-Commerce transactions seem to pose few issues regarding application of GST to taxable importations. If an Australian consumer places an order for goods with a foreign retailer via the Internet and the goods acquired are imported into Australia, then GST will apply unless an exemption applies (such as for low-value goods).

E-Commerce does, however, readily provide for the transformation of certain types of goods into digital form—so that they no longer take the form of "goods." For example, a book could be converted into digital form and sent to an Australian consumer in electronic as opposed to physical form. Accordingly, because there is no importation of "goods," there would be no taxable importation to which GST would apply.

C. Taxable Supplies

1. What Is a "Taxable Supply"? More e-commerce issues occur for "taxable supplies" that are subject to GST. A "taxable supply" is made if

1. A supply is made for consideration;
2. It is made in the course or furtherance of carrying on an enterprise;
3. The supply is connected with Australia; and
4. The supplier is registered or required to be registered (§ 9-5, GST Act).

A "supply" is widely defined to include supplies of goods, services, providing advice or information, and creating, granting, transferring, assigning, or surrendering any right (§ 9-10, GST Act). It would clearly apply to most supplies made in respect of e-commerce transactions. Enterprise is also widely defined to be an activity, or series of activities, done, for example, in the form of a business, or in the form of an adventure or concern in the nature of trade, or on a regular or continuous basis, or in the form of a lease, license, or other grant of an interest in property (§ 9-20, GST Act).

2. When Is a Supply "Connected with Australia"? An important question is whether the supply is "connected with Australia." Whereas Australia's jurisdictional exercise of taxing authority for income tax relies on concepts of residence, source, and the provisions of a DTAA where one applies, whether Australia has jurisdiction to impose GST is determined by whether the supply in question is "connected with Australia." Section 9-25 of the GST Act specifies when supplies are connected with Australia. In the case of real property, it will be connected with Australia if it is situated in Australia (§ 9-25(4), GST Act).

There are specific rules concerning "goods," which are defined to mean "any form of tangible property" (§ 195-1, GST Act). As a corollary, intangible property such as contractual rights and intellectual property will not be "goods." However, the dividing line between the two is often not clear cut. For example, in the case of software, it may be acquired by a purchaser in an Internet transaction and supplied on a disc or in some other tangible form. The ATO considers this to be a supply of goods (GST Ruling 2003/8). However, if the consumer in the Internet transaction downloaded the software to his or her computer, it would not be treated as a supply of goods. The distinction is important because of the different rules for determining whether goods are "connected with Australia."

A supply of goods will be connected with Australia

1. If the goods are delivered, or made available, in Australia to the recipient of the supply;
2. If the goods are removed from Australia; or
3. If the goods are brought to Australia and the supplier either imports the goods into Australia, or installs or assembles the goods in Australia (§ 9-25(1), GST Act).

The ATO considers that goods are delivered in Australia if the goods are physically delivered in Australia and physically made available there, such as goods that the supplier has acquired domestically or imported. If the recipient imports the goods into Australia, the supply is not connected with Australia (Ruling GSTR 2000/31 at ¶¶ 45–49).

Goods will be considered removed from Australia if they are physically taken out of Australia. However, in certain circumstances the export of goods for consumption outside Australia may be treated as GST-free under GST Act § 38-185.

For supplies other than goods or real property, such supplies will be connected with Australia

1. If the thing is done in Australia; or
2. If the supplier makes the supply through an enterprise that the supplier carries on in Australia; or

3. If the above two tests do not apply, the supply is of a right or option to acquire another thing and the supply of the other thing would be connected with Australia (§ 9-25(5), GST Act).

The supplies to which § 9-25(5) of the GST Act can potentially apply are wide ranging. It will apply to intangible property and also to services—both of which are capable of being supplied in an e-commerce transaction. "Thing" is defined in § 195-1 of the GST Act to mean anything that can be supplied or imported, which could include a service, advice, information or a right.

The ATO is of the view that if the "thing" being supplied is a service, this will typically be done where the service is performed. The issues discussed above concerning the supply of services via the Internet will be relevant in this context. In ruling GSTR 2000/31, the ATO provided its views as to when supplies of certain things will be connected with Australia:

1. A service may involve both work being done and the creation of a product as a result of that work—for example, an architect engaged to prepare architectural plans. The service will be done where the work is performed, that is, where the plan is prepared or drawn. The product of the service, the plan, is not treated as a supply separate from the service (¶¶ 69–70).
2. In the case of services comprising the provision of advice or information, it will be considered done where it is produced, prepared or created (¶ 71).
3. Where advice or information is provided instantaneously (such as by telecommunications), it is considered done where the advice or information is provided (¶ 73). When an Australian client phones a UK lawyer for advice, for example, that advice will be provided in the United Kingdom.
4. If the supply is the creation, grant, transfer, assignment, or surrender of a right, the creation of that right in another, the granting, transfer, or assignment of that right or surrender, is done where the right is created in that other person, granted, transferred, or assigned to that other person, or surrendered (¶ 74). If the right is granted under an agreement, then the grant will be considered to be done where the agreement is made. The discussion above at paragraph II.C.3 will be relevant for determining where an agreement is made in the context of an e-commerce transaction.

Where a supplier is in Australia and supplies a thing other than goods or real property for consumption outside Australia, that supply may qualify as being GST-free under GST Act § 38-190. For example, if an Australian accountant provides advice via e-mail to a nonresident that does not have a presence in Australia, that supply would typically qualify as being GST-free under § 38-190.

Even if a supply of a thing other than goods or real property is not connected with Australia because the thing is not taken to be done in Australia, it will be treated as being connected with Australia if the supplier makes the supply through an enterprise that the supplier carries on in Australia. An enterprise will be treated as carried on in Australia if the enterprise is carried on through a permanent establishmen t in Australia, as that term is defined in ITAA36 § 6(1), or a place that would be a permanent establishment if paragraphs (e), (f), or (g) of that definition did not apply.

The ITAA36 § 6(1) definition has elements of similarity to the definition used in the DTAA's and the discussion above will be relevant in this regard. The opening part of the definition refers to "a place at or through which the person carries on any business" and includes various places, including "a place where the person has, is using or is installing substantial equipment or substantial machinery." The exclusions of ITAA36 § 6(1) paragraphs (e), (f), and (g) of the definition in the GST context relates to that part of the definition that excludes dealings through an independent agent in the ordinary course of the agents' business, dealings through an agent that has no authority to enter into contracts, and a place maintained solely for purchasing goods or merchandise. Accordingly, for GST purposes, a wider definition of "permanent establishment" is used. The ATO does acknowledge that guidance as to the meaning of "permanent establishment" may be obtained from the parts of the OECD Commentary dealing with this term in the e-commerce context.[61]

D. Registration

Having determined whether a supply is connected with Australia, the final element to establish if a supply is a "taxable supply" is whether the supplier is registered or required to be registered. The supplier must be registered if its GST turnover is A$75,000 or more (or A$150,000 in the case of nonprofit bodies). Certain supplies, such as supplies that are not connected with Australia, are disregarded in determining whether the registration turnover threshold is met.

E. Reverse Charges

Division 84 of the GST Act can impose GST on a supply of something other than goods or real property that is, in general terms, not connected with Australia if the recipient (being registered or required to be registered) acquires that thing in connection with an enterprise carried on by the recipient in Australia but not solely for a creditable purpose.[62] In this situation, the GST is payable on a reverse charge basis by the recipient of the supply. If, for example, a registered financial institution carrying on business in Australia accesses computer services from a foreign provider, and those services are not connected with Australia, the financial institution would have to pay GST.[63]

---

61 Ruling GSTR 2000/31 at ¶ 85 (2000).

62 There will be a creditable purpose if the thing is acquired in the course of carrying on an enterprise, but not if the acquisition is of a private or domestic nature, or in making input taxed supplies (such as financial supplies)(GST Act, § 11-15).

63 In ATO ID 2001/578, the ATO considered the application of Division 84 in the case of Internet subscription services acquired from a foreign provider.

Division 83 of the GST Act provides the other situation where a reverse charge can apply. This division applies to a taxable supply made by a nonresident to a registered recipient to which Division 84 does not apply. The supplier and the recipient can agree that GST will be payable by the recipient. This is designed to overcome practical difficulties associated with collection of GST where the foreign supplier does not have a presence in Australia. The supplies to which Division 83 apply are not taken into account in determining whether the supplier's registration turnover threshold is met. The recipient would be entitled to an input tax credit for the GST paid, so the result is usually tax neutral so far as the recipient is concerned.

Accordingly, for nonresidents, there is no clear-cut determinant of whether GST will apply to e-commerce transactions in which they are the supplier. Nonresidents will need to self-assess whether they are making "taxable supplies" and whether, as a consequence, they need to be registered or a reverse charge is applicable. Typically, the most important issue that will need to be investigated is whether the supply made is "connected with Australia," which as indicated above can pose challenges with e-commerce transactions.

PART IV

Europe

Chapter 8

France: Invoicing and E-Commerce: What Are the Tax Constraints? Is Electronic Invoicing the Best Solution?

Gwenaëlle Bernier
Fidal

I. INTRODUCTION

When companies decide to engage in e-commerce, they generally expect to be able to enjoy two advantages over "traditional" commerce:

1. They hope to make all borders disappear: their goal being to sell to the greatest number of customers worldwide (especially goods or services that can be downloaded off the Internet).
2. They hope to be able to work in a virtual, paper-free environment in which all administrative paperwork obligations are replaced by electronic processes.

When a company reaches the point where all its transactions are conducted on the Internet (prospecting, selling, and, for intangible services or goods, even delivering), the temptation grows even stronger to think that it can simply do away with all its paper-filing requirements and other obligations that compel it to issue paper documents (e.g., invoices) to its customers.

In reality, and focusing here solely on the tax obligation to issue invoices, one can see that this obligation does not simply evaporate in the Internet environment. Not only does it still represent one of the primary, day-to-day tax obligations for companies engaged in e-commerce, but its dematerialized form (electronic invoicing) is subject to a very strict set of rules that apply in addition to—and not in lieu of—the traditional rules governing "paper" invoicing.

Section II of this chapter will look into the reasons and issues that explain why all the European Union (EU) member states are so attached to the invoicing requirement, in contrast to other jurisdictions such the United States. However, while the invoicing requirement is considered, for value-added tax (VAT) purposes, as a universal rule to which virtually no exception or leniency is allowed in B2B (business-to-business) transactions, section III of this chapter will show that, in B2C (business-to-consumer) transactions, there are certain exceptions wherein the invoicing requirement disappears entirely. As will be seen below, however, this observation must be qualified for businesses engaged in cross-border sales of goods by mail order, and consequently for certain e-businesses.

Then, turning to the more frequent scenarios in which an e-business is required to issue an invoice, section IV of this chapter will explore the reasons why the use of electronic means to perform cross-border commercial transactions makes it even harder to comply with invoicing requirements, a fact that partly stems from the obligation to apply the "right" VAT treatment to each transaction carried out on the Internet. This will provide the occasion to address the issue of VAT fraud and see why, even for companies acting in perfectly good faith, such fraud seems even harder to spot and combat in a virtual environment.

In the end, however, section V will address how, for B2B transactions, and thanks to the accompanying safety mechanisms, electronic invoicing can be a good solution to the problems evoked above, although a thorough European harmonization in this area would greatly encourage businesses to adopt electronic invoicing on an international scale and finally relieve them from some of the invoicing burdens currently imposed on e-commerce.

II. WHY IS INVOICING A TAX REQUIREMENT?

A. What Are the Stakes Involved in Invoicing?

Invoices have multiple dimensions, not all of which are primarily tax-related. Indeed, an invoice is

- A legal document evidencing the existence of a commercial transaction;
- An accounting document serving as original evidence in support of the accounting entry of the transaction in the company's books;
- A tax document constituting original evidence of the collection and deductibility of VAT, as well as original evidence of the accounting entries, and hence the tax result; and
- A business document that is a supporting document for cost accounting purposes and for validating and circulating financial and management information in the company (e.g., delegations of power, strategic management of purchases, a logistics document reflecting withdrawals from inventory, etc.).

The obligation to invoice is vital from a VAT standpoint, because the invoice allows the taxable person (in principle, the seller) to demonstrate that it has duly fulfilled its tax collection obligation on behalf of the state. In the end, it is the invoice that evidences the public treasury's receivable against the taxable person. And it is the original invoice that, conversely, allows the (business) customer to prove its receivable against the state (i.e., its right to obtain a VAT refund on its purchase). While the invoice is a necessary and important document for many non-VAT-related reasons as well (e.g., the fight against undeclared work and transactions, etc.), for present purposes this discussion will be limited to VAT-related considerations, which by themselves are sufficient to justify the invoicing requirement imposed on companies. To the extent that a country's tax revenue is dependent on it, the obligation to invoice is necessarily strict and strictly enforced, giving rise to severe penalties for violations.

In France, for example, a failure to issue a sales invoice is punishable by a fine of up to 50 percent of the price of the transaction (French Tax Code [FTC], art. 1737-1-3). Each formal error or omission on the invoice is, moreover, punishable by a fine of €15 per error or omission, capped at one-fourth of the stated invoice price (FTC art. 1737-II).

In countries that do not have a VAT system like that of the European Union, such as the United States, the stakes involved in having each transaction trigger an invoice to be drawn up according to tax laws are lower, since the above-mentioned phenomenon of receivables/debts toward the state simply does not exist. This observation is true for all countries (which now represent a small minority) that have not introduced a VAT system wherein the invoice takes on the status of a key document upon which the entire corresponding taxation and deduction system depends. In addition to the United States, such countries include Hong Kong and certain states of India, Africa (with the notable exception of the North African countries and South Africa), and the Middle East.

B. What Are the Main Obligations?

Given the interests at stake in the issuance of an invoice in Europe, invoicing has become a highly regulated formality, from both a substantive and a formal standpoint. As the cornerstone of the entire VAT system, invoices must be as complete as possible, a necessity well illustrated by French regulations. The invoicing requirement is an old one in French tax law. It was updated following the adoption of the VAT directive on invoicing (Directive no. 2001/115/EC of December 20, 2001), which was to be transposed into the member states' legislation by no later than January 1, 2004. This directive is aimed, in particular, at harmonizing invoicing rules within Europe. In France, the directive was transposed by the Amended 2002 Finance Act (Law no. 2002-1576 of December 30, 2002), applicable as from July 1, 2003.

In France, the obligation to issue invoices on all business transactions is codified in Article 289-I-1 of the FTC, which transposes the VAT directive: "Every taxable person shall ensure that an invoice is issued, either by himself or, in his name and on his behalf, by his customer or by a third party: in respect of goods or services which he has supplied or rendered to another taxable person [. . .]." Moreover, Article 59 of the Amended 2007 Finance Act (no. 2077-1824) of December 25, 2007, carves out an exemption from the invoicing requirement for taxable persons who perform transactions that are VAT-exempt for reasons other than the application of territoriality rules (FTC art. 261-261E). This exemption applies primarily to VAT-exempt banking and finance transactions. Without delving into too much detail here on the scope of VAT, the invoicing obligation can be summarized as follows: every B2B transaction (whether industrial, commercial, crafts-related, or professional) that is subject to VAT must give rise to an invoice issued by, or on behalf of, the seller of the good or service.

Where the issuance of an invoice is mandatory, it must also contain certain mandatory items of information, which have been more or less harmonized at the European level and which, for France, are listed under Articles 289 and 242*nonies* A of Annex II of the FTC,

- The full name and address of the taxable person (seller) and its customer;
- The VAT identification number under which the seller carried out the sale of the good or service (and that of its tax representative, if any);
- The customer's VAT identification number (for certain intra-EU transactions, to the exclusion of domestic transactions);
- The date of issuance or transmission (for electronic invoices) of the invoice;
- A single number, based on a chronological and continual sequence, on one or several series, which singularly identifies the invoice;
- The quantity and type of the goods delivered or the extent of the services rendered;
- The tax base for each rate or exemption, the unit price excluding tax, as well as any rebates not included in the unit price;
- The date on which the supply of goods or services is performed or completed, if said date is determined and different from the date of issuance of the invoice;
- The VAT rate applied;
- The amount of VAT due (save for exceptional cases where VAT is assessed on the margin, e.g., for used goods or travel agents) and, per VAT rate, the total tax-exclusive amount and the corresponding VAT;
- In cases of VAT-exemption, of self-assessment or of application of the "VAT on the margin" regime, the reference to the relevant regulation of the country in which the transaction is performed or the corresponding provisions of the VAT directive (2006/112), or to any other indication showing that the transaction qualifies for such treatment; and
- In the case of an intra-EU supply of a new means of transportation, special additional items must also be inserted.

These French regulations are representative of how the EU member states have, as a whole, made the invoice a vital document that is full of tax information about the underlying transaction. This approach toward invoicing certainly enhances the transparency of (and the ability to audit) transactions carried out by businesses in the European Union. Nonetheless, certain exceptions have arisen to take into account specific business realities.

III. EXCEPTIONS TO THE INVOICING REQUIREMENT: HOW DO THEY APPLY TO E-COMMERCE?

A. Sales to Private Consumers Are, In Principle, Excluded

The tax obligation to issue invoices does not apply to sellers who sell goods or services[1] to private consumers (FTC art. 289-I-1 pf, *a contrario*). Of course, nothing prevents sellers from voluntarily electing to issue invoices to such consumers.

---

1 Commercial law runs somewhat counter to tax law on certain points, however, particularly where the former requires the issuance of an invoice to private consumers for services of over €15.24 (Decree no. 8350 [Oct. 3, 1983]).

French law has, however, created numerous exceptions to this exclusion from the invoicing requirement, thus making invoices mandatory even on sales to private consumers. Generally speaking, certain of these exceptions—for example, relating to real estate construction work or certain sales of fruit and vegetables in the agricultural industry—will have only a slight impact on e-businesses, because they cover lines of business that are rarely conducted via e-commerce. The same, however, cannot be said of cross-border distance sales of goods (cf. section 2 below) or of the sale of goods in public auctions, to which the invoicing requirement remains applicable even if the customer is merely a private person. Indeed, many e-businesses are directly engaged in such activities.

In the end, what types of business transactions can a seller still conduct with a private consumer without having to issue an invoice?

- All sales of services (distance sales and auction sales involve sales of goods), which also include any products that, thanks to the Internet, have "dematerialized," for example, music, films, certain software, trips, airplane and train tickets.
- Sales of goods that take place in France, that is, sales for which the good is transported from one location in France to another.

B. Special Case of Distance Sales and Public Auction Sales

1. Distance Sales (B2C) "Distance sales" consist of sales of goods (as opposed to sales of services) that are sent or shipped, by or on behalf of the seller, from one EU member state to a private individual domiciled in another member state (FTC art. 258 and 258B[2]). To illustrate the point, these provisions have traditionally applied to businesses engaged in mail-order sales (catalog sales). Now, by extension, they apply to most e-businesses located in the European Union that send goods sold over the Internet to private consumers residing in a different EU member state.

Of course, even if they do not qualify as "distance sales," sales of goods to France by e-businesses established outside the European Union (e.g., the United States), are not entirely exempt from the invoicing requirement either: such businesses must import the goods into France (customs clearance) and therefore provide the customs authorities with at least one document—in lieu of an invoice—that states the value of the goods, in order to pay the corresponding customs duties and taxes. Such e-businesses are, however, subject to lighter invoicing obligations; since the document in question is for customs purposes only, it does not need to comply with French invoicing standards (not all of the above-mentioned mandatory items are required). If, on the other hand, the U.S. company were to dispatch the goods to France from a warehouse containing products that have already cleared customs located somewhere in the European Union (e.g., the Netherlands), the above requirements for distance sales will be applicable to the seller, regardless of nationality.

---

2 Transposition into French law of Directive 2006/112, art. 33 (Nov. 28, 2006).

2. Sales in Public Auctions Organizers of public auctions of used goods, works of art, collectors' items or antiques, as well as their principals, are required to issue an invoice to the buyer, even if he or she is a private consumer. When the sale takes place in France, the invoice must comply with French tax law. This invoicing requirement clearly applies to e-businesses that sell through public auctions on the Internet, provided, however, that the sale takes place "in France." This chapter will not elaborate on all the issues surrounding the determination of Web sites location for tax purposes. These issues are addressed in other chapter in this publication, to which the author kindly refers the reader.

III. THE DIFFICULTIES OF FULFILLING THE INVOICING REQUIREMENT IN A VIRTUAL ENVIRONMENT

The discussion will now focus solely on the situation wherein the seller, operating through electronic commerce, is subject to the obligation to issue a sales invoice (e.g., a private consumer in Belgium orders a good on a French Web site, and the good is physically delivered by the French postal service to the customer). Two problems can arise:

1. Since the seller does not know or see its customer, and (most often) cannot verify his or her identity, will the seller be able to ascertain whether the customer is a business, to which it must therefore issue an invoice, or merely a private consumer? This distinction is truly hard to make, for the seller must rely on the customer's statements alone. Most e-businesses therefore take the cautious approach of issuing invoices on every transaction, regardless of customer, even if the invoice may be electronic (see below).
2. The second problem is more critical, since, still for the same reasons (the difficulty of identifying the type of customer involved, as well as his or her address), the seller will sometimes have trouble applying the right VAT treatment to its transactions, whether it be a question of the right VAT rate or the proper application of an exemption. If, however, the seller mistakenly applies an exemption and is subsequently reassessed, the impact in terms of the price and margin can be substantial.

A. How to Issue a "Fiscally Correct" Invoice to a Virtual Customer

Here, the focus is solely on the case in which the seller is required to issue invoices regardless of whether its customer is a business or a private consumer.

The customer's tax status (for VAT purposes) is key to determining (1) what the contents of the related invoice should be, (2) what items should be indicated thereon and, above all, (3) the rate and amount of the applicable VAT. On the Web, however, the seller does not know who its customer is. The best it can do is to base its invoicing policy on its customer's own online statements—which are not always verifiable—regarding his/her/its main identifying details: name and address, VAT identification number, and confirmation of status as a business or private individual.

If the customer states that it is a business established in an EU member state other than that of the seller and provides its VAT identification number online, the seller should be able to issue a VAT-free invoice (for purposes of this example, assume a sale of statistical data or consulting services). But even if this transaction is VAT-exempt, the seller nonetheless remains the legally taxable person in the event of a subsequent audit. In the interest of good tax management, therefore, the seller would, before issuing its VAT-exempt invoice, like to verify whether this customer does indeed hold the intra-EU VAT number he or she stated on the Web site. However, such verification is, at present, impossible (at least in France and most other EU countries). Indeed, the European Commission's VAT Information Exchange System (VIES) only allows one to confirm the validity and existence of a VAT number, not to trace the identity of its holder. The VIES site is expected to be improved in the upcoming years, but for the time being the risk of a VAT reassessment lies entirely with the e-seller, who has but a limited view of the situation and no means of effectively checking its customer's identity.

B. Is the Risk of VAT Fraud Greater in This Type of Commerce?

On January 1, 2007, France adopted a new arsenal of anti-fraud measures, which the tax authorities have commented on in an instruction published on November 30, 2007. The system is based on three types of penalties applicable in the event of VAT fraud: forfeiture of the exemption on intra-EU supplies of goods, forfeiture of the right to recover input VAT, and the customer's joint liability for the payment of the evaded VAT. Not limited to cases of "carousel" fraud, these new anti-fraud measures cover all types of VAT fraud:

- The nonpayment of VAT invoiced by a supplier and deducted by the customer
- All types of false intra-EU supplies

This anti-VAT fraud apparatus has been reinforced by Article 15 of the Amended 2007 Finance Act, which, as of January 1, 2008, institutes the offense of "flagrant" tax fraud.[3] The introduction of this flagrant tax fraud offense should enable the tax authorities to track down, *inter alia*, hidden activities and cases involving the issuance of either fake invoices or invoices relating to carousel-type VAT fraud.[4] The tax authorities are thus seeking to amass the tools they need to win the race in the fight against fraud, in which time is of the essence (due to quickly disappearing front companies, the destruction of evidence, etc.).

3 French Tax Procedure Code, New Article L16-0 BA, I (as of March 2008).

4 The finding of a flagrant tax offense takes place during very specific, surprise audit procedures conducted on the taxpayer's premises (e.g., tax searches, exercise of investigative rights, surprise on-site audits).

E-Commerce could find itself especially targeted by these new measures, for the following reasons:

- The seller's difficulty in ascertaining who its "virtual" customer is (and what his/her/its tax status is) undermines the seller's ability to detect the commission of a fraudulent sales scheme.
- The vast number of customers makes any audit by the seller illusory.
- The seller should, to be able to collect VAT on distance sales in the customer's country, voluntarily register for VAT in another EU member state. Sellers often face the practical obstacle of not being familiar with their obligations in other EU jurisdictions, because the VAT system is complex and ill-fitted to e-commerce, which demands the application of simple and efficient tax rules.

These new rules thus call upon businesses to "take whatever reasonable steps are in their power, in the course of the ordinary running of their business, to ensure that their transactions with other operators are not implicated in any such fraud schemes" (§ 8 of the VAT fraud instruction of November 2007). In this context, in the event of a tax audit, the tax authorities, who in principle have the burden of proving fraud, may attempt to shift this burden by asserting that the audited company failed to take "reasonable" steps to avoid being implicated in a fraud scheme. It will then be up to the company in question to demonstrate the opposite.

In practice, companies should, within their business relationships, set up internal, preventive audit measures that show they have taken all "reasonable steps" to make sure that their business partners are engaged in a genuine business and that no fraud is being committed. In concrete terms, this would involve setting up an internal audit procedure and a substantive set of documents aimed at demonstrating that the company is acting reasonably and that its behavior shows no indication that it could have been aware of any fraudulent situation. Otherwise, the tax penalties can be very heavy for companies that neglect to take such precautions. Indeed, in addition to the VAT liability, and depending on the degree of negligence involved, a 40 percent penalty for deliberate failures, and possibly an 80 percent penalty for fraudulent conduct, could apply.

V. IS ELECTRONIC INVOICING THE ANSWER TO ALL OF THESE EVILS?

Businesses engaged in e-commerce are quite naturally drawn to any paper-free solutions that hold out the promise of simplifying management and generating cost savings. The average cost of processing a paper invoice (excluding disputes) is estimated at €24: €14 for the purchaser and €10 for the supplier. By comparison, the average cost of processing a dematerialized (i.e., electronic) invoice is reportedly €7: €4 for the purchaser and €3 for the supplier.[5] Moreover, from a tax standpoint, electronic invoicing makes it possible to (1) enhance the reliability of invoices (by ensuring that the mandatory items

5 Source: the GS1 Web site.

are correctly inserted) and (2) ensure the proper identification of the customer (who must have given his or her prior consent to receive such invoices). It would thus seem to be the ideal tool for fighting (VAT) fraud and securing and simplifying invoice management, through the automation of certain processes.

Given these two combined factors, the advantages of a genuinely dematerialized invoicing system, wherein the entire process becomes paper free, look quite compelling. But is tax law flexible enough in practice to allow companies to set up solutions that truly achieve the goal of issuing correct and proper electronic invoices? This is the question addressed below, while at the same time highlighting the special constraints involved in using e-invoicing solutions for cross-border transactions.

A. What Is E-Invoicing?

In practice, electronic invoices differ from paper invoices by both their medium (intangible) and their means of transmission (electronic data interchange, electronic signature); nonetheless, they remain legal documents that must, regardless of the means of transmission, contain the mandatory items of information. The objective of implementing an e-invoicing solution is to be able to manage all the "dimensions" of the invoice at once, by completely replacing the paper invoice with an electronic invoice. If all the conditions for setting up such a system are fulfilled, and if the electronic document complies with all the legal and tax requirements applicable to invoices, it will no longer be necessary to issue a paper document.

The European tax administrations, including France, accept the use of electronic invoices as long as such use does not conflict with their objectives of fighting VAT fraud. A complete computerization of the invoicing process could, however, cause them to fear a less effective management of the VAT process (i.e., lack of control over the IT tool, dissociation between the issuance of the electronic invoice and the underlying physical transaction). In principle, on the seller's side, any VAT collected on an invoice must correspond to what is paid to the public treasury. On the purchaser's side, and bearing in mind that the invoice constitutes a receivable against the state for the amount of the input VAT, tax administrations want to ensure that these receivables are bona fide: Do they reflect transactions that were actually performed? Do they constitute the original supporting documents?

The guarantees required by all the EU member states thus pertain to:

- The integrity of the contents of the invoice (nonalteration)
- The authenticity of the origin of the invoice (the issuer)

The documents issued/received must be "invoices" within the tax or legal meaning of the term (presence of mandatory items).

1. Formats Allowed Under French law, companies may choose from between two e-invoicing systems:

- Electronic data interchange (EDI)
- Electronically signed invoices

Each of these e-invoicing methods is fit for specific and separate needs, which will be analyzed below. Their only real common ground is that, in either case, the electronic invoice cannot be used without the customer's formal and prior consent to receive invoices under such a format. This is certainly one of the major distinguishing characteristics between paper and electronic invoices: sellers are not yet free to invoice electronically unless they have obtained the customer's express consent. On the other hand, it should be pointed out that, since January 1, 2006, no prior notice to the tax authorities is required.

In Europe, the European Directive of 2001 authorizes member states to allow electronic invoices to be sent "by other electronic means"—in addition to the above two means—provided that the procedure used guarantees the authenticity of the origin and the integrity of the data. In practice, most member states have authorized the same e-invoicing systems as France, and only a small number of states, including the United Kingdom, Sweden, and Finland, have authorized other means of transmission.

2. *Main Mechanisms*

A. IN EDI MODE The main advantage offered by the EDI mode of e-invoicing is that it constitutes an integrated management system that automatically integrates the entire process from A to Z. Once installed, it undeniably reduces the costs tied to invoicing (i.e., issuing, dispatching, processing, and archiving). The invoice data processing system is automatically integrated into the company's accounting and financial system. This makes it possible not only to cut invoice issuance and handling costs but also to secure the invoicing process by reducing the risk of clerical mistakes and improving the VAT treatment of transactions, since the formal aspects of the invoices are better controlled and managed by the invoicing software. Lastly, EDI invoicing generally helps improve supplier-customer relations by shortening the steps involved in accounting for invoices: routing, processing, and payment authorization.

However, these very advantages also come with certain constraints inherent in the system: its implementation requires not only a strict contractual framework formed within a stable business relationship but also a technologically complex and costly computerized invoice-transmission structure. Lastly, by its very nature, as well as due to the absence of interoperability between the seller's and buyer's computer systems, this solution is primarily reserved for bilateral relationships between one seller and one purchaser.

B. IN ELECTRONIC SIGNATURE MODE In light of its flexibility and relatively low setup costs as compared with EDI, the electronic signature mode is especially appropriate for suppliers who wish to set up safe, high-volume e-commerce (i.e., with numerous sales to multiple customers). It does not require the installation of an EDI system, because most exchanges are transmitted by e-mail. In principle, however, it does not allow the invoice data to be automatically integrated into the purchaser's accounting records (in general, the invoices transmitted are not specifically formatted), and the invoice image must therefore be handled (i.e., entered, validated) manually. This solution will thus be chosen in situations where, due to the number of customers, the EDI solution proves unsuitable or difficult to implement.

Pioneered by information technology (IT) solution providers, a third approach seems to have gained a strong following: that of setting up a system that makes it possible to exchange electronically signed and specifically formatted invoices. From a tax standpoint, the French tax authorities seem to have recognized that such systems satisfy the requirements of Article 289V of the FTC (electronically signed invoices) and therefore that the summary list of invoices and file of business partners is not required. The relevant administrative doctrine (BOI 3 CA, no. 136 of August 7, 2003) is, however, silent on this point.

C. COMMON POINT TO BOTH MEANS OF TRANSMISSION Insofar as the electronic "messages" in question constitute original invoices, they must contain all the mandatory items of information required by VAT regulations (FTC art. 242*nonies* A of Annex II). In practice, this means that the software must generate compulsory fields for the information required by the invoicing rules (both upon issuance and upon receipt). For example, the software must generate a "field" for such information as (i.e., a space to be filled in) the date of the invoice, the invoice number, the seller's and purchaser's names and addresses, a description of the goods sold, the applicable VAT rate, the amount excluding tax, and the amount of VAT.

On the other hand, the invoicing software does not, for the time being, need to ensure that the fields are actually filled in correctly; if the seller makes a mistake when entering the customer's address or the VAT rate applicable to the goods sold, it will be the seller's responsibility, not the software producer's. This situation is currently a source of misunderstanding between sellers and e-invoicing software suppliers, the former believing that the latter are responsible not only for electronically issuing the invoices but also for ensuring that they show all the right information and VAT treatment, although no such assurances are provided by most software currently available on the French market.

3. Securing the Invoicing Process (to Improve VAT Compliance) Regardless of what type of electronic files are transmitted or received, businesses hope that, by setting up an e-invoicing solution, they will be better able to manage and reduce the tax risks involved in invoicing:

- With respect to direct taxes (corporate income tax, taxes on industrial or commercial earnings), this means ensuring the traceability and consistency between the accounting entries and the original documents.
- With respect to VAT, it means being able to automate compliance with the mandatory information requirements, so as to avoid the €15 penalty per error/omission on an invoice.

B. Can E-Invoicing Be Used at the International Level?

1. What Is Allowed The VAT directive on invoicing (Directive no. 2001/115/EC of December 20, 2001), was adopted in 2001, and was to be transposed into the member states' domestic law no later than January 1, 2004. This directive is aimed, in particular, at harmonizing the invoicing rules in Europe and at allowing invoices to be issued either on paper or electronically, without discrimination and regardless of type of transaction: the directive therefore authorizes the use of such invoices for the payment of international transactions.

In France, the directive was transposed by the Amended 2002 Finance Act (Act no. 2002-1576 of December 30, 2002), effective as of July 1, 2003. This act introduced a new Article 289V into the French Tax Code, dedicated to the transmission of electronically signed invoices, and it is henceforth possible to use e-invoicing for cross-border transactions. The French tax authorities commented on this reform in a lengthy instruction, dated August 7, 2003, which undoubtedly constitutes the reference document on e-invoicing in France (BOI of August 7, 2003, 3CA, no. 136) (BOI).

While, in principle, each EU member state was to have transposed the directive by January 1, 2004, the transposition was not uniform from one state to the next. On cross-border transactions, therefore, not only must the minimal European invoicing legislation be satisfied but also the specific rules imposed by each country.

2. The Constraints (Lack of Legislative Harmonization between the Issuer's Country and the Receiver's Country) On the seller's side lies the burden of tax obligations relating to the (electronic) invoice. Under VAT law, it is the seller who bears the obligation to (1) issue a correct and proper invoice in accordance with French law, (2) apply the VAT treatment appropriate to the transaction (exemption, rate, base, etc.), and (3) pay the input VAT to the public treasury.

In addition, pursuant to the European directive on invoicing (Directive no. 2001/115/EC of December 20, 2001), the seller should be able to use a single model invoice for all its invoicing flows, regardless of its customer's nationality (provided the customer is established in the European Union). In practice, however, many countries require that certain supplementary items be inserted in addition to those required by French law; it is therefore advisable to ensure that the single model e-invoice used does indeed take into account the other countries' specific information requirements (e.g., reference to the delivery slip in Greece, date of payment in the Netherlands).

On the purchaser's side, that is, upon receipt of the electronic invoice, the main concern for the French customer is to receive, within the meaning of the VAT rules, an original electronic invoice in order to protect its right to recover the tax.

Despite all these precautions, a foreign customer may still be somewhat reluctant to use an e-invoicing system that, while compliant with French law, has not been validated or recognized by its own domestic tax authorities. In addition, the procedures used to check and reject invoices may vary from one country to another or from one customer to another. These elements must be taken into account when selecting the overall invoicing solution.

At present, the administrative doctrine on e-invoicing legislation in many European countries (including France) is not clear enough to allow taxpayers to easily ascertain whether one EU country's tax authorities will recognize the validity of a system already approved by another's. Moreover, virtually none of the national tax authorities issue rulings on this subject anymore, with the exception of Spain and the Netherlands (where it generally takes over a year to obtain a ruling).

VI. CONCLUSION

By the end of 2008, the European Commission is expected to issue a report, and possibly a proposal, to modify the conditions of electronic invoicing in the European Union in order to take into account the technological progress that has been made in this area. The ultimate goal is to reach an agreement on a consistent, harmonized e-invoicing system for all the EU member states. This would enable e-commerce businesses to have, at last, access to invoicing systems that are both simpler to manage and more effective and reliable in applying the relevant VAT rules.

Chapter 9

Germany: German Tax Implications on E-Commerce Activities

Patrick Sinewe
Bird & Bird

I. INTRODUCTION

E-Commerce—that is, commerce transacted by means of electronic networked communication systems—has recorded enormous rates of growth throughout the world and, in particular, within Germany. According to the statement of the Federal Association of Mail Order Membership Corporation (*Bundesverband Versandhandel e.V.)*, the mail order business alone handled €6.1 billion e-commerce orders of goods and services over the Internet in Germany in 2005.

While Germany does not have a statutory tax or legal definition of the term "e-commerce," the term is generally used for German tax law purposes for all commercial transactions that are initiated or conducted via electronic networks and in which the parties are exchanging goods or electronic services for payment. This broad definition of e-commerce includes so-called offline business volume as well as net online business volume, for which the distinction is also crucial for tax purposes.

The term "offline-business volume" means the consignment of items or the supply of a service, which are ordered in an electronic way and performed in a conventional way—for instance, mailing a book or pair of theatre tickets ordered over the Internet or the booking of theatre tickets over the Internet. Here, the Internet merely replaces the personal order or the order by phone or fax. Online business volume, however, refers to commercial transactions that are conducted exclusively online, where the presentation of products, order, delivery, and, as the case may be, performance and payment are all carried out over the Internet. Examples include the downloading of music in return for payment, the provision of legal or medical advice over the Internet, and so-called application service providing, for example, the license of software with service for use. It is in the context of net online-business volume that the main issues concerning (corporate) income tax as well as value-added tax (VAT) arise.

From a German tax law perspective, the legislature decided to classify e-commerce business under the rules of common transaction types. New tax law provisions were implemented on the basis of EU regulations, in particular the E-Commerce Directive 2002/38/EG dated May 7, 2002, which was adopted into German tax law with legal effect as of June 1, 2003. It should be pointed out that at the level of the Organization for Economic Cooperation and Development (OECD), a supplement to the tax commentary on paragraph 5 of the OECD Model Convention was enacted, which also affects German tax treatment of e-commerce activities.

Because there are no specific provisions for e-commerce within the income tax or corporate income tax regimes, the main income tax issues associated with e-commerce activities include

- The clarification of income deriving from cross-border services and deliveries of digital products per download.
- The question whether an Internet server can be classified as a permanent establishment (hereinafter referred to as "PE") and the extent to which earnings can be allocated to such PE.
- The classification of an Internet presence (homepage) that has to be maintained and enhanced and that causes substantial business expenses as well as the tax treatment under German GAAP (General Accepted Accounting Principles) which is currently not certain—in particular, whether a homepage can be booked as a capitalized asset in the balance sheet.

These issues are considered in the discussion below.

II. GERMAN INCOME TAX IMPLICATIONS

A. Domestic Business Transactions

As a general rule, income derived from electronic business is subject to German income tax and corporate income tax. Provided that both the supplier and the recipient have their business location and, as the case may be, their tax residence in Germany, the tax principles do not differ from other business transactions. This means that an individual merchant is fully liable for German taxes by way of unlimited taxation if he or she maintains either a place of residence in Germany (*Wohnsitz*) or a habitual abode (*ständiger Aufenthalt*) in Germany.

A place of residence can be assumed if the individual maintains a residence under certain circumstances that indicate that the individual will keep and use it on more than a temporary basis. This is determined on such facts as if his or her family lives at the same place, if he or she owns the apartment, or if the apartment is furnished. In addition, a customary place of abode can be assumed if the individual is physically present for an extended period of time under circumstances that indicate that he or she intends to stay there nontemporarily. German tax law presumes that such a customary place of abode exists if the individual continuously stays in Germany for more than six months. The nationality of the individual is irrelevant for German taxation purposes. A corporate entity will be resident in Germany for tax purposes if the entity's registered office or place of management (i.e., where the day-to-day-business decisions are made) is in Germany. Therefore, if an individual or a corporate entity (such as a limited liability company (*GmbH*)) with a registered office in Germany performs services within the scope of electronic business to customers resident in Germany or abroad, any earnings arising from such transactions are subject to unlimited taxation.

E-Commerce may also be subject to the additional tax burden of local, municipal, and trade taxes. It should be noted that commercial income generated through e-commerce is only subject to German trade tax (at a tax rate of approximately 14 percent) if the supplier of e-commerce activities maintains a fixed place in Germany (constituted by an Internet server, see below). Hence, an additional trade tax burden should be avoided when structuring cross-border e-commerce activities in order to mitigate commercial disadvantages.

B. Cross-Border Business Transactions

Apart from any potential trade tax burden, tax issues may arise on income from cross-border e-commerce operations in inbound and outbound scenarios. Inbound cases occur where the recipient of services is a resident of Germany and receives services by a supplier resident abroad. Outbound cases are situations when a German resident supplier supplies to a customer resident abroad. In such cross-border transactions, the issue is in which country the supplier has to pay income taxes on electronic services.

In *outbound scenarios,* an unlimited tax liability arises for the German supplier. German tax law principles establish that a taxpayer resident in Germany is subject to German income tax or corporate tax on its worldwide taxable income, that is, a supplier resident in Germany pays tax on all profits generated through outbound business activities. However, a different result can arise through the application of double taxation conventions (DTCs), when the right to tax e-commerce operations lies with the country where the service is obtained (i.e., income has to be exempt from German taxation).

In *inbound scenarios*, a supplier resident abroad who supplies services to German residents may also become liable for German taxation. Limited tax liability may be triggered not only where a German PE is maintained but also where individuals who have neither a permanent residence nor an ordinary place of business within Germany realize income from German sources. Similarly, corporate entities that have neither their registered office nor their place of management in Germany are liable to limited corporate tax on their German source income.

C. Specific Inbound Transactions

For the right to tax income pertaining to e-commerce operations, the existence of a PE is a matter of importance. In particular, for commercial income German limited tax liability depends on the existence of a PE or a permanent representative in Germany. In addition, in most DTCs the right to tax is awarded to the country where a PE is situated.

1. Business through a German PE Every fixed business facility or installation serving a business purpose is a PE within the meaning of German tax law. This facility must be fixed as to location, and the business activity must be exercised therefrom. However, any actual or apparent fixture to the surface of the earth is not necessary. Furthermore, the business must have a definite, and not merely temporary, ability to use the facility. A fixed business facility must have a degree of permanence. It will be deemed permanent whenever it lasts for longer than six months. The list of facilities as set out under the German Fiscal Code (providing the legal definitions of a PE) is not exhaustive and includes place of corporate management, branch office, business office, manufacturing plant or workshop, warehouse, points of sale or purchase, as well as mines/quarries or other locally continuous or floating points of extraction of mineral resources.

In general, a DTC will define a PE in order to provide a basis for allocating the right to tax business profits and business assets between the treaty states, for attributing dividends, interest, and royalties to a PE, for allocating the right to tax capital gains from the sale of business assets from a PE and for other income. Whilst the wording of the DTC requires that business activities must be carried out from the fixed facility, German tax law sees a PE wherever the fixed facility (or installation) serves the purposes of the business. The DTC's PE definition is, in essence, the same as that of national law, although it is narrower regarding the nature of the activities. In either case, the business facility must serve the business interests with a degree of permanence that is for longer than six months. Standard examples of PEs in DTC terms are, *inter alia*, a branch office or a business office. Auxiliary or preparatory business facilities, such as delivery stores or purchasing or information offices, do not, however, rank as PEs under the DTC because they are merely supportive. Hence, e-commerce activities conducted through a German fixed place will lead to commercial income subject to German income and trade taxes.

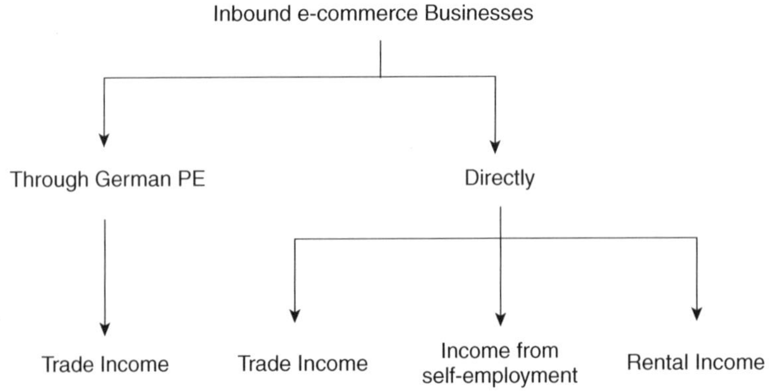

Neither German tax courts nor the tax authorities have made clear statements up to now regarding whether servers can qualify as PEs. However, the German Federal Tax Court held in a decision in 1996 that a pipeline constitutes a PE, because it has a sufficient nexus to Germany even though the foreign company had no personnel or place of business in Germany. Based on that court ruling, the German tax authorities have issued an official circular stating that servers that allow or enable the orders of goods only provide preparatory and auxiliary services and, therefore, are insufficient to constitute a PE. This tax circular was partially overruled by the OECD guidelines on e-commerce activities, which should be applicable, *mutatis mutandis*, to Internet servers. Moreover, there is a common ground between the "pipeline" decision of the Federal Tax Court and e-commerce activities.

The OECD Committee on Fiscal Affairs issued clarifications (dated December 22, 2000) for the taxation of profits generated by or associated with servers. These clarifications were implemented in Article 5 of the OECD Model Commentary. The German tax administration follows the guidelines of the OECD when determining whether a server qualifies as a PE.

According to the guidelines, a PE can be found if equipment (also without any personnel) is located in Germany (physical presence), as long as that equipment performs an essential and important part of a company's business. However, the PE issue may be avoided or at least mitigated if German servers are used by foreign companies performing e-commerce activities but those companies do not own or lease them.

In addition, any potential exposure to double taxation by the country where the supplier is resident and the country where the PE is situated, in which the server is located, makes it necessary to apportion the income from the e-commerce operation between the parent company and the PE of the server. According to German tax law, the duty to record and the duty to document the apportionment of profits between the parent company and PE are laid down in § 90, ¶ 3 German Fiscal Code and the regulation for apportionment and documentation of profit (*Gewinnaufzeichnungsverordnung*) from November 13, 2003, must be taken into consideration. According to these rules, the direct method for splitting profits prevails—that is, the PE is treated virtually as a legally independent company, and the profit attributed to it is determined by creation of a special balance sheet for the PE.

2. Business Activities Directed Toward German Customers In general, earnings derived from e-commerce operations within Germany may qualify as commercial income,[1] rental income,[2] other income from using know-how,[3] or—with increasing relevance—income from self-employment.[4]

A. COMMERCIAL INCOME For example, income from the sale of goods over the Internet is considered commercial income under German income tax law. In determining

1 GERMAN INCOME TAX CODE, § 1, 49, Para. 1 No. 2.
2 *See Id.* § 49, Para.1 No. 6.
3 GERMAN INCOME TAX CODE, § 49, Para.1 No. 9.
4 *See Id.* § 49, Para.1 No. 3.

whether a particular EU country has the right to tax such income, one must consider the difference between offline and online turnover on the one hand and inbound and outbound scenarios on the other hand.

i. Income from Online Business Activities The transfer of title of standard software by download in return for payment without granting intellectual property rights can, for instance, lead to commercial income. In an inbound scenario (i.e., a foreign entrepreneur offers such service to domestic customers in return for payment), the foreign entrepreneur's income is subject to German limited tax liability when he or she maintains a German PE or has appointed a permanent representative in Germany.

According to the prevailing tax opinion, a PE can also be constituted by establishment of a server. For example, a Web-hosting service can be appointed as a permanent representative, whereas Internet service providers, home pages, or similar facilities are not permanent representatives. If a foreign entrepreneur, who derives online income in Germany, does not maintain a PE in Germany and has not appointed a permanent representative, the limited income tax liability does not apply to the online turnover made in Germany.

In an *outbound case*, there are basically no limits to a domestic suppliers' tax liability on its commercial income from net online earnings under § 15 of the German Income Tax Act. But when a supplier resident in Germany maintains a server in a country that has entered into a DTC, the service can be deemed a PE. In this case, the right to tax the PE profits lies with the state where the PE is situated. Only profits that are attributable to marketing performance and not the profit (or proportion of profit) attributable to previous development of the product is attributed to the foreign PE.

ii. Offline Turnover One function of the Internet as a channel of distribution is to support sales that generate offline turnover. However, the processing of the transactions—for example, the delivery of ordered goods—is carried out "traditionally," that is, by mail or a forwarding agent. A PE should not be constituted when a foreign supplier installs a server in Germany or when a domestic supplier installs a server in a foreign country, because the Internet merely functions to support the sale. This is in line with the interpretation of the law concerning e-tailing operations at cipher 42.7 and 42.9 of Article 5 of the OECD Model Convention. As a result, profits generated by offline business transactions are generally taxed where the supplier is domiciled.

B. INCOME FROM SELF-EMPLOYMENT Income from self-employment would include, for example, income from online advice rendered by lawyers or tax advisors via e-mail. In inbound business transactions, the income from such consultancy services is subject to limited German tax liability, if the use of the consultancy service is made in Germany or if the foreign advisor maintains a PE or a fixed place in Germany. For example, tax consultants or international law firms generally meet the foregoing requirements.

In outbound scenarios (where profits are generally taxed in Germany), one must consider that the qualification of income from the German law perspective differs from the DTC, according to which income from consultancy services that were rendered over the Internet are to qualify as commercial profits. Hence, a foreign country only has the right to tax such profits if they are realized through a foreign PE. Where no DTC country is involved, consultancy services are taxed in Germany—irrespective of PE—if the recipient of such service is a German resident.

C. RENTAL INCOME Income from rent includes earnings from the sharing of custom-made or system software, in circumstances where the copyright is assigned for a limited period of time. However, under German law, the temporally unlimited sharing of such software gives rise to commercial income. The same applies if copyrights are assigned for a limited period of time but long enough that the copyright is worthless at the end of the period. Income from the use of customized or system software with a temporally limited assignment of the copyrights is subject to German limited tax liability if the software is used in a PE (maintained by the supplier or a third party) or rights related to such license are registered in Germany.

Under most DTCs, the income from the temporary use of customized or system software is associated with copyrights, which is likely to qualify as royalty income under Article 12 of the OECD Model Convention and therefore must be taxed at the domicile of the supplier, unless the profits can be allocated to a PE. In these cases, the taxation right of the state of residence of the person to whom the service is supplied (according to OECD Model Convention art. 12, ¶ 3) exists only if the supplier maintains a PE in that state.

If the supplier does not use a PE or the services are supplied to a non-DTC state, the unlimited tax liability on income from these services, generated by outbound activities, is kept in the supplier's state of residence.

III. GERMAN VAT IMPLICATIONS

According to the German Value-Added Tax Act (*Umsatzsteuergesetz*), deliveries and services performed in Germany are subject to German taxation. For German tax purposes, VAT is only due if the place where the service is rendered or where deliveries are made is within Germany.

A. Offline Businesses

As already stated, there are no specific VAT issues concerning offline turnovers. This means that any deliveries of goods that are actually ordered over the Internet and subsequently shipped by mail are deemed under German VAT law to be performed at the place where the supply starts. Offline turnovers also apply to services where online activities are merely used for order purposes and performed by the person to whom the service is supplied and a contract for rendering the services is concluded (or procured). The services are performed in a conventional way—for example, a show in the theatre, which is carried out offline. In such case, the place of the performance is the place where the entrepreneur operates his or her business.

B. Online Businesses

Until the EU E-Commerce Directive was implemented, the place of performance for online services was determined based on the general VAT rule, according to which services are rendered where the person providing the service is located. As of June 1, 2003, the place of performance for *other services performed in an electronic way* is deemed to be, as a rule, where the recipient of such services is domiciled.

The term "services performed in an electronic way" is not defined by law but rather is given in a circular issued by the Federal Ministry of Finance dated June 12, 2003. According to this circular, the following services, *inter alia*, are considered electronic services:

- Providing Web sites, Web hosting, remote maintenance of software and hardware
- Providing software and its updates
- Providing pictures
- Providing text and information
- Providing databases
- Providing movies and games, including gambling and lottery
- Providing broadcasts and events from the scope of politics, culture, art, sports, science, and entertainment
- Providing services for distance study
- Online auctions (as far as it is not already services of Web hosting) by automated databases with input of data by the person to whom the services are supplied, which need little intervention by a human
- Internet service packs that provide more than just access to the Internet

When performing such service for payment, the VAT analysis is based (1) on the residence of the supplying entrepreneur and the recipient as well as (2) the recipient's position as entrepreneur or customer. This analysis should be clarified by means of the following examples from the perspective of a supplier resident in Germany:

1. Domestic Recipient, B2B and B2C Operations In business-to-business (B2B) activities where the suppliers as well as the recipient are entrepreneurs pursuant to German VAT law, the place of performance is the domicile of the corporate or individual recipient, that is, in this case, Germany. The service is subject to German VAT at a tax rate of currently 19 percent. The supplier must remit any VAT amount to the German tax authorities and is obliged to issue an invoice stating the amount of German VAT. The same applies to so-called business-to-consumer (B2C) activities where only the supplier is an entrepreneur liable to charge German VAT.

2. B2B- Commercial Operations Toward a Recipient Who Is Resident within or Outside the European Union Services are performed where the recipient maintains his or her business, either within or outside the European Union. This kind of service is not taxable in Germany, so that the service is charged without German VAT. The person liable to pay tax is the person to whom the service is supplied. In addition, this means that services are not burdened with VAT if the country of residence will not levy turnover tax.

3. B2C- Business Operations Toward a Recipient Who Is Resident Outside the European Union B2C service is subject to tax, where the (non-entrepreneur) recipient is resident. The service is not taxable in Germany, so that the invoices are charged without German VAT.

A. EXAMPLE Practical difficulties can arise by the following situations:

A tourist from the United States is vacationing, in Germany. There he visits an Internet cafe and uses the Internet access to surf the World Wide Web for several hours. The place of performance is deemed to be in the United States, because the U.S. tourist is a third-party resident not conducting business activity. A legal applicable taxation by the German owner of the Internet cafe is hardly possible in practice, because the owner will not ask every customer whether he receives the service as an entrepreneur in terms of VAT law or not. In practice, this problem is going to be solved by estimation.

4. B2C- Commercial Operations Toward a Recipient Who Is Resident within the European Union The place of performance of such services is where the supplier maintains its business, that is, in this case, Germany. The supplier is liable for German VAT and has to include the VAT amount according to the pricing ordinance when offering services within the EU.

C. Liability for German VAT

German VAT law provides for a so-called reversed-charge procedure. According to this procedure, any VAT liability on services rendered in an electronic way by a domestic entrepreneur toward an entrepreneur resident abroad (i.e., the procedure is not applicable toward a consumer) is transferred to the domestic recipient.

1. Example A merchandising firm resident in Frankfurt engages a software developer resident in France to establish and maintain a home page. All activities required on this are performed in France. After setting up the home page, the developer will update the home page in the future via the Internet from France. Such electronic services that relate to such electronic activities by the French corporation are rendered domestically and are subject to German VAT, because the recipient in its capacity as an entrepreneur is a German resident. The merchandising firm located in Germany falls within the reversed-charge procedure and is liable for the VAT amount. The result should be the same if the offering software corporation is residing outside the European Union, for instance in the United States.

However, the tax analysis would differ if the recipient of the services is not an entrepreneur. Only individual or corporate recipients are subject to the tax liability, which are regarded as entrepreneurs under the German VAT Act. An entrepreneur is a person

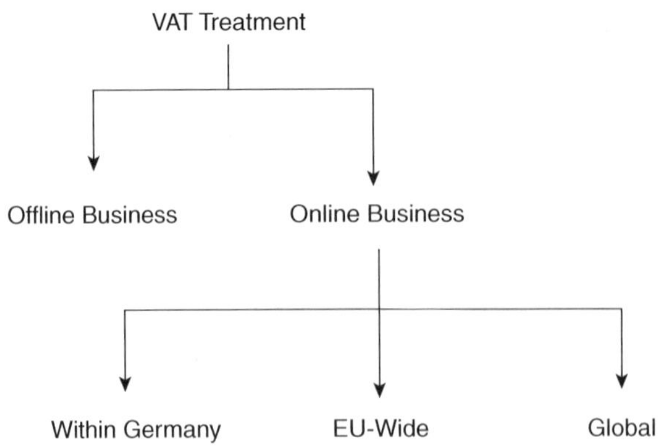

who performs a commercial or business activity independently, continuously, and with the intention to generate earnings. If the supplier is resident in another EU state (as in this case here), the place of performance would be in that member state. If the supplier is resident outside the European Union and conducting business within the European Union, he has to be registered for VAT purposes in Germany.

IV. GERMAN GAAP IMPLICATIONS

According to several rulings of the German Federal Fiscal Court, not only tangible or intangible assets can be shown as a balance sheet item, but also noncash benefits.

Based on this tax classification, for instance, software can also be booked as a single intangible asset if it is appraisable on a standalone basis. Specific provisions apply for system software (i.e., machine-oriented (low-level) software that is independent of the specific software present to the user and that makes the utilization possible) and tailor-made software (software that is required for accomplishing specific tasks for the user).

According to current legal opinion prevailing in Germany, system software has to be classified as an independent intangible asset when it is acquirable as an operating system for fair market value and when it is implemented in hardware that was acquired without an operating system. A dependant part of the hardware (and therewith not independently able to capitalize) in contrast is system software that is individually fitted to the customer's devices and firmly installed (so-called firmware). Also, in the case of so-called bundling—where the system software is delivered in combination with the hardware without specific charging and separate payment—the characteristic of being an independent intangible asset is not assigned to the software.

Tailor-made software is, as a general rule, an independent intangible asset. Admittedly, the German tax authorities exempt so-called trivial software, which is assigned to the associated hardware as a dependant part. Notably, for complex software solutions the separation of single mutually independent modules from each other as independent assets can play a role. However, the German Federal Ministry of Finance defined in a tax circular dated November 18, 2005, that, based on a narrow uniform interrelationship in application and function, modules that belong to a system are to be regarded as one intangible asset that must be capitalized.

Provided that software is an intangible asset, the German Income Tax Act establishes that intangible assets cannot be shown in the balance sheet unless the assets are acquired (or unless it is manufactured for sale and therefore considered as working capital).[5] In this case, the cost of producing the software is instantly deductible as an operational expense. In contrast, any acquisition of software or an Internet presence from a third party will lead to capitalizing each intangible asset as fixed assets in the balance sheet.

The criteria outlined for software also apply to a home page which, in general, is an (authorized) intangible asset when it is dedicated to a long-term Internet presence. The German Federal Fiscal Court held in a decision dated October 10, 2006, that an Internet presence is treated as a nondepreciable intangible asset. Please note that in cases where domains are continuously traded, an Internet presence represents a current (capitalized) asset that may be subject to depreciation.

V. FINAL REMARKS

While offline e-commerce business does not implicate specific tax treatment, companies may be faced with tax exposures when performing online e-commerce activities in inbound and outbound scenarios. Inbound scenarios generally result in German limited tax liability for the foreign supplier or servicer who renders services to persons resident in Germany. German outbound transactions are likely to result in unlimited tax liability for the German entrepreneur. Tax displacements may occur if the entrepreneur maintains a PE in a DTC country from which supplies or services are rendered. Because a server may constitute a PE, it seems to be tax wise to use a server maintained by a third-party service provider in order to mitigate any tax risks.

Because a definitive VAT burden may lead to competitive disadvantages, the VAT treatment on online services in particular must always be considered. Online e-commerce activities are predominantly taxed for VAT purposes in the country where the recipient of such services is domiciled, unless Europe-wide B2C activities are performed.

Finally, the balance sheet treatment of software and similar assets generally complies with general tax principles. However, tax classification issues may arise when analyzing whether software represents an independent intangible asset or a dependent part of the hardware. When capitalizing such intangible assets, it has to be taken into account that only fixed assets that are acquired from third parties can be capitalized.

5 German Income Tax Code, § 5 ¶ 2.

Chapter 10

Greece: Electronic Transactions and the Boundaries of National Tax Legislation

Theodoros Skouzos
Iason Skouzos & Partners

I. INTRODUCTION

Whilst the Internet and other electronic tools facilitate the efficient allocation of global resources, taxing Internet use struggles to retain national character and is an obstacle to the development of e-commerce. E-Commerce increasingly involves the international sharing of tax revenues. According to this argument, failure of the applicable international and local laws to tackle the increased role of e-commerce in global business will result in revenue losses for some countries and revenue increases for others, but also, potentially, to double taxation of the same revenues. The result will vary not only according to the way in which the issue is handled by internationally applicable rules but also more importantly by local laws, to the extent that taxation retains its national character. The increased role of electronic transactions facilitates tax competition between states. On the other hand, the power of a state to impose tax is now challenged by the fact that the traditional rules defining the country to which one is subject to tax, such as the notion of permanent establishment, were not originally designed to accommodate e-businesses.

The impact of e-commerce on taxation is mainly seen in two broad situations: (1) the liability to a country's tax, and (2) the computation of business profits. The present study analyzes the way the Greek tax system treats these issues so that the reader can assess Greece's readiness on e-commerce and its taxation policy.

According to Article 28, ¶ 1 of the Greek Constitution, international tax treaties, like all other international treaties, after their statutory ratification and their coming into effect, become an integral part of the Greek legal system and prevail over possible contradictory provisions of other statutes.

Greece is a member of the OECD (Organization of Economic Cooperation and Development) and as a result, in its negotiations with other states, whether members of

OECD or not, Greece uses as its legal base the OECD Model Tax Convention of 1977 and 1992. Any reference in the present study to the OECD Tax Convention is in relation to the model treaty and not to individual tax treaties signed by Greece, for reasons of simplicity. Obviously, in examining specific cases, the relevant treaty provisions are going to be considered, although, in principle, the provisions relating to the issues in question will not deviate substantially from the model treaty.

Still, tax treaties are not as comprehensive as domestic business practices, and sometimes their precepts do not suffice if the tendency of a state is to interpret new business practices in a narrow tax-collecting approach.

II. INTERCOUNTRY ALLOCATION OF TAXING RIGHTS OVER BUSINESS PROFITS—THE LIABILITY TO GREEK TAXES

A. Place of Establishment and the Avoidance of Double Taxation

States, in the exercise of their power to tax, impose taxes based on different criteria. For instance, some governments impose taxes on the basis of either the residence of the taxpayer, whether natural person or legal entity, or the source of income, or both. Greek tax legislation applies both of these criteria. According to the Income Tax Code, Law 2238/1994 (hereafter ITC), Article 2 ¶ 1, every natural person who resides in Greece is subject to tax on his or her worldwide income, regardless of nationality. Also, every natural person, regardless of nationality or residence, is subject to tax in Greece on income that has its source in Greece. Similarly, according to Article 99, ¶ 1a of the ITC, Greek legal persons of a profitable nature, meaning corporations formed in Greece under Greek law, are taxed on their worldwide income. Finally, foreign corporations are subject to Greek tax for income produced in Greece. The latter rule applies to the permanent establishment of a foreign corporation in Greece, which will be analyzed separately later.

The simultaneous application of the above two criteria—residence and source of income—by different countries inevitably raises the issue of double taxation, that is, the imposition of tax on the same person for the same income by two or more states. For example, when a Greek taxpayer declares his or her worldwide income, he or she will be taxed on income derived from a source located in a foreign state, which could also tax the same income on the basis of the source criterion (legal double taxation). Or a tax may be equally claimed for the same income by two different taxpayers who reside in different states. Double taxation is a fear that tends to restrict the development of intercountry business, and this fear needs to be extinguished in light of the booming development of e-commerce. To that end, measures have been taken and are continuously being developed at an international (OECD, United Nations) and national level.

At a national level, Greek tax legislation restricts double taxation via the following provisions.

1. Tax on the Income of Natural Persons (ITC Article 9, ¶ 8b) According to the provisions of Article 9, ¶ 8b of the ITC, any tax that has been paid abroad on income derived abroad will be set off against the tax payable on the taxpayer's total worldwide net income, up to the amount of Greek tax that is attributable to the same income. Tax paid abroad is not set off if the taxpayer has been taxed in Greece for that income according to the provisions of ITC Article 12, which provides for withholding t ax on interest payments and similar tax issues.

2. Tax on the Income of Legal Entities (ITC Article 109, ¶ 4γ) ITC Article 109, ¶4y, provides that Greek tax authorities will deduct or set off from the total taxable income of a corporation any tax paid abroad for income derived abroad that is subject to tax. That will be deducted from dividends received by a Greek mother company from its foreign daughter company, whether corporate income tax or withholding tax on dividends, whether imposed on the daughter company or a more distant affiliate of a lower category, to the extent that such tax is attributable to the same dividends payable to the Greek mother company. In order to prove the amount of tax that has been paid abroad for these dividends received by the Greek mother company, a certificate issued by the country that imposed the tax, or by a certified auditor, or by any other competent public authority is required. The tax to be set off may not exceed the tax attributable to the same income in Greece.

The above provisions are the legislative tools used by Greece for the avoidance of double taxation. Yet, it is important to note that these deductions are subject to the general rule of "non-deduction of tax exceeding the tax attributable to the same income in Greece."

B. Permanent Establishment of Foreign Legal Entities in Greece

For purposes of Greek income tax law (ITC), a permanent establishment of a foreign business or corporation in Greece is deemed to exist if the foreign business entity

1. Has one or more shop(s), establishment(s), agency (ies), branch (es), office(s), warehouse(s), factory (ies), workshop(s), and/or facilities designed to extract natural resources; or
2. Engages in the industrialization of raw materials or processes agricultural products in its own facilities, or through the use of the facilities of others in Greece acting under the orders of the foreign company or on its behalf; or
3. Conducts business in Greece or provides services through a representative, who is authorized to and can negotiate and conclude contracts on behalf of the foreign legal entity, as well as when the business or services are offered without a representative, provided that they are related to the drawing up of studies or projects or the conduct of research in general or provided that these works and services are technical or scientific in general; or
4. Keeps a stock of merchandise from which it executes commercial orders on its own name or in its own name on its behalf; or
5. Participates in a "personal company" or a limited liability company that is resident in Greece.

To determine the net profit produced in Greece by the permanent establishment of a foreign business, the charging of the permanent establishment in Greece with general management expenses and other organizational and operational expenses incurred and undertaken by the head offices of the business abroad cannot exceed 5 percent of the managerial and operational expenses incurred in Greece by the permanent establishment of the foreign business, as these expenses appear in the annual financial statements of each given tax year. Decrees issued by the minister of finance establish the necessary certificates, requirements, and documents requested for the recognition of these expenses.

The purpose of the ITC is to determine the taxable profits of the permanent establishment of a foreign business entity in Greece. According to article 100 of the ICT, a foreign legal entity in Greece is treated as an independent business entity with independent legal personality.

Hence, a permanent establishment is subject to the ITC and the specific provisions relating to the taxation of business entities that have legal personality. Expenses incurred abroad in the name of the "mother" entity relate in different proportions (depending on the nature of the business, the distance, the way that the group is structured, and many other criteria) to the permanent establishment. These expenses may be, for example, marketing expenses, payroll, transportation, software development, and central management. Information technology and globalization tend to allocate business resources worldwide, and the modern trend of outsourcing business activities adds more examples to the list of expenses that are attributable to the group as a whole.

The legal paradox of treating a permanent establishment as an independent business entity for the purpose of these deductions is not an exclusive Greek concept; many other countries have implemented similar rules for the deduction of such expenses. This was a natural legal development because, from the other side of the argument, that is, the taxation of the mother entity or the headquarters, it would not be fair to allow deduction of expenses attributable to branches and establishments abroad. The issue is whether the provision of Article 100, ¶ 2 of the Greek ITC, and especially the 5 percent threshold, is fair and in line with the model tax convention of the OECD.

Article 24 of the OECD Model Convention provides that taxation of a permanent establishment that an enterprise of one contracting state has in another contracting state, shall not be less favourably levied in that other state than the taxation levied on enterprises of that other state carrying on the same activities. Interest, royalties, and other disbursements paid by an enterprise of a contracting state to a resident of another contracting state shall, for the purpose of determining the taxable profits of such enterprise,be deductible under the same conditions as if they had been paid to a resident of the first-mentioned state. Similarly, any debts of an enterprise of a contracting state to a resident of the other contracting state shall, for the purpose of determining the enterprise's taxable capital, be deductible under the same conditions as if they had been incurred by a resident of the first-mentioned state.

According to the above, Greece is obliged to recognize the analogous deduction of expenses realized by the "mother" entity without any limitation or restriction other than the ones imposed on local businesses. In other words, the limitation included in

Article 100, ¶ 2 of the ITC is contrary to the model convention. Although the convention provisions should prevail, per the constitutional rule, in practice Greek tax authorities narrowly apply the statutory provisions, often forcing the taxpayer to seek judicial remedy.

The minister of finance, according to Article 100, ¶ 2, is empowered to issue decrees providing details and implementation rules for these provisions. The purpose for granting such a power was to establish of a framework by which it could be easily assessed whether these expenses are real, whether they refer to the overall operations of the business group, and the extent to which they relate to the operation of the permanent establishment in Greece. Yet, the only relevant ministerial decision, issued in Article 1131/22.4/1997, provides that general management expenses and the various expenses for the organization and operation of a foreign business's permanent establishment in Greece, which are made abroad by the "mother" foreign company, may be deducted from the permanent establishment's gross income of the same fiscal year, according to Article 100, ¶ 2 of the ITC—subject to the condition that, up to the date of the tax audit of the mother company, the latter will produce to the Greek tax authorities a certificate from the competent authority or other public authority of the country where the mother company is based. This certification must show the following:

1. The total sum of expenses made by the mother company abroad during that fiscal year and that were included in the mother company's accounting books as a debt of the Greek permanent establishment;
2. The portion of these expenses that relate to the general management expenses and other organizational and operational expenses that the mother company realized exclusively for the operation of the permanent establishment.

Obviously, these conditions render the deductibility of such expenses an extremely difficult exercise. They are contrary to the very nature of such expenses. An international business organization that applies universal methods and criteria for the operation of its branches throughout the world cannot easily estimate the degree to which an expense should be attributable to the operation of the Greek branch. For example, the expense for the development of central Enterprise Resource Planning (ERP) software that will benefit the group and the expense of designing the shops of a multinational clothing business may all be centralized for cost-cutting purposes and may thus not be safely attributable to local establishments with the criteria imposed by Greek law.

In conclusion, it may be argued that both Article 100 and the ministerial decision issued for its interpretation are contrary to the principles of the OECD model treaty and the relevant guidelines.

C. Additional Rules Governing Liability for Greek Taxes

The Greek business community has increased its use of offshore entities, thanks to information technology and globalization. Not that offshore companies were unknown before; Greek shipowners have been using them for decades. However, in the nineties, they became more familiar among medium- and small-scale businesses as a tool to increase anonymity and reduce the tax bill. Moreover, forming an offshore entity is a very simple procedure compared to the bureaucratic incorporation processes in Greece. According to data from the Ministry of Finance, offshore companies are mostly used in Greece for the passive possession of land and/or recreational boats, such as yachts and cruisers. There is, however, considerable use of offshore companies for the transfer of taxable income abroad through the manipulation of transfer prices, in the same way as they are used in other countries. This latter abuse of offshore entities is of interest to e-business.

In Greece, the most important legislation limiting the potential abuse of the tax system through the use of offshore companies was adopted in 2000. This legislation supplements the general tax provisions, both in defining liability for Greek taxes and in measuring profits. First, Article 15, ¶ 3 of Law 2992/2002, Article 107, ¶ 1 of the ITC was modified to the effect that every foreign legal person in possession of or owning land in Greece is obliged to submit an income tax return regardless of whether income is produced from such land. Although this provision is not related to e-commerce, it is indicative of the tax system's offensive policy against the use of offshore companies; it does not tax the possession or ownership of land, but it obliges the owner to declare possession or ownership, rendering the tax audit easier against possible nondeclaration of income produced by such land possession or ownership.

Second, Law 3052/2002 modified certain provisions of the Code of Books and Records (CBR), Presidential Decree 186/1992. CBR is the law that governs the issuing of invoices, the recording of taxable transactions, and similar activities, of all natural and legal persons earning income. A natural or legal person is subject to the CBR if that person exercises a business or a profession. In other words and generally speaking, CBR catches all income earners apart from the "passive" ones. For reasons of simplicity, this chapter shall refer to income earners subject to the CBR as "professionals."

Law 3052/2002 introduced two important rules. First, it imposes the CBR obligations on foreign legal entities that acquire real property in Greece, regardless of whether or not income is produced. Second, it imposes the obligations of CBR to foreign entities if they have a physical/actual presence in Greece, regardless of whether or not such a presence is considered a permanent establishment for income tax purposes.

Law 3052/2002 is definitely of interest for e-commerce, and this is why it is analyzed in the statute and the explanatory guideline 1271/12.12/2002 issued by the Ministry of Finance. According to these provisions, as of January 1, 2003, excepting persons that are considered as having a permanent establishment according to the general provisions, the following persons are also considered professionals and subject to the obligations of the CBR (book keeping, submission of tax returns and forms):

1. Foreign natural or legal persons who have a real physical establishment (office, shop, agency, warehouse, plant, etc.), regardless of whether such establishment is deemed a permanent establishment by the general provisions;

2. Foreign entities that own or have interests in land. The above two groups of persons have the same book-keeping requirements as their Greek equivalents.

The above provisions do not apply to foreign natural or legal persons that are obliged to keep accounting books under 1174/2002, which governs the procedure for declaration and payment of value-added tax (VAT) by persons established in another member state of the European Union. According to Law 1174/2002, persons who are subject to VAT, that are established in a member state of the European Union, and that perform activities subject to VAT from the place of their establishment, are obliged to appoint a representative for the fulfillment of their obligations in Greece, according to the Greek VAT Code, and under the condition that these actions do not constitute a permanent establishment of such person according to other provisions of the VAT Code. Such an appointment must take place before the realization of taxable activities for which VAT is payable in Greece. The obligation to appoint a VAT representative in Greece does not apply in the following cases:

1. For transactions for which VAT is payable by the recipient of goods or services according to the VAT provisions;
2. In cases of exportation of goods by a seller established in Greece who acts in the name and on behalf of a buyer who operates within the European Union and is subject to VAT.

The appointment of the representative takes place with the signature of a document that expressly declares that the representative is the only one appointed in Greece and specifies the actions he or she is authorized to perform. The representative appointed may be a natural or legal person who is subject to tax and has a permanent establishment or registered seat in Greece. Such a person may be an accountant, tax advisor, or any other person who must be accountable, reliable, and fully capable of acting. If such person is a legal person, he or she must operate legally and must not have been guilty of serious tax violations. The representative must sign a document whereby he or she accepts the appointment. The representative must submit on behalf of the principal a declaration for the commencement of taxable activities to the tax office overseeing the area where the representative is based.

Natural or legal persons subject to the requirements have all the book-keeping (CBR) plus VAT rights and liabilities of persons established in Greece. As an exception to those rights and liabilities, they may issue invoices in the country of their establishment. If the natural or legal persons issue invoices in their country of establishment, the invoices must mention, in addition to all the necessary data of the main establishment, the tax registration number acquired in Greece by the tax representative, the value of the transaction, and the VAT payable according to the Greek rates. Copies of those invoices must be sent to the representative so that the latter can file them and record the relevant data in the accounting books.

The above deviations from the permanent establishment definition are not compatible with the OECD principles. Article 5, ¶ 4 of the OECD Model Tax Convention provides that a permanent establishment is deemed to exclude the use of facilities or premises solely for the purposes of (1) storage, display, and delivery of merchandise; (2) purchase of goods or collecting information; (3) maintenance of goods of the enterprise for the purpose of processing by another enterprise; or (4) a combination of the above activities where overall activity resulting from this combination is of a preparatory or auxiliary character. The above deviations mention neither these nor other exceptions, nor any criterion like the "auxiliary nature" criterion proposed by the OECD.

III. MEASUREMENT OF PROFITS

When a business chooses the country where it will establish all or part of its operations, it may do so for reasons relating to payroll costs, infrastructure, distance, and language. Yet, the decision in many occasions can very well be purely tax-driven. Tax avoidance and tax evasion are not very easily distinguished from one another. Within the goal of achieving efficiency, businesses tend to seek the optimum tax treatment of their operations. To that end, multinationals choose the country of establishment of all or part of their activities in favorable tax regimes, shifting their tax obligation, to the extent that this may be permissible in the country where they are based. This creates tax competition between states, which in turn, leads the tax authorities of different countries to look into the economics of a business that goes far beyond merely answering the question of whether a specific business is taxable but challenges the amount of profits that will be subject to it. The opportunities created by new technologies to shift operations are no longer only a privilege of multinationals and big enterprises but are only a click away for small businesses and solo traders.

A. The Arm's-Length Principle in the Greek ITC

Transfer pricing under the Greek ITC is covered by Article 39 of Law 2238/1994, which is titled "Over-invoicing and under-invoicing." Article 39 provides that when a contract is concluded for the sale of goods or the provision of services between two Greek businesses or a Greek business and a foreign business, in which the consideration is unreasonably higher or lower than would have been agreed to under market conditions between two independent parties, the difference between the market price and the agreed price is deemed as profit of the business that received lower or paid a higher consideration accordingly. This difference would be added to the net business profits without any consequence in relation to the overall validity of its accounting books. This rule applies if (1) a Greek company is controlled by the foreign company due to the latter's participation in the capital or the management of the first; and (2) in the case of Greek companies, if one exercises direct or indirect material managerial or financial dependence or control over the other.

The resulting difference, according to the above provision, is added to the gross income of the business, as this appears in its accounting books, so that this income is taken into account for computation of all other direct and indirect taxes, duties, and charges imposed by other provisions. The business at fault is subject to a fine of 10 percent on the difference. This fine is imposed regardless of the imposition of any other additional taxes, supplementary charges, and other penalties provided in other statutes.

The unreasonable consideration rule does not apply in the following circumstances:

1. If the consideration has been set by virtue of a contract between Greece and the foreign entity and said contract has been ratified by law;
2. If the contracting businesses prove that the over-invoicing or under-invoicing did not take place with the purpose of avoiding direct or indirect taxes.

The provisions of Article 39 apply accordingly to rights and compensation paid by foreign businesses and organizations for the use of technical expertise, patents, drawings, musical works, industrial methods, intellectual property rights, and similar rights in Greece.

Article 39 has not gone far in tackling illegal transfer pricing practices. This is so because the nonfulfilment of both conditions of the rule, that is, the relation between the contracting companies and the difference between the agreed-on and the market price, will result in the nonapplication of the rule (Accord, Council of State 3803/1988, 660/1995, 4464/1997). These conditions, apart from being vague in principle, are also difficult to prove. Furthermore, even if the conditions are satisfied, the "escape" provision that allows the taxpayer to avoid any consequences by proving that the purposes of transfer pricing was not tax avoidance, often leads to litigation. Instances where the courts have accepted the satisfaction of the escape provision include those in which the taxpayer can prove that the overall tax obligation would not differ if the prices accepted by the tax authorities were adopted in the transaction.

The above difficulties have, in practice, directed the tax authorities to seek enforcement of other rules against transfer pricing, rules that leave them greater discretion and that have simpler criteria.

B. Rules That Deal with Mock Invoicing and Their Overlap with Transfer Pricing Rules

Notwithstanding the above-mentioned provisions of Article 39 of the ITC that deal with transfer pricing tactics, there are recent provisions that are much easier and stricter in their application, and the tax authorities no longer have to resort to applying Article 39. In brief, under these new provisions there is no need to get into the details of the relationship between the contracting parties, and it is irrelevant whether the taxpayer intended to avoid tax. These provisions are set forth in Law 2523/1997, which deals with tax evasion, tax fraud, and provides for criminal and administrative penalties. The administrative penalties are dealt with in Article 5, ¶ 10. This article provides that the issue of mock or counterfeited invoices, their acceptance, and/or their recording in the accounting books is subject to a fine equal to twice the amount of the invoice. If the value of the invoice is partly incorrect, the fine is imposed for that incorrect portion. When it is not easy to estimate the incorrect value (over-invoicing or under-invoicing) half of the above-mentioned penalty is imposed.

In addition to the administrative penalties, the use of false invoices is a crime. According to Article 19 of Law 2523/1997, "Crime of tax evasion through the issuance or acceptance of counterfeited or mock invoices," whoever issues counterfeited or mock invoices and whoever accepts those, regardless of whether he or she avoids the payment of tax through that action, is subject to imprisonment of at least three months. When the total value of these invoices exceeds the amount of €235,000, apart from the above penalties, the wrongdoer may face the closure of his or her business for up to one month.

A mock invoice is one that is issued for a transaction that is fictitious in its entirety or part thereof, or is issued by different persons than the persons appearing on the invoice. Invoices that mention a value higher or lower than the real value attributable to the transaction fall under the definition of mock invoices.

C. Dealings with Offshore Companies and the Measurement of Profits

Law 3091/2002 contains the most recent definition of an offshore company under Greek law. According to this law, offshore companies are companies that are not active in the country where they have their registered seat and shares, which are usually anonymous (to the bearer). These countries are often referred to as "tax havens," for obvious reasons.

Most countries' tax authorities are suspicious when they come across an invoice issued by a business located offshore. Since 2002 when Law 3190 was passed in Greece, Greek tax authorities no longer have to be apprehensive of these invoices. Two important provisions have been added to the ITC by virtue of Article 5, ¶¶ 7 and 9, which render dealings with offshore companies unattractive.

Article 5, ¶ 7 states that "the depreciation of fixed assets that have been bought by an offshore company is not recognised for deduction from its gross income." Article 5 ¶ 9 reads, "Expenses that the business incurs for the purchase of goods or the receipt of services by an offshore company as well as rights and compensation paid to the offshore company for the use in Greece of technical assistance, patents, copyright, drawings, secret industrial methods and formulas, intellectual property and other similar rights may not be deducted from its gross income."

The law takes into account three criteria to classify a company as an offshore company:

1. That the corporate seat of the company is located abroad;
2. That the activity of such company is restricted to any other country than the one where it has its registered seat; and
3. That the company is subject to a very advantageous tax regime in the country where it has its registered seat.

The country where the company has its registered seat is the main criterion for applying these strict rules of nondeductibility. The provision regarding the corporate seat ignores the following facts:

1. The factor of a company's real seat;
2. The possibility that a company that has its corporate seat abroad can be active in Greece only; and
3. The possibility that, instead of an offshore company, the expense is payable to a natural person residing offshore.

The provisions of Law 3091/2002 on offshore companies also ignore the so-called productivity factor, a general tax principle that considers the deductibility of an expense. According to the Greek Constitution and the general principles of Greek tax law, the tax authorities are not allowed to look into the purposes or the limit of an expense incurred by a business but only into the legality of such an expense, which is covered if there is sufficient proof of such an expense according to CBR principles.

The result of the above is that real expenses that may be necessary for the operation of a business may not be deducted simply because the same expenses are the income of a company that enjoys favourable tax treatment elsewhere.

All the above are in breach of Article 4 of the Constitution of Greece, which provides that all Greeks contribute to taxes according to their capacity. The legislature has evaded the constitutionally protected right for equality in tax treatment in order to combat tax evasion. And this is done without any referral to tax evasion or transfer pricing issues; instead it follows only some formal requirements. Apart from the incompatibility of such an approach with tax treaties, these rules prohibit the internationally acceptable transfer of tax obligation within a global economy, which is sound tax competition.

The effect of the above strict rules on e-commerce with Greek businesses is not so obvious but still very important. Businesses that trade online or sell digitalized products or provide services electronically are very commonly established offshore, for reasons that are not solely tax-driven.

IV. CONCLUSION

Although the Greek ITC has a rigid definition of permanent establishment of a foreign business, which has been sufficient for decades, the development of modern business models has forced Greece to adopt additional rules imposing tax obligations on other forms of business presence in Greece. This was done without modifying the definition of permanent establishment. In practice, however, there is not much difference in the sense that businesses are not interested in words and labels but in the pecuniary or practical consequences resulting in their business presence in Greece. In other words, even if a business that has dealings with customers in Greece is far from satisfying the requirements of a permanent establishment, this does not necessarily mean that it will not incur tax liability, that it will be free from bureaucratic dealings with the tax authorities, and that it will be free from reporting and filing tax forms. In recent years, Greek tax law has not redefined permanent establishment but has cancelled out its practical importance by extending tax obligations to businesses that deal in different ways with Greece, without questioning if they are established or not.

The limit imposed by the Greek legislature on the amount of expenses that may be recognized for deduction for a permanent establishment is unfair by definition. Why should there be a limit at all? It is purely a weakness of the system, which cannot look into the accounting of a multinational as a whole. In any case, if the only (conventional) solution is the imposition of a limit, notwithstanding the relevant incompatibility with OECD rules, 5 percent certainly does not reflect the reality of a multinational that has spread its activities and resources internationally.

Once it has been established that a share of a business's profits originates from a country, and that country should be allowed to tax them, it is necessary to have rules to determine the share of profits that should be subject to such tax. Tax is imposed on profit, which is income minus expenses. In calculating the taxable profit of a business, the Greek tax authorities have a very wide discretion when defining "expenses," and this is the main issue in most tax audits that take place in Greece. Greek tax authorities, for reasons that are attributable to the way that Greek society operates in general, tend to be preoccupied that everybody is tax-evading. This is reflected very simply by the provisions that literally prohibit expenses payable to offshore entities. As with the rest of transactions, they retain a purely subjective method, without even referral or recourse to the arm's-length principle, of challenging the value agreed for a transaction, even if the transacting parties are totally independent the one from the other.

The actual "prohibition" of dealings with offshore companies, even if it is somehow justified, has an impact on e-commerce in Greece to the extent that the contracting party in electronic transactions is very likely to be based offshore. Sometimes it is hard to define where it is actually located. The fear of nondeductibility of an expense may very well prevent Greek businessmen from dealing electronically.

The above rules and practices are of a catch-all character. They are not only incompatible with internationally -accepted rules of tax fairness, such as the OECD principles, but serve as an obstacle for businesses operating in Greece to enter into electronic transactions with other states.

E-Commerce lets businesses participate to a significant degree in the economic life of a country through automated functions without the need for a physical presence that would fall under the definition of a permanent establishment. To that extent, it may no longer be appropriate to base tax liability on whether business activities are carried out in a specific country, because e-commerce has clearly changed the nature of physical requirements necessary to conduct business in a local jurisdiction.

There are three ways a tax system may adapt to the new economy:

1. Catch-all formalistic regulation, which is tax-collecting in principle and leads to unfair results.
2. Source taxation, such as withholding taxes on interest and royalties. It efficiently taxes payments but also produces unfair results, if one considers fairness to be taxation on profit rather than taxation on transactions.

3. Unitary taxation or formulary apportionment of profits. Of course, such a method would also raise questions of fairness, especially if they are not adopted in a uniform way between the countries involved.

E-Commerce has made the world increasingly more complex. What is happening today certainly poses a challenge to the long-term viability of the arm's-length standard and the traditional definition of permanent establishment. The increasing role of digital products and services and the expanded degree of licensing and transferring of know-how are challenging the traditional trade patterns globally. Differing corporate taxes create or maintain inefficiencies in an otherwise harmonized business environment. A globally accepted method of unitary taxation seems like a good solution for eliminating such inefficiencies. To the extent that this is not achieved, Greece, together with other states, will naturally seek to interpret new methods and business practices with a tax-collecting mentality.

Chapter 11

Hungary: Trends in Hungarian E-Commerce Taxation and Administration

Jacques Bernard de Servigny & Szabolcs Erdős
Gide Loyrette Nouel

I. INTRODUCTION

This chapter aims to provide a general overview of current tendencies in Hungary toward e-commerce and an Internet-friendly taxation environment, as well as their underlying legal framework. The authors wish to outline the major electronic procedures available in Hungary for taxation purposes, and to provide the reader with some insight from a Hungarian taxation perspective into a few typical transactions that are carried out by electronic means.

The first part of the chapter will elaborate on general Hungarian electronic public procedures and their advantages. The discussion will then focus more closely on the Hungarian administrative and procedural aspects of e-commerce taxation, such as the use of electronic contracts, electronic signatures, electronic invoices, and the ability to store taxation documents in an electronic format.

The second part of the chapter will provide examples of certain Hungarian indirect tax aspects of the supply of goods and services provided by electronic means, especially through the Internet, to both taxable and nontaxable entities. This part will also scrutinize certain issues of interest and practical difficulties that often arise when such transactions are carried out.

II. E-COMMERCE

A. What Is E-Commerce?

Generally speaking, e-commerce consists of the buying and selling of products or services over electronic systems such as the Internet or other computerized networks.

The notion of e-commerce is more specifically defined under Act CVIII of 2001 on Electronic Commerce, whereby e-commerce means the sale, purchase, or exchange of goods and services through electronic systems, normally for financial consideration. In practice, electronic commercial services are provided at a distance and normally at an individual request made by the prospective recipient of the goods or services.

While it sounds like a modern notion, e-commerce dates back at least three decades. The commonly-known technology of electronic data interchange (EDI) and electronic funds transfer (EFT) were introduced in the 1970s, to be utilized by businesses to send commercial documents such as purchase orders or invoices electronically. E-Commerce then progressed with the introduction of credit cards, automated teller machines (ATMs), and telephone banking systems in the 1980s, and has become more and more increasingly widespread through the 1990s, and into the twenty-first century.

Although current statistics reveal that only a relatively low portion of Hungarian population has access to computers and to the Internet, there is an ever-increasing tendency toward e-commerce, a process that is further accelerated by the developing legal framework for such electronic procedures.

B. Main Characteristics

1. Use of Electronic Equipment for Processing, Storing, and Transmitting Data First and foremost, e-commerce is undoubtedly linked to the use of certain electronic equipment for processing, storing, and transmitting data. More often than not, the data is transmitted, conveyed, and received by wire, by radio, by optical means, or by similar other electromagnetic means. But most important of all, the use of the Internet has led to an extraordinary growth in trade conducted electronically in Hungary, just as in many other places around the world. A wide variety of commerce is conducted this way, such as EFT, supply chain management, Internet marketing, or online transaction processing, as well as inventory management systems and automated data collection systems.

2. Connection and Communication between the Parties It is quite a unique feature of e-commerce that the parties taking part in such transactions most often do not meet in person but conclude their contracts, make payments, and communicate by electronic means. This characteristic makes it possible for countless suppliers and purchasers to do business together, who would most probably never encounter each other without an electronic environment.

3. Specific Legislation As a result of the increasing importance of e-commerce, the need to govern this field has gradually arisen. E-Commerce law was created in Hungary in 2001, with the introduction of laws on e-commerce and electronic signatures. This legislation makes it possible to undertake such tasks as signing contracts electronically, and also provides grounds for filing tax returns through the Internet, using electronic invoices, or registering companies or patents online.

4. Special Security Measures The nature of e-commerce entails and increases the possibility of dissatisfaction of the parties and the failure of such transactions. Therefore, special security measures are necessary. These affect confidentiality, the safety of electronic payments, the mutual identification of the parties, the identification and clear presentation of the goods or services offered for sale, and protection against crackers and hackers. These potential problems or difficulties require appropriate legislation and a technical background.

III. GENERAL ELECTRONIC PROCEDURES

A. General Procedural Rules

The wide range of public administrative procedures is primarily governed by Act CXL of 2004. In addition, there are a number of other laws and regulations construing various procedures that can be managed by electronic means. These include automobile registration, passport applications, and public procurement procedures or filing tax returns (this latter will be dealt with in more detail later on in this chapter). Furthermore, even companies can be founded electronically at the Registry Court, as long as the founders turn to an attorney with a certified digital signature (*minősített elektronikus aláírás*—to be outlined later on in greater detail) and using the services of a time-stamp provider.

In other words, practically all procedures other than civil law and criminal law proceedings are governed by this act. Obviously, these services may affect almost all private individuals and other entities in Hungary. Therefore, the fact that the law provides for the possibility of electronic procedures in public administration is a huge step toward a more user-friendly legal environment in Hungary. Electronic procedures are not only more convenient for all parties involved, but even their time-frame is considerably shorter than that of regular procedures.

In principle, the law allows for an electronic public procedure, unless expressly prohibited by legislation, which means that electronic procedures are basically equivalent to "traditional" procedures in terms of their legal effect. Given the nature of the vast majority of these procedures, private individuals can benefit from electronic administrative procedures more often than companies.

1. Eligibility for Electronic Procedures In order to benefit from the above advantages, it is necessary to be registered before the electronic procedure can commence. There are two possible alternative methods for this registration. One option is the identification of the person taking part in the electronic procedure by means of a so-called secure digital signature (*fokozott biztonságú elektronikus aláírás*), provided that the applicant already has such a digital signature (note that there are various types of electronic signatures under Hungarian law, which will be discussed later on). In addition, the issuer of the digital signature must verify once again, if requested by the authority, the "real" (as opposed to the "virtual") identity of the applicant with a digital signature.

As a result, the identity of the applicant will become established via a digital signature. Subsequently, the final step is registration with the Client Portal system (*Ügyfélkapu*) through the Internet. This system will also be touched upon later in this chapter.

Using a digital signature for personal identification as described above is comparatively rare in international practice, but not entirely unheard of; a similar system is in place in Austria. Experience shows that this form of registration is less frequent in practice in Hungary than the other type of registration described below.

The second method is used much more widely in practice. This solution requires the applicants to present themselves at the local municipality's relevant office where identity cards, passports, and other such forms of documentation are issued (*okmányiroda*), in order to prove their identity. By virtue of this step, the applicant becomes registered with the Client Portal system, and receives an identification code, which is then used to generate a personal user name. This personal user name will be valid for up to five years, to be used in electronic procedures.

Note that it is possible for one person to obtain access to the Client Portal and to be authorized by various other persons to file the tax returns of all these individuals through his or her Client Portal access. In other words, an accountant, for example, may electronically submit the tax returns of all of his clients through his own Client Portal access, providing that his clients have authorized him for this purpose and this fact has been registered with the Tax Authority beforehand.

2. Access to and the Use of the Client Portal Once the registration process is finished, the Client Portal system can be reached at the Web site www.magyarorszag.hu. This is a very useful and versatile Web site. In addition to providing access to the Client Portal, it gives detailed explanations on multiple public procedures (including those that cannot be managed electronically). For example, tax returns may be filed electronically through this Web site, corporate entities can access the pension data of their employees, and even trademarks may be registered through this Web page. Moreover, there is an even wider range of services available to private individuals, such as requesting a passport or seeking legal information on various matters, since current Hungarian legislation is made available to the public here.

There are specific provisions in the law regulating the means of sending electronic requests to various public authorities, the time when they are considered to be delivered, and the related deadlines. The law also provides a list of requests that can be made electronically to an authority, such as a request for an appeal or for the consideration of evidence. But even some communications from the authority toward clients may be in an electronic format, such as the notification of a deadline, or a decision in a certain matter. Legislation provides that certain electronic decisions of the authority must be in the form of a document signed by a secure digital signature, for example, official certificates or permits issued by specialised authorities.

It is a particularity of the Hungarian system that the authentication of a person for an electronic procedure automatically authenticates all the actions taken by this person during a Web-based administrative process, including sending documents, even if the client is not in possession of a secure digital signature. Therefore, it is crucial to bear in mind that the client is liable for damages caused by revealing his or her identification data to third parties.

B. Electronic Contracts

Electronic contracts have the same legal effects as traditional hard-copy contracts. They only differ from their hard-copy counterparts in terms of their form. However, an electronic contract must meet additional conditions to be legally binding, primarily to deal with consumer protection and security issues that boil down from the special nature of these contracts.

As with other countries around the world, purchasing goods and services on the Internet has becoming increasingly popular amongst Hungarian customers as well. This fact led to the need to enact a separate act to govern e-commerce and the underlying electronic contracts in adequate detail.

In Hungary, Act CVIII of 2001 on e-commerce lays down the fundamental rules for providing services and concluding contracts online. This act typically governs civil law contractual transactions. For this reason, the scope of this act excludes administrative procedures and personal electronic communications. In brief, the act is built around two major notions, e-commerce and e-contracts.

E-Commerce services are defined as information technology services whose main purpose is facilitating the sale of goods or services. As a general condition, the provider of e-commerce services is required by law to disclose various pieces of information on his or her Web site—such as his or her address details, tax registration number, the price of the goods and services to allow potential customers to identify the supplier before they enter into an e-contract to purchase goods or services.

While Hungarian legislation provides no explicit definition of an e-contract, it does put forth a set of rules for concluding binding agreements online without having face-to-face interaction. From this it can be concluded that an *e-contract* is basically a means of conducting e-commerce transactions. It is also accepted as true that an e-contract is a traditional contract that differs from a hard-copy contract only in the way it is entered into: there is no personal meeting between the two contractors, but they only communicate through a Web page. Additionally, there is often a third party to the transaction, namely the host of the Web site through which the contract is concluded.

Pursuant to the specific nature of e-contracts pointed out above, there are additional legal requirements that do not apply to traditional contracts, in order to adequately protect the rights of both contractual parties. These additional requirements specified under the act are largely in line with corresponding EU legislation. The most important of these requirements are the following:

- The general terms and conditions of the contract must be made available online so that the customer can download, retrieve, and get acquainted with them;
- Information must be provided, for example, regarding the language of the contract or the correction of orders made erroneously or mistakenly; and

- The seller must acknowledge receipt of the order by the customer; if the seller fails to reply within at most two days, the customer will be released from any contractual obligations derived from his order.

In addition to the above, it is an important feature of e-commerce activities that both the provider of the e-commerce service (i.e., the seller) and the provider of the intermediary service (i.e., the company hosting the Web site) are responsible for the content of the offers publicized on the Web site. However, the provider of the intermediary service can be relieved of this responsibility with regards to third parties if the provider proves that he or she had no active part in publishing the offending content.

C. Electronic Signatures

These days, electronic signatures are more and more widely used to provide security for various types of electronic transactions, since in electronic procedures a manual signature is obviously impossible and an abuse of this "defect" requires a remedy to protect the rights of the parties involved.

Electronic signatures play an important role in the Client Portal registration procedure, for example, or e-contracts as outlined above, even though it is not explicitly indispensable. For instance, the use of an electronic signature is an option for the taxpayer, in addition to the compulsory use of his or her personal user name and password when he or she manages certain tax procedures through the Client Portal system. However, in the case of electronic invoices (to be discussed later in detail), an electronic signature is an absolute must.

Three types of electronic signatures are recognized in Hungary, as defined under Act XXXV of 2001 on digital signatures. Each of them has a different legal force, and a different level of security and identification.

1. Simple Digital Signature The "simple" digital signature is a mere indication of the name of the author on a digital document, such as a signature at the end of an e-mail message. This type of electronic signature is insecure and can easily be abused. Therefore, it is not used for legally binding electronic documents.

2. Secure Digital Signature A secure digital signature (*fokozott biztonságú elektronikus aláírás*) has to conform to four requirements:

1. It has to be capable of identifying the signatory;
2. It is to be uniquely linked to the signatory;
3. It has to be created under the signatory's sole control; and
4. It has to be linked to the document in such a manner that all changes made to the document after digitally signing it will be detectable.

This type of electronic signature is created by an algorithm using the public-key infrastructure system, and is, therefore, much safer than a simple digital signature. If a legal instrument requires a written format for a document (e.g., a real estate sales contract), documents signed by a secure digital signature are considered to be equivalent to a traditional written signature.

3. Certified Digital Signature A certified digital signature (*minősített elektronikus aláírás*) has to conform to all requirements for a secure digital signature, as well as the following two additional requirements:

1. It has to be created by a device used for the creation of secure digital signatures, and
2. It has to be certified by a qualified entity empowered to certify digital signatures.

This kind of electronic signature has the highest level of security: in this case, a trusted third party certifies the identity of the signatory. As a result, the certified digital signature is equivalent to signing a document by hand. If a document is signed by a certified digital signature, there is a presumption that its contents have not changed since signing.

As a result, such a document is considered to be a document of full probative power (*teljes bizonyító erejű magánokirat*); that is, the document is legally identical to a nondigital document where the signature is either witnessed by two individuals or countersigned by an attorney or a public notary. Furthermore, if prepared by a court or authority acting in such a capacity, an electronic document equipped with a certified digital signature qualifies as a public document (*közokirat*).

4. Obtaining an Electronic Signature Those wishing to obtain a secure or certified electronic signature must be in the possession of a computer program that generates the algorithms necessary for the encryption, and they must also subscribe to a digital signature service provider. In other words, an electronic signature is not as easy to "create" as a traditional signature, because it has to be purchased along with the evidence that it is authentic and unique.

Providers who offer digital signature services are registered with the National Communications Authority (*Nemzeti Hírközlési Hatóság*), where there is a short list of providers empowered to issue secure or certified digital signatures that can be used in electronic administrative procedures.

IV. ELECTRONIC TAXATION PROCEDURES

A. Electronic Invoices

Under the rules of the act on value-added tax (VAT, invoices may be issued in a hard-copy format or electronically, upon the decision of the taxpayer (note that a simple receipt—*nyugta*—can only be issued in a hard-copy format). This is a significant relief as opposed to earlier legislation where a hard-copy invoice had to be issued even if an electronic invoice was prepared, that is, the electronic invoice was a mere duplicate of a regular hard-copy invoice. This rigid rule greatly limited the advantages of electronic invoicing.

Therefore, the new rules allowing for the total replacement of hard-copy invoices by electronic invoices is a significant step toward a modern tax environment in Hungary.

By definition, an electronic invoice is the transfer or provision of data or digitally compressed data to the recipient of the goods or services by electronic means through a telephone, radio, optical, or other electromagnetic network, providing that it is done for the purpose of an electronic process of the data.

Under the act on VAT, the most important requirement for an electronic invoice is that the authenticity of the completeness and originality of both the invoice and the data contained therein are assured. If this requirement is not met, the electronic invoice cannot be acknowledged for taxation purposes. If this requirement can be met, there are two alternatives for the electronic issuance of invoices:

1. The invoice may take the form of a document signed by at least a secure digital signature and equipped with a time-stamp provided by a certified service provider;
2. The invoice is exchanged by the parties concerned in an EDI system.

In the latter case, that is, when the invoice is exchanged through an EDI system, the person responsible for issuing the invoice and the recipient of the goods or services are obliged to previously agree in writing that that the EDI system will be applied and used. In this case, there is another requirement that a monthly summary be prepared in hard copy about all the invoices issued in a given month. This has to be handed over to the recipient of the goods or services.

Other than the above, electronic invoices fall under the same rules as normal hard-copy invoices in terms of their statutory content and the period for which they have to be kept. As for their storage, however, they have to be retained in an electronic format. That is, it is not possible to print electronically issued invoices and only store the printouts. The storage has to be managed by the issuer of the electronic invoice, or by another party that specializes in storing such electronic data.

If a tax audit takes place, electronic invoices—as with traditional hard-copy invoices—have to be presented to the tax officers within three days. For this purpose, the necessary software and/or hardware also have to be made available for the tax audit, so that the electronic invoices can be viewed.

Finally, the reader should note that the use of electronic invoices is not exclusively acknowledged by Hungarian VAT legislation. For example, the rules for simplified entrepreneurial taxation also allow the issue of electronic invoices. In this case, the prerequisites for their use are similar to those set out for VAT purposes.

B. Accounting Documents, Storage of Documents Electronically

Under Act C of 2000 on accounting, electronic documents may be used as accounting documents if they have been equipped with at least a secure digital signature and a time stamp, and if they meet the general requirements for an accounting document as specified under the accounting law.

Electronic accounting documents must be stored in digital form in a way that all data can be retrievable and continuously accessible without delay, and any retroactive modifications should be fully impossible.

It is of note that the act on accounting makes it possible to retain hard-copy documents in an electronic format. This possibility is clearly an advantage for entities subject to Hungarian accounting rules, given that these documents have to be kept for a period of eight years, which may result in the volume of these documents taking enough space to fill an entire warehouse in the case of a large company. However, it is important to point out that the underlying decree for the electronic storage of hard-copy documents has not yet been enacted. Therefore, this possibility will be usable in practice only in the future.

C. Electronic Auctions in Tax Collection Procedures

Under Hungarian tax procedure rules, if a taxpayer has outstanding tax liabilities and is reluctant to pay them, it is possible within strict statutory limits to sell certain properties of this taxpayer through an auction and cover the outstanding liabilities from the revenues generated. Experience shows, however, that such auctions were mostly unsuccessful, since there were few people interested in taking part.

In order to make auctions more efficient, it has been possible, since January 1, 2008, for the Hungarian Tax Authority to organize auctions electronically. This way the auction is publicized through the official Web page of the Tax Authority (https://arveres.apeh.hu), which is easily reachable by anyone interested in purchasing the movable properties offered for sale. The only prerequisite to becoming a bidder in such an auction is that the potential purchaser has to be registered with the Client Portal system. Even though the new electronic auction system was introduced only recently, it can already be seen that it will be far more popular and successful than traditional Tax Authority auctions have so far ever been.

V. VALUE-ADDED TAXATION OF E-COMMERCE TRANSACTIONS

The newly codified Hungarian act on VAT (Act CXXVII of 2007) is largely in line with the EU VAT rules specified in the 2006/112/EC directive. Accordingly, Hungarian VAT rules regulate in detail certain transactions that typically constitute electronic transactions. Below are demonstrated two characteristic transactions: distance selling of goods and the sale of electronic services.

A. Distance Selling of Goods

The electronic supply of goods often constitutes distance selling where goods are typically sold to a nontaxable purchaser in another EU member state, usually via the

Internet. The main feature of a distance sale from a VAT perspective is that it is subject to "special place of supply" rules. The reason for this distinctive treatment lies in the different nature of such supplies of goods.

In the absence of distance sale rules, the general rules for the supplies of goods would apply. Namely, the supplier in one member state would have to charge VAT under his or her jurisdiction on supplies made to nontaxable entities in another member state, since the purchasers do not hold a community VAT number to qualify for a tax-exempt intracommunity supply of goods. This situation would put the country of the supplier in a disadvantageous position compared to countries where domestic VAT rates are lower, since the purchaser would obviously prefer to purchase goods in member states where VAT exposure is minimal. To eliminate this potential discrimination and distortion of competition, the place of the supply is where the goods are delivered, that is, the country of the purchaser, if all the conditions for a distance sale are met. By virtue of this special provision, the purchasers are subject to their domestic VAT, regardless of the source country of the goods they purchase.

In principle, a distance sale constitutes a sale where the goods are transferred from one member state to another as a consequence of a sale, and are bought by one of the following:

1. A taxable legal entity carrying out supplies but without the right to deduct VAT;
2. A taxable legal entity performing agricultural activities; and
3. A nontaxable legal entity.

Purchases by these three groups of entities qualify as a distance sale if their intracommunity purchases (from all EU member states altogether) do not exceed €10,000 (excluding tax) during the year and the preceding year. In addition to the above, a distance sale is also manifested if the purchaser is a nontaxable private individual or organization, regardless of whether or not the €10,000 benchmark is exceeded.

As mentioned, for supplies of goods that do not qualify as a distance sale, the place of supply is where the goods are situated when the transportation is *commenced.* This means that if the goods are sold by a Hungarian entity to an Austrian purchaser, the place of the supply of the goods is in Hungary. Notwithstanding this general rule, the place of the supply for a distance sale is where the goods are delivered or situated *at the end* of their transportation.

A typical example of a distance sale is when a private individual orders a certain item through the Internet, whereby the goods are delivered through the postal service upon the order of the supplier or a third party. In such transactions, the purchaser is often not taxable for VAT purposes. However, due to distance sales rules, the VAT on supply is triggered in the country of the purchaser. Nevertheless, it would be unreasonable to force such people to self-charge VAT in their countries, as would be the case for a normal intracommunity acquisition of goods. Therefore, in such cases the law requires the supplier to obtain an appropriate tax number in the country and charge VAT there to the purchaser. This taxation method naturally imposes significant additional administrative burdens on the supplier.

So to further ease international transactions—including the electronic supply of goods—and thus the situation of such a supplier, the supplier does not have to charge VAT in the country of the customer, if the sales he or she makes do not exceed the value of €35,000 (excluding tax) both during the year and in the preceding year, and the goods supplied do not qualify as excise goods. If these requirements are met, then the supply is subject to the general place of supply rules, that is, it will be subject to VAT in the country of the supplier.

Note that the purchaser (excluding a nontaxable entity or organization) may opt out of distance selling rules also below the €10,000 benchmark and use regular intracommunity place-of-supply rules, if he or she reports this option to the Hungarian Tax Authority beforehand. In this case, the purchaser has to obtain a Hungarian tax registration number, which results in the transaction being treated as an intracommunity acquisition of goods in Hungary, whereby the purchaser has to self-charge and may deduct VAT as well. This is financially more favourable for the purchaser, but entails VAT taxpayer status and involves administrative obligations, such as the preparation of VAT returns. The purchaser's choice may not be withdrawn for a period of two years.

Similar to the above, the supplier may choose to register for VAT in the country of the destination of the goods even below the €35,000 benchmark, if this is reported to the Hungarian Tax Authority beforehand. This option is advantageous if the relevant VAT rate is lower in the purchaser's country than in the supplier's. This option may not be changed for a period of two years.

As can be seen from the above, the place of taxation and the consequent tax administrative obligations (e.g., registration, invoicing) are largely contingent on two values, one for the supplier and one for the purchaser. In order to make it easier to observe the taxation rules in the case of a specific transaction, the following table may be useful.

B. Provision of Electronic Services

The new act on VAT, effective as of January 1, 2008, widely regulates the VAT treatment of services rendered by electronic means, that is, electronic services. Electronic services comprise first and foremost the following, as long as they are provided and received through a global information network:

	Purchaser is below EUR 10,000	Purchaser exceeds EUR 10,000 or opts out of distance sale
Supplier is below EUR 35,000	The supplier charges VAT in his own country to the purchaser.	The purchaser registers for VAT in his own country, the supply generally qualifies as an intra-Community supply of goods: the supplier charges no VAT, the purchaser self-charges and deducts VAT in his own country.
Supplier exceeds EUR 35,000 or opts out of distance sale	The supplier registers for VAT in the country of the purchaser and charges VAT to the purchaser there.	In this case, the transaction should qualify as an intra-Community supply and is treated as described above.

- Provision of electronic storage;
- Home page storage and operation;
- Monitoring and maintenance of programs and equipment;
- Provision and upgrade of software;
- Provision of images, text, and information and access to data banks;
- Transmission of music, movies, and games (including gambling), political, cultural, artistic, sporting, scientific, and entertainment events, and the broadcast thereof; and
- Distance education services.

The above list is not exhaustive; it is only to provide guidance as to the range of electronic services. However, the lawmaker makes it clear that the mere communication between the provider and the recipient of a service by electronic means (e.g., ordering goods or services over electronic channels) does not qualify as an electronic service. Accordingly, if a person orders a book on the Internet, the transaction will qualify as a supply of goods rather than an electronic service.

The significance of electronic services from a VAT point of view lies in the fact that the place of the supply is determined differently from the general rules. Specifically, there are three rules:

1. The place of supply is where the *taxable recipient* has economically settled down, or has a permanent home or habitual abode, providing that this country is different from the one where the provider of the service has economically settled down or has a permanent home or habitual abode.
2. The place of supply is where the *recipient—whether taxable or not*—has settled down, or has a permanent home or habitual abode, providing that this place is outside the European Union.
3. The place of supply is where the *nontaxable recipient* has settled down, or has a permanent home or habitual abode if this place is within the European Union, and the provider of the service has economically settled down, or has a permanent home or habitual abode outside the European Union.

The main point of the above is to shift the place of taxation to the country of the recipient of the electronic service whenever possible. Point 1 above can be considered as the general place of supply rule for electronic services, where the VAT will be triggered in the country of the taxable recipient, who will charge VAT him- or herself.

Points 2 and 3 above extend the general place of supply rule to nontaxable entities as well for special reasons. Under point 2, the provider of the electronic service is basically relieved from the obligation to charge VAT in the country of a third-country recipient, even though the recipient is a nontaxable entity, that is, unable to handle VAT in its own country itself. This measurement relieves both the provider and the recipient of the service from an unnecessary VAT burden in cases where the destination of the service is outside the European Union. Point 3 is the opposite of point 2 in the sense that, in this case, is it the provider of the service who is a resident outside the European Union, and the nontaxable recipient is an entity within the European Union. In this case, the law forces the third-country service provider to register for VAT in the European Union and charge EU VAT to the recipient of the service.

As already partly touched upon above, the VAT raised in the country of the recipient can be charged in two different ways, depending on the taxable or nontaxable status of the recipient of the service. These two alternatives are the following:

1. If the recipient is a taxable entity, it has to reverse-charge VAT in his or her own country. This VAT can also be deducted in the same assessment period, on the condition that all relevant statutory obligations (e.g., the possession of a proper invoice) are fully met. That is, the taxable recipient will have no ultimate VAT payment obligation if the deduction is allowed.
2. If the recipient is a nontaxable entity, it will be the provider of the service who charges VAT in the country of the recipient. This means that the provider of the service will have to obtain a tax registration number in the country of the recipient to charge VAT there.

Notwithstanding the above, there is a beneficial rule for the case described in point 3, that is, when the recipient of the service is a nontaxable entity resident in the European Union and the provider is resident outside the European Union. If such a provider renders services to several nontaxable recipients resident in different EU countries, the provider would have to register for VAT in each of these countries under the general rules. However, this provider may register in one of these countries for a special status of a taxable entity exclusively providing such services. In this case, the service provider has to file a tax return in only one of the EU member states in which he or she provides services, and is entitled to reclaim any input VAT as a foreign entity (i.e., not in his or her tax return but under an Eighth Directive procedure).

The condition for this beneficial regime is that the provider of the service may not become subject to VAT in any EU member state on any supplies of goods or services. Another requirement is that the special registration has to be initiated before any services are rendered within the European Union.

VI. THE PERMANENT ESTABLISHMENT CONCEPT IN CROSS-BORDER E-COMMERCE TRANSACTIONS

Commercial activities carried out through the Internet are becoming increasingly common in Hungary. Such activities are often managed by special software and operated on the server of an Internet service provider. Consequently, determining the place and form of the corporate taxation of income derived from such Internet-based business activities is obviously of fundamental importance. It entails extra considerations of the Internet service providers' activities and those of the e-commerce businesses. Below there is a brief outline of the major factors considered to determine the corporate taxation place for e-commerce businesses, particularly, the "permanent establishment" concept specified in double-taxation treaties that follow the Organization for Economic Cooperation and Development (OECD) commentaries.

Under the vast majority of over 1000 existing bilateral double-taxation treaties concluded worldwide, the concept of "permanent establishment" was created to allocate the right to impose tax to a given jurisdiction when a nonresident enterprise conducts business through a certain degree of physical presence. In essence, one of its effects is that business profits generated by an enterprise resident in one country through its permanent establishment situated in another country will be taxable in the country where the permanent establishment is located, inasmuch as the business profits are attributable to this permanent establishment.

Hungary's double-taxation treaties are based on the OECD Model Tax Treaty. Accordingly, Hungary adopted the OECD definition of permanent establishment, "a fixed place of business through which the business of an enterprise is wholly or partly carried on." There is a permanent establishment in Hungary if the business activities are carried on through the premises, equipment, or machinery of an enterprise situated at a distinct location but with a somewhat permanent physical presence in Hungary. While the above definition may look fairly straightforward at first sight, in practice, it often gives rise to conflicting interpretations. Indeed, application of the permanent-establishment test can become problematic when the "physical presence" through which business is conducted merely comprises automated computer equipment such as a server with no personnel. When business income is generated through automated computer equipment comprising both software and hardware elements, the commentary to the OECD Model Tax Convention provides that a strict distinction needs to be made between computer equipment, that is, hardware that is installed and situated at a certain location, and the software or data stored or used by the computer equipment. This distinction is also required under Hungarian law to determine whether permanent establishment exists when physical presence is only found through automated computer equipment.

A. Computer Equipment

Computer equipment such as a server is of a tangible nature and may be regarded as a fixed place of business. Therefore, it may be viewed as a permanent establishment for double-taxation treaty purposes if other relevant conditions are fulfilled. Whether an e-commerce business operates the server, that is, whether it is entirely under its control, or the server is operated by another party—an Internet service provider, which is quite often the practice—are important questions to determine a permanent establishment. If the server is operated by a third party, usually under hosting agreements, only certain disk space is granted to the enterprise to operate its Web site; thus, no fixed place of business and no permanent establishment can be claimed because in such a case the server is not at the total disposal of the entity. If, however, the server is operated by the enterprise itself, it may qualify as a permanent establishment regardless of whether the enterprise owns or rents the server.

The treaty definition of permanent establishment also requires that the server be "fixed;" that is, it has to be located at the same place for a sufficient period of time. Additionally, a permanent establishment is raised only if business activities are carried on through this fixed base and activities are not merely of a preparatory or auxiliary nature but constitute the core functions of the business, such as selling, making payments, concluding contracts with clients, and arranging delivery of products.

B. Data and Software

A Web site comprising software and electronic data is not in itself tangible. Therefore, it cannot constitute a fixed place of business and does not result in a permanent establishment by itself. As a consequence, if an entity carries on business through a Web site, a fixed place of business can only be established if the server through which the Web site is maintained is also operated by this entity, as explained above. Mere data and software do not establish physical presence and cannot lead to a permanent establishment.

Chapter 12

Italy: Taxation of Products (Including Digital Products) and Services in the Digital Environment

Enrico Fadani
NCTM Studio Legale Associato

I. INTRODUCTION

Not even twenty years ago, globalization was simply understood as a process of integrating national economies into an international one through trade, foreign direct investment, capital flows, migration, and spread of technology.[1] Today technological development and increasing broadband Internet capacity, finding its peak in the latest innovation push called "Web 2.0," have redefined the understanding of how globalization makes the world a unique market and production place.

While in the past, global companies still operated in a well-defined environment, today the borders are becoming more and more transparent. Outsourcing, offshoring, work-flow software, video conferences, and digitalization have enabled new production techniques and even new types of products and services. Services and products such as iTunes, podcasting, You-Tube, Google, and Yahoo have introduced new economic realities, unknown to the principals of the old economy. Imagine the impact of virtual data rooms, allowing lawyers sitting in their offices in New York and Frankfurt to review documents of a Chinese company, uploaded by London-based consultants to a document server located in Canada and managed by a company residing in Luxembourg. This is not science fiction but rather today's reality. Thinking about this scenario, it is not difficult to understand the challenge of defining the nature of services rendered and allocating the respective income earned therefrom. The allocation of costs becomes even more difficult if you imagine production scenarios with

1 Jagdish Bhagwati, In Defence of Globalization (New York: Oxford University Press 2007).

departments of the same company distributed around the world and connected simultaneously by workflow software to the same project.[2]

In light of these developments a question must be raised: are the current principles of taxation, which are based on the dogma of local jurisdictions, still applicable? Is it possible to catch the profits of these new products and services with the existing provisions? How can internationally disparate projects correctly be taxed?

This article will discuss the application of income taxation, value-added tax (VAT), and customs duties on e-commerce scenarios and to identify, in an international environment, innovative approaches to these new challenges. While the discussion focuses on Italy, it will also analyze how the Italian provisions merge with the international system of taxation developed by international bodies such as the European Union and the Organization for Economic Cooperation and Development (OECD). Enlightened and meaningful judgements of the European Court of Justice have contributed to the understanding of these challenging questions. Italian taxation of e-commerce can therefore only be analyzed in the light of both Italian and international understandings.

The term "electronic commerce" refers to the use of computer networks to facilitate transactions involving the production, distribution, sale, and delivery of goods and services in the marketplace. Not only does e-commerce streamline the relationship between customer and business, it also encourages more efficient business processes within a company and even between different companies.[3]

Applications of e-commerce are many and varied. They include the paperless exchange of business information from business computer to business computer using electronic data interchange (EDI) technology, electronic mail (e-mail), electronic bulletin boards and conferencing software, electronic funds transfers, and many other technologies. In addition, the term "electronic comme rce" includes an online approach to conducting business with customers including advertising, marketing, order entry and processing, payment, and customer support.

In addition to the buying and selling of goods and services over the Internet, the definition of e-commerce includes other aspects of e-business, such as the transmission or receipt of information to improve the convenience and lower the cost of payment systems and tax compliance, and direct consumer marketing.

More generally, e-commerce is a new way of doing business, and it already affects such large sectors of the economy as business services, communications, finance, and retail trade. Currently around 80 percent of total e-commerce activity is between or among businesses.[4] The growth of e-commerce has had far-reaching consequences for the structure of the economy, especially in the retail sector. This opens up additional opportunities for new products and production schemes, trade, and the international division of labor in general, because distance plays a diminishing role.

---

2 Please see several examples in Thomas L. Friedman, The World Is Flat (2006).

3 This scenario refers in particular to the type of offshoring and outsourcing processes that integrate the supplier into a company's production process.

4 Enterprise and Industry Directorate General by Empira Gesellschaft für Kommunikations und Technologieforschung mbH, published on behalf of the European Commission, The European e-Business Market Watch 2006.

The growth of e-commerce has been and continues to be exponential. Estimates of annual growth for the next few years range from 40 to 125 percent.[5]

Since the establishment of the World Wide Web[6] in 1993, the Internet[7] has developed into a global medium for telecommunication and information exchange within the space of just few years. While access to the Internet, and in particular broadband access, is still not widely available in southern Italy, central and northern Italy are developing an infrastructure that is comparable to other European countries. Historically, the communications infrastructure has not provided integrated voice, data, and video services. For example, a business user requiring voice, data, and video conferencing might have to use three separate networks.

In contrast to long-established (proprietary) business-related networks, the Internet's nonproprietary character has proved to be a crucial competitive advantage: there is no centralized ownership controlling access by requiring licences and imposing charges for its use.[8]

The rapid diffusion of modern information and communication technologies, particularly in the most developed economic regions (i.e., North America, Western Europe, and Japan), has established the preconditions required for a broad-based use of e-commerce.[9] The major importance of the Internet lies in the fact that it has transformed e-commerce from just a process of data transmission to a real business activity in two different forms:[10]

1. Direct e-commerce, where the entire transaction is electronic, for example, online ordering, reception, and payment of services, and
2. Indirect e-commerce, where electronic ordering and payment result in physical goods being dispatched.

---

5 Jonathan Coppel, *E-Commerce: Impacts and Policy Challenges,* Economic Department Working Paper No. 252, http://www.oecd.org/eco/eco.

6 The term "World Wide Web" is sometimes used interchangeably with the term "Internet." More accurately, the Web is a navigation tool for locating and accessing information presented in graphic form available on the hard drives and other storage facilities of computers known as Web servers on the Internet. Users can access the Web through Web-browser software, such as Microsoft's Internet Explorer or Mozilla Firefox, and can travel from site to site easily by using a pointing device (e.g., a mouse) to click on a link to another constituted by a word or picture.

7 Originating in the 1960s in the United States, the Internet was initially developed as a computer network between government offices, research laboratories, and academic institutions. Its extremely decentralized network architecture reflected strategic military considerations: even if some important parts of the network were to be disabled, communication could continue automatically via the remaining components in use.

8 S. Bach, M. Hubbert & W. Müller, Taxation of E-Commerce: Persistent Problems and Recent Developments (Vierteljahrshefte zur Wirtschaftsforschung 69 Jahrgang, Heft) 657–678 (2000).

9 Jonathan Coppel, **E-Commerce: Impacts and Policy Challenges** (2000).

10 P. Valente & F. Roccatagliata, I Principi del Diritto Fiscale Internazionale 15 (Rassegna di fiscalità internazionale, 5) (2001).

The Internet has also made it possible to provide services (intangible commercial transactions) electronically.

How the availability of e-commerce has changed the means by which business is conducted can be described in many different ways. For example, business-to-business (B2B) operations might be distinguished from business-to-consumer (B2C) operations and consumer (C2C) transactions. The analysis provided by Don Tapscott, David Ticoll, and Alex Lowy in *Digital Capital*[11] is as good as any for capturing the breadth of new business organizations.[12]

To the extent that some businesses have become quite mobile due to significant developments in telecommunications and data capabilities and the fact that their value derives from intangible goods and services—rather than physical goods and traditional face-to-face services—existing rules regarding residence for tax purposes and antideferral provisions may need to be reexamined. Over the last few years, several state bodies and expert committees have raised concerns and highlighted that new business structures built around faster and more efficient networks may require a complete reconsideration of fundamental principles of international tax law. In order to start such a process, Tapscott, Ticoll, and Lowy in their book *Digital Capital*, have tried to elaborate a useful framework for the structural changes occurred to business forms:[13]

- *Agora*—An agora describes a business that facilitates exchanges directly between buyers and sellers. It is a "space" where buyers and sellers can get together to negotiate and consummate deals. Traditionally, this has been the function of physical structures such as stock exchanges, job fairs, and trade shows. Now, businesses like eBay (http://www.ebay.com) or FreeMarkets (http://www.freemarkets.com), an online business procurement site, bring buyers and sellers together. Transactions are made online, with buyer, seller, and agora facilitator typically in different jurisdictions.
- *Aggregation*—In an aggregation, the intermediary offers an assortment of goods and services to customers. Retailers and wholesalers are aggregations. Aggregations can take a variety of forms. Some businesses aggregate traditional product categories, creating value out of efficiency. For example, in a B2C context a company like Webvan (http://www.webvan.com) functioned as a digital grocer that aggregated groceries.
- *Value chain*—Whereas an aggregator pulls together a variety of goods and services for customers, a value-chain company integrates the output of producers to meet the customers' needs. A value chain produces goods as specified by customers. For example, Cisco Systems (http://www.cisco.com), which sells routers and other networking products, does not directly manufacture the components it sells but rather designs technologies and coordinates their implementation. However, other

---

11 Tapscott, Ticoll & Lowy, Digital Capital (Harvard Business School Press 2000).

12 Richard L. Doernberg, Electronic Commercial and Multi-Jurisdictional Taxation 38 (Kluwer Law International 2001).

13 *Id.*

participants in the value chain carry out specific functions according to Cisco's specifications.

- *Alliance*—In a more traditional way, alliances have been formed virtually by companies, on both horizontal and vertical capabilities, using work-flow software and redefining production-chain layouts.
- *Distributive network*—The most visible impact can be traced to the massive evolution of the existing distribution channels. Online order platforms,[14] integration of global delivery services,[15] and real-time ordering systems[16] are today a substantial part of the economic life.

II. RELEVANCE OF E-COMMERCE TAXATION

While business goes global electronically, taxation remains physically local, at least to a large extent. This phenomenon is called "new age fiscal"[17] and arises from a combination of sociology, economy, and digital technologies.[18] As e-commerce has developed, experts on international taxation have started to investigate and monitor the different types of e-commerce. While the majority accept the challenge to push the rules of the game toward new boundaries, a few authors still believe that the impact of Internet and e-commerce may be addressed with the existing principles and rules.[19] It is this author's view that the authors who still continue to apply basic principles of taxation may not fully appreciate the dematerialized content of e-commerce.

The nature of e-commerce and its related business structures makes it difficult to correctly apply the consecrated principles of taxation for classifying commercial transactions. Television streaming for a worldwide audience may be different than selling a container of oranges. While nobody will challenge the classification of oranges as products, what is television streaming? Is it an electronic product, or is it a service? Where is the place that the service (if it is a service) is rendered: the server of the content provider, the user's Internet service provider, or the place where the user watches the streamed television content? What about the same content offered on mobile phones?

---

14 The turnover generated by e-commerce giants as Amazon has easily overrun the turnover of traditional home-delivery entities. Even a long-established reality like the German-based Quelle had to admit that the part of turnover generated by orders placed on its Internet platform had largely surpassed the turnover from classic mail orders.

15 Thomas Friedman offers in his book The World Is Flat a superb example of this type of integration by describing the outsourcing of the repair services from Dell Computers to the global delivery company DHL.

16 The most efficient and most developed system may have been introduced by the U.S.-based international supermarket chain Wal-Mart, which generates automatically real-time orders based on sales in individual stores.

17 R.O. Asorey, *El impacto del cibercomercio en los principios fiscales*, in Corso di diritto tributario internazionale (v. Uckmar ed. Padova: CEDAM 2002).

18 L. Hinnekens, *New Age International Taxation in the Digital Economy of the Global Society*, 25(4) Intertax 116 (1997).

19 F.M. Hornes & J. Owens, *Tax and the Web; New Technologies, Old Problems*, 50(IV) Bulletin of International Fiscal Documentation 12 (1996).

The concept of taxation involves the concept of jurisdiction. From the Boston Tea Party Rebellion in which tea was taxed as it physically landed on American shores, to sophisticated concepts of international taxation, a government's authority to tax has always been based on territory and jurisdiction.

With the Internet, a business can easily move to so-called tax-haven jurisdictions and conduct business outside the taxing jurisdiction of any country. While the term "tax haven" is often used as a synonym for tax avoidance, certain tax-friendly jurisdictions, such as the Isle of Man, have started to offer important incentives for information technology (IT) companies that go far beyond a zero tax rate.

The speed at which electronic transactions occur, the fully automated purchase and payment procedure, and the absence of a traditional paper trail, especially with respect to intangible property transmitted by computer such as software, digital music, or books and services, make it very difficult, if not impossible, to apply traditional rules in order to determine which jurisdiction—if any—is competent to tax such transactions. These aspects generate new challenges for taxation systems, especially as far as the adaptation of new tax rules is regarded. Legal provisions governing domestic and international taxation will need to adapt to the new economic-technological environment of e-commerce. The institutional and technical implications of cyberbusiness have already had tremendous impact on taxation procedures. For example, in February 2006 the OECD launched a project aimed at providing guidance for governments on applying value-added taxes (VAT) or goods and services taxes (GSTs) to cross-border trade. The current lack of international "rules of the game," according to the OECD, leads to uncertainties, unintended double taxation, or unintended double nontaxation, which can be harmful for the development of international trade, in turn affecting both businesses and governments.

In order to better understand the type and nature of the new challenges arising from taxation of the Internet, this discussion will first focus on criteria to distinguish between national and international transactions. Next, the chapter will move to analyze legal and illegal actions of taxpayers and discuss the taxation problems connected to the new electronic economy. Due to the technical, financial, and economic characteristics of the Internet, tax evasion becomes easy and bears low risk.

III. TRADITIONAL INTERNATIONAL TAXATION PRINCIPLES

Cross-border transactions may be subject to taxation in multiple jurisdictions. The multijurisdictional framework for both income taxes and consumption taxes are overviewed in this section. Necessarily, e-commerce demands an extensive change of paradigm regarding concepts such as "product," "service," or "use of intangible."[20] There are three fundamental principles applicable to international taxation: neutrality, equity, and nondiscrimination.

20 T.A. O'Donnel & P.A. Di Sagro, *United States Tax Policy on Electronic Commerce*, 25(12) Intertax 429 (Kluwer Law International).

A. Neutrality

The principle of neutrality means that revenues and turnover related to e-commerce must be taxed in the same way as traditional commerce. The underlying reason is to refrain from introducing different forms of taxation for new categories of commerce.[21] Neutrality is a fundamental principle of taxation. In an international context, it means that the pattern of taxation does not interfere with or affect the taxpayer's choice between investing at home and investing in foreign countries. It also means that functionally equivalent transactions should be taxed in the same way. The principle of neutrality has two dimensions: *capital export neutrality* (CEN) and *capital import neutrality* (CIN).[22] CEN is generally favored by many economists as a prerequisite for worldwide economy efficiency. According to the principle of CEN, the tax system should not distort the choice between investment at home or abroad. To implement CEN, a residence country that taxes a taxpayer's worldwide income should provide a credit for foreign taxes.

On the other hand, according to CIN, all business activity within a given jurisdiction should be subject to the same overall level of taxation. Thus, a country should avoid tax rules that might cause its taxpayers to bear a higher effective tax burden in foreign markets than their competitors from other countries. To implement CIN, residence countries should exempt all foreign-source income from domestic tax, or at least allow the deferral of current domestic taxation on foreign-source income.

B. Equity

Tax equity is another fundamental principle of taxation. In a domestic context, tax equity often refers to taxpayer equity. Taxpayer equity is analyzed in terms of horizontal equity and vertical equity. In an international context, in addition to taxpayer equity, there is also an issue of internation equity—each country receives a fair share of revenue from cross-border transactions.[23]

C. Nondiscrimination

Nondiscrimination[24] is incorporated into most bilateral tax treaties. The most typical nondiscrimination provision of a tax treaty[25] prohibits contracting states from

---

21 Conf. European Ministerial Conference, Global Information Networks theme paper, *Creating a Favourable Environment for Electronic Commerce by Mario Monti*; Bonn, July 6–8, 1997; *Tax Notes Today* 139–40.

22 MUSGRAVE, UNITED STATES TAXATION OF FOREIGN INVESTMENT INCOME, Chapter VII, 1969; KLAUS VOGEL, *Worldwide v. Source Taxation of Income—A Review and Revaluation of Arguments*, INTERTAX (1988/8–9 216, pt. 1), (1988/10 310, pt. 2), and (1988/11 393, pt. 3).

23 See Kaufman, *Fairness and the Taxation of International Income*, 29 L. & POL. IN INT'L BUS. 145 (1998).

24 The principle of nondiscrimination has become a battleship of the European community and the number of cases decided by or still pending in front of the European Community Court is touchable evidence.

25 OECD Model, art. 24 (2001).

imposing tax consequences on individuals or entities who are resident in the jurisdiction of the treaty partner that are less favorable or more adverse than the tax consequences imposed on individuals or entities residing in their own jurisdiction.[26]

This principle has been interpreted not to prohibit differences in the taxation of investment income earned by residents and nonresidents. For example, it has been applied to withholding taxes on dividends, interest, and royalties earned by nonresident individuals or entities at a fixed rate on a gross basis, on the grounds that residence can be considered a relevant circumstance and therefore justifies a different treatment of resident and nonresident individuals and entities.

IV. INCOME TAXATION BETWEEN COUNTRIES OF RESIDENCY

The discussion of the intersection of e-commerce and income tax principles focuses primarily on the implications for content providers, those who use the Internet to sell goods and services. There is also some discussion of the implication for Internet service providers, those who provide telecommunications services and Internet access.

Any discussion regarding these topics must preliminarily take into consideration that, in general, a country exercises jurisdiction for legal and tax purposes based on either *nationality* or *territoriality*.[27] Taxes on income are usually levied according to the world income principle. As a consequence of this basic principle, any taxable individual or entity is to be assessed in the jurisdiction of residence on its entire income, regardless of the place where such income has been generated.[28] This at least holds true for persons or entities subject to unlimited taxation, that is, taxpayers with a domestic place of generation. Meanwhile, foreigners or foreign companies are subject to limited taxation for their domestic income (source country principle).

However, the major problem with Internet taxation is not potential cases of international double taxation but rather imminent taxation shortfalls.[29] The nature of e-commerce and, under certain circumstances, the spatial mobility of a computer used as server as a taxable permanent establishment, allow taxable entities to cause a

---

26 *See* ARNOLD, TAX DISCRIMINATION AGAINST ALIENS, NON-RESIDENTS AND FOREIGN ACTIVITIES: CANADA, AUSTRALIA, NEW ZEALAND, THE UNITED KINGDOM, AND THE UNITED STATES (Toronto: Canadian Tax Foundation 1991); VAN RAAD, NON-DISCRIMINATION IN INTERNATIONAL TAX LAW, (Kluwer 1986); Jones, et al., *The Non-discrimination Article in Tax Treaties,* British Tax Review 395 (1991); and Warren, *Income Tax Discrimination Against International Commerce,* 54 TAX L. REV. 131 (2001).

27 A territorial connection justifies the exercise of taxing jurisdiction because a taxpayer can be expected to share the costs of running a country, which makes possible the production of income, its maintenance and investment, and its use through consumption.

28 This principle is not, however, applied in all jurisdictions worldwide. For example, according to Cap. 112 Hong Kong Ordinance, Inland Revenue Ordinance (in short, IRO) IRO section 14, profit tax shall be charged on profits arising in or derived from Hong Kong.

29 A taxation shortfall exists when a tax object that can be attributed to different states is subject to a lesser tax burden than intended by the tax policy of the country of residence or the source country. Taxation shortfalls can result from legal or illegal tax arrangements or of calculation errors, loopholes in the law, or conflicts of qualification between the national tax laws.

taxation shortfall by legal and illegal measures. The results are distortion of competition, unfair tax burdens, and loss of revenue.

V. TURNOVER TAX BETWEEN THE COUNTRY-OF-DESTINATION AND COUNTRY-OF-ORIGIN PRINCIPLES

As a consumer levy, turnover tax is designed to fall on final consumer expenditure.[30] Normally, the so-called country-of-destination principle is applied on cross-border transactions. The goal of this principle is that the final consumer bears the same domestic turnover tax for all goods supplied and services rendered that he or she consumes in his or her country—regardless of their origin. Within the European Union, where check points at the internal EU borders no longer exist, the destination principle is realized through separate settlement.

When one examines the set of rules applying to sale and purchase transactions entered into by two entities that are registered for VAT in two different member states, a clear principle emerges: while the sale will be exempt from VAT, the purchase will be taxed. This so-called principle of destination is contrary to the principle of origin applied to domestic transaction. Consequently, the purchaser has to pay turnover taxes in the country of destination (where he or she may be entitled to deduct it) and make monthly reports. To comply with this EU-wide tax system, all companies participating in intra-EU trade were assigned a turnover tax identification number, which they have to communicate to their business partners. This information will be shared by the tax authorities of the member states. The country-of-destination principle has been criticized for being difficult to execute administratively within an integrated market without border controls. Massive tax frauds have been investigated in recent years.[31]

Whether the growth of e-commerce will render traditional source-based taxation unusable as a taxing norm is open to question. Source-based taxation principles have been developed in an era when commerce was typically conducted through a bricks-and-mortar presence in a country. However, there are no national borders on the Internet; the Internet fosters direct cross-border shopping, and a wide range of new Internet products can be interpreted as services. The rise of e-commerce opens the source-based principle to re-examination.

---

30 Within the OECD countries, the concept of VAT has prevailed against other systems and was established more or less homogeneously in the European Union. The turnover tax is levied on all turnovers of enterprises on all stages of production and distribution. The input tax is refunded by the tax authorities. This system is called an input tax deduction system. An older kind of turnover tax, with diminishing relevance, is the sales tax, only imposed on sales to non-taxpayers (consumers). In the United States or Canada there are still sales taxes at the state level. However, most of the east European countries in transition have decided to apply the VAT system as well.

31 The triangle transactions with a car dealer in Germany have been largely dealt with in the press and the title "VAT Carousels" may be recalled.

VI. SERVER AS PERMANENT ESTABLISHMENT

In e-commerce the central production tool is a computer, or more accurately a server, which produces and delivers electronic products or manages the purchase procedure. Considering that a server can be easily placed anywhere, managed on a remote basis and needs basically no physical space or human resources, there are key questions concerning its role in international taxation.

Article 4 of the OECD Model Tax Convention on Income and on Capital[32] (the convention) clearly states that an entity shall be deemed resident by reason of its domicile, residence, place of management, or any other criterion of a similar nature. Article 7 states that profits of an enterprise shall be taxable only in the state where it is resident, unless the enterprise carries on business in another state through a permanent establishment situated therein.

Article 5 of the OECD convention defines "permanent establishment" as a "fixed place of business through which the business of an enterprise is wholly or partly carried on." The problem of its application to any Internet-based business is easily understandable.

Internet servers usually have to be placed in a building and wired, which means that they are—as a rule—firmly attached to the ground. The firmly installed Internet server thus seems to meet the requirements of durability and therefore to possess the characteristics of a fixed place of business as described in Article 5, section 3 of the OECD convention. Even if the server is only leased by a content provider, under the prevailing doctrine it would be a permanent establishment.[33]

The situation may be different where the content provider does not run the Internet server but uses an Internet service provider (ISP) to manage its home page and store relevant data. In this case, the content provider has no disposing power, or even any joint disposing power, over the server's location or the server itself.[34] In this case, there is no permanent establishment. The OECD Expert Group has considered that a Web site does not constitute a permanent establishment due to the absence of a natural person.

In order to better understand the application of these principles to e-commerce, assume that a certain company, G.M. Corp. installed a server in country M. If now G.M. Corp., through its employees or another agent, operates and maintains this server for its own account, the server shall be deemed a permanent establishment of G.M. Corp in M. It may not even be necessary for employees or agents to be present in

32 Model Tax Convention on Income and on Capital, condensed version July 15 (2005), commented by the OECD Committee on Fiscal Affaire.

33 A. Lovisolo, *La «stabile organizzazione»*, in Corso di diritto tributario internazionale (V. Uckmar ed. Padova: CEDAM 2002).

34 I. Lejeune, B. Vanham, I. Verlinden & A. Verbeken, *Does Cyber Commerce Necessitate a Revision of International Tax Concept?* in Bulettin for International Fiscal Documentation 53 (pt. I and pt. II 1998).
"The question which remains is the kind of functionality that can be allotted to a computer. It cannot conclude a contract, it cannot think (. . .). Everything a computer does, however has been initiated by natural person who may or may not be located in the country were the server is located."

country M to come to the same conclusion. However, if the server was installed "solely for purpose of storage, display, or delivery of goods or merchandise,"[35] it would not be considered a permanent establishment. If the server merely provides advertising for G.M. Corp., the advertising should be considered auxiliary and preparatory in nature—not enough by itself to constitute a permanent establishment.

In a different scenario, the Web server might merely act as a clearinghouse that receives a request issued by a customer's browser for specified data that is situated on a server located outside of country M, say in country U, and fills that request by securing the information from the country U computer and forwarding it to the customer. In this case, much of the computer processing occurs in country U, where the data server is located. The Web server situated in country M acts only as an intermediary, and customers do not directly access G.M. Corp.'s data server. However, if G.M. Corp.'s Web server in country M provides not only advertising and other information concerning G.M. Corp.'s products but also carries advertising for other companies for which G.M. Corp. receives a fee, then the server may possibly constitute a permanent establishment.

Italy has implemented the OECD recommendations by amending ¶¶ 4 and 5 of Article 162 of the Italian Income Tax Code and introducing these principles to Italian internal tax law, and these principles now apply to transactions entered with entities residing in both treaty and nontreaty jurisdictions. The new language of the Italian Income Tax Code highlights the server's functional role and provides that a server shall not be deemed a permanent establishment in Italy as long as the server's main function is purely of a preparatory or auxiliary character, such as the collection of data and information needed for a subsequent transaction.

In the case of a French company supplying game-downloading services in Italy, the Italian Tax Agency recently denied the preparatory and auxiliary character of its servers and therefore assessed the income in Italy. In this case,[36] the French company offered to its customers the ability to download a client application and to play online videogames through the company's servers. To reduce connection costs, the company "mirrored" its French server on a server situated in Italy and managed by an Italian ISP. The Italian Tax Agency concluded that, in this case, the server located in Italy carried on the company's core business by allowing Italian costumers to access and run the online video games. Because the mirroring of the Web site reduced, in the opinion of the Tax Agency, the Italian ISP's pure maintenance role, it found that the French company asserted full control of the Italian server.

The fundamental principle emerging from this interpretation by the Italian tax authorities is that a server is considered a permanent establishment of a foreign entity in Italy if the following conditions apply: (1) the server is controlled by the foreign entity; and (2) the server's role does not have a preparatory and auxiliary character for the foreign entity's core business.

When examining tax issues arising from Italian entities' establishing servers outside Italy, one must consider the Italian rules regarding controlled foreign companies (the

---

35 OECD Model Tax Convention, art. 5(4) (2001).

36 The case has been reported by Italian Tax Revenue Office in the Resolution No. 119/E issued on May 28, 2007.

Italian CFC rules). The tax consequences of the presence of an Italian entity's subsidiary in specific jurisdictions are governed by the Italian CFC rules contained principally in Article 167 of Decree No. 917/1986 (the Italian Income Tax Code). The CFC rules allow Italian tax agencies to consider companies that are incorporated in specific low-tax-regime jurisdictions identified by ministerial decree[37] and commonly known as the "Black List" as resident in those jurisdictions for tax purposes.[38] Because low-tax-rate jurisdictions do attract entities solely seeking tax benefits, antiavoidance provisions will look through corporate structure to determine effective residence for tax purposes. Therefore, it will not be sufficient to incorporate in a low tax jurisdiction a company to own and run a Web server, in order to benefit from this tax rate without a proper structure. Corporate entities simply managed by a corporate service provider, without offices, employees, or local directors, will not be considered "resident," and neither will the Web server, even if the requirements of a permanent establishment are met.

VII. REPRESENTATION BY A PERMANENT AGENT

The task of a permanent representative is to serve the enterprise and to promote its economic activities.[39] A permanent representative or agent, and thus a permanent establishment, is recognized if the following criteria are fulfilled:

- The agent is a legal or natural person, not independent from the enterprise;
- The agent has power of attorney to conclude contracts for the enterprise; and
- The agent regularly exercises this power.

---

37 The current version of the ministerial decree identifies, *inter alia*, the following jurisdiction having an unfair low tax regimes: Alderney, Andorra, Anguilla, Netherlands Antilles, Aruba, Bahamas, Barbados, Barbuda, Belize, Bermuda, Brunei, Cyprus, Philippines, Gibraltar, Pjibouti (ex Afar and Issas), Grenada, Guatemala, Guernsey, Herm, Hong Kong, Isle of Man, Cayman, Cook, Marshall, Turks and Caicos, British Virgin Islands, U.S. Virgin Islands, Jersey, Kiribati (ex Gilbert), Lebanon, Liberia, Liechtenstein, Macao, Maldives, Malaysia, Montserrat, Nauru, Niue, New Caledonia, Oman, French Polynesia, Saint Kitts and Nevis, Solomon, Samoa, Saint Lucia, Saint Vincent and Grenadine, Sant'Elena, Sark, Seychelles, Singapore, Tonga, Tuvalu, and Vanuatu. Further, jurisdictions such as Switzerland are included under specific circumstances.

38 The budget law of the 2007 recently amended the Italian Income Tax Code to substitute the "Black List" with a "White List" of jurisdiction granting a sufficient exchange of information. Because the "White List" has not been published yet, the tax agencies continue to apply the existing "Black List."

39 *See* ONU, Department of International Economic and Social Affairs, *United Nations Model Double-Taxation Convention between Developed and Developing Countries*, par. 5 (New York 1980) ("Notwithstanding the provisions of paragraphs 1 E 2, where a person—other than an agent of an independent status to whom paragraph 7 applies—is acting in a Contracting state on behalf of an enterprise of the other contracting State, that enterprise shall be deemed to have a permanent establishment in the first-mentioned Contracting State in respect of any activities which that person undertakes for the enterprise, if such person: [. . .] b) Has no authority to conclude contracts in the name of the enterprise, but habitually maintains in the first-mentioned state a stock of goods or merchandise from which he regularly delivers good or merchandise on behalf of the enterprise.")

With regard to the Internet, it is understood that a permanent representative must be a natural person; a server; therefore, does not qualify as a representative. An ISP that is only responsible for management of data highways also does not qualify as a permanent representative of a foreign content provider. This basic understanding has not been challenged by Italian authorities.

VIII. EU VAT

> The principle of the common system of Value Added Tax involves the application to goods and services of a general tax on consumption exactly proportional to the price of the goods and services, whatever the number of transactions which take place in the production and distribution process before the stage at which tax is charged. On each transaction, Value Added Tax, calculated on the price of the goods or services at the rate applicable to such goods or services, shall be chargeable after deduction of the amount of Value Added Tax borne directly by the various costs components. The common system of Value Added Tax shall be applied up to and including the retail trade tax.[40]

A common VAT system is in place in all EU member states. It will also be applied, as an integral part of the *acquis communautaire*, in the eastern European countries that are candidates for accession to the enlarged community.[41]

On June 28, 1998, the European Commission consulted the Economic and Social Committee,[42] under Article 198 of the Treaty Establishing the European Community. The commission identified the current EU VAT taxation system as the most appropriate form of taxation for e-commerce. Specifically, it is applicable, regardless of the means of communication or commercial mode used, "to all supplies of goods and services for consumption within the EU, as well as to imports of goods and the purchase by businesses of most services from sources outside the EU."

However, the European Union is also at the forefront of searching for new ways to apply the VAT to e-commerce transactions. In Council Directive 2002/38/EC of May 7, 2002, the European Council stated,

> until now, the uniform basis of assessment provided for by the common system of value-added tax (VAT) has not adequately addressed the supply of services delivered electronically because the supply of services in this way was simply not envisaged when the existing tax system was set up.

As a result, the application of the prior VAT rules to these transactions produced perverse and discriminatory results. Previously, electronically delivered services originating within the European Union were generally subject to VAT irrespective of the

---

40 First EC Directive (1967). In its 1996 Report on Taxation in the European Union (Monti Report), the European Commission referred to 1980–1994 statistics confirming that the European average of the implicit tax rate (consumption tax revenues divided by tax base) rose from 13.1% to 13.8%.

41 VAT represents 44% of the European Community's own resources.

42 On the *Communication from the Commission: Electronic Commerce and in Direct Taxation.*

place of consumption, while those from outside the European Union were notsubject to VAT even when delivered within the European Union. The absence of a clear and fair tax regime was a disincentive to investment and put EU businesses at a competitive disadvantage. The goal of the above directive is to introduce new harmonized rules and thus eliminate distortions in competition for radio and television broadcasting services and electronically supplied services within the European Union.

One of the main changes in the uniform basis of assessment provided for by the common system of VAT regards the place of taxation for services supplied in electronic form over electronic networks. Under the rules provided by the above directive, electronically supplied services include "services such as cultural, artistic, sporting, scientific, educational, entertainment, information, and similar services as well as software, video games, and computer services generally." Therefore,

1. For certain electronically delivered services that are supplied by a non-EU operator to an EU customer, the place of taxation is within the European Union; accordingly the services are not subject to VAT;
2. When these services are provided by an EU operator to a non-EU customer, the place of taxation is where the customer is located and services are not subject to EU VAT;
3. When an EU operator provides these services to a business in another member state, the place of supply is the place where the business customer is established; and
4. Where the EU operator provides these services to a private individual in the European Union or to a taxable person in the same member state, the place of supply continues to be where the supplier is located.

The directive provides also that non-EU operators are required to register for VAT purposes only when their business involves sales to final customers.[43] Non-EU businesses are able to register with a tax authority in a member state of their choice. They are required to charge VAT to nonbusiness customers in the European Union according to the standard tax rate in the member state where the customer lives.

The request for interpretation filed by the Hoge Raad der Nederlanden (Supreme Court of the Netherlands) to the European Court of Justice[44] regarding the Sixth Council Directive 77/388/CEE of May 17, 1977, on the harmonization of the laws of the member states relating to turnover taxes, is an example of the uncertainty that rules all over Europe in applying VAT to e-commerce. The main issues in this case concerned the tax treatment of the service elements contained in e-commerce supplies. The court examined the issues under the Sixth Council Directive 77/388/EEC, as amended by Council Directive 2002/38/EC of May 2002.[45]

43 If they supply to EU businesses, they face no obligations at all because the business customers account for the VAT themselves on a self-assessment basis under the "reverse charge mechanism."

44 Case registered under C-41/04

45 Council Directive 2002/38/EC of May 7, 2002, temporarily amending Directive 77/388/ECC, introduces into Article 9(2) special provisions on the place of supply of electronically supplied

The advocate general argued that the acquisition of standard software on a data carrier and the subsequent customization thereof to meet the customer's requirements must be regarded as a single supply within the meaning of the Sixth Directive. Under a uniform basis of assessment where the subsidiary supplies are so closely linked, when such supplies are examined in isolation, they do not have the necessary practical benefit for customers. In assessing this issue, it is irrelevant whether separate prices have been agreed to and separate invoices have been made out for the subsidiary supplies. In fact, under Article 2 of the Sixth Directive, the following are to be subject to VAT: (1) the supply of goods or services for consideration within the territory of the country by a taxable person acting as such, and (2) the importation of goods.

The term "supply of goods" is defined in Article 5(1) of the Sixth Directive as "the transfer of the right to dispose of tangible property as owner." Article 6(1) of the Sixth Directive, meanwhile, makes the following distinction regarding the supply of services: "'Supply of services' shall mean any transaction, which does not constitute a supply of goods within the meaning of Article 5." Such transactions may include, *inter alia*, any assignments of intangible property whether or not it is the subject of a document establishing title.

In February 2006, the OECD launched a project aimed at providing guidance for governments on applying VAT or GST to cross-border trade in order to erase uncertainties, unintended double taxation, or unintended double nontaxation, which can be harmful for the development of international trade, in turn affecting both businesses and governments. OECD countries have agreed on two fundamental principles for charging VAT on internationally traded services and intangibles:

1. For consumption tax purposes, internationally traded services and intangibles should be taxed according to the rules of the jurisdiction of consumption;[46]
2. The burden of VATs themselves should not lie on taxable businesses except where explicitly provided for in legislation.

Converting these fundamental principles into concrete guidelines requires a clearer definition of the meaning of "jurisdiction of consumption." The commission was making an active contribution to the international debate under way on this question within the OECD and World Trade Organization (WTO).

The question regarding the VAT system raises specific cross-border issues. Introduction of a common VAT system based on taxation at origin and providing for a single country of registration[47] reflects the essentially decentralized and international nature of electronic markets. Under the rules of EU VAT, all types of electronic transmissions and all intangible products delivered by such means are deemed services. All transactions taking place within the European Union, using the medium

services. An Annex L was also added to the directive, which contains an illustrative list of services covered.

46 Luxembourg expressed a reservation on this principle.

47 Where an operator would both account for and deduct tax in respect of all his EU VAT transactions.

of e-commerce and resulting in consumption within the European Union are subject to VAT. However, the main issue is where the VAT on intangible products shall be taxed.

Based on the guidelines proposed by the OECD and European Commission, a number of options may be envisaged.[48] One of the main issues involves the carrier stage, when the electronically transferred goods become tangible and are physically delivered. The next question is whether the goods or services transferred physically to a private individual are subject to VAT. Many of these products could also be purchased by other means, such as diskettes, CD-ROMs, or books; it follows that they may be compared with products supplied by conventional trade, which must pay VAT. In conclusion, any failure to tax products delivered by e-commerce would distort competition between sellers.

Over the last years, several significant legislative reforms in Italy have marked an important turning point that involved both the material tax law and its procedural rules. Legislative Decree No. 273, containing specific electronic commerce rules, came into force to implement the EU Directive No. 2002/38/CE of May 7, 2002. This legislative decree introduced significant amendments to the rules regarding application of VAT, provided several changes to the Article 7 of Decree No. 633 of October 26, 1972, and introduced Article 74-quinquies, which contains specific rules applicable to services carried out through electronic means by an agent domiciled or resident outside the European Community to EU agents that are not identified as VAT taxpayers in Italy.

Italy meanwhile removed the reasons for changing the VAT application arising from the general territoriality principle provided by the above-mentioned Article 7, with reference to the proper localization of the commercial transaction. Legislative Decree No. 273[49] introduced a fundamental change to the Italian understanding of e-commerce and its VAT effects by qualifying electronic transactions as the rendering of services and not as the sale of goods. This concept is now applied to all intangible products listed in Annex L of Directive No. 2002/38/CE, including

1. Web site supply, Web hosting, distance maintenance of programs, and equipment;
2. Supply of software, and updating thereof;
3. Supply of images, text, and information (e-books) and making databases available;
4. Supply of music, films, and games, including games of chance and gambling, and of political, cultural, artistic, sporting scientific and entertainment broadcasts and events; and
5. Supply of distance teaching (e-learning)

The second significant innovation regards the introduction of a special tax system with reference to non-EU entities, not identified in the EU for tax purposes, in order to allow them to fulfil VAT duties in the event that they carry out electronic services to a customer not identified as VAT taxpayer.

---

48 Opinion of the Economic and Social Committee of Dec. 28, 1998.

49 Iva S. Capolupo, *Commercio elettronico, fatturazione elettronica e microfilmatura ottica: Una vera rivoluzione*, 15 Il Fisco 1–2197 (April 12, 2004).

In Italy the necessary registration for VAT can be done electronically through the Italian Tax Agency's home page (www.e-services.agenziaentrate.gov.it). Once the registration is completed, the system provides a special VAT identification number to be used for all those transactions listed by the directive. A foreign entity operating around the EU may decide to register for VAT only in one member state. The jurisdiction the entity chooses for purposes of VAT registration represents the jurisdiction with which the agent is obliged to fulfil all its obligations under the VAT rules. This is called the "member state of consumption," and is the jurisdiction of residence of the client to whom the services are rendered. An agent registered within a member state of the European Union for purposes of the special scheme is obliged to add the VAT to the sale price of the services rendered, applying the standard rate in force in the said member state of consumption, and shall electronically submit a VAT report to the member state of its identification. The report must be filed within twenty days from the end of the period it refers to. In Italy, the report can be filed through a specific procedure made available on the Internet site of the tax agencies (www.e-services.agenziaentrate.gov.it).

Legislative Decree No. 52 of February 20, 2004, implementing EU Directive No. 115/2001 of February 20, 2001, introduced several rules regarding electronic invoicing. As has been noted by various experts,[50] the ability to issue electronic invoices is not an absolute innovation for Italy but has been a recognized method of invoicing since 1998. In fact, because Article 21 of the Italian VAT code requires as a general rule that an invoice containing specific details shall be issued for every assessable transaction, the Italian Tax Agency had already specified in Resolution No. 50/E issued on May 29, 1998, that this requirement can be satisfied by electronic invoicing as long as the electronic invoices are printed and physically stored by the company. Therefore, in the period from 1998 to 2004, electronic invoicing referred only to the method of transmission, while the physical document needed to be stored traditionally. The need for physical storage of the invoice was finally left behind by mandate of Legislative Decree No. 52/2004, which contained additional provisions to avoid any risk of fraud or abuse, and provided for the existence of e-commerce and electronic conservation of invoices.

In addition to the above, Article 101 of Law 342/2000 abolished the need to issue an invoice for specific electronic transactions paid online by credit card. This provision states that an invoice, physical or electronic, need not be issued if the transaction is otherwise registered to safeguard the enforceability of the tax payment. The law provides that the Ministry of Finance shall issue specific rules determining the requirements and standards for such registrations. However, because these rules have not been issued yet, this exemption, although provided by a law, is not currently available, and therefore formal invoices must be made for all electronic transaction in Italy.[51]

---

50 *Id.*

51 The Italian Tax Revenue Office has recently confirmed this interpretation with Resolution No 274/E issued on July 3, 2008.

IX. CUSTOM DUTIES

Customs duties have existed since the dawn of international trade. But it can be difficult to apply the system of customs duties, which was developed around the physical transport of goods on boats, to the delivery of digitalized products through data highways. Global e-commerce transactions in goods entail international movement of those goods, which in turn trigger customs duties, and, in some cases, imposition of tariffs.[52]

As a general rule, the government of the importing country or market community imposes customs duties and tariffs. However, international trade is subject to both rules set by WTO agreements as well as domestic rules for the import of goods. If the exporting and importing countries have signed free-trade agreements, certain products, such as products purchased via e-commerce, may be exempted from customs duties, or the customs duties may be substantially reduced. Thus, e-commerce transactions among countries with free-trade agreements offer importing incentives for online buyers who may not have to pay high customs fees for products bought online.

The WTO began considering the implications of e-commerce in 1998,[53] following a decision by the Second Ministerial Conference in Geneva "to examine all trade-related issues relating to global electronic commerce" and "the economic, financial development needs of developing countries." The Fourth Session of the Ministerial Conference in Doha in 2001, noting the progress made by the Work Programme and the importance of creating an environment favorable to the future development of e-commerce, agreed to its continuation. The General Council agreed, following Doha, to maintain the earlier institutional arrangements for handling the Work Programme, namely that the Councils for Trade in Services, Trade in Goods and the Agreement on Trade Related Aspects of Intellectual Property Rights (TRIPS), and the Committee on Trade and Development would examine and report on aspects of e-commerce relevant to their respective areas of competence, with the General Council consenting to keep this process under constant review.

At the 1998 ministerial conference, WTO members agreed to a temporary moratorium on customs duties for all products delivered over the Internet.[54] A key motivation for the moratorium was the difficulty of distinguishing between the physical and electronic delivery of products purchased over the Internet and the blurring of the traditional distinction between goods and services. In fact, products purchased electronically but delivered physically[55] would appear to be subject to existing WTO rules

52 Within the European Union, D.P.R. no. 43/1973 and Regulation EEC no. 2913/1992 regulate the matter of customs duties.

53 *See* Catherine L. Mann & Sarah Cleeland Knight, *Electronic Commerce in the World Trade Organization*, in The WTO after Seattle (Jeffrey Scott ed. Washington, DC: Institute for International Economics 2000).

54 Catherine L. Mann, *Transatlantic Issues in Electronic Commerce*, 11 IAI Quaderni (Oct. 2000).

55 For example, books bought from Amazon.com and delivered physically to customers via DHL.

on trade in goods, while the same product delivered electronically would simply be exempted.

To help clarify these issues, the Geneva Ministerial Conference declaration mandated that the WTO General Council embark on a comprehensive analysis of all trade-related aspects of e-commerce. Based on this mandate, two relevant WTO work areas have been established. The first is the host of relevant negotiations on liberalizing trade in services, including services that allow e-commerce to function better and those that will benefit most from its application. Negotiation on this opened in Geneva on February 25, 2000. The second is the question of developing the Information Technology Agreement (ITA), under which signatories (currently sixty, accounting for over 90 percent of world trade in IT products) accord duty-free treatment to an agreed range of IT products.

The European Union has asserted that "all electronic transmissions consist of services" and, therefore, these products should fall under the scope of the General Agreement on Trade in Services signed in 1995 (GATS).[56] Most countries, including the United States, agree that services delivered over the Internet are covered by GATS, but other products are more like a good or are a hybrid between a good and a service.[57] When confusion exists on the application of these agreements to e-commerce, the most liberalizing treatment should prevail. In some cases, this could mean that electronic delivery of goods and services would be treated more favorably than other modes of delivery as currently scheduled in GATS. For example, digitized software could be sold over the Internet without incurring customs duties, or insurance products could be sold over the Internet even if the physical presence of a foreign insurance firm had not been scheduled for liberalization under GATS.

X. FINAL COMMENTS

Although e-commerce and the Internet have been changing the way business and commercial transactions are conducted for over twenty years, not only the Italian but also the international rules regarding taxation and customs duties lay far behind. The difficult exercise of adapting the existing rules to new business models is still in an embryonic state. While in certain areas, such as the taxation of business profits, a possible adaptation of the existing rules can be envisaged, in other areas, such as customs duties, it is clear that the traditional approach is far too outdated to effectively address e-commerce transactions.

As long as the rules are linked to traditional concepts such as "nations" and "products," the e-commerce and Internet-based business will not be regulated properly. While the Internet becomes a global environment, tax and customs duties remains the playground of national governments or communities. In order to overcome this distortion, a radical reform of the existing principles may be necessary.

---

56 World Trade Organization, *Communication from the European Communities and Their Member States on the WTO Work Programme on Electronic Commerce* (Aug. 9 1999).

57 For example, electronic books and downloaded software.

Considering the impact of the unified European market for VAT and customs duties, the future will show whether the global character of the e-commerce will have the same impact on a more international level. While unification of income tax rules in Europe seems still far away, perhaps e-commerce will push this development farther than politics could have done in the recent years.

Chapter 13

Netherlands: Nexus for Purposes of Imposing Corporate Income Tax

Machiel Lambooij
Freshfields Bruckhaus Deringer LLP

I. INTRODUCTION

This chapter discusses in general terms, without focusing on any specific jurisdiction, the concept of "nexus"[1] with a taxing jurisdiction required for a person (the e-tailer) resident outside that jurisdiction to be subject to tax on its business profits earned in connection with its e-commerce activities.[2] It then discusses specifics about The Netherlands' position. The jurisdiction where the customers of the foreign e-tailer are based is hereinafter referred to as the *source state*. The term nexus refers to the threshold an e-tailer will have to surpass in terms of presence (physical, virtual, or otherwise) in the target jurisdiction in order to become taxable there on its profits. Profit allocation and other tax-base issues, once it has been established that there is sufficient relevant nexus, are not the subject of this article.

The term "nexus" is often used in connection with U.S. state sales taxes, in order to establish whether a state has sales tax jurisdiction in respect of an out-of-state party. U.S. constitutional rules,[3] as interpreted by the U.S. courts, do not permit taxing a party on interstate commerce without that party having a substantial nexus to the taxing jurisdiction. The term "nexus" in this article is instead used in the different context of profit taxation of an out-of-jurisdiction e-tailer, because it is a more generic term than the technical terms "source" and "permanent establishment"[4] (PE) that are usually

1 Latin for "link," or "connection."

2 This chapter will focus on enterprises, and does not make a further distinction between physical persons or unincorporated and incorporated enterprises.

3 U.S. Const. Art. I, § 8. clause 3, the Interstate Commerce Clause.

4 Generally defined as "a (local) fixed place of business through which the business of an enterprise is wholly or partly carried on;" cf., references to various model tax conventions hereinafter. Also sometimes referred to as a local "branch" in a jurisdiction (*the source*

used in this context. Given the subject of this publication, the discussion here is limited to nexus in connection with e-commerce activities.[5] Nexus criteria may be defined by domestic legislation; these are referred to as domestic nexus criteria. Conventions for the avoidance of double taxation (tax treaties) may restrict the right of a jurisdiction to apply its domestic nexus criteria, and use nexus criteria that are defined in the relevant treaty; these are referred to as treaty nexus criteria.

II. NEXUS IN GENERAL

A. Residence versus Source Taxation

A ruling principle of international tax doctrine[6] is that the right to tax rests by default with the residency state; another jurisdiction is normally only entitled to tax a nonresident on certain sources of income from that jurisdiction. In the context of e-commerce, the relevant potential sources of income on which a nonresident may be taxable are business profits and royalty income. Business profits are generally taxable in the residency state, unless there is sufficient nexus with the source state, in which case the source state is entitled to tax the allocable profit. The residency state will exempt such portion of the overall profit, or it may provide for a credit in respect of the source state's tax against the residency state's tax on such profits. Which system for the avoidance of double taxation applies depends on the residency state's rules. In the case of royalty income, the source state often will tax the gross amount of such income with a withholding tax. The residency state will generally include the gross amount of the royalty income in the taxable profit and allow a credit against its taxation in respect of the withholding tax levied by the source state.

These principles are generally recognized in bilateral tax treaties. In situations such as the absence of a tax treaty or the differing application of a tax treaty, a source jurisdiction may claim more taxation rights and a residency state may refuse to provide an exemption or a credit as set out above in respect of income also taxed in the source state. Consequently, double taxation could arise. Alternatively, but less likely in the context of e-commerce, double nontaxation may arise if the source state would not tax certain income while the residency state would exempt such income.[7] In order to avoid such economically and/or politically undesirable situations, it is important that jurisdictions agree on the minimum

---

jurisdiction) different from the jurisdiction where (the head office of) the enterprise is established (*the residency jurisdiction*).

5 For this purpose, the definition of e-commerce provided by the U.S.'s Internet Tax Freedom Act (ITFA; as amended by the Internet Tax Freedom Act Amendments Act of 2007) is used: "any transaction conducted over the internet or through internet access, comprising the sale, lease, license, offer or delivery of property, goods, services or information, whether or not for consideration, and includes the provision of internet access," 47 U.S.C. § 1104(3) (2007).

6 Tax literature, discussions in international tax forums, such as the United Nations and the Organization for Economic Cooperation and Development (OECD), and as generally reflected in model tax conventions.

7 Or provide a fictitious credit.

level of nexus required for a source state to be allowed to tax certain income and that they ensure that a corresponding exemption/credit is available in the residency state.

Clearly, in the absence of a tax treaty or in case of substantial differences in its interpretation and application, an e-tailer involved in cross-border business will run the risk of double taxation, which could seriously impact its business.

Although not the subject of this chapter, apart from the sales tax issues mentioned before, it should be noted that comparable nexus issues arise in the context of value-added tax (VAT). There is considerable debate in the context of e-commerce whether the place of supply or the place of consumption should be the basis for levying VAT. While the place of consumption (destination principle) is generally intended to be determinative of the right to levy such taxes, in the case of e-commerce to private consumers it is often difficult to enforce for practical reasons.

B. Regional Taxation and Nexus

Early discussions on nexus can be found in the context of interactional taxation in Switzerland, in the allocation of the tax base for local tax purposes (*Gewerbesteuer*) in Germany, and in state sales tax issues in the United States. Many of the questions arising in international taxation caused by the globalization of commerce have historic precedents in these regional tax systems. Interestingly, the Swiss case law on interactional taxation is based on nexus tailored to the specific type of business and a fair allocation of the overall (Swiss) tax base between cantons. Oberson[8] mentions, "For train transport companies, in particular, railways and railway stations are characterized as PEs. Profits are attributed in accordance with the frequency of traffic in the various cantons involved. . . . For electrical companies, electrical antennas, transformer stations and other types of similar installations are regarded as PEs in the place in which they are located. The allocation of profits is based on the ratios of production factors (labour and capital) in each of the cantons involved." For e-commerce, he mentions that the allocation factor (for interactional profit allocation) "should probably be the turnover generated by each customer, paying due regard to the functions performed by the head office (praecipuum) and, if any, other PEs." Simple physical presence is apparently already sufficient to provide a right to tax. The allocation key between cantons is tailored to the business involved. Because the overall profit is allocated on the basis of nexus (rather than nexus leading to each jurisdiction determining the allocable profits), the Swiss system should never lead to double taxation, but only to a discussion between tax authorities on the division of the overall tax base. For the taxpayers involved, that is quite a luxurious position compared to their position in the international context.

For sales tax in the United States, a U.S. state traditionally is allowed only to levy sales tax from an out-of-state seller if the seller has a physical presence in that state. Physical presence was traditionally interpreted to mean a retail store, sales office, warehouse, manufacturing plant, or the presence of employees or agents. U.S. states

8 Xavier Oberson, *IFA Cahiers de Droit Fiscal International*, LXXXVIa National Report (Switzerland) 703–704 (2001).

have been very creative in applying the physical presence nexus requirements to telephone, mail-order, and later e-commerce business. States have argued that a Web site running on an in-state server creates a physical nexus. Even the presence of cookies on the computer of the in-state buyer was considered to be a form of physical nexus.[9] To prevent the proliferation of these forms of nexus from stifling further development of e-commerce within the United States, the U.S. Congress has introduced a moratorium on further taxation of Internet activities by passing the 1998 Internet Taxation Freedom Act, which was extended in 2007.

Within the European Union, the right to tax consumers with VAT has also been the subject of extensive discussions on nexus issues. With respect to the sale of physical goods to consumers residing in another EU member state, in many cases, in practice the jurisdiction of the seller determines the applicable VAT system. If a brick-and-mortar mail-order company, however, selling goods from one EU member state, without having a PE in another EU member state, exceeds a certain turnover level in that other EU member state, it needs to account for (and pay) VAT in the jurisdiction of the buying consumers.[10] One could say that in-bound sales volumes exceeding the applicable monetary threshold[11] create a sufficient nexus for the state in which the consumer resides to exercise taxation rights. Recently,[12] the European Union decided to fully apply the principle of taxation at the place of consumption in respect of electronic services to private consumers (with a one-stop-shop compliance system in the member state of residence of the e-tailer[13]). Given political sensitivities, however, and the existing substantial economic interests of Luxembourg in the provision of those services, by way of compromise, this is proposed to be fully effective only as of January 1, 2015. The presence of customers of an e-tailer in a jurisdiction then will be sufficient to create nexus with that jurisdiction for VAT purposes.

C. History of Nexus in International Taxation

Nexus criteria were developed to allocate tax revenue between states. The general principle was that a state was entitled to tax a nonresident's income or wealth that was economically realized in that state. It was considered fair to tax such a nonresident in

9 *See Sales Tax Nexus and Sitting in the Age of Electronic Commerce*, Inf. brief Minnesota H. Rep., (Dec. 1998), http://www.house.leg.state.mn.us/hrd/pubs/nexsitng.pdf.

10 VAT Directive 2006/112/EC, art. 34. (2006) (EU VAT Directive).

11 Interestingly, the member state of the consumer may reduce the level of this threshold to approximately one-third if it fears that otherwise serious distortion of competition would arise. EU VAT Directive, art. 34(2).

12 After a lengthy debate, the EU Council of Ministers decided to shift to the place of consumption principle for business-to-consumer electronic services, not only for non-EU suppliers, but now also for EU suppliers to be effective as of January 1, 2010. Press Release, Council of the European Union, no. 15698/07 (Dec. 4, 2007) (Presse 270).

13 This means that although the e-tailer will have to charge and pay VAT on the basis of the VAT rates applicable in the country of residence of its customers, it reports and pays over all VAT collected to the tax authorities in the member state where it is resident, which then will transfer the tax return details and the VAT payments received to the relevant member states.

those cases because it was benefiting from the source state's infrastructure or causing costs therein. The discussion of residency versus source (and the comparable discussion about place of supply versus place of consumption in the sales tax/VAT context) was (and probably continues to be) substantially influenced by debates on tax-revenue sharing between capital-exporting and capital-importing countries, and specifically between developed and developing countries.[14]

Source countries developed domestic tax rules attempting to tax nonresidents earning profits in their territory through the regular use of local physical infrastructure, although initially a certain level of permanency of a nonresident enterprise's presence was more important than a physical presence on a fixed point. Under domestic rules, countries generally would want to tax a nonresident enterprise that on a more regular, substantial, and continuous basis earns profits in their territory. Different source-based principles applied by states led to double-taxation issues that were considered unacceptable. The jurisdictions involved concluded agreements on the principles and definition of what is currently called the PE,[15] generally restricting the right of the source country to levy tax.

At the end of the nineteenth century, discussions arose between countries and in international bodies on the allocation of tax revenues from cross-border business profits. The focus of the issue was on industries heavily relying on immovable properties, such as mining, industrial factories, and sales operations from offices.[16] From this background, the PE concept was developed as a minimum threshold to allocate tax revenue to the jurisdiction where these business profits arose through that physical presence. Moreover, the fact that the presence of capital goods in the source jurisdiction facilitated the collection of taxes has surely played a role as well.

In the absence of a physical presence, the dependent-agent concept was developed, so as to be able to tax a foreign enterprise doing business in another jurisdiction through a local agent, following its instructions and concluding contracts on its behalf. In order for a local dependent agent to create a fictitious PE for the principal, the agent needs to *habitually* exercise the authority to conclude contracts, which reflects some form of permanency yet again.[17]

These principles were subsequently laid down in early bilateral tax treaties, and later in model tax conventions,[18] which formed the basis for many bilateral tax treaties across the world. The application of these principles is explained in the commentaries

---

14 A very interesting article expressing the views from the capital importing and developing countries is Chang Hee Lee, *Impact of E-Commerce on Allocation of Tax Revenue between Developed and Developing Countries*, 4(1) Journal of Korean Law 19–50 (2004), which is an updated expansion of an earlier version published in Tax Notes International 2569 (1999).

15 Arvid Skaar, Permanent Establishment, Erosion of a Tax Treaty Principle, Chapter 7 (Kluwer 1991).

16 *Id.* at Chapter 6.

17 *Id.* at Chapter 29. *See also* OECD Model, art. 5(5).

18 Draft of a Bilateral Convention for the Prevention of Double Taxation Doc. C.216. M85. 1927 II (Geneva 1927), OECD Model Tax Convention on Income and on Capital 1963, 1977, and 1992–2005 (together, the OECD Model), United National Model Double Taxation Convention between Developed and Developing Countries, 1980 and 2001 (together, the UN Model). Model Tax Conventions to be abbreviated to MTCs. Where no year is mentioned, there is no relevant difference between the various versions of the MTC referred to.

to the OECD Model Tax Conventions, which in practice play an increasing role in the authorities' interpretation of bilateral tax treaties based on these models.[19]

With respect to the right of the source country to levy withholding taxes on royalties, a substantial number of, but not all, OECD member states felt that the source country should not be allowed to tax royalties, while the developing countries felt they should be allowed to do so. On this point, there is an important difference between the OECD Model and the United Nations (UN) Model.[20]

As of today, in many jurisdictions the right to tax nonresident enterprises under domestic legislation exceeds the right to tax under applicable tax treaties.[21] If a non-resident person expands a business into a jurisdiction without an applicable tax treaty, chances are that the target country claims more taxation rights than it otherwise would in a treaty situation. In practice, this translates into a restricting factor in the use of tax-haven entities for cross-border business operations (which in many cases also is the intended effect).

D. Current Nexus Criteria in the Nonvirtual World

Before examining the application of the current nexus criteria to e-commerce, it is useful to consider in general terms the tax treatment under domestic and treaty rules that a nonresident person (*the foreign enterprise*) exercises in conducting a business activity cross-border.

1. Cross-Border Sale of Own Physical Goods without Any Actual Physical Presence In most jurisdictions whose domestic legislation applies the concept of PE, in the absence of such an establishment the foreign enterprise will not be subject to tax. The mail-order enterprise that sells goods to customers in another jurisdiction should therefore be subject to tax on its profits only in the jurisdiction where it is resident. In some countries, a broader ("engaged in a trade or business") test applies under domestic rules. Generally also under those rules, however, a complete absence of any physical presence should not normally result in local taxation. The question then would arise whether, for instance, the distribution of mail-order catalogs and/or advertisements published in that jurisdiction, in combination with sales actually made there, would lead to the conclusion that the nonresident is indeed engaged in local trade or business.

---

19 The exact standing of the Commentary on a Model Tax Convention varies; the OECD in any case believes that it should have an important role in the interpretation of bilateral tax treaties. This is not further discussed as this would go beyond the scope of this publication.

20 The OECD Model allocates the right to tax royalties exclusively to the residency state; in practice, many jurisdictions (including some developed countries) have reserved the right to levy a withholding tax. The UN Model provides for a source country withholding tax on royalties.

21 Either there is a less defined concept of PE in the domestic law, leaving more room for interpretation than the treaty PE concept, or there are more general concepts applied such as "trading within the jurisdiction" (United Kingdom), "effectively connected to a trade or business" (United States), or "complete cycle of operations" (France).

Often, the presence of agents, and certainly the presence of staff, would tip the scale toward taxation in the source jurisdiction.

Under most bilateral tax treaty rules, the territory in which the customers reside will not have the right to tax solely on that basis. The presence of staff to assist in the solicitation of orders (but not the conclusion of contracts), and/or to assist in the delivery of the goods, should not normally lead to a PE by itself. This is usually the case under treaties based on the OECD Model,[22] and differs if the business has staff or enlists the help of external parties that have the authority and regularly exercise that authority to conclude contracts on behalf of the foreign enterprise on a non-independent basis (the dependent-agent concept). Under treaties based on the UN Model, even if the authority to conclude contracts is absent, the presence of a stock of goods from which goods are regularly delivered to customers may already be considered sufficient nexus.[23]

2. Cross-Border Provision of Services without a Physical Presence With respect to the cross-border provision of services, the conclusions would not be materially different from the cross-border sale of goods. However, some countries, and especially the developing countries, also consider the presence of staff for the execution of certain types of services a sufficient nexus for taxation on a profit basis. Under domestic rules, there are jurisdictions that also levy withholding taxes on a gross basis on the payment of fees for the rendering of services by foreign enterprises, either as a final levy or as a pre-levy to profit taxation.

This right to tax under domestic legislation is often disallowed under tax treaties, unless the activities are of a certain nature and have a certain length. The 2001 UN Model, for example, allows taxation in the case of the "furnishing of services, including consultancy services, by an enterprise through employees or other personnel engaged by the enterprise for such purpose, . . . only if activities of that nature continue (for the same or a connected project) . . . for a period or periods aggregating more than six months within any twelve-month period."[24] This definition clearly includes, through the defined minimum period the services are provided locally, some element of permanency in the nexus criterion.

3. Cross-Border Sale of Goods or Provision of Services through Physical Presence If the sale of goods or the provision of services takes place from or involves the use of physical presence, under most domestic nexus rules, this is often considered prima facie a sufficient nexus for the jurisdiction where that physical presence is located.

Under bilateral tax treaties, a physical presence qualifies normally as "a fixed place of business through which the business of an enterprise is wholly or partly carried on." Such a fixed place of business then in principle qualifies as a PE. However, this is different (and in some jurisdictions this exception also applies under domestic nexus rules) if the physical presence has a limited function compared to the core business activities of the enterprise as a whole. Physical presence in the form of merely

22 OECD Model, art. 5(4) (1963). *See also*, OECD Model, art. 5(5) (1977, 1992–2005).

23 UN Model, art. 5(5) (2001).

24 UN Model, art. 5(3)(b) (2001). In this case, the service provision is deemed to constitute a PE.

stocking, storing, displaying, or holding goods for delivery, the purchasing of goods, or the collection of information normally is considered insufficient nexus. This applies under the condition that the combination of local activities performed through local physical presence has a preparatory or auxiliary character.[25] The rationale of this exception is that, for this particular business that meets the preparatory/auxiliary activities test, the profits realized through such physical presence are minimal or even nil. If, however, the purpose of the particular business is the provision of exactly that type of service, then the service will be regarded as a core activity of that enterprise, and the exception will not apply. The type of core business of the enterprise in relation to the business activities carried out locally determines therefore whether a local activity is considered to be of a preparatory or auxiliary nature;[26] a preparatory or auxiliary activity for one enterprise may be a core activity for another enterprise.

4. Royalties Many jurisdictions levy, under their domestic tax rule, a withholding tax on the payment of royalties to a foreign enterprise. Generally, the rationale for this is that royalty payments are normally deductible with the payer and therefore reduce the domestic tax base, while they constitute income for the recipient that, under general principles of benefit, equality, and fairness, should be taxed in the source jurisdiction. For instance, the use of the rights within a jurisdiction for which the royalty is paid establishes sufficient nexus for the source jurisdiction to tax the foreign enterprise. Ideally, from the source country's perspective, the tax rate should equal the tax rate of the tax base against which it is deducted.

Under the OECD Model, this right is in principle taken back, and therefore royalties are only taxable in the enterprise's residency jurisdiction. Some OECD member states, however, have retained the right to tax royalties. As a result, under many bilateral tax treaties, and under the UN Model, the source country retains some right to tax on gross payments on a withholding basis, at a reduced rate; the extent of this taxation is then the result of negotiations between the relevant jurisdictions. In both scenarios, the term "royalties" is defined in the relevant treaty and often is less broad than under domestic legislation. Under the OECD Model it is restricted to payments for the use of certain intellectual property rights.[27] The 1963 OECD Model and the 2001 UN Model added to the definition of royalty payments for the use of or the right to use industrial, commercial, or scientific equipment. The 2001 UN Model also expressly includes payments for films or tapes used for radio or television broadcasting.

Payments arising from the source country that do not fall within the definition of royalties under an applicable treaty (and otherwise do not fall into another category of income in such treaty) should be treated as business profits, which would mean that in

25 OECD Model, art. 5(3) (1963); OECD Model, art. 5(4) (1977/1992–2005); the criterion is whether these activities, in combination, form an essential and significant part of the activity of the enterprise as a whole, and this needs to be considered on a case-by-case basis; Commentary on the OECD Model 1992–2005, ¶ 24.

26 Commentary on OECD Model, art. 5(4), ¶ 24 (2005).

27 OECD Model, art. 12(2): "Payments of any kind for the use, or the right to use, any copyright of literary, artistic or scientific work, including cinematograph films, any patent, trade mark, design or model, plan, secret formula or process or for information concerning industrial, commercial or scientific experience."

the absence of physical presence the source country has no right to tax, due to the absence of sufficient nexus.

V. NEXUS AND E-COMMERCE

A. Existing or New Nexus Criteria?

When e-commerce activities first came onto the radar screen of tax policy makers, concerns were expressed that domestic tax bases could be substantially eroded, either to the benefit of a limited number of technology exporting jurisdictions (principally the United States) or to tax-haven jurisdictions. The fear was that, as a result of disintermediation (direct sales from producer to consumer without the need for local traditional intermediaries such as wholesalers and retailers), not only profit margins realized by these intermediaries would be taken out of domestic tax bases, but also tax compliance and enforcement would be substantially affected. Direct business links would be established between consumers and out-of-country producers, leading to the loss of visibility and therefore control by local tax authorities on cross-border transactions. This would negatively affect the practical ability of countries to charge sales taxes and VAT, but would also potentially lead to a substantial increase in tax evasion, because funds could be more easily held offshore (e-banks) and used for consumption outside the control of the local tax authorities.

It was feared that application of the traditional nexus criteria would lead to a total loss of tax base with regard to e-commerce activities. As a result, on a domestic basis and also later on an international basis, discussions arose whether to apply the traditional nexus criteria to e-commerce or find alternative nexus criteria.

In the United States these issues initially led to a proliferation of states attempting to impose sales taxes on e-commerce activities by out-of-state e-tailers. U.S. Congress felt, however, that this would seriously undermine the growth of these activities and therefore put a stop to it through the Internet Taxation Freedom Act.[28]

Meanwhile, based on the fears arising in the international tax community, the OECD started a discussion in 1997[29] on the subject that eventually led to the adoption by the OECD Committee for Fiscal Affairs of amendments to the Commentary on Article 5 of the OECD Model.[30]

B. The OECD Position

Because a change to the large network of bilateral treaties would take a substantial number of years, the OECD's approach was to attempt to fit e-commerce into the

28 *See* note 3.

29 *International Conference and Business-Government Forum,* Turku, Finland, Nov. 18–21 (1997).

30 OECD Committee on Fiscal Affairs, Clarification of the Application of the Permanent Establishment Definition in E-Commerce: Changes to the Commentary on the Model Tax Convention on art. 5 (Dec. 22, 2000).

available model by adding interpretative language to the existing commentary and in that way influence the application of existing bilateral tax treaties that are based on the model. This necessarily meant that e-commerce activities would have to be made to fit within the existing nexus criteria—specifically, the PE concept and the royalty concept.

The OECD had already concluded early in the process that neither a Web site, even if contracts are concluded on or through it, nor the hosting service can be considered an "agent" in the sense of Article 5(5) OECD Model. The reasoning was that the Web site is not a "person" in the sense of the model, the host only provides technical services and neither has nor exercises the authority to conclude contracts.[31]

Based on the analogy of "gaming and vending machines"[32] already mentioned in the commentary, the OECD found a way to apply the PE concept to local servers. It also reached the important conclusion that, for a PE to be present for direct tax purposes, it is not necessary to have local human intervention. An important basis for the discussion around this subject was the German pipeline case, in which a German tax court decided that local staff did not have to be involved to find the presence of a PE in Germany. In that case the supervision of a pipeline between the Netherlands and Germany was organized automatically from a control center in the Netherlands, and no persons were needed for its normal operation within Germany. The German tax court ruled that nevertheless a PE was present.[33]

At that time, the practice was that in many more substantial e-commerce activities local servers were required and that the presence of those servers equated to physical presence as meant in the classic PE concept. Hence, application of the PE rules would be possible without too many problems. Also, the exception for auxiliary and preparatory activities would apply in many cases for e-commerce-related enterprises not themselves involved in the provision of technical infrastructure but using technical infrastructure to provide other services to their customers. In cases where the enterprise's overall activities were more or less the same as those performed locally on the servers, and analogous to the vending machines that, according to the commentary could lead to a PE, a PE could exist if it did not fall under the exception for preparatory and auxiliary activities. This concept is referred to as the "smart server" concept: all activities, from initial contact to the conclusion of a contract, payment, and delivery of the digital product or services, takes place on the server itself. This led to a finding of sufficient nexus in the case of servers over which fully digital services or products would be marketed, sold, paid, and delivered to local customers. Given the state of e-commerce activities at the time, this was a logical approach, and it served to avoid double-taxation situations.[34]

---

31 Revised draft for comments, March 3, 2000, The Application of the Permanent Establishment Definition in the Context of Electronic Commerce: Proposed Clarification of the Commentary on art. 5 of the OECD Model Tax Convention, ¶ 15.

32 OECD Model Commentary on art. 5(2), ¶ 10 (previously ¶ 9).

33 Bundesfinanzhof, II R 12/92 (Oct. 30, 1996); an English translation is available at http://home.germany.net/101-274850/pipeline.html.

34 Obviously, this requires jurisdictions to follow the OECD approach in their domestic legislation or the interpretation of the PE concept under domestic law and/or under applicable tax treaties. Most OECD member states seem to apply this approach in practice. For the Netherlands approach, see the publication by the Ministry of Finance *Taxes in a World without Distance*,

Currently, many types of e-commerce activities do not really need a local server anymore, due to the availability of highly developed broadband Internet access and substantial cross-border Internet backbone connections. This may (currently) still be different in businesses that require higher-than-normal security (such as e-banking applications) or higher-than-usual bandwidth requirements (such as multimedia gaming applications with many players) that need servers close to the end-customers for performance reasons. However, also in those cases, often regional servers (rather than servers in every jurisdiction) are sufficient to handle these technical needs, and one may expect technological developments that would further reduce the need for local servers. Even in the developing countries, bandwidth availability is likely to substantially increase.[35]

In respect of cross-border payments for e-services, notably in relation to the use of downloaded software and music, an OECD technical advisory group (TAG) advised that in normal business-to-consumer and in most business-to-business situations, these payments are generally not in fact made for the use of copyrights. The copyrights on software and music (and the acceptance of a license agreement by the person downloading such products) serve to protect against illegal copying. In reality, however, a user does not normally pay for the use of the copyright, but for the transmission and use of the product itself. Only if the user actually pays for the use of the copyright (e.g., if a publisher downloads an illustration to include in a book), the payments qualify as a royalty. In other words, the sale of "off-the-shelf" digital products through e-commerce does not, in the view of the OECD TAG, normally constitute a royalty payment, but qualifies as a business profit.[36] This means that under tax treaties a PE is required in order for the target country to have the right to tax the foreign e-tailer.

Another OECD proposal on the taxation of services[37] mentions that, in order for the target jurisdiction to be allowed to tax services provided by a foreign entity under specific services provisions in a bilateral tax treaty, "the provision only applies to services that are performed in a State by a foreign enterprise; these services must also be performed in that State, where for example, an enterprise provides telecommunication services to customers located in a State through a satellite located outside that State, the services performed through the satellite would not be covered by the provision because they are not performed in the State." Clearly, the same should apply to services provided by a foreign e-tailer over the Internet into the target jurisdiction. Without local service provision (physically in the source state) the source state cannot tax the service fees to a foreign e-tailer."

May 1998 (available August 2008 at http://download.belastingdienst.nl/itd/beleid/taxworld.pdf); *see also* the section in this chapter called "The Netherlands: Promotion of a Global Tax Treatment of E-Commerce.

35 *See, Report of the International Telecommunication Union on Telecommunication/ICT Market and Trends in Africa 2007* and the ITU's program "Connect the World" and "Connect the unconnected by 2015," http://www.itu.int.

36 *See* Commentary on OECD Model, art. 12(2).

37 Public Discussion Draft of the OECD on the *Tax Treaty Treatment of Services: Proposed Commentary Changes*, dated December 8, 2006.

The combination of the various OECD positions in practice means that a regular e-tailer is not likely to be taxed in any other jurisdiction than where it is resident or established, unless:

- It has for technical reasons a physical presence close to its customers, and making that technical equipment available is a core business service it provides (this may for instance apply to internet access providers);
- Its business consists of making intellectual property rights available to other business customers that use those intellectual property rights in their own businesses; or
- It is doing business in jurisdictions that do not apply the OECD interpretation under bilateral treaties or, in the absence of a relevant treaty, in their domestic legislation. This may be the case if e-commerce business activities are provided from offshore jurisdictions (because these often are not party to bilateral tax treaties) into jurisdictions that apply broader domestic nexus criteria than treaty nexus criteria.

C. Differing Approaches

The United Kingdom generally takes the position that the presence of a server in the United Kingdom does not create a taxable presence for a foreign e-tailer.[38] As mentioned,[39] in most cases, a server would not create a PE due to the exception for preparatory or auxiliary activities. When a server is part of the core business, it is likely that its presence is required for technical reasons only, and the thinking apparently is that in those cases only a limited profit would be allocable to that technical function. For pragmatic reasons, it then makes sense to exclude servers entirely. Spain and Portugal, however, take the position that even without a physical presence in their respective jurisdictions, a foreign e-tailer should be subject to local taxation on its presence, because these countries take the position that "virtual presence" through a Web site via which a business is carried out in their territory should be sufficient for creating nexus.[40] The underlying idea, at least from a Spanish perspective, is that foreign e-tailers use local infrastructure and markets to earn profits, and on that basis should be taxed if they have some permanent presence in the local market through a Web site and do regular business there (indicators of which are a certain minimum volume of business, specific marketing focussed on that jurisdiction, use of local postal services to deliver goods, use of local conflict resolution techniques, use of local banks, etc.[41]). They have made an appropriate reservation in respect of the amendments to the OECD commentary.[42] However, in practice, they do not appear to be taxing e-tailers on this basis.

---

38 Press release, 84/2000, Inland Revenue (April 11, 2000).

39 *Id.at* ¶ 0.

40 OECD Report, *Clarification on the Application of the Permanent Establishment Definition in E-Commerce: Changes to the Commentary on the Model Tax Convention on Article 5, Paragraph 6* (Dec. 22, 2000).

41 *Informe de la comisión para el estudio del impacto del comercio electrónico en la fiscalidad española*, Ministerio de Hacienda 43 (Oct. 2000).

42 *See* ¶ 6 of the report and observations on the Commentary on art. 5, ¶ 45.6.

India appears to take a stricter stance and apparently feels it should, in principle, be able to tax all foreign e-tailers doing business in its territory without a physical presence; a high-level committee suggested abandoning the PE concept and preferred the "base erosion approach with a withholding tax and an option to be taxed on net income" as an alternative.[43] This clearly does not agree with the OECD approach to PEs and the amended commentary on Article 5 of the MTCs. The approach in practice in India appears to be that "any website which enters into any contract for the sale of a service or a product with a person resident in India is deemed to have finalised the transaction through an office situated in India."[44] In case law and rulings[45] a mix of physical presence, dependent-agent arguments, and Indian views on how contracts are concluded through Web sites is used to tax foreign entities doing business in the Indian territory. A recent example is the Galileo case, where a U,S, entity used a global airline reservation system; the system ran at a U.S.-based computer center, but computer screens and communication networks were made available, through local distributors, to local subscribers. The Indian Appellate Court ruled that Galileo had a source of income in India (the booking fees) and a PE in India formed by the available network and computer screens at the subscribers' sites in India; the court also found that the (independent) distributor qualified as a dependent agent. Consequently, it ruled Galileo to be subject to Indian tax on its profits.[46] Based on the available case description, this seems to be a borderline case, because it could also be easily argued that the presence of the network and computer screens in India would serve an auxiliary communication function only.

More generally, developing countries tend to claim more taxation rights over e-tailer activities than the OECD approach generally allows. This has not yet translated into the UN Model Tax Convention, but suggestions have been made for amendments. The Indian Report alludes to this, and the basis of this position may be found in the article written by Professor Chang Hee Lee,[47] who concludes that the UN Model should be amended so as to permit a developing country to impose a withholding tax on all payments to a foreign e-tailer or, if that country so elects, to any base-eroding payment. He also suggests formula apportionment of e-tailers, that is, profits in the case of a PE or when sales by a foreign e-tailer in the developing jurisdiction exceed a certain monetary threshold (suggesting that in that case there would be sufficient nexus).

In the same context, developing countries appear not to be in agreement with the restrictive interpretation and application of the definition of "royalties" in relation to digital goods. Under the OECD commentary, effectively, payments for all off-the-shelf digitized products that are not themselves used for the production of another good by a business are effectively not considered to be royalties, mainly based on the argument

---

43 Indian Report, *India's High Powered Committee on Electronic Commerce and Taxation* (July 2001).

44 *Taxing E-Commerce India to Set Precedent That Can Boomerang*, (July 2001), http://www.naavi.org.

45 Summaries are included in the annex to the report mentioned in the Indian Report.

46 Tax News Service (Jan. 28, 2008), India; United States, report by Sanjay Sanghi, Khaitan & Co., Mumbai.

47 *See* note 14. The report by the Indian High Powered Commission refers to the publications by Professor Lee.

that the payment is not for the copyright. Various jurisdictions do not accept that restrictive interpretation and wish to tax all such payments for items such as software.[48]

In general, it can be concluded that several e-commerce importing jurisdictions are looking for ways to tax e-tailers' profits in the absence of physical presence. The arguments to support this position essentially go back to the rationale for the introduction of the PE concept in international taxation: a foreign e-tailer doing substantial business in another jurisdiction (where the volume of the business is viewed as an indication for permanence) benefiting from the local market infrastructure (i.e. the Web, the body of Web-based customers, use of local payment systems and local postal services) should be taxed on profits realized through that local market, especially if and to the extent the payments made erode the local tax base. Effectively, a new nexus criterion would then need to be introduced ranging from virtual presence to even the mere presence of the payer of a fee for an e-commerce transaction. This is further discussed below.

D. Nexus per Type of E-Commerce Activity

Where, in practice, do these nexus criteria lead in the context of e-commerce?

1. Ordering Physical Goods over the Internet When a foreign brick-and-mortar business sells physical goods over the Internet to customers in other jurisdictions, the function of the Web site is similar to that of a mail-order catalog with an order form, enhanced with an online payment module. The foreign e-tailer will usually not have any physical presence in the jurisdictions to which it ships the goods. If there is a presence, it would likely be the maintenance of stock for the purpose of quick delivery. In those situations, under the OECD nexus criteria, the e-tailer will not be subject to a tax on its profits in the "target" jurisdiction, because it does not have physical presence there that qualifies as a PE. If stock is kept locally, it would fall under the exception of Article 5(4)(b) of the OECD Model. The key issue therefore in this scenario would be whether the e-tailer would be protected against source-state taxation pursuant to a tax treaty based on the OECD Model or at least under a treaty where the source state accepts in practice the amended commentary relating to e-commerce taxation.

If the e-tailer's jurisdiction of residence is not a party to such a treaty with the source state, or if the source state does not accept the OECD Model Commentary, the domestic nexus criteria of the source state would determine whether the e-tailer would be subject to taxation there. This would likely be the case in jurisdictions that apply a more generic "engaged in a trade or business" rule or have established specific nexus criteria for virtual e-businesses (but in those cases, it is likely that a certain focus on the source jurisdiction would need to be present and/or a certain minimum level of sales would need to be passed before such liability would become effective).

2. E-Services with Physical Presence Where an e-tailer has a physical (technical) presence in another jurisdiction in order to deliver e-services (i.e., the sale of digital

48 *See* the reservations made by Poland, Portugal, and Greece to OECD Model, art. 12(2).

products and digitally provided services) to local customers, in most situations it is very likely that the technical presence qualifies as a fixed place of business through which the business of the enterprise is wholly or partly carried on. This may be different in those jurisdictions that specifically exclude a server from the fixed place of business concept (such as the United Kingdom).[49] The key determinative factor in whether such a fixed place of business would lead to a PE would be the relative function of the local presence compared to the business of the enterprise as a whole. In most cases, the local presence's function will be for communication and/or performance reasons only. If that is indeed the case, and the core business of the enterprise is not about making this technical equipment available to customers (e.g., in the case of an Internet service provider or telecom company providing connectivity through this equipment; in those cases, the enterprise's core business may be operating the technical presence), then the exception for auxiliary activities should normally apply. The exception for auxiliary activities will not apply, according to the OECD Model Commentary, if the activities performed on the server are such that the server qualifies as a "smart server." This may be the case "if the typical functions related to a sale are performed on that location, for example, the conclusion of the contract with the customer, the processing of the payment and the delivery of the products is performed automatically through the equipment located there."[50] This would be applicable to digital products that are made available online and are downloaded and paid for through that Web server. Examples include online gambling, online games, possibly downloading of multimedia content, and viewing of valuable information. In the examples cited, the distinction between core business functions and auxiliary business functions (which would determine whether there is sufficient nexus or not) is a very thin line. Most business types can be dissected in various functions, each of which is to some extent essential in delivering the ultimate product to the customer, and it is debatable what functions or combination of functions can be qualified as the core business function.

As mentioned earlier, in most cases, often the only reason to have a local technical presence is the lack of sufficient bandwidth to the jurisdiction in question, in combination with the bandwidth-intensive nature of the services. If there were sufficient bandwidth, the services could have been provided from the country of residence of the e-tailer. It could be argued that the local technical presence therefore has a mere communication function, which should be qualified as auxiliary and therefore subject to the exception for auxiliary functions. The question that needs to be answered on a case-by-case and country-by-country basis is then whether the fact that the whole sales and delivery process is also running on that server for practical reasons can be disregarded. For the time being, given the OECD commentary on smart servers, most source countries will likely take the position that now that such a process is actually present on that server, that fact should lead to sufficient nexus.[51]

---

49 *See* above.

50 Commentary on OECD Model, art. 5, E-commerce, ¶ 42.9.

51 The subsequent debate would then be about the level of profit allocation, but as mentioned in the introduction to this chapter, this subject is outside the scope of this article.

A good example of this position is a recent Italian case involving a French company offering online video games to Italian customers through two Italian servers, which were maintained for facilitating the connection with its customers and were managed from France. The Italian tax authorities took the position that the server constituted a PE and that the exception for auxiliary activities did not apply to the server because "it is used to conduct electronic commerce aimed at the sale of goods and services downloadable directly from the Company's web site, and all the stages of the business (including the transfer of the product and the payment) are carried out electronically."[52]

In cases where there is a physical presence in the country where the customers reside, the applicability of a tax treaty remains a relevant factor if and to the extent the treaty contains an exception for auxiliary activities while domestic law does not. If the local physical presence clearly qualifies as core business, then for the nexus discussion, normally the treaty would no longer be relevant[53] since also under the treaty there would be sufficient nexus.

3. Fully Digitized Goods/Services and No Physical Presence In the absence of any physical presence, under the current OECD interpretation of the PE clause in the OECD Model, the source country will normally not have the right to tax the foreign e-tailer, except to the extent payments are made for the actual use of copyrights in specific circumstances. In the latter case, if the domestic legislation of the source country provides for a withholding tax on royalties, effective taxation on a gross basis could result, subject to reduction or full exemption under an applicable tax treaty. Most technology importing and developing countries, but also several OECD member states that have made appropriate reservations to the OECD Model, will normally attempt to negotiate the right to levy a withholding tax on royalties.[54] The debate will then be whether payments for the specific type of digital goods and/or services provided will qualify as a royalty or as business profits. As mentioned above, the OECD approach generally is that only in exceptional circumstances such a payment would indeed qualify as royalty. If and to the extent this is followed, the source country will not be able to effectively tax the foreign e-tailer on the provision of digital products.

In the absence of an applicable tax treaty based on the OECD Model, a foreign e-tailer may be taxed by jurisdictions that apply a broad "engaged in a trade or business" approach and take the view that virtual presence would be sufficient nexus. Alternatively, withholding taxes may be levied on cross-border payments; many of the developing countries apply some form of withholding tax on service payments under their domestic legislation. Normally, this will apply only to business-to-business commercial transactions because it would be practically difficult to enforce such taxation on payments for business-to-consumer transactions unless, for example, the help of local financial institutions

52 Quote from Tax News Service (June 5, 2007), discussing Italian tax authorities ruling no. 119, dated May 28, 2007.

53 It may still be relevant in terms of profit allocation, as in case of double taxation of profits, because if the source country allocates more profits than the residency country is willing to exempt, the taxpayer may still benefit from requesting a mutual agreement procedure.

54 Contrary to the OECD Model, the 2001 UN Model provides for such (limited) right.

is enlisted to process consumers' payments. Under the OECD approach in most cases, the digital products, if qualifying as services, will not be performed in the source state.[55]

4. Virtual Presence as New Nexus Criterion? Since the release of the OECD report on PEs, the expected exponential growth in cross-border e-commerce activities has not actually taken place. E-Commerce sales did grow on a material basis, and now e-commerce has clearly become a financially significant industry on its own.[56] A substantial part of customer spending through e-commerce is, however, still coming from the purchase of physical goods from "brick-and-mortar" companies, which are shipped to consumers, triggering sales tax and VAT proceeds.[57] It is also likely that a substantial part of the turnover generated by physical e-commerce sales is realized within the same jurisdiction, for consumer confidence[58] and shipping costs reasons, in which case the profit realized is taxed in the same jurisdiction where the customers reside. This means that cross-border e-commerce to customers in jurisdictions other than where the e-tailer resides should likely still be comparatively limited in value. Within the category of cross-border e-commerce activities, the sale of purely digital goods and other e-services is also possibly[59] still relatively small. Although lately the sale of digital music (e.g., Apple's iTunes Web shop) has substantially increased (Apple reported a fourth quarter 2007 net sales of more than US$800 million on music-related services[60]); the introduction of movie rentals through the Internet may further substantially increase the volume of digital products. The focus of the concerns in this respect currently is with the levying of sales tax and VAT,[61] rather than with the levying of profit taxes in the source jurisdiction.[62] As bandwidth availability grows, the need for local technical presence for e-tailers becomes less and less, and therefore the possibilities in practice for e-tailers to offer e-services from other jurisdictions without the need for local

---

55 *See* note 34.

56 U.S. e-commerce sales for 2006 excluding travel spending: US$102 billion up 24% against the previous year, according to Enid Burns, *E-Commerce Spending Up for 2007 Holiday and Year*, ClickZ Network (Jan 5, 2007).

57 Based on various statistical data published on ClickZ Network, http://www.internetworldstats.com/stats.htm.

58 *See* Eurostat news release 18/2008 (Feb. 8, 2008), including basic statistical data on the number of persons in the 27 EU member states avoiding e-shopping because of security concerns.

59 It is difficult to find any accurate recent figures on this level of detail. International trade statistics do not yet record on a reliable basis digital products/services. A 2001 report made to the OECD in this respect contains some statistical data on UK imports and exports, but these relate to the year 1999 only. OECD Statistics Directorate, National Accounts, International Trade Statistics, Cross-Border Electronic Commerce and International Trade Statistics, STD/NA/ITS (Oct. 24, 2001). *See* for recent statistics about the number of individuals shopping on the internet in the European Union, the Eurostat news release mentioned in note 58.

60 SEC Form 10-Q filed by Apple Inc. for the quarterly period ended December 29, 2007.

61 After a lengthy debate, the EU Council of Ministers decided to shift to the place of consumption principle for business-to-consumer electronic services, to be effective as of January 1, 2010. Press Release, Council of the European Union, no. 15698/07 (Dec. 4, 2007) (Presse 270).

62 This conclusion is also drawn in the OECD Final Report, *Are the Current Treaty Rules for Taxing Business Profits Appropriate for E-Commerce* 72, (Dec. 29, 2007). The report can be found at http://www.oecd.org, topic tax, tax and electronic commerce.

presence will continue to grow. However, developed countries are, given the absence of any further material debate, clearly not that concerned about the loss of revenue. Instead, the concerns come from developing countries, initially in areas where, due to the lack of sufficient infrastructure, certain digital services are provided from outside the jurisdiction by satellite. The pressure to change the nexus criterion from the physical rules of the current PE definition to some form of "virtual presence" criterion therefore comes mainly from these countries.

The OECD produced a report in 2003 on alternative nexus[63] criteria. It discussed and compared the following alternatives: (1) the virtual fixed place of business, (2) the virtual agency, and (3) the on-site business presence. The virtual fixed place of business would lead to nexus if an e-tailer's Web site runs on any server within a jurisdiction. The virtual agency concept relates to contractual arrangements being concluded on a Web site within the jurisdiction. A local "click" on the "I agree" function within the Web site would lead to a contract having been concluded, with the Web site's software acting as a "virtual agent." This looks like a rather artificial context, but if one looks at the history of the dependent-agent concept, it could be argued that it is the logical modern version of that concept if there is sufficient permanency (compare the "habitually" conclusion of contracts above).

The on-site business presence refers to a completely virtual presence. Along these lines, Spain has been arguing[64] that an e-tailer's economic presence in a jurisdiction over the Internet of a certain volume and with a certain level of permanence would then be deemed to be a PE.

Replacing the physical PE concept -at least for electronically provided services-with some form of a virtual presence concept would not be possible by continuing to expand the interpretation of the current definition of PE in most treaties. This would therefore require amendments of the PE provisions in the MTCs and all relevant bilateral tax treaties. It appears extremely unlikely that this will actually happen in the foreseeable future, unless there are dramatic changes in cross-border e-commerce volumes between developed nations and/or extreme cases of abuse (e.g., if large software providers move most of their business offshore).

Digital products and e-services importing jurisdictions are likely to become increasingly frustrated about their inability to tax substantial business from foreign e-tailers and will therefore further attempt to expand their taxation rights under their domestic legislation and create broader nexus criteria; if the e-tailer is not a resident of a treaty jurisdiction (e.g., a tax-haven jurisdiction), they would be able to impose such taxation. If the e-tailer is a resident of a treaty jurisdiction, they would need to find arguments to avoid the claim that their domestic taxation rights are restricted by treaty provisions. The Indian tax cases[65] are a good example thereof: finding a factual basis for the use

63 *Id.*

64 *See* Differing Approaches.

65 *See* the Galileo case mentioned above and several other Indian cases reported: *Foreign TV Channel Companies Selling Airtime for Advertisements Delivered through Satellites into India*, TNS Online (March 1, 2006); *No Tax Liability: AAR Ruling, Business Information Purchased Online in India from Spain, without the Seller Having a Server in India*, TNS Online (Jan. 10, 2005).

of the dependent-agent clause, finding a physical nexus, and/or not adhering to the restrictive interpretation in the commentary to the OECD Model with respect to the PE definition and/or the royalty definition. Should a local court uphold these treaty interpretations, then the tax payer in question will have to request a mutual agreement procedure in order to avoid being subject to double taxation.

IV. NETHERLANDS PROMOTION OF A GLOBAL E-COMMERCE TAX TREATMENT

A. Introduction

The Netherlands Ministry of Finance initially perceived e-commerce developments as a serious threat to the state budget. Two main reasons supported this perception: (1) the possible erosion of the Netherlands' tax base if core business activities move offshore and (2) potential tax avoidance through so-called "digifraud." However, during the early stages of the international discussion on the impact of e-commerce on traditional tax rules, the Netherlands tax policy makers realized that it was in the best interest of the Netherlands to promote a global approach to e-commerce taxation. The state secretary of finance at the time, Willem Vermeend, set up an advisory committee[66] and produced an extensive report analyzing the potential impact of e-commerce on Netherlands taxation principles and how to best deal with the e-commerce tax issue.[67] That discussion concluded that the Netherlands should promote an international and consensual approach to e-commerce taxation, both in the area of direct taxation[68] and VAT. The tax environment should be adapted, where necessary, to avoid double taxation or implement a nontaxation policy in this area. The discussion suggested that the Netherlands should abstain from taking measures that are incompatible with those of other jurisdictions and that it should take a pragmatic approach promoting the development of e-commerce in or through the Netherlands. Maintaining competitive neutrality was also highlighted as a policy goal (avoiding differential tax treatment for physical and electronic goods). This first discussion led to an extensive follow-up report, published in 2000.[69] In addition to domestic discussions on e-commerce taxation, the Netherlands subsequently assumed an active role in international debates both at the OECD and European Union level.

---

66 Decision no. AFP97/498M (Dec. 22, 1997).

67 The 1998 report is available online at http://download.belastingdienst.nl/itd/beleid/taxworld.pdf. The author of this chapter was a member of the advisory committee.

68 *See also* Letter State Secretary of Finance, IFZ97/791, VN 1997/3140 (Aug. 14, 1997), in which the intention of coordination is expressed.

69 A report prepared by a committee of the Netherlands Association of Tax Science, although not a government report, officials of the Ministry of Finance participated in the preparation of this report and the outcome of these discussions were used to determine the Netherlands position in various international discussions. GESCHRIFTEN VAN DE VERENIGING VOOR BELASTINGWETENSCHAP, VERANDERENDE AANGRIJPINGSPUNTEN VOOR DE BELASTINGHEFFING (VAB), no. 213 (Kluwer, Deventer 2000).

B. Corporate Income Tax

Netherlands personal[70] and corporate income tax[71] law does not contain a detailed definition of PE. Rules for the avoidance of double taxation[72] include a definition that conforms to the OECD definition. Traditionally, the Netherlands' tax authorities use the OECD commentary to the various MTCs as guidance, and tax authorities[73] and tax courts[74] frequently apply them; this includes the OECD guidance on the PE issue in the e-commerce context.[75] The tax authorities are likely to apply the OECD transfer pricing guidelines[76] when a PE, in a technical sense, exists. In cases where a PE is considered to be present, it is likely that a functional analysis of the activities performed over a Netherlands-based server at the disposal of a nonresident entrepreneur would lead to a cost-plus approach.

In the Netherlands, there is no relevant published case law about e-commerce-related PE issues on corporate income tax. The reason for this lack of case law could be either (1) taxpayers in borderline cases using a Netherlands resident entity instead of taking their chance on the outcome of a possible PE discussion or (2) the taxpayer and tax authorities pragmatically discussing the issue and coming to some form of agreement when there is certainty as to the existence of PE.

Because the Netherlands does not levy a withholding tax on royalties under its domestic legislation, qualification of e-commerce transactions for such purposes is not generally relevant for direct taxation purposes.

C. Value-Added Tax

The Netherlands implemented the EU directive on electronic services[77]in its domestic legislation.[78]The key issue is to determine the place where electronic services are rendered (place of supply). This requires that the status and identity of the customer are established and that the entrepreneur has sufficient evidence to show that he or she has provided services to customers outside the European Union. With respect to corporeal goods, there are

---

70 Personal Income Tax Act 2001, art. 7.2(2)(a).

71 Corporate Income Tax Act 1969, art. 17(3)(a).

72 Decree for the Avoidance of Double Taxation 2001, art. 2.

73 Explanatory notes to the 2001 Decree for the Avoidance of Double Taxation; Nota van toelichting 31–32; repeating the same position as expressed under the explanatory notes to the 1989 Decree for the Avoidance of Double Taxation.

74 Hoge Raad no. 27 252, BNB 1992/379 (Sept. 2, 1992).

75 OECD Model Tax Convention on Income and on Capital, as amended, Commentary to art. 5, ¶¶ 42.1–42.10.

76 Decision State Secretary of Finance, IFZ2001/295, VN 2001/21.3 (General decision on applicability of OECD Transfer Pricing Guidelines in the Netherlands), ¶ 2.3 (March 30, 2001).

77 Currently included in the EU VAT Directive, 2006/112/EU (Nov. 28, 2006), as amended, art. 56 (1)(k) and 57(1).

78 Turnover Tax Act 1968, art. 6(2)(d)(10°), art. 6(2)(f), and art. 28q–28t; *see* the guidance provided by the tax authorities on http://www.belastingdienst.nl/variabel/buitenland/en/business_taxpayers/business_taxpayers-109.html (Aug. 2008).

specific requirements about their export and how this evidence can be collected; there is quite some case law on this topic. With respect to the provision of electronic services, the Ministry of Finance issued a general administrative ruling in 1998, indicating how entrepreneurs can collect sufficient evidence of electronic services exports.[79] A customer's response to specific questions, location of the e-mail domain, verification of the customer's credit card bank, the IP address, and some other similar indicators are together accepted as evidence. If the e-tailer has taken reasonable measures to determine and record the tax status and residency of his or her customer, tax authorities will usually accept these as sufficient evidence for the determination of the place of supply of the electronic service. In practice, it appears that taxpayers and tax authorities are able to cope with these guidelines, because there is no relevant published case law on these issues.

D. Other Taxes

Taxation of online gambling is a hot topic in the Netherlands. Under the Netherlands gambling regulatory regime, a limited number of state-approved organizations may offer gambling services in the Netherlands. Internet-based nonresident gambling is perceived to be a threat to this monopolistic policy. The government has taken measures to stop the offering of Internet gambling services by unlicensed operators to Netherlands residents. One of the measures is the tightening of gambling tax rules and the increase of the tax rate; a legislative proposal on this topic is currently before parliament.[80] It is unclear, however, how in practice the Netherlands authorities (including the tax authorities) are able to enforce compliance with these rules.[81]

E. The Netherlands: Conclusion

The Netherlands position regarding e-commerce taxation is to follow the OECD/EU approach and be pragmatic, where possible. An exception to this positive attitude toward e-commerce is the tightening of the tax treatment for Internet gambling; this, however, is motivated by an attempt to maintain the government's strict regulatory regime against gambling in general.

---

79 Decision, no. VB98/1785, VN 1998/40.33 (Aug. 14, 1998); this decision was withdrawn by decision no. CPP2006/1796, VN2006/47.17 (Aug. 29, 2006), but this does not appear to have triggered a policy change. The reason for the withdrawal seems to be that the description in the original decision was outdated by current developments and by the specific legislation on electronic services based on EU directives. The author believes that in practice the principles expressed in the 1998 decision can still be applied.

80 Amendment of the Gambling Tax Act in respect of gambling games via the Internet; legislative proposal 30.583.

81 The tax authorities announced that they have set up a trial with a "digital tax inspector" service through a software package called Xenon (a search robot) that scans the Internet for activities that give rise to Netherlands tax consequences. Announcement, Ministry of Finance, no. WT04-12–20 (Dec. 20, 2004). It is unclear whether this trial continues.

V. NEXUS IN GENERAL: CONCLUSION

The treaty nexus criteria for cross-border transactions subjecting enterprises to a tax on their profit in the countries in which they are doing business are currently still, for historical reasons, directly related to a physical presence through which their core business activities are exercised. For e-tailers, however, physical presence in many cases has a communication function only (which would normally qualify as an exception to the PE concept). Where that is not the case, the trend toward increased availability of high bandwidth connectivity is resulting in less and less of a physical presence in "target" jurisdictions. Both factors lead to e-tailers being normally taxed only in their country of residency and not in the country where their customers reside. This is maybe different in cases where the e-tailer is not resident in a jurisdiction that has a tax treaty in place that conforms to the OECD Model and the jurisdiction where the customers reside has a broader domestic nexus concept. It typically is not the case in treaty situations if the e-tailer's core business is the provision of communication services over a local server or the e-tailer's core business is the sale of digital goods or e-services where the complete sale transaction (including payment and delivery) takes place digitally on a local server (the smart server concept). Also, this is not true in those (target) countries that do not accept the OECD commentary to the application of the PE concept.

The conclusion is likely that, in most countries that import digital products and/or e-services, taxation of foreign e-tailers cannot be effected if the e-tailer is resident in a treaty jurisdiction. For the importing jurisdictions, often developing countries with substantial net imports of digital products and services, this situation is becoming less and less acceptable as the net imports grow. They typically react by seeking to extend their domestic nexus criteria, but are then still restricted by treaty nexus criteria. Through detailed fact finding and extensive interpretation, they nevertheless frequently attempt to interpret these treaty nexus rules in such a way that they are allowed to tax e-commerce activities within their territory. This may lead to local litigation and mutual agreement procedures. They will attempt, where they can, to amend treaty nexus criteria for e-commerce in order to effectively extend their taxation rights on the one hand and avoid double-taxation issues for the e-tailers on the other hand. The current network of bilateral treaties has been set up over many years. A complete and consistent change of the treaty nexus criteria for e-commerce will take a long time, if it ever happens. Because the main digital product–exporting countries have an important influence in the OECD and do not currently appear to have an interest in changing the current treaty principles, it is likely that the current approach to nexus in e-commerce situations will remain as it is for many years to come.

Chapter 14

Spain: Permanent Establishment and Electronic Commerce

Ignacio Arráez Bertolín
Castro, Suerio & Varela

I. INTRODUCTION: ELECTRONIC COMMERCE AS A TEST FOR CURRENT TAXATION SYSTEMS

The advent of the digital society gives the impression of being so extraordinarily accelerated that any effort to adapt always seems lame and insufficient.[1] The vast majority of the old rules and regulations, which were drafted to face ancient problems and happened to be adequate for different societies and situations, appears less suitable for the present time.

The implementation and development of newer information technologies are essential factors in the global economy, and overcoming the digital divide may become the main approach to achieving millennium development goals. Not only have digital technologies opened new markets, but they have also reduced dramatically the time spent in transactions. Furthermore, said technologies have radically collapsed distance barriers. Similarly, costs involved in most commercial transactions have been vastly diminished.

Even though this phenomenon is generally considered an essentially positive one, some hindrances are arising. On one hand, it would be impossible to continue as if the current changes are nonexistent, but on the other hand it seems difficult to imagine a reversal in the present course of events. Nevertheless, adjustment and other elements are necessary, especially those regarding economy and law, since aged institutions need updating to fit in this new global economy.

Experts believe that e-commerce calls for a new set of principles and rules, since the application of analogous regulations and ruling on distance selling or telesales are not quite satisfactory in many cases. For tax law purposes, it was evident early on that an international approach to e-commerce would be necessary. Therefore, in the European Union, earnest efforts have been made to harmonize those aspects related to indirect

1 Javier Cremades, El Paraíso Digital (2001).

taxation, particularly regarding value-added tax. On the other hand, the agenda of the Organization for Economic Cooperation and Development (OECD) focuses more on direct taxation as the preferred way to reach the necessary harmonization.

In this respect, given the high risk of tax avoidance, the European Union aims to prevent e-commerce from becoming a tax-fraud and -evasion loophole. However, the United States strongly defends having no taxation on electronic transactions as a means to promote e-commerce. The OECD has traditionally resolved conflicts regarding double taxation through using the institution of permanent establishment.

This chapter will discuss the taxation of e-commerce within the Spanish framework. In particular, the discussion will deal with the concept of permanent establishment and its application to e-commerce, and will attempt to propose options to handle conflicts on taxation that inevitably arise. Another related aspect that will be covered in this article is the role of electronic tax authorities and their challenges in the electronic commerce field.

II. E-COMMERCE IN THE SPANISH LEGAL FRAMEWORK

Before discussing taxation on e-commerce, this section will briefly comment on Spanish contract law.

Depending on their nature, electronic contracts fall either under the Civil Code or the Commercial Code. As a rule, a contract will be considered a commercial one as long as it is carried out by a company or a businessman, with the intention of performing business activities.

According to the principle of antiformalism that prevails in modern legal systems, under Spanish law an electronic contract does not require any previous agreement of the parties on the use of electronic means. Therefore, electronic records are considered perfectly valid evidence of the contract. Consequently, they fulfill the requirement of written form whenever such a form is compulsory, and they will be admitted as documentary evidence. However, those contracts or legal acts that require a specific form to be valid, that require the intervention of jurisdictional bodies or public notaries, or that need public registration to be effective will have to meet their particular requirements, according to the applicable provisions.

To promote and clarify e-commerce in Spain, both the Civil and Commercial Code were revised to establish that in online contracts, consent to the contract is considered given when the acceptance takes place. By contrast, consent to offline contracts under the Civil and Commercial Codes is considered given when the supplier has knowledge of the buyer's acceptance, or when the buyer sends the acceptance to the supplier, as long as there is no possibility that the supplier may ignore it, in accordance with the good-faith principle.

The place where the contract was made is essential to establishing the law applicable to it and to identifying the legal authorities that will solve any possible dispute. On that point, the Information Society and Electronic Commerce Act[2] applies the international

2 Law 34/2002 (July 11, 2002). Corrected by BOE 6 Agosto. Corrección de errores L 34/2002 de 11 Jul. (servicios de la sociedad de la información y de comercio electrónico). Amendments: L 56/2007de 28 Dic. (medidas de impulso de la Sociedad de la Información), L 25/2007

private law rules. This means that contractual obligations are those corresponding to the place where the contract is formalized, unless the parties agree to be under a different jurisdiction. Electronic contracts of civil nature will be deemed made in the place where the buyer has his or her habitual residence. Commercial electronic contracts, meanwhile, will be deemed made in the place where the service provider is established, unless a private pact between the contracting parties provides otherwise.

III. TAXATION OF E-COMMERCE IN GENERAL: THE CONCEPT OF E-COMMERCE FOR TAXATION PURPOSES

Before studying permanent establishment and e-commerce, one must examine how the value-added tax (VAT) interacts with e-commerce. The reason for this first step is that the regulations regarding indirect taxation on e-commerce provide a valuable categorization of electronic transactions. The discussion will focus exclusively on online transactions; that is, only those contracts that are completely carried out by electronic means are considered strictly online transactions.

The Information Society and Electronic Commerce Act defines "contract concluded by electronic means" or "electronic contract" as a contract in which both the offer and the acceptance of that offer are transmitted by means of electronic data processing and storage equipment connected to a telecommunication network.

The challenge that e-commerce represents to application of VAT is essentially limited to online operations. An online operation is one in which all the elements are electronic: the client's request for the goods or services, the supplier's delivery of said goods or services, and, most of the time, the payment, are completely done by electronic procedures.

In some offline operations, only the client's request for the service or product is done by electronic means. If the actual good is provided by physical means, the operation is deemed a delivery, an intracommunity acquisition or a goods importation, which are always offline operations. These types of transactions are not different from the traditional commercial operations, and the process for collecting VAT is the same.

A. Consequences of Qualifying Electronic Operations as Provider of Service

E-Commerce has changed the traditional methods of assessing VAT. The distinction between delivery of goods and provision of services is no longer clear, and therefore controversies on taxation may arise. Some authors suggest as a solution creating a new category of "goods susceptible to be converted into a digital system," which will include not only those goods that are digitalized, but also those that could be. This will establish a unique regime for all goods susceptible to digitalization, including online

---

Oct. 18 (Conservación de datos relativos a las comunicaciones electrónicas y a las redes públicas de comunicaciones), L59/2003 Dic. 19 (firma electrónica), la Ley 32/2003, Nov. 3, General de Telecomunicaciones.

operations. Goods that cannot be digitalized will be taxable under the traditional way. Other experts maintain that e-commerce operations can be handled under the current classification of economic operations subject to VAT. Consequently, under this view there is no need to change these categories.

According to Article 8.1 of the Spanish Value-Added Tax Act (VAT Act),[3] goods are considered delivered when there is a transfer of the power to dispose of physical goods.

3 Law 37/1992 (Dec. 28, 1992). Corrected by BOE 8 Febrero 1993. Corrección de errores L 37/1992 de 28 Dic. (del Impuesto sobre el Valor Añadido). Amendments: L 51/2007, Dic. 26 (Presupuestos Generales del Estado para el año 2008), L 36/2006 Nov. 29 (medidas para la prevención del fraude fiscal), LO 8/2007 Jul. 4 (financiación de los partidos políticos), L 36/2006 Nov. 29 (medidas para la prevención del fraude fiscal), L 26/2006 Jul. 17 (mediación de seguros y reaseguros privados), L 6/2006 Abr. 24 (modificación de la L 37/1992 de 28 Dic., del IVA, para la clarificación del concepto de vehículo destinado al transporte de personas con minusvalía contenido en la misma ley), L 4/2006 Mar. 29 (adaptación del régimen de las entidades navieras en función del tonelaje a nuevas directrices comunitarias), L 3/2006 de 29 Mar. (modificación L 37/1992, del IVA, para adecuar la aplicación de la regla de prorrata a la Sexta Directiva europea), L 23/2005 Nov. 18 (reformas en materia tributaria para el impulso a la productividad), L 22/2005 Nov. 18 (incorpora directivas comunitarias sobre fiscalidad de productos energéticos y electricidad, y régimen fiscal común a sociedades matrices y filiales, y regula el régimen fiscal de aportaciones transfronterizas a fondos pensiones), RDLeg. 4/2004 Mar. 5 (TR Ley del Impuesto sobre Sociedades), L 62/2003 Dic. 30 (medidas fiscales, administrativas y del orden social), L 58/2003 Dic. 17 (General Tributaria), L 62/2003 Dic. 30 (medidas fiscales, administrativas y del orden social), L 36/2003 Nov. 11 (medidas de reforma económica), L 36/2003 Nov. 11 (medidas de reforma económica), L 53/2002 Dic. 30 (medidas fiscales, administrativas y del orden social), L 24/2001 Dic. 27 (medidas fiscales, administrativas y del orden social), L 14/2000 Dic. 29 (medidas fiscales, administrativas y del orden social), L 46/1998 Dic. 17 (introducción del euro), L 6/2000 Dic. 13 (medidas fiscales urgentes de estímulo al ahorro familiar y a la pequeña y mediana empresa), RDL 10/2000 Oct. 6 (de medidas urgentes de apoyo a los sectores agrario, pesquero y del transporte), L 54/1999 Dic. 29 (Presupuestos Generales del Estado para el año 2000), L 55/1999 Dic. 29 (medidas fiscales, administrativas y del orden social), RDL 15/1999 Oct. 1 (medidas de liberalización, reforma estructural e incremento de la competencia en el sector de hidrocarburos), RDL 10/1999 Jun. 11 (IVA. Se deroga la exención del impuesto de las entregas de bienes efectuadas en las tiendas libres de impuestos), L 1/1999 Ene. 5 (entidades de capital riesgo y sociedades gestoras. Regulación), L 50/1998 Dic. 30 (medidas fiscales, administrativas y del orden social), 9/7/1998, L 23/1998 Jul. 7 (cooperación internacional para el desarrollo), L 9/1998 Abr. 21 (modificación de la L 37/1992 de 28 Dic., impuesto sobre el valor añadido), L 66/1997 Dic. 30 (medidas fiscales, administrativas y del orden social), L 65/1997 Dic. 30 (presupuestos generales del Estado para 1998) L 9/1998 Abr. 21 (modificación de la L 37/1992 de 28 Dic., impuesto sobre el valor añadido), RDL 14/1997 Aug. 29 (modificación Ley del IVA), L 17/1997 May 3 (incorpora al derecho español la Directiva 95/47 CE del Parlamento Europeo y del Consejo, Oct. 24., uso de normas para la transmisión de señales de televisión y medidas adicionales para la liberalización del sector), RDL 1/1997 Ene. 31 (incorporación de la Directiva 95/47/CE, sobre el uso de normas para la transmisión de señales de televisión y de medidas para la liberalización del sector), L 12/1996 Dic. 30 (presupuestos generales del Estado para 1997), L 13/1996 Dic. 30 (medidas fiscales, administrativas y del orden social), RDL 12/1995 Dic. 28 (medidas urgentes en materia presupuestaria, tributaria y financiera) L 43/1995 Dic. 27 (impuesto sobre sociedades), L 41/1994 Dic. 30 (presupuestos generales del Estado para 1995), L 42/1994 Dic. 30 (medidas fiscales, administrativas y de orden social), L 23/1994 de 6 Jul. (modificación L del IVA), L 22/1993 Dic. 29 (medidas fiscales, reforma

Article 11 of the VAT Act gives a negative definition of the provision of service, namely, everything that is not considered to be a delivery, intraommunity acquisition, or importation of a good. Leasing real estate or transmitting intangible goods are examples of services.

E-Commerce allows for operations that traditionally have been considered deliveries of goods with a physical component to now lose their physical aspects and be taxed as a service provision. An example of this is the sale of a movie or a book. The available technology allows the acquisition of these products by downloading or electronically transferring a file, without using a DVD, compact disc, or any other physical element. The same is true for the supply of computerized products. According to Articles 8.2 and 11.2 of the VAT Act, these operations can be taxed as a delivery of goods or provision of services. If the goods are uniform computerized products, which do not require any substantial modification to be used by the consumer, they are treated as a delivery of goods. On the other hand, if the computerized products are modified according to the client's requests, they are treated as a provision of service.

The European Union decided that the tax applicable to sales of intangible products should also be applicable to the provision of a service. However, this solution alone does not sufficiently respect the basic principle of tax neutrality. Therefore it is necessary to introduce some supplementary measures. Regarding VAT, this solution requires that goods are treated identically regardless of whether there is a delivery of a physical good or a transfer of electronic data. This distinction becomes more important when we start to consider tax rates and exemptions. The dilemma will be solved if we admit that the applicable rate is linked to the nature of the service or goods, without considering the means used to complete the sale. Only under this criterion will taxes be equally applied both to traditional and electronic commerce.

However, this solution is not available under the current law. The Sixth VAT Directive allows member states to approve a list of goods and services subject to a lesser VAT. The problem is that it also states that services provided by electronic means cannot be included in this list.

Although Spanish law does not mention anything about this particular point, the Spanish General Tax Directorate (*Dirección General de Tributos*) has shed some light on the question. According to the General Tax Directorate, whose criteria are usually binding, sales of books, newspapers, and magazines that are digital and transmitted by electronic means are subject to the general VAT tax rate, even when they are similar or identical to goods supplied in paper format, which are taxed at a reduced VAT rate.[4] As stated above, this official interpretation fails to preserve the principle of neutrality because it applies a different tax regime to e-commerce than to traditional commerce. Consequently, instead of being promoted, e-commerce is in a worse situation than traditional commerce.

---

del régimen jurídico de la función pública y protección por desempleo), L 21/1993 Dic. 29 (presupuestos generales del Estado para 1994), RDL 7/1993 May 21 (IVA. Impuestos indirectos. Medidas urgentes).

4 For instance, we may mention Response 1506-02, by the Spanish General Tax Directorate (Oct. 8, 2002).

Regarding services, the European Union's Sixth VAT Directive does not provide a clear means to identify when a service has been provided electronically; it only states that communications between the supplier and the customer via e-mail are not enough to consider that the service performed is an electronic service. Instead, Directive 2002/38/EC, modifies Article 9.2 (e) of the Sixth VAT Directive, establishing in Annex L an illustrative list of electronically supplied services:

- Web site supply, Web hosting, distance maintenance of programs and equipment;
- Supply of software and updates therefore;
- Supply of images, text, and information, and making databases available;
- Supply of music, films, and games, including games of chance and gambling games, and of political, cultural, artistic, sporting, scientific, and entertainment broadcasts and events; and
- Supply of distance teaching.

The Spanish regulations provide more criteria to determine when services are electronically supplied. Those services in which both initial transfer and reception are done by processing equipment that transfers, transports, and receives them by cable, radio, optical systems, or any other electronic means will be considered electronically supplied. This includes numeric comprehension and data storage. Essentially, the two basic requirements for a service to be considered electronically supplied are (1) the use of processing equipment, to send and receive the message; and (2) the use of electronic means to transmit, transport, and receive that message.

Article 70.1.4 B of the Spanish VAT Act also includes the examples of electronically supplied services set forth in the Sixth VAT Directive.

IV. THE CONCEPT OF PERMANENT ESTABLISHMENT UNDER SPANISH LAW

The concept of permanent establishment has been essential both to highlight and to regulate the controversies and disputes on taxation in the field of international commerce. When all parties to a transaction are taxpayers who reside in the same country and no foreign element is involved, there should be no serious questions regarding the taxing jurisdiction. In such cases, the commercial operation falls under that country's tax sovereignty. On the other hand, in cases where several taxing jurisdictions are involved, tax treaties tend to tax business profits not in the country of taxpayers' residence but rather in the territory where the taxpayer has a permanent establishment.

The presence of several taxing jurisdictions claiming competence over the same transactions calls for a rule of attribution among the countries involved. This international element is more likely to appear whenever Internet and telecommunications are involved. The Internet provides a wider market for goods and services, and, consequently, more chances for foreign players to be involved. Additionally, the location and jurisdiction of Web sites can be easily manipulated. Further complicating the issue is that some countries are quite generous in the assignment of domain names associated with them. For instance, domains names ending in ".tv," which are granted by Tuvalu, do not necessarily mean that the owner of said domain name has a permanent establishment there. At the same time, top-level domain names ending in ".com" or ".org" do not show a direct connection with any country.

In the model double-taxation agreement drawn up by the OECD, a permanent establishment is defined as a "fixed place of business through which the business of an enterprise is wholly or partly carried on." The model gives as examples of permanent establishments places of management, branches, offices, factories, workshops, mines, oil or gas wells, quarries, or any other place of extraction of natural resources. These should only be considered permanent establishments if they are facilities through which business activities are performed in a regular and permanent way.

The administrative controls determining the corresponding tax authorities appear rather complicated. New technologies in general, and the Internet in particular, permit avoidance of tax obligations as well as statutory rights recognized in favor of consumers and other compulsory provisions. In addition to this, it must be taken into account that the Internet promotes small business in a global market. For that reason, discussion of this matter does not only involve tax implications for transnational companies, but also the key fact that the number of international transactions involving medium-sized and small companies is growing.

In 2003, the OECD introduced into the commentaries of Article 5 of the Model Tax Convention a special part dedicated to permanent establishment and e-commerce. In the report presenting the changes to article 5, clarification of the definition of permanent establishment in e-commerce, one of the main questions analyzed is whether sole use of computer equipment in e-commerce could constitute a permanent establishment. In this sense, it is necessary to distinguish between equipment and technology located in an office that could constitute a permanent establishment under certain circumstances and the data and software used or stored in that equipment.

A Web site does not constitute a tangible good; therefore it does not have a location that constitutes a place of business. The server that stores a Web site is a piece of equipment and has a physical location. Consequently, a server may constitute a fixed place of business. Generally, an Internet service provider (ISP) hosts the Web site through which the company operates. As a rule, in these cases, the Web site's owner does not control either the server or the place in which the server is located.

A different situation arises when the company acquires or leases a server to host its Web site. The place in which the server is located could be considered a permanent establishment under the following circumstances:

- The place in which the equipment is located must be a fixed place.
- All or part of the company's business must be carried on in the place in which the server is located.
- No personnel are required—an automatic server can constitute a permanent establishment.
- The business activities carried out on the server are not preparatory or auxiliary.

Certain e-commerce activities are considered preparatory or auxiliary:

- Providing a communications link—much like a telephone line—between suppliers and customers;
- Advertising goods or services;
- Relaying information through a mirror server for security and efficiency purposes;
- Gathering market data for the enterprise; and
- Supplying information.

However, when these activities constitute on their own an essential part of a nonresident company's business activities, or when other basic activities of the company are made through the computer equipment, and the equipment constitutes a fixed place of business, those activities will not be considered preparatory or auxiliary.

Paragraph 5 of the commentaries on Article 5 discusses when use of an authorized agent can constitute a permanent establishment. This discussion, however, is not applicable to ISP. An ISP is not considered an authorized agent of the company that owns the Web site because it does not have power to sign contracts on behalf of the company, does not sign these contracts on a regular basis, and because it is an independent agent—that is, Web hosting is its everyday business.

Spain has expressed reservations to the changes to the OECD's Commentary on the Model Tax Convention on Article 5. Spain, as well as other countries, expressed its doubts regarding the applicability of future ¶¶ 42.1 and 42.10. Therefore, Spain will not necessarily consider these two paragraphs until the OECD finishes its analysis and reaches final conclusions.

Article 13, Chapter 1, section (a), Compilation Text of Nonesidents Income Tax Act,[5] limits the concept of permanent establishment for tax law purposes. Under this act, a person or company will be considered to hold a permanent establishment in Spanish territory when it has installations or work places of any kind in Spain, in which all or part of its activities are regularly carried out. A permanent establishment will also be found when a company acts through an authorized agent with the power to sign contracts on the company's behalf, and said agent habitually exercises this power. This definition of permanent establishment is based on the existence of an economic link between the activity carried on through the business location that constitutes the permanent establishment and the profits that this business produces.

The following situations are given as examples of permanent establishments by the compilation text of the Nonresidents Income Tax Act: the seat of management, branches, offices, factories, workshops, warehouses, stores and other establishments, mines, oil and gas wells or quarries, agriculture, aquaculture, any other place of

---

5 Royal Decree 5/2004 (Mar. 5, 2004). Amendments: L 35/2006 Nov. 28 (Impuesto sobre la Renta de las Personas Físicas y modificación parcial de las leyes de los Impuestos sobre Sociedades, sobre la Renta de no Residentes y sobre el Patrimonio), L 36/2006 Nov. 29 (medidas para la prevención del fraude fiscal), L 22/2005 Nov. 18 (incorpora directivas comunitarias sobre fiscalidad de productos energéticos y electricidad, y régimen fiscal común a sociedades matrices y filiales, y regula el régimen fiscal de aportaciones transfronterizas a fondos pensiones).

extraction of natural resources, and construction projects or installations that last more than six months.

It is also important to point out that any installation that produces economic benefits, even if it does not collect a price for its products, is considered a permanent establishment. It is enough that the installation adds any value to the goods or services produced. For example, establishments in which products are transformed for the use by the mother company are considered permanent establishments and therefore obligated to pay taxes in Spain.

Even though the Spanish tax regulations do not explicitly mention e- commerce, the Spanish Ministry of Finance constituted a commission of experts to study the impact of e- commerce on its tax regime. Their recommendations have been regarded as more innovative than those presented by the OECD. Their suggestions include the following:

- Adapting the current concept of permanent establishment to the problems presented by electronic commerce. In accordance with Article 5 of the Model Tax Convention, the existing concept of permanent establishment is considered valid for traditional commerce but seems insufficient for e-commerce.
- Proposing to the Spanish representatives in the OECD that modifying Article 5 of the Model Tax Convention to include e-commerce should be accomplished in the very text of the article, and not only in the commentaries.
- Studying whether a Web site, under certain conditions, could constitute a fixed place of business (meaning regular, continued, and stable) of variable location. In order to determine whether or not there is a permanent establishment in e- commerce, states should use continued economic activity, instead of permanent physical presence.
- The Spanish representatives in the OECD should defend the idea that the presence of human intervention in e-commerce is not necessary to determine that a nonresident company is operating in a country as a permanent establishment.

V. ELECTRONIC PERMANENT ESTABLISHMENT

In general, the OECD continues to adhere to a physical concept of permanent establishment, even in the field of the e-commerce. Some experts point out that servers may provide this physical aspect and may be the logical adaptation of the traditional tax concept of permanent establishment to newer technology. However, other specialists have argued that servers may easily be established in countries with low taxation. For this reason, many national tax authorities oppose this adaptation. At the end of the day, one cannot forget that the consequence of considering servers or other possible elements as permanent establishments is the attribution of tax incomes among the corresponding taxing jurisdictions involved.

It must be also kept in mind that servers can be mobile. For example, a laptop can be used as a server, and, consequently, such server will lack the necessary permanence in a territory to fulfill the internationally accepted criteria.

In response to this issue, some writers suggest creating a definition of permanent establishment adapted to the specifics of e-commerce that does not rely on physical attributes. One possible approach to determining electronic permanent establishment would use Web sites, which enjoy a virtual permanence in the economy of the source country. Thus, the country that is the source of the corresponding business income would be considered the competent taxing jurisdiction. Spanish experts generally support this position, and, along with tax authorities from several other countries, argue that foreign businesses operating virtually in a country take advantage of many costly services and infrastructure in said countries. For that reason, those businesses should contribute to the costs of these services and this infrastructure.

Obviously, using Web sites as permanent establishments involves some obstacles. The main one seems to be the distribution of business income among the corresponding company and its electronic permanent establishments, on the one hand, and the large number of taxing jurisdictions that may claim competence, on the other.

The guidelines for transfer pricing elaborated by the OECD may offer a solution to the attribution of taxable income. The proposed analysis may consider the Web site as a separate entity from the corresponding company and establish distribution by taking into account assets used and risks assumed by associated companies in controlled transactions and by independent companies in comparable, uncontrolled transactions.

Regarding the large number of taxing jurisdictions involved, the obvious complication is that businesses operating on the Internet may face tax obligations in almost every country where their Web sites are accessible. Medium-sized and small businesses or sole traders would be unable to cope with this unending list of tax obligations and requirements. Even multinational companies would find it extremely difficult to meet the requirements imposed by every taxing jurisdiction in which they are operating "virtually." Moreover, apart from the obligation of paying taxes, many other formal and supplementary requirements may be applicable, creating quite a heavy burden on businesses. Such a heavy burden may commonly limit e-commerce. Even if a limitation on the tax liability is established, for instance, by examining the volume of operations carried out in a particular country, there would be a significant restraint on e-commerce. Tax authorities must come up with an innovative adjustment for e-commerce. Recent developments in that field are discussed below.

VI. "CYBER" TAX AUTHORITIES

This section will first comment briefly on tax authorities and the new role they are called to play on global economy. It is clear that tax authorities should take advantage of new information technology to update and modernize their functions. Automated proceedings, for instance, may save costs on staff and time not only for the tax authority but also for the taxpayers. Furthermore, automated controls on tax returns and on formal obligations may be extraordinarily accurate, as long as the proceedings and forms are sufficiently standardized. Another additional aspect to bear in mind is the savings on paper that electronic forms may provide.

In this respect, the Spanish Tax Agency (*Agencia Estatal de la Administración Tributaria*) has made an enormous effort with the aim of modernizing its procedures. Likewise, businesses operating in Spain have made some effort to update their proceedings and train their personnel for the new electronic procedures. Tax forms on paper are growing less common, and for certain tax forms only the electronic version is valid.

In the European Union, important measures have been taken to improve the functioning of taxation systems in the internal market. The community program called *Fiscalis 2013* pursues reducing the administrative burden on administrations and taxable persons. The total amount to be borne by the community's budget is 156.9 million for the 2008–2013 period. In fact, this program has had previous versions launched in 1998 and in 2002 for 2007. Fiscalis 2013, meanwhile, is a community program to facilitate trade and to combat fraud so as to safeguard the financial and security interests of the European Union and its citizens. The program's main goal is to increase cooperation between national customs administrations, including exchanging risk analysis information. According to the European Commission "the ultimate goal would be to move to paperless customs procedures ('e-customs') where the maximum amount of data is transferred electronically."

Fiscalis 2013 is intended to improve programs that gather together officials from different nationalities in order to share and understand different experiences, problems, and solutions applicable to taxing systems. The officials involved in these programs must be multilingual to participate actively. The new community program also implements training activities for these officials with the objective that they achieve a high level of understanding of community law and its domestic implementation. The program also looks for a continued improvement of administrative procedures. Another tenet of Fiscalis 2013 is the establishment of several communication and information exchange systems. This shall include, among others, common communications networks or common systems interfaces, the value-added tax information exchange system (VIES), excise systems, and any new tax-related communication and information exchange system.

Consequently, modernization, cooperation, and coordination among tax authorities are vital to tackle the challenges arising from e-commerce. Likewise, a self-imposed limitation on national tax authorities' range of authority to tax seems necessary.

VII. CONCLUSIONS

Tax law needs to respond to the challenges and requests that e-commerce presents. These traditional institutions deeply established in international tax law quite often do not offer solutions suitable for the disputes and conflicts that e-commerce causes. Although online commerce is not exempt from the same principles, rules, and regulations applicable to offline transactions, some modifications need to be made. It is quite obvious that there are no disinterested positions on this issue. Some governments may be tempted to promote taxation on source countries, whereas others may prefer to defend tax-free e-commerce. Not surprisingly, those countries in which the headquarters of the companies operating on the Internet are established tend to be more reluctant to favor taxation on the source countries. On the other hand, and neither surprisingly, countries in which fewer electronic businesses are set up find it difficult to accept a tax exemption for e-commerce.

Moreover, governments and national tax authorities will have to adapt their organization, structure, proceedings, and rules, bearing in mind that online transactions with international elements will be more frequent in the future. Tax sovereignty is already highly threatened and, consequently, most countries will find that no other remedy is left for them other than limiting the scope of the operations they decide to control and promoting international collaboration among tax authorities.

In this sense, the European Union is permanently trying to achieve a more transparent and efficient tax law regime. It is seen as essential to pursuing an effective, uniform, and efficient application of community law in the internal markets. This efficient application will allow for a more functional taxation system, will protect the national financial position, and at the same time will combat tax evasion and tax avoidance. In this respect, European Union membership may and should result in a competitive advantage to their members, since they already enjoy a high degree of tax harmonization and because under the Lisbon Agenda, promoting the telecommunications market, digital society, and information industry is considered as one of the key factors in converting the European Union into the most competitive region in the global economy. This ambitious aim will not be accomplished unless all members of the European Union not only modernize and harmonize their tax authorities, proceedings, and rules but also become willing to share and communicate the information they obtain from their taxpayers and public bodies. Promoting mutual understanding among countries and their corresponding tax authorities is absolutely essential to regulate a phenomenon that defies taxing sovereignty.

Chapter 15

United Kingdom: E-Commerce and Taxation: Cases of Goods, Digital Products, and Services

Erika Jupe
Osborne Clarke

I. INTRODUCTION

There are a number of ways in which goods and services can be provided over the Internet, which are, for the purposes of this chapter, categorized into two principal types: the classical model and the modern approach.

The classical model is very similar to a typical brochure or catalog business. The e-business will set up a Web site to advertise its goods, and customers will make purchases online that are then delivered to them. The e-business' Web site is similar to a traditional brochure or catalog. A good example of the classical model would be the original Amazon.com Web site, whereby customers could browse online and purchase a book in hard-copy form, which Amazon would deliver to them by postal service or other similar means.

The development of the modern approach has been encouraged by the increase in available bandwidth and the improvements in hardware and software that have allowed companies to sell digital products to customers over the Internet. A good example of the modern approach is the music download service offered by Apple, where music is purchased by making a digital copy rather than by buying a physical CD.

In addition to business-to-consumer (B2C) transactions, there has been an exponential increase in the rise of business-to-business (B2B) transactions where the Internet has been used as a means of supplying products and services, such as digital invoicing or software solutions.

A. Example

A fictional company, eTunes.com, which traditionally sold CDs and books from its network of shops, has set up in the United Kingdom (UK) as an e-business selling CDs,

DVDs, and books online. The company's Web site is hosted from a server based at its UK office and another server hosted by an Internet service provider (ISP) based in the United States. The Web site has acted as a new sales channel by which the e-business can access customers. However, its products are still sold in tangible form and require physical delivery. In the main, the customers' geographic location can be monitored because this would be dictated, to a large extent, by the addresses to which the goods are delivered. eTunes has now decided to expand into the growing market in digital products such as music downloads, e-books, and software packages (i.e., standard music compilation software and more bespoke products offered to commercial enterprises for commercial exploitation).

Additional tax considerations will arise for eTunes as its business changes from the classical to the modern approach. It will need to consider whether its U.S. presence constitutes a permanent establishment. It will also need to consider whether providing a service to customers that allows them to make a digital copy of the CD/DVD/book constitutes a royalty payment. In addition, eTunes will need to determine the appropriate rate of consumption tax (i.e., value-added tax, or VAT) applicable in circumstances where it sells its products to multiple jurisdictions. This raises the difficulty of trying to determine the physical location of its customers and how it can set up business systems that will capture the information. These issues are considered in detail in the rest of this chapter.

B. Development of the Legal Framework for E-Commerce

Before considering the tax position in detail, it is worth recapping some of the principal developments that have been made toward establishing the legal framework for e-commerce transactions in the United Kingdom.

1. Formation of an E-Contract At the beginning of the dot-com boom, there was concern about whether an electronic signature in an e-contract was sufficient to form the contract, and there was also uncertainty about the place of formation of a contract made online. This could affect which legal rules determine the contract's validity and terms. At the risk of oversimplification, these issues have now to a large extent been resolved at a European Union (EU) level and a UK level.

Under English contract law most agreements can be formed electronically without any written formalities. The view of the UK government is that the great majority of statutory requirements are already capable of being fulfilled by electronic communication. As a result of the partial implementation of the Electronic Signatures Directive (99/93/EC) in the United Kingdom by means of the Electronic Communications Act 2000 (Electronic Communications Act), the UK government may issue regulations that modify existing legislation in order to remove any obstacles to electronic contracting.

The Electronic Commerce (EC Directive) Regulations 2002 (E-Commerce Regulations) provide some statutory guidance on when an e-contract is treated as being formed. Before the introduction of the E-Commerce Regulations, there had been uncertainty as to the time when an e-contract would be treated as formed.

On the one hand, if the contract formation followed the so called "postal rule" the contract would be formed at the time the acceptance of the offer was sent by the acceptor. However, if the rule established in *Entores v Miles Far East Corp.*, [1955] 2 QB 327, [1955] 2 All ER 493, for instantaneous methods of communications applied, acceptance would take place when acceptance was received by the offeror. The place of formation would be determined by the time of acceptance and the location of acceptance of the contract, so that in international transactions there was potential uncertainty as to when and where a contract was formed.

Under the E-Commerce Regulations, an e-business must include in its Web site terms and conditions the different technical steps that must be followed in order to conclude a contract, as well as provide the technical means for customers to identify and correct input errors prior to placing an order. Whilst the E-Commerce Regulations do not expressly state the time at which a contract is formed, the effect of the regulations is likely to remove the uncertainty as to when, and in consequence where, formation takes place.

II. E-COMMERCE VERSUS CONVENTIONAL FORMS OF DOING BUSINESS

One of the key attributes of e-commerce is that the physical reach of a business is no longer a constraint on the reach of its economic activity. Goods can be sold and services provided to customers regardless of the physical location of either the business or the customer. For example, an e-business such as eTunes, discussed above, could establish a Web site through which it makes software and other digital product downloads available to customers throughout the world.

From an indirect or consumption tax (i.e. VAT) perspective this will create a number of tax compliance risks as well as tax-planning possibilities. One possibility (which is considered in detail in the "Going Offshore" section below) is that the e-business could establish its operations in a jurisdiction with a low rate of consumption tax (or alternatively no consumption tax), and thereby achieve an advantage over competitors established in jurisdictions with higher rates of VAT. As will be discussed in section IV.A below, there has been a degree of international cooperation to address cross-border consumption tax issues, and within the European Union there has been a political response to protect EU businesses from potential loss of revenue from non-EU e-businesses that had previously been able to sell digital products into the European Union without charging VAT at the same rates as the EU businesses.

From a direct tax perspective the main business activities of an e-business can be established in a low tax jurisdiction and, provided that its sales fulfillment activities do not amount to a permanent establishment, no direct taxes would be payable offshore. The significant risk of erosion of national tax bases has meant that there has been a raft of developments at the international and national level to try and reduce the risk of nontaxation of e-commerce. The response of international tax authorities to these issues is considered in detail in section III.A.

III. EVOLUTION OF RULES FOR TAXING E-COMMERCE

A. The International Response to E-Commerce Taxation

The challenges posed by global e-commerce to tax systems were discussed at an international level by the Organization for Economic Cooperation and Development (OECD), resulting in the endorsement of the following broad taxation principles at the Ottawa Conference in October 1998.

The same principles that governments apply to taxation of conventional commerce should equally apply to e-commerce, namely:

- *Neutrality*—Taxation should seek to be neutral between e-commerce and conventional business.
- *Efficiency*—Compliance costs to business and administration costs for governments should be minimized as far as possible.
- *Certainty and simplicity*—Tax rules should be clear and simple to understand, so that taxpayers know where they stand.
- *Effectiveness and fairness*—Taxation should produce the right amount of tax at the right time, and the potential for evasion and avoidance should be minimized.
- *Flexibility*—Taxation systems should be flexible and dynamic to ensure they keep pace with technological and commercial developments.

The two most significant conclusions of the OECD were that no new tax rules were currently needed to deal with e-commerce and that existing rules must not discriminate against e-commerce as compared with more conventional forms of doing business.

Following the Ottawa Conference, most national tax authorities have signed up to the central premise of tax neutrality set forth in the Taxation Framework Conditions. In the United Kingdom, Her Majesty's Revenue and Customs (HMRC) has fully endorsed the position taken by the OECD on e-commerce. In its policy paper entitled *E-Commerce—The UK's Taxation Agenda*, issued in November 1999, HMRC recognized that the four broad principles of neutrality, certainty and transparency, effectiveness, and efficiency should apply to the United Kingdom's rules in relation to taxation of e-commerce.

B. Development of Rules on Consumption Taxes

There are essentially two approaches that can be adopted for consumption taxes, namely the "destination" principle and the "origin" principle. Under the destination principle, supplies of goods and services are taxed in the jurisdiction of destination at the consumption tax rate in force in that jurisdiction. For example, if the destination principle applies, exports are generally exempt from consumption taxes in the exporting jurisdiction, and a tax liability will arise when the goods are imported into another jurisdiction. This is generally the approach applied for VAT purposes in respect of supplies of goods under EU rules.

One reason behind a destination approach is that all suppliers to customers in a particular jurisdiction will have to charge the same rate of tax regardless of the jurisdiction from which they make the supply. The downside is that there are conflicting interests between the tax authorities in the jurisdiction of the digital product supplier and the jurisdiction of the customer. The OECD proposes that consumption taxes for e-commerce transactions should be paid in the customer's jurisdiction, that is, a destination-based system.

A destination principle also gives rise to difficulties in terms of collection and administration of taxes where B2C supplies are involved. Where goods are supplied to nonbusiness customers in another EU jurisdiction, this is generally dealt with using the "distance sales" rules, which require an overseas business to register for VAT purposes in the jurisdiction in which its customers are based. This can place a heavy burden on the e-business to account for consumption taxes in all the jurisdictions to which it sells its digital products.

The alternative is the origin-based system, under which consumption taxes are collected by the e-business at the point of the transaction's origin at the rate of consumption tax in the e-business' jurisdiction. The jurisdiction in which the consumption tax charge arises and is payable is clearly that of the e-business selling the products under the origin-based system. This removes compliance issues for tax authorities in terms of the administration and collection of taxes. It is also simpler for an e-business because it does not have to determine the location of its customers and keep up to date with the consumption tax rates in all the multiple jurisdictions to which it supplies products. This is the approach generally adopted in respect of supplies of services for VAT purposes in the European Union.

However, from a political perspective this option can appear unattractive, particularly in the case of e-businesses, because it can distort competition. It may lead to the migration of e-business to the jurisdiction with the lowest rates of consumption taxes, as has been seen with the location of many e-businesses to Madeira and Luxembourg, which have historically had low rates of VAT. This in turn would put an e-business in high-consumption tax jurisdictions at a competitive disadvantage in comparison to those in jurisdictions with low rates of consumption tax.

IV. DIFFICULTIES IN TAXING E-COMMERCE

A. Locating the Transaction and Applying the Appropriate Rate of Consumption Tax

The location of the customer in a "virtual" transaction will often be difficult to determine. For example, when a digital product is downloaded from a server by a customer who is paying through an online payment account, it may be difficult for the e-business supplying the digital product to determine where that customer belongs. The place where the customer belongs may affect the rate of consumption tax to be charged and to which tax authority the tax will need to be accounted for.

At the OECD level it has been accepted that digital supplies should be treated as supplies of services and should result in taxation in the jurisdiction where consumption takes place. In addition, when a business acquires services and intangible property from a nonresident supplier, consideration should be given to the use of a "reverse-charge" mechanism or other equivalents to collect taxes on the supply.

For B2C transactions, the place of supply for the supply of services made cross-border to private customers should be the jurisdiction in which the recipient has their usual residence.

The recommended approach for B2B transactions in cases where the supplying business is registered for consumption tax in a different jurisdiction than that of the recipient is a self-assessment or reverse-charge mechanism consistent with the overall design of that jurisdiction's national consumption tax system. The OECD recognized that the self-assessment or reverse-charge mechanism has a number of key advantages that make it effective: the tax authority in the country of consumption can verify and enforce compliance; the compliance burden is on the recipient and not the supplier; and it reduces the revenue risks associated with the collection of tax by nonresident suppliers.

For B2C transactions the recommended approach for collection is a registration system where the nonresident supplier would register in the jurisdiction of the recipient. This is in part due to the possibility of distorting competition where the consumption tax charged is at the rate of the supplier's jurisdiction (i.e., suppliers of digital products may be encouraged to transact from the jurisdiction with the lowest rates of consumption tax). Such registration requirements of a tax authority should ensure that the potential compliance burden is minimized and should seek to apply registration thresholds in a nondiscriminatory manner.

In terms of practical recommendations, the OECD recognized that further work would be required on an ongoing basis in relation to the collection and administration of consumption taxes and, in particular,

- For B2C transactions, identification and verification of the customer's jurisdiction (the customer's jurisdiction of residence entitled to tax the transaction);
- Identification and verification of the status of the customer (to identify between business and private consumers);
- Registration thresholds (in the UK for the supply of goods these are currently set at £67,000);
- Technology-based and technology-facilitated collection mechanisms (possible trusted third party methods of collection are discussed below in section V.A.1).

These recommendations have been adopted within the EU for the purposes of applying VAT to digital services. When a business in one EU member state makes a supply to a business customer in another member state, it is not required to charge VAT in its home jurisdiction. However, the customer is required to account for VAT on the supply under the reverse-charge mechanism.

B. Differences between VAT Treatment of Goods and Digital Products

1. Where Does the Customer Belong? Subject to certain exceptions, some of which are discussed below in section VI.B, a supply of services is generally treated as made for VAT purposes where the supplier belongs. A supplier "belongs" in the jurisdiction in which it has its business establishment or some other fixed establishment. The business establishment will usually be the headquarters or "seat" from which the business is run. A fixed establishment is an establishment other than a business establishment and includes an overseas branch of a business; It does not usually include the temporary presence of staff or equipment in another jurisdiction. However, a fixed establishment could exist in the United Kingdom where an overseas business that contracts with UK customers to provide services and incorporates a subsidiary in the United Kingdom to act in its name to provide those services, where the UK subsidiary is not functionally and organizationally independent of its parent. If the supplier is established in more than one country, the supplier "belongs" in the jurisdiction in which it has the establishment that is most directly concerned with the supply in question.

However, the place of supply for digital products will in many cases be the jurisdiction in which the recipient "belongs." This can present an e-business with the problem of trying to establish the physical location of its customers only from the details obtained from a "virtual" transaction.

C. Tax Residence and Competing Claims to Share the Tax Base

As explained above, the basic premise is that a company carrying on business overseas will be subject to taxation not only at its place of residence, but it may also be liable to tax overseas if its overseas presence amounts to a permanent establishment. In its report entitled "Are the Current Treaty Rules for Taxing Business Profits Appropriate for E-Commerce," the OECD concluded that to provide for the exemption of such multiple taxation, priority would be given to source taxation (i.e., no permanent establishment), the jurisdiction where the permanent establishment is located, and residual taxing rights given to the state of residence.

The conditions to determine whether a business is resident in a particular jurisdiction are set out in Article 4 (Residence) of the Model Tax Convention (Article 4). Article 4, ¶ 3 is the tie-breaker rule that ensures that a business will have only a single jurisdiction of residence for purposes of the Model Tax Convention, and this shall be where the effective place of management is situated. In recognition of the impact that new forms of distance communications technology may have on the ability of individuals to operate a company from a different jurisdiction, the OECD set out proposals to amend the tie-breaker rule in a further discussion draft of the "Place of Effective Management Concept: Suggestions for Changes to the OECD Model Tax Convention." The first proposal was for a "refinement" of the "place of effective management" concept to distinguish between the places where a board of directors makes key decisions and where these decisions are approved. The proposal sought to address situations in which managers making decisions are based in a different jurisdiction to the business, which merely approves these decisions. Under the second proposal, "hierarchy of tests," the residence of the business would be determined in the following order of priority (1) the jurisdiction with which its economic relations are closest, (2) the jurisdiction in which its business activities are primarily carried on, and (3) failing determination by either of these two, by mutual agreement between the tax authorities in each jurisdiction in which the business may be resident. This is in effect an extension of the refinement proposal, in that consideration would be made of where the key management and commercial decisions necessary for the conduct of that business are made in substance, rather than merely "rubber stamped." This approach works in part to limit some tax-planning opportunities to locate e-commerce activities in low tax jurisdictions whilst effectively running the business from a high tax jurisdiction.

D. Taxation of Business Profits from International Transactions

1. Permanent Establishment In taxing business profits that stem from international transactions two questions arise, namely, in what circumstances a country should have a legitimate claim to tax the business profits of a foreign enterprise and what the appropriate basis is for deciding which part of the business profits of a foreign enterprise should be taxed in a country.

In determining where the profits of an e-business are taxed it is necessary to determine the following:

- Where the e-business has its primary liability for taxation;
- Whether it has a permanent establishment in any other jurisdiction;
- Attribution of the profits between the permanent establishments and resident taxpayer (head office); and
- Where there are competing claims to the same business profits, the rules for sharing the tax base.

From a theoretical standpoint the principal considerations are whether business profits are taxed from where the profits originate (source) or where the wealth or profits are spent (residence). There is a wide international consensus that business profits can be taxed on both residence and source, subject to source profits reaching a defined threshold (i.e., the permanent establishment threshold). Because an e-business can set up operations in jurisdictions without the need for the same level of physical presence that would have been required for more traditional forms of commerce, it has become possible for more transactions to be carried out remotely from where the physical offices of a supplier are located. For example, to what extent are the profits from a Web site hosted on a server in one jurisdiction taxable in that country or in the country from where the e-business has its head office or principal operations?

The basic definition of "permanent establishment" in Article 5 of the Model Tax Convention (Article 5) is "a fixed place of business through which the business of an enterprise is wholly or partly carried on." The definition incorporates a geographical requirement (i.e., a fixed physical location) and time requirement (the presence of the enterprise in the relevant jurisdiction must be more than merely temporary). There are generally exceptions for facilities used for the storage, display, and delivery of goods and for activities that are of a preparatory or auxiliary character. The definition of permanent establishment includes an agent that carries on business in a country for a nonresident business if that agent habitually exercises an authority to conclude contracts in the name of the nonresident business. This part of the definition specifically excludes an independent agent acting in the ordinary course of its business.

The OECD has clarified how it considers the definition of permanent establishment should apply to e-commerce operations:

- A Web site cannot, in itself, constitute a permanent establishment.
- Web site-hosting arrangements typically do not result in a permanent establishment for the enterprise that carries on business through the hosted Web site.
- Except in very unusual circumstances, an ISP will not be deemed to constitute a permanent establishment for the enterprise to which it provides services. It is possible that where an e-business uses a payment solutions provider to host its Web site, conclude contracts, and process payment on its behalf this may constitute a permanent establishment.
- The functions performed at a place where computer equipment or a server is based must go beyond what is merely preparatory or auxiliary for it to constitute a permanent establishment. What constitutes auxiliary functions is set out in Article 5(4), which include activities such as providing a communications link or relaying information through a mirror server, advertising, gathering market data, or supplying information. However, if these activities represented the core functions of an e-business, then the server or Web site may give rise to a permanent establishment. A number of jurisdictions, such as Spain and Portugal, take a contrary view on this issue and have expressed reservations on this part of the OECD commentary.

The development of e-commerce has meant that many multinational enterprises can integrate their business functions that are located in different jurisdictions. Where the profits of one of these functions are to be taxed at source, the rules for computing the profits are based on the notional separate-entity basis and arm's-length principles. This means that the branch and head office of a multinational enterprise are treated as separate entities for the purposes of the computation of profits under tax treaties. In determining the profits of the branch, the profits can be readjusted to reflect the price that would have been paid at an arm's length between two independent enterprises.

The ownership and use of intellectual property presents particular difficulties in the transfer pricing context. It can be hard to determine the extent to which the head office or permanent establishment owns certain intangible property belonging to a multinational enterprise. For example, this will include software that has been developed and used by the business for commercial exploitation as well as marketing intangibles such as the brand. The head office would in many cases be treated as the owner of such marketing intangibles; however, there may be circumstances in which the permanent establishment collects customer information or advertises the brand to the extent that it can be said to be the owner of or has contributed to the value of these intangibles.

In its paper on the attribution of profit to a permanent establishment involved in e-commerce transactions, the OECD considered the following four scenarios in respect of the attribution of profits to a permanent establishment:

1. A standalone server with no personnel where the Web site is hosted on the server and is used to advertise the e-business, process orders, and allow customers to download digital products from the server.
2. Multiple servers where the same tasks are performed as in the example above, except that the Web site is hosted over several servers in different physical locations with identical tasks carried out between the servers (i.e., mirror servers).
3. A server deployed with personnel based at the permanent establishment to maintain the server, repair the hardware, and provide a technical troubleshooting service to customers.
4. Personnel based at the permanent establishment to develop the hardware and software used to host the Web site.

The OECD report concluded that the amount of profit to be attributed to the permanent establishment should be related to the functions it performs (taking into account the assets used and risks assumed), and which part of the multinational enterprise "owns" or has created the intangible assets used by the permanent establishment.

In examples 1 and 2 (a standalone server or mirror servers), the permanent establishment is unlikely to own the assets operating the Web site, so it is likely that all the substantial assets and risks would be with the head office. As such, the majority of the profit will be attributed to the head office. In example 3 (personnel to maintain the server), any profits attributable to the permanent establishment would be commensurate with those that independent service providers would be expected to earn in similar situations. In example 4 (in-house development), this would produce a more substantial attribution of profits to the permanent establishment because it would assume sufficient development risk to be considered owner of the intangible property developed to operate the server and Web site.

During the actual commercial exploitation of the assets (including the intangible assets) any profits due to the operation of the hardware and software could be attributed to the permanent establishment on the comparable uncontrolled price (CUP) basis since this would be owned by the head office. However, for any e-commerce marketing intangibles it would be necessary to determine to what extent these are owned by the head office or owned by the permanent establishment, because the value of the brand may be more clearly related to the operation of the Web site. When this is the case, the permanent establishment would be treated as owning, to an extent, some of the marketing intangibles associated with this development of the brand. Under the interpretation of the commentary to the Model Tax Convention in Article 9 (Associated Enterprises) and Article 7, when making a deduction in its profits attributable to using the marketing intangibles, the permanent establishment is treated as having the right to use the marketing intangibles owned by the head office at an arm's length. However, in accordance with the current interpretation of Article 7, this is on a book value basis rather than the market value of the marketing intangibles. As such, any value attributable to these marketing intangibles as a result of developments made by the head office will not be calculated in determining the arm's-length price. This will be beneficial because it will give rise to a lower profit for the permanent establishment than if market value for the marketing intangibles were to be used.

2. Business Profits or Royalties?

A further issue in relation to an e-business that supplies goods and digital products is whether the revenue for these transactions should be treated as business profits or royalties. This can have a significant impact on the amount of tax payable in the context of international business. If an e-business is selling digital products such as music available in download format (i.e., music in MP3 format that has been purchased from a Web site), then in some jurisdictions this may be regarded as the licensing of copyright to the customer—for example, if the customer has been granted a right under the contract to make one or more copies of the digital content. In the United Kingdom (as is the case with many other countries), there is an obligation to withhold tax from royalty payments for copyright. It therefore becomes necessary to identify the consideration for the payment, in other words, identify the extent to which the customer is granted use of the copyright in the digital product and whether this would require the customer purchasing it to withhold any tax from this royalty payment. This is a question of fact and law, and the response may vary from jurisdiction to jurisdiction.

These issues were considered by the OECD with a view to providing necessary clarifications in the commentary of the Model Tax Convention. Under Article 7 of the Model Tax Convention (Article 7), business profits are to be taxed only in the jurisdiction where the enterprise is resident for tax purposes unless that enterprise carries on business in another jurisdiction through a permanent establishment. In such circumstances the permanent establishment is liable to tax only on the profits properly attributable to the permanent establishment. However, the wording of paragraph 7 of Article 7 states that "where profits include items of income which are dealt with separately in other Articles of [the] Convention, then the provisions of those Articles shall not be affected by the provisions of this Article."

Article 12 of the Model Tax Convention (Article 12) deals with the payment of royalties, which are defined in paragraph 2 of Article 12 as being "payments of any kind received as a consideration for the use of, or the right to use, any copyright of literary, artistic or scientific work including cinematograph films, any patent, trade mark, design or model, plan, secret formula or process, or for information concerning industrial, commercial or scientific experience."

The OECD's conclusion was that where the essential consideration for a payment was something other than the use of, or right to use, a copyright (such as to acquire other types of contractual rights, data, or services), this would not be treated as a royalty payment. Accordingly, limited rights to acquire the rights necessary to download, store, and operate the product on the customer's computer or other storage device would be disregarded for the purposes of applying Article 12. For example, when payment is made by a customer to download and copy a digital product (i.e., music download) onto their computer, although the act of copying the digital signals (i.e., the music download) may technically constitute the use of a copyright by the customer, this is merely an incidental part of the essential supply, that is, the process of downloading the digital product and storing it for future use.

The OECD considered the income categorization of 27 different types of typical e-commerce transactions. This is an overview of the provisions that may affect an e-business such as eTunes (transacting in both the classical model and modern approach), in terms of the OECD's conclusions on the income characterisation in of the following transactions:

- *Sale of a tangible product*—The e-business advertises CDs, DVDs, or other tangible products from a catalog hosted on its Web site, and a customer purchases these items, which are then physically delivered to the customer, for example, using a postal carrier. There is no separate charge to the customer for using the online catalog.
- *Sale of a digital product*—The e-business advertises music downloads, software downloads, or other digital products from a catalog hosted on its Web site that the customer purchases and downloads to his or her computer hard disk or other media that store a copy, for example, on an iPod or other similar devices. There is no separate charge to the customer for using the online catalog.
- *Provision of digital products for commercial exploitation*—The e-business advertises digital products from a catalog hosted on its Web site that the customer purchases and downloads onto his or her computer hard disk or other storage device. The customer then has the right to commercially exploit the copyright in the digital product. In the example of eTunes, it may distribute music downloads for commercial exploitation, that is, if the business became involved in distributing artists' work to promotional suppliers who will in turn distribute this through other retail outlets.
- *Software downloads*—The e-business sells software or other digital products (i.e., music or videos distributed as rental copies) that are downloaded by the customer but for which the customer receives a license to use that software or digital product for a period of time that is shorter than the useful life of the product. On expiry of the licence period, the software or digital product will be deleted or unusable.

In the case of the sale of a tangible product, the consideration is not for the use of a copyright, and therefore falls within Article 7 and is taxable as a business profit. No issue of withholding tax on royalty payments will arise. In the case of the sale of a digital product, the OECD concluded the service provided would be the download of the digital product for the customer's enjoyment, and any use of copyright to perform this download would be incidental to the essential supply. To the extent that the customer then copied the digital product onto another storage device, this would not be treated as changing the classification of the income for Model Tax Convention purposes, because the copying of the product is merely incidental to the main supply.

When the e-business provides a digital product to a business customer for commercial exploitation, then any payment will constitute a royalty. In the example given of the copyright in music downloads made available for reproduction and sale to retail outlets by the customer (either by adding it to a CD or by distribution of digital downloads), it is clear that the customer will obtain the right to use the copyright in order to commercially exploit this digital product. In many jurisdictions, such as the United Kingdom, the customer is required to withhold tax on the royalty payments to the e-business, particularly if the payment is made overseas. This form of commercial exploitation will invariably be carried out by a person or business acting in the course of business, so they would be expected to have the necessary capabilities to deduct and account for withholding tax made on any payment.

When the e-business is supplying software with a limited license, the OECD concluded that such a limited licence should be treated as business profits in the same way as the sale of a tangible product or digital product.

V. RESPONSE OF TAX AUTHORITIES

A. Problems with Tax Collection and Administration

1. Using Technology The nature of e-commerce and the underlying technology is such that whilst it creates problems in identifying where the tax charge may arise on cross-border transactions, it also brings about opportunities to use the new technologies to assist taxing authorities in their tax administration. The OECD has noted general trends, such as the move by taxing authorities from paper communications to electronic communications, from checks or cash to electronic funds, from manual responses and a segmented service to an integrated service with automated voice and mail facilities and, perhaps optimistically, the metamorphosis from taxpayer to customer!

In the European Union, all member states have been required to allow electronic cross-border invoicing since January 1, 2004, under the terms of the EU Invoicing Directive (2001/115/EC), which sets out some common requirements for electronic invoicing.

In its report entitled "Emerging Trends in Taxpayer Service Industries Using New Technology," the OECD identified four consumption-tax collection models: the self-assessment option (i.e., reverse charge); the registration option (i.e., nonresidents are obliged to register in the jurisdiction into which they are selling and then to charge, collect, and account for consumption tax); the tax-at-source option (i.e., e-businesses collect consumption taxes on exports to nonresidents and account for this to their tax authorities, who in turn account for this to the tax authority of the nonresident consumer); and the trusted third-party/clearinghouse option (i.e., a third party would be engaged to collect consumption taxes on payments and account for this to the tax authorities of the country of consumption).

The self-assessment model is what is currently in place for EU VAT in relation to most B2B transactions; however, from a B2C perspective this is unworkable. The registration option, which applies for most B2C supplies, has high costs for nonresident e-businesses supplying products across multiple jurisdictions for nominal amounts that would be a high burden. This option is therefore unattractive to business. The tax-at-source model would require intergovernmental agreement as to how tax authorities would collect, transfer, and account for consumption taxes in addition to the problem of how the jurisdiction of the customer is to be verified (the so-called clearinghouse system). The trusted third-party model involves the same processes as the tax-at-source model, but this is done by a third party rather than the tax authorities. The OECD, whilst recognizing that this was an effective solution, noted that there was still a question as to how feasible it would be to transfer the tax-collecting burden onto a third party, e.g., financial institutions or an ISP.

B. EU Approach to VAT and Electronically Supplied Services

There have been various political and economic considerations affecting this change to VAT policy. On the one hand, within the European Union, it has been difficult to achieve unanimous agreement to any proposed changes, due to what is sometimes referred to as the "Luxembourg problem." Under the current VAT rules governing the place of supply of telecommunications, broadcasting, and electronically supplied services (i.e., digitized services), where a business is established in the European Union and supplies digitized services to private consumers who are also resident in the European Union, the supply takes place in the member state where the business is established. The supplier must charge VAT at the rate applicable in that member state. This can give companies established in EU countries with a low VAT rate, such as Luxembourg, an economic advantage.

However, if the supplier is established outside the European Union, the supply takes place where the private consumer is resident (subject to certain exceptions relevant to telecommunications and broadcasting, where the supply is where the effective use and enjoyment takes place). This change was designed to ensure that EU businesses were not at a competitive disadvantage compared with their non-EU counterparts. The rules mean that if a non-EU business makes supplies of digitized services to an EU nonbusiness customer, it is required to register for VAT purposes in the European Union to simplify the registration process; the business is only required to register in one EU jurisdiction (known as the one-stop-shop scheme), but is still required to chase and account for VAT at the rates prevailing in each jurisdiction in which it has customers. For example, if a U.S. business makes digitized supplies to private consumers based in Italy and France, it may be registered in the United Kingdom for VAT purposes, but it will be required to charge French VAT on supplies to French customers and Italian VAT on supplies to Italian customers.

Conversely, if a UK business makes supplies of digitized products to private consumers based outside the European Union, it is not required to charge VAT. These rules are subject to "use and enjoyment" provisions that state that if a supply would otherwise be treated as taking place outside the European Union, but effective use and enjoyment takes place inside the European Union, the supply is treated as taking place in the European Union. Conversely, if a supply would be treated as taking place inside the European Union, but effective use and enjoyment takes place outside the European Union, the supply is treated as taking place outside the European Union.

The EU Commission has been concerned that, in the absence of harmonization of VAT rates, the current place of supply rules encourage EU businesses to relocate to member states with low VAT rates and non-EU businesses to establish a presence in such member states. For example, the VAT rates in Luxemburg are 15 percent compared with rates of 25 percent in Sweden and Denmark.

In July 2005, the EU Commission issued a proposal for a directive to amend the VAT rules governing the place of supply of "digitized services" to private consumers. These changes are designed to bring the "supply of digitized services" rules into line with the distance-selling rules that apply to the supply of goods and prevent businesses from effectively "choosing" the rate of VAT they charge on such services.

The proposed changes to VAT rules mean that all EU and non-EU businesses would need to register for and charge VAT based on each customer's place of residence, creating huge administration and compliance costs. Under a separate proposal, a single registration scheme, or one-stop shop, may provide a way for EU and non-EU businesses, such as U.S. firms who trade in the European Union through a subsidiary, to minimize these additional compliance costs. The single registration scheme will allow a supplier to register for VAT only once, in the supplier's home member state (or if established outside the EU, in a host member state), and use that VAT registration for all supplies throughout the European Union. Further, the process will allow VAT declarations to be submitted electronically to a single portal, which would then distribute the declarations directly to the applicable member states. However, it remains unclear how the single registration process can operate effectively without full EU-wide harmonization of the VAT rules.

The EU Commission had proposed that the directive should enter into force on July 1, 2006. However, the proposal must first be adopted unanimously by member states, and it has been delayed while political negotiations continue. The council of the European Union, however, has now adopted draft legislation to change the place of supply for digitized services, but implementation has been deferred to an unspecified later date. In their press release of December 3, 2007 the council stated that, where they apply, application of the new rules will be deferred until January 1, 2015.

VI. TYPICAL DIRECT AND INDIRECT TAX ISSUES

A. Direct Taxes

1. Connecting Factors/Taxable Presence Most jurisdictions seek to tax businesses if there is a "connecting factor" with or a "taxable presence" in that jurisdiction.

The most common types of "connecting factor" are either the place of incorporation or formation (in the U.S. and civil law jurisdictions) or the place of tax residency (in the UK). In most cases, a country will seek to tax the worldwide profits of a company with a connecting factor with that jurisdiction. The most common types of "taxable presence" are either a branch or agency or a permanent establishment. If the entity has a taxable presence in a jurisdiction, that country is likely to seek to tax the profits earned in that jurisdiction that are connected with that taxable presence. For example, a U.S. trading company that opens a branch in the United Kingdom will be liable to UK corporation tax on profits and gains connected with that branch.

For UK tax purposes, UK resident companies are liable to UK corporation tax on worldwide profits and gains, with credit being available for taxes paid overseas. Nonresident companies will be liable to UK corporation tax if they carry on trade in the United Kingdom through a permanent establishment.

2. Permanent Establishment In the United Kingdom, the position set out by HMRC in their Press Releases of April 11, 2000, and February 12, 2001, is that regardless of whether a server is owned, rented, or otherwise at the disposal of a business, the server or Web site will generally not be treated as a permanent establishment for UK direct tax purposes. This is obviously helpful for non-UK businesses using the services of UK-based ISPs or using UK servers. The narrower OECD position may still be of importance to UK businesses that are operating using overseas servers or the services of overseas ISPs; UK companies should check with local tax advisers on whether an overseas server or ISP will create a permanent establishment in an overseas jurisdiction.

3. Transfer Pricing In the United Kingdom, the transfer pricing regime broadly seeks to ensure that transactions between companies under common control are entered into at arm's length. These rules will apply to large group companies (and in certain circumstances medium-size groups where there are fewer than 250 staff but more than 50, and turnover of less than €50 million but more than €10 million, or balance sheets of less than €43 millionbut more than €10 million). Under the transfer pricing rules, connected companies are treated as earning an arm's-length price on the transactions between them and pay tax on this amount. A UK company that has established a permanent establishment or subsidiary in another jurisdiction, or a non-UK company that establishes a UK branch or subsidiary, will need to ensure that it complies with UK transfer pricing rules in the United Kingdom. Although there are no specific guidelines for e-commerce, the discussions at the OECD level, and in particular the OECD Transfer Pricing Guidelines and commentary, will be highly relevant in determining transfer prices in the United Kingdom.

In the United Kingdom, HMRC has adopted a self-assessment system in respect of any transactions where transfer pricing considerations might apply. An e-business liable to corporation tax in the United Kingdom that has a Web site selling digital products from a standalone or other relatively unmanned server based in a permanent establishment situated overseas may as such be faced with difficult questions as to how to value the use and development of its brand in respect of transactions between its UK head office and permanent establishment.

B. Indirect Taxes

A liability to VAT may arise if a business has a taxable presence in the United Kingdom or its customers are resident in the United Kingdom. A liability may also arise if customers are present in a jurisdiction, for example, VAT rules on supplies of electronic services by non-EU companies. The test for where a business "belongs" for UK VAT purposes is discussed above in the "where does the customer belong?" section.

1. Goods or Services? There are significant differences between supplies of goods and services for UK VAT purposes. The distinction between whether something is a supply of goods or services has an impact on the place of supply, and consequently the rate of UK VAT that may be charged on a transaction. Certain types of supply are expressly defined as goods or services. Whilst the meaning of "goods" is defined, a supply of services is anything done for a consideration that is not a supply of goods. Most supplies of digital products will be treated as supplies of services for VAT purposes. The requirement for something to be done for a consideration means that the distribution over the Internet of free software available to download will not be subject to UK VAT, although apportionment issues arise where "free" software is combined with a wider fee-paying service.

2. Place of Supply The place of supply of goods is generally determined by the location of the goods when the goods are sold. There are a number of exceptions to this general rule, for example, for imports and exports to and from outside the European Union and supplies between member states (known as "acquisitions").

For supplies of services, the general rule is that the place of supply is where the supplier belongs. This is subject to certain exceptions, including in the case of digitized services, which are treated as supplied where they are received if supplied outside the European Union or to a business customer based in another EU jurisdiction (see VATA 1994, Sch. 5 ¶¶ 1–8 ["Schedule 5 Services"]). Schedule 5 covers supplies of intellectual property, such as made-to-order software, as well as supplies of telecommunications services. Paragraph 7C of Schedule 5 deals with supplies of digital products, including software, images, and information. Paragraph 7C is subject to "effective use and enjoyment" provisions, where the supply is made to a business customer, which means that if the supply would otherwise be treated as supplied in the European Union, but effective use and enjoyment takes place outside the European Union, the supply is treated as taking place outside the European Union. Similarly, if the supply would otherwise be treated as supplied outside the European Union, but effective use and enjoyment takes place in the European Union the supply is treated as taking place in the European Union. For example, if a UK company supplies digital information to a U.S. company, which is used solely by employees whilst traveling in the United Kingdom, the supply is treated as made in the Untied Kingdom and the UK supplier will need to charge VAT.

For supplies made by a UK supplier to consumers based in other EU member states, the place of supply of digital products is still where the supplier belongs. This means that if a UK business supplies digital products to a consumer based in, say, France, it will be required to charge UK VAT on the supply. However, where a supplier based outside the European Union makes supplies of digital products to consumers based in the European Union, it is liable to charge VAT in each jurisdiction in which it has customers. The non-EU business will also be required to register for VAT purposes in the European Union, but it will be able to use the simplified registration system for non-established traders, which will require it to register for VAT purposes in a single member state, although it will still be required to collect VAT in respect of each jurisdiction in which it has customers.

When the customer is a UK-VAT registered business and receives Schedule 5 services from an overseas supplier (either EU or non-EU), it must account for these under what is known as the "reverse-charge" procedure. This is, in effect, a self-assessment procedure in which the UK business receiving the supplies will account for UK VAT on receipt of the service (input VAT). It is entitled to recover this amount as output tax in the usual way, that is, for a UK business that is fully taxable under VAT, the VAT would "wash through" its accounts. Under the reverse charge, businesses will treat services brought in from outside the United Kingdom in the same way as services that are actually supplied in the United Kingdom, and the same rate of VAT will apply.

3. VAT Treatment of Supplies of Software The distinction between goods and services for VAT purposes has raised issues as to the correct treatment of a supply of computer software. The question of whether this is a supply of goods or services will have an influence on the place of supply for UK VAT purposes in international transactions.

In the United Kingdom, computer software is recognized as carrying an element of both goods and services. The goods are the tangible carrier medium on which the software resides, such as a CD, and the services comprise elements such as the data, programs, and/or instructions. The UK VAT treatment of these goods and services is determined by whether they are "normalized" (i.e., off-the-shelf) or "specific" (i.e., custom-made) software. For example, a supply of normalized software purchased from the Web site of a U.S. e-business and shipped to a UK business may have different UK VAT treatment than the same supply of software if it was downloaded from the same Web site.

"Normalized" software includes mass-produced items available freely to all customers who would use the software independently and with limited training. This would include software such as Microsoft Office products or similar packages available on a standardized basis to a wide retail market. "Specific" software would include items made to a customer's requirements or enhancements to software already made to a customer's requirements. It would also encompass enhancements to normalized software programs where these enhancements had been supplied under a contractual obligation to customers who had bought the original software program. Where "normalized" software is imported into the United Kingdom and the goods and services elements (i.e., carrier medium and program) are not separately identified, this would be treated as an importation of goods and UK VAT and customs duties would be payable. If the goods and services element of normalized software can be identified, UK VAT is only payable on the cost of the carrier medium, and the reverse-charge procedure is followed with respect to the supply of services (i.e., the program). With respect to specific software, the carrier medium is treated as a supply of services, and no customs duties are imposed. If the customer is a UK VAT registered business, they will need to account for UK VAT under the reverse-charge procedure.

The VAT rules governing electronically supplied services set out a detailed guide on what constitutes "digitized services," which includes "digital products." Examples of digital products include music, videos, and software. Unlike the UK VAT rules on importation of software carried on a physical medium, which distinguish between the goods and services element of software dependent on whether it is "normalized" or "specific," the definition of a digital product in the directive includes software that is off the shelf (i.e., normalized) or customized (i.e., specific). Supplies of digital products will be treated as a supply of services and not goods so that no customs duties will be chargeable within the European Union.

4. Taxation of E-Books The manner in which a transaction is carried out (i.e., downloaded or hard-copy purchase) may also alter the UK VAT treatment of a supply of services, as illustrated by two UK VAT cases. In *Emphasis Ltd.*, [1995] VATDR 419 (VAT Decision 13759), a catering company took orders for sandwiches, confectionary, and drinks by e-mail. The commissioners of HMRC had argued that this was a supply of catering services and so was standard rated and liable to UK VAT at the standard rate of 17.5 percent. The VAT and Duties Tribunal, however, found that it was akin to a telephone ordering service and so could be zero-rated (i.e. 0% rate), since this was the rate for equivalent food services. *Emphasis Ltd.* is a good example of the classical model in which a business is using the Internet as an extension of its existing operations, such as the supply of tangible items, to provide an additional channel to contract with customers. In this case, the way the product was supplied did not alter the VAT treatment.

In *Forexia (UK) Ltd.*, (1999) VAT Decision 16041, the company supplied a foreign-exchange and currencies newsletter to its clients by fax, by e-mail, and by making it available for download on its Web site. This was held to be a supply of information and so was standard-rated for UK VAT, in contrast with the supply of a tangible book, which would be zero-rated. Although the newsletter may have been printed off onto paper (i.e., a physical object) on receipt by the customers, it was the manner in which it was supplied that determined the VAT liability.

Following the *Forexia* case, HMRC issued guidelines on the zero rating of books in their Notice 701/10 published in August 2003. The notice covers the zero rating of items in VATA 1994, Sch. 8, Group 3 (Group 3 items) such as books, pamphlets, newspapers, journals, and printed music, which are derived from Article 5 of the EU Sixth VAT Directive. The notice sets out that the words used for Group 3 items are used in "their everyday sense," which means they are restricted to "goods produced on paper and similar materials such as card," so that most qualifying items will be products of the printing industry. The result is that written works in book or booklet form or newspapers or journals that consist of several large sheets of paper or as paper-bound publications will be zero-rated for UK VAT purposes, whereas the same written works in digital form would be standard-rated. Notwithstanding any customer preferences, an e-business of the classical model offering physical books for sale over the Internet would as such have a tax advantage over an e-business of the modern approach offering e-books or e-journals. Given the increasing popularity for customers of downloading digital products from the Internet and the improving capabilities of e-books, it is questionable whether this distinction is viable in the long-term, especially given increasing environmental sensitivities to the amount of paper that is used in producing physical books, newspapers, and journals. This also offends the concept of tax neutrality between e-commerce and conventional transactions that was put forward by the OECD.

VII. GOING OFFSHORE

Given the geographical flexibility of e-businesses, they should be ideally suited to being carried on from low-tax or no-tax jurisdictions. This final section considers some of the benefits and pitfalls of going offshore.

A. Taking Advantage of VAT Exemption on Low-Value Goods

Due to the cost of compliance in calculating and administering the collection and remittance for any VAT due on supplies of goods, the European Union introduced the Low-Value Consignment Relief whereby any goods imported from outside of the European Union with a value under £18 are exempt from VAT. The VAT exemption for small consignments (containing physical goods) does not apply to digital products.

This VAT exemption has been used as a tax-planning opportunity by certain businesses established in the Channel Islands. These businesses had used this exemption to avoid VAT on sales of CDs and DVDs into the United Kingdom. (Although the Channel Islands are within the customs territory of the European Community, they are outside the European Union for VAT purposes.) This allowed some digital businesses established in the Channel Islands to achieve a significant tax-saving advantage over competitors. The Jersey government has imposed restrictions to avoid large retailers such as Tesco plc., establishing a nominal offshore presence in the Channel Islands in order to use the VAT exemption. Now only bona fide, established retailers can continue to supply such goods from the Channel Islands. In the European Court of Justice (ECJ) decision in the case of *Dollond & Aitchison Limited*, ECJ Decision (C-491/04), the ECJ held that where Dollond & Aitchison Limited (D&O) had established a subsidiary in the Channel Islands that was within the D&O VAT group to dispense contact lenses to customers in the European Union in connection with the supply of ophthalmic services, which included annual eye examinations, this was a mixed supply. The offer of ophthalmic services and the imported goods (below the VAT exemption) was a "global offer in respect of which a single payment was made." The transaction value therefore included the value of the goods and the services provided, which was over the de minimis limit so that import VAT was due. Whilst this case was decided on its particular merits, it shows the limitations of certain forms of tax planning with regard to this particular VAT exemption.

B. Direct Tax Planning

One of the most significant benefits of running a digital business offshore is that profits may be liable to reduced rates of corporate income taxes. One potentially attractive option for a business engaged in e-commerce would be for it to set up a subsidiary in a low-tax jurisdiction that carries on the e-commerce activities of the group.

In order to be benefit from this type of tax-planning strategy, it will be necessary to ensure that the subsidiary is not resident in a high-tax jurisdiction (see section IV.C) and does not have a permanent establishment in a high-tax jurisdiction (see section IV.D.1). Even if these two requirements can be satisfied, many jurisdictions (including the UK) have adopted "controlled foreign company" or "passive foreign income" rules (CFC rules) which are intended to prevent the diversion of profits overseas. In the United Kingdom, if the CFC rules apply then the UK parent will be liable to UK corporation tax on the profits of the overseas subsidiary as they arise and not when they are transferred to the parent. There are certain exceptions to these rules, but they are likely to require either the majority of the overseas companies' profits to be distributed to the United Kingdom or for the overseas company to earn significant trading profits in the overseas jurisdiction.

Based on the decisions on the Cadbury Schweppes case, such a structure may be more successful if the business is set up in a low-tax EU jurisdiction, such as Ireland or Luxembourg, and that has a genuine business presence in the relevant jurisdiction. In such cases it may also be possible to rely on an applicable provision in a double-taxation treaty to ensure that any presence in the customer's jurisdiction, such as a warehouse or marketing activities, does not amount to a permanent establishment.

Chapter 16

Ukraine: E-Commerce Taxation in Ukraine

Olena V. Losevska
International Law Offices

I. THE NATURE AND EXTENT OF E-COMMERCE DEVELOPMENT IN UKRAINE

Recently, Ukraine has observed an unprecedented increase of Internet users. Today, practically every Ukrainian family has a PC connected to the World Wide Web. The spread of Internet use among the population has led to more and more users buying goods on the Internet, in online shops and through Internet auctions, and acquiring e-products. The use of Internet technology in business life has become standard for Western and Ukrainian domestic companies. However, Western companies use the Web not only for mailing and accessing information but also to perform specific commercial transactions, from which stems e-commerce. Development of such technologies promotes loss reduction, accelerates business procedures, and, as a result, increases a company's profitability.

In its broadest sense e-commerce is regarded as the sale of material and nonmaterial (such as information) goods and services via the Web. The e-commerce system includes not only the sale process itself but also an opportunity to expand the demand for products and services, computerize managerial functions related to sales and processing orders, and enhance the exchange of information between partners. The e-commerce process can be schematically divided into the following steps: (1) online marketing, (2) order processing or conclusion of transactions, (3) making payments, and (4) delivery and information support.

Unfortunately, due to the practically total absence of proper laws and regulations, business-to-business (B2B) models so far are scarcely developed in Ukraine and seldom employed by companies in their daily activities. In spite of a number of e-commerce-related laws adopted in Ukraine (such as those relating to electronic digital signatures, electronic documents, and electronic document circulation), e-commerce essentially has no legal regulation at all, or is regulated by basic juridical norms applied to non-electronic bargains. In particular, matters such as electronic settlement agreements, rules on the execution of electronic contracts, tax procedures and auditing of tax payments on Internet transactions, and the necessity of documentary proof for a company's actual existence, remain unaddressed.

Presently, there is no clear procedure about how electronic digital signatures should be used, and the Ukrainian government has not approved the state program on the introduction of electronic documents using electronic digital signatures. The absence of these real mechanisms not only restrains the development of e-commerce in the country but also impedes the interaction between citizens, companies, and public/local authorities. The current state of affairs does not of course enhance e-commerce's popularity among Ukrainian companies.

E-Commerce is a powerful instrument to stimulate economic activity and expand the market for products and services at the domestic and international levels. For this reason, Ukraine needs to adopt appropriate laws and create state programs that regulate this field, so that Ukrainian companies can become rightful participants in the electronic market.

This chapter will review current Ukrainian law applicable to e-commerce transactions and their taxation. This review will consider both positive and negative aspects of the legislative development in this field, as well as examine particular issues concerning e-commerce and taxation that are specific to Ukraine.

II. UKRAINIAN LEGISLATION ON E-COMMERCE TAXATION

A. Brief Review of Ukrainian E-Commerce Law

1. The Definition of E-Commerce There is no specific law in Ukraine that defines e-commerce. However, legislators cannot ignore the rapidly increasing number of Ukrainian Internet users.

Ukraine has adopted a number of laws containing definitions and interpretations of concepts related or ancillary to e-commerce, such as the Law of Ukraine "On Information," No. 2657XII (Oct. 2, 1992); the Law of Ukraine "On Protection of Information in Automated Systems," No. 80/94-BP (July 5, 1994); the Law of Ukraine "On Telecommunications," No. 1280-IV (Nov. 18, 2003); the Law of Ukraine "On Electronic Digital Signature," No. 852-IV (May 22, 2003); and the Law of Ukraine "On Electronic Documents and Electronic Documents Circulation," No. 851-IV (May 22, 2003).

Thus, under the Law of Ukraine "On Electronic Digital Signature," an electronic signature shall be the data in electronic form attached to other electronic data or logically related to them and identifying the one who signs such data.[1]

Article 9 of the Law of Ukraine "On Electronic Documents and Electronic Documents Circulation" defines the circulation of electronic documents as the combination of the processes of creating, sending, transferring, receiving, storing, using, and destroying

---

1 Law of Ukraine "On Electronic Digital Signature" no. 852-IV, art. 1 (22/05/2003).

electronic documents, along with confirming their integrity and, if necessary, confirming the document's receipt.

The Law of Ukraine "On Telecommunications" defines the Internet as a worldwide information system of common access that is based on a protocol determined by international standards.[2]

The "Instruction on Filling State Statistic Observation Forms Regarding Trade and Restaurant Networks" gives a definition of trade via Internet: a type of trade independent of shops where offers and orders are provided through the Internet.[3]

The definition of the "electronic trading system" is interesting: the combination of organizational, technological, and technical means used by a stock exchange to provide for the conclusion of stock deals and creation of stock contracts for securities and other financial instruments. This definition is included in the "Regulation on Functioning of Stock Exchanges."[4]

Based on the above interpretations of concepts related to or involving e-commerce, it is possible to infer a general, conceptual definition for it under Ukrainian law as follows: e-commerce is a type of trade effected through the Internet's worldwide information system, using a combination of organizational, technological, and technical means to provide sale offers and orders, as well as to conclude and perform agreements and contracts based on electronic documents and using electronic digital signatures.

2. Ukraine's Challenges and National Approach to E-Commerce Taxation Unlike a number of countries, where special e-commerce taxation rules have been established, Ukrainian aw does not have any particular rules on the taxation of e-commerce transactions. E-Commerce transactions are taxed under the same general rules provided for regular commercial operations.

Applying the so-called direct laws (general taxation laws) to Internet transactions results in certain problems:

A. THE PROBLEM OF IDENTIFYING A TAXPAYER The anonymity of an Internet user secures the anonymity of an e-transaction for tax purposes. There is a widespread practice in the Ukrainian Internet environment where a company will reside in one country, register its Web site address in another country, and locate the server hosting the site in a third country. As a result, it is often impossible as a practical matter to identify the subject of taxation.

B. EXTRATERRITORIALITY OF AN ELECTRONIC DEAL Due to the nonstationary nature of the Internet, often there is no connection between an Internet address and a company's

2 Law of Ukraine "On Telecommunications," no. 1280-IV, art. 1, (18/11/2003).

3 Trade via Internet, telephone, and TV are types of trade independent of shops where offers and orders are provided by means of Internet, telephone, and TV. (Item 3.3.8 of the "Instruction on Filling State Statistic Observation Forms Regarding Trade and Restaurant Networks" approved by the Order of State Statistics Committee of Ukraine no. 327 (24/10/2005)).

4 Item 1 of the "Regulation on Functioning of Stock Exchanges" approved by the Decision of State Commission on Securities and Stock Market no. 1542, (19/12/2006).

physical location (or a physical person), which does not allow one to determine a taxpayer's location, and consequently his or her mode of taxation (resident or nonresident). For example, while a company may register its domain name under Ukraine's country code top-level domain (.ua), the company itself may or may not be resident in Ukraine.

C. THE NONPHYSICAL NATURE OF AN E-COMMERCE DEAL E-Commerce allows traditional legal and tax documents to be prepared in electronic form, which cannot be considered and checked by public and tax authorities due to the absence of proper control mechanisms and the technical ability to realize such control.

Because there are no legislatively approved mechanisms allowing for real-time, online payments, Ukrainian Internet shops today are in fact acting as electronic "shop-windows" or order bureaus. In most cases Internet shops process electronic orders, and goods are physically delivered, with the payment being settled in cash to the delivery courier or by prepayment through a bank.

In Ukraine, Internet sales are performed as follows:

1. A potential customer visits an Internet shop site, chooses goods, and makes an order.
2. The buyer chooses a mode of payment so that the order can be processed. When the customer chooses prepayment, he or she either prints out the corresponding invoice, if the shop offers this option, or contacts the shop-keeper by phone or e-mail and receives this invoice from him or her.
3. Depending on the terms specified by the seller, the goods are delivered to the buyer by mail or courier service.
4. All the necessary paperwork for the goods is performed by courier on-site or before the goods are dispatched by mail to the customer. In the case of mail delivery, only advanced payment through the bank is available; courier delivery allows the customer to pay for the goods in cash to the courier.

As was noted above, the Laws of Ukraine "On Electronic Digital Signature" and "On Electronic Documents and Electronic Documents Circulation" passed in 2004 do not have any practical legal effect since the required implementing legislation was never adopted. As a result, documentary processing procedures for Internet transactions are in fact non-existent today (except for bank operations under the Customer-Bank system). Consequently, trade via the Internet is currently among the most risky areas of business in Ukraine.

For the above reasons, buyers of goods via Internet are mainly individuals. However, in this case and because of the legislatively unregulated documentary basis for such operations, conflicts often arise between a seller and a buyer. The most common are the seller's failure to deliver the goods paid for by the buyer, or the buyer's refusal to pay for the delivered goods. At this point, it is practically very difficult to settle these problems using the existing e-commerce laws because neither the fact of advanced payment for goods by a buyer nor the order receipt by a seller with a guarantee of further payment is supported by documents that have a legal status. Hence, proving such transactions before a court seems impossible.

Thus, since the laws regarding electronic documents and digital signatures are not yet implemented, Ukrainian e-commerce entrepreneurs have to follow traditional book-keeping and tax-accounting practices. Indeed, virtually all the necessary documents for e-commerce transactions are made on paper, as if the transactions were realized through an ordinary shop. In this way e-commerce entrepreneurs can avoid problems and claims from the Ukrainian tax authorities. Consequently, under this scenario, Ukrainian tax inspectors have no ability to control the volume of sales made through the Internet and determine whether they were taxed correctly. Sellers often report to the tax authorities the transactions they deem pertinent, while fiscal authorities have no technical resources to control the volume of sales made by an Internet shop.

Delivery of virtual goods or services (news, consultations, access to online games, etc.) is provided, obviously, via the Web. However, payment for such products (services) is not usually made in an electronic way. Thus, tracing the delivery of online products and fixing it by tax authorities seems impossible in Ukraine for the time being.

There are currently about a dozen electronic payment systems used by Ukrainians when buying goods or services over the Internet. The use of so-called virtual money (Web money) is currently the most popular form of payment and can be used through the following Web site: webmoney.ru. Web-money transfer (WMT) allows payments in real time by way of special units. The control of such virtual money is in the user's hand via WMT's software. The system supports several types of virtual money secured by various assets and kept in a corresponding electronic purse (Web purse). An online purchaser may only transfer Web money from his or her purse to an Internet shop or seller. Online buyers and Web-money users should first replenish their purses via the methods discussed below. Once the purse is replenished, online buyers can pay for their goods or services through transfers from their purse to the seller's.

There are several ways to replenish a purse on the Web-money site:

- By a Web-money card offered for purchase in Ukrainian and CIS cities;
- By special prepaid cards and vouchers;
- By purchase from an authorized dealer acting in the region;
- By bank or mail transfer, as well as transfer via special systems of swift money transfer;
- By cash in automates or automatic cash terminal;
- By exchanging the electronic currency of other payment systems;
- By exchanging cash for Web money in any of the certified exchange offices; and
- By obtaining funds from other users of the system as payment for goods, services and labor performed.

Any of the methods mentioned above allows for exchanging funds for Web money as well as exchanging Web money for cash. The system also provides for replenishing the virtual purse from a bank account and returning the funds back to the same account if they are not used.

These forms of electronic payment are rather new for Ukraine, and the law in force has no definition of the term "virtual money." Moreover, there are no laws that regulate the issuance of virtual money and revenue procedures. Yet, there are several viewpoints regarding the nature of virtual money and its legal use in sale contracts.

Electronic payments in Ukraine are regulated by the Law of Ukraine "On Payment Systems and Funds Transfer in Ukraine," No. 2346-II (Apr. 5, 2001) (hereinafter Law on Payment Systems). The Law on Payment Systems defines "payment system" as follows: it is a payment organization, and a member of the payment system, and the integrity of relationships arising between them during the transfer of funds. The transfer of funds is an obligatory function of the payment system.[5]

Legal entities or physical persons can participate in a payment system provided that they are part of a relationship engaged in the transfer of funds. A member of a payment system is a legal entity properly formed and licensed that renders services concerned with the provision of transfer of funds and, in accordance with Ukrainian law, is entitled to render such services within Ukrainian territory.[6]

Currently, there are only two types of companies in Ukraine entitled to accept payments for third parties: commercial banks duly licensed by the National Bank of Ukraine (NBU), and nonbank financial institutions bearing a financial company certificate as well as a license for the transfer of funds. It is quite obvious that sites such as webmoney.ru are not commercial banks having an NBU license, and rarely will a financial institution obtain a financial company certificate together with the license for transfer of funds.

Therefore, if one considers the system of payment on the Internet for goods and services by virtual money as a kind of credit card payment, the Law on Payment Systems is not observed in this situation. If, however, one deems the virtual money not a means of payment but as a symbolic notation of goods or services defined by special units, a kind of barter system can be determined here: the buyer pays for received goods or services with goods or services as well. Unfortunately, this system contradicts Ukrainian law because the use of barter and off-set is prohibited in transactions between individuals, who are the payers of the single tax, as will be discussed below. Moreover, in spite of its popularity and convenience, the use of this kind of payment is also legally risky for Ukrainian companies.

3. Taxation of Operations Connected with the Sale of Goods/Services via Internet (Business to Customer) In the absence of dedicated laws regulating transactions on the Internet, Ukrainian law regards the sale of goods/services over the Internet as a normal sales-purchasing operation subject to regular taxation rules.

The procedures for VAT taxation on the sale of goods/services are regulated by the Law of Ukraine "On Value-Added Tax," No. 168/97-BP (Apr. 3, 1997), as amended (the VAT Law). According to the VAT Law, the taxation rate amounts to 20 percent and is levied upon the contractual price of goods/works/services. The date when the tax is charged is the date of the event: either the date the goods/works/services were accepted, or when

---

5 Law on Payment Systems and Funds Transfer in Ukraine, no. 2346-II, art.1, item 1.29 (05/04/2001).

6 *Id.* at art.1, item 1.43.

payment for such goods/works/services is received[7]. Thus, the levying date can occur even when the seller has only handed over the goods but has not yet received payment.

In accordance with ¶ 3.1.1 of the VAT Law, the object of VAT taxation shall be the taxpayer's operations related to the delivery of goods and services, with the place of their transfer or grant within the customs territory of Ukraine. Moreover, if goods are forwarded or transported by the seller or buyer or a third person, the place of the goods' delivery shall be regarded as the place where the goods are at the moment of dispatch or transportation.[8] However, the VAT Law stipulates that if goods are sold via the Internet, regardless of the location of the domain registration, the seller's location or residence shall be regarded as the place of the goods' delivery in this case.[9]

Under Ukrainian law, a buyer who purchases goods over the Internet should pay the seller the VAT as included in the goods' price, and the seller is obliged to transfer the VAT amount to the state. In this regard, one of the critical features and problems of the trade in goods and services through the Internet in Ukraine is that Internet traders must register for VAT regardless of the volume of their taxable operations. As soon as a subject of economic activity starts working and opens an Internet shop, he or she is already under obligation to register as a taxpayer for VAT.[10] This rule does not apply to persons whose taxation is handled through the simplified taxation procedures discussed below.

As for rendering services to customers with the use of computer networks, the place where the services are delivered will be the place of the seller's registration. When such services are rendered by nonresidents to residents of Ukraine, the place of delivery is Ukraine, and the services are subject to a 20 percent VAT. In accordance with ¶ 2.3.3 of the VAT Law (*see* note 10), a nonresident providing such services must register his or her permanent representative's office in the territory of Ukraine to handle VAT payments.

Unfortunately, this rule seems to be inapplicable in practice. Many foreign companies render services through the Internet to both Ukrainian companies and physical persons. Most often, these are the so-called content services, such as providers of software, consulting, advertising, designing, and other similar services. Technically, having

---

7 The date of commencement of the tax obligations as to the sale of goods/works/services shall be the date, within the relevant tax period, when any of the following events occurs first (earlier): either the date of transfer of funds from the buyer (customer) to the taxpayer's bank account as payment for goods/works/services for sale, and in the event of sale of goods/works/services for cash; the date when the cash is received by the taxpayer's cash office and if there is no such cash office; the date when cash is received by the banking institution servicing the taxpayer; or the date of goods shipment, and for works/services, the date of the drawing up of the document certifying the fact of fulfillment of works/services by the taxpayer. Ukraine Law "On Value-Added Tax," no. 168/97-BP as amended, art. 7, ¶ 7.3.1, item 7.3 (03/04/1997).

8 *Id.*, at art. 6, ¶ a, item 6.4.

9 *Id.*, at art. 6, ¶ d, item 6.4.

10 A person subject to obligatory registration as a payer of VAT is defined as the following:

> A person supplying goods or services in the customs territory of Ukraine with the use of global or local computer networks; moreover, a non-resident person is entitled to exercise such activities only through his permanent representative office registered in the territory of Ukraine.

Ukraine Law "On Value-Added Tax," no. 168/97-BP as amended, art. 2, ¶ 2.3.3, item 2.3 (03/04/1997).

rendered such a service and been paid for it, a foreign company is obliged to register a permanent representative's office in Ukraine to pay the VAT. To open a permanent representative's office in Ukraine, however, would require certain expenses. Yet, this fact notwithstanding, a foreign company rendering Internet services to a great number of persons and companies would in practice likely not, as a rule, register a permanent representative's office in Ukraine to pay VAT.

Ukraine regulates taxation of the profit earned from Internet sales of goods or services based on several factors:

1. What taxation system is used by the entity that earned the profits;
2. Whether this entity is a legal entity or physical person; and
3. Whether the entity is a resident or a non-resident of Ukraine.

The basic method of taxing profits is the "common" profit taxation system as set up by the Ukraine Law "On Enterprise Profit Tax," No. 334/94-BP (Dec. 28, 1994) (hereinafter Enterprise Profit Tax Law). This system taxes profits—that is, the difference between a taxpayer's gross income and gross expenses—at a rate of 25 percent. The key issue for this basic taxation method is the date when tax liability arises for a taxpayer. As for the VAT, this is either the earlier of the date the goods/works/services were delivered or transferred, or the date payment was received for them.[11] Therefore, as soon as an Internet trader delivers goods or renders services or receives payment for either, the profits of this transaction should be included in the taxpayer's gross income for the relevant tax period.

A number of problematic issues arise when applying the provisions of the Enterprise Profit Tax Law to Internet traders. Inasmuch as the main buyers of goods and services through the Internet are physical persons who usually pay for such goods/services in cash handed over to a courier delivering the goods, Internet traders can include income from these operations in the tax period when they expect the largest gross expenses, thereby showing the lowest profit gained. It is very difficult for the tax authorities to check, and furthermore prove, the real date of levying for a particular taxpayer. It is unlikely that Ukrainian couriers have cash machines on hand to note the transaction and hand a bill to the customer on-site. And, to compare the date of the goods' order with the date of their shipment from the Internet shop's warehouse is rather difficult as well. Therefore, an Internet trader has the ability to control its profits in any given tax period, and consequently pay less tax.

On the other hand, under the Enterprise Profit Tax Law an Internet trader may well encounter, say, the problem of the "usual price" rule applying[12]. According to this law,

---

11 *See* Ukraine Law on Enterprise Profit Tax, no. 334/94-BP, art. 11, ¶ 11.3.1, item 11.3 (28/12/1994).

12 "Usual price" is defined as a contractual price of goods or services, if otherwise is not stipulated by law. The usual price is deemed to be a fair market price, unless proven otherwise. The fair market price is a price at which goods/services are transferred to another person, provided that (1) the seller is willing to transfer such goods/services; (2) the customer is willing to obtain them without any constraints; (3) both parties are independent legally and de facto; and (4) the parties possess sufficient information about such goods (services), as well as market prices for

the tax authorities bear the burden of proving that the contractual price does not satisfy the "usual price" requirement is placed on the tax authorities. During an audit, the tax authorities are entitled to make an inquiry, and the taxpayer should provide evidence of the level of contractual prices or refer to the sub-item 1.20.1 (that the contractual price is a fair market price; see note 12).

Since there is an opportunity to reduce business expenses while trading goods via the Internet (no need to pay rent for premises, to keep a big staff, to buy special machinery, etc.), such goods are often cheaper than those in bricks-and-mortar shops. This is the main reason buyers prefer Internet shopping. In such a situation, an Internet trader would be obliged to provide support for his or her prices to the tax authorities, which is undesirable, since such evidence would have to reflect all aspects of the trader's activities, which could ultimately result in additional penalties for him or her.

Because the Enterprise Profit Tax Law's provisions are not really appropriate for the specific conditions of e-commerce, both taxpayers and controlling authorities face challenges, which mostly do not come out in favor of the Internet traders.

In addition to the basic taxation system in Ukraine, there is a simplified taxation system regulated by the provisions of the Decree "On the Simplified System of Taxation, Accounting and Reporting for Small Business Entities," No. 727/98 (as amended by the Decree of President of Ukraine, No. 746/99, dated June 28, 1999), dated July 3, 1998. For legal entities[13] the simplified taxation system provides two options:

1. Paying the single tax at the rate of 10 percent, without VAT being levied and paid; or
2. Paying the single tax at the rate of 6 percent, with VAT being levied and paid by the common rules. In this case, the base of taxation will not be profits but total income—specifically, the receipts from goods/works/services realization.[14] Settlements in this situation must be done only in cash; no exchange (barter) or other mutual

---

identical (or homogeneous) goods (services). Ukraine Law on Enterprise Profit Tax, No. 334/94-BP, art. 1, item 1.20, sub-item 1.20.1 (28/12/1994).

The usual price is determined based on comparable data for sales of identical or homogeneous goods/services or public data on conditions of sale. Where prices for goods/services are regulated by the state, the usual price is that established by the state (except for the case when the state establishes minimum sale prices). Where there are no transactions with identical or homogeneous goods/services, or where it is impossible to determine the price because the comparable information is absent or is not publicly available, the contractual price shall be deemed to be the usual price.

13 The simplified system of taxation, accounting, and reporting is introduced for legal entities—subjects of the economic activity of any kind of organizational-legal form or ownership having an average number of registered employees not exceeding fifty persons and the quantity of receipts from the production and sale of goods/works/services sale does not exceed UAH$1 million per year. Presidential Decree "On the Simplified System of Taxation, Accounting, and Reporting for Small Business Entities," item 1, ¶ 1, (as amended by the Decree of President of Ukraine, no. 746/99, dated 28/06/1999).

14 The receipts from the realization of the production and sale of goods, works, or services is considered the amount actually received by the subject of the economic activity in its current bank account and/or in the cash box for performing sale operations. *Id.*, at item 1, ¶ 3.

settlements (off-set) can be applied with this form of taxation. The date of tax levying is defined by the cash-box mode, that is, by the date of payment in cash received.

For physical persons who are subjects of entrepreneurial activity (hereinafter physical persons-SEA),[15] this system envisages monthly payment of a fixed amount, with a maximum of UAH$200, or US$40. Such a taxpayer can earn income up to UAH$500,000 (US$100,000) per year with no additional tax levied. Exchange bargains (barter) and mutual settlements (off-set) are prohibited for this system of taxation.

This taxation system is the most common and popular in Ukraine in the small business sphere. Apart from the minimum tax rates, the physical persons-SEA who are single taxpayers (hereinafter physical persons-SEA STP) enjoy additional advantages; in particular, they do not have to use digital cash-control machines to settle with customers; they are not subject to most of the obligatory payments to the government; and they are entitled to use simplified procedures of accounting and reporting.

The simplified taxation system for physical persons is widely used in the e-commerce field due to its advantages. In particular, services such as Web design, Web-site creation, online consulting, small Internet shops (whose maximum income is UAH$500,000 per year), and many other Internet projects prefer to proceed under this mode of taxation.

There are also many variations on when a physical person-SEA STP can provide for payments and other necessary operations when he or she is just a part of a larger Internet project. Unfortunately, these are not always suitable for large Ukrainian companies acting around the country or who place their shares stock exchanges.

4. Taxation of Bargains Concluded via Internet (Business to Business) When two companies carry out commercial transactions with the help of Internet, their commercial relations can reach a new level and their partnership can be enhanced. E-Commerce also gives companies more opportunities for activities in the global market. The B2B pattern may be open (i.e., visible to and visited by users or other possible partners) or closed (i.e., existing only for certain partners or working groups and performing only certain technological functions). B2B systems often reflect fully automated interactions between two companies' business processes. From a legal standpoint, to secure such activities it is necessary to have a legal basis for electronic document turnover, which allows for providing settlements through the Internet and is a vital condition for providing transactions within the Web.

It is worth noting that realization of such projects as trading and concluding bargains between companies in electronic media is currently the most problematic issue for Ukrainian business. Apart from the insufficient level of management development and

15 "Physical persons" means individuals who perform economic activity without creating a legal entity and who do not employ more than ten employees per year, including members of their families, as well as whose amount of receipts from production realization does not exceed UAH$500,000 UAH per year. *Id.*, at item 1, ¶ 1.

automation of most Ukrainian companies, as well as other technical and managerial reasons, B2B transactions are subject to a number of problems in the legal sphere:

1. The large number of legal requirements for concluding transactions between legal entities (certain proceedings, notary verification etc.).
2. The tax authorities' lack of special technical facilities to audit taxation of such bargains. Ukrainian law requires that the result of every trade bargain must be shown in the company's tax accounting in a prescribed way.
3. The distrust of Internet companies themselves because this sphere of trade is practically unregulated, and if any problems arise, the claiming party will have difficulty proving anything.
4. Complex procedures when a nonresident is involved in these Internet transactions, because Ukrainian law stipulates that a nonresident is entitled to conduct activities in the country only if he or she registers a permanent representative's office there.

At first glance, the bargain procedure for Internet transactions is mostly the same as the common one set forth in the Civil Code of Ukraine. If a bargain proposal on the Internet contains all the essential conditions of a contract and shows the contractors' intention to be bound if the offer is accepted, such a proposal has all the features of an offer. Usually, a customer fills in an electronic order form and then sends it back. Acceptance in this case is regarded as the act of filling in and sending back the form to the offeror.[16] However, there are some distinctions between e-contracts and "regular" contracts that cause collisions with current law:

- The mode in which the bargain is concluded, that is, the exchange of electronic data via the Internet;
- The contract's format.

Under Ukrainian civil law, bargains between legal entities must be concluded in written form;[17] bargains made through written electronic communication are permitted.[18] However, the law also requires that a bargain concluded by a legal entity must be signed and stamped. The bargain must be signed by the person authorized to do so under the entity's constituting documents, power of attorney, legal norms, or other civil law acts, and stamped.[19] The electronic offer and the form of its acceptance provide for use of a certain analogue to the personal signature of "regular" contracting parties. Only in this case is the bargain deemed valid and having legal force. According to the Ukraine Law "On Electronic Digital Signature," an electronic digital signature is used by physical persons and legal entities to identify the undersigned and verify the

16 Ukraine Civil Code, no. 435-IV, art. 641, 642 (16/01/2003).

17 *Id.*, at Art. 208, item 1, ¶ 1.

18 The bargain is considered as performed in written form if the will of the parties is stated by way of teletype, electronic or another technical means of connection. *Id.*, at Art. 207, item 2, ¶ 1.

19 Ukraine Civil Code, no. 435-IV, art. 207, item 2, ¶ 2 (16/01/2003).

integrity of the electronic data, but its use shall not alter the procedure for signing contracts and other documents as legally required for bargaining in writing.[20]

Therefore, based on the above, one could conclude that the form of a contract concluded via Internet (by exchanging documents through electronic communications) is the type of written form of contract that meets the law's requirements with regard to bargains concluded by legal entities, provided such a contract has an authorized person's proper electronic digital signature. Unfortunately, in Ukraine there are no properly registered certification parties for electronic signatures necessary for this procedure at this time. Besides, there is no regulation of the procedures for identifying electronic documents, defining the dates of their sending, and other necessary procedures for securing the electronic document turnover as has been provided by the Ukraine Law "On Electronic Documents and Electronic Documents Circulation."[21]

The matter of notary verification for bargains concluded on the Web not is solved either. Although the Law of Ukraine "On Electronic Documents and Electronic Documents Circulation" allows for such a possibility,[22] there is no legislatively stipulated procedure for providing such verification at this moment.

If a bargain is concluded with a nonresident, then it is also necessary to consider the provisions of the Law of Ukraine "On Foreign Economic Activities" (hereinafter the FEA Law), No. 959-XII (Apr. 16, 1991); provisions of Chapter VII of the Economy Code of Ukraine (hereinafter ECU); and those of the Regulation "On Foreign Economic Contracts" (Agreements) form as approved by the Order of the Ministry of Economy and European Integration Issues of Ukraine, No. 201 (Sept. 6, 2001).

The FEA Law requires that a foreign economic contract (agreement) should be concluded by an FEA subject or its representative in a simple written form if an international agreement of Ukraine or its law do not otherwise provide. The content of a foreign economic agreement (contract) is quite strictly regulated by the law, and the contract may be deemed invalid in court if it fails to meet the requirements of the law of Ukraine or its international agreements. The law regulates not only the issues that must be included in an FEA agreement but also the content of its clauses.

As was mentioned in section 3 above, besides the requirements for the form of an agreement, it is also necessary to consider the provisions of the VAT Law and Enterprise Profit Taxation Law when bargaining with a nonresident, namely, those regarding the obligatory registration of a permanent representative's office in Ukraine for a nonresident conducting business activities and earning income in the country.

Analyzing the law governing the conclusion of bargains and signing of contracts by legal entities shows that this process is too complicated and laborious to be smoothly

20 Ukraine Law "On Electronic Digital Signature," no. 852-IV, art. 4, ¶¶ 2, 3 (22/05/2003).

21 The procedure for electronic circulation shall be determined by the state bodies, local authorities, enterprises, institutions, and organizations of all types of ownership in accordance with the law. Ukraine Law "On Electronic Documents and Electronic Documents Circulation," no. 851-IV, art. 9, ¶ 2 (22/05/2003).

22 The notary verification of a civil agreement concluded by means of electronic document(s) creation is performed according to the procedure stipulated by law. *Id.*, at Art. 8, ¶ 4.

transferred into the electronic format, even once the public procedures for electronic signature use and electronic document turnover are developed and implemented.

Given how the conclusion of electronic bargains appears in a company's tax accounting and how the fiscal authorities audit these records, it is necessary to admit that none of the existing forms and control techniques in Ukraine are tailored for taxation of Internet transactions. The reasons for this were discussed above. Nonetheless, the tax authorities are already working on a system for taxing e-commerce companies, since these companies' activities are of great interest to them.

The tax authorities more and more actively use online search systems and other resources that allow them to gather information on Web sites and their owners or to trace the paths up to the final end-user's PC. By examining the links, one can discover "connected" sites and can reveal affiliated resources and services' payment conditions. As a result, once they discover details of income earned by Internet companies, the tax authorities may demand from banks confirmation of gains by a particular entity or person. Thus, with the absence of clear legislative norms regulating various aspects of companies' activities via Internet, tax authorities could discover violations in tax accounting and payment by even the most cautious companies. Consequently, such a company may be assessed considerable penalties by the Ukrainian government.

In Ukraine the real e-commerce process will only be possible when a normative system of securing such bargains and a system of controlling settlements on such bargains appear. Only under these conditions would companies have the ability to proceed correctly with and document a bargain, while tax authorities would be able to easily check the activities of those companies within a set of legally defined rules for auditing.

III. DEVELOPMENT PROSPECTS OF E-COMMERCE AND LEGISLATION CONNECTED WITH E-COMMERCE TAXATION IN UKRAINE

In 1996 the United Nations (UN) General Assembly adopted a model law on e-commerce that was developed and approved by the UN Commission on International Trade Law (UNCITRAL). This law should be applied to any kind of information in the data-exchange format used for trade activities. The term "data exchange" refers to the information prepared, sent, received, or kept via electronic, optical, or similar means, including the electronic exchange of data, e-mail, telegraph, telex, or telefax.

According to the UN Model Law, the basic legal principle of e-commerce (for both international and national markets) lies in the following: parties who conclude an electronic bargain cannot dispute it only on the basis that it was concluded electronically (i.e., with the use of electronic techniques), was not based upon traditional paperwork, and was not accompanied by the traditional personal signature.

In 2007, a draft law on e-commerce (hereinafter the draft) was submitted to the Verkhovna Rada (Parliament) of Ukraine. Article 1 of the draft mentioned in particular that "the purpose of this Law is to provide legal conditions for E-commerce: securing the rights and liabilities of the parties providing E-commerce, setting up rules to perform transactions using electronic documents as well as admitting electronic documents as evidence in court" On the whole, the draft submitted is based on the UN Model Law, but is adapted to national conditions. Considering the prospects for e-commerce development in Ukraine, it is worth considering the draft's following provisions.

A. Electronic Documents and Their Contents

According to the list of definitions referred to in Article 3 of the draft, an electronic document is defined as a document whose information is conveyed as electronic data containing, inter alia, obligatory details such as an electronic signature, and that can be formatted, transferred, processed, stored on a physical storage device, and transferred or restored to a form of presentation readable by humans. In other words, the symbols and ways they are comprehended and manipulated are not an electronic document if they cannot be perceived visually.

Electronic documents are necessary to carry out electronic trade. The draft defines electronic documents as documents concluding civil deals as well as identifying other business rights and liabilities through electronic means. According to the draft, the right to conduct e-commerce is granted to any entity involved in economic activities. Such a right originates from the moment of a legal entity or physical person-SEA registers with the state and requires no additional licensing.

B. Concluding and Acknowledgment of Electronic Contracts

The draft suggests that e-commerce contracts can be concluded only by the exchange of electronic-documents exchange where it is clearly demonstrable that a document is sent by a contract party, while an offer may be forwarded either by the offeror him- or herself or by an automatic information system programmed by the offeror or on his or her behalf. In this case the contract would be deemed concluded from the moment the offeror receives an acceptance, while the acceptor's confirmation of the offer's receipt would not be deemed an acceptance if the confirmation does not so provide, the offer does not mention it, nor is it envisaged by an additional agreement between the parties.

Also, the draft suggests regulating the matter of time and place of conclusion of an e-contract. A document should be deemed as sent at the moment when it passes into the information system and is beyond the document signer's control. The receipt time for such a document should be deemed the moment when it passes into the information system as defined by the receiver, and if it is not defined, the moment the document is received by the receiver. The place of conclusion of an electronic contract may be assigned by the parties on their own judgment. Otherwise, the document's origin should be the sender's usual location, and the destination the receiver's usual location. Thus, if a contract is to be concluded at the moment the offeror receives the acceptance, the place of the deal will be the offeror's usual location.

The contract itself must contain certain provisions set forth in Ukrainian civil law, as well as some other essential obligatory provisions. The latter are the techniques for concluding a contract, the mode and procedure of acceptance, and the mode of storage and presentation of electronic documents, the conditions of electronic access to such documents, as well as the procedures for providing hard copies.

The draft states that an electronic document cannot be copied in electronic format but only on paper, with all the electronic copies electronically signed being the originals.

Also under the draft, any documents may be electronically formatted, but they must bear an electronic signature. The electronic signature is the electronic data attached to other data and logically related to them and used for confirming their authenticity as well as the identity of the undersigned. The electronic signature can be simple, substantial (connected to the signer only using a signature creation tool), or qualified (created with the use of a personal key having the key-substantiating certificate and by way of a reliable signature creation tool). To prove the key's identity and authenticity, the key is subject to certification by a keys certification center, and its certificate is the electronic data connecting the key and possibly some other data elements to a particular person or object and certifying the key's possession by a particular person or object.

The electronic signature must be valid. An electronic signature is valid unless an unauthorized key or a key with an invalid certificate is used when the signature is created, or if the signature creation key does not conform to the signature verification key, or if the integrity of the key certificate data is broken or the key is used without permission, as well as in any other case where the key verification was negative. The draft suggests conferring the burden of proving key invalidity on a person who disputes its originality.

C. Particular Issues on the Legality of Electronic Documents

The draft provides rules regarding validity or invalidity of certain documents. According to the current civil legislation, certain kinds of contracts are subject to notary verification. Thus, a rule that would allow for notary verification of electronic documents by affixing notaries' personal electronic signatures has been proposed. It should be noted that this creates certain problems for notary verification of some transactions, because not every notary has an electronic signature. At the same time, the draft ignored the issue of the procedure for state registration of an electronic contract that is subject to such registration.

Electronic contracts, like contracts on paper, are recognized as admissible evidence in the court. Such evidence is to be presented in the original unless the court considers the paper copy sufficient.

Unfortunately, due to existing deficiencies, the introduced draft cannot be considered a sufficient legislative base for further development of e-commerce in Ukraine. Perhaps the Verkhovna Rada will eliminate the above-mentioned deficiencies during the discussion process. Additionally, it is necessary to develop a number of procedures and to implement serious measures providing state bodies with due technique maintenance. Such measures are essential for the efficacy of norms stipulated by the Ukraine Laws "On Electronic Digital Signature" and "On Electronic Documents and Electronic Documents Circulation," as well as for implementation of the draft provisions.

The first steps have already been made. In 2007 the Verkhovna Rada created the Draft Law of Ukraine "On State Program of Implementation of Electronic Document Circulation with the Use of Electronic Digital Signature." When it comes into effect, electronic document circulation will receive not only legislative regulation but also a program for implementation and development at the national level.

In Ukraine the legal regulation of e-commerce has not yet been implemented. Once the above-mentioned draft laws are adopted, the system will develop an interrelated set of rules at the international and national levels. It would be reasonable to involve companies conducting e-commerce and the organizations that provide the work of the Web itself in the development of the improved civil law. It will be important for Ukraine not to lag behind the processes happening in the electronic business sphere when creating corresponding international legislation and integrating into the world economy.

In sum, e-commerce can considerably facilitate the activities of domestic businessmen: they can perform operations with their business partners even without leaving the office or traveling to meetings. This will save time and let home businesses reach a new level in the national economy.

PART V

Latin America

Chapter 17

Argentina: E-Commerce Taxation in Argentina

Alfaro Abogados*
Buenos Aires, New York, London Madrid

I. E-COMMERCE IN ARGENTINA

E-Commerce taxation in Argentina must be understood within the context of its market evolution. In this sense, e-commerce in Argentina has developed at a slower pace than other countries in the region. Despite a strong growth during 2006 and 2007, Argentina is still behind its Latin American neighbors in terms of e-commerce sales and gross domestic product (GDP). In 2007, e-commerce in Argentina represented 0.3 percent of the GDP, compared to 0.43 percent in Chile and 0.38 percent in Brazil. The Argentine Web-site share in the e-commerce market is of 50 percent, compared to 70 percent in Brazil.[1] Reasons for this situation are attributed to (1) the 2001 economic crisis that created certain financial and economic constraints in Argentina and (2) the existence of broadband users with low data transfer speed—an average speed of 512 kilobits per second—which initially inhibited new users. Since 2006, however, e-commerce in Argentina has grown 167 percent to an annual total amount of US$739 million, accompanying a 9 percent average growth of the economy per year and an increase in consumer confidence. The Internet, now positioned as a mandatory channel for commercialization of products and services, is becoming one of the most valuable business models, and it is expected to replace other traditional commercial channels in the years to come. Nevertheless, as it will be discussed in this article, e-commerce tax legislation and jurisprudence is still incipient. E-Commerce tax cases are solved by application of traditional taxation rules.

---

* alfaro@alfarolaw.com

1 Mercedes García Bartelt, *Negocios por Internet,* LA NACION 23 (Aug. 25, 2008).

E-Commerce in US$ Million[2]

	2003	*2004*	*2005*	*2006*	*2007*
Brazil	757	1289	2270	3541	4899
Mexico	296	504	567	868	1377
Venezuela	85	140	253	490	821
Argentina	83	162	281	619	739
Chile	79	104	243	472	687

II. GENERAL OVERVIEW OF THE ARGENTINE TAXATION SYSTEM

A. Different Jurisdictional Levels of Taxation

Argentine taxes are levied at three different jurisdictional levels: federal, provincial, and municipal. Federal taxes, especially value-added tax (VAT) and social security contributions yield most of the state revenue. In addition to those taxes, the federal government levies the income tax, the assets tax, excise taxes, tax on personal assets, custom duties, and tax on financial transactions. Provinces levy taxes primarily on gross receipts (turnover tax), stamp taxes, and taxes on real estate. Together with municipalities, they also levy fees for services.

The federal income tax is 35 percent; VAT, in general, is 21 percent on sales of goods and services, with some reduced exemptions according to the activity involved; gross income tax is levied at provincial level at rates of 1.5 percent or higher.

B. Double-Taxation Treaties

Argentina has signed twenty double-taxation treaties that, according to the National Constitution, have a higher authority than local legislation. Treaties have been signed with Australia, Austria, Belgium, Bolivia, Brazil, Canada, Chile, Denmark, Great Britain, Finland, France, Germany, Netherlands, Italy, Norway, United States of America, Spain, Sweden, Switzerland, and Russia.[3] Argentina's double-taxation treaty model follows in general terms the Organization for Economic Cooperation and Development (OECD) model, even though the country is not a member of this organization. On the other hand, double-taxation treaties with Latin American countries follow the Andean group model.

III. TAXATION OF E-COMMERCE IN ARGENTINA

A. Absence of Legal Framework

Argentina has no specific legal framework applicable to taxation of electronic transactions, and therefore general tax rules apply. Hence, as it occurs in the rest of the

2 Mercedes Garcia Bartelt *Negocios por Internet*, LA NACION 23 (Aug. 25, 2008).)

3 The Argentina treaties with United States and Russia are not in force yet.

countries, the special characteristics of e-commerce, including detachability from location, relative anonymity, mobility of the parties involved, are challenging the usefulness of traditional territory-based tax principles to address e-commerce transactions.

B. Direct Taxation: Income Tax

1. Taxation and Residence Pursuant to the Argentine Income Tax Law (ITL), Argentine residents are taxed on their worldwide income, whereas nonresidents are subject to withholding tax only on their Argentine-source income at different effective rates, depending on the type of income derived. To determine taxable income, taxpayers are allowed to deduct their ordinary and necessary business expenses, including (with some restrictions) royalties, technical assistance fees, and interest. There are two main concepts that determine *residence* in Argentina: nationality and permanence in the country. Natural persons are considered residents if they are Argentine nationals and do not stay abroad for more than 12 months. On the other hand, foreigners, will be considered Argentine residents if they stay in Argentina for more than 12 months. Companies are considered residents in Argentina if they are incorporated in Argentina or if they have a permanent establishment in the country. For e-commerce purposes, the most important issue is the delimitation of the concept of "permanent establishment" that defines the possibility of the local tax authorities to tax the worldwide income involved.

In Argentina, the lack of a clear criterion regarding the taxation of e-commerce generates a conflict of jurisdiction that leads either to a double taxation or to a lack of taxation of such activities. Traditional rules for determining which country has jurisdiction to tax a company's worldwide income-based on the principle of residence by reference to the place of formation, the place of registered office, or the place of effective management—are more difficult to apply to taxpayers engaged in e-commerce. Indeed, the parameters established in tax treaties for the purpose of apportioning tax powers among states in case of conflicts,—most of which are based on the place of effective management principle, are overridden in an area such as e-commerce, where the company's managing bodies can be mobile and located in different jurisdictions during a fiscal year. In this regard, it can be extremely difficult to determine which place is the company's place of effective management. As mentioned above, this situation creates the potential for double taxation or no taxation at all.

2. Permanent Establishment The ITL does not apply the term "permanent establishment," as used internationally by the OECD, but rather uses the term "stable establishment" without providing a clear definition for this term. This lack of legal definition, together with a lack of unified legal precedents and regulatory decisions, prevents codification under Argentinean law of common criteria for what should be considered a "permanent establishment." The following criteria are used by the Argentinean jurisprudence and doctrine to determine "stable establishment."[4]

---

4 Carlos A. Forcada, *El Comercio Electronico*, Aspectos Impositivos del Comercio Electrónico, xxiii Jornadas Latinoamericanas de Derecho Tributario, Relatoría Nacional (2006).

A. ARGENTINE INCOME TAX CRITERIA Law 25,063 included the term "stable establishment" in section 128. This regulation was originally created to regulate Argentinean residents conducting business abroad through stable establishments. Since there is no definition or regulation applicable to nonresidents conducting transactions in the country, the definition in section 128 is also applicable to nonresidents. The term "stable establishment" has the following characteristics: (1) it must be an organization, (2) the organization must constitute a company, and (3) the company should be permanent or stable. This last expression of stability is considered to be similar to the international concept of permanent establishment. Argentine tax authorities also consider that (1) permanent establishment (PE) implies a head office and an activity developed in it or through it; (2) the PE has to be organized as a company, which implies the existence of certain management, structure, and capital; and (3) the PE requires stability which implies the intention to last or remain.[5]

B. PRESUMED MINIMUM INCOME CRITERIA The Argentinean tax laws include rules on "presumed minimum income." Taxation on presumed minimum income incorporates a broader definition of stable establishment that also includes mere groundwork or auxiliary activities. Under the presumed minimum income rule, stable establishment is defined as the usage of facilities with the purpose of acquiring, storing, exhibiting, or delivering merchandise or the maintenance of a fixed place of business to gather information for publicity purposes, scientific investigations, or the like. The only activity beyond the scope of this definition would be the activity of independent contractors acting as agents or intermediaries during the ordinary course of their business.

C. DOUBLE-TAXATION TREATY, OECD, AND UN MODEL CRITERIA Except for the treaties signed with Bolivia and Chile—both based on the "source criteria"—all other treaties use the term "permanent establishment" based on the concept derived from the OECD model and United Nations (UN) model. Besides the application to companies from countries that are parties to the treaties, the criteria based on these models is also a useful interpretative tool for the Argentinean domestic legislation, and courts have used it in certain cases.[6]

D. OTHER STANDARDS In some cases, courts have rejected the idea of PE by considering necessary the existence of a "head office" and decision-making executives with legal duties and responsibilities within the national territory. In a number of cases, tax authorities have also requested the idea of "risk assumption" to configure the PE concept.

E. COMPARING THE OECD MODEL TEST FOR PE WITH THE STABLE ESTABLISHMENT DEFINITION UNDER THE ARGENTINE SYSTEM According to the OECD model and comments, a finding of PE for e-commerce purposes requires complying with certain tests. The following

5 118/99 DAL.
6 *Pesquera Santa Elena S.A. Fish Managemnt S.A.*, UTE, TFN, Sala "B" (Feb. 2, 2004).

sections compare Argentine law regulations with respect to those OECD tests when applying the stable establishment definition.[7]

i. Place of Business Test: Permanent Establishment Must Be a Place of Business Argentine legislation applies the principle that the stable establishment must also be a place of business. In this respect, section 128 of the income tax law clearly provides that stable establishment has to be an enterprise for the development of business activities. Under Argentine law, the business concept requires a place where business is actually conducted, meaning that place where business activities and goals are met. In this regard, Argentine law is similar to the OECD model, and the model's conclusions may apply.

ii. Location Test: Fixed Place of Business Argentine legislation does not provide any requirement on a fixed or nonfixed place of business. In fact, it could be said that the Argentinean model expressly excludes any requirement of being "fixed." For example, vessels traveling through Argentina's continental shelf are considered PE.

iii. Human Presence Test Although some controversies arise with respect to the necessity of human presence to configure PE, Argentine law, for this purpose, does not provide for any requirement with respect to human presence.

iv. Right of Use Test: Activity Effectively Developed in the Place of Business It is clear under Argentine law that the place of business and the activities developed therein are commercial activities. Therefore, under Argentine law, the place of business must be an enterprise.

v. Permanence Test: Minimum Requirement Place of Business Usage With respect to the permanence test, Argentine law follows the UN six-month minimum requirement. Applying this test to e-commerce transactions in Argentina is complicated due to several circumstances: (1) is difficult to establish a connection between location and software unless a business could completely unify "server" to its "software;" (2) most of the electronic processes do not require human presence; and (3) it is not possible to determine the duration of a Web site on its server. In Argentina, therefore, the following guidelines have been implemented:

1. A Web site by itself cannot constitute a PE.
2. A server by itself cannot constitute a PE.
3. The place where the server is placed could possibly be considered a PE.
4. The server located in a place managed by any third party but where the service provider has control (even when the provider does not manage it), could be considered a PE.

---

7 Marcos Gabriel Gutman, El Concepto de Establecimiento Permanente: Análisis del Articulo 5 del Modelo de la oecd con Relación al Comercio Electrónico, 62–31 (Revista del Derecho Informático, no. 29) (2000).

C. Indirect Taxation: VAT

E-Commerce taxation is mainly concerned with online or digitally delivered products such as books, software, movies, and music, which are products a consumer downloads onto his or her computer in real-time. This e-commerce form differs from Internet sales in which products sold online are subsequently delivered by using conventional means of transportation. This latter e-commerce model poses fewer technical difficulties in relation to VAT because it still involves the physical supply of tangible goods to which traditional VAT concepts apply. With respect to taxation of digitally delivered products, the most common approaches are (1) the European Union (EU) approach, under which any electronic transaction involving intangible product is considered a service for VAT purposes; and (2) the U.S. approach, which considers inappropriate a change in the essence of the transaction to simplify application of taxation laws. Despite the lack of legislation and judicial precedent on taxation of digital products in Argentina, the author considers that the real nature of the transaction should be the main factor to determine the taxable event.

The *sale* of intangibles such as e-books and MP3 music because they are not considered movable goods, is in principle, not subject to VAT in Argentina unless (1) they constitute financial services or a concession of commercial or industrial exploitation; or (2) they are attached to a service subject to VAT (i.e., know-how). Author's rights are not subject to VAT.

Services rendered by electronic means are subject to VAT depending on each case. Argentina levies taxes on services effectively used or exploited in Argentina following the principle of "place of effective use" or "place of exploitation of the service." Still, there is no unified legal criterion on this topic.

Therefore, services rendered in Argentina destined to be used abroad are not subject to VAT (i.e., telecommunication services). On the contrary, services rendered outside of the country effectively used in Argentina are, in principle, subject to VAT provided that the service involved is a taxable event and the recipient is not a final consumer or exempted individual or entity. Moreover, similar to the EU approach, foreign e-commerce service providers rendering local services in Argentina must be registered before the tax authorities in case their services are VAT taxable. In practice, there is no possibility to enforce this obligation for foreign providers because no withholding or tax substitution system has been instrumented.

IV. UNCERTAINTY ON TAXATION

The absence of a specific legal framework and the lack of a solid jurisprudence provide uncertainty on taxation of e-commerce in Argentina, specifically with regard to digitally delivered products. E-Commerce activities have come to challenge territory-based taxation principles. With respect to income tax, the special characteristics of e-commerce make the traditional rules on determining which country has jurisdiction to tax a company's worldwide income more difficult to apply.

Within its legal framework, Argentine applies the concept of PE, but it is unlikely that under Argentinean law a "server" could possibly constitute PE. Jurisprudence and regulatory proceedings are scarce, but existing criteria refer to the notion of business organization with its main characteristics, organization, personnel, decision-making executives, and other components, as main requisites to find PE.

With respect to VAT, the legislation ambiguities that exclude taxation of sale of intangibles (i.e., software) together with the impossibility of enforcing taxation of services rendered abroad when there is no PE in the country create a complex scenario. This situation has worsened by the inexistence of unified criteria on the rule of "the utilization or exploitation within the country" that applies to international services.

In addition, it is unclear yet whether Argentina will need to adopt new tax schemes or simply adapt the existing ones for businesses using electronic means. However, it is clear that no new rule could possibly work if it breaks constitutional domestic principles. It is therefore advisable to take into account the real nature of the transaction (i.e., what the parties have foreseen when executing the electronic transaction) instead of focusing on negligible factors to generate "source" jurisdiction.

Income tax and VAT represent more than 55 percent of the overall national tax revenue. If the Internet replaces commercial channels and Argentina does not enact clear tax policies toward e-commerce, many transactions will remain untaxed, thereby affecting the administration's revenue.

V. PRIVACY AND INTERNET SECURITY

Argentina has enacted several laws[8] that widened the scope of the criminal code to protect intangible objects such as e-commerce, electronic communications, software, Web pages, electronic data, and any other applications used through electronic means. Within this context, it also punishes computer fraud, through manipulation of electronic/computing systems, hackers, and other forms of electronic sabotage.

A. Information through New Communication Technologies

The criminal code protects any information derived from electronic means or sent through communication technologies with the same level of protection the national constitution gives to traditional ways of communication, such as mail, telephone, or other forms of private correspondence (Criminal Code, sections 153, 153bis, and 155).

B. Personal Data Protection

Law 25,326 and Law 26,388 added section 157bis to the Criminal Code. This section has intensified the legal protection with respect to any personal information inserted in

8 Law 25,326 (2000); Law 26,388 (2008).

a file or personal data file, thereby punishing its unauthorized transmission, illegitimate interference, and/or diffusion.

> A punishment of jailing from one month to two years shall be imposed upon: 1. Any person who knowingly and illegitimately, or in violation of confidentiality and security data systems, obtains information from a personal data file in any way. 2. Any person who reveals to another information registered in a personal data file which, pursuant to law, he is obliged to maintain confidential. 3. Any person who illegitimately inserts data in a personal data file. (Law 26,388). In case the author is a public official, limited disqualification from one to four years shall also be imposed.

The law's main purpose is to protect the integrity of any type of information referred to persons or entities, stored in archives, databases, or registries, under any technical means, and to guarantee privacy and access to personal information. With respect to this section, the law defines three different situations according to the activity the offender performs.

1. Illegitimate Access to Data Files The law punishes the person that "knowingly" or "illegitimately" *accesses* a site where the information is stored or copied (backed up), thus violating confidentiality and the security systems. It is important to point out that *appropriation* of information is not an element of the crime; the sole act of accessing the system constitutes crime and deserves the protection of law.

2. Disclosure of Personal Data The law punishes the "illegitimate disclosure" of private information contained in a personal data file when the personal data file is protected by law and when law imposes a special protection duty to the offender.

3. Insertion of Data The law punishes any person who illegally inserts information into a personal data file. To constitute a wrongful behavior, the wrongdoer's action must present two elements: (1) it must be done without any prior authorization by the affected person; or (2) it must be done in disregard of legal procedures.

C. Manipulation of Electronic Systems: Fraud

Law 26,388 introduced subsection 16, and Law 25,930 introduced subsection 15 to the Criminal Code section 173. Accordingly, section 16 provides as a special case of computer fraud: "Any person who defrauds another by use of any means of manipulation of computing programs which may alter the normal functioning of a system or data transferring" commits the crime. The main characteristic of this provision is given by the term "manipulation of a computing program." In this case, the offender, through fraud, uses a program or a system with the sole purpose of obtaining certain economic advantage. To categorize this conduct as electronic fraud, the manipulation has to necessarily alter the system or produce the transferring of data. Subsection 16 is related to subsection 15 and punishes fraud through the "unauthorized use of data obtained by any means or through the use of an automatic system from credit or debit cards."

D. Hackers and Other Forms of Sabotage

Paragraph 2, section 183 of the Argentine Criminal Code, introduced by Law 26,388, widens the scope of crimes against property, thereby protecting data, documentation, programs, and electronic systems when illegitimately targeted by offenders. The Argentine law punishes any activity intending to introduce any computer virus, thereby unlawfully altering computing programs. This section punishes "electronic sabotage" when it states that "any person who alters, destroys, or disables data, documentation, programs, or systems" belonging to third parties, and including software and Web pages is sanctioned with time in prison and fines. The law also punishes "hackers" when it says that anyone "who sells, distributes, transfers or introduces in a system, any program destined to cause damages" is sanctioned with time in prison and fines. In this case, the law punishes the offender when distributing, transferring, or introducing a virus even when it produces no damage.

VI. DIGITAL SIGNATURES

Through Law 25,506, Argentina has regulated the use of electronic and digital signatures and documents. This law provides electronic signatures and records with the same validity as traditional paper signatures and documents. Some exceptions apply to the use of electronic signatures; for example, electronic or digital signatures are not valid in inherited rights, family law matters, real estate property rights, and any other specifically mentioned private matters. In general, Argentinean digital signature law follows the proposed UNCITRAL rules on digital signatures.

VII. ONLINE GAMBLING

A federal law enacted in 2000 introduced the possibility of Internet gambling in Argentina. However, gambling is regulated at a local level in the country, and it is Argentina's 23 provinces and the autonomous city of Buenos Aires, rather than the national government, that are empowered to grant gambling operating licenses within their respective territories. Certain operators have so far been able to obtain online gambling licenses from provincial authorities, but Buenos Aires has yet to introduce its own regulations governing the activity.

Chapter 18

Brazil: E-Commerce Taxation in Brazil

Rossana Neaime Bonaldo
Optimizers Consultores

I. INTRODUCTION

The development of the Internet and, correspondingly, the increasing frequency of e-commerce transactions, have fostered the emergence of many legal questions, including tax issues surrounding this new method of conducting business. The world's governments are slowly responding to the Internet and its effect on commerce by enacting modern tax laws that take into consideration the latest medium on which the transactions are taking place. Some governments, like Brazil's, have responded more slowly than others. Brazilian law does not include particular provisions governing the taxation of e-commerce. Thus, e-commerce transactions will be taxed under the same law as traditional transactions.

II. DOMESTIC TAX LAW

A. Introduction

The Federal Constitution of Brazil and the National Tax Code (*Código Tributário Nacional* or CTN) establish the principles of taxation, including jurisdictional limitations and competence across the government's territorial divisions.[1] Thus, through their administrative political autonomy the Union (federal government), the states, the federal district, and the municipalities may collect a wide range of taxes from income and revenue, property, production of goods and services, and cross-border transactions.

The Union may tax foreign trade, income and earnings, industrialized products, financial operations, and rural land and property. The Union may also levy a value-added

1 Law no. 5172/66.

tax (VAT) on manufactured goods.[2] The states and federal district may tax inheritance and gifts, circulation of goods, and transportation and communication services, in addition, the can levy a VAT on goods in general, including automobiles and some specific services.[3] The municipalities and the federal district may tax urban land and property (IPTU), real estate conveyance (ITBI), and services (ISS), except those subject to ICMS.[4]

The Brazilian tax system is divided between two categories of taxes, fund raising and regulatory. The majority of taxes are fund-raising taxes that collect revenue for government activities. Regulatory taxes are used as instruments for economic development and social policy enforcement.[5]

B. Income Tax

1. In General Brazil has a progressive personal taxation system under which individuals are taxed up to a maximum 27.5 percent on their worldwide income, regardless of whether they are Brazilian nationals.[6] Taxable income is composed of any and all compensation and benefits paid by a Brazilian employer for employees' services. Corporations are taxed at 15 percent on net profits, with adjustments. An additional tax of 10 percent is levied on adjusted net profits exceeding BRL$240,000. A social contribution of 9 percent is also applicable to net profits. Brazil taxes income derived from Brazilian sources regardless of the residence of the income beneficiary.[7] The agency permanent establishment provisions of the Organization for Economic Cooperation and Development (OECD) Model Convention are applicable to the income taxation of nonresidents, according to income tax regulations.[8]

2. Tax Jurisdiction Under the tax code, the following persons are taxable:

1. Brazilian citizens and naturalized foreigners who reside in Brazil;
2. Foreigners holding a permanent visa (resident as of the date of entry into Brazil with the visa);
3. Foreigners holding a temporary visa with a local employment contract (resident as of the date of entry into Brazil with the visa); and
4. Foreigners holding a temporary visa without a local employment contract.

---

2 Constituição Federal [CF] [Brazil Const.] art. 153, I, VI.

3 CF art. 155 (Braz.).

4 CF art. 156 (Braz.).

5 Receita Federal (Federal Revenue Service), Taxes and Taxing Powers, http://www.receita.fazenda.gov.br/principal/Ingles/SistemaTributarioBR/BrazilianTaxSystem/powers.htm (last visited Aug. 27, 2008).

6 Law No. 7713/88.

7 Codigo Tributario Nacional [CF] [Tax Code], Law no. 5,172, art. 43–45; Mariza Delapieve Rossi et al., *Brazil*, in Cahiers de Droit Fiscal International: Taxation of Income Derived from Electronic Commerce 291–305 (2001).

8 Regulamento do Imposto de Renda [RIR], art. 539 (Decreto 3.000/99); OECD Model Convention art. 5, ¶¶ 5–7.

Unless a double-taxation treaty (DTT) is applicable, foreign nationals who are tax residents in Brazil are required to pay tax on their Brazilian and overseas-generated income.[9]

Foreign nationals become subject to tax-residence status if they stay in Brazil for more than 183 days in any 12-month period, and this status applies for 12 months after their last departure from Brazil.[10]

C. Residency

1. Definitions

A. RESIDENT A company may acquire resident status for tax purposes under domestic law if it is incorporated under Brazilian law. If a nonresident has a branch, representative offices, and/or agents operating in Brazil, that company may be treated as a resident.

B. NONRESIDENT Brazilian domestic law has not developed formal regulations defining what constitutes a permanent establishment of a nonresident doing business in Brazil. In the absence of an applicable tax treaty, nonresidents doing business in Brazil, who lack an established legal presence in Brazil, are taxed on their gross income. Brazil does not have a mechanism for taxing nonresidents on net income, such as the "effectively connected income derived from the conduct of a trade or business" mechanism used by the U.S. government, which takes into account revenues and expenses when taxing net income.[11] A nonresident may file a request with the Ministry of Commerce, Industry, and Development for a branch to conduct business out of, which is then treated as a taxable corporation.

C. TAXATION BASED ON RESIDENCY STATUS A nonresident with a branch formally registered in Brazil must self-assess its own income tax liability under the rules applicable to resident companies. Nonresident companies without a branch in Brazil, but deriving Brazilian-source income, are subject to income tax withholding.

Nonresident owning assets and rights in Brazil, for example, real estate, vehicles, share participations, bank accounts, and investments in the Brazilian financial and capital markets, must register as taxpayers with the Brazilian federal tax authorities. Such nonresidents must also appoint a local representative in Brazil and notify the federal tax authorities of the appointment. Foreign nationals who are not tax-resident are only required to pay tax on their income from Brazilian sources, at a rate of 25 percent on earned income and 15 percent on unearned income, and do not have to file an annual tax return.

---

9 *Taxation, from Brazil: An Expratriate Guide*, http://www.expatfocus.com/expatriate-brazil-taxation (last visited Aug. 27, 2008).

10 Nonresident status for tax purposes is regulated by R.I.R., art. 18–20.

11 Interview by Rossana Neaime Bonaldo with Roberto Greco de Souza Ferreira, associate with Stroeter, Royester & Ohno-Avaogados (associated with Steel Hector & Davis LLP), Brazil.

2. Source Rules

A. IN GENERAL Nonresidents are not subject to tax in Brazil when they supply goods manufactured abroad to Brazilian residents. Taxability of a nonresident's income derived from the sale of intangible goods, including digitized products, (e.g., e-books, videos, and music) distributed through the Internet, to residents of Brazil is still an undecided question.

B. ROYALTIES Brazil's withholding tax rate on royalty payments made to nonresidents is 15 percent.[12] Royalty payments include fees paid for the transfer of technology and for technical, administrative, and scientific assistance.[13] In addition to the withholding tax, royalties paid to a nonresident for the transfer of trademarks, patents, and technology and for the supply of administrative, technical, or scientific assistance, are also subject to the contribution for intervention in the economic domain (CIDE). The contribution is not withheld at the source, as other taxes on royalties are. CIDE is levied on the Brazilian payor.[14] CIDE contributions are not levied on payments for a license to use software; however, the contribution will be applied to transfers of technology, for example, the acquisition of software rights.[15]

3. Withholding Tax A withholding tax is applicable to the income and other gains of nonresidents derived from Brazilian sources. Withholding tax payments are due at the time income is paid, credited, delivered, employed, or remitted by a domestic source to a nonresident. The withholding tax base is the gross amount of the payment made by the resident payer. The Brazilian payor has sole responsibility for paying the withholding tax, and must make the tax payment even if the payor did not withhold tax from the payment to the nonresident.[16]

D. Customs

1. In General Internet purchases imported into Brazil through the mail are subject to a simplified taxation system (RTS).[17] The taxation rate is 60 percent of the price stated on the commercial invoice, including the transport and insurance costs if they were not included in the merchandise total price. The maximum value of the good allowed to be imported through this regime is US$3,000.[18]

---

12 The rate will be 25% if the nonresident recipient of an interest on net equity payment is in a low-tax jurisdiction.

13 Law No. 10,332/01.

14 Law No. 10,168/00.

15 Law No. 11,452/07 art. 20.

16 Regulations, art. 682, 695, 713, 717, 722, 725.

17 Frequently Asked Questions, Regime de Tributação Simplificada [RTS] 096/1999 [Simplified Taxation Regime], http://www.receita.fazenda.gov.br/principal/Ingles/faq.htm (last visited Aug. 27, 2008).

18 Normative Instructions on the Implementation of the RTS, available at http://www.receita.fazenda.gov.br/Legislacao/Ins/Ant2001/1999/in09699.htm

There are exceptions to the tax on goods imported through the mail. Goods valued at less than US$50 are exempt from the tax if shipped between individuals.[19] Additionally, medicines shipped into the country for individual consumption are taxed at a zero rate.[20] An additional 18 percent VAT (ICMS) is added to goods imported using an international express courier.

The customs value of off-the-shelf software shipped by mail into Brazil will be the value of the media (e.g., CD-ROM) on which the software resides and not the total value of the software if the shipping invoice lists the value of each part separately. Thus, software that is, instructions on physical media will only be taxed at the 60 percent rate if the value of the software is not stated separately from the value of the media on the shipping invoice.[21]

2. Place of Payment When goods imported through the mail have a value up to US$500, the recipient may pay the import tax at the post office, without customs formalities. When the value of the goods received exceeds US$500, the recipient must present the simplified import declaration (DSI) upon retrieving the package.[22] When goods are imported into Brazil through an international express courier, the courier is in charge of collecting the respective tax. Thus, the total amount due from the recipient of the goods will include the import taxes.[23]

III. GUIDING PRINCIPLES FOR DEVELOPMENT OF E-COMMERCE REGULATIONS

A. Brazil Chamber of E-Commerce

Brazil's Chamber of E-Commerce—Camara-e.net—promotes digital businesses in Brazil.[24] The organization includes over 160 members, including 80 percent of online retailers, major software companies, law firms, and consulting companies.

B. Brazil and the OECD

Brazil is not a member of the OECD; however, in most cases it follows the OECD Model Tax Convention. Therefore, Brazil is not obligated to follow the OECD view on the definition of permanent establishment in the context of e-commerce but may borror some principles from the OECD definition.

---

19 *Id.* at Art. 1, § 2.
20 *Id.* at Art. 1, § 1.
21 Receita Federal (Federal Revenue Service), Decision no. 96 (May 25, 2004).
22 Frequently Asked Questions, *supra* note 17.
23 *Id.*
24 Brazilian Chamber of E-Commerce, http://www.camara-e.net/english/index.asp. (last visited Aug. 27, 2008).

Although Brazil's bilateral tax treaties prevail over its domestic law, Brazil's domestic courts have exclusive jurisdiction to interpret tax treaties. Brazil has not released guidance clarifying most important tax issues surrounding e-commerce. The government has, however, created the Executive Committee of Electronic Commerce to examine the legal issues arising in the e-commerce environment. Unfortunately, the committee has not issued guidelines on whether servers and Web sites may constitute permanent establishments in Brazil.[25]

IV. TREATY LAW

A. In General

Brazil is a signatory to a treaty for the prevention of double taxation with many countries all over the world: Argentina, Canada, China, France, Germany, Italy, Japan, Netherlands, Norway, and Spain, among others. DTT generally follow the OECD model. There is currently no such agreement between Brazil and the United States.

A double-taxation prevention treaty enables offsetting tax paid in one of two countries against the tax payable in the other, to prevent double taxation. The grant of an exemption or tax at a reduced rate on certain receipts, such as interest, royalties, dividends, capital gains, and others that are connected with a transaction, may be carried out between parties associated with the double-taxation prevention treaty. When certain income is taxable under the Brazilian Income Tax Ordinance but there is an applicable exemption, commonly reduced tax, under any taxation treaty, the income may taxed, but only according to the provisions of the taxation treaty.

V. ISSUES IN E-COMMERCE

A. Privacy

The Brazilian Constitution guarantees the right to privacy and recovery from breaches of privacy.[26] Further, the Brazilian Consumer Protection Code protects the privacy of Brazilian consumer's databases and makes it a criminal act to violate the privacy of personal information.[27] Currently, the code is silent about the application of this to cookies; but this rule may be extended to apply when and if the privacy violation damages personal information. The only legal violation of the protection of e-commerce may occur when a judge issues a court order to aid and further a criminal investigation.

A Brazilian law passed in 1990 protects children and adolescents from the unauthorized disclosure of private information, be it personal or legal.[28] The law was amended

25 Interview with Roberto Greco de Souza Ferreira, *supra* note 11.

26 CF, art. 5.

27 Law no. 8,078, art. 43 (Sept. 11, 1990).

28 Law no. 8,069 (July 13, 1990).

in 2003 to include the Internet as a medium for the disclosure or publication of child pornography.

The Brazilian Civil Code recognizes the individual's right to privacy and charges the courts with protecting that right.

In addition the general right to privacy, the Telecommunications Act of 1997 provides that users of telecommunications services have a right to privacy with respect to personal data.[29]

The Financial Institutions Secrecy Law explicitly requires financial institutions to preserve the privacy of their customers in all the institutions' operations. There are exceptions for the exchange of information between institutions, responses to information requests by the Federal Revenue and Customs Secretariat (Secretaria da Receita Federal), and for reporting illegal activity to the authorities. Confidentiality can also be breached during any phase of an inquiry into illegal activity or action at law.

Two proposed laws would protect the privacy of personal data on the Internet. If passed, Bill No. 3,360/2000 will protect the privacy of network users by providing that a user's information may only be collected if the individual is given prior notice, the individual permits disclosure, and the data is only used for the purpose for which it was collected. Violation of the rule may result in a fine.[30] Finally, proposed Bill No. 4,906/2001 would impose a limit on information that may be that may be requested from a customer in a commercial Internet transaction, and requires that all personal data be held in strict confidentiality.[31]

B. Cybercrime and Penalties

The Federal Penal Code criminalizes data breaches. For instance, introducing false data into an information system is punishable by a term in sentence of two to twelve years.[32] Unauthorized alteration of an information system may be punished by imprisonment from three months to two years. Likewise, the Federal Penal Code and Federal Procedural Penal Code were amended in 2003 to escalate sanctions for copyright violations and the unauthorized distribution of copyrighted works through any electronic system.[33] The Federal Procedural Penal Code introduced rules to expedite searches and seizures as a measure to protect copyright holders. The loosening of the search and seizure requirements has allowed the Brazilian Association of Record Producers (ABPD) to initiate criminal proceedings against individuals suspected of illegal distribution of music on the Internet.

The Brazilian Supreme Court has issued a decision curtailing the right to privacy. The court held that the seizure of stored e-mails under a court order is a privacy issue and not an issue relating to protection of electronic communications. Because Brazil's

29 Law no. 9,472 (July 16, 1997), Book 1, art. 3, IX. (Telecommunications Act).

30 Bill no. 3,360/2000.

31 Bill no. 4,906/2001.

32 Law no. 9,983 (July 14, 2000).

33 Law no. 10,695 (July 1, 2003).

privacy rights are not absolute, they may be mitigated in favor of other, more pressing, policy concerns.[34]

C. Gambling

While online gambling is not explicitly illegal in Brazil, some cities have taken action to reduce gambling by individuals under the age of 18. In 2004, the City of São Paulo mandated that cybercafés involved in online computer gambling register patrons under 18 years of age. The cybercafés face civil penalties of up to BRL$6,000 and business license revocations if they fail to do so.[35]

D. Digital Crimes Bill

On July 10, 2008, the Brazilian Senate passed the Digital Crimes Bill, which defines cybercrimes and provides penalties for violations. The bill is awaiting approval by the House of Representatives.[36] The bill incited uproar on Internet blog sites, with users complaining that many individuals would violate the provisions of the bill unknowingly and that the bill was passed without public debate. In response to the public's dissatisfaction with the bill, the Senate Press Relations Office issued a press release clarifying that the bill defines 13 new crimes:[37]

1. Unauthorized access to an information device;
2. Obtaining, transferring, or providing unauthorized data or information;
3. Disclosing or misusing personal information or data;
4. Destroying, making unusable, or degrading objects or electronic data belonging to another person;
5. Distributing and introducing viruses;
6. Damaging a system by distributing or introducing a virus into the system (results in enhanced penalties);
7. Electronic deception (e.g., phishing);
8. Electronically attacking public utility and security services;
9. Interrupting or disrupting telephone service, computer, or other electronic services;
10. Forgery of electronic public data;
11. Forgery of private electronic data (e.g., credit card cloning).

---

34 Supremo Tribunal Federal [STF], no. 373.058-4 RS; Agravo Regimental no Recurso Extraordinário, no. 373.058-4—RS.

35 Law no. 13,720.

36 *Paula Goes, Brazil: Bloggers question the 13 New CyberCrimes*, http://globalvoicesonline.org/2008/07/17/brazil-bloggers-question-the-13-new-cyber-crimes// (last visited Aug. 27, 2008).

37 Senate Press Relations Office, *Understand the Draft law of Crimes Committed through Computers* (*Entenda o projeto de lei dos crimes cometidos por meio de computadore*) (Jul. 10, 2008), available at http://www.senado.gov.br/agencia/verNoticia.aspx?codNoticia=76844&codAplicativo=2.

12. Disseminating racist content over a computer network; and
13. Receiving or storing child pornography.[38]

In addition to the foregoing amendments to the Criminal Code, the bill will also amend the Military Penal Code to include similar prohibitions.

E. Internet Pornography

The social networking site Orkut—owned and operated by Google—has 11 million users registered in Brazil and is Brazil's most popular Web site. According to prosecutors and nonprofits, the site has become a popular vehicle for child pornographers, pedophiles, and racist and anti-Semitic groups.

The aforementioned Digital Crimes Bill constitutes the Brazil's first attempt to police online child pornography. Previously, the only recourse against child pornography on a site was to manually delete offensive and illegal profiles from the site. At one point, a group of Brazilian hackers formed a vigilante group, hacking into sites promoting child pornography. But legislators worried that erasing sites simultaneously erased evidence needed for prosecution.[39] Google initially refused to cooperate with Brazilian authorities when asked to provide information about the sites, including IP (Internet protocol) addresses. Without this information, it was virtually impossible for the government to track down child pornographers. Google eventually reached agreement with the Brazilian government and will use filters to block illegal content and will also assist police and prosecutors gathering evidence relating to offenses against children and teens on the site.[40]

---

38 *Id.*

39 SaferNet Brasil, *Orkut Angels Delight in Fight* (Mar. 16, 2006), http://www.safernet.org.br/twiki/bin/view/SaferNet/Noticia20060316021702 (last visited Aug. 27, 2008).

40 Reuters.com, *Google in Deal with Brazil to Fight Child Porn* (July 2, 2008), http://www.reuters.com/article/internetNews/idUSN0237672120080702 (last visited Aug. 27, 2008).

Chapter 19

Colombia: Value-Added Tax on Online Content

Carmen Sanabria Gomez
Cárdenas & Cárdenas Abogados Ltda.

I. INTRODUCTION

The analysis of value-added tax (VAT) on online content is relevant for two reasons. First, e-commerce[1] has and will continue to have a tremendous growth during the coming years,[2] especially direct e-commerce or online commerce, with the online supply of intangible products expected to have the greatest growth. Second, an increase in e-commerce results in a decrease in tax collection derived therefrom, to such a point that it has been said that the main tax problem originated from the online supply is the decrease of tax collection, especially regarding VAT.[3] This decrease in tax collection is caused by existing difficulties, such as qualification of the revenues obtained, as well as the difficulty in controlling the operations carried out through the use of e-mail and the Internet.

II. WHAT IS ONLINE CONTENT?

It is important to differentiate the two major categories of e-commerce: (1) national and international *indirect* e-commerce, consisting of electronic orders for the

1 In 1998 the World Trade Organization stated that e-commerce should be defined as the production, advertisement, sale, and distribution of products through telecommunications networks. However, in several discussions, e-commerce refers only to Internet and other commerce modes based on networks. UNIVERSIDAD DE LOS ANDES, INTERNET, ELECTRONIC COMMERCE AND TELECOMMUNICATIONS. TAX ASPECTS OF ELECTRONIC COMMERCE 295 (1st ed. Legis 2002).

2 The Josten Report published in 1999 estimates that during the year 1998 the volume of economic transactions in the network amounted to US$7–8 billion, estimating that this amount in year 2003 may be near to $108 billion. *See* R. Josten, E-COMMERCE TAXATION: ISSUES IN SEARCH OF ANSWERS, EXECUTIVE SUMMARY (Sept. 1999).

3 RAMIRO CUBILLOS VELANDIA & ERICK RINCÓN CÁRDENAS, INTRODUCCIÓN JURÍDICA AL COMERCIO ELECTRÓNICO 141 at note 36 (Ediciones Jurídicas Gustavo Ibáñez 2002).

acquisition of tangible goods;[4] and (2) national and international *direct* e-commerce, consisting of the online supply of services, technology, and intangible goods.[5]

This latter category, direct e-commerce, refers to the supply of various products—for example, books, movies, software, music—transmitted telematically in a digital form, in such a manner that the purchaser "download" the product directly into his or her computer, once he or she has accessed the Web page of the seller company and has paid for the product, normally through a credit card.

This new way of supply is possible because e-commerce allows for the application of rights and obligations in a new dimension. E-Commerce allows transactions to be accomplished through electronic and computer devices, independently from their location in real time (online) and represented by means of a text, by illustration, and by multimedia.[6]

III. MAIN PROBLEMS OF ONLINE CONTENT[7]

As established in the experts' doctrine, the main problems of online content are (1) the qualification of the income obtained and of the operations to be carried out through e-commerce, and (2) the difficulties in locating the commercial activities in the electronic environment and the identification of the domicile of the taxpayers.

A. The Qualification of the Operations to be Carried out in E-Commerce

The majority of international treaties and laws assign a diverse tax treatment for payments, depending on whether they relate to the delivery of physical products, the use of an intangible good, or the rendering of a service.[8]

For example, a newspaper sale would be deemed as the sale of a physical product. However, if the way in which it is delivered changes from the printing copy of the newspaper to the delivery of such to the customers' computer, would this imply that the transaction changes from the sale of a physical product to the rendering of a service or to the licensing of an intangible?[9]

The foregoing example leads to the following question: does the transmission of digital information involve the assignment of a right to use, or does it relate to the acquisition of a good? In the first case, there would be a payment for the use or

4 José María Obando Márquez, Aspectos Impositivos de la ley de Comercio Electrónico en Colombia 128 (Universidad Externado de Colombia 2000).

5 *Id.* at 128.

6 Rafael Oliver Cuello, Tributación del Comercio Electrónico 13 (Tirant Lo Blanch 1999).

7 José María Obando Márquez, Aspectos Impositivos de la ley de Comercio Electrónico en Colombia 13 (Universidad Externado de Colombia 2000).

8 Adriana Nuñez, Comercio Electrónico: Aspectos Impositivos, Contables y Tecnológicos 9 (La ley, Buenos Aires 2002).

9 *Id.* at 11.

granting of a right, and in the second a consideration for the acquisition of a good or the rendering of a service. This matter obviously raises another question: does the tax result from a sale depending on the distribution channel used,[10] and thus should a different tax treatment apply?

The Organization for Cooperation and Economic Development (OECD) has stated that, by virtue of the principle of neutrality, similar treatment should be granted to business transactions independently from the fact that they are carried out through Internet or otherwise.[11] Namely, a different treatment should not be given to any specific transaction simply because it is carried out through telematic means. Thus, e-commerce is not as new from the tax point of view. But what is innovative is the new manner in which transactions are carried out, the new ways products are advertised, the new ways of communicating with clients and suppliers and of rendering services, among others.[12] In fact, basically, essential differences offered by e-commerce with respect to other types of commerce may be summarized as follows: (1) it has allowed new services to emerge through the use of the Web; (2) new "digital products" and some formerly tangible products may now be sent through the Web; and (3) business can now operate in a remote manner.

The National Tax and Customs Authorities of Colombia (DIAN) stated in its Opinion 15727 of 2001[13] that "[t]here is no special tax regulation for electronic transactions, but concerning their tax effects, it is deemed that they correspond to the same effects produced by similar operations carried out in a traditional manner. Electronic commerce is an additional mean through which activities and transactions are carried out and, consequently, those are subject to general tax provisions since no special regulation exists to grant them a different treatment."

The European Union, in the communication from the commission to the Council of Ministers, to the European Parliament, and to the Economic and Social Committee of June 19, 1998, on "electronic commerce and indirect taxation "set forth that operations on goods and services must be qualified, with no differentiation, as the rendering of services or selling goods on the web (*online* supplies)."

Why then, if no significant differences exist, should a good physically delivered to the client through traditional channels require customs duties while the digital delivery of the same goods sent through the network would not require customs duties?[14]

---

10 *Id.* at 11.

11 *Are the Current Treaty Rules for Taxing Business Profits Appropriate for E-Commerce?*, Public Discussion Draft 47, (Nov. 23 2003).

12 Adriana Nuñez, Comercio Electrónico: Aspectos Impositivos, Contables y Tecnológicos 76 (La ley, Buenos Aires 2002).

13 In accordance with the provisions of Article 264 of Law 223 of 1995 the taxpayers acting based on the written opinions of the Legal Su-Directorate of the National Tax and Customs Directorship may support their acts before the administration and the courts based on them. During the time of enforceability of the mentioned opinions, the tax acts carried out under their provisions may not be objected by the tax authorities. If the National Tax and Customs Directorship changes the position assumed in an opinion previously issued, such change must be published.

14 Adriana Nuñez, Comercio Electrónico: Aspectos Impositivos, Contables y Tecnológicos 76 (La ley, Buenos Aires 2002).

B. Difficulties in Locating the Commercial Activities in the Electronic Environment and in the Identification of the Taxpayer's Domicile

Online supplies have created difficulty in applying the criteria of the "economic activity address" and have generated doubts as to whether the servers or Web pages may be deemed as permanent establishments of the seller when that server is located in the purchaser's country.

Regarding the identification of the taxpayer's domicile, Colombian Law 527 of 1999 on e-commerce does not refer to the tax treatment thereof. Notwithstanding, Article 25 the referred of Law 527 of 1999 establishes that should no different agreement be reached by the initiator and the addressee, the data message shall be understood as issued from the place where the initiator has its own establishment and as received in the place where the addressee has his or her own domicile. If the initiator or addressee has more than one establishment, its establishment should be the one keeping a closer relationship with the underlying operation; or if there is no closer place to its underlying operation, the place will be its principal establishment. If the initiator or the addressee has no establishment, its customary residence will be taken into account.

Additionally, direct e-commerce has made the problems of technical nature visible, especially the difficulties for tax administrations to locate the subjects who take part in an electronic transaction. Remember that a domain name does not necessarily correspond with a geographical location, and it is possible to be anonymous when acting as an Internet purchaser.[15]

IV. ANALYSES OF ONLINE INTANGIBLE SALES OR IMPORTS, LICENSING, AND RENDERING OF SERVICES VIS-À-VIS THE SALES TAX IN COLOMBIA

A. Sales or Import of Incorporeal Goods

Article 420 of the Colombian Tax Code establishes that VAT applies to the sale and import of corporeal goods that have not been expressly excluded. This is why incorporeal goods are excluded from VAT. Consequently, the sale of a trademark, patent, or copyright, or the right to exploit them (licensing) in Colombia, would not be subject to VAT.

On July 12, 2004, Decision 599 of the Andean Community Commission was issued to harmonize essential and procedural aspects of taxes, such as the VAT of the member countries (Colombia, Peru, Ecuador, and Bolivia). Pursuant to the provisions of Article 40 of Decision 599, this Andean decision shall be included in the internal legislation of each member country whenever the respective constitutional provision is established so, and it shall be enforceable on the first calendar day immediately

15 Rafael Oliver Cuello, Tributación del Comercio Electrónico 78 (Tirant Lo Blanch 1999).

following the date of the latest deposit of the corresponding instrument at the general secretariat of the Andean Community. Notwithstanding the above, Decision 635 of the Andean Community Commission, dated July 19, 2006, repealed Article 40 of Decision 599 and established that Decision 599 would only become enforceable on January 1, 2008.

Article 5 of Decision 599 provides that VAT is accrued on the sale or transfer of goods, and thus the sale of incorporeal goods in transactions between individuals of the country members of the Andean Community of Nations (CAN) shall be subject to VAT as from January 1, 2008. However, such provision requires a procedure of incorporation into the Colombian internal legislation, which has not yet taken place, and therefore, until such transposition or incorporation takes place, this provision will not be applicable. Hence, the sale of intangible goods between residents or individuals domiciled in the CAN member states will be subject to VAT only from the time of Colombia's incorporation of this Andean Decision into its internal legislation.

Regarding VAT, an interesting matter to be analyzed is the sale of copies by electronic means: the intangible goods that result from the rights of the original intangible may also be subject to sale, as the sale of a compact disc containing a musical work. Such sale may be carried out as a tangible good (book or record) or intangible good (a copy of the record or book through electronic means). If the sale of the record or book[16] is made electronically, pursuant to the above provisions, such sale would not be subject to VAT in Colombia.

In order to understand the copyright legal regime protecting intangible goods, and the transactions that can be carried out with them, it is worth remembering that, pursuant to the provision under Article 3 of Law 23 of 1982, which regulates copyrights in Colombia, the economic rights of the work's author are, among others (1) the right to dispose of its work gratuitously or for a consideration, and (2) the right to take advantage of the work for profit or otherwise, through printing, recording, hard copies, phonogram, photograph, cinematographic film, and videogram and through the execution, speech, representation, translation, adaptation, display, transmission, or any other means of reproduction, multiplication, or disbursement known or to be known.

In accordance with the aforementioned, we should point out that there are two categories of intangible goods: (1) trademarks, patents, literary works, and other copyrightable works, and (2) the rights derived from such works (to which we referred in item (2) above) that may give rise to the production of other tangible or intangible goods.

Each one of those intangible goods may be the subject matter of juridical transactions:

1. The intangible good as such may be subject matter of sale, as when a trademark is sold.
2. Any of the rights derived from the intangible good may be subject to licensing, as in the case of a sale of the reproduction right of a literary work, or of sale, for example, of the right to perform adaptations to its work.

---

16 Article 478 of the Tax Statute establishes that scientific and cultural books and magazines are exempt from VAT, which includes the ones published in electromagnetic means, as expressly established by Article 2nd of Law 98 of 1993.

3. Finally, intangible goods arising from the rights of the originary intangible good may also be subject matter of sale, as in the case of the sale of a compact disc containing a musical work, which may be a tangible good (book or record) or intangible good (copy of the record or book through electronic means).

Pursuant to the above, the DIAN established in its Opinion 88305, dated November 17, 1998,[17] that the assignment of intangible goods would not be included within the facts/transactions that accrues VAT. However, the sale of a copy of a musical work as compact disc is subject to VAT; this leads one to conclude that, depending on the distribution channel used, the same transaction in one case would be subject to VAT and on the other would not. This double standard violates the neutrality principle established by the OECD as the fundamental principle for applying the tax provisions to e-commerce.

Concerning advertising recorded on videotapes (advertising spots), the Colombian Council of State through Decision 9784 of April 28, 2000, declared the DIAN's Opinions 0013 of February, 1998, and 006 of February 24, 1999, void. Through these, DIAN had stated that a TV advertisement was merchandise subject to payment of customs duties upon import, whereby the intangible (advertising spot) protected under copyright was mistakenly taxed according to the means in which it was transmitted. The Colombian Council of State based the nullity of these DIAN opinions on the fact that the TV advertisement is not merchandise but rather an intangible good, to the extent that there is neither inventiveness nor creativity (which is the intangible good). Therefore, intangibles do not become tangibles simply because of the media on which they are contained.

Regarding know-how matters, under Opinion 69743 of August 1, 2001, DIAN established that if the transfer of know-how (an intangible good), through any title, is made from abroad, and the user or beneficiary of the service is within Colombian territory, the service is to be taxed in Colombia at the rate of 16 percent. This opinion is contradictory because, as has been noted before, the sale of an intangible good is not subject to VAT in Colombia.

Although there should be no difference between taxation of intangible goods contained in a physical medium and those supplied online, in reality there is a practical difference between them. The sale of intangible goods contained in physical media requires nationalization of goods, which implies, in the case of software, payment of customs duties and VAT. In this case, the customs assessment of the software is made solely over the cost or the value of the computer support, provided that its cost is distinguished from the cost or value provided in the commercial invoice, as established by Article 214 of DIAN Resolution 4240 of 2000. Notwithstanding the above, under Opinion 51 of July 31, 2001, DIAN established that the foregoing provision applies only to imports of software to be used in computers. Consequently, a machine or a

17 The DIAN opinions issued prior to 2003 are no longer enforceable since the enforceability of the VAT Unified Opinion No. 1 of 2003. However, in those matters where there exist subsequent opinions, those opinions have been included to show the position that DIAN has assumed regarding certain matters.

piece of equipment that requires software for its operation shall be subject to a valuation assessment by using the valuation methods, starting from the "transaction value." "On the other hand, the massive consumption software is valued on the basis of the total value of the transaction, with it being understood that in these cases, the intangible is incorporated into the tangible mean, in such a manner that both are considered to be one unit."[18]

B. Licensing of Intangible Goods

Licenses are legal transactions where one party, the owner of a good or right, authorizes the other party to use such good or right in such a manner that the other takes economic advantage thereof. Licenses may have as purpose the use or exploitation of an intangible good. The first case (license of use) occurs, for example, when authorization is given to download a program (intangible product) or to obtain such program through physical means for an individual use. The second case (exploitation license) occurs when an authorization is granted to obtain benefits from the rights inherent to an originary intangible good, as occurs, for example, with the securing of a license to use a trademark for commercial exploitation.

For VAT purposes, a service is understood as any activity, labor, or work rendered by an individual or legal person, or by a de facto company without the existence of a labor relationship between the one who contracts the execution and the one who undertakes such execution, regardless of the fact that the material or intellectual factor rules and that a consideration in money or in kind is generated independently from the denomination or type of remuneration.[19]

Consequently, the following licenses are subject to VAT within the definition of services:

- Licenses that rest on originary intangible goods, such as licenses on copyright, patents, and trademarks granted online;
- Licenses that rest upon rights on such intangible goods, such as the license to adapt or to reproduce a work granted online; and
- Licenses that rest on copies of intangible goods, such as licenses on software copies granted online.

In this same sense, DIAN, under Opinion 67804 of October 17, 2002, established that, in legislation, licensing is considered to be the rendering of a service and, consequently, subject to VAT. Therefore, whoever grants the license of use online is responsible for VAT.

Subparagraph 3 of Article 420 of the Colombian Tax Code establishes that certain services, such as licenses and authorizations for use and exploitation of any title,

---

18 Catalina Hoyos Jiménez, *Tributación de intangibles en Colombia*, XXIX Jornadas colombianas de Derecho Tributario Memorias 174, 2005.

19 Regulatory Decree 1372, art. 1 (1992).

intangible or incorporeal goods, rendered from abroad in favor of users or addressees located within the national territory, are to be understood as rendered in Colombia and are consequently subject to VAT.[20]

When applying the above provision, DIAN in its Opinion 66280 of 2001 determined that when a foreign corporation without domicile in Colombia receives payments for granting the use of software to users in the country, those payments are for services subject to VAT.

In Opinion 025826 of 2001, it became evident that the DIAN had confused the sale or assignment of intangible goods, which is not subject to VAT because to the extent such sale or assignment is considered by law to be a transaction not subject to this tax (as was explained above), with the exploitation of an intangible good by virtue of a license. The DIAN established, through this opinion, that the assignment of a license of copyrights generated VAT if the assignee exploited the license within the country, because this exploitation is considered a service rendered from abroad by a nonresident or nondomiciled party in Colombia in favor of a user or addressee located in Colombia. In fact, the sale or assignment of an intangible good is not subject to VAT, since the sale of intangible goods does not accrue VAT under Colombian law.

In the same way, under Opinion 1933 of January 15, 2002, when answering the question as to whether a newspaper from abroad delivered through electronic means to users located within the national territory was subject to VAT, DIAN established that such cases were the rendering of a service that should be understood as rendered in Colombia and that, consequently, was subject to VAT. In fact, as in the previous case, this constitutes the sale of intangible goods not subject to VAT.

1. Licensing of Software At an international level, both the Agreement on Trade-Related Aspects of Intellectual Property Rights (TRIPs Agreement) and the World Intellectual Property Organizations (WIPO) Treaty regarding copyright (WCT) of 1996 provide that the computer software are source programs or purpose programs, protected as literary works.

In this same sense, Andean subregional legislation provides in Article 23 of Decision 351 of the Cartagena Agreement that computer software is protected along the same terms as literary works. Such protection extends both to operational programs and to application programs, whether by way of a source code or purpose code.

As established above, in accordance with the provisions of subparagraph 3 of Article 420 of the Colombian Tax Code, certain services, including exploitation of intangibles through license agreements, are subject to VAT when rendered from abroad to an addressee in Colombia. When applying such provision, under Opinion 62356 of June 9, 2001, the DIAN determined that whoever acquires a computer software program via the Internet, even in the event that the service is executed from abroad, is

---

20 Similarly, Decision 599 established that services, within which licenses and authorizations for the use and exploitation at any title of incorporeal or intangible goods are expressly listed, shall be subject to tax in the country of destination.

subject to VAT because, following the principle of territoriality of Colombian tax laws, when the user or addressee is located within the national territory, it is understood that the service is located in Colombia.

Based on this background, it is worthy to analyze two controversial topics concerning software licensing: the acquisition of online software copies and the acquisition of personalized software for the purchaser.

Regarding the purchase of software copies, two questions arise that require a current solution:

1. Should the acquisition of computer products of massive consumption be deemed as a purchase of a good or as an exploitation of an intangible good?
2. Does this qualification change, or should it be changed, if the acquisition of such product is carried out online?

In connection with musical works, which are also subject to copyrights, the DIAN has established that the transfer of music through electronic means represents an exploitation of an intangible good. Notwithstanding the above, it also sets forth that when a compact disc that contains a musical work is purchased abroad, the transaction is a sale that is not subject to VAT because it is deemed to be a purchase of a corporeal movable good abroad. This again generates confusion because a single operation (purchase of a musical work) cannot be qualified in a different manner depending upon the distribution mode: that is through the acquisition of a compact disc or through the acquisition via electronic means (online).

In the new drafting of the comments on Article 12 of the OECD model agreement regarding double taxation, which pretends to clarify, in principle, the tax treatment of software either as royalty or as entrepreneurial benefit product from the purchase and sales it is emphasized that tax treatment is not affected by the act of supplying the product through the network (online supply).[21]

In connection with software, the DIAN has expressed that anyone who purchases a computer product of massive consumption abroad, without acquiring any right to exploit the intangible good, is carrying out an exploitation of an intangible good. This DIAN opinion is problematic because there should be no difference between the purchase of massive-consumption software to be used at home and the purchase of a compact disc to listen to music; in both cases they refer to the purchase of a physical product containing copyrighted works.

The OECD has provided that every operation should be investigated to determine the reason for which the payment is received, and if such payment does not correspond to the right to use or exploit a copyright, it is not to be considered a royalty. For example, if the purchaser of software is allowed to make copies thereof, but such is a means for the purchaser to benefit from the software and it is not the essential reason for the payment, then in this case the payment is not a royalty because the main reason for the payment thereof is not the licensing or right to use or exploit the intangible good.

21 Rafael Oliver Cuello, Tributación del Comercio Electrónico 32 (Tirant Lo Blanch 1999).

Here is another example of a payment that would not qualify as royalty. In a business that allows the client to electronically download digital products (e.g., images, sound, text) for the client's own use, payments are made for the *acquisition of data* digitally transmitted, in which case, the payment would not be made as a royalty for the exploitation or use of the intangible good.[22] Using this same idea, Oliver states that "the principles of jurisprudence allow an understanding that, in the case of the purchase of standard computer programs, namely, 'product' or 'merchandise' offered in a massive manner or by commercial mass production, the existence of income qualified as royalties must be discarded, since there is no assignment of intellectual property rights . . ."[23] Likewise, just as it has been set forth under Appendix II regarding the analysis of several categories of typical transactions of e-commerce, the electronic purchase orders and delivery of digital products are deemed entrepreneurial benefit, since the purpose of the payment is the acquisition of information transmitted electronically.[24]

Copying or saving the product on the hard drive of the purchaser's computer is an incidental part of the business, which is not of consequence for its classification, since it is not the main reason for such payment (acquisition of information transmitted digitally). However, when the essential consideration for payment is the granting the title of the right to use a digital product that is electronically downloaded for such purpose, royalties shall be paid for the licensing of an intangible good. This is the case, for example, of a book editor who pays to acquire the right to reproduce a picture that shall be electronically downloaded for the purpose of including it on the book cover. In this case the payment is made for the right to reproduce and distribute such picture and not only for acquiring the digital content.[25]

Pursuant to the aforementioned, it is evident that the acquisition of copies of online software is not subject to VAT, so long as the reason for the payment is not the licensing of a good, even in the event that the purchaser may be allowed to make copies of the purchased software pursuant to the agreement. Likewise, it is not subject to VAT when the seller allows the purchaser access to some software program component in order to install, execute, or operate other program, for example, having access to support and maintenance post-sale services for the acquisition of (intangible) data digitally transmitted.

The DIAN in its Opinion 125326 of 2000 established that copies of products that are protected by copyright provisions cannot be the subject matter of sale. For this reason, acquisition of music, publications, and software that are commercially available to the public from the Internet is subject to VAT because such acquisition constitutes the exploitation of intangible goods. In Colombia, such operations, including the sale of software as package for massive consumption, represent, according to DIAN, the rendering of qualified services. Therefore, pursuant to DIAN, when a resident of Colombia

---

22 OECD, *Taxation and Electronic Commerce: Implementing the Ottawa Taxation Framework Conditions*, 88 (2001).

23 Rafael Oliver Cuello, Tributación del Comercio Electrónico 46–47 (Tirant Lo Blanch 1999).

24 OECD, *Taxation and Electronic Commerce: Implementing the Ottawa Taxation Framework Conditions*163 and following (2001).

25 *Id.* at 89.

receives from abroad a technological package that has not been designed especially for him or her (tailored), to be installed in his/her computer for the execution of certain programs (application software), or for the operation of equipment (operative software), this purchase would be subject to VAT to the extent that it is originated in the exploitation of computer programs.

Regarding the acquisition of tailored software, the DIAN has understood that such acquisition relates to a license for exploitation of intangible goods subject to VAT if the execution of the software is made from abroad in favor of a user or addressee located in Colombia. Notwithstanding the above it is important to remember that in this type of agreement, the person who pays for the software acquires a technological package that he or she therefore owns, and if he or she pays for a license of use, this license is not the main reason for the payment but rather an incidental fact to the payment for the production of software of specific characteristics. This, therefore, becomes a payment for the rendering of a technical service, which when being rendered abroad does not accrue VAT.

All of this leads to the conclusion that the DIAN has disregarded the above-mentioned consideration when analyzing the several operations on intangible products supplied online, and has mistaken the true nature of the transactions, submitting operations to VAT that are not subject to such tax. The DIAN has understood, as established by Opinion 67804 of October 17, 2002, that the only transactions that apply to software are (1) the sale of economic rights inherent to intellectual property of the software by its owner, exercising the right of disposal; and (2) the licensing and authorization for its use, without transferring of economic rights over intelligent development or logical support.

The confusion of the DIAN is such that the DIAN has supported in Opinions 4948 of 2002, 3133 of 2002, and 57,378 of 2000, that the export of software and of magazines and booklets contained on disc is to be considered an export of services.

C. Rendering of Services

Article 420 of the Colombian Tax Code establishes that VAT is applicable to the rendering of services in the national territory. Concerning the territoriality of VAT, the same legal provision establishes that services are deemed to have been rendered in the place of business of that person who renders the service.

Article 91 of Law 633 of 2000 provides that in Colombia, all Web pages and sites in the Internet whose economic activity is of a commercial, financial, or service-rendering character must be recorded in the mercantile registry and must submit to the DIAN the information over its economic transactions.

The Constitutional Court, through decision C-1147 of October 31, 2001, established that such obligation must be complied, in a professional manner, by those who carry out economic activities over the Internet through the Web pages of Colombian origin and that the foregoing is compatible with the principle of neutrality that governs taxation of e-commerce. Pursuant to this decision, taxation shall not be affected in any manner due to the virtual means used to carry on commercial activities, in order to avoid discrimination between electronic and traditional commerce.

Among the most common electronically rendered services are those for software maintenance; consultancy provided by professionals; computer professional services (related to outsourcing agreements), such as the use of equipment for limited time period; files and database consultations; computer marketing studies; technical and computer documentation for preventive, corrective, and preservation maintenance; data management; audit and diagnoses; development of feasibility studies; and investment or acquisition of goods or information technologies.[26] Consequently, if a company domiciled in Colombia or an individual residing in Colombia renders online services of software maintenance to another company domiciled in Colombia or to another individual residing in Colombia, such service shall be subject to VAT.

Pursuant to the provisions of letter (e) of Article 481(e) of the Colombian Tax Code, the export of services is VAT exempt.[27] Consequently, if a service of data management is rendered online by someone domiciled or resident in Colombia to benefit someone domiciled or resident abroad always provided that the use, advantage, or exploitation of the services is located abroad, despite that the rendering of the service is carried out in the country of export such service would be exempted from VAT.

However, the following services carried out from abroad that benefit users or addressees located in the national territory shall be understood to have been rendered in Colombia, and consequently are subject to VAT according to general rules:

1. Licenses and authorizations for the use and exploitation, at any title, of incorporeal or intangible goods;
2. Consultancy, advisory, and auditing professional services[28];
3. Lease of movable corporeal goods, except for those corresponding to vessels and aircraft and other movable goods destined to international transportation services by companies engaged in such activity;
4. Services of translation, correction, or drafting of texts;
5. Insurance, re-insurance, and co-insurance services, except those expressly exempted;
6. Those carried out in movable corporeal goods, except those directly related to the rendering of international transportation service;
7. Satellite connection or access services, regardless of the location of the satellite; and
8. The satellite television service received in Colombia, for which the taxable basis shall be represented by the total value billed to the user in Colombia.

Given the difficulty of determining where the services rendered online are used, the OECD states that in transactions benefiting companies, the consumption place for the

26 Rafael Oliver Cuello, Tributación del Comercio Electrónico 76 (Tirant Lo Blanch 1999).

27 Article 24 of Decision 599 establishes that the exported services shall be subject to the zero-rate regime.

28 In the community system, Article 24 of Decision 599 of CAN adopted the principle of imposition of services in the country of destination. Among the services subject to tax in the country of destination, one can find licenses and authorizations for the use and exploitation at any title, of incorporeal or intangible goods, as well as professional services of consulting, advisory, and auditing.

rendering of services and intangible goods is the place where the addressee has business presence. For Transactions in favor of individuals, the place for the rendering of services and intangible goods shall be that where the addressee has his or her customary residence. Until now, the DIAN has not issued an official position on this matter.

In addition, a professional consultancy or advisory service, in which technical assistance[29] is included, will be subject to VAT when rendered online abroad by a company without domicile in Colombia or by an individual without residence in Colombia. On the other hand, if the service rendered online abroad were is purely a technical service,[30] it would not be subject to tax in Colombia, given that, according to decisions dated February 12, 2004, and December 7, 2004, from the Fourth Section of the Council of State, technical services are not included among consulting services.

Although there is no legal statutory definition of technical services in Colombia, there is a definition provided by case law, pursuant to which technical services involve the direct application of technique by an operator or the application of special knowledge.[31] The DIAN has understood that the services on which technology is a means for the rendering of such services are considered technical services as well; such is the case of Web-hosting services or leasing of spaces for Web sites (and that would apply for many other types of services, including the offer of online games). The DIAN, in Opinion 076974 of 2002, stated that these digitally transmitted services were technical services "of intangible virtual character," given that the supplier has technological knowledge concerning the infrastructure that is the means for rendering the service.

The Web-hosting service is an "ISP (internet service provider) service that allows the server to memorize the client's page in a machine located near the user and permanently connected to Internet,"[32] namely, a "lease of a virtual space," which implies the lease of an incorporeal good. Thus, it is the rendering of a common service and not a technical service, which is the one that implies the use of a technological knowledge; and for this reason, if this service is rendered from abroad, it will not be subject to VAT.

In contrast, the OECD has stated that payments for allowing the access to one or more software applications and for Web hosting do not require application of special skills or knowledge but merely require the necessary equipment and software rights to make it available.[33]

---

29 Article 2 Regulatory 2123 of 1975: Technical assistance shall be understood as the advisory given through an agreement for the rendering of incorporeal services, for the use of technological knowledge applied by the exercise of an art or a technique. Such assistance comprises also the training of persons for the application of the expressed knowledge.

30 Writ dated July 26, 1984, and judicial decisions of April 29, 1988, and February 12, 2004, from the Council of State. Technical services imply to directly apply technique by an operator or to apply special knowledge.

31 Writ of July 26, 1984, and judicial decisions of April 29, 1988, and February 12, 2004, from the Council of State.

32 Piergiogio Valente, La Fiscalidad del Comercio electronicO (CISS: Praxis 2002).

33 OECD, *Taxation and Electronic Commerce: Implementing the Ottawa Taxation Framework Conditions* 166 (2001).

Likewise, concerning services of data processing, the DIAN is mistaken in its interpretation regarding qualification of these services for tax purposes. The DIAN established in Opinion 054967 of 2000 that the payments made by a company to its parent company abroad for the service of data processing through software are subject to VAT to the extent it is considered a technical service, when in fact it relates to an ordinary service that is rendered outside Colombia, and thus not subject to VAT.

Finally, pursuant to the provisions of Article 430 of the Colombian Tax Code, artistic and cultural services provided online from abroad are understood to be rendered in the place where they are physically carried out. Therefore, if these types of services are rendered online, the question that arises is whether the service should be considered to be rendered through the computer support of the user in Colombia or in that of the supplier abroad.

V. CONCLUSIONS

E-Commerce in Colombia is subject to general tax provisions, since no special regulation exists to grant it a different treatment.

Because incorporeal goods are excluded from VAT, supplies online have a treatment that lacks neutrality in that certain transactions are subject to different rules than those applied to the same transaction if carried out through traditional means.

Decision 599 from CAN corrects the prior imperfections of the Colombian VAT regime by including the sale of intangibles as a transaction that accrues VAT and by applying VAT to the import of services in the place of destination. This incorporation to Colombian internal law will ensure more neutral treatment to online commerce.

Some of the opinions by the DIAN regarding software licensing, online sales of intangible goods, and rendering of services in which technology is used are clearly mistaken, in this author's opinion, because they do not take into account the provisions on copyrights or the OECD analysis on those topics.

PART VI

Middle East

Chapter 20

Israel: Direct Taxation of E-Commerce Transactions in Israel

George Rosenberg
Rosenberg, Keren-Polak & Co., Advocates

I. INTRODUCTION

The sale of goods and services via the Internet has raised a number of regulatory issues, among them the matter of determining the basis of taxation of such transactions. This chapter will examine the Israeli tax system and its handling of direct taxation of Israeli residents and nonresidents. An overview of e-commerce in Israel will be provided. As is the case with many countries, Israel has also has opted not to enact specific tax rules for e-commerce transactions. This chapter will examine the possible reasons for this inaction.

Since specific rules have not been enacted to date, the subject of direct taxation of e-commerce in Israel will be treated by analyzing the Israeli Income Tax Ordinance, the published circulars of the Israeli Tax Authority, and Israel's treaties for the avoidance of double taxation.

In the course of the above, the chapter will examine the various issues arising from e-commerce, such as determining the origin of the transaction, income classification, dual residence, and others.

II. E-COMMERCE: AN OVERVIEW

A. E-Commerce Transactions in General

Electronic commerce (i.e., the sale of goods and services via the Internet) is a relatively new way of doing business. In traditional commerce it is fairly simple to ascertain the specifics of the transaction, such as the place of the transaction and the contracting parties. E-Commerce, in contrast, occurs in the virtual and borderless world of the Internet, via a network of computers.

The use of the Internet ignores national geographic borders and has enabled businesses to advertise, market, and sell their products and services using innovative and cost-efficient means available through the Internet. These new alternatives have caused businesses to rethink their corporate structure and reestablish their businesses in an effort to create a cost-efficient structure. The Internet also provides many businesses with a relatively easy way to manage their business ventures in various countries. For example, a business may manufacture a product in one country and create marketing venues in another country. This grants the company versatility in managing its business. Also, because of the customers' ability to order remotely via the Internet, a business is no longer required to have a fixed place of business in order to transport products or a service to its customers.[1]

E-Commerce has many advantages—notably the simplicity of the transaction—since the sale does not require the use of intermediaries such as agents, banks, and other financial institutions. The Internet also allows for accessibility to a large number of potential consumers simultaneously in many countries. The Internet has undeniably provided companies with an unprecedented and cost-efficient way to connect with their customers.

Confusion and uncertainty in the domestic law system, however, have been byproducts of the Internet's "global village" aspect. The new method of commerce raises fundamental regulatory concerns and has required governmental and multinational treatment in areas such as intellectual property, consumer protection, contract law, dispute resolution, and, of course, the imposition of tax.[2]

B. E-Commerce in Israel

E-Commerce in Israel only started to develop in 1999, and the amount of e-commerce transactions has since increased in a relatively slow pace, in comparison with other advanced economies. At the end of 2005, the market size of e-commerce transactions was estimated at approximately NIS 1.5 billion.[3]

According to surveys, a growing number of Israelis have been using the Internet. It is estimated that over 80 percent of households are currently connected to the Internet, compared with 67 percent in 2005.[4] Israelis are becoming accustomed very quickly to the idea of buying via the Internet, using online stores, and the governmental, banking, and investment online services.

The five major Internet service providers (ISPs) providing Internet access in Israel are Gold Lines, Internet Gold, Bezeq International, Barak, and Netvision.

---

1 Shai Dotan and Meir Shimra, *Taxation of Internet Transactions: Main Issues inCconnection with VAT*, 106 ISRAELI TAXATION QUARTERLY, available at http://www.mof.gov.il/museum/hebrew/internet.htm (in the Hebrew language).

2 Adv.(CPA) Ronen Arviv and Adv. Udi Schuster, *Electronic Commerce: Taxation Aspects*, at http://www.altertax.co.il/article_details.aspx?articleID=1428 (in the Hebrew language).

3 The Economist Intelligence Unit, Global Technology Forum, *Israel: Overview of E-Commerce* (Sept. 2006).

4 *Id.*

The telecommunications industry in Israel has been affected by the increasing convergence of the telecom, Internet, and broadcast cable service sectors. In recent years, large telecommunications companies have undergone a restructuring and consolidation process. Recent examples of this can be seen in the ISPs that have entered the telephony market, offering long-distance phone calls via the Internet (i.e., VoIP, or voice-over Internet protocol). Moreover, cable companies have entered into the domestic telephone market. By 2006 these companies had launched an all inclusive, "one-stop shop" type of telecom service package, including Internet, broadcast cable, and telephone services.[5]

The surge of online advertising is yet another indicator of the Internet's rising popularity in Israel: according to industry estimates, the market size of Internet advertising had reached approximately US$50 million in 2006, constituting more than 5 percent of the advertising market in Israel. In earlier years, the online advertising market had risen dramatically by 50 percent in 2003, to US$21–25 million, compared with US$13–17 million in 2002.[6]

The five leading Web portals in Israel are Walla!, MSN Israel, Y-net, Nana, and Tapuz; these leading portals take in over 70 percent of the advertising revenue.[7]

III. CHARACTERIZATION OF E-COMMERCE TRANSACTIONS

In order to understand the taxation problems arising from e-commerce, it is necessary to characterize or define e-commerce. To do so, one must first understand how the Internet works.

The Internet is a title for the transferring of information in the form of text, pictures, and music from one computer to another computer. The method used to do this is using binary codes transferred from one computer to another and decoded by "browsers" such as Microsoft Internet Explorer.

When a customer knows which product he or she wishes to order on a business's Web site, he or she must type in an address in the browser on his or her personal computer, and this address reaches the Web site. This process of connecting between the customer's wishes and the desired Web site is accomplished by an ISP. The customer's request, entered in the desired Web address, is transferred from the customer's personal computer through the ISP into a server that stores all of the Web site's information.

After receiving the request, an answer is transferred from the Web site to the consumer using the same path in reverse. The final result is that the consumer receives the contents of the Web site on his or her personal computer.[8]

5 *Id.*

6 *Id.*

7 Page Wunder and Lauren Rapaport, *The Information Technology Landscape in Israel, "Electronic Commerce,"* http://www.amercian.edu/carmel/nk3791a/Ecommerce.htm.

8 *See* footnote 1 above.

E-Commerce transactions can be divided in two main groups:

- Transactions using the Internet for ordering and purchasing *tangible* products and services (travel tickets, books, etc.) (hereinafter tangible transactions). In this case, the Internet is simply a device for purchasing the product, and the product itself is sent by mail or courier, or the service is provided tangibly.
- E-Commerce transactions in their pure form, wherein the product or service is intangible and may only be received via the Internet (hereinafter digital transactions). Such transactions are for digital goods (software, information, music, etc.) or services (search-engines, games, banking, etc.).

IV. REGULATION OF E-COMMERCE TAXATION IN ISRAEL

A. General

As is commonly the case with other countries, the current trend in Israel is not to enact specific laws regulating the taxation of cross-border e-commerce, but rather to adapt the existing law system to this relatively new medium.[9]

The Israeli Tax Authority (the Tax Authority) has published circulars referring to e-commerce in connection with double-taxation avoidance treaties, the classification of software transactions, and control and management issues. Often, the Tax Authority has quoted the position of the Organization for Economic Cooperation and Development (OECD), as will be elaborated on in section IV.

There may be several reasons for Israel's non-enactment of specific regulations pertaining to taxation of e-commerce:

- *Recent tax reform*—In 2003 Israel enacted a very significant tax reform. This tax reform changed the Israeli tax system from a territorial/remittance-based system of taxation to a personal system, wherein residents are taxed on a worldwide basis and nonresidents are taxed on a territorial basis. Fresh with this new worldwide system, the regulator's view may well be that any transaction undertaken by an Israeli resident, regardless of the jurisdiction in which such transaction is undertaken or which borders it crosses, is prima facie subject to tax in Israel.
- *Parity of income*—Another reason may be the notion, common to many other countries, that new or additional taxes are not needed in order to regulate e-commerce, since all income should be treated equally, regardless of whether such income is derived via electronic or more "traditional" commerce methods. It appears that the Tax Authority shares this view. An income tax circular published by the Tax Authority has stated explicitly that for the purposes of classifying certain electronic transactions,

---

9 Arthur J. Cockfield, *The Rise of the OECD as Informal 'world tax organization' through the Shaping of National Responses to E-commerce Tax Challenges*, YALE JOURNAL OF LAW AND TECHNOLOGY (forthcoming).

the Tax Authority makes no distinction between transactions performed traditionally and electronic transactions (the Software Circular).[10]

- *International tax treaties*—Israel's domestic nonregulation may stem from the view that since the nature of the e-commerce transaction is intrinsically cross-border and international, the natural arena for determining taxation of such transactions may be more properly the international forum within the context of international tax treaties. It is in this context that the Tax Authority frequently cites the OECD position on e-commerce taxation,[11] since the multinational OECD, in responding to the need for definitive principles on e-commerce taxation, has dealt with issues relating to determination of the source of the transaction and to income classification.[12]

B. Tax Liability According to Israeli Income Tax Ordinance

1. Israeli Tax Reform Israeli tax law has recently undergone major reform when the Knesset (the Israeli Parliament) adopted the Law to Amend the Income Tax Ordinance, No. 132 (2002) (hereinafter the Tax Reform), which came into force on January 1, 2003.

Prior to the Tax Reform, the tax system in Israel was based largely on a territorial/remittance basis: Ordinary income was taxed if it was accrued, derived, or received in Israel, largely without regard to the residency of the taxpayer (i.e., both Israeli residents and nonresidents were taxed on this basis).

The Tax Reform changed the tax system in respect of international taxation from a territorial one to a personal one based on residency, that is, taxation of Israeli residents on ordinary income earned worldwide (as was always the case in respect of capital gains). Nonresidents, as before, continue to be taxed on Israeli-sourced income only.

The Tax Reform has been followed by a series of related amendments of the Income Tax Ordinance (hereinafter the Tax Ordinance), which serve to fine-tune the major reform of 2003.

2. Who Is Considered an Israeli Resident for Tax Purposes? An "Israeli resident" is defined in the Tax Ordinance, in respect of an individual, as a person whose life is centered in Israel. Center-of-life of an individual is determined according to specific criteria set in the Tax Ordinance.[13]

In respect of a body of persons (e.g., a company), such body is resident in Israel if it is incorporated in Israel or if its business and management are controlled from Israel.

---

10 Classification of Income from International Software Transactions, Income Tax Circular 13/2001, 1 (Dec. 27, 2001).

11 Israel has recently been admitted to the OECD on the usual trial basis.

12 For an elaboration on this, *see* Chapter IV.

13 The center-of-life test takes into consideration the financial, economic, and social ties of the individual, including the location of the individual's permanent home; the place of residence of the individual and his or her family; and the location of his or her regular activities, jobs, assets and investments, clubs, unions, and institutions of which he or she is a member. (Tax Ordinance § 1).

3. Determining the Place Where Income Is Produced Setting clear rules for the determination of the source of the income, that is, the place in which income is accrued, is important in a personal taxation system in order to determine the jurisdiction that has the right to enforce its tax rules on its residents. This is also important with regard to entitlement to tax credits against foreign tax payments. Tax credits will be granted on account of foreign taxes paid by an Israeli resident—only if the place in which the income is deemed to be produced or accrued is outside of Israel.[14] In the case of non-residents, the determination that the transaction is sourced in Israel is important in order to determine Israel's right of taxation.

The place where certain kinds of income are produced is determined by the Tax Ordinance as follows:

- The source of income with regard to *business income* is determined according to "the place where the income-yielding business activity takes place."[15]
- In respect of payments *for use of an asset*, the place of income is where the asset is used.[16]
- In respect of *gain or profit, including royalties that stem from an intangible asset*, the place of income is determined according to the taxpayer's place of residence.[17]

4. Determining the Place Where Income Is Produced in E-Commerce Transactions Given the virtual and borderless nature of the sale of e-commerce goods and services, it is difficult to decide where exactly the "income-yielding business activity" actually takes place.

If the e-commerce transaction is between two Israeli residents, the e-commerce nature of the transaction is actually irrelevant since the personal tax regime dictates that residents are taxable, even if the server through which the transaction takes place is situated outside of Israel, and/or the goods/services provided in the transaction are delivered from abroad. For instance, say an Israeli travel agency sells an electronic ticket of a foreign airline to an Israeli resident, via a server based outside of Israel. This transaction will be classified as business income in the hands of the travel agency, which will be taxed accordingly.

What is the situation; however, if part of the sale occurs in a jurisdiction outside of Israel, that is, one of the parties to the transaction is a nonresident? And is there a difference, in such case, if the server is situated outside of Israel or not? Is the source of the income produced by the transaction now shifted to a jurisdiction where the non-resident resides or where the server is located, so that such jurisdiction may claim a right to tax?

---

14 Israeli Tax Authority Circular no. 21/2002, *The Income Tax Reform: International Taxation*.

15 Tax Ordinance § 4A(1).

16 *Id.* at § 4A(6).

17 *Id.* at § 4A (7).

C. Application of the Tax Rules to Tangible Transactions or Digital Transactions

1. Tangible Transactions In transactions which may be characterized as tangible transactions (see section III above), the e-commerce aspect of the transaction (i.e., the use of the Internet) is only the facilitator for the transaction and not the transaction itself.

Thus, when one orders a book from Amazon over the Internet, the entire sale process—order, payment, and delivery—is basically the same as any remote sale processes that had been in use prior to the introduction of the Internet, for example, purchasing a book via the mail. As such, there is no difficulty in applying the existing tax rules to such a tangible transaction.

In the Amazon example above, the income earned by Amazon is sourced in the place where Amazon has its residence. Although Amazon is doing business with a book purchaser who resides elsewhere, Amazon is not doing business in the place of residence of the purchaser, unless it has a permanent establishment in such place (see below in section IV). Therefore, the right to tax ought to be in the jurisdiction where Amazon resides.

The tax liability is no different if the purchaser in one jurisdiction sends a letter, or telephones, with his or her credit card details, to a bookstore in another jurisdiction and asks that the book be delivered by mail or courier.

2. Digital Transactions In digital transactions it is difficult to apply these rules in the same way, mainly because it is more difficult to classify the type of income. As pointed out above, there are no specific domestic tax provisions in Israel dealing with the classification of income in connection with digital transactions, in general. Nevertheless, since the object of many digital transactions is software—whether as the asset itself that is being sold or as the platform on which a digital sale is to take place—it is useful examine the Software Circular,[18] which was published by the Tax Authority and deals with classification of income, both in respect of domestic transactions and international transactions. The circular may be summarized as follows.

A. OUTRIGHT SALE AND A LICENSE TRANSACTION "Outright sale" is a transaction for the sale of the *total* software asset, including all rights appertaining thereto. "License transaction" is a transaction granting a *license for a limited use* of the software asset. The software asset may be a copyright of the software, or a software copy.

B. OUTRIGHT SALE OF COPYRIGHT OF THE SOFTWARE This type of outright sale is a sale of the copyright itself and all related rights, characterized by a preponderance of the following characterizations:

- Transfer and waiver of the essential share of owner's copyright;
- Transfer of or providing access to the source code;

18 *See* note 10.

- Purchaser is entitled to carry out any modifications, adjustments, or applications in the software;
- Purchaser is entitled to prepare unlimited copies of the software;
- Purchaser is entitled to publicly distribute the software by sale, lease, or loan;
- Purchaser is entitled to exhibit the software publicly; and
- No requirements to destroy or return the software after a defined period of time.

C. OUTRIGHT SALE OF A COPY OF THE SOFTWARE This is a sale of a copy of the software usually without any other rights such as copyright (e.g., sale of a book), and is characterized by a *preponderance* of the following characterizations:

- Purchaser buys the copy for his or her personal use only, or marketing purposes only.
- Period of use is unlimited, or limited for the life period of the copy.
- Length or extent of the use period does not affect the payment.
- No undertaking on the purchaser's part to return or destroy the copy.
- Copy may be used "as-is," and requires no special adjustments.
- Purchaser is entitled to transfer the "license" to another person, or copy was purchased under an anonymous license agreement (even if such license includes a prohibition on the transfer of the copy to another person).

D. LICENSE—COPYRIGHT OR COPY OF SOFTWARE Any transaction that does not fall within an outright sale (copyright or copy) transaction, as defined above, is a *license* transaction, either of software copyright or copy, as the case may be.

A high component of support services may indicate that the transaction is a license transaction.

From the above Software Circular, the following conclusions may be drawn regarding the classification of income generated by software.

If the transaction in question is for *the outright sale of the software* (copyright or a copy of software), then the income may be classified either as

- Ordinary income from a business, if it is carried on in the ordinary course of business of the seller, and accordingly it will be subject to tax in the place where the business activity, which produces the income, is carried on, that is, the place where the sale is consummated, where the software is delivered for use;[19] or
- Capital gain, if it is a capital transaction not carried out in the ordinary course of business of the seller, and accordingly it will be subject to tax in accordance with the special provision in the Tax Ordinance dealing with capital gains.[20]

19 Tax Ordinance § 4A(a)(1).

20 Tax Ordinance, Chapter V: Residents are subject to capital gains tax on a worldwide basis; nonresidents are subject to tax if the asset was situated in Israel or if the asset sold was a right to an asset in Israel. The tax rate for capital gains is fixed at 20%, or 25% if the taxpayer owned 10% of more of the asset sold (substantial shareholder).

If the transaction may be classified as *the grant of a right of use* in the software, that is, a "license," then the income will be deemed as income from "royalties," or "income from gain or profit that stem from an intangible asset," or "fees for the use of an asset" and will be subject to tax in Israel if the *payer* is resident, or the asset is *used*, in Israel.[21]

The above classifications ought to hold true notwithstanding that the services offered via the server may originate from a server situated in a place other than where the business activity took place or where the payer is resident.

3. International Transactions The above domestic rules are applicable generally, *mutatis mutandis*, to cross-border international transactions as well. In such transactions, the classification of income will first be carried out in accordance with the domestic rules, as above, and then the provisions of the relevant convention for the avoidance of double taxation (tax treaty), if there is one, will be applied.

In applying the tax treaty, the links, which the cross-border nature of e-commerce typically creates between Israel and other jurisdictions, must also be considered. These links may raise the following issues, among others:

- Which links, with regard to e-commerce, will be considered as granting the source country right of taxation? (That is, which link, for example, will constitute a permanent establishment?)
- Dual-residence issues—What if the Israeli resident is also considered a resident of the foreign jurisdiction (i.e., the source country)?
- Upon determining that the transaction is, in fact, liable to tax in the source country, then at what rate, and which part of the transaction will be taxed?

Answers to these matters may be found in the tax treaties to which Israel is a party (see below), the OECD commentary on tax treaties, and tax circulars published by the Tax Authority.

V. TAX TREATIES

A. General

In general, a tax treaty determines the relative rights of two countries to tax a transaction that—according to the respective domestic tax laws of the two countries—gives rise to a tax liability in both countries. The provisions of tax treaties normally override the domestic laws of both contracting countries.

In determining the relative rights of the two countries, tax treaties set conditions whereby the transaction is deemed to be sourced in one country or the other, as well as the applicable tax rates. Tax treaties also outline a tax credit mechanism in order to avoid double taxation when the taxpayer is liable to taxes in both countries. Such treaties

21 Tax Ordinance § 4A(a)(7) and (6).

also grant exemptions or reduced tax rates on certain income such as royalties, dividends, and interest.

Israel is a signatory to 45 tax treaties that are in force.[22] Tax treaties were also signed, but not yet ratified, with Portugal and Latvia.

Most of Israel's tax treaties are based on the OECD Model Tax Convention on Income and on Capital (OECD Model Convention). Some of the treaties also include provisions from the UN Model Double-Taxation Convention between Developed and Developing countries.

After signature, each state needs to ratify the tax treaty. In Israel, the ratification is done by the Knesset, and afterward by the government. After concluding ratification procedures, the Israeli Minister of Finance issues regulations[23] that give effect to the treaty. Under Israeli tax law the provisions of tax treaties override any domestic tax legislation.

B. Applicability of Tax Treaty Rules to E-Commerce

1. Concept of Residence Tax treaties to which Israel is party are binding on Israeli residents and residents of the contracting country. The residence is determined according to each contracting country's internal law.[24] What happens, however, in a case in which two countries claim a person or body of persons as resident?

In case of dual residence of a company, this situation is resolved by a "tie-breaker" rule. In most of Israel's tax treaties, the tie-breaker rule determines that the country where the company has its effective or actual management is the country in which that company is resident for tax purposes.[25] This is in line with the OECD

22 The countries with which Israel has double-taxation avoidance treaties, as of November 2007, are Austria, Belarus, Belgium, Bulgaria, Brazil, Canada, China, Croatia, Czech Republic, Denmark, Ethiopia, Finland, France, Germany, Greece, Hungary, India, Ireland, Italy, Jamaica, Japan, Latvia, Lithuania, Luxembourg, Mexico, Moldova, Netherlands, Norway, Philippines, Poland, Romania, Russia, Singapore, Slovakia, South Africa, South Korea, Spain, Sweden, Switzerland, Thailand, Turkey, Ukraine, United Kingdom, United States, and Uzbekistan.

23 Tax Ordinance § 196.

24 Israeli Tax Authority Circular 8/2002, *Permanent Residence* in Tax Treaties. The circular specifies criteria for determining residence of *an individual*, but such criteria are less relevant for the purposes of this article. According to recent Israeli case law (*Israeli District Court: G-Tech Technologies Ltd. v. Kfar Saba Tax Assessor*, T.A 1255/02 (April 7, 2005)), the assessed person (resident of either contracting parties) may request with regard to a specific matter, to enter into the mutual agreement procedure set in the tax treaty. In such case, the application should be filed with the appropriate authority in the residence country. Such authority shall determine the assessed person's claim and whether the imposed tax was in accordance with the treaty. The judgment further held that the mutual-agreement procedure set in the tax treaty was part of the auditing procedure, and, therefore, the mutual-agreement procedure should first be exhausted so long as the residence country's courts have not rendered a final tax judgment.

25 *See* Israeli Tax Authority Circular 4/2002. Note that this circular deals with the issue of management and control in general, and states in its conclusions that "at this stage" the circular does not deal with this issue in the context of e-commerce that is currently being examined within the framework of the OECD.

Model Convention.[26] According to this criterion, the place in which the entity is managed in actual fact, and in which substantively all the important strategic decisions are resolved, is the place of effective management and, therefore, tax residence.

The "place of effective management" criterion is similar to the "control and management" concept in Israeli tax law. According to the Tax Ordinance, apart from the residence test based simply on incorporation in Israel, a body of persons is also resident in Israel if its business and management are controlled from Israel.

The declared policy of the Tax Authority is to include in the concept of "control and management" not only the place from where the everyday business of a company is carried on but also the place where the strategic decisions and long-term planning are carried on. This is in line with one of the options suggested by the OECD Model Convention, to wit: the place where the majority of senior executive decisions are taken and where the corporate headquarters are located.[27]

The Tax Authority, however, has extended the above policy to mean that the place of *residence* of the persons, who operate the company and/or make the strategic decisions, is the place of residence of the company. In other words, if such decisions are made by an Israeli *resident*, regardless of the place where they are made, the Tax Authority takes the position that the company is resident in Israel.

This is a doubtful extension and position—not as yet challenged in the courts—of the definition of residence of a "body of persons" in the Tax Ordinance. Such definition attributes Israeli residence to any foreign body corporate (body of persons) if "the control and management of its business are exercised from Israel."[28] In other words, the *residence* of the person who is exercising the management and control is not relevant. What is relevant is the *place* from where such management and control are exercised. Thus, contrary to the interpretation of the Tax Authority, the exercise of control and management of the business of a foreign company by an Israeli resident, where such exercise takes place outside of Israel, ought not to result in the company being deemed an Israeli resident. Conversely, where a nonresident exercises the management and control of a foreign company from within Israel, such company ought to be deemed resident in Israel.

Moreover, in the Internet age, determining the "place of effective management" may be more complicated. Before the advent of Internet technology, directors held face-to-face meetings in order to make business decisions and resolve operational issues. Current technological advancements, such as video conferencing and e-mail exchanges, may cause difficulties in determining place of effective management. Maintaining a physical head office may no longer be needed because directors and managers, who maintain residences in different jurisdictions, are able to attend meetings without leaving

26 Section 4 of the OECD Model Convention states, "Where by reason of the provisions of paragraph 1 a person other than an individual is a resident of both Contracting States, then it shall be deemed to be a resident only of the State in which its place of effective management is situated."

27 Arthur J. Cockfield, *The Rise of the OECD as Informal "World Tax Organization" through the Shaping of National Responses to E-Commerce Tax Challenges*, Yale Journal of Law and Technology (forthcoming).

28 Tax Ordinance § 1.

their desks. This increases the difficulty for high-tax countries to assert that corporations are residents of their jurisdictions.[29]

As the use of new communication technologies opens up the possibility of avoiding residence in high-tax jurisdictions, such as Israel, the ability to escape tax liability, both in respect of domestic law and relevant tax treaty provisions, is made easier. It appears, therefore, that the criterion of "effective place of management" must be redefined to take into the account the use of new communication devices.

2. Income Classification under Tax Treaties in General The domestic rules of income classification that have been examined above must now be reexamined in the context of the tax treaties as they apply to e-commerce. The importance of the classification stems from the fact that the domestic tax laws of most countries and all the tax treaties impose different taxes on various classes of income.

In the context of international e-commerce and tax treaties, it is often important to distinguish between payments classified as "business profits" and those classified as "royalties."

3. Business Profits Income derived from tangible transactions is considered business profits. Since e-commerce transactions involving online advice, communications with technicians, use of database, and so forth are considered *provision of tangible services* rather than know-how, the income derived from these transactions would also be considered business profits.

Income derived from digital transactions may also result in business profits, although when digital goods are downloaded in order to exploit copyright relating to the digital goods, this may be classified as royalties rather than business profits.

The current rules do not distinguish between the methods of transaction—traditional or digital—and make an effort to treat substantively similar sales of services/products in the same manner regarding income classification. Thus, business profits, which under domestic Israeli rules would normally be taxed at source, under Israel's tax treaties are not taxed at the source country unless a permanent establishment exists (see below). This is in line with the OECD Model Convention, which states that business profits may be taxed in the source country "but only so much of them as are attributable to that permanent establishment."[30]

4. Royalties In the event that the digital transaction involves the transfer of the *right to use the copyright in a digital product*, then the payments will be considered royalties.

"Royalties" usually pertain to payments for use of copyright and other intangible assets. In most of Israel's tax treaties, and in accordance with the OECD Model Convention, the term "royalties" is defined as "payments of any kind received as

---

29 Dr. Doron Herman, Adv., S. Fridman & Co, *E-commerce: The Online Challenge for Tax Rules*, in ANNUAL SUMMARY (2000) at http://course_materials/Skira-eCommerce_2000.doc (in the Hebrew language).

30 OECD Model Convention, "Business Profits," art. 7.

consideration for the use of, or the right to use, any copyright of literary, artistic or scientific work including cinematograph films, any patent, trademark, design or model, plan secret formula or process, or for information concerning industrial, commercial or scientific experience."

In most instances there is a fixed rate of withholding tax deducted by the source country, such rate being less than the normal rate payable under the domestic law. Conversely, the tax treaties typically allow the recipient's country to impose a tax at the normal tax rate on the royalty received. Thus in the case of Israel, where an Israeli resident receives royalties from a resident of a treaty country, the Israeli resident will be subject to the full marginal tax rate in the case of an individual[31] or the corporate tax rate in the case of company[32], subject to a credit for the withholding tax paid in the source country.

5. Disagreement as to Classification When the residence country and the source country do not agree on the classification of the transaction, then there may a case of double taxation, since the residence country might not recognize the tax that was already paid in the source country, for the purpose of tax credits.

6. OECD Position Since cross-border transactions performed via the Internet raise income classification issues, the OECD has offered its position on the characterization of income produced by the e-commerce sale. For software transactions via the Internet, the OECD has distinguished between the underlying copyright in the program and software that incorporates a copy of the copyrighted program. This position is reflected in the Software Circular of the Tax Authority, referred to above.

The OECD commentary on the OECD Model Convention (the commentary) now clarifies that e-commerce transfers of all digital products should attract the same treatment as software payments, *and that the technological method of transfer is not relevant.*

7. Permanent Establishment in E-Commerce As discussed above, a tax treaty applies only to the residents of both contracting countries, but for the purpose of apportioning the tax between the two countries, it is the country in which the person receiving the income resides that constitutes the *residence country*. The *source country*, by contrast, is determined in most tax treaties according to the place where the income-producing activity takes place. The apportionment of the taxes between the residence country and the source country may vary, however, in those cases, where the recipient of the income (the residence country) has some presence in the source country. The issue whether such presence is sufficient to cause a variance in the tax apportionment is settled, typically, in tax treaties by determining whether the recipient of the income has a "permanent establishment" in the source country, through which he or she conducts the business that produces the income.

Most tax treaties define "permanent establishment," in general, as "the fixed place of business through which business is conducted," and in particular most of Israel's

31 The rate for 2008 is 47%.

32 The rate for 2008 is 27%.

tax treaties and in the OECD Model Convention define "permanent establishment" as follows:[33]

The term 'permanent establishment' includes especially:

1. a place of management;
2. a branch;
3. an office;
4. a factory;
5. a workshop; and
6. a mine, an oil or gas well, a quarry or any other place of extraction of natural resources.

The OECD Model Convention then goes on to exclude certain actions as *not constituting* a permanent establishment, among them, activities that are of a "preparatory or auxiliary character."

Dependent agents who have the authority to sign contracts on behalf of a principal company are also deemed permanent establishments.

The Commentary on Article 5 of the OECD Model Convention, which is similar to the typical article regarding permanent establishments in Israel's tax treaties, reads as follows: "The definition, therefore, contains the following conditions . . . the carrying on of the business of the enterprise through this fixed place of business. This means usually that persons, who, in one way or another, are dependant on the enterprise (personnel), conduct the business of the enterprise in the State in which the fixed place is situated."

Can the situation be different in the case of e-commerce? Can a company have a permanent establishment in a jurisdiction even though it does not own any office premises, nor does it employ any personnel, in the jurisdiction in question?

The commentary, in discussing permanent establishment in relation to e-commerce,[34] takes the following position:

- No human intervention is required for a permanent establishment to exist.
- A Web site cannot, in itself, constitute a permanent establishment.
- While a place where computer equipment is located may in certain circumstances constitute a permanent establishment, this requires that the functions performed at that place be significant as well as an essential or core part of the business activity of the enterprise.
- For computer equipment to constitute a permanent establishment it must be
  - *Tangible property*—Therefore, the data and software that is used by, or stored on, that equipment will *not* be considered permanent establishment;
  - *At the disposal of the enterprise*—For example, the enterprise should own or lease and operate the computer equipment;
  - *Fixed*—That is, the equipment is located at a certain place for a sufficient period of time; what is relevant is not the possibility of it being moved, but whether it is in fact moved.

---

33 OECD Model Convention, art. 5, § 2.

34 Commentary on Article 5, ¶ 42.

Moreover, even where computer equipment is used only for "preparatory or auxiliary activities" (e.g., provision of a communications link, much like a telephone line, between suppliers and customers) and therefore, prima facie, may not constitute a permanent establishment, nevertheless "where such functions form in themselves an essential and significant part of the business activity of the enterprise as a whole, or where other core functions of the enterprise are carried on through the computer equipment, these would go beyond such preparatory or auxiliary activities.[35]

Pursuant to the above, the commentary indicates that a server will constitute a permanent establishment if (1) the server performs integral aspects of a cross-border transaction;[36] (2) the server is owned or leased by the nonresident firm;[37] and (3) the server is fixed in a location for a sufficient period of time.[38] Therefore, installing a server that complies with the above specifications of a permanent establishment may well attract tax liability in that jurisdiction, for better or for worse.

Notwithstanding the above position of the OECD on servers, there is a school of thought that opposes this position for the following reasons:[39]

- A server is simply a computer networked to the Internet much like millions of other computers, all of which, therefore, theoretically could be regarded as permanent establishments.
- The specifications required for a server to be a permanent establishment focus on the function of the server, that is, on its software content. While creating the original software has a high cost, the cost of copying it and moving it from server to server is negligible. Thus to tax in the place where copied software is used in a server is contrary to the doctrine that income tax should be levied at the place where the value is added or where the goods or services are consumed.
- It is too easy a tool for international tax planning to enable tax avoidance by transferring servers from a high-tax jurisdiction to a low-tax one.
- Contrary to the traditional definition of permanent establishment, which focuses on fixed installations, difficult to move (factories, building sites, etc.), that is not the case with servers that can easily be moved.
- The method to be used by tax authorities to attribute profits to servers is unclear since this is in the realm of cross-border trade in intangible assets. As such, this may lead to double taxation.

As mentioned, however, despite the weight of these arguments against the permanent-establishment/server OECD rule, it would appear that the Tax Authority would follow

35 Commentary on Article 5, ¶ 42.8.

36 *Id.*

37 Commentary on Article 5, ¶ 42.3.

38 Commentary on Article 5, ¶ 42.4.

39 *See* Arthur J. Cockfield, *The Rise of the OECD as Informal "World Tax Organization" through the Shaping of National Responses to E-Commerce Tax Challenges*, Yale Journal of Law and Technology (forthcoming).

the OECD rule since, to date, it has clearly followed the OECD guidance in tax treaty matters.

Although to date there has been no Israeli jurisprudence regarding the permanent-establishment/server issue itself, the courts have also adopted the OECD commentary as an inherently necessary interpretive tool. Such adaptation is exemplified in recent Israeli case law[40] which held as follows:

> The position of the [OECD] organization, although it is not binding on the Israeli courts, does have great persuasive and interpretive value; among other reasons, because it expresses the attitudes of the countries that are members in the organization, and sets forth the desired interpretation for countries requesting to join the organization. Clearly it is enough that one of the contracting parties is a member of the organization in order to cause an expectation between two contracting states of a treaty based on the OECD model, that such treaty will be interpreted according to the [OECD] commentary, as these are published from time to time. Uniform interpretation by the courts of the contracting states in implementing tax treaties based on the OECD model, is an actual necessity that is inherent in the implementation of the treaty that is in it a contractual act that becomes law within countries that ratify the treaty . . .[41]

VI. TAXATION OF INCOME OF NONRESIDENTS IN E-COMMERCE TRANSACTIONS IN ISRAEL

A nonresident of Israel is defined in the Tax Ordinance as a person who is not a resident as defined in the Tax Ordinance.[42] Nonresidents are taxed in Israel on income accrued or produced in Israel.[43]

The criteria for determining whether income was accrued or produced in Israel differ with regard to different types of income: *business income* depends on the place in which the income producing activity takes place, whereas *royalties from an intangible asset* are determined according to the place of residence of the payer. Thus, the same source rules which apply to Israeli residents,[44] apply conversely to taxation of nonresidents in Israel.

For example, if a nonresident company has a permanent establishment situated in Israel, then income from its e-commerce transactions that constitute *business profits* will be taxable in Israel, regardless of whether the payer is an Israeli resident or nonresident, and notwithstanding the fact that the tax treaty between Israel and the country where the nonresident company is resident exempts business profits from tax in Israel.

---

40 *Yanko-Weiss Holdings v. Holon Tax Assessment Officer*, District Court Decision 005663/07 (Dec. 30, 2007).

41 *Id.* at 8.

42 For the definition of an Israeli resident, *see* Chapter III, § 2.

43 Tax Ordinance § 2.

44 *See* Chapter III, § 2.

Here is another example: if a nonresident company has no permanent establishment in Israel, and the transaction involves the payment of *royalties* to the nonresident company, nevertheless, such royalties, payable by an Israeli resident, will also be taxable in Israel.

Once the nonresident's tax liability is determined according to the Tax Ordinance as in the two above scenarios, then Israel will be deemed the "source country" for the purposes of the application of the tax treaty between Israel and the country of residence of the nonresident.

The analysis in section IV with regard to tax treaties and income classification is also relevant, *mutatis mutandis*, in the case of taxation of nonresidents.

VII. CONCLUSION

By and large, the taxation of e-commerce in Israel is not regulated by any tax provisions that specifically relate to e-commerce. Thus, one must look at the general taxation provisions of the Israeli Income Tax Ordinance and apply these to e-commerce transactions, whether they are tangible transactions or digital transactions. This relates particularly to the issues of residence and classification of income.

Because of the cross-border nature of most e-commerce transactions, tax treaties play an important role in determining the tax liability of these transactions. While here, too, the text of the law normally does not regulate the taxation of e-commerce specifically, nevertheless, thanks to the OECD and its commentary on the OECD Model Convention, there is certain guidance to the taxation of e-commerce. Israel, by and large, has adopted this guidance.

The Israel Income Tax Authority has also published definitive rules for classifying software transactions, both domestically and internationally. In addition, the Tax Authority has postulated that for the purpose of classifying income and applying the rules that correspond to each class of income, there should be no difference between traditional transactions and e-commerce ones. The OECD has stated a similar position.

The chapter has shown that in the case of direct taxation Israel has chosen, similarly to other countries, to classify e-commerce transactions as to their substance rather than technical form, and not to afford e-commerce transactions special treatment differing from traditional ones.

Notwithstanding the above position of the Tax Authority, it is difficult to believe that there will be no specific Israeli tax legislation in the future dealing with certain aspects of e-commerce. E-Commerce is still relatively new, but considering Israel's very prominent role on the global high-tech scene, and the high percentage of Israeli residents who use computers; there will be a steady rise in e-commerce activity. This fact, together with ever-increasing number of Israeli companies who are developing e-commerce, will force the Tax Authority, sooner or later, to confront the subject of taxation of e-commerce with specific legislation.

Chapter 21

Turkey: Development of E-Commerce Legislation and Taxation of Revenues from Online Content in Turkey

Orhan Yavuz Mavioğlu and Onur Ulusakarya
ADMD Law Office, Turkey

I. INTRODUCTION

Activities such as production, presentation, sales, insurance, distribution, and payment of goods and services are possible via computer networks with e-commerce. E-commerce presents major physical differences from conventional commerce, and therefore many arguments have been raised regarding the problems of regulating and taxing e-commerce under the old commercial and tax regimes applicable.

As e-commerce evolved rapidly, Turkey began to customize the current tax systems and take major legislative measures. Along with these legislative decisions, an Internet Tax Office was established, enabling taxpayers to access their own declarations and make submissions accordingly. This chapter will try to analyze these and other electronic adaptation measures taken by Turkey and the administrative bodies who regulate such measures.

II. E-COMMERCE COORDINATION COMMITTEE AND INTERNET SUPREME COUNCIL

In 1997 the High Council for Science and Technology of the government established a special committee dealing with e-commerce issues, and a special administration for science and technology called TUBITAK and the undersecretary of foreign trade of the prime ministry were assigned to this project. The E-Commerce Coordination Commission (ETKK) held its first meeting in 1998, and three different work groups were formed to draft necessary resolutions for the government to regulate e-commerce.

The first target of ETKK was to promote e-commerce security and legalization via digital signature verifications according to applicable global standards. In addition, the project aimed to provide a secure zone with privacy and integrity of information on the Web so that this secure zone would abolish the technical, legal, and financial limitations of e-commerce in Turkey.

The researches of ETKK proved that development of e-commerce was directly related to the validity of agreements between individuals, the conditions of these agreements, and the ability to prove capacity of consent. Therefore, as stated above, the significance of signatures in e-agreements under the provisions of the Turkey Code of Obligations and the "proof capacity in e-agreements" under the provisions of Code of Civil Procedure, the Turkish Commercial Code, and the Criminal Code became the focus of attention by the Turkish authorities when adapting its legislation to e-commerce transactions. The European Union (EU) and the United Nations Commission on International Law (UNCITRAL) standards were the main sources for this legislative work in Turkey. Specifically, the government of Turkey used the Austria's Electronic Signature Code and related Austria Regulations, dated May 2000. After numerous studies and reports, ETKK enacted the main regulations on e-commerce in Turkey, which will be covered later in this chapter.

In 2001, the Ministry of Communication organized an Internet Supreme Council (ISC) to deal with issues related to the Internet and its effects. The ISC's primary duties were the planning, coordination, and monitoring of the Internet infrastructure and its operations in Turkey. Accordingly, the ISC also cooperated with ETKK and other administrative bodies of the government in updating the Turkish legislation.

III. E-SIGNATURE

The Law of Electronic Signature No. 5070, dated January 15, 2004, is the most important legislation on e-commerce in Turkey. This main regulation provides validity to e-signatures for all legal transactions and provides commercial security for e-commerce activities in general.

UNCITRAL published the ground-setting arrangements on e-signature by drafting the UNCITRAL Model Law on Electronic Signatures in 2001. ETKK made studies and proposed that the Turkish government and the parliament adapt this model law into the Turkish domestic legislation.

The UNCITRAL Model Law was drafted to cover the concepts of declaration of intent such as the legal offer and acceptance in electronic transactions. Likewise, electronic data was described as information that is created by electronic, optic, or similar tools and then, sent, received and stored. The UNCITRAL Model Law defined an electronic signature as any symbol, process, or voice that is attached to an electronic record as proof of signature.

An e-signature depends on technologies of public-key cryptography and asymmetric crypto system to provide high security. The concept of e-signature under Turkish law is very general, and its description includes scanned and digitize handmade signatures of people; recorded biological features of people, such as retina, fingerprints, or voice;

and numerical signatures. Numerical signatures differ from signed text, and they are required by using mathematical functions.

According to Article 3 of the Turkish E-Signature Law, "Electronic signature is a data which is annexed to another electronic data or a related electronic data for identification purposes." Thus, the law aims to provide flexibility on the electronic identification of parties and their consents, subject to available technology that evolves almost every day.

The same principles of offer and acceptance for general transactions among parties found in the Turkish Law of Obligations are applicable to e-commerce transactions. If signature verification is not sought for a non-electronic transaction to become valid, e-signatures will not be subject to verification in electronic transactions. The law aims to harmonize the standards applicable for electronic or non-electronic transactions. Therefore, agreements that require an attached signature under the Law of Obligations will require an e-signature if they are made in electronic format.

In e-commerce, validity of identification of the parties, their consents, and security of information among them must be guaranteed by the technical and legal infrastructure. The most important tool for such purpose, therefore, is an e-signature.

According to Article 4 of the Turkish E-Signature Law, a secure electronic signature shall have the following:

1. Exclusivity for connection verification to the signature holder;
2. A secure electronic-signature generator tool;
3. A qualified electronic certificate to identify the signature owner; and
4. Security for the e-signing data of the signature holder after the date has been signed.

In Turkish law, the value of a signature is generally designated in the Law of Obligations in Article 13 which states that "written agreements have to possess the signature of the party undertaking such obligation; unless otherwise stipulated, a signed letter or a telegraph signed by such party may fulfill this requirement." According to a former Article 14 of the Law of Obligations, titled "Signature," a "[s]ignature has to be handwritten by the one who assumes obligation." In order to satisfy such signature requirement, the E-Signature Law amended the above-mentioned clause, and a new clause was added to Article 14 stating that "[h]andwritten signatures have the same evidence power as secured electronic signatures." Therefore, e-signatures are granted the same legal value as handwritten signatures under Turkish law.

The E-Signature Law not only triggered changes to the traditional Law of Obligations, as above mentioned, but also Article 295/A of the Code of Civil Procedure was amended in order to provide electronic signatures and relevant documentation data the value of a legal instrument that could be presented as proof in legal proceedings.

The E-Signature Law also developed requirements for security and verification tools for e-signatures as follows:

1. Security generator tools shall have unique generation data.
2. Recorded generation data of electronic signature cannot be taken out of such generation tool and shall be private.

3. Generator tools shall be preserved from any third-party access and be protected against counterfeiting.
4. Generator tools shall not allow anyone except the signature owner to change data to be signed and shall allow viewing of that data before the actual e-signing.
5. Signature verification tools shall show data for verifying signature party.
6. Verification tools shall operate secure and accurate verification processes and shall show verification results without change to signature holder.
7. Verification tools shall store and present the signed data securely.
8 Verification tools shall determine reliability and validity of the electronic certificate used for signatures and shall present the results to the verifying person.
9. Verification tools shall present identity of the owner of signature to verifying person.
10. Verification tools shall provide conditions for determining any changes made after signature that may affect the verification.

Hence, even if the above conditions are present, e-signature cannot be used for all transactions according to Turkish law. Article 5 of Turkish E-Signature Law establishes that legal transactions that require a mandatory formal ceremony or a mandatory format cannot be verified by e-signature. For instance, the actual sale or commitment to sell real estate property in Turkey could not be concluded electronically, since such a transaction is governed by specific legal ceremony to be concluded before a designated legal authority.

IV. INTERNET TAX OFFICE

The Turkish Internet Tax Office (ITO) has been in service since 1999 as part of the Tax Office Full Automation Project (VEDOP). The ITO is one of the government offices created to achieve transparency of public administration and individuals' access to government records. The ITO, online at www.gelirler.gov.tr, allows tax subjects to track down their tax processes and their own information online. This Web site also allows taxpayers to make their private consumption tax payment online.

The ITO consists of corporate tax administration, income tax administration, and motor Vehicles tax administration offices. Individuals could search for information at the Web site such as tax identity information, certification numbers, notices of assessment and revenues, matured and nonmatured tax information, additional notifications regarding terms and assessment, revenue information, electronic processes of tax collection, and prohibitions to travel abroad for nonpaying individuals.

Taxpayers could also search for vehicle information registered to automated tax administrations, information on motor-vehicles tax due, traffic ticket information, and all other collections of information from the mentioned Web site. Daily information of the automated tax administrations is transferred to the central database via VEDOP.

Electronic Bank Collection Project (EBTIS) also evolved within the structure of VEDOP. EBTIS helps process tax-payment transfers through banks. Accordingly, electronic banking payments eased the processing of over ten million tax-payment receipts.

The ITO also enables searching for motor vehicles that are registered to automated tax offices for traffic ticket information, vehicle tax information, and other such information.

The ITO has been in service for corporate taxpayers since 2000 and for income taxpayers since 2001. Since 2006, corporate tax declarations and valued-added tax (VAT) returns are totally automated, and all such services are handled online.

V. ELECTRONIC TAX STATEMENTS

In early 2004, the Ministry of Finance proposed some tax amendments that were later adopted in the Tax Procedure Code No. 213. The amendment allowed taxpayers to submit their tax declarations and statements in electronic format to achieve efficiency. The goal was to allow taxpayers to use available electronic technology for simple, quick, and inexpensive tax submissions, and to allow tax administrations better access to their own filings for auditing purposes.

The Communiqué of Tax Procedure Code No. 376 published by the Ministry of Finance in October 2007 is the most recent legislation introducing a significant legal change in Turkey. Tax Procedure Code No. 376 allowed income and corporate taxpayers, taxable due to their commercial, agricultural, and professional activities, to submit their withholding tax returns, VAT returns, and temporary income tax statements online.

Corporations or individuals submitting their tax statements and tax payments online must, themselves or through their accountants, obtain an access password from the respective tax office. Then, the tax office issues a document titled "Electronic Statement for Interagency Authorization Application Form and Covenant" (ESIAA) to evidence the commitment between the tax subject and the tax administration. This document also serves for identification purposes. In addition to facilitating tax submissions and payments online, taxpayers in Turkey are now offered free software for tax-statement filing, which was developed by the tax administration to ease taxpayers' electronic tax submissions.

VI. CONSUMER RIGHTS IN E-COMMERCE

The Law for the Protection of Consumers No. 4077 is one of the most important e-commerce regulations enacted by the government of Turkey and an important tool to facilitate e-commerce transactions. Yet, the customer protection afforded by this law was limited, and it was only expanded by Law No. 4822 from 2003, which amended Law No. 4077.

The amendments made in 2003 were very significant and became a boost for e-commerce in Turkey. The new law redefined the definition of e-commerce "goods" to include software, audio, video, and other such abstract goods that are traded on the Internet, along with other conventional goods and services. The law also reclassified online agreements as "long-distance agreements" and provided consumers with the most advantageous protection measures for online transactions.

Long-distance agreements are defined by Article 9/A of Law No. 4822. This article defines long-distance agreements as those made by using written paper, phone, and electronic forms, without coming face-to-face with consumers, in order to provide goods or services either immediately or with delay. Law No. 4822 requires that all shopping Web sites and firms that sell goods or services on Internet provide to their consumers information such as their firms' commercial name, open address, the details of the quality and quantity of the goods or services provided, their prices of goods including all relevant taxes, duration of validity of the price, shipment charges, return conditions, and access to a complaint system, among other things.

With the reclassifications and expanded definition of long-distance agreements, consumers now have the right to return the goods and services that they purchase via Internet within seven days of the day of purchase and without any reason. According to this law, providers of services or goods are obliged to return the money received from online sales within ten days after the return of the sold goods.

VII. SECURITY IN E-COMMERCE

Since online customers do not commonly use digital certificates in Turkey, customers cannot easily verify the identities of the vendors. Entrepreneurs are still trying to develop an easy and secure access system for this purpose. Currently, online security is obtained through encryption provided by security protocols for submitted information. The most popular of these protocols are SSL (Secure 128) and SET. These systems use key-algorithms to provide a secure communication for e-commerce.

SLL standard is used for secure communication of customers. Sellers register with an electronic Web site identity that is obtained from the approved institution. SLL provides security of the communication between customer and vendor, checks whether the vendor that is reached on the Internet is real or not, and encrypts the data transferred.

The security of communication between vendors and banks for the payment intermediation is provided by SET protocol. The payment information (credit card) taken from customer with SLL is sent to the bank with encrypted SET protocol by the seller. If customer's account is adequate, then the bank approves the shopping and sends provision information to the seller.

These security protocols used by e-commerce subjects are supposed to conform with the E-Signature Law mentioned above. Certification for online security is regulated by the Telecommunications Authority via a communiqué issued. However, since auditing of e-commerce is almost impossible, and consumers in Turkey are not well-informed on such protocols, the actual security is still dependent on the credibility of the firms who use and develop these protocols.

VIII. PROTECTION OF PERSONAL DATA

Collection, use, and verification of personal data in e-commerce has become a must in today's environment. Therefore, the concept of the protection of privacy raises new issues in the e-commerce environment.

The Turkish legal system provides rules for the protection of privacy under its Civil Code. The protection starts from the integrity of body and the privacy of residence, family life, and personal communications. At this time, the protective measures and penalties against violations of privacy are not specifically defined for personal data submitted online for purposes of e-commerce; thus, protection of personal information still constitutes a problem.

Although Turkey is a party to EU Council Agreement No. 108, titled "Protection of Individuals against Automatic Process of Personal Data," dated 1981, Turkey has not yet adopted a local legislation for this purpose. In 2006, Turkey's legislative body drafted a proposal to domestically adopt this EU law. This draft law is titled "Law for the Protection of Personal Data" and is expected to be enacted in 2008.

The draft law for the protection of personal data regulates the processing and storing of personal data, establishes a high council for the supervision of such activities, and designates a ground rule for open consent by the submitting party for the sharing of the information provided.

IX. DETERMINING A DEFINITION FOR E-COMMERCE

The development of e-commerce has changed the manner of making business, and distinguishing physical goods, online goods, and services from each other is getting harder day by day. Commercial transactions are not completely set onto physical bases anymore. Besides the difficulty of classifying goods in Internet-based transactions, classifying revenues that are earned from these transactions is no longer simple because present taxation rules do not recognize specific characteristics of digital transactions.

Since e-commerce is a new concept, there is no single definition for the term at this time, which is critical before moving on to taxation issues. According to some definitions, all transactions that are done via electronic instruments are accepted as e-commerce; however, others transactions and payments done only in open networks are considered to be e-commerce as well. Examples of such different definitions by various international organizations are noted below.

According to the definition of the World Trade Organization (WTO), e-commerce is performing production, advertisement, selling, and distribution of goods and services over telecommunication networks. However, for the Organization of Economic Cooperation and Development (OECD), e-commerce activities are those transactions that associations and individuals perform, that are related to trade, and that are grounded in transmission of digitized data, such as text, audio, or video, over open or closed networks. United Nations Centre for Trade Facilitation and Electronic Business (UN-CEFACT) defines e-commerce as the sharing of business information, structured or unstructured, in order to conduct business, management, and consumption activities, between producers, consumers, public bodies, and other organizations, over electronic instruments (e-mail, instant messages, and electronic bulletin boards), World Wide Web technology, smart cards, electronic funds transfer, and electronic data interchange. UNCITRAL defines e-commerce as exchange of every kind of data message in the scope of commercial activities.

According to definition of the European Commission in 1997, e-commerce is simply performing operating activities by electronic means. This activity is based on processing and transfer of text, sound, and video data by electronic means. Therefore, e-commerce includes digital payment of goods and services as well.

X. CLASSIFICATIONS OF E-COMMERCE REVENUES

Revenues earned from electronic transactions are classified as royalties or commercial earnings according to tax applications of the OECD states and the United States (U.S.). Subject to those general tax practices of the OECD countries, including Turkey, royalties are the total sum of the money or benefits paid regularly to an author, an inventor, or a publisher in consideration of transferring their own rights.

The transactions that are considered "commercial earnings" are downloading and updating digital products, making additions to digital products, using digital products, downloading one-use software, storing data, submitting advertisements, and providing online consulting services, data delivery services, technical data services, sound, music and image broadcasts. The tax base revenue that is considered royalties is the income generated from the sale of downloaded software, the service and use of hidden technical services, and the sale of contents that are eligible to be published by Web site owners.

A. Commercial-Earnings Transactions

The following transactions are considered commercial earnings:

- *Downloading digital products*—The profit that is gained from downloading a digital product, such as software, music, video, or book, is accepted as commercial earning. Customers have the right to make a copy of the digital products they purchased.
- *Update and attachment of digital products*—Software updates and attachments realized via the Internet are classified as downloads of software.
- *Using digital products*—Income that arises from the temporary use of digital products is considered commercial earning. Temporary use means using a digital product for less time than its beneficial period without right to copy.
- *Downloading single-use software*—The profit that is earned from downloading single-use software is also considered commercial earning.
- *Web site accommodate firms*—Earn profits from allowing users to store and access data on the web through third-party content and software.
- *Storage of data*—According to view that is accepted by OECD countries, profits that are earned from the storage of data are considered commercial earnings.
- *Data technical assistance*—Profits earned from online technical assistance are commercial earnings.
- *Search results*—Profits earned from search results over any online database are commercial earnings.

- *Advertisement*—Profits associated with transactions of advertising over Internet Web sites are commercial earnings.
- *Online consulting services*—Profit generated from providing services such as law, accounting, consulting over the Internet are considered commercial earnings.
- *Data delivery services*—Profits earned from data delivery services are commercial earnings.
- *Web site membership* Web site subscription systems are considered services to customers and are taxed as commercial earnings.
- *Online accommodations*—Earnings of online accommodation services are commercial earnings.
- *Audio, music, and video broadcast*—Profits generated from broadcast of audio, music, and video over the Internet are considered commercial earnings.

Royalties Transactions

The following transactions are considered royalties:

- *Downloading and operating*—If any software is downloaded from the internet, and if any commercial earning is generated from selling or reproducing this product, then these profits are considered royalties.
- *Use of secret technical information*—Profits earned from serving and using secret technical information are considered royalties. The fees that are paid for transfers of this kind of information are not considered royalties unless they include use of information more than once.
- *Use of patented content*—Earnings that are generated from contents that are brought out by Web site owners against a copyright fee are deemed royalties.

XI. TAXATION OF ONLINE CONTENT

In the present Turkish tax system, the first determination to make is what income should be taxed. This is called the "origin" or "source of income" rule of taxation. Description of earned income and determination of the origin is realized in accordance with income elements.

Under the framework of Article 7 of the OECD Model for taxation, a contracting state cannot tax the earnings of the other contracting state unless these earnings are derived through a business establishment located in that state. In other words, taxation of a foreign establishment in the state that it is established is related to having a business establishment only in that state. When there is no business establishment, income is taxed only by the resident state. According to Article 12(1) of the OECD Model, "royalties arising in a Contracting State and beneficially owned by a resident of the other Contracting State shall be taxable only in that other State." Therefore, the right of the taxation power is only given to the state of residence. However, the United Nations (UN) Model anticipated that shared connection and royalty is bonded to the authority of the residence state, and the origin state would continue to apply reduced taxation rates.

Turkey made a reservation for Article 12 of OECD Model and therefore reserved the right to tax royalties in the origin state. Thus, in practice and in Turkish tax agreements, origin states continue cutting taxes in the royalties. For this reason, the description of royalties and whether this description includes income from e-commerce has special importance in Turkey.

The concept of "royalties" is described as payments of any kind received as a consideration for the use of, or the right to use, any copyright of literary, artistic, or scientific work, including cinematograph films, any patent, trademark, design or model, plan, secret formula or process, or for information concerning industrial, commercial, or scientific experience. Royalties and such payments that arise from patents and such assets are incomes that arise from leasing operations.

For digital products there is a classification problem in determining whether the payment that is paid for limited use of digital products is an income that is earned from the right to use or just use of the industrial, commercial, or scientific equipment. In these occasions, a customer buys the right to use software or another digital product for a shorter time than the actual use time of the product. The product is downloaded electronically or delivered in a material instrument, such as a CD or DVD. When the term of the license expires, the copies of the digital product are deleted or become useless (OECD Treaty Characterization Report, Annex 2, Category 5). Then, the next problem is whether the digital product is equipment, and if so, whether it is industrial, commercial, or scientific.

Because the term "equipment" is applied to material products, digital products cannot be thought of as equipment. The fact that digital products are obtained over a material instrument does not change the other fact that a transaction is made to buy the right to use digital content, not the right to use a material asset. The term "equipment" can be used for an asset that could be an instrumental item; in this electronic context, it is not used to imply a good such as a music or video CD or DVD. Digital products cannot be considered "industrial, commercial, or scientific" when they are provided for the use of individual consumers. When these products' characteristics and the users' purchasing purposes are taken into consideration, products such as games, music, or videos cannot be considered industrial, commercial, or scientific. Payments made for such transactions are not payments made for the use of or the right to use a product, because these concepts are not applied to payments made when buying goods for a short term of use. Buying a video game CD or DVD that is not going to be used after a period of time is an example for such intent of temporary use.

XII. ADOPTING INCOME ELEMENTS TO E-COMMERCE IN TURKISH TAX LAW

Turkish Revenue Code Article 7 and Value-Added Tax Code Article 12 designate the separation of income elements of "limited tax subjects" and income generated in or from Turkey. As noted in such regulations, the "limited tax subjects" (taxpayer) must have a physical location or a permanent representative in Turkey, and income must be generated by these establishments or by the representatives to become taxable in Turkey.

According to Value-Added Tax Code Article 24, commercial, agricultural, and other incomes and returns of limited corporate taxpayers are taxable in Turkey. Tax rates of these are 25 percent on fees, 20 percent on self-employment income, 20 percent on returns on immovable properties, 25 percent on copyright, privilege, invention, enterprise, trade name, trademark, and sales, transfer, and conveyance of other similar intangible rights.

Pursuant to agreements on avoidance of double taxation, the mentioned tax rates may be reduced (for instance 10 percent on intangible rights) or entirely ignored by the tax authority in Turkey.

Please note that the OECD does not differentiate between commercial income and self-employment income anymore, and the OECD qualifies them both as business income. Although, it is agreeable to think that most e-trade income should be considered the product of sales and services and, therefore, should be considered business income, Turkish tax authorities do not make the same conclusion, and there are different classifications applied for commercial earnings, royalties, and appreciation earnings.

A. Software—Digital Products

The differentiation in earnings brings the related issue of determining whether income is originated from Turkey. Qualification of commercial earnings leads to an examination of the business establishment; and qualification of royalties leads to the determination of the place of use of real assets, the type of rights transferred, the place of payment, or place of register according to measure of valuation in Turkey. In that last case, the origin of income generally leads to the conclusion that income is originated in Turkey.

1. Personal Use According to Turkish tax laws, supply of software or digital products by downloading them via the Internet is considered "package programs" or other goods in trade transacted in traditional ways. In other words, that income is considered commercial earning. (Corporate Tax Law, art. 12/1; Income Tax Law, art. 37).

2. Commercial Use There are two alternative in this case, either copyrights are rented or sold.

A. RENTING AND SALE IN OWNER OF WORK CAPACITY The earnings generated from rent or sale of copyrights by their owners or their inheritors are considered professional service earnings. (Income Tax Law, art. 70/6 and 80/3). According to Income Tax Law Article 18, these kinds of earnings are exempted from income tax.

Within the framework of intellectual property laws, the owner of a copyrighted works is the one who generates the work. (Turkish Intellectual Property Law, art. 8/1). Thus, publishers, producers, and legal entities are not considered the owners of the copyrighted work (product). Additionally, since legal entities have no intellectual activity, they cannot create intellectual products under Turkish law. In fact, according to the modified clause 1/B(b) of the Intellectual Property Law, the owner of a copyrighted work is the individual who creates the work. Therefore, works created by an employee, officer, or vassal in the course of employment belong to the employee. However, because work is the subject of a service agreement, moral rights belong to the employee and the right of using financial rights belong to the employer, according to legal provisions.

B. RENTING AND SALE IN THIRD PERSON CAPACITY According to Turkish tax laws, earnings generated from renting copyrights by persons and institutions other than authors are considered royalties (Income Tax Law, art. 70/6; Corporate Tax Law, art. 24). Earnings from disposal of copyrights and patents by third persons other than the authors, inventors, and their legal heirs are considered appreciation earnings, and these are subject to various ratios of income tax based on the taxable amount and/or 25 percent corporate tax.

With respect to agreements on avoidance of double taxation to which Turkey is a party, renting copyrights on software and digital products for commercial purposes are subject to shared taxation as royalties according to (most commonly Article 12) these agreements. In other words, Turkey can tax payments that are made as the origin state; however, this rate is generally limited to 10 percent. There are two alternatives in the sale of the copyrights for commercial purposes.

c. Technical Data (Know-How) Technical data (know-how) is regulated under the Article 70/5 of Income Tax Law as rights associated with data, based on experience obtained in the industry, commerce, and science areas. The revenues provided by know-how, if rented, are considered royalties and are subjected to advance corporate tax at the rate of 20 percent. According to avoidance tax agreements, revenue is transacted as a royalty, and the applicable advance tax rate in Turkey is at maximum 10 percent.

PART VII

North America

Chapter 22

Canada: E-Commerce: Canadian Considerations of Residency, Carrying on Business in Canada, Permanent Establishment, and the General Anti-Avoidance Rule

David W. Chodikoff
Heenan Blaikie LLP

I. INTRODUCTION

There are no special Canadian income tax rules applicable to electronic commercial transactions.[1] Undoubtedly, this will change in the not-too-distant future. In the short term however, current federal income tax laws provide one framework for federal e-commerce taxation.[2] There are a number of concepts and provisions applicable to the Income Tax Act[3] and Canada's tax treaties that will continue to be the subject of intense discussion and review by Canadian legislators and bureaucrats in order to develop more precise and efficient ways to tax and administer e-commerce transactions. Central to these deliberations is the necessity for tax policy makers and specialists to fully understand the concepts of Canadian tax residency, carrying on business in Canada, the permanent establishment principle, and the application of the general anti-avoidance rule (GAAR). This chapter examines the current state of Canadian case law in relation

---

1 This chapter would not have been possible without the collaborative effort of Angie Wynn, student-at-law, Heenan Blaikie LLP.

2 A couple of general comments about this chapter are in order. This chapter is not intended to be an exhaustive review of the law. The author has endeavoured to highlight current legal thinking on the subject areas covered in this paper. The chapter does not cover in detail the goods and services tax and e-commerce transactions. For more reading on this topic, *see*, e.g., Brent Jay, GST and E-Commerce: Planning and Risk Management (Toronto: CCH Canadian Ltd. 2006); and Steven K. D'Arcy, Non-Residents, Cross-Border Transactions and the GST (Toronto: CCH Canadian Limited 2005).

3 R.S.C., 5th Supp., c.1 as amended (1985) [referred to herein as the "Tax Act"].

to these subjects and the implications for e-commerce transactions from a Canadian perspective.

II. CANADIAN TAX RESIDENCY

Canada taxes its residents on their worldwide income.[4] Residence is used as the primary connecting factor to determine tax liability on the theory that a person who enjoys the economic benefits of association with a country should bear his or her appropriate share of the costs of association.[5]

A. The Problem That E-Commerce Poses[6]

The nature of e-commerce is such that an entity's residence or physical location need not bear any relationship to the e-commerce in which the taxpayer engages.[7] Accordingly, the traditional approach to the inquiry of corporate residency may not result in a clear determination. Moreover, the growing mobility of multinational corporations increases the risk that they will be viewed as dual-resident entities.

B. Canadian Interpretation of Residency[8]

Residence for tax purposes refers to the legal and economic nexus that an individual has with Canada.[9] It is determined in one of three ways: under statutory rules, at common law, or in accordance with a tax treaty.

---

4 *Id.* at § 2(1) provides that "An income tax shall be paid ... on the taxable income for each taxation year of every person resident in Canada at any time in the year."

5 Vern Krishna, *The Fundamentals of Canadian Income Tax,* in TORONTO: THOMSON CARSWELL, 99 (9th ed. 2006).

6 For further information regarding the issue of e-commerce taxation in Canada, *see*, e.g., JINYAN LI, INTERNATIONAL TAXATION IN THE AGE OF ELECTRONIC COMMERCE: A COMPARATIVE STUDY (Toronto: Canadian Tax Foundation 2003); Jack Bernstein, *Canadian Taxation Issues for Electronic Commerce*, in 21 TAX NOTES INTERNATIONAL 263 (2001); Pierre J. Bourgeois and Luc Blanchette, *The Internet, Electronic Commerce, and Taxes—Some Reflections: Part 1*, 45 CAN. TAX J. 1127 (1997), available at Income_taxes.ca.com; Pierre J. Bourgeois and Luc Blanchette, *The Internet, Electronic Commerce, and Taxes—Some Reflections: Part 2,* 45 CAN. TAX J. 1378 (1997), available at Income_taxes.ca.com; *International Fiscal Association 2110 San Francisco Congress Cahiers de droit fiscal international Volume LXXXVIa Taxation of Income derived from electronic commerce National Reporters Canada* (Rotterdam: International Fiscal Association) (2001).

7 United Nations, Secretariat, *Tax Considerations for Electronic Commerce Companies*, Ad Hoc Group of Experts on International Cooperation in Tax Matters (Geneva: UN 2001).

8 For a detailed review of Canadian corporate residency *see* ROBERT COUZIN, CORPORATE RESIDENCE AND INTERNATIONAL TAXATION (Amsterdam: International Bureau of Fiscal Documentation 2002).

9 *Supra* note 3 at 11.

1. Statutory Residence The Tax Act deems a corporation incorporated in Canada to be resident in Canada for tax purposes.[10] This rule applies to all corporations incorporated in Canada after April 26, 1965, regardless of where they are managed or controlled.

2. Common-Law Residence Under the common law, a corporation is resident in the country in which its central mind and management are exercised. This concept of corporate residence was developed in the United Kingdom and adopted by Canadian courts. The *De Beers* formulation of central management and control is the seminal decision.

A. *DE BEERS CONSOLIDATED MINES, LIMITED V. HOWE (SURVEYOR OF TAXES)*[11] De Beers, a South African mining company, maintained its head office and was registered in the Colony of the Cape of Good Hope. The company also maintained an office in London. The issue was whether De Beers was a resident of the United Kingdom for income tax purposes.

The House of Lords rejected the proposition that the test for residency was the place of incorporation since this factor could be easily manipulated. Rather, the proper method to establish a test for corporate residence was by analogy to a natural person, and central to the test was where the corporation carried on business.

In applying the conception of residence to a company, one ought, in this author's view, to proceed upon the analogy of an individual. A company cannot eat or sleep, but it can keep house and do business. One ought, therefore, to see where it really keeps house and does business.[12]

Thus, the proper test to determine corporate residence is where the "real business" of the corporation is carried on, and the real business is carried on where central management and control actually abide.

The House of Lords held that De Beers was a resident of the United Kingdom, despite the fact that the company's operations, head office, and general meetings were located in South Africa. It based this determination on the finding that a majority of the directors lived in the United Kingdom, and it was in United Kingdom where the real control was exercised in practically all the important business of the company, except its mining operations. In essence, the House of Lords defined corporate residency as the locus of financial, administrative, and policy decision making.

3. Treaty Residence As a result of the *De Beers* analysis, a corporation can have more than one residence. For example, if a corporation is incorporated in Canada but its central management and control are located elsewhere, it will be resident in two jurisdictions. Bilateral tax treaties, where they exist, impose a tie-breaker rule to determine which country has taxing jurisdiction over such a corporation.[13]

---

10 *Supra* note 3 § 250(4)(a).

11 5 TC 198 (HL) (1906) (hereinafter *De Beers*).

12 *Id.* at 212–213.

13 The main focus of double-taxation conventions is to avoid double taxation, which, if not addressed, may impede cross-border flows of trade, investment, and capital. Double taxation is

The Organization for Economic Cooperation and Development (OECD)[14] Model Tax Convention on Income and on Capital (the OECD Model Convention)[15] is the basis for the concept of treaty residence in modern Canadian tax treaties.[16] In *Crown Forest Industries Ltd. v. Canada*,[17] the Supreme Court of Canada confirmed that, in interpreting treaty provisions, a court may refer to extrinsic materials, including model conventions.[18] The Supreme Court referred to the OECD Model Convention specifically as being of high persuasive value.[19]

Under the OECD Model Convention, the "place of effective management test" is used to determine the residence of a dual-resident corporation. "Resident of a contracting state" is defined as "any person who, under the laws of that State, is liable to tax therein by reason of his domicile, residence, place of management or any other criterion of a similar nature, and also includes that State and any political subdivision or local authority thereof. This term, however, does not include any person who is liable to tax in that State in respect only of income from sources in that State or capital situated therein."[20] There are three elements to this definition: (1) a corporation must be liable to tax in the relevant state; (2) such liability must be by reason of a connecting factor; and (3) the connecting factor must fall within the list of domicile, residence, place of management, or any other criterion of a similar nature.

The OECD Model Convention is accompanied by commentary (the Model Commentary) which is intended to reflect the consensus of the member nations on the interpretation and the application of the Model Convention.[21] The Model Commentary provides guidance on the effective management test:[22]

> The place of effective management is the place where key management and commercial decisions that are necessary for the conduct of the entity's business are in substance made. The place of effective management will ordinarily be the place where the most senior person or group of persons (for example a board of directors) makes its decisions, the place where the actions to be taken by the

---

discussed in Jinyan Li, Arthur Cockfield, J. Scott Wilkie, *International Taxation in Canada* (Markham: LexisNexis 2006).

14 The OECD has been described as an informal world tax organization; see Arthur J. Cockfield, *The Rise of the OECD as Informal "World Tax Organization" through the Shaping of National Responses to E-Commerce Tax Challenges*, 8 YALE J.L. & TECH. 136 (2006).

15 OECD, Committee on Fiscal Affairs, Model Tax Convention on Income and on Capital (Paris: OECD, 2005).

16 *See, e.g.,* Convention between the Government of Canada and the Government of the United Kingdom of Great Britain and Northern Ireland for the Avoidance of Double Taxation and Prevention of Fiscal Evasion with Respect to Taxes on Income and Capital Gains, Canada and the United Kingdom, September 8, 1978, as Amended by Protocols Signed on April 15, 1980, October 16, 1985, and May 7, 2003.

17 CanLII 103 (S.C.C.) (1995).

18 *Id.* at ¶ 54.

19 *Id.* at ¶ 55.

20 *Id.* at note 12 art. 4.

21 David E. Spiro and Kate Lazier, *Permanent Establishment and the Challenges of Electronic Commerce*, in TAXATION & VALUATION OF TECHNOLOGY (J. L. Horvath and D. W. Chodikoff eds. Toronto: Irwin Law 2008).

22 *Id.* at note 12, Commentary on Article 4.

entity as a whole are determined; however, no definitive rule can be given and all relevant facts and circumstances must be examined to determine the place of effective management.

Recently, in the case of *Wood v. Holdon (Inspector of Taxes)*,[23] the U.K. Court of Appeal articulated that there is no difference between the common-law test of corporate residence and the treaty concept of place of effective management.

A. HOLDON The Woods owned shares in a UK company (Greetings). Upon receiving tax advice, the Woods transferred their shares of Greetings to another UK company (Holdings), on a rollover basis. Forty-nine percent of Holdings was owned by CIL, a Virgin Islands company. CIL incorporated a Netherlands Company, Eulalia, the directors of which were resident in the Netherlands. CIL sold its shares of Holdings to Eulalia. The Woods expected that both CIL and Eulalia were nonresidents, and therefore the gain on the sale would not be attributable to them under an exemption for disposals between members of a nonresident group of companies. They were reassessed on the basis that Eulalia was really resident in the United Kingdom because the directors, who were a Dutch Trust Company, did not in fact make decisions. Rather, the trust company did what it was told to by Mr. Wood or accountants on his behalf. The Court of Appeal confirmed that a corporation is resident where the evidence shows that the decisions of the board of directors are actually made. Under Article 4(3) of the double-taxation convention, Eulalia would be deemed a resident of the state "in which its place of effective management is situated." It is not clear—at least, not clear to most—whether the Article 4(3) test differs in substance from the *De Beers* test.[24] Accordingly, Eulalia was found to be a resident of the Netherlands.

C. Application of Canadian Law to E-Commerce

E-Commerce and technological improvements are allowing companies to become increasingly mobile. For example, a company can incorporate in another jurisdiction and conduct its e-commerce business over the Internet through corporate employees, managers, and directors located in Canada. Under the place of incorporation test, such a company will not be subject to taxation as a resident of Canada.[25]

The place of central management and control is equally mobile. Face-to-face meetings of a board of directors may be replaced by virtual meetings, organized by conference calls, and conducted through video conferencing. As a result, there may no longer be a physical place for meetings between directors, shareholders, and managers; minds may meet in cyberspace. The location of central management and control is difficult to establish in this context. Moreover, even if it were possible to pinpoint the physical presence of such meetings, this place is subject to manipulation.

---

23 EWCA Civ. 26 (2006) (hereinafter *Holdon*).

24 *Id.* at ¶ 6.

25 Note that a company may still be subject to taxation on Canadian source income, which will be discussed in further detail in section III, "Nonresidents Carrying on Business in Canada."

D. Conclusion

Canada taxes its residents on their worldwide income. Corporate residents include those that are incorporated in Canada as well as those corporations whose central management and control are exercised in Canada. Where a corporation is considered a dual resident of Canada and another country, a tax treaty will generally provide a tie-breaker determination of which country has taxing jurisdiction based on the place of effective management. A corporation may more readily manipulate the application of these tests in the e-commerce context.

III. NONRESIDENTS CARRYING ON BUSINESS IN CANADA

In addition to residents, Canada also taxes nonresidents on their Canadian source income. Specifically, nonresidents who carry on business in Canada are taxed.[26]

A. The Problem That E-Commerce Poses

An issue arises as to whether commerce carried on electronically can bring a nonresident within Canada's taxing jurisdiction. That is, can the presentation of goods or services over a Web page be considered carrying on business in Canada? This question is difficult to resolve by reference to traditional criteria. The concept of carrying on business has developed under, and therefore reflects, the conventional manner of doing business through physical bricks-and-mortar locations. Consequently, even though a foreign entity may engage in e-commerce transactions with Canadian customers, it is not clear whether such an entity is carrying on business in Canada.

The factors currently used to determine whether a nonresident is carrying on business in Canada reflect the conventional manner of doing business; interaction with customers through Web sites with minimal human involvement presents challenges for determining whether a nonresident is considered to be carrying on business in Canada.

B. Canadian Interpretation of "Carrying on Business"

The meaning of "carrying on business" is determined under the common law, and certain activities will be deemed to constitute carrying on business in Canada.[27]

---

26 *Id.* at note 1 § 2(3). Note that Canadian taxation also extends to nonresidents who are employed in Canada or disposed of taxable Canadian property.

27 For further review, *see* W. Jack Millar, *Carrying on Business in Canada and Permanent Establishment: GST Considerations* (Canadian Tax Foundation Conference Report 21:1 2006); Jas Hayre, CA, *Non-Residents Carrying on Business in Canada*, 2002 British Columbia Tax Conference (Vancouver: Canadian Tax Foundation 2001) 12:1

1. Common-Law Meaning of Carrying on Business Courts have developed a number of factors to determine whether a nonresident is carrying on business in Canada, none of which is determinative. The Federal Court of Appeal in *The Queen v. Gurd's Products Company Limited,*[28] reiterated what was said in the United Kingdom in 1881 in the case of *Erichsen v. Last*:[29]

> I do not think there is any principle of law which lays down what carrying on of trade is. There are a multitude of incidents which together make the carrying on of a trade, but I know of no one distinguishing incident which makes a practice a carrying on of trade, and another practice not a carrying on of trade. If I may use the expression, it is a compound fact made up of a variety of incidents.

These factors can be categorized into the place in which the contract is made and the location from which profits arise.

A. PLACE OF CONTRACT In determining whether a nonresident is carrying on business, the place where a contract is made is considered to be the paramount factor in the United Kingdom and has been adopted by Canadian courts.[30] The place of contract is determined in accordance with contract law. In the case of instantaneous two-way communication, the place of contract is the place in which acceptance is received.[31]

B. LOCATION FROM WHICH PROFITS ARISE In some cases, the courts have considered the location from which profits arise as the most important factor in determining whether a nonresident is carrying on business in Canada. The following factors have been cited as relevant in determining the location from which profits arise: the place of delivery; the place of payment; the place of manufacture or production; the nature of the activities; the substance of the transactions; the place from which transactions are solicited; the location of inventory; the location of a bank account; the place where the nonresident's name and business are listed in a directory; whether individuals in Canada assist the taxpayer; the reasons for the taxpayer's existence; whether activities in Canada are merely ancillary to the main business; the degree of supervisory or other activity in Canada; and the location of employees or dependent agents.[32]

The Canada Revenue Agency (the CRA) has considered the meaning of carrying on business for purposes of the goods and services tax (GST) and, in the e-commerce context, has indicated its preference for the location where profits arise.[33] The CRA has also indicated that new factors particular to e-commerce may become relevant and suggested that the place where the computer is located may become an additional factor to consider.

---

28 85 DTC 5314.

29 IV T.C. 422 at 423 (1881).

30 *See, e.g.,* Geigy (Can) v. Commissioner, Social Services Tax, C.T.C. 79 (1969).

31 Brinkibon Ltd. v. Stahag Stahl and Stahlwarenhandelsgesellchaft m.b.H, 2 A.C. 34 (HL) (1983).

32 *Id.* at note 3, 1371.

33 CRA, GST/HST Policy Statement P-051R2, *Carrying on Business in Canada* (April 29, 2005).

2. Extended Meaning of Carrying on Business in Canada In addition to the common-law meaning of carrying on business, the Tax Act deems a nonresident to be carrying on business in Canada under certain circumstances. Where a nonresident solicits orders or offers anything for sale in Canada, through an agent or servant, whether the contract or transaction is to be completed inside or outside Canada or partly in and partly outside Canada, the nonresident is deemed to be carrying on business in Canada.[34] The terms "solicit" and "offer" are not defined in the Tax Act. This provision, however, was interpreted in *Sudden Valley Inc. v. The Queen.*[35]

A. SUDDEN VALLEY Sudden Valley Inc., a U.S. corporation, sold land in Sudden Valley, Washington. In an effort to attract Canadian buyers, Sudden Valley commenced an advertising campaign in Vancouver. Canadians visited Sudden Valley and ultimately acquired property there. The sales contracts were drawn up and executed, and payments were made in Washington. At issue was whether Sudden Valley was carrying on business in Canada. The court found that the advertisement did not offer the land for sale nor did it use words from which an intention could be implied. Rather, it was merely an inducement to visit Sudden Valley. The court held that a mere invitation to treat did not fall within the phrase "soliciting orders or offering anything for sale." The expression "offers anything for sale in Canada" was limited to offers that, if accepted, would create a binding contract.

C. Application of Canadian Law to E-Commerce

An enterprise conducting e-commerce via a Web site will likely be considered to be carrying on business in Canada. In a typical situation, a nonresident's presence in Canada will be limited to the viewing of its Web site. However, through a Web site, a vendor is able to provide detailed product information, solicit orders for those products, provide a means of ordering, accept and process payments, and deliver its products.

Under the place-of-contract test, the place of contract is the location in which acceptance is received. In the case of e-commerce, the place where acceptance is received will depend on whether a Web page constitutes an offer for sale. If it is merely an invitation to treat, then a customer in Canada will be considered to have made an offer to a nonresident vendor. If the offer is accepted, the vendor will communicate acceptance over the Internet to the customer, and acceptance will be received in Canada. Accordingly, the place of contract will be Canada, and the nonresident vendor will be carrying on business there. On the other hand, if the Web site constitutes an offer, the Canadian customer will accept the offer in Canada and communicate acceptance over the Internet to the vendor. The place of contract therefore, will be outside Canada, and the vendor will not be carrying on business in Canada.

---

34 *Id.* at note 1, § 253(b).

35 76 DTC 6448 (hereinafter *Sudden Valley*).

A Web site that provides detailed information about products and a way to order them will likely be considered an offer, and the place of contract will therefore be Canada. Accordingly, a nonresident vendor will be carrying on business in Canada. The application of this test, however, is unclear. Moreover, a nonresident can easily avoid carrying on business in Canada merely by choosing to conclude contracts outside Canada. These considerations suggest that courts may look to the location where profits arise.

When considering the location from which profits arise, factors such as the place of delivery, the place of payment, the nature of the activities, and the reasons for the taxpayer's existence suggest that a nonresident vendor will be carrying on business in Canada. The place from which transactions are solicited, whether activities in Canada are merely ancillary to the main business, and the degree of other activity in Canada may point in the other direction.

Factors such as the location where the nonresident's name and business are listed in a directory and the location of warehouses, manufacturing, production, and employees reflect the traditional manner of doing business and have limited application to e-commerce.

The extended meaning of carrying on business is broader than the common-law test. The solicitation or offer must be done through an agent. It is not clear whether the agent must be physically present in Canada. As discussed in further detail in section IV, an Internet service provider who hosts a nonresident's Web site will not ordinarily be considered its agent.

Sudden Valley limits the application of this provision to offers that would create a binding contract. Accordingly, the analysis regarding place of contract applies, and a Web site that provides a detailed description of products, pricing and shipping information, and a means for customers to order products will be considered an offer. Therefore, a nonresident vendor will be carrying on business in Canada. However, if the activities of a nonresident vendor are limited to a passive solicitation of business via a Web site, the Tax Act will not deem the nonresident to carry on business in Canada unless the activities are carried out through an agent.

D. Conclusion

A nonresident conducting e-commerce through a Web site will likely be considered to be carrying on business in Canada and therefore be subject to taxation. However, taxation is limited through bilateral treaties to enterprises that have a permanent establishment in Canada.

IV. THE PERMANENT-ESTABLISHMENT PRINCIPLE

The permanent establishment concept is widely used in modern tax treaties as the main way to establish tax jurisdiction over the business activities of a nonresident carried out in a country. In the absence of a permanent establishment, a country where goods or services are sold has no jurisdiction to tax the resulting profits. Historically, the permanent-establishment principle was created to avoid double taxation. Jurisdictions agreed on a common standard to determine which jurisdiction had the right to tax the business profits of an entity. The permanent-establishment principle provided sufficient evidence that a foreign company's business within the source country was substantial enough to justify the imposition of tax on the foreign company. The OECD states the policy rationale in the following terms:

> It is perhaps sufficient to say that it has come to be accepted in international fiscal matters that until an enterprise of a State sets up a permanent establishment in another State it should not properly be regarded as participating in the economic life of that other State to such an extent that it comes within the jurisdiction of that other State's taxing rights.[36]

This concept satisfied the requirements of certainty and predictability of tax law in that it provided multinational companies with clear rules to determine whether and in what way foreign tax authorities would tax their activities abroad.[37] As a result, a typical bilateral tax treaty provides that a contracting state is authorized to tax only those business profits of a nonresident that are attributable to a permanent establishment in the contracting state.[38]

---

36 *Id.* at note 3, Commentary on Article 7.

37 *Id.,* Revised Commentary on Article 7. The principles of certainty, predictability, and fairness in tax law are considered fundamental tax policy objectives. These principles were cited recently by the Supreme Court of Canada in *The Queen v. Canada Trustco Mortgage Company* SCC 54 (2005) (hereinafter *Canada Trustco*).

38 *See*, e.g., Article V of the Convention between Canada and the United States of America with Respect to Taxes on Income and on Capital, Canada and United States of America, September 26, 1980, as Amended by Protocols Signed on June 14, 1983, March 28, 1984, March 17, 1995, and July 29, 1997, T.I.A.S. no. 11,087, which provides

1. For the purposes of this Convention, the term "permanent establishment" means a fixed place of business through which the business of a resident of a Contracting State is wholly or partly carried on.
2. The term "permanent establishment" shall include especially: (a) a place of management; (b) a branch; (c) an office; (d) a factory; (e) a workshop; and (f) a mine, an oil or gas well, a quarry or any other place of extraction of natural resources.
3. A building site or construction or installation project constitutes a permanent establishment if, but only if, it lasts more than 12 months.
4. The use of an installation or drilling rig or ship in a Contracting State to explore for or exploit natural resources constitutes a permanent establishment if, but only if, such use is for more than three months in any twelve-month period.
5. A person acting in a Contracting State on behalf of a resident of the other Contracting State—other than an agent of an independent status to whom paragraph 7 applies—shall be deemed to be a permanent establishment in the first-mentioned State if such person has, and habitually exercises in that State, an authority to conclude contracts in the name of the resident.
6. Notwithstanding the provisions of paragraphs 1, 2 and 5, the term "permanent establishment" shall be deemed not to include a fixed place of business used solely for, or a person referred to in paragraph 5 engaged solely in, one or more of the following activities: (a) the use of facilities for the purpose of storage, display or delivery of goods or merchandise belonging to the resident; (b) the maintenance of a stock of goods or merchandise belonging to the resident for the purpose of storage, display or delivery;

A. The Problem That E-Commerce Poses

From a tax administration perspective, the most recognized problem with e-commerce is that an entity is able to carry on business through a virtual, rather than physical, presence in a country. This poses a challenge to the historical understanding of the permanent-establishment principle, given that an enterprise no longer requires a physical presence within a country to transact substantial business there.

The problem of lack of physical presence has been widely recognized. In 1998 the OECD adopted a mandate to assume leadership in coordinating international efforts regarding e-commerce taxation. To this end, it established a working group to conduct a detailed examination of the permanent-establishment principle. The group aimed to balance the need to allow e-commerce to flourish while maintaining the tax base. A range of proposals were examined, and the group considered whether and how existing principles could apply to e-commerce. The working group recommended that the status quo be maintained but broadened the concept of permanent establishment to accommodate e-commerce. The OECD accepted these recommendations.[39]

Within Canada, a policy paper on the relationship between e-commerce and the permanent-establishment principle was produced outlining the position that e-commerce fits comfortably within the existing principles of international taxation.[40] However, the Canadian judiciary was yet to examine this issue.

B. Canadian Interpretation of "Permanent Establishment"

Canadian tax treaties generally mirror the OECD Model Convention and provide for two types of permanent establishment, both of which are applicable to e-commerce

---

(c) the maintenance of a stock of goods or merchandise belonging to the resident for the purpose of processing by another person; (d) the purchase of goods or merchandise, or the collection of information, for the resident; and (e) advertising, the supply of information, scientific research or similar activities which have a preparatory or auxiliary character, for the resident.

7. A resident of a Contracting State shall not be deemed to have a permanent establishment in the other Contracting State merely because such resident carries on business in that other State through a broker, general commission agent or any other agent of an independent status, provided that such persons are acting in the ordinary course of their business.
8. The fact that a company which is a resident of a Contracting State controls or is controlled by a company which is a resident of the other Contracting State, or which carries on business in that other State (whether through a permanent establishment or otherwise), shall not constitute either company a permanent establishment of the other.
9. For the purposes of the Convention, the provisions of this Article shall be applied in determining whether any person has a permanent establishment in any State.

39 OECD, Centre for Tax Policy and Administration, *Are the Current Treaty Rules for Taxing Business Profits Appropriate for E-Commerce? Final Report* (Paris: OECD, 2005).

40 Minister's Advisory Committee on Electronic Commerce, *Report of the Committee on Electronic Commerce* (April 1998).

transactions: (1) a "fixed place of business through which the business of an enterprise is wholly or partly carried on"; and (2) agency permanent establishment.

1. Fixed-Place-of-Business Permanent Establishment Permanent establishment is defined in Canadian tax treaties and the OECD Model Convention to mean a fixed place of business through which the business of a resident of a contracting state is wholly or partly carried on.[41] There are three elements to this definition: (1) the existence of a "place of business;" (2) the place of business must be "fixed"; and (3) business must be carried on through this fixed place of business.

The Model Commentary provides that the term "place of business" refers to a facility such as premises or, in certain instances, machinery or equipment. The place need not be owned or rented, and it may belong to a related party, a client, or even be occupied illegally.[42]

For a place of business to be "fixed," the Model Commentary indicates that there must be a link between the place of business and a specific geographical point, and there must be a degree of permanence.[43] Canadian tax treaties and the OECD Model Convention provide the following examples of permanent establishments: a place of management; a branch; an office; a factory; a workshop; and a mine, an oil or gas well, a quarry, or any other place of extraction of natural resources.[44] Each of these examples, with the exception of place of management, refers to a physical location. However, since these examples must also meet the definition of permanent establishment, a place of management must be a fixed place such as an office.

Finally, "through which" is given a wide meaning in the Model Commentary so as to apply to any situation where business activities are carried on at a particular location that is at the disposal of the enterprise for that purpose.[45]

2. Agency Permanent Establishment In addition to having a permanent establishment through a fixed place of business, a corporation may be deemed to have a permanent establishment in a country in which it has a dependent agent.[46] The Model Commentary provides that a company has a permanent establishment where a person who acts on behalf of a company has and habitually exercises the authority to contract on the company's behalf.[47] Canadian tax treaties and the OECD Model Convention provide an exception if the agent is limited to preparatory activities.[48] Similarly, the

---

41 *Id.* at note 12, art. 5; *id.* at note 13, art. V; *id.* at note 34, art. V.

42 Minister's Advisory Committee on Electronic Commerce, *Report of the Committee on Electronic Commerce* (April 1998) at note 12, Commentary on Article 5.

43 *Id.*

44 *Id.* at note 12, art. 5(2); *id.* at note 13, art. V, § 2; *id.* at note 34, art. V, § 2.

45 *Id.* at note 12, Commentary on Article 5.

46 *See* Minister's Advisory Committee on Electronic Commerce, *Report of the Committee on Electronic Commerce* (April 1998) at note 12, art. 5(4); *id.* at note 13, art. V, § 4; *id.* at note 34, art. V § 4.

47 *Id.* at note 12, Commentary on Article 5.

48 *See* Minister's Advisory Committee on Electronic Commerce, *Report of the Committee on Electronic Commerce* (April 1998) at note 12, art. 5(3)(e); *id.* at note 13, art. V, § 3(e); *id.* at note 34, art. V, § 3(e).

activities of a broker, general commission agent, or any other agent of an independent status are exempted from this deeming rule, provided that such persons are acting in the ordinary course of their business.[49]

The relevance of the OECD Model Convention and Model Commentary in interpreting Canadian tax treaties is not yet well established by Canadian jurisprudence, particularly in the case of a treaty entered into before the relevant Model Commentary was adopted.[50] In determining the definition of "permanent establishment," Canadian case law is also relevant. The leading Canadian case on the meaning of "permanent establishment" is the Supreme Court of Canada's decision in *Sunbeam Corporation (Canada) Ltd. v. M.N.R.*[51]

A. *SUNBEAM CORPORATION (CANADA) LTD. V. MNR* Sunbeam maintained its head office and manufacturing plant in Ontario but sold its products in Quebec through sales representatives located in Montreal. The issue was whether Sunbeam had a permanent establishment in Quebec. The sales representatives did not have authority to conclude contracts on behalf of Sunbeam; they were required to pay their own expenses, to work exclusively for Sunbeam, and to follow Sunbeam's instructions. They kept a small number of Sunbeam products for display purposes, but the orders were filled from Sunbeam's Ontario plant. The sales representatives maintained offices and office equipment in their residences, but they did not receive any rent or compensation for doing so. The Supreme Court indicated that the fact that Sunbeam had employees in Quebec was not sufficient to conclude that Sunbeam had a permanent establishment in Quebec. The Court stated that the word "establishment" contemplates a fixed place of business of the corporation, a local habitation of its own. The word "permanent" means that the establishment is a stable one, and not of a temporary or tentative character.

B. *THE QUEEN V. DUDNEY*[52] In Dudney, the Federal Court of Appeal upheld a Tax Court of Canada ruling on the meaning of "fixed base" within the context of the Canada-U.S. Treaty.[53] The issue was whether the appellant had a fixed base regularly available to him in Canada. Dudney, a U.S. resident, was hired as an independent contractor by a U.S. company that provided technical training services to PanCanadian Petroleum Limited (PanCan), a Canadian corporation. All services Dudney provided were performed on PanCan's premises, and Dudney could not conduct any other business from PanCan. He was not even permitted to use the telephone for non-PanCan purposes. Dudney had no letterhead or business cards that identified him as working at PanCan or elsewhere in Canada. The Tax Court compared the terms "fixed base" and "permanent establishment" and concluded that "there is little, if any, real difference in

49 *See* Minister's Advisory Committee on Electronic Commerce, *Report of the Committee on Electronic Commerce* (April 1998) at note 12, art. 5(5); *id.* at note 13, art. V, § 5; *id.* at note 34, art. V, § 5.

50 *Id.* at note 18.

51 Sunbeam Corporation (Canada) Ltd. v. MNR, 62 DTC 1390 (hereinafter *Sunbeam*).

52 The Queen v. Dudney, DTC 6169 (2000) (hereinafter *Dudney).*

53 Minister's Advisory Committee on Electronic Commerce, *Report of the Committee on Electronic Commerce* (April 1998) at note 34.

meaning between the two expressions as used in the Convention."[54] The Federal Court of Appeal noted that the OECD Model Convention does not define the term "fixed base regularly available to him" and referred to the Model Commentary on permanent establishment to determine its meaning:

> These commentaries indicate that an enterprise has a "permanent establishment" where it has a "fixed place of business," an identifiable location with a certain degree of permanence in which the business of the enterprise is being carried on.[55]

The Federal Court of Appeal then described the factors to be considered:

> The factors to be taken into account would include the actual use made of the premises that are alleged to be his fixed base, whether and by what legal right the person exercised or could exercise control over the premises, and the degree to which the premises were objectively identified with the person's business. This is not intended to be an exhaustive list that would apply to all cases, but it is sufficient for this case.[56]

The appellate court concurred with the findings of the Tax Court judge in that the PanCan premises did not constitute a location through which Dudney carried on his business, since he could only use the premises during business hours and only for the purpose of performing the contracted service for PanCan. Accordingly, the Federal Court of Appeal concluded that Dudney did not have a fixed base regularly available to him.

Following the *Dudney* decision, the CRA announced its position as to when it would follow the *Dudney* reasoning. The CRA stated that legal control alone is not sufficient in making a determination of permanent establishment, then stressed that, while the court identified three factors to consider, it also indicated that the factors were not exhaustive. The CRA also stated that it was unnecessary for a nonresident to carry on all aspects of business in Canada in order to have a permanent establishment there, given the definition of permanent establishment in Canada's treaties. Finally, the CRA said that it would determine whether a permanent establishment exists by examining all of the facts of the given situation in light of the particular treaty, jurisprudence and the OECD Model Commentary.[57]

C. *TORONTO BLUE JAYS BASEBALL CLUB V. MINISTER OF FINANCE (ONTARIO)*[58] In the *Toronto Blue Jays* case, the Ontario Court of Appeal considered the meaning of permanent establishment under the Employer Health Tax Act (Ontario) (EHTA). The question was whether dressing rooms and other facilities used by the Toronto Blue Jays, the Toronto Maple Leafs, and the Toronto Raptors during away games outside of Ontario

54 Minister's Advisory Committee on Electronic Commerce, *Report of the Committee on Electronic Commerce* (April 1998) at ¶ 11.

55 *Id.* at note 48, ¶ 16.

56 *Id.*¶ 19.

57 CRA Income Tax Technical News no. 33 (Sept. 16, 2005).

58 Toronto Blue Jays Baseball Club v. Minister of Finance (Ontario), DTC 5360 (2005) (hereinafter *Toronto Blue Jays*).

constituted permanent establishments of the teams for purposes of the EHTA. The court considered the business of professional sports teams and determined where these activities took place. The court found that the contracts entered into with the players, the selling of tickets, the licensing of concessions, the negotiations of sponsorships, advertising, and television and radio broadcasting rights were fundamental to the professional sports business and that all of these activities took place at the team's home venues. The space used at the non-Ontario locations was comparable to possession of a hotel room. Accordingly, the court concluded that the teams' connections with and control over non-Ontario venues was transitory and therefore could not be viewed as a fixed place of business.

The CRA has indicated that the *Toronto Blue Jays* decision is only of persuasive value because it was not decided by a federal court, it involved provincial legislation, and the EHTA definition of permanent establishment is not identical to the definition of permanent establishment in the majority of tax treaties. However, it is notable that the definition of permanent establishment for purposes of the EHTA contains the same components as the tax treaties' definition. The definition requires the employer to have a business, the business must be in a fixed place, and, by virtue of deeming rules in the legislation, the definition encompasses places where the employer wholly or partly carries on the business. Accordingly, it is arguable that *Toronto Blue Jays* provides further guidance on the issue in the international tax context.

To summarize, the term "permanent establishment" contemplates a fixed place of business and requires a degree of permanence. The factors to be considered include the actual use made of the premises, whether and by what legal right the enterprise exercises control over the premises, and the degree to which the premises are identified with the enterprise's business. Finally, a permanent establishment can be found where it can be said that the business activities of an enterprise take place.

C. Application of Canadian Law to E-Commerce

Given the nature of e-commerce, attention has been largely focused on Web sites and servers for their possible qualification as a permanent establishment and therefore a source of taxation. Since Canada has not renegotiated any of its tax treaties to take e-commerce into account, and jurisprudence does not directly address these issues, guidance can be taken from the Model Commentary, statements by Canadian courts, and the CRA in related contexts.

1. Web Sites A Web site is a collection of Web pages, images, videos, or other digital assets that are hosted on one or several Web servers. It is a document that is almost always accessible via a protocol that transfers information from a Web server to display in the user's Web browser.

According to the OECD, a Web site cannot be considered a permanent establishment. In 2000, in addition to Model Commentary on the phrase "permanent establishment" generally, the OECD published additional guidance specific to e-commerce issues.[59] In the case of Web sites, the Model Commentary suggests that a Web site does not itself constitute tangible property and therefore does not have a location that can constitute a place of business, because there is no facility such as premises or machinery or equipment.

The CRA has commented on this issue for the purposes of the Excise Tax Act (ETA).[60] While the ETA is not identical to Canada's tax treaties, the CRA's approach mirrors the OECD's approach for income tax treaty purposes. Therefore, comments of the CRA provide helpful guidance. The CRA has also concluded that a Web site will not constitute a permanent establishment:

A Web site, which merely consists of software and electronic data, is not tangible property, and therefore does not have a location that can constitute a place of business. As a result, the Web site of a nonresident person, including a Web site that is being hosted in a typical Web-site-hosting arrangement, does not, in itself, constitute a permanent establishment of the nonresident person for GST/HST purposes.[61]

Given that the *Sunbeam* and *Dudney* decisions require that the there be a fixed place of business in Canada, Canadian jurisprudence supports the position that a Web site does not constitute a permanent establishment. Moreover, *Toronto Blue Jays* suggests that a permanent establishment will not be found unless the business activities of the enterprise are carried out from the same location as the Web site.

2. Computer Servers By way of contrast, the server on which the Web site is stored and through which it is accessible may be considered a permanent establishment. A server may be distinguished from a Web site in that it is a piece of equipment having a physical location, and such location may thus constitute a fixed place of business of the enterprise that operates that server.

The Model Commentary provides that when a server within a country is at the disposal (i.e., owned or leased) of an enterprise carrying on business through a Web site, the enterprise carries on business functions through it for a sufficient period of time, and those functions are significant as well as an essential or core part of the enterprise's business activities, it may be considered a permanent establishment. In addition, computer equipment may only constitute a permanent establishment if it meets the criteria of being fixed. Accordingly, in order to constitute a fixed place of business, a server will need to be located at a certain place for a sufficient period of time so as to become fixed. The Model Commentary also clarifies that where an enterprise operates computer equipment at a particular location, a permanent establishment may exist even though no personnel of that enterprise are required for the operation of the equipment.[62]

---

59 OECD, Committee on Fiscal Affairs, *Clarification on the Application of the Permanent Establishment Definition in E-Commerce: Changes to the Commentary on the Model Tax Convention on Article 5* (Paris: OECD 2000).

60 R.S., c. E-15 (1985).

61 CRA GST/HST Policy Statement, document number P-208R (Mar. 23, 2005).

62 Minister's Advisory Committee on Electronic Commerce, *Report of the Committee on Electronic Commerce* (April 1998) at note 55, ¶ 42.6.

The Model Commentary also provides that a permanent establishment will not be found where e-commerce operations carried on through a server at a given location are restricted to preparatory or auxiliary activities.[63] Examples of these activities include providing a communications link between suppliers and customers; advertising; relaying information through a mirror server for security and efficiency purposes; gathering market data; and supplying information. However, where such functions form an essential and significant part of the business activity of the enterprise, a permanent establishment may be found.

The CRA's comments in relation to the ETA mirrors the Model Commentary and provides that a server must constitute an "essential and significant part of the business activity of the non-resident as a whole."[64] The CRA has provided the following example: a nonresident company is in the business of supplying goods to customers worldwide, leases a server that is permanently located in Canada, and uses the server to store its business records, including billing information. The CRA does not consider that the server in this example constitutes a permanent establishment in Canada. While the server is at the disposal of the nonresident because it is leased and used by the nonresident and is a fixed place of business of the nonresident, it is not a fixed place of business through which the nonresident makes supplies, because the function carried out through its operation is auxiliary to the nonresident's business of selling goods.[65]

Canadian jurisprudence also supports that a server may constitute a permanent establishment when it is owned or leased by a nonresident enterprise. According to the Federal Court in the *Dudney* decision, the following factors are relevant in the determination of whether a permanent establishment exists: the actual use made of the premises, whether and by what legal right the enterprise exercises control over the premises, and the degree to which the premises are identified with the person's business. In addition, a server will meet the requirements imposed by the Supreme Court in *Sunbeam* if it is a fixed place of business with a degree of permanence. A permanent establishment also can be found where it can be said that the business activities of an enterprise take place. In the case of a server, it is equipment and therefore requires a physical location. When it is owned or leased by an enterprise, it meets the requirement that the enterprise has a legal right to and exercises control over the premises. Finally, where the functions carried out by the server are fundamental to the enterprise's business, the requirement that the business activities of the enterprise take place at the premises of the server is also met. Accordingly, it is likely that a server that an enterprise owns or leases will satisfy the Canadian test for permanent establishment.

To summarize, for a server to constitute a permanent establishment, it has to meet the following requirements: the server on which the Web site is hosted and its location have to be at the foreign enterprise's disposal, meaning that they are owned or leased and operated by the enterprise rather than Web-hosted; the server must be located in the taxing state to meet the requirement of a fixed place of business; and core business

---

63 *Id.* at ¶ 42.7.

64 *Id.* at note 57.

65 *Id.*

activities, not preparatory or auxiliary functions, must be performed through the server.

3. Internet Service Providers (ISPs) An ISP provides individuals and businesses with access to the Internet and related services. It is also common for an ISP to provide Web-site-hosting services for other enterprises on their servers.

The Model Commentary considers whether an ISP could constitute an agency permanent establishment. It provides that a nonresident person who has its Web site hosted on a server of an ISP would not generally be regarded as having a permanent establishment because an ISP is not an agent for the enterprise—an ISP will not have the authority to conclude contracts on the business' behalf or will constitute an independent agent acting in the ordinary course of business, as evidenced by the fact that it hosts the Web sites of many different enterprises. Therefore, the use of an ISP will not lead to the conclusion that the enterprise has a deemed permanent establishment in the ISP's jurisdiction.

The CRA's comments in relation to ETA mirror the OECD Model Commentary.[66] The CRA has provided the following example: a nonresident business enters into an agreement with an independent Canadian ISP for its Web site to be hosted on the ISP's server. The Web site provides detailed information about the nonresident's business and its products. The ISP charges a hosting fee on the basis of bandwidth usage to store the software and data required by the Web site. The CRA considers that the nonresident in this example does not have a permanent establishment in Canada. The Web site itself does not constitute a permanent establishment since it is not tangible property that has a physical location and therefore cannot constitute a place of business. The server on which the Web site is stored is tangible property and therefore can constitute a place of business. However, it will not be considered a permanent establishment because it is not at the nonresident business disposal.

Jurisprudence also supports that an ISP would not likely constitute a permanent establishment in Canada. The *Dudney* decision highlights that whether and by what legal right the enterprise exercises control over premises is a factor in determining whether a permanent establishment exists. In the case of a hosting agreement with an ISP, an enterprise does not exercise legal control over the server. Furthermore, a server owned by an ISP is not typically identified with the enterprise's business. In addition, the business activities of an enterprise that contracts to have its Web site hosted by an independent ISP do not take place at the location of the server. Thus, according to the reasoning in *Toronto Blue Jays*, a Web site hosted by an ISP will not constitute a permanent establishment.

To summarize, the OECD and CRA share the similar view that neither a Web site nor a hosting arrangement with an independent ISP will constitute a permanent establishment in Canada. On the other hand, Canadian jurisprudence supports the proposition that a server that is located in Canada and is at the disposal of a nonresident will constitute a permanent establishment when the enterprise carries on significant

---

66 Minister's Advisory Committee on Electronic Commerce, *Report of the Committee on Electronic Commerce* (April 1998).

and essential or core business functions through it for a sufficient period of time. As a result, foreign persons doing business on the Internet or through a Web site have the potential to conduct extensive commercial activities in Canada without establishing a permanent physical presence. They can avoid having a permanent establishment simply by ensuring that they do not have a server at their disposal through the use of an ISP to host their Web site.

D. Conclusion

The OECD has considered whether and how the existing principle of permanent establishment could apply to e-commerce and has chosen to incrementally enlarge its scope. The benefits of this option are ease of implementation and administration. However, to equate a permanent establishment with the location of a server seems highly vulnerable to manipulation. While it is not clear what direction the Canadian judiciary will take on this issue, it is likely that in initial test cases it will follow the OECD Model l Commentary.

V. THE GAAR AND INCOME TAX CONSIDERATIONS

In Canada, there has been a developing "mini-tax cottage industry" concerning the application of the GAAR. Tax specialists have written books about it, and the subject is now a regular staple feature at the Canadian Tax Foundation's annual conferences.[67] Certainly, there are more situations assessed and reassessed by the CRA wherein the GAAR has been applied. Consequently, the number of GAAR cases has increased over the last several years.[68] To date, however, there is no pure application of the GAAR to an e-commence transaction or transactions. Unquestionably at some future point in time, the CRA will apply the GAAR to some e-commence transaction that the CRA considers offensive. In fact, there has been some conjecture that GAAR will first be applied to a GST-based transaction rather than one that comes within the ambit of the Tax Act. Time will be the judge of which prognosticator has it right. The fact remains that the Canadian tax community is still waiting to see where the CRA will take its first stand against an e-commerce transaction that it says runs afoul of the GAAR. This final section of the chapter will outline the GAAR and provide some further observations on the potential application of the GAAR to e-commerce-based transactions.

67 *See. e.g.*, David G. Duff & Harry Erlichman, Tax Avoidance in Canada after Canada Trustco and Mathew (Toronto: Irwin Law 2007); Alan M. Schwartz, GAAR Interpreted: The General Anti-Avoidance Rule (Toronto: Thomson Carswell, Looseleaf 2006).

68 At the 2007 Annual Canadian Tax Foundation, it was reported that as of August 31, 2007, the GAAR was considered by the CRA in over 749 cases and applied in approximately 500 cases, 2007 Annual Tax Conference, Canadian Tax Foundation presentation by Ed Croft.

A. Background

The rationale for GAAR was simple. It was implemented by the Canadian Ministry of Finance and the CRA implemented it because these state agents believed that there was a need for a statutory tool to prevent the proliferation of aggressive tax-avoidance transactions. In late 1987, the Canadian government proposed several tax measures, including a revised anti-avoidance rule. During the early part of 1988, the government fine-tuned the GAAR provisions, and on September 13, 1988, Bill C-139, which included the GAAR, received Royal Assent.[69] The GAAR was supposed to eliminate all of the trouble earlier judicial anti-avoidance doctrines had caused and implemented the step transaction doctrine modified by a purpose test. The "bona fide purposes" test was intended to permit a sweeping approach to analyze the purposes of transactions to determine whether the transaction was primarily tax motivated. GAAR could now be applied to any avoidance transaction. From the Ministry of Finance's point of view, the GAAR was simple, provided a method of stabilizing tax revenues, and accordingly promoted fairness in the Canadian tax system.[70]

Similar to so many other good intentions, the Ministry of Finance's perspective has not been exactly correct. Even though there have been an increasing number of cases where the GAAR has been applied, we have yet to see the Canadian courts be consistent in their approach to its application. This is troubling not only for the Ministry of Finance, the CRA, and tax specialists but, most importantly, for taxpayers.

B. Basic Principles: *The Canada Trustco* and *Mathew Cases*

In October 2005, the Supreme Court of Canada delivered its first decisions concerning the application of the GAAR. In unanimous decisions, the Court dismissed the Crown's appeal in *Canada Trustco Mortgage Co. v. Canada (Canada Trustco)* and the taxpayers' appeal in *Mathew v. Canada (Mathew)*.[71]

In Canada *Trustco*, the taxpayer was a financial institution holding a basket of loans and leases to government agencies and large companies. The taxpayer entered into a number of different transactions with other parties. The transactions were prearranged, and intended to obtain additional Capital Cost Allowance (CCA) deductions, to shelter anticipated leasing income. The entire arrangement was structured so that there would be minimal economic risk to the taxpayer. In reality, the economic risk was all but eliminated because the funds used to buy the equipment were effectively repaid on the day the loan was made. The Minister of National Revenue argued that the GAAR

69 For the lead up to the final measures *see* Canada, *Supplementary Information Relating to Tax Reform Measures* 101–102 (Ottawa: Queen's Printer, Dec. 1987).

70 D.A. Dodge, *A New and More Coherent Approach to Tax Avoidance*, 36 Canadian Tax Journal 1 at 3 (1988).

71 *Id.* at note 37; The Queen v. Canada Trustco Mortgage Company, SCC 54 (2005); Mathew v. The Queen, SCC 55 (2005) (sub nom. *Kaulius v. Minister of National Revenue*) (hereinafter Mathew).

should apply to restrict the cost for CCA purposes to the true "economic" cost of the acquired property. The taxpayer countered with the argument that the cost for CCA means legal cost, and absent an "at risk" rule, there was nothing in tax policy that said "cost" meant "economic cost." The Tax Court of Canada agreed with the taxpayer, and both the Federal Court of Appeal and the Supreme Court of Canada concurred with the Tax Court's ruling.

The outcome was just the opposite in *Mathew*; there, the taxpayer lost at every level of court. In *Mathew*, the taxpayers were individual and corporate investors who acquired interests in a partnership, which, in turn, had acquired a 99 percent interest in another partnership to which the Standard Trust Company (Standard) had transferred a number of mortgages, the value of which was much less than their original cost. Essentially then, there were a series of transactions that resulted in the transfer of a loss in respect of the loan portfolio from Standard (an insolvent company) to arm's-length taxpayers through the interposition of a partnership. The idea was to rely on subsection 18(13) of the Tax Act, which apparently, and according to the tax planners' thinking, permitted and preserved and accrued loss on the transfer of assets to a partnership by a transferor that, after the transfer, held a majority interest in the partnership. The Minister of National Revenue denied the losses allocated to the members of the partnership and deducted in computing their respective incomes. The Minister of National Revenue's position was that the various transactions were nothing more than a series of transactions that resulted in a tax benefit in the form of the deductions claimed by the taxpayers. The Minister of National Revenue argued that the primary purpose of the acquisition of partnership interest was to obtain a tax benefit. The Crown further submitted that the transactions resulted in a misuse of subsection 18(3) of the Tax Act (as it read then) and an abuse of the scheme of the Tax Act. The Tax Court agreed with the Crown's arguments, and both appellate courts concurred with the Tax Court's ruling. As a result, the taxpayer was denied the loss.

In the two decisions, the Supreme Court of Canada provided a detailed analysis and explanation of how the GAAR should be understood and applied. Before doing so, however, the Court examined the general principles of statutory interpretation. The Court affirmed the modern approach to statutory interpretation. In other words, "the words of an Act are to be read in their entire context and in their grammatical and ordinary sense harmoniously with the scheme of the Act, the object of the Act, and the intention of Parliament."[72] The court added that

> the interpretation of a statutory provision must be made according to a textual, contextual and purposive analysis to find meaning that is harmonious with the Act as a whole. When the words of a provision are precise and unequivocal, the ordinary meaning of the words plays a dominant role in the interpretive process. On the other hand, where the words can support more than one reasonable meaning, the ordinary meaning of the words plays a lesser role. The relative effects of ordinary meaning, context and purpose on the interpretative process may vary, but in all cases the court must seek to read the provisions of an Act as a harmonious whole.[73]

---

72 *Id. Canada Trustco* at ¶ 10.

73 *Id.* at ¶ 10.

The Supreme Court tempered these statements with others that give greater depth to the analytical approach that should be adopted when considering provisions of the Tax Act and the GAAR. In particular, the Court stated that the provisions of the Tax Act must be interpreted in a manner that achieves "consistency, predictability and fairness so that taxpayers may manage their affairs intelligently."[74] Not surprisingly, the Court in its judgment repeated the Duke of Westminster principle that taxpayers are entitled to arrange their affairs to minimize the amount of tax payable. Moreover, the Court emphasized that "*[A]bsent a specific provision to the contrary*, it is not the courts' role to prevent taxpayers from relying on the sophisticated structure of their transactions arranged in such a way that the particular provisions of the Act are met, on the basis that it would be inequitable to those taxpayers who have not chosen to structure their transactions that way [Emphasis added]."[75]

The Court further qualified its statutory pronouncements when it considers an analysis under subsection 245(4) of the Tax Act. When a court applies the misuse and abuse analysis, it must do more than merely accept a provision's clear and unambiguous language:

> The first part of the inquiry under s. 245(4) requires the court to look beyond the mere text of the provisions and undertake a contextual and purposive approach to interpretation in order to find meaning that harmonizes the wording, object, spirit and purpose of the provisions of the *Income Tax Act*. There is nothing novel in this. Even where the meaning of particular provisions may not appear to be ambiguous at first glance, statutory context and purpose may reveal or resolve latent ambiguities. "After all, language can never be interpreted independently of its context, and legislative purpose is part of the context. It would seem to follow that consideration of legislative purpose may not only resolve patent ambiguity, but may, on occasion, reveal ambiguity in apparently plain language" . . . In order to reveal and resolve latent ambiguities in the meaning of provisions of the *Income Tax Act*, the courts must undertake a unified textual, contextual and purposive approach to statutory interpretation.[76]

Turning to the application of the GAAR, the Supreme Court stated that there were three basic requirements.[77] First, there must be a tax benefit resulting from a transaction or part of a series of transactions. Second, there must be an avoidance transaction. The Court indicated that it must be an avoidance transaction "in the sense that it cannot be said to have been reasonably undertaken or arranged primarily for a bona fide purpose other than to obtain a tax benefit."[78] Third, there must be abusive tax avoidance. Once again, the Court clarified its meaning by adding that abusive tax avoidance means that "it cannot be reasonably concluded that a tax benefit would be consistent with the object, spirit or purpose of the provisions relied upon by the taxpayer."[79]

---

74 *Id.* at ¶ 11.
75 The Queen v. Canada Trustco Mortgage Company SCC 54 (2005), ¶ 12.
76 *Id.* at ¶ 47.
77 *Id.* at ¶ 17.
78 *Id.* at ¶ 17.
79 *Id.* at ¶ 17.

The Court then considered each constituent element of the GAAR length. A tax benefit is a factual determination initially made by the Minister of National Revenue and, on review, by the courts. At this stage of the analysis, the size of the tax benefit is not relevant. If, however, a "deduction against taxable income is claimed, the existence of a tax benefit is clear, since a deduction results in a reduction in tax."[80] In other cases, it may only be possible to establish the existence of a tax benefit by comparing the situation to an alternative arrangement.

Turning to the second requirement for the application of the GAAR, the Supreme Court held that, to determine whether the transaction is an avoidance transaction, the Court must objectively assess the parties' relationships and the transactions that were executed between them.[81] Finally, the Court must find that the transaction is truly abusive under subsection 245(4) of the Tax Act.[82] Subsection 245(4) requires a single, unified approach to the textual, contextual, and purposive interpretation of the specific provisions of the Tax Act that the taxpayer relies upon in order to determine whether there was abusive tax avoidance. This involves a two-step inquiry. First, the object and spirit of the particular provision in issue must be considered utilizing a textual, contextual, and purposive approach. Second, following the interpretation of the relevant provisions, the Court must determine whether permitting the tax benefit would defeat the particular object and spirit of the provisions. As the Court stated, "the GAAR may be applied to deny a tax benefit only after it is determined that it was not reasonable to consider the tax benefit to be within the object, spirit, or purpose of the provisions relied upon by the taxpayer."[83]

The *Canada Trustco* court also addressed the burden of proof. The court restated that the initial burden is on the taxpayer to "refute" the Minister of National Revenue's factual assumptions by "disproving" the existence of a tax benefit or, alternatively, by demonstrating that a bona fide nontax purpose primarily motivated the transaction.[84] However, insofar as the inquiry into abusive tax avoidance under subsection 245(4) is concerned, the Supreme Court of Canada has concluded that it is for the "Minister who seeks to rely on the GAAR to identify the object, spirit or purpose of the provisions that are claimed to have frustrated or defeated, when the provisions of the Act are interpreted in a textual, contextual and purposive manner."[85]

VI. CONCLUSION

The CRA has been applied the GAAR to a wide variety of issues, including interest deductibility, surplus strips, tax treaty avoidance, loss creation, and RRSP strips. Some of the CRA's resulting assessments and reassessments have in turn led to a handful of

80 *Id.* at ¶ 20.

81 The Queen v. Canada Trustco Mortgage Company, SCC 54 (2005), ¶ 30.

82 *Id.* at ¶ 36.

83 *Id.* at ¶ 62.

84 The Queen v. Canada Trustco Mortgage Company, SCC 54 (2005), ¶ 63.

85 *Id.* at ¶ 65.

taxpayer court challenges.[86] These cases are slowly making their way through the Canadian court system. Yet, there are still no court cases strictly dealing with the application of the GAAR to an e-commerce transaction.

At the present time, the Canadian government appears to be quite prepared to rely upon the "tried and the true" as principles for taxing e-commerce transactions. The problem is that there are no current Canadian tax decisions that can tell us whether this reliance is well-placed or ill-founded. Canadian policy makers have been slow to implement a coherent overall strategy to tax e-commerce transactions. While this situation may be pleasing to the business community, it is one that is at the potential expense of the whole Canadian society.

86 See also Evans v. The Queen, DTC 1762 (2005); Univar Canada Ltd. v. The Queen, DTC 1478 (TCC) (2005); Desmarais v. The Queen, DTC 2376 (TCC) (2006); Overs v. The Queen, DTC 2196 (TCC) (2006); Lipson et al. 2006 DTC 2687 (TCC), aff'd 2007 FCA 113, on appeal to the SCC; Ceco Operations Ltd. v. The Queen, DTC 3006 (TCC) (2006); MIL (Investments) SA v. The Queen, DTC 3307 (TCC) (2006), aff'd 2007 FCA DTC 5437; McMullen v. The Queen, T.C.C. 16 (2007); MacKay v. The Queen, T.C.C. 94 (2007); Copthorne Holdings Ltd. v. The Queen, DTC 1230 (TCC) (2007). On January 8, 2009, the Supreme Court of Canada released its reason for judgment in Earl Lipson v. Her Majestic The Queen, and Jordan B. Lipson v. Her Majestic The Queen. This reason may shade new and further light to the interpretation of section 245 of the Tax Act.

Chapter 23

Mexico: Electronic Commerce and the Concept of Permanent Establishment

Graciela M. Diedrich
Baker & McKenzie

I. INTRODUCTION

International commerce has spread in multiple forms, booming particularly through the Internet, where is widely known as electronic commerce, or e-commerce. This new form of conducting cross-border business activities presents the question of whether or not the income derived from said activities should be taxed by the source country. This chapter explores the different circumstances under which e-commerce activities lead to the existence of a permanent establishment.

Nonresidents may be taxed in Mexico only in two cases: (1) when they have Mexican source income, and (2) to the extent that business profits are attributable to a permanent establishment located in Mexico.

This chapter discusses when e-commerce activities lead to the existence of a permanent establishment in Mexico; however, it will not discuss the issues related to taxation of a nonresident when it obtains Mexican source income.

II. THE CONCEPT OF PERMANENT ESTABLISHMENT UNDER DOMESTIC LAW

Pursuant to domestic law, a permanent establishment may exist under different tests. The Income Tax Law establishes what can be identified as the place-of-business clause, the dependent-agent clause, and the independent-agent clause, among others.

A. The Place-of-Business Clause

Under the place-of-business clause, a permanent establishment is any place of business where business activities are carried on or independent personal services are rendered, totally or partially.[1]

The following two elements are thus required for a permanent establishment to exist under the place of business clause:

1. The existence of a place of business, and
2. The nonresident must carry on business activities or render independent personal services through such place of business.

B. The Dependent-Agent Clause

A permanent establishment also exists when a nonresident acts in Mexico through a person, other than an independent agent, who exercises powers to execute contracts on behalf or on account of the nonresident in order to carry out the activities of the nonresident in Mexico, with respect any activities said agent carries out for the nonresident.[2]

C. The Independent-Agent Clause

Likewise, a permanent establishment exists when a nonresident acts in Mexico through an individual or entity that is an independent agent, if such agent does not act in the ordinary course of its activities.[3]

III. THE CONCEPT OF PERMANENT ESTABLISHMENT UNDER TREATY LAW

Under treaty law, the concept of permanent establishment is somewhat different. Mexico has extensive tax treaty network. As of the time of drafting this article, Mexico has executed treaties to avoid double taxation with the following countries:

- Australia
- Austria
- Argentina
- Belgium

---

1 Income Tax Law, art. 2. (Published in the Federal Official Gazette on Jan. 1, 2002, as last amended on Oct. 1, 2007).

2 *Id.*

3 *Id.*

- Brazil
- Canada
- Chile
- China
- Czech Republic
- Denmark
- Ecuador
- Finland
- France
- Greece
- Germany
- Indonesia
- Ireland
- Israel
- Italy
- Japan
- Luxembourg
- Korea
- Netherlands
- New Zealand
- Norway
- Poland
- Portugal
- Romania
- Russia
- Singapore
- Slovakia
- Spain
- Sweden
- Switzerland
- United Kingdom and North Ireland
- United States of America

Mexico has also executed treaties to avoid double taxation with India and Venezuela, but said treaties have not been published in the Federal Official Gazette, which is a requirement for their application. Mexico also is in the process of negotiating treaties to avoid double taxation with Hungary, Iceland, Malaysia, Nicaragua, Panama, South Africa, Thailand, and Ukraine.

Most of the treaties to avoid double taxation executed by Mexico follow the Organization for Economic Cooperation and Development (OECD) Model Tax Convention on Income and on Capital (the OECD Model Convention); some provisions, however, are inspired by the Model Double-Taxation Convention between Developed and Developing Countries of the United Nations (the UN Model Convention).

As mentioned before, the concept of permanent establishment is somewhat different under the treaties to avoid double taxation and domestic law.

A. The Place-of-Business Clause

Under treaty law, the term "permanent establishment" means a fixed place of business through which the business of an enterprise is wholly or partly carried on.[4]

When comparing the definition of permanent establishment under the place-of-business clause pursuant to treaty law and domestic law, some important differences can be noted. First, under to the treaties to avoid double taxation, the activities carried out at the place of business are limited to business activities; that is, the rendering of independent personal services is excluded. Second, under treaty law a third element is required for the existence of a permanent establishment. This third element is that the place of business must be fixed.

In summary, under the treaties to avoid double taxation, the three elements for a permanent establishment to exist under the place of business clause are

1. The existence of a place of business,
2. The place of business must be fixed, and
3. The nonresident must carry on business activities through such place of business.

B. The Dependent-Agent Clause

Permanent establishment is the place where a person—other than an agent of an independent status—is acting on behalf of a nonresident enterprise and has, and habitually exercises in Mexico, an authority to conclude contracts in the name of the enterprise.[5]

When compared to domestic law, the difference under the dependent-agent clause is that under treaty law the authority to conclude contracts has to be habitually exercised by the dependent agent. Thus an occasional or isolated activity by a dependent agent would not create a permanent establishment pursuant to treaty law.

C. The Independent-Agent Clause

When a nonresident acts through an agent of an independent status and such agent acts in the ordinary course of its business, the nonresident will not have a permanent establishment.[6] The contrary result is obtained when such independent agent does not act in the ordinary course of business. As the OECD commentaries to Article 5 clarify:

> Where an enterprise of a Contracting State carries on business dealings through a broker, general commission agent or any other agent of an independent status, it cannot be taxed in the other Contracting State in respect of those dealings if the agent is acting in the ordinary course of his business (cf. paragraph 32 above). Although it stands to reason that such an agent, representing a separate enterprise,

4 OECD Model Convention, art. 5, ¶ 1.

5 Model Convention, art. 5, ¶ 5.

6 Model Convention, art. 5, ¶ 6.

> cannot constitute a permanent establishment of the foreign enterprise, paragraph 6 has been inserted in the Article for the sake of clarity and emphasis.[7]
>
> A person will come within the scope of paragraph 6, i.e. he will not constitute a permanent establishment of the enterprise on whose behalf he acts only if *a*) he is independent of the enterprise both legally and economically, and *b*) he acts in the ordinary course of his business when acting on behalf of the enterprise.[8]

IV. WHICH REQUIREMENTS MUST BE APPLIED?

To decide which requirements must be applied to determine whether a permanent establishment exists when e-commerce activities are carried out, one must find out whether a treaty to avoid double taxation has been executed by Mexico. If such a treaty is in place, the issue then becomes to determine which requirements must be applied: the stricter requirements established in domestic law or those established in the corresponding treaty. Resolving this issue is of the utmost importance, since the results of a case may be quite different under treaty law and local law. For example, pursuant to the place-of-business clause of treaty law, the requirement establishing that the place of business must be fixed has to be satisfied in order to have a permanent establishment in Mexico. The opposite result is obtained under domestic law, since the fixed element is not required; thus, even if the period of time is insufficient under international principles, a permanent establishment may be found to exist under domestic law. Another case would that of the dependent-agent clause, because under treaty law said agent must exercise its authority to conclude contracts habitually and not merely occasionally to create a permanent establishment for the nonresident.

The Mexican Constitution provides that the constitution, the federal laws derived thereof, and the treaties signed by the president of Mexico and approved by the Senate are the supreme law of the union.[9] The interpretation given to this provision by the Mexican Supreme Court of Justice has changed over the time. The current and previous positions of the Mexican Supreme Court of Justice are illustrated in the following binding precedent:

> THE HIERARCHY OF INTERNATIONAL TREATIES IS HIGHER THAN THE FEDERAL LAWS AND LOWER THAT THE FEDERAL CONSTITUTION. Doctrine has persistently presented the question regarding the hierarchy of the norms laws in our legal system. It is unanimous that the Federal Constitution is the fundamental law and even though in principle the expression ". . . shall be the Supreme Law of the Union . . ." seems to indicate that not only the constitution is the supreme law, the objection has been overcome by the fact that the laws must derive from the Constitution and be approved by . . . the Federal Congress and that the treaties must be in agreement with the Fundamental Law, which clearly indicates that only the

---

7 OECD commentaries to Article 5 of the Model Convention, ¶ 36.

8 *Id.*

9 POLITICAL CONSTITUTION OF THE UNITED MEXICAN STATES, art. 133 (Published in the Federal Official Gazette on Feb. 5, 1917, as last amended on Nov. 13, 2007).

Constitution is the Supreme Law. The problem regarding the hierarchy of the other norms of the legal system, has found in the jurisprudence and doctrine different solutions, among which: the supremacy of the federal law versus local law. . . . Notwithstanding, this Supreme Court of Justice considers that the international treaties are in a second level immediately under the Fundamental Law and above the federal and local laws. This interpretation of article 133 of the Constitution derives from the fact that these international compromises are assumed by the Mexican State as a whole and bind all authorities before the international community; . . . the interpretation of article 133 leads to consider in third place federal and local laws . . . This High Court had adopted a different position in the thesis P. C/92 . . . entitled: "FEDERAL LAWS AND INTERNATIONAL TREATIES. HAVE THE SAME LEGAL HIERARCHY;" however, this full court deems it is time to abandon such criterion and assume the one that considers the higher hierarchy of the treaties even with regard to the federal law.[10]

Under the current position of the Mexican Supreme Court, because international treaties prevail over federal law, when a treaty to avoid double taxation is in place, the requirements provided in the treaty to have a permanent establishment must be met.

To interpret the treaties to avoid double taxation executed by Mexico, one may resort to the commentaries of the OECD Model Convention. For several years now, the Tax Miscellaneous Resolutions have followed said commentaries to discern the meaning of the treaties to avoid double taxation. The Tax Miscellaneous Resolution for 2007 provides that

> For the interpretation of the treaties to avoid double taxation concluded by Mexico, the commentaries of the model convention for the avoidance of double taxation and the prevention of fiscal evasion, referred to in the recommendation adopted by the Organization For Economic Cooperation and Development, on September 21, 1995, or the one replacing it, are applicable, as long as such commentaries are congruent with the provisions of the treaties concluded by Mexico.[11]

V. E-COMMERCE AND THE PLACE-OF-BUSINESS CLAUSE

In 2000, the commentaries to the OECD Model Convention were amended to address the issue of whether or not e-commerce activities could fall within the definition of permanent establishment.

---

10 *Sindicato Nacional de Controladores de Transito Aereo*, Amparo in review 1475/98 (May 11, 1999). Unanimity of ten votes. Absent: Jose Vicente Aguinaco Aleman. Justice: Humberto Roman Palacios. Secretary: Antonio Espinoza Rangel. The full court, in its private session held on October 28, approved the previous thesis with number LXXVII/1999 and determined that votes are the requirement to create jurisprudence. Mexico City, Federal District, October 28, 1999. Note: This thesis abandons the criterion sustained in the thesis P. C/92, published in *Federal Laws and International Treaties Have the Same Legal Hierarchy*, 60 Federal Judicial Weekly Gazette Number 27, (8th Era Dec. 1992).

11 Tax Miscellaneous Resolution for 2007, Rule 2.1.1 (in effect at the time of writing this chapter) (Published in the Federal Official Gazette on April 25, 2007, as last amended on April 2, 2008).

Below is an analysis of each of the elements required for the existence of a permanent establishment under treaty law in light of the commentaries of the OECD.

A. Place of Business

The first requirement to have a permanent establishment is the existence of a place of business. In general terms a place of business may be premises, facilities, installations, or equipment used precisely to carry out the business of the enterprise.

The OECD position with regard to the place of business in the context of e-commerce is summarized below:

- A place of business may be situated in the business facilities of another enterprise.[12] It is immaterial whether the premises, facilities, or installations are owned or rented by or is otherwise at the disposal of the enterprise.[13]
- A location where automated equipment is operated by an enterprise may constitute a permanent establishment in the country where it is situated.[14]
- A Web site in itself cannot constitute a permanent establishment, because as an intangible it cannot have a physical presence, and thus it cannot constitute a place of business.[15]
- If an enterprise carrying on business through a Web site has the server at its own disposal for example, it owns (or leases) and operates the server on which the Web site is stored and used the place where that server is located could constitute a permanent establishment of the enterprise if the other requirements of the article are met.[16]

B. Fixed

The second requirement to have a permanent establishment is that the place of business be fixed. To be fixed, a place of business must be located at a specific geographical point and be used with certain degree of permanence. Because a computer server is a piece of equipment that has a physical location, such location may be a fixed place of business of the enterprise that operates such server.[17]

What is relevant in the case of a server is not that the server *may* be moved, but whether the server *is* in fact moved. To be fixed, the server must satisfy the permanency requirement, that is, the server has to remain in its location for a sufficient period of time so as to become a fixed place of business.[18]

---

12 Model Convention, commentary to art. 5, ¶ 4.

13 *Id.*

14 *Id.* at ¶ 42.2.

15 *Id.* at ¶ 42.2.

16 *Id.* at ¶ 42.3.

17 Model Convention, commentary to art. 5, ¶ 42.4.

18 *Id.*at ¶ 42.4.

When the activities are carried out recurrently, it is necessary to consider each period of time together with the number of times that place is used. When the activities constitute a business that is carried on exclusively in a particular country, the business may have short duration because of its nature, but since it is wholly carried on in that country, its connection with that country is stronger.[19]

In summary, two elements thus must be satisfied in order to determine whether a place of business, such as a server, can be considered as being fixed: (1) if in fact such server will remain at the certain facilities in Mexico without being moved to other locations, and (2) if the server will be located at such facilities for a sufficient period of time so as to become fixed. As to the time requirement, the OECD commentaries indicate the following:

> Whilst the practices followed by Member countries have not been consistent in so far as time requirements are concerned, experience has shown that permanent establishments normally have not been considered to exist in situations where a business had been carried on in a country through a place of business that was maintained for less than six months (conversely, practice shows that there were many cases where a permanent establishment has been considered to exist where the place of business was maintained for a period longer than six months).[20]

In the reservations to Article 5 (permanent establishment) of the Model Convention, the Czech Republic and the Slovak Republic, whilst agreeing with the "fixed place of business" requirement of paragraph 1 (i.e., "the term 'permanent establishment' means a fixed place of business through which the business of an enterprise is wholly or partly carried on"), reserved the right to propose in bilateral negotiations specific provisions clarifying the application of this principle to arrangements for the performance of services over a substantial period of time.[21] Given that Mexico did not make any reservation or observation in this regard, as the Czech Republic and the Slovak Republic did, it appears that Mexico adheres to the six-month threshold.

C. Business Activities Carried on through a Fixed Place of Business

In general, the treaties to avoid double taxation establish the following rule regarding terms not defined under such treaties:

> As regards the application of the Convention at any time by a Contracting State, any term not defined therein shall, unless the context otherwise requires, have the meaning that it has at that time under the law of that State for the purposes of the taxes to which the Convention applies, any meaning under the applicable tax laws of that State prevailing over a meaning given to the term under other laws of that State.[22]

---

19 *Id.*at ¶ 6.
20 Model Convention, commentary to art. 5, ¶ 6.
21 *Id.* at ¶ 60.
22 OECD Model Tax Convention on Income and on Capital, art. 3, ¶ 2.

Pursuant to the Mexican tax laws, business activities include commercial, industrial, agricultural, cattle, fishery, and forestry activities.[23] To determine whether or not e-commerce may create a permanent establishment, first it is necessary to determine whether it is valid to carry out business electronically in Mexico.

Although Article 75 of the Mexican Commercial Code, which is the core section to define commercial activities, does not make reference to e-commerce, other sections of the Commercial Code refer to e-commerce. It was not until May 2000 that the Mexican Commercial Code was amended to recognize the phenomena of e-commerce, with one of the provisions establishing that commercial contracts and agreements may be entered electronically.[24]

In conclusion, because e-commerce is considered a business activity, it may lead to the creation of a permanent establishment if the other requirements of the definition are met.

VI. PREPARATORY AND AUXILIARY ACTIVITIES

One of the exceptions of permanent establishment arises when preparatory or auxiliary activities are carries out exclusively in the fixed place of business. Thus, the issue is to determine whether e-commerce operations carried on through computer equipment at a given location are restricted to the preparatory or auxiliary activities. In this respect, the OECD commentaries indicate that providing a communications link—much like a telephone line—between suppliers and customers would generally be regarded as preparatory or auxiliary.[25] Other expressly listed activities that generally would be considered as preparatory or auxiliary within the electronic commerce context are[26]

- Advertising of goods or services;
- Relaying information through a mirror server for security and efficiency purposes;

---

23 Federal Fiscal Code, art. 16 (Published in the Federal Official Gazette on Dec. 31, 1981, as last amended on Oct. 1, 2007). Commercial activities are those that federal laws consider as commercial and are not deemed as industrial, agricultural, cattle, fisheries, or forestry activities. Industrial activities are understood as extraction, conservation, or transformation of raw materials, finishing of products, and the manufacture of consumer goods. Agricultural activities include activities for sowing, cultivation, harvest, and first sale of the products obtained that have not been subject to industrial transformation. Stockbreeding activities consist of the raising and fattening of livestock, domestic poultry, and animals, as well as the first sale of the products thereof which have not been subject to industrial transformation. Fishery activities include raising, cultivation, development, and reproduction care of all kinds of marine and freshwater species, including aquaculture, as well as capture and extraction thereof, and the first sale of the products thereof which have not been subject to industrial transformation. Forestry activities consist of cultivating forests or woodlands, as well as raising, conserving, restoring, developing, and making use of the vegetation thereof and the first sale of the products thereof which have not been subject to industrial transformation.

24 Commercial Code, art. 80 (Published in the Federal Official Gazette from October 7 to Dec. 13, 1889, as last amended on June 6, 2006).

25 *Id.*at ¶ 42.7.

26 *Id.* at ¶ 42.7.

- Gathering market data for the enterprise; and
- Supplying information.

Whether the activities are preparatory or auxiliary has to be determined on a case-by-case basis, based on the facts and circumstances surrounding the specific case. The decisive criterion is whether or not the activity carried out in the fixed place of business is a core business activity. For example if the activity carried out at the fixed place of business is identical to the activities of the home office, then such activity cannot be said to be preparatory or auxiliary but rather is a core activity.[27] What constitutes the core activity is somewhat clarified by OECD Commentary 42.9 to Article 5:

> 42.9 What constitutes core functions for a particular enterprise clearly depends on the nature of the business carried on by that enterprise. For instance, some ISPs [Internet service providers] are in the business of operating their own servers for the purpose of hosting web sites or other applications for other enterprises. For these ISPs, the operation of their servers in order to provide services to customers is an essential part of their commercial activity and cannot be considered preparatory or auxiliary. A different example is that of an enterprise (sometimes referred to as an "e-tailer") that carries on the business of selling products through the Internet. In that case, the enterprise is not in the business of operating servers and the mere fact that it may do so at a given location is not enough to conclude that activities performed at that location are more than preparatory and auxiliary. What needs to be done in such a case is to examine the nature of the activities performed at that location in light of the business carried on by the enterprise. If these activities are merely preparatory or auxiliary to the business of selling products on the Internet (for example, the location is used to operate a server that hosts a web site which, as is often the case, is used exclusively for advertising, displaying a catalogue of products or providing information to potential customers), paragraph 4 will apply and the location will not constitute a permanent establishment. If, however, the typical functions related to a sale are performed at that location (for example, the conclusion of the contract with the customer, the processing of the payment and the delivery of the products are performed automatically through the equipment located there), these activities cannot be considered to be merely preparatory or auxiliary.

In other words, a Web-site-hosting arrangement will not generally constitute a permanent establishment for the guest enterprise, but if the host company is in the business of operating its servers to host Web sites, such activity cannot be considered as preparatory or auxiliary and may constitute a permanent establishment if the other requirements of Article 5 are met.

The Committee on Fiscal Affairs has clarified that the example provided in OECD Commentary 42.9 is merely illustrative and should not be considered to determine the point at which the preparatory or auxiliary threshold is exceeded. As indicated, where a function carried out by the computer equipment is an essential and significant part of the business activity of the enterprise as a whole, such function cannot be considered as one of the exemptions for a permanent establishment to exist, because it goes beyond a mere auxiliary activity.

---

27 OECD Model Convention, commentary to art. 5, ¶ 24.

VII. E-COMMERCE AND THE AGENCY CLAUSE

The chapter has already established that for a place of business to constitute a permanent establishment, the enterprise using it must carry on its business, in whole or in part, through such place. Because the business of an enterprise is generally carried out through the personnel of that enterprise, one may think that no permanent establishment exist in cases where an employee operates a server but does not have authority to conclude contracts on behalf of the enterprise. However, the OECD commentaries to the Model Convention clarify that in case of automated equipment, such as computers and servers, no human intervention is required.

The OECD Commentary 2 to Article 5 provides that

> The paragraph [1] defines the term "permanent establishment" as a fixed place of business, through which the business of an enterprise is wholly or partly carried on. This definition, therefore, contains the following conditions: . . . the carrying on of the business of the enterprise through this fixed place of business. This means usually that persons who, in one way or another, are dependent on the enterprise (personnel) conduct the business of the enterprise in the State in which the fixed place is situated. However, where an enterprise operates computer equipment at a particular location, a permanent establishment may exist even though no personnel of that enterprise are required at that location for the operation of the equipment. The presence of personnel is not necessary to consider that an enterprise wholly or partly carries on its business at a location when no personnel are in fact required to carry on business activities at that location. This conclusion applies to electronic commerce to the same extent that it applies with respect to other activities in which equipment operates automatically, e.g. automatic pumping equipment used in the exploitation of natural resources.[28]

Another question is whether an Internet service provider (ISP) that provides hosting services to Web sites of other enterprises on its own servers may constitute a permanent establishment of the guest enterprise. The OECD commentary illustrates that the hosting company will generally not be an agent of the enterprises to which the Web sites belong, because it will not have authority to conclude contracts in the name of these enterprises and will not regularly conclude such contracts or because it will constitute an independent agent acting in the ordinary course of its business, as evidenced by the fact that it hosts the Web sites of many different enterprises.[29]

VIII. PROCEDURAL REQUIREMENTS TO APPLY TREATY BENEFITS

Regarding the procedural aspects established by domestic law, OECD Commentary 26.2 to Article 1 of the Model Convention provides the following:

> 26.2 A number of Articles of the Convention limit the right of a State to tax income derived from its territory. As noted in paragraph 19 of the Commentary on Article 10

28 *Id.* at ¶ 42.6.

29 *Id.* at ¶ 42.10.

as concerns the taxation of dividends, the Convention does not settle procedural questions and each State is free to use the procedure provided in its domestic law in order to apply the limits provided by the Convention. A State can therefore automatically limit the tax that it levies in accordance with the relevant provisions of the Convention, subject to possible prior verification of treaty entitlement, or it can impose the tax provided for under its domestic law and subsequently refund the part of that tax that exceeds the amount that it can levy under the provisions of the Convention. As a general rule, in order to ensure expeditious implementation of taxpayers' benefits under a treaty, the first approach is the highly preferable method. If a refund system is needed, it should be based on observable difficulties in identifying entitlement to treaty benefits. Also, where the second approach is adopted, it is extremely important that the refund be made expeditiously, especially if no interest is paid on the amount of the refund, as any undue delay in making that refund is a direct cost to the taxpayer.

Accordingly, the Income Tax Law provides that the benefits of the treaties to avoid double taxation may only be applied to taxpayers that prove they are residents of a country that executed a tax treaty with Mexico and that comply with the provisions of the treaty in question and the procedural provisions contained in the Income Tax Law, including obligations related to registration, filing reports, and appointing representatives.[30]

Obviously, the above means that it is necessary to comply with such requirements only when the obligation is applicable under local law. It would be contrary to reason and logic to pretend to impose to nonresidents the obligation to register with the federal taxpayer registry, obtain reports, and appoint representatives if such obligations are not established in the domestic law. Consequently, the above provision means that nonresidents must to comply with such requirements when the obligation is imposed by domestic law if they want to avail themselves to the benefits provided in the treaties to avoid double taxation.

Nonresidents may prove their tax residence in a country with which Mexico has executed a treaty to avoid double taxation with certificate of residence or a certificate attesting that they have filed their tax return for the preceding year.[31] These certificates must be issued by at competent tax authority and shall be effective during the calendar year in which they are issued.[32]

30 Income Tax Law, art. 5. (Published in the Federal Official Gazette on Jan. 1, 2002, as last amended on Oct. 1, 2007).

31 Regulations to the Income Tax Law, art. 6 (Published in the Federal Official Gazette on Oct. 17, 2003, as last amended on Dec. 4, 2006).

32 *Id.*

Chapter 24

United States: Sales and Use Taxation of Telecommunications Services Including Voice-Over Internet Protocol

Raymond P. Carpenter, Sr.
Holland & Knight LLP

I. INTRODUCTION

The sales and use tax on telephone calls and telecommunications services provides significant tax revenues for state, county, and municipal governments to fund infrastructure projects and other general revenue obligations. The value of this tax as a revenue source can be illustrated by the fact that some states that do not impose a sales tax on general retail transactions in the state impose a special sales tax on telecommunications services. Some states that do impose a general sales tax impose a special sales tax with a higher tax rate on telecommunications services. As a result, governmental entities become very concerned when new technology is introduced that threatens to erode the base of telephone calls or telecommunications services subject to tax in their jurisdictions. The advent of voice communication over Internet technology is the latest innovation in the manner in which telecommunications services are provided to a broad range of customers. This technology and the next generation of technological change (Wi-Fi, for example) will challenge the ability of governments to continue to capture these transactions in their jurisdictions and may well see reductions in the amount of tax revenues that can be expected from these types of services.

This chapter will discuss the sales and use tax as currently applied to telephone calls and telecommunications services in various jurisdictions, to illustrate the diversity in approach to taxation of these services. The chapter will look briefly to national policy at the Federal Communications Commission (FCC) and Congress to identify the policy considerations that drive whether telecommunications services are subject to regulation and ultimately taxation. Recent litigation will also be reviewed on the characterization of voice communications completed over the Internet and how the courts and the policy makers determined to proceed in the taxation and regulation of this area. The chapter will review how the larger states define telecommunications services and how aggressively they have included telephone calls provided over advanced technology in their tax definitions. Finally, there will be a discussion of the activity of the State Streamlined Sales Tax Project (SSTP) to determine whether its approach will provide answers that all states may adopt.

II. CURRENT SALES AND USE TAXATION OF TELECOMMUNICATION SERVICES

The sales tax (and its complement, the use tax) are designed to capture fairly straightforward exchanges of goods and services between buyers and sellers, generally who are in the same taxing jurisdiction at the time of the exchange. When they are not in the same place at the same time, the use tax seeks to require that the buyer, who may have left the state to avoid the tax, pay the tax as if the transaction had occurred in the state. This is accomplished by placing the burden of the tax on the seller, if the transaction occurs in the taxing jurisdiction, and on the buyer, if the otherwise taxable transaction occurs outside the taxing jurisdiction but the beneficial enjoyment or use of the goods or services are enjoyed in the taxing state. So long as the taxing state has a sufficient "nexus" with the transaction so that constitutional considerations under the commerce clause and the due-process clause are satisfied, the dual prongs of the sales and use tax will capture the transactions described above.[1]

In the taxation of telecommunications services, Illinois sought to tax interstate telephone calls as if certain calls occurred only in Illinois. (*See*, *Goldberg v. Sweet*, 488 U.S. 252 (1999)). Interstate calls are calls that may be originated in one state but completed in a different state. With telephone technology being what it was, the court noted that there may be several states involved in the connection of interstate calls before the final connection is made in the caller's home state. To resolve this issue, the Illinois telecommunications excise tax imposed a gross-receipts tax on long-distance or interstate telephone calls if the call was originated or terminated in Illinois and was billed to an Illinois service address. The location of the service address was the location of the telephone equipment used to originate or terminate the call.

The question framed by the court was whether Illinois had fairly apportioned the tax so as to avoid violation of the Commerce Clause as interpreted in *Complete Auto Transit v. Grady*,[2] which set out a four-prong test to determine whether a state law placed an undue burden on interstate commerce. Illinois clearly had a sufficient connection or "nexus" with the call, being the location of either the maker or recipient, but had Illinois demanded value beyond that connection to the call? In addition, what

---

1 *See* discussion of constitutional concepts in *Complete Auto Transit v. Brady*, 430 U.S. 274 (1977). This case established a four-prong analysis that must be satisfied before any transaction that touches interstate commerce is lawful.

2 *Id.*

would occur if another state also assessed its tax on the same call? The court was persuaded that two of the three points of presence outlined in the statute would give Illinois sufficient basis for exercising it authority to tax the call and, parenthetically, the statute contained a credit if the taxpayer could show that a competing jurisdiction had assessed its tax on the same call. This formulation, that is, whether the call originates or terminates in the jurisdiction and is billed to a service address in the jurisdiction, has been adopted by most jurisdictions as the basis for their taxation of interstate telephone calls.

Prior to deregulation of telephone service in 1986, states imposed a gross-receipts tax on the telephone service revenues generated by the monopoly provider AT&T and its subsidiaries. AT&T would then collect the tax from its customers as a percentage of their bill and remit it to the taxing jurisdiction. After deregulation, most jurisdictions changed to a sales and use tax imposed on the purchaser of the telephone service, or alternatively on the buyer and seller, in order to make sure that the tax was not avoided.

A recent survey[3] revealed that of the 45 states that impose general sales and use tax, 40 of those states impose that tax on some form of telecommunications service typically provided by regulated local-exchange carriers. Thirty-eight states impose a sale tax on intrastate sales of interexchange carriers. Only 21 states impose sales and excise taxes on interstate and international services provided by interexchange carriers. Of the five states that do not impose general sales and use tax, four states enacted a specific excise or gross-receipts tax levied on telecommunications services. Two states, which impose general sales tax, only tax local services (Georgia and Michigan). Three states, while taxing telecommunication services under the general heading of sales and use taxes, apply a differential rate, generally higher to telecommunications services. In some states, the tax is applied only against companies that are regulated by the public-service commission.

Connecticut, for example, imposes a 6 percent sales tax on sales of all telecommunications services, including interstate and international calls. This tax includes in the tax base all wire line, wireless, computer-related, television and video programming, and miscellaneous telecommunications services. The Massachusetts tax applies to intrastate, interstate, and international calls. The tax includes wireless communications devices. The Illinois tax is a separate telecommunications excise tax that is imposed on intrastate, interstate, and international calls and wireless calls. The international and interstate calls are apportioned to the state. The Texas sales tax is also a comprehensive sales tax imposed on all intrastate, interstate, and international calls, along with wireless calls. Computer-related calls are included in the sales tax base.

A. What Is a Telecommunication Service

The Communications Act of 1934 established a comprehensive federal regulatory framework governing "... all interstate and foreign communications by wire or radio." The Communications Act of 1996 now uses the term "telecommunications" to define

---

3 The Telecommunication Tax Taskforce of the Council on State Taxation (COST), 2004 State Tax Study and Report on Telecommunications Taxation (CCH Incorporated).

the transmission, between or among points specified by the user, of information of the user's choosing, without change in the form or content of the information as sent and received. (*See*, 47 U.S.C. § 153 (43)). Telecommunications services are defined as "the offering of telecommunications for a fee directly to the public." This was distinguished from "information services," which is the offering of a capability for generating, acquiring, storing, transforming, processing, retrieving, utilizing, or making available information via telecommunications. (*See* 47 U.S.C. §§ 153 (20) and (46).) Providers of telecommunication services are common carriers subject to regulation by the FCC, and providers of information services are not.

For state sales and use tax purposes, the term has a more specific definition:

- *Florida*—Communications services means the transmission, conveyance, or routing of voice, data, audit, video, or any other information or signals including cable services to a point or between or among points by or through an electronic, ratio, satellite, cable, optical, microwave, or other medium or method now in existence or hereafter devised, regardless of the protocol used for such transmission or conveyance.[4]
- *Illinois*—Telecommunications includes but is not limited to messages or information transmitted through use of local, toll, and wide-area telephone service, channel services, telegraph services, teletypewriter service, computer exchange services, private line services, specialized mobile radio services, or any other transmission of messages or information by electronic or similar means between or among points by wire, cable, fiber optics, laser, microwave, radio, satellite, or similar facilities. The term also includes wireless telecommunications services.[5]
- *New York*—Telephony or telegraphy or telephone or telegraph service, including but not limited to any transmission of voice, image, data, information, and paging through the use of wire cable, fiber optic, laser, microwave, radio wave, satellite, or similar media or any combination thereof and shall include services that are ancillary to the provision of telephone service (such as, but not limited to, dial tone, basic service, directory information, call forwarding, caller identification, call waiting, and the like) and also include any equipment and services provided therewith. Provided, the definition of telecommunication services shall not apply to separately stated charges for any service which alters the substantive content of the message received by the recipient from that sent.[6]
- *Texas*—The term telecommunications services is defined to mean: the electronic or electrical transmission, conveyance, routing, or reception of sounds, signals, data, or information utilizing wires, cable, radio waves, microwaves, satellites, fiber optics, or any other method now in existence or that may be devised, including but not limited to long-distance telephone service. The term does not include "(1) the storage of data or information for subsequent retrieval or processing . . ., or (3) Internet access services."[7]

---

4 Fla. Stat. § 202.11(2).
5 Ill 35 ILCS 630/3 and 4 and 86 Ill. Admin Code 436, 100 et. seq.
6 N.Y. Tax Laws § 1105(b)(1)(B).
7 Tex. Tax Code Ann. 3151.010(R(6); Tex. Admin. Code § 3.44(b).

Clearly these definitions are designed to capture the widest range of telecommunications transactions possible regardless of technology. The language is broader than the language contained in the federal telecommunications acts and could indicate a taxing policy at variance with federal policy in this area. This was clearly the issue when telephone service became connected or accessed from the World Wide Web or the Internet.

III. TAXATION OF INTERNET ACCESS AND SERVICES PROVIDED OVER THE INTERNET

If the telephone call had remained a relatively simple end-to-end voice transmission conducted by copper wires and managed by a national monopoly, there is little likelihood that telecommunications services as we know them would ever have developed. However, the breakup of the Bell monopolies in 1986 brought on a wave of innovation in the voice communication field that is continuing unabated today. The first change was in the telephone itself. No longer was a caller tethered to a black box fixed in a single room of the house. Telephone equipment erupted into a band of colors and styles reflecting pent-up creative demand. Not only was equipment available in virtually every color of the rainbow, but the telephone design now included football telephones, pet phones, vegetable phones, and automobile replica phones produced not by the telephone company but by independent companies who, before the 1986 breakup, could not compete in the equipment market. In addition to the equipment came enhanced or ancillary services such as incoming caller identification, call waiting, call back (*69), single-digit dialing, three-way calling, and expanded 800 and 900 dialing.

These features were introduced without a significant change in technology. When fiber-optic cable began to replace copper wires, the amount of data that could be transmitted expanded exponentially. The cable industry first recognized that the "pipeline" into the home could carry much more than just voice, or just data, or just entertainment. All of these services and more could be brought into the home simultaneously. When the Internet became a possibility, cable and the remaining telephone companies began a race for supremacy in the provision of any and all of these services to the homes and businesses.

It was the Internet that accelerated this trend. Dial-up Internet access reflected the demand for access to the Internet, but this technology was maddeningly slow and subject to interruption. When access to the Internet became possible at increased speed over broadband technology, the competition took on a new sense of urgency. And when voice became available over the Internet, and the quality issues were addressed, clearly the changes presaged a quantum shift in the way that communication services would be provided and enjoyed. Suddenly, voice, data, entertainment, interactive video games, movies and television, and movies on demand became the standard for communication services to homes and businesses.

The FCC recognized that these services, variously called "enhanced" or "ancillary services" were not "telecommunication services" under the terms of the Communications Act of 1934 and its 1996 amendment. These services were defined as "information services" and, as such, were not subject to regulation by the local public utility commission (PUC) and not subject to the federal excise tax that was in effect at that time. Telecommunications services, on the other hand, were subject to regulation by local PUCs and were subject to sales and use tax already. Enhanced services would have to be taxed separately if at all.[8]

A. Internet Tax Freedom Act

On October 31, 2007, President Bush signed the Internet Tax Freedom Act Amendments Act of 2007, Public Law 110-108, which extended the federal moratorium on Internet taxes until November 2014. The moratorium applies to any tax on Internet access, regardless of whether the tax is imposed on a provider of Internet access or a buyer of Internet access and regardless of the terminology used to describe the tax. The 2007 amendments defined "Internet access" to include a home page, e-mail, or instant messaging (including voice- and video-capable e-mail and instant messaging), video clips, and personal electronic storage capacity that is provided independently or not packaged with Internet access.

Sales of telecommunications to Internet service providers for use in the provision of Internet access (such as DSL service) are not taxable. The Internet Tax Freedom Act Amendments Act keeps in effect provisions retroactive to November 1, 2003, that amend the definition of Internet access to clarify that the moratorium does not extend to a tax on telecommunications services, except to the extent such services are purchased, used, or sold by a provider of Internet access to provide Internet access. According to committee reports, the federal legislation was amended in 2003 to recognize the technological developments in the methods used to access the Internet since the time that the act was first enacted in 1998. The amendments were designed to ensure that all methods of Internet access, whether in the form of dial-up, DSL, cable, satellite, wireless, or any other technology platform, as well as components used to provide Internet access, are covered by the Internet access tax moratorium and, therefore, are exempt from state and local taxation.[9]

The moratorium has not and will not apply to the imposition of tax on a charge for voice-over Internet protocol (VoIP) audio or video programming, or other products and services that use Internet protocol and any successor protocol, regardless of whether the charge is separately stated or aggregated with the charge for listed Internet services.

If charges for Internet access are aggregated with and not separately stated from charges for telecommunications or other charges that are subject to taxation, then the charges for Internet access may be subject to taxation unless the Internet access provider can reasonably identify the charges for Internet access from its books and records kept in the regular course of business.[10]

---

8 *See*, FCC Amendment of Section 64.702 of the Commission's Rules and Regulations, Final Decision, 77 FCC 2d 384 (1980) (Computer II) affirmed sub. nom. Computer and Communications Industry Ass'n v. FCC, 693 F.2d 198 (D.C. Cir. 1982) (CCIA), cert. denied, 462 U.S. 938 (1983).

9 Public Law 110–108, 34.

10 Public Law 110–108, 35.

So contrary to some interpretations, the Internet Tax Freedom Act does not and has never been a barrier to the taxation of VoIP when manifested in a telephone call or other enhanced services provided to telecommunications consumers or by telecommunications service providers or others. While the act has always prohibited taxation of "Internet access charges," that term has never included a telecommunications or telephony-based service. However, the debate on this subject continues in some states as to just what impact this statute would have on this service or any service that uses this protocol. As will be shown, the service providers who provide VoIP exclusively have always argued that the purpose of the moratorium was to allow this type of service to flourish prior to it assuming the same burdens as switched-based services. While this is not an unreasonable argument, Congress has clearly removed it from consideration. Because the FCC has prohibited regulation of VoIP in the same manner as switched services, there is still some vitality to the argument. However, more states are applying their own analysis to the issue and either taxing the service or exempting it based on how their own laws approach the taxation of telecommunications generally.

1. New York New York imposes as a sales and use tax on sales of "telephony and telegraphy and telephone and telegraphic services" except when such sales are for resale. Excluded from the tax are sales of interstate and international telephony and telegraphy and interstate and international telephony services and telegraph services. The terms "telephony" and "telegraphy" includes the use or operation of any apparatus for transmission of sound and sound reproduction, coded, or other signals.[11] These services are not taxable services if they are incidental to the purchase of a different service.[12]

A telecommunications excise tax is imposed on the gross receipts from the sale of telecommunications services. For these purposes the excise tax is imposed on telephony or telegraphy, or telephone or telegraph service, including, but not limited to, any transmission of voice, image, data, information, and paging, through the use of wire, cable, fiber-optic, laser, microwave, radio wave, satellite, or similar media or any combination thereof and shall include services that are ancillary to the provision of telephone service (e.g., but not limited to, dial tone, basic service, directory information, call forwarding, caller identification, and call waiting) and also include any equipment and services provided therewith. (*See* Tax Law § 186-e.1(g)).

The sales tax is imposed only on receipts from intrastate calls. The telecommunications excise tax is imposed on the gross receipts from intrastate telecommunication services, interstate, and international telecommunications services if the service originates or terminates in New York and is charged to a service address in New York and private telecommunication service attributable to New York.

2. Florida In any discussion of the state tax on telecommunications services, Florida has always had a special place. The cumulative tax on these services in Florida, when considering sales tax, gross receipts tax, franchise fees, and other local levies has been in the area of 17 to 18 percent of the customer bill. In addition, it was always very

11 N.Y. Tax Law § 1105(b)(1)(B).
12 N.Y. C RR 20 § 527.2(d)(4).

difficult to determine just which taxes and fees applied to a given call. In 2001, the Florida legislature sought to clear up some of this confusion and at least simplify the imposition of these taxes. The Communications Services Tax Simplification Law was effective October 1, 2001. Under this scheme, the state communication services tax on telecommunications replaced the sales tax on telecommunications services, and was combined with the gross receipts tax on telecommunications to services to produce a single state tax on communications services.

The communications services tax is imposed on the business of selling communications services at retail in Florida. The tax rate was 6.8 percent and applied to the sale price of communications services that originate and terminate in Florida, or originate or terminate in Florida and are charged to a service address in Florida, when sold at retail, computed on each taxable sale for the purpose of remitting the tax due.

In addition to the state communications tax, each county, municipality, and school district locality has the option of imposing a local communications services tax as well. This tax, which is in addition to the state tax, is imposed on calls subject to the tax in the state but that also originate or terminate within the locality or that originate or terminate within the locality and are billed to a service address in the locality. The maximum tax rate of 5.1 percent may be supplemented by fees for rights of way and other permits of up to 0.24 percent. The school board rate is in addition to the local governmental rates.[13]

3. California California does not impose a sales tax or a communications excise tax on the sale at retail or telecommunication services or telephony. Even when telecommunication services are sold "bundled" with the sale of a communication "device," the sales tax or excise tax applies only to the unbundled price of the device and under no circumstances to the cost of the service.[14]

4. District of Columbia The District of Columbia imposes a sales and use tax on local telephone service only. Toll telephone service (or long-distance service) and wireless communications services are exempt from the sales tax; however, telecommunications providers are subject to the gross receipts tax on the provision of toll and wireless communication services in lieu of the sales tax.

"Local telephone services" is defined as the access to a local telephone system and the privilege of telephonic quality communication with substantially all persons having telephone or radio telephone stations constituting a part of such local telephone system, as well as any facility or service provided in connection with the local telephone service.

With regard to bundled services, the term "sales price" does not include a charge for nontaxable services that is made in connection with a sale of taxable communication service if the vendor can reasonably identify the charges not subject to tax from its books and records maintained in the normal course of its business activity.[15]

---

13 Fla. Stat. § 202.12, Sales of Communications Services.

14 Cal. Code Regs. 18, 31501.

15 D.C. Code Ann. § 47–2001(N)(1)(G)(i) and (ii).

IV. TELECOMMUNICATION SERVICES PROVIDED BY THE USE OF VoIP

VoIP is the convergence of voice and data into a single bit stream, according to the National Cable Television Association (NCTA), which enables the provision of innovative offerings that integrate the two in ways not possible using the traditional circuit-switched technology. Voice communications are digitized into packets and routed in that form over managed IP (Internet protocol) networks or over the public Internet to the desired location using IP addressing. VoIP then is really not a new service so much as it is a new technology that allows voice traffic to packetized and transported or routed over privately managed networks as data packets. Because most telephone subscribers continue to be served by local exchange carriers using circuit switched technology, VoIP-based calls will continue to travel over the public switched networks at some point during their routing. As VoIP technology becomes more prevalent however, the likelihood is that the need for the local exchange carrier (LEC) and the switched network will diminish over time.

The term "VoIP" encompasses many other services, including voice-enabled instant messaging, chat and voice-enabled gaming (such as X-Box Live), unified messaging (where users have a single message platform for e-mail, voice-mail, faxes, and the like), personal portals for caller ID on televisions sets, talking e-mail, customized dial tones, and greetings. VoIP may also make possible advanced videoconferencing, including a combination of voice video and data delivery. In an example offered by the then-chairman of the FCC, ". . . you may make an Internet call to your doctor's office to make an appointment. The doctor's office calls up your medical records, your medications and your last visit and instantly displays them. It also brings up the appointment times available, allows you to select one and then calls you back or sends a text message to your cell phone the day of the appointment to remind you." Clearly a great deal is already possible under the name of VoIP. However, for purposes of this chapter, the term is probably most useful as a telephone call completed over the Internet because that is where the discussion is at this point. When more interactive services are included within the accustomed term telecommunication service, then the discussion will focus on whether there is sufficient connection to the taxing jurisdiction and whether this is the type of transaction to which the sales tax should apply.

The Internet Tax Nondiscrimination Act made clear that while charges for Internet access were prohibited from state taxation, VoIP was not "Internet access," and, as such, state taxation of VoIP was not prohibited by these federal acts. States had been reluctant to extend their telecommunications taxes to VoIP for fear that this service either represented nontaxable Internet access or untaxed and unregulated information services. This issue was addressed by the Eighth U.S. Circuit Court of Appeals and the FCC in the same proceeding arising out of Minnesota.

On July 15, 2003, the Minnesota Department of Commerce filed a complaint with the Minnesota Public Utilities Commission (MPUC) arguing that digital voice services VoIP offered by an unregulated company called Vonage Holdings Corp., which utilized VoIP technology, was actually "telephone service." The complaint argued that Vonage was providing these services without complying with state regulations governing the provision of telephone services, such as obtaining a service permit and filing a tariff listing the prices for the telephone services, applicable taxes, and conditions for provision of digital voice.

In response, Vonage filed a petition with the FCC requesting that it preempt the order of the MPUC for two reasons. First, they argued that digital voice was not a traditional "telecommunication service" as that term was defined in the Communications Acts of 1934 and as amended in 1996, but was in fact an "information service," specifically not subject to state regulation under the acts. The second argument presented by Vonage involved the "impossibility exception" contained in 47 U.S.C. § 152:

> (b). This exception allows the FCC to pre-empt state regulation of a service which would otherwise be subject to dual federal and state regulation where it is impossible or impractical to separate the services' intrastate and interstate components, and state regulation interferes with valid federal rules or policies.

At the same time, Vonage filed a suit against the MPUC in Federal District Court in Minneapolis requesting a cease-and-desist Order and a permanent injunction to ban the MPUC from enforcing its order for Vonage to comply with the regulation in Minnesota. The District Court in fact granted the injunction against the MPUC from enforcing its order and decided that digital voice was in fact an "information service," not a telecommunication service, and therefore not subject to regulation by the MPUC. The MPUC was without authority to subject Vonage to common carrier regulation under the act. (*See*, *Vonage Holding Corp. v. Minnesota Public Utilities Commission*, 290 F. Supp 2d 993, at 999 (D. Minn. 2003).) The MPUC appealed those order to the Eighth Circuit Court of Appeals in January 2004.

While the Eighth Circuit appeal was pending, the FCC took up the Vonage petition. On March 10, 2004, the FCC released a Notice of Proposed Rule Making (NPRM) regarding Internet protocol–enabled services and invited public comment seeking guidance on which classes of IP-enabled services, if any, are telecommunications services under the act and which, if any, are information services.

After several public hearing and a great deal of public comment, the FCC issued an order that adopted Vonage's alternate argument. The FCC ruled that regardless of whether the service is defined as a telecommunication service or an information service, it is appropriate to preempt state regulation because it is impossible or impractical to separate the intrastate component of VoIP service from its interstate components. "The practical inseverability of other types of IP enabled services having basic characteristics similar to digital voice would likewise preclude state regulation." *In Re Vonage Holdings Corp*, 19 F.C.C.R 22404, 22424 at ¶ 32 (2004); 2004 W.L. 2600194 at ¶ 11.

After the FCC order, a number of parties filed petitions seeking direct review of the order in various federal District Courts of Appeals, one in the Second Circuit (New York) one in the Sixth Circuit and Ninth Circuit and two in the Eighth Circuit. The cases were consolidated at the Eighth Circuit with the Vonage Petition and resolved as one.

There were a number of compelling issues raised by the parties in their petitions. The Eighth Circuit determined, however, that the "impossibility exception issue" was dispositive of the case. The court agreed with the FCC that it was impossible or impractical to separate the intrastate features from interstate features of digital voice. Therefore, the exception applied. Its application in this case was neither arbitrary nor capricious by the FCC, and the court would defer to the position of the FCC because of the high level deference due on such fact-specific issues. The court did not determine that digital voice was either an information service or a telecommunication service. It did not need to reach this issue since the impossibility exception made further inquiry unnecessary.

State legislatures have, nonetheless, determined that VoIP is a telecommunication service for sales and use tax purposes and have extended their telecommunications services taxes to cover the expanded technology whether provided by a traditional LEC or an unregulated entrant into the market, such as Vonage. The FCC decision established that Vonage's VoIP services and those of other VoIP service providers will be regulated, if at all, on a uniform basis at the federal level and not under an inconsistent regimen at fifty-state public utility commissions. The FCC explained in its order that VoIP calls are more similar to wireless calls than traditional switched services with fixed geographic locations for users. Wireless calls were exempted from state regulation by Congress in 1992. The FCC acting under the congressional mandate of the Telecom Act of 1996 § 230 stated, "It is the policy of the United States to preserve the vibrant and competitive free market that presently exists for Internet and other interstate computer services unimpeded by federal or state regulators." State governments have nonetheless rolled the services into their existing telecommunications services taxable under their sales and use tax statutes.

A. New York's Treatment of VoIP

New York defines VoIP service as a service that enables a user to make and receive calls to and from any domestic telephone number. The services may be billed either on a call-by-call basis or on a flat fee basis. On either basis, the service provider may have the ability to distinguish intrastate from interstate calls. The service is often bundled with other services (e.g., Internet access, voice mail, and the like) or with the purchase of tangible personal property such as equipment. Because VoIP enables the user to make and receive telephone calls, the services constitute the use or operation of equipment for the transmission of sound and other signals, using principles of telephony or telegraphy within the terms of the sales and use tax statute. As a result, the service constitutes "telephony and telegraphy and telephone and telegraph service" within the meaning of the sales and uses tax statute and is subject to the tax. The use of the Internet or Internet routing protocols for the transmission of all or part of the call does not change this result.

Because the VoIP service is often bundled with other services that may or may not be subject to the sales tax and sold to the customer for a single charge, the entire charge is subject to the New York sales tax unless the charge for the nontaxable property or service is reasonable and separately stated on the invoice or other statement of price provided to the customer. In order to be reasonably identified, such charges must be objective and verifiable and reasonable in relation to the total charge.

New York, therefore, treats the VoIP telephone call as any other telephone call regardless of the technological protocols which allow the call to be completed. Because

New York exempts interstate and international calls, the bill received by the customer should clearly reflect any interstate or international calls, or the entire bill will be subject to the sales tax. The reach of the tax is no respecter of the company that provides the service. In some states, only telephone companies regulated by the public service commission are taxed. In New York, the service provider who provides the taxable service is charged with the collection and remittance of the tax if the provider provides a service defined in the statute. In this instance, there is nothing to distinguish the VoIP service from other telephony or telegraphic service.

B. Florida's Treatment of VoIP

"Communications services" is defined to include the transmission, conveyance, or routing of voice, data, audio, video, or other information or signals, including cable services, to a point, or between or among points, by or through an electronic, radio, satellite, or cable, optical, microwave, or other medium or method now in existence or hereinafter revised, or regardless of the protocol used for the transmission or conveyance. In addition, the term includes such transmission, conveyance, or routing in which computer processing applications are used to act on the form, code, or protocol of the content for purposes of transmission, conveyance or routing without regard to whether such service is referred to as VoIP services or classified by the FCC as enhance or value added. (Fla. Statute § 202.11.)

It is clear that the definition of communication service is meant to include VoIP; however, the tax was not immediately applied to this service. The state sought to include VoIP under a services provided under a "substitute communications" definition, which would have covered services originally designed to bypass the local telephone service network by establishing private telecommunications networks, for example. Collection of the communications tax on VoIP has been sporadic because most of the original providers were not telephone companies and were not regulated by the public service commissions. While this tax was originally designed to create a more user-friendly tax system, the eventual tax rate of 14 percent was only slightly better than the rates that had been replaced, and the confusion of what was taxable has not yet been ironed out. VoIP is clearly subject to tax under this new regimen, but enforcement against VoIP providers has been hampered by the state confusion on whether the Internet Tax Freedom Act would prohibit this levy on these service providers. As a result, the issue is still largely unsettled in Florida.

C. Pennsylvania's Treatment of VoIP

Pennsylvania, in sales tax Bulletin No. 2005-02, issued January 28, 2005, defined VoIP as ". . . real time audit or data transmitted and/or received in a digital format through the use of Internet protocol data packet transmission, or any similar or successor protocol transmission." Calls may be made between users of the same VoIP service as well as between users and those with landline or mobile telephone service. Some VoIP services work only over a computer or special VoIP telephone, but others allow use of a traditional telephone with an adapter.

The Pennsylvania tax is imposed on

> Any one-way transmission or any two-way, interactive transmission of sounds, signals or other intelligence converted to like form which effects or is intended to effect meaningful communications by electronic or electromagnetic means via wire, cable, satellite, light waves, microwaves, radio waves or *other transmission media*. The term includes all types of telecommunication transmissions, such as local, toll, wide-area or any other type of telephone service; private line service; telegraph service; radio repeater service; wireless communication service; personal communications system service; cellular telecommunication service; specialized mobile radio service; stationary two-way radio service; and paging service. (Emphasis added). 72 P.S. § 7201(rr).

The bulletin concludes that "Clearly, VoIP falls under the statutory definition."

The Pennsylvania statute goes on to state,

> Since VOIP utilizes computer-processing applications solely for the management, control or operation of a telecommunications system or the management of a telecommunications service, it does *not* come within the enhanced telecommunication service exclusion from sales and use tax. VOIP utilizes Internet Protocol that permits the transmission of packeted data across a network or across multiple networks, but does not interact with the information it transmits; it merely serves to address and route the information.
>
> The federal moratorium, the Internet Tax Non-Discrimination Act P.L. 108–435, or ban on taxing Internet access specifically excludes VOIP, freeing states to tax it as a telecommunication service.
>
> The Federal Communications Commission ("FCC") has ruled that digital voice is not subject to state public utility regulation; however, the FCC has expressed no opinion on state taxation of the service.
>
> **Conclusion**
>
> VOIP is a taxable telecommunication service subject to Pennsylvania state and local sales tax.

V. STREAMLINED SALES TAX PROJECT (SSTP)

State conflicts over interjurisdictional transactions were at the heart of the congressional prohibition on new sales and use taxes on transactions that occur over the Internet. The Internet Tax Freedom Act prohibited, after 1998, any new taxes on transactions that occur over the Internet. While this ban was aimed at sales of tangible personal property and services, it had a chilling effect on state efforts to tax not only sales of merchandise but Internet-based services as well. The states, however, could foresee, in the development of the Internet, a vast new marketplace where traditional sales activities might migrate if it would mean avoiding the sales tax. Congress, too, recognized that while the states would forfeit sales tax revenue for the time being, the period necessary for the Internet market place to develop would bring rewards to everyone.

In December 2000, a group of state representatives voted to approve a Uniform Sales and Use Tax Administrative Act and the Streamlined Sales Tax Agreement. These agreements require legislative ratification in each state. The goal of the Agreement is to provide states with a streamlined sales tax system suitable for use by both "Main Street businesses" and those conducting business predominately or exclusively on line. The primary features of the system can be summarized below:

- *Uniform definitions of tax terms used in sales tax laws*—State legislatures in member states will be required to adopt the same tax terms in order to participate in the project. While it is recognized that changes in definitions of taxable items will result in some loss of revenue to the states, the loss is expected to be minimized by the increase in the tax base from the use of the use of uniform terms.
- *Rate simplification*—States will be allowed one general sales tax rate and one special rate for special items such as food and drugs. In addition, each local jurisdiction will be allowed one tax rate regardless of the number of local taxes now in effect. The general rate must be applied uniformly to all the sales within the tax base. Currently, telecommunications services, for example, are often taxed at a different rate than the normal tax rate. Under the SSTP, such differentiation will not be allowed.
- *State-level administration of all sales taxes*—States that now allow local administration of sales tax, such as Virginia, Louisiana, and Alabama, will be required to use only a state single point of administrative interpretation and reporting. Local governments will be required to adopt the same tax base.
- *Uniform sourcing rules*—States will adopt a single rule on sourcing of sales of tangible personal property for sales tax purposes. The destination/delivery determination has been adopted (as opposed to the origination/sale alternative), although special sourcing rules may be allowed when justified by unique industries. Since most local jurisdictions adopt the origination/sales sourcing rule, it will require major reordering of sales tax sourcing at the local level.
- *Simplified exemption administration*—The project has already adopted a uniform form to be used in applying for sales tax exemptions. All exemptions will be "entity" based to avoid further complication.
- *Uniform audit procedures*—States will conduct joint audits of multistate businesses to assure uniformity of tax interpretation. Use of proprietary reporting technology should limit the scope of most audits.

The SSTP for its purposes has adopted a uniform definition of the term "telecommunication service." For these purposes, the term means the electronic transmission, conveyance, or routing of voice, data, audio, video, or any other information or signals to a point, or between or among points. The term "telecommunications service" includes such transmission, conveyance, or routing in which computer-processing applications are used to act on the form, code, or protocol of the content for purposes of transmission, conveyance, or routing without regard to whether such service is referred to as VoIP services or is classified by the FCC as enhanced or value added.

The term is defined to exclude data processing and information services, installation or maintenance, tangible personal property, advertising, billing and collection, Internet access or radio and television broadcasting, any ancillary services, or digital products.

It is safe to say that outside of the SSTP, no state has adopted this definition for its own tax laws. Some states have determined that VoIP does constitute telephone service, and some states have specifically determined that no decision has as yet been made on this subject. While this definition seeks to take a broad leap forward to capture the new technology and avoid telecom services that may have been lost because of more advanced technology, it is clear that this definition will have to be amended for the next great leap forward in technology.

VI. SUMMARY AND CONCLUSIONS

The sales and use tax on telecommunications services is a popular tax among all levels of government. Virtually every state and many local jurisdictions tax some segment of the telecommunication service spectrum under their general retail sales and use tax, under a gross-receipts tax on local exchange carriers, or under a special excise tax on telecommunications separate from the general retail sales tax at a higher rate of tax. The sales and use tax has largely replaced the gross-receipts tax on telephony services imposed upon the Bell companies when the telephone business was a regulated monopoly. The Internet Tax Freedom Act and the Internet Nondiscrimination Act were necessary to prohibit states from throttling the development of the vital Internet marketplace by a stifling array of inconsistent and burdensome state and local taxes.

VoIP grows out of expanded technological capabilities to provide one-way or interactive communication services to the home. The courts and the FCC are not in agreement as to whether VoIP should be removed from regulation at the state level as an information service; however, they are in agreement that the local public service commissions do not have the authority to regulate VoIP as a local exchange common carrier. Nonetheless, VoIP is not exempt from the sales and use tax as a taxable telecommunications service for tax purposes. The SSTP will cement this determination in local sales tax law and potentially spread it to other states that have taken no position on VoIP taxation.

Finally, new technologies will continue to challenge even the most forward-looking statutory definitions formulated by the states to protect their sales and use tax base. But states have proven resourceful in adapting their statutes to technological innovation to protect this important revenue source.

Chapter 25

United States: E-Commerce Tax Administration and Compliance

J. Richard Duke
Duke Law Firm

I. INTRODUCTION

Electronic commerce (e-commerce) presents unique tax problems under the U.S. Internal Revenue Code (I.R.C.) but traditional tax laws can be applied to e-commerce transactions in most cases.[1] Tax issues, as well as tax compliance issues, include

1. Federal, state, and foreign taxation; and
2. Accounting for costs of acquiring, creating, and operating e-commerce enterprises.

Some form of verifiable digital identification (ID) must be presented when the identity of a party to a transaction is required. One ID system uses trusted intermediaries to issue verified digital IDs. The intermediary identifies the identity of the person seeking the digital ID, and, once verified, the digital ID is issued in a form that can be independently verified and is not subject to tampering. The U.S. Treasury anticipates the use of digital IDs that will permit tax returns to be filed electronically. Congress passed a law requiring the Internal Revenue Service (IRS) to develop such a system.[2]

Worldwide access to consumers is available through e-commerce where the parties, such as a buyer and seller, are physically located in different jurisdictions or locations. The parties to a transaction must know the location of the other parties for purposes of complying with the federal and state tax laws. As a result, parties to an Internet-based transaction may not know the location or identity of the other party, which raises issues

1 For a thorough discussion of the issues and planning regarding e-commerce taxation, *see* DAVID E. HARDESTY, ELECTRONIC COMMERCE: TAXATION AND PLANNING (Warren, Gorham & Lamont 2003), available at http://ria.thomsonreuters.com/EStore/detail.aspx?ID=ECTMP-SK.

2 Department of Treasury, *Selected Tax Policy Implications of Global Electronic Commerce* (Nov. 1996), available at http://www.treas.gov/offices/tax-policy/library/internet.shtml.

of how the tax obligations can be determined and the tax compliance and reporting requirements be properly met.

The U.S. payor of income to a nonresident alien or foreign corporation may be classified as a withholding agent under the I.R.C. A withholding agent is required to pay over, on certain types of income payments to nonresident aliens or a foreign corporation, a 30 percent withholding tax. And a withholding agent is personally liable for failure to pay over these taxes and file the required tax returns. Failure to properly act as a withholding agent may result in the personal liability for payment of tax, plus interest and penalties.[3] The withholding agent may avoid these penalties if he or she has reasonable cause for failure to withhold. The withholding agent claims reasonable cause by demonstrating that an underpayment was due to reasonable cause and not due to willful neglect. In order for an argument to prevail, it must be shown that the withholding agent exercised care and prudence in determining that the payment was not being made to a nonresident alien or foreign corporation. The problem is that the identity of foreign vendor-payees may be difficult or impossible as a result of the many online transactions that occur each day.

A. State Sales Tax

States generally require collection of sales tax that are due on taxable sales by a vendor, and when the vendor or seller fails to collect, interest and penalties may be imposed for any unpaid tax. Also, in general, penalties may be waived if the vendor shows reasonable cause for the failure to collect sales taxes. Because of the potentially large amount of interest and penalties for unpaid sales tax, it is recommended that online vendors require buyers in e-commerce to identify their states of residence, or counties and cities of residence.

The identity or location of a buyer is not required when digital goods are sold and delivered directly online. It is generally necessary to know the state, city, or county in which a buyer lives to accurately determine any sales tax liability. The Internet Protocol (IP) number associated with an Internet user can now be used to identify the country, and even the state, in which a party to the transaction is located.

B. Web-Based Businesses

One area in which tax issues under the current laws in the I.R.C. are not clear is the effect of the server location on tax compliance issues. The location of a server in a jurisdiction may not cause a nexus for taxation, but the location of company employees almost always results in nexus in that jurisdiction. For example, the location of a server in California does not affect the determination of a company's nexus for sales or income tax in that state.

---

3 I.R.C. §§ 6656(a) and 6672(a) (as amended in 1998).

Web-based businesses choose e-commerce jurisdictions that are friendly, such as California, and financial centers such as Bermuda. These friendly jurisdictions have laws or rules that provide that a server in that jurisdiction results in nexus. Web-based businesses avoid jurisdictions where the tax policies on the nexus issue are not clear or are not certain.

C. Digital Cash Reporting Requirement

In the course of a trade or business, any person receiving more than US$10,000 in cash in one transaction, or in two or more related transactions, must report the transaction within 15 days. This transaction is reported on IRS Form 8300.

Cash includes coin and currency of the United States or any other country.[4] Cashier's checks, bank drafts, traveler's checks, or money orders with a face amount of not more than US$10,000 are included as cash if received in either of the following:

1. A transaction that a recipient knows is being used in an attempt to avoid the reporting requirements; and
2. Certain retail sales of consumer durable goods, collectibles, or travel/entertainment activities.[5]

Digital cash is not mentioned in the Treasury Regulations (Treas. Regs.), but it appears that the definition of "cash" will be interpreted to include digital cash, cybermoney, and similar forms of Web-based payment.

E-Commerce activities encourage U.S. persons[6] to use foreign banking systems in business transactions and for holding and managing investments. Furthermore, it is easy for U.S. persons to open foreign bank accounts through the Internet or other means. The ease of opening online foreign bank accounts generally results in U.S. persons falling into international tax-reporting requirements. Such foreign bank accounts are subject to the filing of a Form TD F 90-22.1[7] and disclosure on Schedule B, Part III, Form 1040, which are discussed in greater detail later in this chapter.

D. Accounting Records

Accurate and complete accounting records must be maintained by a vendor.[8] Substantial accuracy-related penalties apply, as well as criminal penalties, for failure to maintain such records.[9] Furthermore, the IRS is authorized to reconstruct a vendor's income if adequate books and records are not maintained. Also, the IRS may issue a third-party

4 Treas. Reg. § 1.6050I-1(b) (as amended in 2001); *see* Instructions to Form 8300.
5 I.R.C. § 6051I(a) (as amended in 1996); Treas. Reg. § 1.6050I-1(c) (as amended in 2001).
6 U.S. persons for IRS purposes include citizens or legal residents.
7 31 C.F.R. § 103.24 (as amended in 1987); instructions to Form TD F 90-22.1.
8 I.R.C. § 6001 (as amended in 1982).
9 I.R.C. §§ 662(a) (1986), 7203 (as amended in 1990).

summons to the vendor's bank, credit reporting service, and other third-party record keepers in order to obtain records to reconstruct the vendor's income.[10]

A number of states are in the process of adopting the Federation of Tax Administrators (FTA), March 1996 Proposed Model Record-Keeping and Retention Rules, which require the following:

1. Electronic records must be maintained in sufficient detail to identify individual transactions.
2. Electronic record-keeping systems must be reliable in order to be subject to audit examination.

The regulations also require the vendor to maintain hard copies of records produced in the ordinary course of business.

Record-keeping requirements for automatic data processing (ADP) systems are required by the IRS[11] for all types of data processing systems, including "a mainframe computer system, stand-alone or networked microcomputer system, Data Base Management System ('DBMS'), and a system that uses or incorporates electronic data interchange ('EDI') technology or an electronic system." The Revenue Procedure also covers Internet-based record-keeping systems, although not stated in said Revenue Procedure. Failure to maintain the required records may result in penalties. The IRS can issue a Notice of Inadequate Records pursuant to Treas. Regs.,[12] if records are not properly retained. Accuracy-related penalties[13] and potentially possible criminal penalties[14] may apply for failure to keep records.

E. Systems for Electronic Imaging

The IRS proposed new rules for maintaining books and records with respect to electronic-imaging record-keeping systems. Imaging systems use electronic technology to prepare, record, image, index, preserve, retrieve, and reproduce books and records, the original of which are in the hard-copy format of active books and records. In addition, the originals are kept in hard-copy format.[15] The proposed requirements are similar to the requirements for a normal record-keeping system. But the electronic-imaging record-keeping system must include reasonable controls to "prevent the unauthorized creation of, addition to, alteration of, deletion of, or deterioration of any image document."

F. Sales and Use Tax Reporting

Proper systems must be used in order to determine the sales and use taxes among various states, for example. If only one or two states are involved, some companies are

10 I.R.C. §§ 7602(a) (as amended in 1998), 7609(a) (as amended in 1998).

11 Rev. Proc. 98-25, 1998-1 C.D. 998.

12 Treas. Reg. § 1.6001-1(d) (as amended in 1990), pursuant to this Rev. Proc.

13 Under I.R.C. § 662(a) (1986).

14 Under I.R.C § 7203 (as amended in 1990).

15 Notice 96-10, 1996-1 C.B. 363 (1996).

developing their own systems. But if sales and use taxes involve numerous states, then a commercial complete e-commerce package must be purchased in order to maintain adequate records with respect to sales and use tax obligations.

II. FOREIGN CORPORATIONS OWNED BY U.S. PERSONS

Prior to e-commerce transactions, U.S. persons commonly formed corporations in tax-haven jurisdictions in an attempt to defer taxation of income until the earnings were repatriated to the United States. Many abuses occurred during the pre-e-commerce era, and those abuses continue both in non-e-commerce transactions as well as e-commerce transactions. A U.S. person cannot simply incorporate a foreign corporation and defer income without meeting the requirements of the most complex rules in the I.R.C., which consist of

1. Transfers of appreciated assets to foreign corporations
2. The rules for controlled foreign corporations
3. The subpart F income taxation rules
4. The credit for foreign taxes paid rules
5. Tax treaties, if applicable

The first question with respect to income generated by a corporation is whether the source of income is inside or outside the United States. If the source of income is inside the United States, then it is taxed in the United States. If the source of income is outside the United States, it is taxed outside the United States. But it is possible that the foreign-source income is also subject to taxation in the United States, or the income is taxed to the U.S. shareholders of a foreign corporation, U.S. partners of a foreign partnership, or U.S. owners of other types of entities. U.S. persons are taxed on worldwide income without regard to source. A statutory exemption permits U.S. citizens an annual exclusion of income derived from services rendered outside the United States by those citizens if certain conditions are met under I.R.C. § 911 (as amended in 1997). The exemption is up to US$82,400 of earned income from income taxes in any one year for a U.S. citizen who lives outside the United States for a full year. Nonresident alien individuals are taxed on U.S.-source income effectively connected with a trade or business in the U.S. under I.R.C. § 872 (as amended in 1994).

A foreign corporation with U.S.-source income that is formed by one or more U.S. persons is subject to U.S. income taxation. In addition, if that foreign corporation does not form a subsidiary corporation in the United States, a branch-profits tax will apply, as discussed later in this chapter.

A foreign corporation, whether owned by U.S. shareholders or foreign shareholders, may be subject to U.S. income taxation the same as a nonresident alien with U.S.-source income.

If the foreign corporation has U.S.-source business income that is effectively connected with the conduct of a U.S. trade or business, or if the foreign corporation has a permanent establishment in the United States, then it is subject to U.S. taxation.

The foreign corporation, with or without U.S. shareholders, files a Form 1120-F and pays U.S. corporate income taxes on its U.S.-source income from a trade or business in the United States. If the foreign corporation is subject to U.S. income taxation and also has U.S. shareholders, then later distributions to those shareholders, if treated as dividend distributions, will be subject to an additional personal income tax (double tax since the corporation receives no deductions for dividends paid).

Foreign corporations and nonresident aliens with income that is not effectively connected with the conduct of a U.S. trade or business will have income that is passive income. Such passive income is called "fixed or determinable annual or periodical income from a U.S.-source" and is subject to withholding on payments from the United States. Such income includes interest, dividends, and gains from the sales of real property, annuities, and similar kinds of income.

U.S.-source income includes income derived from the operation of a U.S. trade or business in which the foreign corporation has a fixed place of business in the United States, has an employee in the United States, or an agent in the United States, who can conclude contracts on behalf of the corporation. The following are general rules as to the source of income:

1. Interest income is generally U.S.-source income if paid by a U.S. entity or person to a foreign person or entity.
2. Dividends paid by a U.S. corporation are U.S.-source income.
3. Compensation for services provided in the United States is U.S.-source income.
4. Rents or royalties on property located in the United States is U.S.-source income.
5. Gains from the sale of U.S. realty are U.S.-source income.

Whether income is U.S.-source or foreign-source is important for several reasons under U.S. international tax law. For example, foreign tax credits are available only where foreign taxes are paid on foreign-source income.[16] Foreign tax credits (or deductions) are available under specific rules if the foreign taxes are paid on foreign-source income. Proper planning is necessary to ensure receipt of this tax credit in order to avoid double taxation. An example of the problem is where foreign taxes are paid under appropriate foreign laws, but the United States deems this income to be of U.S. source. In such a case, the tax credit is not available because of the U.S source determination.

A. The *InverWorld, Inc.* Case

The Internet makes it possible to run a business from a server located in another country without being present in that country. The hope is that by forming a corporation in a foreign jurisdiction that does not tax that corporation, U.S. income taxation can be avoided. In general, a foreign corporation operated from the United States is taxable in the United States, and a fixed place of business in the United States may result taxation of both U.S.-source and foreign-source income. In the well-known case

16 I.R.C. § 904(a) (as amended in 2002).

of *InverWorld, Inc. v. Commissioner*,[17] the party involved was InverGroup, a related group of investment management and financial services. Those related groups included InverWorld, Ltd., incorporated in the Cayman Islands, InverWorld, Inc., a U.S. corporation, InverMexico, a Mexican corporation, and other companies. The court analyzed the activities that occurred in Texas, Mexico, and the Cayman Islands and found that most of the operating activities took place in Texas. The court found that the management fee income, loan interest, commissions, and various other types of income of InverWorld, Ltd. were effectively connected with the conduct of a U.S. trade or business and subject to taxation in the United States.

A key question concerns how income in a transaction is characterized. For example, the nature of the transaction may mean that a sale occurs or, in the alternative, a license arrangement is entered into. Depending on the transaction, the source of the income is different. For example, rental income from the use of intangible property is sourced in the place of its use by the licensee; a transaction characterized as services is sourced where the services are performed; a sale of U.S. manufactured goods is allocated between the United States and the country where the sale is made; the source of inventory sales is determined by the place of sale, which is determined by the place in which title passes. Thus, if taxes are paid in both the United States and a foreign country, the transaction must be structured so that the foreign taxes are paid on foreign-source income under U.S. law; otherwise, the foreign tax credit is not available, and double taxation results.

Because U.S. corporations are taxed on worldwide income, their direct activities offshore may be subject to current U.S. tax, as well as foreign-country tax. Indirect foreign activities in a foreign country may not attract foreign-country tax if such indirect activities do not rise to the level of "engaging in business" in that foreign country. For example, use of an unrelated distributor may be substantially conducted from outside the foreign country so that no income generated from sales is considered to be sourced inside the foreign country. Use of a sales representative also may result in the foreign country imposing no tax. However, this result depends upon the role of the particular sales representative and whether the activities of the representative cause the U.S. company to be treated as engaging in business in the foreign country.

A distributor takes title and, typically, possession of products from the seller. A sales representative does not take title to the property. A distributor then makes his or her profits on the resale of the goods. A sales representative, however, earns his or her profits in the form of commission for services rendered. Another major distinction is that the distributor assumes the credit risk in connection with the sale of the goods to the foreign customer. The primary drawback to the use of distributors is that the U.S. supplier is unable to participate in the profits generated from sales by the distributor to the foreign customer.

A sales representative generally does not take title to or possession of the goods that are drop-shipped directly to the ultimate customer. The sales representative bears no credit risk with respect to the sales; however, the practical risk is that a sales representative who aggressively sells products to nonpaying customers is soon out of a job.

17 InverWorld, Inc. v. Comm'r, 1996 RIA TC Memo. 1996-301 (1996).

From a tax perspective, the actions of an ordinary sales representative employed by a U.S. manufacturer may be imputed to the U.S. company as its principal. If the sales representative's activities rise to the necessary level under foreign law, a trade or business may exist. If a trade or business does exist in that foreign jurisdiction, the income generated by the activities of the sales representative may attract a foreign income tax. In general, this result does not occur if the sales representative is independent and acts on behalf of multiple suppliers. Also, if the sales representative does not have the authority to conclude a contract in the foreign country, it is unlikely that these activities attract a foreign income tax. These are matters of foreign law that require foreign tax counsel.

A U.S. entity may establish a branch operation in a foreign country. The branch brings the assets of the U.S. entity under the jurisdiction of the foreign court system. For this reason alone, many U.S. companies prefer to establish a foreign subsidiary to limit their exposure to legal liability. The local presence of a foreign subsidiary may provide better business opportunities and an access to the local court system in the event of a legal dispute. The use of a foreign subsidiary, however, results in higher costs and administrative duties and may involve the requirement for local country shareholders in the subsidiary entity.

The use of distributors or sales representatives involves little, if any, direct physical presence in the foreign country. The establishment of a branch or other physical presence indicates a much higher degree of commitment to conducting business in the foreign country. The decision of whether to have a real physical presence in a foreign country is generally dictated more by business considerations than tax considerations. However, once this decision is made from a business perspective, tax considerations come to the forefront.

When a business has operations or facilities in more than one country, the source of the income of the business could be manipulated for tax advantages. Because income taxes are imposed on net income after deductions for expenses and the costs of the products or services, the allocation of such expenses or costs between branches or subsidiary companies in different countries afford opportunities for tax misallocations. To prevent such misallocations, the IRS is given the power to reallocate income, deductions, or credits between two or more related entities if they are controlled or owned by the same interests.[18]

B. Branch Profits Tax

A foreign corporation doing business in the United States is required to pay a corporate income tax on taxable income from U.S.-sources the same as a domestic corporation.[19] If the foreign business operates as a U.S.-based corporation, there is a withholding tax of 30 percent on dividends paid to the foreign parent corporation or other shareholders. But if the foreign corporation merely operates as an unincorporated branch through an

18 I.R.C. § 482 (1986).

19 I.R.C. § 882 (as amended in 1988).

employee or agent located in the United States, distributions of after-tax profits to the foreign owners would not be subject to the withholding tax on dividends.

Partly to equalize the treatment of a branch operation and a corporation owned by foreign persons, and mostly to prevent avoidance of the withholding tax on dividend distributions, I.R.C. § 884 (as amended in 1996) imposes a special tax on the profits of a branch of a foreign corporation doing business in the United States.

The branch profits tax is equal to 30 percent of the "dividend equivalent amount," which is basically a 30 percent tax on the after-tax earnings by a foreign corporation's U.S. branch to the extent the earnings are not reinvested in assets connected with a U.S. trade or business. The rate of tax may be lower if the branch operation is owned by a corporation based in a country with which the United States has a treaty. Treas. Regs. restrict this exception to foreign corporations that meet certain tests to determine foreign residency of the corporation.

Various foreign companies impose a similar tax on the earnings of a noncorporate business activity within their borders. If a foreign corporation is owned by U.S. shareholders and has income that is effectively connected with a trade or business in the United States, it will also be subject to the branch profits tax on earnings that are not reinvested in the U.S. business.

III. CONTROLLED FOREIGN CORPORATIONS AND SUBPART F INCOME

The United States does not have the legal authority (jurisdiction) to impose taxes on foreign corporations unless those corporations have U.S.-source income or are engaged in a trade or business in the United States. But the United States does have the authority to impose a tax on U.S. persons (individuals and entities) who are shareholders of foreign corporations. The Revenue Act of 1962 introduced what is now known as "subpart F" of the I.RC.[20] These provisions require U.S. shareholders of controlled foreign corporations to include earnings and profits of the foreign corporation in the income of U.S. shareholders.

Only U.S. persons who meet the definition of U.S. shareholders are subject to the subpart F rules. Generally, the rules only apply to those shareholders who own 10 percent or more of the stock of the foreign corporation by vote or value. The law refers to such shareholders as "U.S. shareholders."

A. Definition of a Controlled Foreign Corporation

A controlled foreign corporation (CFC) is a foreign corporation that is controlled by U.S. shareholders. Control means that the U.S. shareholders own or control more than 50 percent of the foreign corporation, by vote or value.

---

20 I.R.C. § 962 (as amended in 1988).

For this purpose, a U.S. shareholder is a U.S. person[21] who owns,[22] or is deemed to own,[23] 10 percent or more of the stock or the combined voting power of all classes of stock of a foreign corporation.

Only U.S. persons can be U.S. shareholders. I.R.C. § 957(c) (1986) refers to I.R.C. § 7701(a)(30) (as amended in 1997) for the definition of a U.S. person that is very broadly defined to include individuals, partnerships, corporations, trusts, and estates.

A U.S. shareholder, for purposes of determining whether there is a CFC, is one who owns 10 percent or more, by vote, of the foreign corporation.[24] In determining the 10 percent or more ownership, the attribution rules (described below) of both I.R.C. §§ 958(a) and 958(b) apply.

Once it is determined—through direct ownership, indirect ownership under I.R.C. § 958(a) (as amended in 1996), or constructive ownership under I.R.C. § 958(b) (as amended in 1996) that, in the aggregate, U.S. shareholders own more than 50 percent by vote or value in the foreign corporation, it is classified as a CFC.

Only those shareholders that own (directly or indirectly) 10 percent or more of the foreign corporation stock are included in the "more than 50 percent" ownership test. Thus, a foreign corporation with twenty U.S. shareholders with equal shares of 5 percent of the foreign corporation is not a CFC. Or, if a foreign person legitimately owns 50 percent or more of the corporation, then no combination of U.S. persons can own "more than 50 percent" of the foreign corporation. If one U.S. person owns 40 percent of a foreign corporation, and ten U.S. persons each own 6 percent, it is not a CFC, even though U.S. persons own 100 percent of the stock. Only one of those U.S. persons is a "U.S. shareholder" as defined for this purpose.

Each U.S. person's ownership percentage is determined by taking into account the attribution and constructive ownership rules. A 10 percent or more shareholder of a corporation or a 10 percent or more partners in a partnership are deemed to have a proportionate interest in any corporate stock owned by the corporation or partnership.[25] Thus, ownership of a foreign corporation is derived from the direct ownership of the taxpayer plus any indirect ownership arising from the attribution and constructive ownership rules.

B. Constructive Ownership

The determination of whether a U.S. person is a U.S. shareholder of a CFC depends on both direct ownership and indirect ownership of the foreign corporation.

Direct ownership is simply the number of shares of stock (or the ownership interest in a foreign limited liability company (LLC)) the individual or parent corporation owns. Constructive ownership includes shares of stock attributed to the individual that is owned

---

21 As defined in I.R.C. § 957(c) (1986).

22 As defined in I.R.C § 958(a) (as amended in 1996).

23 By applying the rules of ownership of I.R.C. § 958(b) (as amended in 1996).

24 I.R.C. § 951(b) (as amended in 1997).

25 I.R.C. § 958(b)(3) (as amended in 1996).

by estates or trusts in which the individual is a beneficiary, or shares owned by a partnership or corporation in which the individual or corporation owns 10 percent or more.

I.R.C. § 318(1)(a) (as amended in 1997) provides that

> An individual shall be considered as owning the stock owned, directly or indirectly, by or for:
>
> (i) his spouse (other than a spouse who is legally separated from the individual under a decree of divorce or separate maintenance), and
> (ii) his children, grandchildren, and parents.

I.R.C. § 318(a)(2) (as amended in 1997) provides that stock owned by an individual shall be attributed from a partnership, estate, trust, or corporation.

> (A) From partnerships and estates
> Stock owned, directly or indirectly, by or for a partnership or estate shall be considered as owned proportionately by its partners or beneficiaries.
> (B) From trusts
> (i) Stock owned, directly or indirectly, by or for a trust (other than an employees' trust described in chapter 401(a) that is exempt from tax [. . .]) shall be considered as owned by its beneficiaries in proportion to the actuarial interest of such beneficiaries in such trust.
> (ii) Stock owned, directly or indirectly, by or for any portion of a trust of which a person is considered the owner under subpart E of part I of subchapter J (relating to grantors and others treated as substantial owners) shall be considered as owned by such person.
> (C) From corporations
> If 50 percent or more in value of the stock in a corporation is owned, directly or indirectly, by or for any person, such person shall be considered as owning the stock owned, directly or indirectly, by or for such corporation, in that proportion that the value of the stock that such person so owns bears to the value of all the stock in such corporation.

However, I.R.C. § 958(b)(3) (as amended in 1996) provides that "in applying subparagraph (C) of I.R.C. § 318(a)(2) (as amended in 1997), the phrase '10 percent' shall be substituted for the phrase '50 percent' used in subparagraph (C)."

I.R.C. § 318(a)(3) (as amended in 1997) provides that stock owned by an individual shall be attributed to an entity in which the individual has an interest.

> (A) To partnerships and estates
> Stock owned, directly or indirectly, by or for a partner or a beneficiary of an estate shall be considered as owned by the partnership or estate.
> (B) To trusts
> (i) Stock owned, directly or indirectly, by or for a beneficiary of a trust (other than an employees' trust described in chapter 401(a)) shall be considered as owned by the trust, unless such beneficiary's interest in the trust is a remote contingent interest.
> (ii) Stock owned, directly or indirectly, by or for a person who is considered the owner of any portion of a trust under subpart E of part I of subchapter J (relating to grantors and others treated as substantial owners), shall be considered as owned by the trust.

(C) To corporations

If 50 percent or more in value of the stock in a corporation is owned, directly or indirectly, by or for any person, such corporation shall be considered as owning the stock owned, directly or indirectly, by or for such person.

I.R.C. § 958(b) (as amended in 1996) does not change the 50 percent test under I.R.C. 318(a)(3)(C) (as amended in 1997).

For example, John Jones is a beneficiary of a trust that owns 5 percent of the stock of a CFC. His wife owns 3 percent, and he owns 60 percent of a partnership that owns 5 percent of the stock of the foreign corporation. Jones is a U.S. shareholder because he is deemed to own the shares held by the trust, by his wife, and 60 percent of the shares owned by his partnership. He is therefore deemed to own 11 percent of the stock of the CFC.

As explained below, the definition of a related party, under I.R.C. §§ 958(a) and (b) (as amended in 1996), provides that stock of a foreign corporation owned by a nonresident alien individual (other than a foreign trust or foreign estate) shall not be considered as owned by a citizen or by a resident alien individual. Thus, if a parent, child or spouse is a nonresident alien and owns 50 percent of the stock of a foreign corporation in which the U.S. individual owns 50 percent, the corporation will not be a CFC.

The interaction of I.R.C. § 318 (as amended in 1997) and § 958 (as amended in 1996) can produce some very ambiguous results and must be studied in detail in the context of a particular ownership pattern.

C. Subpart F Income

U.S. shareholders (as defined above) are subject to current taxation on certain types of income (after deducting expenses properly allocable to such income) of a CFC. The kinds of income that are subject to current taxation by the U.S. shareholders are described in I.R.C. § 952 (as amended in 1997) through § 954 (as amended in 2002) and are referred to as "subpart F" of the I.R.C. Hence, these forms of income are referred to as "subpart F income."

The five categories of subpart F income under I.R.C. § 952 (as amended in 1997) include

1. Insurance income;[26]
2. Foreign base company income;[27]
3. Income from countries subject to international boycotts;[28]
4. Illegal bribes, kickbacks, and similar payments;[29] and
5. Income from countries where the U.S. has severed diplomatic relations.[30]

---

26 As defined at I.R.C. § 953 (as amended in 2002).

27 As defined under I.R.C. § 954 (as amended in 2002).

28 I.R.C. § 999 (as amended in 2000).

29 I.R.C. § 162(c) (as amended in 2003).

30 I.R.C. § 901(j) (as amended in 2000).

The major category applicable to most foreign corporations is "foreign base company income," which is defined to include

1. Foreign personal holding company (FPHC) income (I.R.C. § 954(c) (as amended in 2002))
2. Foreign base company sales income (I.R.C. § 954(d) (as amended in 2002))
3. Foreign base company services income (I.R.C. § 954(e) (as amended in 2002))
4. Foreign base company shipping income (I.R.C. § 954(f) (as amended in 2002))
5. Foreign base company oil-related income (I.R.C. § 954(g) (as amended in 2002))

FPHC income is basically income from passive investments such as interest, dividends, certain rents, royalties, and capital gains.

"Foreign base company sales income" is defined by I.R.C. § 954(d) (as amended in 2002), but it generally includes income from buying or selling personal property from a related person.

"Foreign base company services income" is defined as "income" (whether in the form of compensation, commissions, fees, or otherwise) derived in connection with the performance of technical, managerial, engineering, architectural, scientific, skilled, industrial, commercial, or like services.

Subpart F income, to the extent of the earnings and profits of the corporation, is taxable each year (whether distributed or not) to shareholders owning 10 percent or more of the stock, determined by direct ownership or the attribution rules under I.R.C. § 958(a) (as amended in 1996), but not I.R.C. § 958(b) (as amended in 1996).

D. Tax Treatment of U.S. Shareholders in CFCs

Generally, only those foreign corporations in which U.S. shareholders own more than 50 percent of the stock of the foreign corporation are subject to tax at the shareholder level. Subpart F income includes passive investment income, income from personal service contracts, income from transactions with related U.S. persons or entities, and income from certain industries such as insurance, banking, mining, and others.

To add to the confusion, exceptions apply to many of these general rules:

- If a U.S. shareholder is required to include any subpart F income in his or her (or its) tax return, the income is treated as dividend income; but it is generally not eligible for the reduced tax rate of 15 percent (or 5%) for "qualified dividends."
- If the foreign corporation has losses for the tax year, they are not deductible by the U.S. shareholders.
- Any gain on the subsequent sale of CFC stock is treated as dividend income to any U.S. shareholder who owns 10 percent or more of the stock at any time within five years before the sale of the stock. This dividend treatment is only applicable for gains to the extent of the accumulated and undistributed earnings and profits of the corporation. The dividend income is not a "qualified dividend." Thus, the tax-deferred earnings of a CFC will eventually be subject to tax as ordinary income, rather than

as a capital gain or qualified dividend. For 10 percent or greater shareholders, it does not matter if the earnings of the foreign corporation are distributed as dividends or if the stock is sold at a gain.[31]

- Gains from the sale of stock by shareholders who do not directly or indirectly own 10 percent of the company are eligible to be treated as a long-term capital gain rather than being taxed as ordinary income.[32]
- Although U.S. shareholders of a CFC may be subject to current tax on the subpart F income of the CFC, losses are not passed through as deductions to the shareholders.
- Where a U.S. shareholder formed a CFC in order to invest in a foreign security, no loss was available to the shareholder when the security became worthless because the security was owned by the corporation instead of by the shareholder. In order to secure a capital loss deduction, the foreign corporation has to be liquidated. There is a realization of gain on any appreciated assets held by the liquidating corporation.
- Foreign taxes paid by the CFC can be claimed as a tax credit (or deduction) by a corporate shareholder but not by an individual shareholder, partnership, estate, or trust.

IV. TAX FILING REQUIREMENTS OF A FOREIGN CORPORATION

U.S. shareholders of a CFC are required to file Form 5471 with their personal tax return, even if the CFC has no subpart F income. Form 926 is used to report transfers of property (including cash) to a foreign corporation. Because a foreign corporation will have some kind of foreign bank or financial account, the U.S. shareholders who have control, signatory authority, or a financial interest over the account must file Form TD F 90-22.1 by June 30 of the year after the calendar year ends. If the foreign corporation's shareholders have made an election to have the corporation treated as a disregarded (noncorporate) entity for U.S. tax purposes, then the shareholders must file a Form 8865 for a foreign partnership and a Form 8858 for a foreign disregarded entity. In order to make an election to be treated as a disregarded entity, a Form 8832 must be filed. If the foreign corporation has made an investment in any passive foreign investment companies, or if the foreign corporation is a passive foreign investment company (PFIC), then the U.S. shareholders may be required to file a Form 8621 to report their share of the income of the PFIC or the gain on any dispositions of PFIC shares. If the foreign corporation has any U.S.-source income, it files a Form 1120-F. In the event of the purchase or sale of a foreign corporation, the buyer and seller file a Form 8883, which is an Asset Allocation Statement. If the shareholders or the corporation rely on a treaty that overrides a provision of the I.R.C., a Form 8833 must be filed to reflect a treaty based return position. Depending on the nature of the business of the corporation, other forms may be required.

31 I.R.C. § 1248 (as amended in 1996).

32 If the foreign corporation is a passive foreign investment company, shareholders who own less than 10% of the stock will be subject to the tax rules for PFIC distributions and share dispositions.

A. Form 5471 for U.S. Shareholders of Foreign Corporations

Form 5471 is the "Information Return of U.S. Persons Regarding Certain Foreign Corporations." It is required to be filed at the time that a person's corporate or personal tax return is filed, including any extended filing date. A second copy must be sent to the Philadelphia office of the IRS.

A person must determine whether he or she is required to file IRS Form 5471 if

That person is (1) a shareholder, director, or officer in a foreign corporation; (2) the grantor of a trust that has formed a foreign corporation (also referred to as IBCs in financial centers); or (3) an individual whose U.S. corporation or partnership owns shares in a foreign corporation.

Five categories of persons are required to file this form:

1. a U.S. citizen or resident who is an officer, director, or a 10 percent shareholder of an FPHC (passive investment income);
2. a U.S. citizen or resident who is an officer or director of a foreign corporation in which a U.S. person has acquired stock that meets the 10 percent ownership requirement;
3. a U.S. person (defined below) who acquires stock in a foreign corporation, which when added to any stock owned meets the 10 percent ownership requirement;
4. a U.S. person who had control of a foreign corporation for an uninterrupted period of at least thirty days during the accounting year of the corporation; and
5. a U.S. shareholder who owns stock in a foreign corporation that is a CFC for an uninterrupted period of thirty days or more during any tax year and who owned that stock on the last day of the year.

A "U.S. person" includes a citizen, permanent resident, domestic partnership, domestic corporation, domestic trust, or domestic estate.

Depending on which of the five categories apply to a required filer, different schedules must be completed. An officer of director of a CFC who is not an owner of the CFC will be required to file under category 2, where certain U.S. persons have acquired additional stock in the corporation. A category 2 filer is required only to complete page 1 and Schedule G. Where a U.S. corporation is the 100 percent owner of a foreign corporation that is not a FPHC, the corporation could be classified as a category 3, 4, and 5 filer. In this case, all of the schedules except Schedule A, Part II and Schedule O, Part I may be required.

The penalties for a failure to file the return are severe, and it is not necessary that the corporation have any profits for the penalties to apply. A return must be filed even if there is no taxable income to report. Complete details of the applicable penalties are provided in the Instructions to Form 5471, but in general, the penalty is $10,000 per year for failing to file the form. In addition, if the form is not filed, one's personal income tax return is deemed to be incomplete, and the statute of limitations does not begin to run until the information required by Form 5471 is filed.

This form is required to be filed by April 15 or the extended due date of the personal or corporate tax return.

B. Reporting Requirements—Transfers to Foreign Corporations

The tax-free transfer rules under I.R.C. § 351 (as amended in 1999), with respect to controlling shareholders exchanging property for stock in that corporation without taxation, do not apply for transfers to foreign corporations. The transfer of property to a foreign corporation is taxable based on the value of the property transferred, unless exceptions apply,[33] requiring a valuation. The transfer of cash is not taxable.

An exception includes assets transferred to a foreign corporation that are used in foreign business activities.[34] All of the following requirements must be met to qualify for the exception:

1. The foreign corporation must be involved in an active trade or business.
2. The trade or business must be conducted outside the U.S.
3. The transferred property must be held for use in an active foreign trade or business.[35]

C. Transfers of Intangibles to Foreign Corporations in Exchange for Stock

Special rules apply to transfers of intangibles to foreign corporations in exchange for stock.[36] Under these rules, transfers are not immediately taxable (as under the above-discussed rules for transfers of other assets to foreign corporations). Instead, transferors are required to recognize ordinary income (taxable in the U.S.) from the intangible asset for the life of the asset, up to a maximum of twenty years.[37] Basically, the transferor is treated as having sold the property to the foreign corporation in exchange for payments that are contingent upon the productivity, use, or disposition of the property, that is, a royalty.

The I.R.C. imputes income to the transferor that

1. Reasonably reflect the amounts that would have been received annually in the form of payments over the useful life of the property (up to a maximum of 20 years); or

---

33 I.R.C. § 367(a) (as amended in 1999). (If in connection with any exchange described in §§ 332, 351, §354, 356, or 361, a United States person transfers property to a foreign corporation, such foreign corporation shall not, for purposes of determining the extent to which gain shall be recognized on such transfer, be considered to be a corporation).

34 I.R.C. § 367(a)(3) (as amended in 1999).

35 Temp. Reg. § 1.367(a)-2T(b)(2) (1986).

36 According to I.R.C. § 367(d)(1) (as amended in 1999), these rules apply to intangibles within the meaning of I.R.C. § 936(h)(3)(B) (as amended in 1996), including (1) a patent, invention, formula, process, design, pattern, or know-how; (2) a copyright, literary, musical, or artistic composition; (3) a trademark, trade name, or brand name; (4) a franchise, license, or contract; (5) method, program, system, procedure, campaign, survey, study, forecast, estimate, customer list, or technical data; or (6) any similar item that has substantial value independent of the services of any individual.

37 *See* J. Kuntz & R. Peroni, U.S. International Taxation, vol. 1, ¶ A3.07[3] (Warren, Gorham & Lamont 1992).

2. In the case of a disposition of the property, reasonably reflect the amounts that would have been received at the time of disposition; and
3. That is commensurate with the income attributable to the intangible.[38]

This special rule does not apply to a transfer of foreign goodwill or going-concern value,[39] nor to a copyright, including a software copyright, transferred by

1. The creator of the copyright; or
2. A person whose basis in the copyright is determined by reference to the basis in the hands of the creator.[40]

The transferor is required to report these transfers as ordinary income.[41]

D. Form 8832—Check-the-Box Entity Classification

If the CFC rules cannot be avoided and a particular business venture does not meet an exception to the immediate taxation to the U.S. shareholders under subpart F, the U.S. shareholder or shareholders may avoid CFC status and the requirements to file a Form 5471. For a single-owner CFC in a country that is not on the "per se" list described in Treas. Reg. § 301.7701-2(b)(8) (as amended in 2007), the corporation can elect to be a "disregarded entity" for tax purposes. Generally, the "per se" list includes corporate statutes referred to as Sociedad Anonima. International Business Companies (IBCs) and foreign LLCs[42] will be classified for tax purposes as foreign corporations unless an election is made by filing Form 8832 to be treated as a disregarded entity or a foreign partnership.

A summary of the income, expenses, assets, and debts of the foreign entity is reported on a Form 8858 (see below). The net income of the entity would then be included in the Form 1120 of a domestic corporation that is the sole owner of the CFC or on the Form 1040 of an individual who is the sole owner of a CFC.

Although the Form 5471 is not required to be filed for a disregarded entity, it is not clear whether the Form 926 is required to be filed with respect to transfers to the disregarded foreign entity.

A Form 8832 can be filed by two or more owners electing to treat a foreign corporation or foreign LLC as a foreign partnership. A foreign partnership must file a Form 8865,

---

38 I.R.C. § 367(d) (as amended in 1999); Temp. Reg. § 1.367(d)-1T(a) (as amended in 1998).

39 Temp. Reg. § 1.367(d)-1T(b) (as amended in 1998).

40 Temp. Reg. §§ 1.367(d)-1T(b) (as amended in 1998), 1.367(a)-5T(b)(2) (1986). In addition, the rule does not apply to (1) a literary, musical, or artistic composition, a letter or memorandum, or similar property held by a taxpayer whose personal efforts created such property; (2) a letter, memorandum, or similar property held by a taxpayer for whom such property was prepared or produced; or (3) a taxpayer in whose hands the basis of such property is determined, for purposes of determining gain from a sale or exchange, in whole or in part by reference to the basis of such property in the hands of a taxpayer described in (1) or (2) above.

41 I.R.C. § 367(d)(2) (as amended in 1999).

42 Treas. Reg. § 301.7701-3(b)(2)(i) (as amended in 2006).

which in general is more complicated than a Form 5471. But, flow-through tax treatment and other tax disadvantages of the CFC may be avoided by a foreign partnership. An election to treat a foreign entity as a foreign partnership does not avoid the complications and cost of the Form 5471 for a foreign corporation with multiple owners, because the owners must file a Form 8865. But easy flow-through tax treatment applies, and some tax disadvantages of the CFC may be avoided by a foreign partnership.

Form 8858 requires identifying information for a single-member foreign disregarded entity, a summary of the income and deductions, a very brief balance sheet, a number of questions, and a brief summary of the earnings and profits of the foreign entity. The third page of the form is a matrix of transactions between the entity and various related parties, including the owners of the entity. This page substantially duplicates the information required by Form 926.

A penalty of $10,000 applies for a failure to file this form "within the time prescribed," which is the due date of the tax return of the owner(s) of the disregarded entity including any extensions of time to file.

E. Form 8865—Return of U.S. Persons with Respect to Certain Foreign Partnerships

Where there are multiple owners of a foreign partnership, certain U.S. owners of the entity must file a Form 8865. This form is a combination of the Form 1065 for domestic partnerships and the Form 5471 for CFCs. Because of the complexity of partnership tax law, the foreign partnership return is more complex than the foreign corporation return, but the instructions to the Form 8865 are just ten pages as compared to 15 pages for the foreign corporation return.

The filing requirements are somewhat similar to those for the U.S. owners of a CFC and also serve to identify which of the various schedules must be submitted by different types of filers.

A category 1 filer is a U.S. person who owns 50 percent or more of the partnership. Because of the rules for constructive ownership and attribution of ownership, there can be more than one 50 percent owner of a foreign partnership.

A category 2 filer is a U.S. person who owns a 10 percent or greater interest in the partnership. However, if the partnership had a category 1 filer, no other partner would be required to file as a category 2 filer.

A category 3 filer is a U.S. person who has contributed property to the partnership during the tax year and who owns a 10 percent or greater interest after making that contribution or whose contribution had a value (on the date of the transfer) in excess of $100,000.

A category 4 filer is a U.S. partner who had an acquisition, disposition, or change in his or her proportionate partnership interest during the tax year.

A schedule K-1 is required to be prepared for each U.S. partner to report the partner's share of the income, deductions, and credits of the partnership.

A Form 8865 must be filed with the income tax return of the U.S. partners who are required to file the form. In some cases, this could include all of the partners; in other cases, it might include only a 50 percent or greater partner.

A $10,000 penalty applies for a failure to file a timely return. A reduction in foreign tax credits will be imposed for an incomplete return filed on time.

F. Form 8833—Treaty-Based Return Position Disclosure

The provisions of a treaty usually override the provisions of the I.R.C. When a taxpayer relies on a provision of a treaty that is different from the position of the I.R.C., the position must be disclosed on Form 8833. However, Treas. Reg. § 301.6114-1(c) (as amended in 2006) provides a list of treaty-based return positions that do not require disclosure on Form 8833. This is a one-page form, but it may require extensive attachments.

G. Form 8883—Asset Allocation Statement

This two-page form is not unique to the area of international taxation. It is required where there is a purchase or sale of the assets of a business in which the purchase price must be allocated among the various assets.

H. Form 1120-F—Income Tax Return of a Foreign Corporation

This is the tax form that is filed by a foreign corporation with income from U.S.-sources. If the foreign corporation is engaged in a trade or business in the United States, it will not be subject to withholding on its U.S.-source income, but it will pay a corporate income tax on such income. If the foreign corporation is not engaged in a trade or business in the United States, then its U.S.-source income may be subject to withholding by the U.S. payor. In that case, the amounts withheld may be claimed as a credit on Form 1120-F.

The U.S.-source income of a CFC is not also subject to tax by U.S. shareholders as subpart F income. The U.S.-source income must be accounted for separately so that when it is distributed, it is treated in the same manner as distributions from a domestic corporation.

A penalty for a late-filed return is 5 percent for each month of the unpaid tax up to a maximum of 25 percent of the unpaid tax.

I. Miscellaneous Reporting Interests in Foreign Accounts

1. TD F 90-22.1—Report of Foreign Bank and Financial Accounts A TD F 90-22.1 is filed by a U.S. person who has a financial interest in, or signature authority or other authority over, any financial accounts, including bank, securities or other financial accounts, in a foreign country exceeding US$10,000 in the aggregate at any time during a calendar year.[43] A U.S. person means a citizen or resident of the United States,

43 Required by 31 U.S.C. § 5314 (1982).

a domestic partnership, a domestic corporation, or a domestic estate or trust.[44] A "financial account" generally includes any bank, securities, securities derivatives, or any financial instruments accounts. Such accounts generally also encompass any accounts in which the assets are held in a commingled fund, and the account owner holds an equity interest in the fund. The term also means any savings, demand, checking, deposit, time deposit, or any other account maintained with a financial institution or other person engaged in the business of a financial institution.[45] An account in a foreign country includes all geographical areas located outside the United States, Guam, Puerto Rico, and the Virgin Islands.[46] A "financial interest" includes a financial interest in a bank, securities, or other financial account in a foreign country and means an interest described in either of the following two paragraphs:

1. A U.S. person has a financial interest in each account for which such person is the owner of record or has legal title, whether the account is maintained for his or her own benefit or for the benefit of others, including non-U.S. persons. If an account is maintained in the name of two persons jointly, or if several persons each own a partial interest in an account, each of those U.S. persons has a financial interest in that account.
2. A U.S. person has a financial interest in each bank, securities, or other financial account in a foreign country for which the owner of record or holder of legal title is (a) a person acting as an agent, nominee, attorney, or in some other capacity on behalf of the U.S. person; (b) a corporation in which the U.S. person owns directly or indirectly more than 50 percent of the total value of shares of stock; (c) a partnership in which the U.S. person owns an interest in more than 50 percent of the profits (distributive share of income); or (d) a trust in which the U.S. person either has a present beneficial interest in more than 50 percent of the assets or from which such person receives more than 50 percent of the current income.[47]

Signature or other authority over an account means a person having signature authority over an account if such person can control the disposition of money or other property in it by delivery of a document containing his or her signature (or his or her signature and that of one or more other persons) to the bank or other person with whom the account is maintained. Other authority exists in a person who can exercise comparable power over an account by direct communication to the bank or other person with whom the account is maintained, either orally or by some other means.[48]

---

44 Instructions for TD F 90-22.1, General Definitions, 1. Exceptions to filing the TD F 90-22.1 include the following: (1) if the foreign bank account is in a U.S. military banking facility or a U.S. military finance facility operated by a U.S. institution designated by the U.S. government to serve U.S. government installations abroad; and (2) under certain circumstances, to employees of commercial banks and to employees and officers of large public domestic corporations, if the individual has no personal financial interest in the account.

45 Instructions for TD F 90-22.1, General Definitions, 1.

46 Instructions for TD F 90-22.1, General Definitions, 1.

47 Instructions for TD F 90-22.1, General Definitions, 1.

48 Instructions for TD F 90-22.1, General Definitions, 1.

The TD F 90-22.1 is filed on or before June 30 for the previous calendar year and is mailed to U.S. Department of the Treasury, P.O. Box 32621, Detroit, MI 48232-0621.

Form 1040, Schedule B, Part III, line 7a asks "did you have an interest in or a signature or other authority over a financial account in a foreign country, such as a bank account, securities account, or other financial account?" Line 7a of this schedule must be answered in the affirmative for a foreign grantor trust. Line 7b of this schedule then requires entering the name of the foreign country where the foreign account established by the trust is located. Line 8 of this schedule asks "did you receive a distribution from, or were you the grantor of, or transferor to, a foreign trust?" This also must be answered in the affirmative, since the person who establishes the trust is both a grantor and a transferor to the trust. Line 8 then states, with respect to an affirmative answer, that "you may have to file Form 3520." Answering lines 7 and 8 of this schedule in the affirmative clearly requires the filing of Form TD F 90-22.1. Answering line 8 in the affirmative also requires the filing of Form 3520.

2. FinCENT Form 104 FinCEN Form 104 is a currency transaction report that is filed for deposits, withdrawals, exchange of currencies or other payments or transfers of more than US$10,000 per year.

3. FinCENT Form 105 FinCEN Form 105 is a report that is filed for international transportation of currency or monetary instruments.

4. Withholding Forms New withholding Treas. Regs. went into effect January 1, 2001.[49] These Treas. Regs. permit foreign institutions to become qualified intermediaries (referred to as QIs).[50] The withholding Treas. Regs. apply to U.S.-source income of foreign persons and require U.S. persons who are treated or classified as owners for tax purposes or have beneficial interests in foreign trusts and entities to provide a Form W-9 to the withholding agent, generally the foreign bank or banks holding the assets.

For example, if a foreign trust has U.S.-source income, the settlor and any beneficiaries (who receive distributions) are required to file Form W-9 (Request for Taxpayer Identification Number and Certification) that is used to certify to certain payors that the individual, corporation, partnership, or trust has a U.S. taxpayer ID number. A Form W-9 is required for a trust that is treated as either a grantor trust or a U.S. trust for U.S. tax purposes. In addition, other forms may be due, such as Form W-8BEN (Certificate of Foreign Status of Beneficial Owner for United States Tax Withholding); W-8ECI (Certificate of Foreign Person's Claim for Exemption from Withholding on Income Effectively Connected with the Conduct of a Trade of Business in the United States); W-8EXP (Certificate of Foreign Government or Other Foreign Organization for United States Tax Withholding); or W-8IMY (Certificate of Foreign Intermediary, Foreign Partnership, or Certain U.S. Branches for United States Tax Withholding).

---

49 Treas. Reg. §§ 1.1441-1 (as amended in 2007) through 1.1441-9 (as amended in 2000).

50 Treas. Reg. § 1.1441-1(e)(5)(ii) (as amended in 2007).

Chapter 26

United States: The Allocation and Sourcing of Service Income in E-Commerce for State Income Tax Purposes

Stanley R. Kaminski
Duane Morris LLP

I. INTRODUCTION

Currently, there are 45 states (and the District of Columbia) in the United States that impose some form of corporate income tax,[1] as well as 4 states that impose a type of gross or adjusted gross revenue/receipts tax.[2] While many of these taxes are similar in kind, there are exclusions, terminology, interpretation, and application differences that impact how these taxes are imposed. As to the taxation of income from the sale of services, differences in the sourcing or allocation of such services also arise depending on the type of service being sold. Nevertheless, income from the sale of services is generally sourced or allocated based on either (1) the location at which the service is performed (commonly cost of performance is used for this analysis); or (2) the location of the benefit of the service to the customer (sometimes customer receipt or billing location is used for this purpose).

For e-commerce services that are supplied, received, or utilized through the Internet, the same general allocation and sourcing rules apply in most states. Yet, some

1 Alabama, Alaska, Arizona, Arkansas, Colorado, Connecticut, Delaware, Florida, Georgia, Hawaii, Idaho, Illinois, Indiana, Iowa, Kansas, Kentucky, Louisiana, Maine, Maryland, Massachusetts, Minnesota, Mississippi, Missouri, Montana, Nebraska, New Hampshire, New Jersey, New Mexico, New York, North Carolina, North Dakota, Ohio, Oklahoma, Oregon, Pennsylvania, Rhode Island, South Carolina, Tennessee, Utah, Vermont, Virginia, West Virginia, and Washington D.C.

2 As of 2008, the states of Ohio, Michigan, Texas, and Washington have imposed a business gross or adjusted gross revenue/receipts tax, and notably the states of Michigan and Ohio have both a corporate income and business adjusted gross receipts tax. Ohio is currently scheduled to phase out its corporate income tax at the end of 2009.

states have modified their allocation and sourcing rules to handle the unique nature of these Internet services. In doing so, a few states have issued special regulations or rules on how to source such service income for tax apportionment purposes. These special rules usually focus on the receipt, access location, or business\residence location of the customer.[3]

II. GENERAL BACKGROUND OF SERVICE INCOME ALLOCATION AND SOURCING

A. Sourcing of Service Income

In determining how to source income from services, whether in e-commerce or otherwise, one must first look at how a state classifies the service income for income tax purposes. Under the Uniform Division of Income for Tax Purposes Act (UDITPA), a general framework was set up over fifty years ago to provide some uniformity in the apportionment of income for tax purposes among the various states. Many states have adopted all or part of the UDITPA provisions. However, over the years a significant number of states have added or revised their sourcing formulas to differ with UDITPA.

The UDITPA classifies income into two general types: business income and nonbusiness income. For nonbusiness income, such income is "allocated" to a state usually based upon where the property generating the income is located or, for intangible property, generally the commercial domicile of the seller/taxpayer.[4] On the other hand, UDITPA "apportions" business income among the various states using a formula made up of three different factors: the sales factor, the property factor, and the payroll factor.[5] For purposes of determining whether the income falls within the numerator of the sales factor, the income is then "sourced" to a specific state. (Notably, an increasing percentage of states weigh these three apportionment factors differently, and some only use a single sales factor.)

"Services" are included under the general category of sales of intangibles for UDITPA purposes. Therefore, services are usually lumped together as the sale of any other intangible. UDITPA does exclude from this general "intangible" category services provided by financial institutions, public utilities, and certain purely personal services by an individual.[6] Nevertheless, when it comes to the vast majority of services, they are treated as intangibles to be allocated or sourced to a state under the sales factor using the "income-producing activity" test. In those states that do not follow UDITPA for service income sourcing, the customer's access or benefit location is normally used in determining the sourcing of such services.

---

3 *See e.g.* New York Department of Taxation and Finance, TSB-A-99(16)C (Subscription fees to receive market data).

4 UDITPA § 6.

5 *See* UDITPA § 9.

6 *See* UDITPA § 2.

While most states start with the UDITPA classification of services as intangibles and allocate or source such services income based upon the sourcing of other intangibles, a growing number of states have separated out various types of services from the general intangibles allocation formula, and a minority of states have even broken out all services from the intangible classification to source them as a separate criteria altogether. Because of this, the first step in determining where a service will be sourced (whether purchased in e-commerce or otherwise) for a particular state, one must first determine whether that state (1) treats such service as the sale of intangibles; (2) treats such service as a separate service classification different from intangibles; or (3) separates out such service as a separate industry category altogether to be sourced differently from other types of services and intangibles.

It should be noted that the Multistate Tax Commission (MTC) has also set forth detailed allocation and apportionment regulations on how various services and service industries should have their income apportioned or sourced for state income tax purposes.[7] Following UDITPA, these regulations also classify income as either business or nonbusiness income. Moreover, like UDITPA, services are treated as a type of intangible and are allocated based upon where the income-producing activity occurred as determined by the location where the "cost of performance" takes place. Unlike UDITPA, however, special rules have been developed for airlines, construction contractors, financial institutions, railroads, trucking companies, television and radio broadcasting, and publishing.

Once it is determined how a state classifies a service for purposes of allocation and sourcing of its income or even gross receipts tax, this will then indicate the criteria the state will use in allocating or sourcing that service income to the state. As mentioned before, this generally means for most services that the income will be sourced either depending upon where the services were performed or where the benefit of the services is received, except for those special industry services that have their own unique sourcing rules, such as the telecommunications industry or the transportation industry that may allocate that service income by possibly origination or delivery locations, miles traveled through the state, relay points, or other criteria.

For e-commerce-acquired services that are supplied, received, or utilized either fully or partially through the Internet itself, the allocation or sourcing of these services becomes even more difficult. While some states will still treat these services like normal services under their general apportionment and sourcing rules, other states have developed, either by rule or regulation, a unique allocation or sourcing rule for such services. An example is New York's corporation franchise (income) tax, which generally sources most services to where the income-producing activity of the service takes place, that is, the place the service is performed.[8] For certain Internet-provided services, however, the location where the customer accessed the service has been held to be sourcing location by the New York Department of Taxation and Finance.[9]

---

7 MTC Allocation and Apportionment Regulations, adopted February 21, 1973, revised August 2, 2007 (MTC Regs.).

8 N.Y. Tax Law §§ 210(3)(a)(2)(B) and (6); N.Y. Reg. 4-4.3.

9 TSB-A-00(15)C (Internet access to databases).

B. Allocation of Service Income

While allocation in the normal income tax context refers to "nonbusiness" income assigned to a state for direct taxation purposes,[10] it sometimes refers to that state to which the income is being sourced for sales-factor apportionment purposes. In such cases, the income is not being totally allocated to and taxed instate, but is merely part of the sales factor that determines that portion of the pool of income (including the service income) that will be apportioned and taxed by the state. For example, when service income is considered business income under an income-based tax, its allocation to a state refers to the location where the income is being sourced for sales-factor purposes. As such, it is merely another term for "sourced." Service income also may be referred to as being "allocated" depending on the nature of the tax at issue. Thus, when service income is viewed in relation to some gross receipts/revenue taxes, allocation refers to the state to which the service income should be assigned for direct taxation purposes. In such instances, it is not being simply used in a sales formula to determine the percentage of all income to be taxed, but rather the entirety of the service income is subject to tax in the state to which it is allocated.

III. TYPES OF SERVICES ACQUIRED IN E-COMMERCE

Services purchased in e-commerce are much more than just the purchase of Internet access services or Internet gaming services, but can involve (1) services performed by the seller or its designee at the location of the buyer (e.g., warranty service purchased online for in-home repair); (2) services performed at the seller's location and delivered to the buyer's location (e.g., accounting service where raw data is sent over the Internet and where completed work is sent back to buyer either in the mail or back through the Internet); (3) services performed at multiple locations and benefit the buyer at multiple locations (e.g., Internet advertising service or a computer data storage service in which service is performed at one or more locations); or (4) services utilized by buyer through the Internet (e.g., computer time-sharing services, Internet telephone service). This fourth category is a growing area, and in many instances it is difficult to source or even determine where the actual service is performed. Moreover, the benefit locations of the services to the buyer can be numerous. This has resulted in some states developing special rules for services supplied or utilized solely through e-commerce.

A. Services Performed at Buyer's Location

A number of services sold or acquired through e-commerce may be performed at the location of the buyer. This includes, but is not limited to, in-home computer warranty services, equipment repair services, consulting services, computer maintenance services, training services, auditing services, management services, administrative services, and security services. The seller may even partially utilize the Internet in performing the

---

10 *See* MTC Regs. § IV.2(a), Definitions.

service (e.g., computer maintenance services). These types of services are generally sourced using the normal sourcing rules for sales of services or intangibles.

B. Services Performed at Seller's Location and Delivered to Buyer's Location

Services acquired through e-commerce can include services performed at a seller location but then delivered to the buyer either through the Internet or by other means. These types of services may include transportation services, data-processing services, accounting services, various professional services, credit search services, certain transportation services, certain brokerage services, certain financial services, design services, certain management or administrative services, certain insurance-related services, certain investment services, certain computer software services, and other services. Generally, these services will be sourced to the various states under the usual sourcing rules for sales of services or sales of intangibles. Yet, some of these services may be sourced under special provisions, such as transportation services, financial services, and insurance services. Likewise, to the extent a service is almost totally supplied and utilized through the Internet (*see* section III.D, below), a state may have made a special sourcing rule for that service.

C. Services Performed at Multiple Locations and That Benefit the Buyer at Multiple Locations

Another type of service that can be purchased in e-commerce may have multiple performance locations or multiple-benefit locations. These types of services include certain transportation services, financial services, advertising services, administrative services, computer and professional services, among many others. The same source rules that apply to the sourcing of other services (or intangibles) generally will apply here. As a result, the state where the service is predominantly performed will generally be considered the state in which the service will be sourced.[11] However, some states source certain categories of services under special rules, such as transportation, financial, brokerage, and advertising services. Moreover, in the states that source sales of intangibles or services using the benefit location of the buyer, sourcing becomes even harder when more than one benefit location is involved (e.g., advertising service performed in state A for advertising in states B, C, and D).

D. Services Utilized by Buyer through the Internet

Common services acquired and utilized over the Internet include Internet access, time-sharing services, VoIP (voice over-the-Internet protocol) phone services, online data-processing services, electronic information services, Internet daily credit update

11 *See* UDITPA § 17; MTC Regs. § IV.17.4(A).

services, automatic online storage and retrieval data services, various Internet membership services, Internet marketing services, online bill-processing services, Web design services, and research services, among others. Like most services, income from these services are either sourced or allocated using the same general sourcing rules that apply to other services, or sometimes by special rules designed for that specific service.

IV. DIFFERENCES BETWEEN THE SOURCING OR ALLOCATION OF SERVICE INCOME AND TAX "NEXUS"

The sourcing or allocation of service income concerns how a state will tax such income under its state income tax (or gross receipts tax) laws. "Nexus," on the other hand, is a jurisdictional principle that refers to whether the state has the jurisdiction to tax the person, property, or transaction it is targeting.[12] Hence, even though income from a service may be sourced to a state under its tax law, if the person it seeks to tax does not have nexus with the state, such sourcing becomes irrelevant. For example, assume a Web provider of Internet advertising has customers in state B but has all of its presence, such as its place of business, employees, agents, property, and services in state A, and has no presence in state B. Even if state B sourced such advertising income to state B, it would be meaningless since state B would not have tax "nexus" with the Web providers to allow it to tax the Web provider. (Note: Some states could try to assert economic nexus over the Web provider if the Web provider actively markets in their state or has intangible property in their state.)

With respect to tax nexus, states are always pulling at its limits. A service provider must therefore be aware of its protections under the United States Constitution Commerce and/or Due Process Clauses. As to the Due Process Clause, it requires "some minimum contacts" between the state and the service provider before nexus is established.[13] Nevertheless, marketing to customers of a state is generally sufficient to satisfy that test.[14] The Commerce Clause requires "substantial nexus" between the state and the service provider, but the term is undefined.[15] As a result, many states are expanding their reach and asserting that purely economic nexus is sufficient (i.e., the presence of customers usually accompanied with advertising, marketing, or intangibles in the state) to satisfy these tests.[16] In this regard, the Michigan Department of Treasury has taken an ultra-aggressive position for its new Michigan business tax, which asserts that the ability of a Michigan resident to purchase an item on an out-of-state Web site of a seller is sufficient in itself to create nexus for that out-of-state seller.[17]

---

12 Allied-Signal, Inc. v. Director, Division of Taxation, 504 U.S. 768 (1992).

13 National Bellas Hess, Inc. v. Dept. of Revenue of Illinois, 386 U.S. 753 (1967).

14 Quill Corp. v. North Dakota, 504 U.S. 298 (1992).

15 Complete Auto Transit, Inc. v. Brody, 430 U.S. 274 (1977).

16 Geoffrey, Inc. v. S.C. Tax Commission, 437 S.E.2d 13 (S.C. 1993); Lanco, Inc. v. Dir. Div. of Tax'n, 879 A. 2d 1234 (N.J. Super. Ct. App. Div. 2005), *affirmed*; A&F Trademark, Inc. v. Folson, 605 S.E.2d 187 (N.C. Ct. App. 2004); Tax Comm'r of the State of W. Va. v. MBNA, 640 S.E.2d 226 (W. Va. 2006).

17 Michigan Revenue Administrative Bulletin 2007-6 (Dec. 27, 2007).

Notably, unlike many sellers of tangible personal property (i.e., goods), services businesses in e-commerce or otherwise do *not* have the protection of Public Law 86-272, a federal law that requires more substantial presence before a state can impose an income tax on a person.[18] Under Public Law 86-272, solicitation or the presence of salesmen in a state who only solicit business will *not* create nexus.

On the flip side, just because tax "nexus" is present, that does not mean that the service income will be sourced to a particular state. Using the previous example, if a Web provider of advertising service did have nexus with state B, but performs all of its services in state A, no portion of such services will be sourced to state B if state B uses the performance location as its sourcing test. Therefore, even though nexus is present, there may be no income taxable in state B.

V. SOURCING OR ALLOCATION OF SERVICES INCOME FOR STATE INCOME TAX PURPOSES

As previously mentioned in this chapter, sourcing or allocation of income from the sale of services for state income tax purposes usually centers on either the performance location of the service or the benefit location to the buyer. This section will concentrate on how such service income is sourced by the various states under the various methods used by such states. Because nonbusiness service income is very uncommon, the allocation of nonbusiness service income, which is generally allocated to the state of commercial domicile of the seller, will not be discussed.[19] In this regard, most states still follow with UDITPA formula for the sourcing of services (i.e., the sale of intangibles) when it comes to state income taxes. However, to provide a better understanding of how the services purchased in e-commerce may be sourced in the various states, some general differences between the states will be pointed out.

A. Performance Location Rule

In determining where the income from the purchase of a service should be sourced, the most prevalent rule used is the performance location rule.[20] Under this rule, the "income-producing activity" is looked at to determine where the service is performed and thus sourced for income tax purposes. Generally, when the income-producing activity is performed within a number of states, but the greater proportion is performed in one particular state, that state will be considered the location in which the income should be sourced. In implementing this rule, most states have also adopted the "cost of performance" test in determining where the income-producing activity takes place. This test becomes more difficult to apply where (1) there are multiple performance locations, (2) the services are bifurcatable between states; or (3) independent

18 15 U.S. Code (U.S.C.) § 381.

19 *See* UDITPA § 6(c).

20 *See* UDITPA § 17; MTC Regs. IV.17.

contractors or agents perform part of the service. In such cases, states differ on how to treat these variables in sourcing the service income. For example, the MTC Regulations now include as part of cost of performance those payments to agents or independent contractors in performing personal services that gave rise to the production of income.[21] However, other states have held that third-party contractors or agents cannot be included in the cost-of-performance calculation.[22]

1. Cost-of-Performance Test The cost-of-performance test is a test normally used by most states in determining where the income-producing activity of a service is located. This test is necessary in these states to determine where the income-producing activity principally takes place, and therefore where to source the income from such services. As explained in the MTC Regulations, the term "cost of performance" means "direct cost determined in a manner consistent with generally accepted accounting principles and in accordance with accepted conditions or practices in the trade or business of the taxpayer to perform the income-producing activity which gives rise to the particular item of income."[23]

In applying the cost-of-performance rules, direct costs, such as compensation paid to employees, property costs, travel costs, and other direct costs, should be included to determine in which state the predominance of these costs were incurred. As noted above, there is a debate among a number of states as to whether costs paid to third parties or agents who performed parts of the services should also be included in the factor. Recently, in the case of *General Motors Corp. v. Commonwealth of Virginia*, 602 S.E.2d 123 (Va. 2004), the Virginia Supreme Court disagreed with the Virginia Department of Revenue, which tried to exclude payments by GMAC (the financial-services subsidiary of the General Motors Corp) to third parties from the cost-of-performance ratio. The court held that under Virginia statutes, direct cost should not be limited by only direct costs incurred by GMAC, but would include any costs paid by GMAC to third parties to perform services on its behalf. Applying the above rules to purchases in e-commerce, it becomes imperative to evaluate where the services that are purchased are actually being performed. Understanding whether the state includes third-party services in the cost of performance is also essential depending upon the service involved. For example, if an accounting service is being purchased, and that service is being performed in state A for a customer in state B, none of the service income will be sourced to state B if state B follows the cost-of-performance rule. However, if the accounting service is performed primarily by the accounting service's agent in state B, then an issue arises as to whether state B includes such agent's costs in the cost-of-performance rule.

Another example is the state of Texas, which does not actually follow the cost-of-performance rule, but does look at the performance location of the service in determining where to source the service income. In that regard, the Texas Comptroller's

---

21 MTC Regs. IV.17(3); *e.g.*, Virginia Code § 58.1-418.

22 *See*, e.g., Arizona Department of Revenue Reg. § 15-2D-806 and California Board of Equalization Reg. 18 CCR § 25136.

23 MTC Regs. § IV.17(3).

Tax Policy News, Vol. XIII, Issue 8 of August 2003, explained how the gross receipts on various Internet service activities should be sourced under the Texas franchise tax. One of the examples it gives is a taxpayer earning revenue for providing advertising links to customers to purchase items. The Texas Comptroller held that the gross receipts from these transactions are the performance of a service and are "apportioned to the location where the taxpayer maintains the server that provides the link to the customer." The server location was, therefore, the location of the performance of the service. Likewise, the Texas Comptroller held that for a Web site development service, this service was performed "where the employee creates the website." As one can see, under the performance-location rule (whether cost-of-performance or another test is used), where the service activity itself is taking place is the overriding criteria, rather than the benefit or receipt of the service by the customer.

2. Multiple Performance Locations In many instances, services are performed in multiple locations for a buyer. This can occur with respect to Internet advertising, telecommunication services, as well as a number of other services. The sourcing of these services again depends upon the sourcing test used by the state. Under the traditional income-producing activity (or cost-of-performance) test used by most states, the income from the service is sourced to *that* state where a "greater proportion of the income-producing activity is performed."[24] Nevertheless, not all states follow this rule. Texas Comptroller Regulation 3.557(e)(33) specifically provides that when "service are performed both inside and outside of Texas, then such receipts are Texas receipts on the basis of fair value of the services that are rendered in Texas." Therefore, in Texas, part of the receipts would always have to be sourced to Texas for Texas tax purposes. For example, if a taxpayer providing banner advertising does so through servers located in a number of states, including Texas, or has employees in Texas in developing the banner advertising, a portion of the service income may be allocated to Texas for Texas franchise tax purposes.

In addition, if the service is logically broken down into multiple components, such as an hourly charge for computer maintenance or security services, a state can take the position that these separate hourly amounts should be specifically allocated to the state in which the service for that hour occurs. Moreover, the MTC Regulations state that when the services performed in each state "constitute a separate income-producing activity," then even though one price is paid for the service, "the performance of service attributable to this state shall be measured by the ratio which the time spent in performing the services in the state bears to the total time spent in performing the services elsewhere."[25] Under this regulation, an example is provided that instructs that if a public opinion survey is provided and 600 hours are spent in total, and 200 hours of those are expended in state A, then one-third of the income of the service would be sourced to state A.

---

24 UDITPA, § 17(b).

25 MTC Regs. IV.17(4)(B)(c).

B. Benefit-of-Service Rule

A number of states have adopted a benefit rule in determining how to source income from the sale of services. This rule is prevalent in Georgia, Iowa, Illinois, Maryland, Minnesota, Wisconsin, and Maine. A couple of other states have applied conflicting rules as to whether benefit or cost of performance is the appropriate test for certain services. In the benefit states, services are sourced to those locations where the customer either benefits from the service or, termed another way, received the service. An example of this is in the new statute passed by the state of Illinois. For years ending on or after December 31, 2008, Illinois switched from a cost-of-performance state to a receipt state with respect to the sourcing of service income.[26] Under this Illinois provision, sale of services are sourced to a state if "the services are received in the state." Interestingly, and like other states that have applied the receipt rule, this sourcing of income is also limited to only those states where the corporation, partnership, or trust receiving the service has a fixed location. Similarly, Georgia provides that gross receipts from the sale of intangibles are sourced to Georgia when "the receipts are derived from customers within the state."[27] Likewise, Minnesota provides that "receipts from the performance of services must be attributable to the state where the services are received."[28] Notably, the new Illinois sourcing of services provision is virtually identical to the Minnesota sourcing statute.

1. Benefit of Customer As you can see, under the benefit or receipt rule of sourcing service income, where the service is performed or the costs incurred is meaningless. The customer's location is all that matters. Applying this rule to a purchase of a service in e-commerce would demonstrate that if a service is performed in state A and transmitted to the purchaser in state B, the fact that the purchaser received the service in state B would be all that would be necessary to make such service source to state B for tax purposes. This assumes, of course, that state B adopts the benefit or receipt rule for the sourcing of services.

2. Multiple Benefit Locations In those states that have adopted the benefit or received rule of sourcing services, it becomes more difficult to determine where the source of service is when such service may be received or the benefit obtained in more than one state. Minnesota and Illinois attempt to eliminate this problem by both stating in their laws that if the state where the services are received is not readily determinable, then the services are sourced at the location of the office of the customer from which the services were ordered. Presumably, this was an attempt to solve the issue of whether the receipt could be at multiple locations, thus eliminating the question of sourcing such service income to more than one state. However, this does not mean that certain service income cannot be sourced proportionally in some instances, such as when the service is bifurcatable among states or where special sourcing rules are used.

---

26 Illinois Public Act 95-0707 (amended 35 ILCS 5/304(a)).

27 Code of Georgia, Title 48, art. 2, § 48-7-31.

28 Minnesota Statutes, ch. 290, § 290.191.

One the other hand, Iowa specifically provides by rule that the service income shall be sourced to Iowa "if the recipient of the services receives all of the benefit of the service in Iowa."[29] And, if the recipient of the service has received "some of the benefit of the service in Iowa," then the income from such service shall be sourced to Iowa based on the proportion of the service the recipient receives the benefit of in Iowa. As you can see, this Iowa rule specifically proportions the sourcing of the service income depending upon where the benefit is received. An example of the application of this proportional sourcing requirement can be found in the same rule. This example provides

> A corporation located in State A performs direct mail activities for a customer located in State X. The corporation has nexus with Iowa due to other activities of the unitary business. The direct mail activities include the preparation and mailing of materials to households throughout the United States. The corporation, located in State A, printed and mails direct mail materials to households on a mailing list prepared by the direct mailing company in State A. Five percent of the direct mailing went to addresses within Iowa. Five percent of the gross receipts related to the direct mail contracts are attributable to Iowa and included in the numerator of the apportionment factor.

The sourcing of service income in states that apply the benefit rule can therefore be quite tricky when multiple benefit or receipt locations are involved. The sale of Internet advertising or other Internet services can thus be difficult to source depending upon the wording of the state law and how the state's department of revenue or taxation applies its sourcing rules.

C. Special Sourcing Rules, Including E-Commerce Service Rules

As previously mentioned, a number of states provide special rules for various industries and services apart from the normal sourcing rules applied for services generally. Transportation companies, financial companies, brokerage businesses, insurance companies, telecommunications companies, advertising agencies, and cable companies are among a growing list where special apportionment is become more common. For example, states like Connecticut require brokerage services to source their commissions and profits based upon where their customers are domiciled.[30] Likewise, in Illinois, telecommunications services are sourced to Illinois in most instances if the customer's service address is in the state.[31] Another example is New York, where receipts from radio and television programming are allocated based upon the number of listeners or viewers in each state.[32] In a ruling by the New York Commission of Taxation and Finance, it was also held that video-on-demand services should be allocated based upon the location of subscribers.[33]

29 Iowa Department of Revenue Reg. 701-54.6.

30 *See Conn. Gen. Stat.* § 12-218(g).

31 35 ILCS 5/304(a).

32 New York Dept. of Taxation and Finance Reg. 4-4.3.

33 New York Commissioner of Taxation and Finance, NYT-G-07(1)C (Jan. 17, 2007).

Similarly, in a New York advisory opinion, the New York Department of Taxation and Finance held that a company that provided marketing data services to its subscribers through electronic transmissions was required to source its income from such activity based on the subscriber's location. Significantly, the New York Department of Taxation and Finance appeared to classify the service as something different than an actual service, but rather, termed its receipts as "other business receipts."[34]

Like New York, the Texas Comptroller has also classified the purchase of membership rights to services as being the sale of an intangible and not the sale of a service for Texas sourcing purposes. Sales of intangibles are sourced based upon the location of the customer, while the sale of a service is sourced based upon where the service is performed under Texas law.[35]

In evaluating any sourcing issue for a service purchased in e-commerce, any special sourcing rules should always be reviewed in the state at issue to determine whether they are applicable to the service that is being acquired.

D. Throwback, Double-Throwback, and Throwout Rules

In developing their sourcing rules, many states have created special sourcing methods for certain types of sales or for those situations in which the seller has no tax nexus in the state the income would be sourced under the normal sourcing rules. Under these special rules, the income may either be re-sourced or allocated to a different state or excluded from the sales factor altogether in certain situations. These special re-sourcing rules are usually classified as throwback or throwout rules.

While throwback and double-throwback rules are much more common for sourcing sale of tangible personal property, it is possible that some states may try to apply them when sales of services are involved. Similarly, throwout rules may also be applied by a state when sourcing services income. Currently most states do not apply these rules to sales of intangibles or services, but that practice could change in the future.

1. What Is Throwback or Double Throwback? Throwback is a rule that was developed decades ago to address the situation where sales of tangible personal property are made for delivery to a customer of another state, and the state of sale has determined that the basic sourcing rules should not apply. This normally occurs when sales are made to the federal government or are being shipped to a state where the seller is not subject to that state's income tax. Throwback generally refers to the act of throwing back or re-sourcing the sale back to the state where the office, store, or warehouse, or other place of business from which the property was shipped.[36] Generally, throwback does not apply to the sale of services, since it is a concept used in the sale of tangible personal property. Moreover, except in a few states, sales of services are normally sourced based upon the performance location and not receipt location of the service.

---

34 *New York American Title Exchange*, TSB-A-99(16)C (Apr. 7, 1999).

35 Texas Comptroller Reg. 3.557.

36 *See* UDITPA § 16.

Therefore, throwback has little application when the sale of services is involved, but as the benefit or receipt location becomes more prevalent among the states, such a throwback rule may be developed or applied by the state.

In the same regard, double throwback is concept used when the normal throwback rule does not result in the sourcing of the sale to a state in which the seller is subject to taxation. In the case of *GTE Automatic Electric, Inc. v. Allphin*, 369 N.E.2d 841 (Ill. 1977), the Illinois Supreme Court applied a type of double-throwback rule when GTE was taxable on its sales neither in the state the product was delivered to, nor in the state from which the product was shipped. GTE was a Delaware corporation with its commercial domicile in Illinois. The court concluded that Illinois could source the sale to Illinois "to effectuate the legislative intent of avoiding either an overlap or gap in allocating and apportioning all of the business income of plaintiff's multistate operations." No doubt, if applied to a service transaction where the service is performed in a state that has a receipt test and received in a state that has a performance test, a question arises whether a third state can claim the sourcing of such service for taxation purposes.

2. What Is Throwout? Similar to the throwback and double-throwback rules that are commonly applied in sales of tangible personal property, a throwout rule has been developed by some states to throw out of the sales factor altogether those sales to customers in states to which the seller is not subject to taxation. An example of this rule can be found in Illinois, which throws out of the sales factor receipts from services where the seller is not taxable in the state the service in received.[37]

As a side note, in Maine (which uses the receipt rule), rather than throwing out the sales from services from the sales factor, if the purchaser receives the service in a state the seller is not taxable, then Maine law switches from a receipt state to an income-producing activity (performance of a service) state for purposes of sourcing the service.

E. Alternative Apportionment Rules

Virtually every state has an alternate apportionment rule for the sourcing of sales, including sales of services when the taxpayer claims that the state's apportionment rules do not fairly reflect the income apportioned within the state. States are generally very stingy at applying these rules in favor of taxpayers. Nevertheless, if under the normal sourcing rules there is a substantial distortion of the amount of income that should be sourced to a state, the alternative sourcing rules of the state should be reviewed to see if a modification could be achieved. Generally, this requires filing a petition with the state's taxing authority requesting alternative apportionment. A proposal of what alternative apportionment is desired and the reasons therefore should be explained in detail.

---

37 35 ILCS 5/304(a).

VI. SOURCING OR ALLOCATION OF SERVICES FOR GROSS OR ADJUSTED GROSS REVENUE/RECEIPTS TAXES

The states of Ohio, Texas, Michigan,[38] and Washington impose gross or adjusted gross receipts/revenue taxes. The Washington State tax, which is called the business and occupation tax, has been around for decades. The Ohio, Texas, and Michigan taxes are fairly new, with the Ohio tax being the oldest, coming to existence in 2005. These taxes source service income for purposes of direct taxation by the state. Significantly, Washington's business and occupation tax and the Texas franchise (margin) tax are worded so that service income is only sourced to the state if the service is performed in the state. However, the Washington Department of Revenue has an odd way of defining where a service is performed and has been in a great deal of litigation over that issue. The Texas franchise tax has been around for a long time, even though it has now been revamped from a capital and income-based tax to an adjustable gross receipts tax. It sources service income based upon where the service is performed; however, if the service is performed in multiple states, it apportions that service income among those various states.[39]

The Michigan business tax and the Ohio commercial activity tax also sourced service income, but they do so based upon the benefit or receipt rule. Therefore, the customer location is looked at to determine whether the service income should be sourced to these states for taxation.

VII. CONCLUSION

In determining how income from the sale of services should be allocated or sourced in e-commerce, it must be understood that such sourcing or allocation is not consistent among the states. There are multiple ways that states use to source or allocate service income. While the service-performance location is still used in most states to source service income, the benefit or receipt rule is becoming more popular among the states. Significantly, a state's taxing department may even interpret its state's sourcing rules to re-source the service income in a manner that may not be clearly statutorily authorized. What should be remembered is that sourcing is becoming an evolving rule that will likely change in the future. Therefore, it is important to perform a thorough analysis of the sourcing rules of the states the service is both performed and received to fully understand how such service income will be sourced or allocated for state income tax purposes.

---

38 Note: Michigan also imposes an income tax.

39 Texas Tax Code § 171.103(a)(2).

Chapter 27

United States: Tax Effects of Internet Telecommunications Services

*Warren G. Lavey**
Skadden, Arps, Slate, Meagher & Flom LLP

I. INTRODUCTION

It is popular to say both that "the Internet changes everything" and that "death and taxes are inevitable." According to this framework, it may be tempting to think about the issue of taxes on Internet telecommunications services as a new, unstoppable force (the Internet) meeting an immovable object (taxes). However, this framework is flawed in that both telecommunications services and taxes applicable to telecommunications services have been changing for at least a century, long before the advent of the Internet.

Government authorities have proven quite adept at adopting legislation and revising regulations to make new telecommunications offerings and providers subject to high, industry-specific taxes. Since the spread of Internet telecommunications services, there have been changes in some of the taxes applicable to these and other telecommunications services. Yet, the processes of adapting taxes to new telecommunications technologies, offerings, and market structures have shown their resiliency with regard to the growing revenues of Internet telecommunications services and the growing demands for tax collections.

In the United States, federal, state, county, and municipal governments have found political support for differential taxing of telecommunications services and providers. Landline voice telephone services, their successors (including mobile services and data services), and diverse telecommunications services providers continue to be targeted

---

* Partner, Skadden, Arps, Slate, Meagher & Flom LLP, Former Assistant to the Chief, Common Carrier Bureau, Federal Communications Commission. B.A. and M.S., Harvard University; Diploma in economics, Cambridge University; J.D., Harvard Law School. I am grateful for the assistance of Anthony Oettinger, Ted Carlson, Cary Pugh, Toshihiro Kuwahara, and Oren Sachar. Errors are mine alone.

for a wide variety of industry-specific and service-specific taxes, not just general sales, income, and property taxes. Some of the political support for this is based on viewing telecommunications services as luxury items—such as the federal communications excise tax that was first adopted in 1898 and, with various revisions in legislation and regulations, survives today, as well as the high state and local taxes on mobile services. Other political support has been based on viewing telecommunications providers as public utilities; some industry-specific taxes were initially adopted in the era of regulated telephone monopolies, and, after some expansions and modifications, the taxes survive with political claims that these services still face little loss of demand as tax burdens increase.

Telecommunications services have for several decades been converging with products and services from the information content, computer services, consumer electronics, and other industries. These other industries, products, and services have a different heritage of competitive, unregulated markets as well as lower taxes. There continues to be political support for lighter taxes on these industries. With the ongoing political support for heavier taxes on telecommunications services, the tasks of line drawing for taxes by service and provider are difficult and face new challenges as technologies, offerings, and markets change.

By the time that Internet telecommunications services emerged, U.S. governmental entities had adopted a variety of taxes giving them a huge stake in how these services were characterized. According to a study sponsored by the telecommunications industry, in 2004 the average effective rate of federal, state, and local transaction taxes for telecommunications services was 18.17 percent, compared to 6.12 percent for general businesses nationwide.[1] A study by Ernst & Young "found that of the $18.1 billion in state and local taxes paid by telecommunications companies in 1999 (accounting for 9.1 percent of total telecom revenue), 39 percent—or $7 billion—constituted 'excess taxes' (taxes in excess of those generally imposed on other industries)."[2] The federal communications excise tax alone raised about US$5.8 billion in 2003.[3]

---

1 Testimony of Steven P.B. Kranz before the House Committee on Judiciary, Subcommittee on Commercial and Administrative Law, Hearing on State and Local Telecommunications Taxation, *Framing the Debate Over the Need for Federal Legislation: Addressing State and Local Taxation of Telecommunications Services* at 3 (June 13, 2006). For a contrasting analysis, *see* National Association of Counties, et al., *Local Government Perspective on Telecommunications Taxes: A Response to Industry's* 2004 COST Study (Summer 2006). Another study in 2004 concluded that the weighted average of all taxes on wireless customers was 16.2% as compared to 6.93% for other goods and services. S. Mackey, *The Excessive State and Local Tax Burden on Wireless Telecommunications Service*, State Tax Notes 181, 184 (July 19, 2004).

2 M. Sullivan, *Will VOIP Telephone Services be Subject to Telephone Taxes?*, Tax Notes 458, at 466 (Jan. 26, 2004) (Sullivan) (citing study by R. Cline of Ernst & Young, *Telecommunications Taxes*: 50-State *Estimates of Excess State and Local Tax Burden*, State Tax Notes 930 (June 3, 2002)).

3 Internal Revenue Service, 24(3) Statistics of Income Bulletin, Table 21 at 345 (Fall 2004) (figure is before the refunds pursuant to Internal Notice 2006-50, 2006-25 I.R.B. 1141 (June 19, 2006) (*IRS Notice*)).

As revenues from telecommunications services grew (to about US$332 billion in the U.S. in 2006)[4], these activities continued to be a politically attractive source of funding for governments through higher, industry-specific, and service-specific taxes. While changes in technologies, service offerings, and providers required governments to revisit these taxes at various times, the political consensus for differential taxing of telecommunications services generally remained.

The legal and political focus on the scope, burdens, and effects of a tax rises with the occurrence of problems in applying statutory or agency definitions of what constitutes the taxable services and providers. Some technology changes that had important consequences for telecommunications offerings—such as replacing rotary, analog dialing with push-button, digital handsets; adding facsimile capabilities to local and long-distance transmission services; or implementing packet-switched data services—had little impact on the imposition of most telecommunications taxes. On the other hand, some other technology changes—such as mobile wireless services and Internet-based voice and data services—disrupted the definitions used in many telecommunications taxes, leading to court cases, legislation, and new regulations.[5] Even with the swirl of Internet-driven changes to economic and social activities, including in the structure, technologies, and offerings of the telecommunications industry, the differential approach to taxing telecommunications services continues to thrive in many forms.

The Internet led to rapid changes in the technologies used to provide telecommunications services, the suppliers of telecommunications services, and how these services were priced. Two Internet services gained prominence with regard to taxes. One service, broadband or high-speed Internet access, is a line connecting a home or business to the Internet above some threshold transmission speed, including cable modem service offered by cable operators and digital subscriber lines (DSL) offered by telephone local-exchange carriers. The Federal Communications Commission (FCC) reported that the number of high-speed Internet access lines increased from 4.1 million in 2000, to 15.7 million in 2002, to 31.9 million and 2004, and to 64.6 million in 2006.[6] Another service, voice over Internet protocol (VoIP), has various forms and definitions, including generally "an internet application utilizing 'packet-switching' to transmit a voice communication over a broadband internet connection."[7] VoIP services in the United States,

---

4 Citigroup Analyst Report, *Telecommunications Services: EMT Conference and 4Q Preview—Signals for a Telecom Renaissance*? 1 (Jan. 4, 2007).

5 *See generally* W. Lavey, *Pitfalls in Taxing Telecommunications Services and Equipment*, 3 Telematics 3 (Jan. 1986) (*Pitfalls*).

6 Federal Communications Commission, *High-Speed Services for Internet Access: Status as of June 30, 2006*, Table 1 and note 1 (Jan. 2007) (*FCC Internet Access Report*) (data for June of each year; "high-speed lines are connections to end-user locations that deliver services at speeds exceeding 200 kbps in at least one direction").

7 Minnesota Public Utilities Commission v. Federal Communications Commission, 483 F.3d 570 (8th Cir. 2005) (*MPUC*). *See also* W. Nagel & A. Lev, *VoIP: The Second Battle of the Internet Tax Wars*, Tax Notes 289, at 290 (July 19, 2004):

> VOIP services mimic traditional telephony and aim to bring to the customer the quality and ubiquity of traditional wire-line voice telephone calls. The key technological difference is that VOIP establishes no dedicated circuit between caller and receiver, whereas traditional telephone calls generally occur by creating such a dedicated circuit. Using VOIP,

according to one analyst, grew from less than US$200 million in 2004 to over US$1 billion in 2005 and to US$2.6 billion in 2006.[8]

The emergence and growth of Internet telecommunications services has spurred reforms in U.S. taxes and related regulatory contributions. Because the lines between Internet telecommunications and other offerings are unclear, these technology and market developments led (or contributed) to changes addressing both the charges imposed on these new Internet services as well as the treatment of other, substitutable telecommunications services.

In recent years, the Internal Revenue Service (IRS) ceased applying the federal telecommunications excise tax to long-distance and bundled services (including VoIP services), and federal laws preempted state and local governments from taxing Internet access services. On the other hand, the growing revenues from Internet telecommunications services have been an attractive target for many state and local governments, especially in light of the declines these services cause in the revenues of some heavily-taxed, traditional telecommunications services; several jurisdictions have updated their telecommunications taxes to sweep in Internet telephony services and other technology advances. Moreover, the FCC expanded the contributors to the Universal Service Fund (USF) to include certain VoIP services.

Section II of this chapter describes some of the line-drawing difficulties in characterizing Internet telecommunications services relevant to their tax treatment. Next, section III considers some developments in federal tax laws related to Internet telecommunications services. Section IV follows with a description of some state and local taxes related to Internet telecommunications services. Then, section V analyzes the FCC's decision to expand USF contributions to include VoIP services. Finally, section VI summarizes some lessons for taxes on telecommunications services.

II. LINE-DRAWING DIFFICULTIES IN CHARACTERIZING INTERNET TELECOMMUNICATIONS SERVICES

Services providing electronic transmissions of information come in a wide range of subtly different flavors. Services can be distinguished based on the technologies used, service capacity and other features, pricing, bundled marketing, providers, whether and how they interconnect with other services, and other criteria. Drawing lines distinguishing, or not distinguishing, among these services is important in applying various regulations as well as in applying various taxes.[9] Before considering how Internet telecommunications

---

the digitized voice—rendered in separate bursts of data called "packets"—is sent into the Internet. Information is transmitted on the Internet by thousands of "routers," each of which examines the packet and decides which router to send the packet to next. The standardized programming rules that enable this system of routers to operate is known as the "Internet Protocol," hence the name, "Voice Over Internet Protocol."

8 Light Reading, *U.S. VoIP Revenues Triple* (Mar. 7, 2006) (study by TeleGeography); New Telephony, *TeleGeography: VoIP Hits Mainstream Stride* (Sept. 7, 2007).

9 *See, e.g.*, *Private Line Rate Structure and Volume Discount Practices*, 97 FCC 2d 923, 924 (1984) ("We seek to avoid having two similarly-situated customers who demand the same

services have been characterized for purposes of taxes and USF contributions, a short overview of some other regulatory developments helps illustrate the line-drawing difficulties for these services.

A. Internet Access Services

Two areas of recent FCC regulation demonstrate the many flavors of Internet access services and how they overlap with other telecommunications offerings.

First, the FCC collects and publishes data about broadband availability and deployment throughout the nation to assess the success of its broadband policies, in light of the statutory mandate to "encourage the deployment on a reasonable and timely basis of advanced telecommunications capability to all [Americans]."[10] The January 2007 report reflects high-speed lines ("connections to end-user locations that deliver services at speeds exceeding 200 kbps in at least one direction") and the subset of advanced services lines (speeds exceeding 200 kilobits per second [kbps] in both directions).[11] The subcategories based on technology platform are ADSL (asymmetric DSL), SDSL (symmetric DSL), traditional wireline, cable modem, fiber-optic, satellite, fixed wireless, mobile wireless, and power line and other. The report also reflects subcategories of advanced services based on speed in the faster direction, with thresholds at 2.5 megabits per second (mbps), 10 mbps, 25 mbps, and 100 mbps. Another classification in this report divides residential from business users. In April 2007, the FCC issued a notice of proposed rulemaking regarding possible revisions to this data collection, including raising the minimum speed threshold of 200 kbps, and collecting data on wireless broadband access services designed for devices that have their own browsers ("full Internet browsing").[12]

Second, the FCC issued a series of orders declaring certain technology-based Internet access services to be "information services" (as defined in the Communications Act of 1934, as amended by the Telecommunications Act of 1996[13]), thus falling outside of many of the regulatory requirements applicable to telecommunications services. These orders covered cable modem services (in 2002), wireline services (in 2005), broadband-over-power-line services (in 2006), and wireless broadband services (in 2007).[14] While the FCC stated in its 2005 and later orders that it was acting to further

---

service from the same carrier (such as ten, full-time, voice-grade private lines between points A and B) charged different rates, *i.e.*, unlawful discrimination.").

10 47 U.S.C. § 157 (1996).

11 *FCC Internet Access Report, supra* note 6.

12 *Development of Nationwide Broadband Data to Evaluate Reasonable and Timely Deployment of Advanced Services to All Americans*, 22 FCC Rcd 760, at paras. 14, 19 (2007). *See also Inquiry Concerning the Deployment of Advanced Telecommunications Capability to All Americans in a Reasonable and Timely Fashion*, 22 FCC Rcd 7816 (2007).

13 47 U.S.C. § 153(20) (2006).

14 *Inquiry Concerning High-Speed Access to the Internet over Cable and Other Facilities*, 17 FCC Rcd 4798 (2002), *aff'd*, Nat'l Cable & Telecomms. Assn v. Brand X Internet Services, 545 U.S. 967 (2005); *Appropriate Framework for Broadband Access to the Internet over*

the goal of "developing a consistent regulatory framework across platforms by regulating like services in a similar functional manner,"[15] the phased approach reflects an ability of government authorities to draw lines among Internet access services based on technology with regulatory consequences.

In the order on wireline Internet access services, the FCC did not apply a technology distinction that it used just one year earlier in deciding that some wireline broadband services (including copper loops) would be subject to an unbundling requirement but others (including fiber-to-the-home loops in Greenfield [initial coverage] situations) would not.[16] On the other hand, the FCC's order characterizing wireline Internet access services as information services did not encompass various wireline broadband access services, such as stand-alone asynchronous transfer mode (ATM) service, frame relay service, gigabit Ethernet service, and other high-capacity special access services; the FCC stated that carriers and end users traditionally have used these services for basic transmission purposes, although they could be used for high-speed Internet access.[17] Moreover, the voice-grade copper loops that many people use for dial-up Internet access do not fall within the FCC's category of wireline Internet access services that are information services.

B. VoIP Services

Similar to Internet access services, VoIP services come in many varieties and are not easily defined and distinguished from other telecommunications services. Again, two areas of FCC regulation illustrate these points on line drawing.

In one set of cases, the FCC preempted state regulation of certain VoIP services after determining that it would be impractical, if not impossible, to separate the intrastate and interstate portions of these services, and state regulation would conflict with federal rules and policies.[18] The FCC decisions worked through several possibly critical characteristics of a range of services using Internet protocol (IP) transmissions, such

---

Wireline Facilities, 20 FCC Rcd 14853 (2005) (*Wireline Broadband Order*), *aff'd*, Time Warner Telecom v. FCC, No. 05-4769 (3d Cir. 2007); *United Power Line Council's Petition for Declaratory Ruling Regarding the Classification of Broadband over Power Line Internet Access Service as an Information Service*, 21 FCC Rcd 13281 (2006); *Appropriate Regulatory Treatment for Broadband Access to the Internet over Wireless Networks*, 07-53 (2007).

15 *Wireline Broadband Order, supra*, 20 FCC Rcd at 14855.

16 *Unbundled Access to Network Elements, Review of Section 251 Unbundling Obligations of Incumbent Local Exchange Carriers*, 20 FCC Rcd 2533, 2541 (2004), aff'd, Covad Communications Co. v. FCC, 450 F.3d 528 (D.C. Cir. 2006).

17 *Wireline Broadband Order, supra*, 20 FCC Rcd at 14909. *See also Petition of the Embarq Local Operating Companies for Forbearance under 47 U.S.C. Sec. 160(c)*, FCC 07-184, ¶¶ 7–8 (2007).

18 *Vonage Holdings Corp.*, 19 FCC Rcd 22404 (2004), *aff'd, MPUC, supra note7; IP-Enabled Services*, 19 FCC Rcd 4863 (2004); *Petition for Declaratory Ruling that pulver.com's Free World Dialup Is Neither Telecommunications nor a Telecommunications Service*, 19 FCC Rcd 3307 (2004); *Petition for Declaratory Ruling that AT&T's Phone-to-Phone IP Telephony Services are Exempt from Access Charges*, 19 FCC Rcd 7457 (2004).

as whether the call originates at an IP address tied to an identifiable geographic location ("fixed" VoIP service); the call can be originated using a broadband Internet connection anywhere in the world ("nomadic" VoIP service); the caller can communicate only with other VoIP subscribers, or rather can also communicate with subscribers of traditional circuit-switched telephone service ("interconnected" VoIP service); the call applies IP conversion and transmission only to link originating and terminating ends using traditional landline connections ("backbone" IP or "phone-to-phone" transmissions); and the service features entail accessing different Web sites or IP addresses during the same communication.

Another proceeding in 2005 required the FCC to decide what types of VoIP services, if any, must provide automatic caller location information for calls to emergency services (E-911).[19] The FCC previously required that traditional landline and wireless carriers provide this capability. The FCC decided to apply this requirement to VoIP services that permit users generally both to originate calls to and to terminate calls from the public switched telephone network (PSTN). The FCC did not exempt nomadic VoIP services, even though caller location information was harder to provide than for fixed VoIP service. On the other hand, the FCC did not require that services limited to VoIP-to-VoIP transmissions (noninterconnected VoIP services) offer this capability.

III. FEDERAL AGENCY ACTIONS AND LEGISLATION

Internet telecommunications services have contributed to substantial federal tax activity, including IRS actions and legislation. This section describes the narrowing of the federal communications excise tax and its relationship to VoIP, as well as the adoption and extension of the federal moratorium on state and local taxation of Internet access services. The congressional decisions on these taxes—to allow federal tax revenues to be eroded by changes in how providers price services, and to preempt state and local governments from collecting revenues from services that substitute for traditionally taxed offerings—were unusual and reveal interesting political considerations.

A. VoIP and the Federal Communications Excise Tax

The federal communications excise tax was adopted as part of the Spanish War Act of 1898 as a temporary, luxury tax. The current form of the statute imposes a 3 percent tax on local telephone service, toll telephone service, and teletypewriter exchange service, including services acquired by means of prepaid calling cards.[20] The statutory definition of "toll telephone service" requires "a toll charge that varies in amount with the distance and elapsed transmission time of each individual communication."[21]

19 *IP-Enabled Services, E911 Requirements for IP-Enabled Service Providers*, 20 FCC Rcd 10245 (2005), *aff'd*, Nuvio Corp. v. FCC, 473 F.3d 302 (D.C. Cir. 2006).

20 I.R.C § 4251 *et seq* (1998).

21 *Id.* at § 4252(b)(1).

As developed for many cellular and traditional landline calling plans, VoIP charges often did not vary in amount with distance and elapsed transmission time. Although VoIP calling plans have offered a range of pricing and other terms, one popular provider offered these monthly plans in 2004: US$34.99 for unlimited calling (without regard to distance, elapsed transmission time or number of individual communications); US$14.99 for up to 500 minutes of calling anytime to anywhere in the United States and Canada (without regard to distance); and US$24.99 for unlimited local and regional calling and 500 minutes of long-distance calling.[22] Additionally, for a nomadic VoIP call (between two IP addresses without fixed geographic locations), it is difficult for a provider to determine whether the call would fall within the category of local telephone service (originating and terminating in the same service area) or toll telephone service.

A series of five decisions by circuit courts of appeals—none of which dealt with a VoIP calling plan or provider—held that the tax did not apply to telephone communications for which there was a toll charge varying with elapsed transmission time but not with distance.[23] Decisions adverse to the IRS in these court cases were the thrust behind the IRS's action in 2006 to narrow the application of this tax by excluding long-distance service and bundled service (plans that do not separately state the charge for local telephone service).[24] Nevertheless, VoIP played a prominent role in the IRS's guidance as well as in the lack of legislation on this issue.

Prior to the IRS's 2006 guidance acknowledging the narrower application of this tax, the IRS addressed a form of Internet telephony explicitly only once. An IRS Technical Advice Memorandum (TAM) issued in 2003 applied this tax to a provider using the Internet only for "backbone transmissions" (to connect phone-to-phone communications, between callers and called parties connected to intercity transmission facilities via traditional voice-grade telephone lines rather than broadband Internet access lines).[25] The IRS found that the taxpayer was providing communications services to its customers who were using telephones, not a nontaxed information service; it was irrelevant that the taxpayer used the Internet as an interexchange transmission medium. This ruling did not address other forms of VoIP using broadband Internet access lines on both ends and just one end.

22 Sullivan, *supra* note 2, at 459–60 (describing Vonage offerings).

23 Nat'l R.R. Passenger Corp. v. United States, 431 F.3d 374 (D.C. Cir. 2005) (holding that the tax did not apply; "Taxing all 1965 long-distance service, however, is a far cry from taxing all long-distance service today. Not only does AT&T no longer hold a monopoly on long-distance service, but today's multitude of long-distance carriers offers far more rate structures."); Am. Bankers Ins. Group v. United States, 408 F.3d 1328, 1332 (11th Cir. 2005) ("there is nothing in the statutory context to suggest that 'and' is used in the provision as meaning 'or'"; long-distance services purchased from AT&T); OfficeMax, Inc. v. United States, 428 F.3d 583 (6th Cir. 2005) (holding that the tax did not apply to long-distance services provided by MCI at a flat per-minute rate for all domestic interstate calls); Fortis v. United States, 447 F.3d 190 (2d Cir. 2006) (holding that the tax did not apply); Reese Bros. v. United States, 477 F.3d 229, 241 (3d Cir. 2006) ("The Government would have us extend the reach of the federal communications excise tax beyond its text.").

24 *IRS Notice, supra* note3.

25 TAM 200343001 (Dec. 2003-23011, 2003 TNT 207-20).

The application of this tax to VoIP and other new telecommunications technologies continued to trouble the IRS. In mid-2004, the IRS published an advanced notice of proposed rulemaking on this tax.[26] The IRS noted that the applicable form of the statutory provisions was enacted in 1965, and numerous changes in communications services and methods of transmission had occurred since then. The notice sought comments and suggestions "describing the various technologies, services, and methods of transmission currently available for transmitting data and voice communications and how they should be treated" under this tax. Several telecommunications industry sources viewed the notice as indicating that the IRS intended to apply, or at least was considering applying, the tax to VoIP.[27]

The burden of addressing the application of the federal communications excise tax to VoIP did not fall entirely on the IRS. Congress had amended this statute 14 times from 1965 to 2004.[28] In January 2005, the staff of Congress's Joint Committee on Taxation issued a report analyzing the VoIP developments and presenting three options for further legislative changes.[29] The report discussed the options in the context of the following observations about VoIP and other developments in telecommunications technologies:[30]

> The proliferation of wireless communications technology and the Internet, and in particular broadband access, has blurred the lines between "data" and "voice" and between the functions of transmission and application. Consequently, service providers have found it increasingly difficult to determine which services are taxable communications services and which are nontaxable information services. . . . Any excise tax distorts consumer decisions, and taxing new services and technologies makes them more expensive, and, therefore, may slow their development. . . . [T]echnological changes and practices . . . may make certain nontaxable data services a close substitute for taxable voice services. . . . Voice and data are becoming interchangeable and integrated parts of modern communications. . . . As voice phone service migrates to using Internet protocol, there may be no way to distinguish "packets" of voice and "packets" of data. It is also expected that users will integrate their Internet data and voice applications.

The report also cited complications from VoIP developments that became evident during the recent legislative debates relating to the regulation and the state and local taxation of VoIP services.[31]

The staff report's first option for legislative change would impose the tax on voice telephone services, regardless of whether the charges are fixed or vary with distance,

---

26 Announcement 2004-61, 2004-29 I.R.B. 67, 64 Fed. Reg. 40345 (July 2, 2004) (advanced notice of proposed rulemaking).

27 *See, e.g.*, D. McCullagh, *IRS Eyes Net Phone Taxes*, CNET News (July 8, 2004); G. Kunkle, *Regulatory Update*, STC Lines (Society of Telecommunications Consultants) (Oct. 2004) 4; A. Nellen, *Internet Business, Local Taxation & Nexus* 27 (Oct. 20, 2004) (presented at the California Municipal Revenue and Tax Association Annual Conference).

28 Techlawjournal.com, *IRS Publishes Advance NPRM Regarding Expanding the Excise Tax on Telephones to Include New Technologies* (July 2, 2004).

29 Staff of the Joint Committee on Taxation, *Options to Improve Tax Compliance and Reform Tax Expenditures* 368–78 (JCS-02-05, Jan. 27, 2005).

30 *Id.* at 371–72, 376, 378.

31 *Id.* at 371–72 n. 827.

elapsed transmission time, both, or some other criteria. The report noted this change would not address whether VoIP is a taxable communications service or a nontaxable information service, or the application of the tax to services provided through a mixed use of new technologies such as VoIP.[32] The second option would make voice communications services taxable regardless of the technical form, including voice services using VoIP. However, the report observed that this option depends on the voice/data dichotomy that was under pressure from VoIP and would create an economic distortion.[33] Finally, the third option was to expand the tax base to all voice and data communications. Even this broad sweep was subject to making the increasingly difficult distinction between communications and information services.[34]

In part because of the difficult line-drawing issues surrounding VoIP and political concerns about slowing its development, Congress did not amend this statute in 2005 or 2006. When the IRS announced a narrower application of this tax in June 2006, it also addressed VoIP. In defining the nontaxable "bundled service," the notice states, "Bundled service includes, for example, Voice over Internet Protocol service, prepaid telephone cards, and plans that provide both local and long distance service for either a flat monthly fee or a charge that varies with the elapsed transmission time for which the service is used."[35] In the IRS's notice "Telephone Tax Refund Questions and Answers," intended to provide guidance for individual taxpayers, VoIP services are discussed in three answers.[36]

While developments in the case law precipitated the narrowing of this tax, there can be little doubt that the interpretive challenges associated with VoIP contributed to the decisions by the IRS and Congress and, as a consequence, VoIP emerged outside the scope of this tax. In summary, the status of VoIP after the IRS Notice was as follows: a

1. The IRS ruled that this tax applied to services using the Internet only for backbone transmissions, but did not rule on other forms of VoIP.
2. Many VoIP offerings, like some other communications services, did not fit into the statutory category of toll telephone services because the charges did not vary with distance and, under some plans, did not vary with transmission time.

---

32 *Id.* at 377 ("Future controversies will almost certainly develop as technologies are developed and implemented and the market changes. Since these changes are occurring now, Option 1 is likely to be only a short-run measure.").

33 *Id.* at 373–75, 377–78.

34 *Id.* at 375, 378.

35 *IRS Notice*, *supra* note 3, at Section 3(a).

36 Internal Revenue Service, *Telephone Tax Refund Questions and Answers* (last updated April 12, 2007):

> Question: What is the telephone tax refund? Answer: . . . It is available to anyone who paid such taxes on landline, wireless, or Voice over Internet Protocol (VoIP) services.Question: What is a refund-eligible bundled service? Answer: . . . If Voice over Internet Protocol service (VoIP) provides both local and long distance service and the charges are not separately stated, such service is bundled service. Question: Do Internet long-distance plans qualify for the refund? Answer: Yes. If you paid the federal excise tax on your long-distance Internet plan, you can request the telephone tax refund. Internet long distance plans include broadband VoIP long-distance plans.

3. The IRS and staff of the Joint Committee on Taxation recognized that changes in telecommunications technologies and offerings may require revisions to the tax, with VoIP posing difficulties in drawing lines between voice and data communications services as well as between communications and information services.
4. Congress did not find the political support to broaden or eliminate this industry-specific and service-specific tax.
5. In announcing the narrower application of this tax, the IRS included VoIP in its definition of nontaxable bundled services and nontaxable long-distance plans.

B. Moratorium on State and Local Taxes for Internet Access Services

The preceding discussion of the federal communications excise tax dealt with a tax that was enacted decades before the advent of the Internet, applied to a wide range of landline and wireless communications services, and changed because of developments in various technologies and offerings, including VoIP. In contrast, the following discussion of the Internet Tax Freedom Act of 1998 and its three extensions addresses a federal law that was Internet-specific from its inception. Nevertheless, this legislation also encountered difficult issues of distinguishing among Internet-related offerings. While congressional inaction led to a favorable result for VoIP under the federal communications excise tax, Congress repeatedly developed an unusual consensus against state and local taxes on Internet access services.

The Internet Tax Freedom Act of 1998 (the 1998 Act) was a federal government response to the growth in state and local taxes on Internet access services and Internet-based sales. As the Clinton administration stated, it was important that such state and local taxes "not impede this promising economic opportunity," but also important that the Internet "not become a tax haven that drains the sales tax and other revenues that our cities and States need."[37] The 1998 Act had two major provisions.[38] First, it established the Advisory Commission on Electronic Commerce (ACEC) to report to Congress within 18 months on the effects of, and its legislative recommendations regarding, state and local taxation on Internet access and Internet transactions. This group had representatives from local, state, and federal governments as well as from the e-commerce industry. Second, the legislation maintained the status quo pending this report and any congressional action pursuant thereto. The act prohibited state and local authorities from imposing taxes on Internet access and multiple or discriminatory taxes on e-commerce, except for states that had already imposed taxes on Internet access prior to October 1, 1998. (Ironically, this grandfathering provision in the 1998 Act and each extension thereof rewarded those early-mover jurisdictions that imposed taxes on an emerging telecommunications offering.[39])

---

37 Office of Management and Budget, *S. 442—Internet Tax Freedom Act* (Oct. 1, 1998).

38 Internet Tax Freedom Act, Title XI of the Omnibus Appropriations Act of 1998, P.L. no. 105-277, 112 Stat 2681 (1998).

39 *See* Congressional Budget Office, *Cost Estimate: Internet Tax Freedom Act Amendments Act of 2007* at 2 (Oct. 12, 2007) (estimating that eight states and several local jurisdictions in those states were collecting taxes on Internet access services under the grandfathering provision).

The 1998 Act defined Internet access as "a service that enables users to access content, information, electronic mail, or other services offered over the Internet, and may also include access to proprietary content, information, and other services as part of a package of services offered to users. Such term [Internet access] does not include telecommunications services."[40] This legislation permitted taxes on voice-grade telephone lines used for dial-up Internet access (traditional telecommunications services) but banned taxes on e-mail and instant messaging bundled by providers as part of their Internet access package.[41]

The ACEC's report to Congress recommended extending the moratorium on multiple and discriminatory taxation of e-commerce for five years, and making permanent the moratorium on Internet access taxes, including barring the taxes that were grandfathered in the 1998 Act.[42] Regarding Internet access taxes, the report stated, "This proposal is another crucial initiative, targeted to reduce the price of Internet access, and to close the digital divide [in access to information technologies between rich and poor people]." The report did not address the scope of Internet access services that should be subject to the tax moratorium.

In 2001, Congress renewed the moratorium through November 2003 without changing the definitions of the covered services.[43] On signing the legislation, President George W. Bush stated, "The Internet is an innovative force that enables such applications as distance learning and precision farming. Government must do its part to make access to these services affordable. It should not raise costs through additional taxation."[44]

With the growth in Internet access services and the exclusion of telecommunications services from the tax moratorium, several problems emerged that Congress sought to address in the Internet Tax Nondiscrimination Act of 2004 (the 2004 Act). In addition to renewing the moratorium for three years, this legislation changed the definitions. First, three states had imposed taxes on DSL service—an offering by telephone companies that competed with cable modem service as a high-speed Internet access connection primarily for residential customers—by classifying it as a telecommunications service.[45] In clarifying the preemption of state taxes on DSL service, the 2004 Act excluded from the term "Internet access" telecommunications services "except to the extent such services are purchased, used, or sold by a provider of Internet access to provide Internet access."[46] Second, the 1998 Act did not address bundled pricing for

---

40 Internet Tax Freedom Act, *supra* note 38, at § 1101(e)(3)(D)(1998).

41 United States Government Accountability Office, *Internet Access Tax Moratorium: Revenue Impacts Vary by State* 23 (2006).

42 J. Gilmore, III on behalf of the ACEC, *Letter of Transmittal* (Apr. 3, 2000). The ACEC also recommended eliminating the federal communications excise tax.

43 Internet Tax Nondiscrimination Act, P.L. No. 107-75, 115 Stat 703 (2001).

44 President George W. Bush, *Statement on Signing the Internet Tax Nondiscrimination Act* (Nov. 28, 2001).

45 B. Krebs, *House Approved Internet Tax Moratorium*, Wash. Post (Sept. 17, 2003) (Alabama, Florida and Kentucky) (Krebs). *See also* D. Castro, *The Case for Tax-Free Internet Access: A Primer on the Internet Tax Freedom Act* 4–5 (June 2007) (published by The Information Technology & Innovation Foundation).

46 Internet Tax Nondiscrimination Act, P.L. No. 108-435, 118 Stat 2615, § 2(c)(1) (2004) (2004 Act).

Internet access and telecommunications services. At least 15 states had enacted legislation to tax Internet access when it was bundled with traditional voice services,[47] which could result in taxing Internet access services. On the other hand, providers could try to use bundles of Internet access and telecommunications services to evade taxes on telecommunications services. The 2004 Act adopted an accounting rule for bundled services based on the reasonable identification of the charges for Internet access from the provider's books and records.[48] Third, the 2004 Act addressed VoIP as being a taxable service, except for VoIP services that are incidental to Internet access.[49]

Most recently, the Internet Tax Freedom Act Amendments Act of 2007 was signed into law on November 1, 2007.[50] Opponents of this legislation claimed that it was "disruptive of and poses long-term dangers for state and local fiscal systems," and quoted a study by the Government Accountability Office finding "that imposition of taxes was not a statistically significant factor influencing the deployment of broadband."[51] Again, the extension of the moratorium (this time for seven years) came with modifications to the definition of Internet access services to reflect changes in offerings. With the growth of video distribution over the Internet or using IP, Congress clarified the definition of Internet access to exclude such products and services, allowing them to be taxed.[52] Next, the new legislation specifically provided for certain incidental offerings included in Internet access, including a home page, e-mail, and instant messaging (including voice- and video-capable e-mail and instant messaging), video clips, and personal electronic storage capacity.[53] Additionally, the 2007 legislation struck the provision adopted in 2004 that classified VoIP as a taxable service except for VoIP services that are incidental to Internet access, leaving the federal legislation silent on state and local taxation of VoIP.[54]

---

47 Krebs, *supra* note 45.

48 2004 Act, *supra* note 46, at § 4(a) ("If charges for Internet access are aggregated with and not separately stated from charges for telecommunications services or other charges that are subject to taxation, then the charges for Internet access may be subject to taxation unless the Internet access provider can reasonably identify the charges for Internet access from its books and records kept in the regular course of business.").

49 *Id.* at § 6.

50 P.L. No. 110-108 (2007). *See* U.S. Department of Treasury Press Room, *Secretaries Paulson and Gutierrez Call for Permanent Extension of Internet Tax Moratorium* (Oct. 16, 2007) ("Preventing the taxation of Internet access and keeping the Internet free of multiple or discriminatory taxes will help sustain an environment for innovation, help ensure that consumers continue to have affordable access to the Internet, and strengthen the foundations of electronic commerce as a vital and growing part of our economy.")

51 Testimony of Harley T. Duncan, Executive Director, Federal Tax Administrators, before the Senate Committee on Commerce, Science, and Transportation, *Extension of the Internet Tax Nondiscrimination Act and Collection of Tax on Remote Sales* at 1, 2 (May 23, 2007) (quoting Government Accountability Office, "Telecommunications—Broadband Deployment is Extensive throughout the United States, but it is Difficult to Assess the Extent of Deployment Gaps in Rural Areas" (GAO-06-426) (2006)).

52 *Id.* at § 4.

53 *Id.*

54 *Id.* at § 5.

The federal Internet tax moratorium legislation illustrates several points relevant to this article. First, Internet access services were able to win a highly unusual bar on state and local taxation even years after these services were well-established and widespread, and when they represented a substantial amount of revenues similar to those derived from the telecommunications services, which were heavily taxed by state and local governments. As benefits from making these services available tax-free, the executive branch pointed to these services as promoting innovation and U.S. competitiveness as well as closing the gap between digital "haves" and "have-nots." This series of federal acts is consistent with the analysis of the staff report of the Joint Committee on Taxation regarding the federal excise tax—taxing new services and technologies may slow their development. On the other hand, the Government Accountability Office challenged the significance of this claim.

Second, the line-drawing between Internet access services versus telecommunications and other taxed services required revisions as new offerings and technologies emerged. The tax moratorium provided a strong financial incentive for providers to make offerings classified as tax-free Internet access services. The tax moratorium also provided a strong incentive for state and local governments to find ways to characterize offerings as taxable services falling outside of Internet access services.

IV. SOME STATE AND LOCAL TAXES ON INTERNET TELECOMMUNICATIONS SERVICES

The preceding discussion of the federal Internet tax moratorium highlighted the issue of state and local taxes on Internet telecommunications services. In addition to the federal legislation, the growth of Internet telecommunications services caused many state and local governments to respond with the application of (or failure to apply) various taxes. Without attempting a complete catalog of these actions, this section describes three types of state and local developments: (1) rulings by tax agencies that preexisting statutory and agency definitions of taxable telecommunications services encompass VoIP and certain other Internet-based offerings; (2) legislation to expand the scope of taxable services; and (3) loss of tax revenues to VoIP without expansion of the scope of taxable services.

A. Rulings That Taxable Services Encompass VoIP and Certain Other Internet-Based Offerings

Several jurisdictions have analyzed their broad definitions of taxable telecommunications services that were adopted before the advent of the Internet and issued interpretations that the taxable services encompass VoIP and certain other Internet-based offerings.

For example, Pennsylvania in 2005 issued a Sales Tax Bulletin finding that VoIP services are taxable telecommunications services.[55] That definition of telecommunications

55 Pennsylvania Department of Revenue, *Sales Tax Information Bulletin Relating to the Application of Sales and Use Tax to Telephone Calls Using Voice Over Internet Protocol or VOIP Telecommunications Services* (Sales Tax Bulletin 2005-02) (Jan. 28, 2005).

service is "[a]ny one-way transmission or any two-way, interactive transmission of sounds, signals or other intelligence . . . by electronic or electromagnetic means via wire, cable, satellite, light waves, microwaves, radio waves or other transmission media." The statutory definition had been updated to include specifically cellular service, but the Pennsylvania Department of Revenue found no need for the legislature to address the application of this definition to VoIP. Although the statute excludes enhanced telecommunication services from this definition (with Internet access specified as an enhanced service), the agency found that VoIP does not fall within this exclusion because the computer-processing applications are solely for routing transmissions.[56] (Recall, however, the observation of the staff of the Joint Committee on Taxation quoted in section III.A above, that lines between the functions of transmission and applications have blurred.) The Pennsylvania interpretation did not distinguish between VoIP calls that connect computers versus VoIP calls that connect traditional telephones; between VoIP calls that employ broadband Internet access versus calls that use traditional telephone lines and IP in the backbone transmission; or VoIP calls with service features that entail accessing different Web sites or IP addresses during the same communication.

Similarly, New York issued an interpretation in 2007 finding that VoIP transmitted via landline or wireless facilities constitutes a taxable telecommunications service.[57] As in Pennsylvania, the New York agency looked at VoIP in terms of routing transmissions, not as an application providing users with enhanced features. While the statutory definition of a taxable mobile telecommunications service in New York requires interconnection with the PSTN, the New York interpretation does not limit the application of the tax on telecommunications services to those VoIP services that are interconnected with the PSTN.

B. Legislation Expanding the Definition of Taxable Telecommunications Services

The growth of VoIP contributed to legislation in several states that expanded the definition of taxable telecommunications services. The two examples discussed below intend to make VoIP taxable regardless of the configuration of lines, equipment, and users.

---

56 "Since VOIP utilizes computer-processing applications solely for the management, control or operation of a telecommunications system or the management of a telecommunications service, it does *not* come within the enhanced telecommunication service exclusion from sales and use tax. VOIP utilizes Internet Protocol that permits the transmission of packeted data across a network or across multiple networks, but does not interact with the information it transmits; it merely serves to address and route the information." *Id.*

57 New York State Department of Taxation and Finance, Office of Tax Policy Analysis, Technical Services Division, *Application of Telecommunications Excise Tax to VoIP and Wireless VoIP* (NYT-G-07(3)C) (June 21, 2007) ("Both VoIP and Wireless VoIP involve the 'transmission of voice . . . through the use of wire, cable, fiber-optic, laser, microwave, radio wave, satellite *or similar media or any combination thereof*.' Tax Law § 186-e.1(g) (emphasis supplied) . . . The use of the Internet or Internet routing protocols for transmission of all or part of the call does not change this result.").

In 2004, Tennessee amended its telecommunications tax law.[58] The new definition of taxable services specifically includes "transmission services in which computer processing applications are used to act on the form, code, or protocol of the content for purposes of transmission, conveyance, or routing without regard to whether such services are referred to as enhanced or value added services." The Tennessee Department of Revenue stated that VoIP and electronic data interchange are examples of enhanced services that are subject to tax.[59] On the other hand, the statute excludes Internet access service from the term "telecommunications services."

Another example of an updated state statute occurs in Virginia in 2006.[60] Prior law provided that specific communications services were subject to one or more of a series of nine state and local communications taxes and fees. The new system involves a centrally administered communications sales and use tax, and a uniform statewide E-911 tax on landline telephone service. In the new law, "communications services" are defined to include VoIP: "the electronic transmission, conveyance, or routing of voice, data, audio, video, or any other information or signals . . . regardless of the protocol used for the transmission or conveyance." The guidelines and rules issued for this tax describe VoIP as a taxable communications service.

C. Growing Erosion of Tax Revenues without Expansion of the Definition of Taxable Service

Not all jurisdictions have applied telecommunications taxes to VoIP services. The result of this approach is an erosion of tax revenues as users substitute VoIP for traditional telephony services, as well as a tax incentive favoring the new services.

An illustration of this approach is the utility users' tax (UUT) in California. This tax is imposed on the monthly utility bills paid by customers for electricity, gas, telephone, and certain other utilities, and its scope is defined by the local government. UUT was collected by more than 140 cities and counties and yielded more than US$1.7 billion in 2004.[61] The City of Los Angeles observed in 2006 that providers do not collect UUT on VoIP calls (apparently including interconnected VoIP services), and cited the shift to VoIP and mobile services as a challenge to future revenue growth.[62] Nevertheless, Los Angeles estimated that UUT receipts from telephone users would be US$6.8 million more in 2006 than in the prior year.

Apparently, only one California city or county collecting UUT attempted to expand the scope of this tax to encompass VoIP. In a March 2007 election, 59.5 percent of the voters of the city of Covina voted against an extension and updating of the UUT at the

---

58 Tennessee Chapter no. 782, House Bill no. 3479 (2004).

59 Tennessee Department of Revenue, *Sales & Use Tax Notice #04–13* at 4 (July 19, 2004).

60 Virginia Tax Commissioner, *Guidelines and Rules for the Virginia Communications Taxes* 3–4 (CT-2) (Nov. 1, 2006).

61 V. Vasquez, *Phone Pork: The Government Spoil of Local Telephone Taxes* 7 (San Diego Institute for Policy Research Policy Report) (June 2007) (Vasquez).

62 Letter from L. Chick, Controller, City of Los Angeles, to Mayor A. Villaraigosa (Mar. 1, 2006) at 9 (revenue projections).

prevailing rate of 6 percent.[63] The proposed measure would have provided a functional definition of telecommunications services that would have been technology-neutral and included the use of Internet protocol, broadband services, and private networks. Some analysts point to a general "growing utility tax revolt" in California,[64] including opposition to expanding the scope of the UUT. If cities and counties cannot win voter approval for updating and expanding telephone utility taxes, the substitution of VoIP for traditional telephone services may lead some government entities to attempt to interpret the existing taxes on telephone utility services as including some forms of VoIP services and offerings by some VoIP providers.

The analysis of state and local actions in taxing Internet telecommunications services may be summarized as follows:

1. VoIP and other developments in technologies and offerings have led many jurisdictions to adopt broad, technology-neutral definitions of taxable telecommunications services, leading to less distortion in consumers' choices among substitutable services and a growing revenue base, but also a burden on emerging technologies and offerings.[65]
2. In the states with broad definitions of taxable services, there has been political support for the higher tax collections on telecommunications transmission services but not on information services.
3. In attempting to distinguish between communications services and untaxed enhanced or information services, some jurisdictions are confronted by the blurring of transmission and application functions and other convergences.
4. The federal grandfathering of certain state and local taxes imposed prior to the moratorium in 1998 rewarded early movers (about eight states and several local authorities in those states) in taxing emerging Internet offerings.

V. FCC'S EXPANSION OF CONTRIBUTORS TO THE USF TO INCLUDE VOIP SERVICES

In 2006, the FCC decided that interconnected VoIP services must contribute about 7 percent of their revenues to support the federal USF.[66] The FCC's approach to definitions and its

---

63 League of Women Voters of California Education Fund, *Measure Covina-A: Utility User Tax City of Covina* (May 3, 2007).

64 Vasquez, *supra* note 61, at 8.

65 See W. Lavey, *Innovative Telecommunications Services and the Benefit of the Doubt*, 27 Cal. W. L. Rev. 51 (1990).

66 *Universal Service Contribution Methodology*, 21 FCC Rcd 7518 (2006) (USCM), *aff'd*, Vonage v. FCC, 489 F.3d 1232 (D.C. Cir. 2007). The FCC ordered that interconnected VoIP providers must contribute to the USF on all their interstate and international end-user telecommunications revenues. While VoIP providers may rely on traffic studies, the FCC established a safe harbor that 64.9 percent of the providers' total revenues are subject to such contribution. *USCM*, *supra*, 21 FCC Rcd at 7545. The FCC determines the USF contribution factor quarterly; the factor was 11.0 percent for the fourth quarter of 2007. FCC Public Notice, *Proposed Fourth Quarter 2007 Universal Service Contribution Factor* (DA 07-3928) (Sept. 13, 2007).

policy reasons for imposing this charge are interesting from the perspective of the developments in federal, state, and local taxes described earlier in this chapter.

A. Background on USF

The USF is a program established by the Telecommunications Act of 1996 to support telecommunications and Internet access services for rural and high-cost areas as well as low-income households, schools, and libraries.[67] The USF was designed as an explicit support mechanism (albeit not a tax) to replace a series of regulated procedures within the telecommunications industry intended to make telephone service available and affordable nationwide. Such procedures reflected the era of monopoly long-distance and local telephone services. The implicit, intra-industry support mechanisms were based on jurisdictional cost allocations, averaged (pooled) charges and revenues, rate structures for use of local lines, and switches in long-distance calls (access charges), among other things.

B. Definitions

Three statutory categories are relevant for this analysis. First, "[e]very telecommunications carrier that provides interstate telecommunications services" must contribute to the USF. "Telecommunications service" is defined as "the offering of telecommunications for a fee directly to the public."[68] Second, upon finding that "the public interest so requires," the FCC may require "[a]ny other provider of interstate telecommunications" to contribute to the USF. A "provider of interstate telecommunications" provides "the transmission, between or among points specified by the user, of information of the user's choosing, without change in the form or content of the information as sent and received."[69] Third, providers of information services do not contribute to the USF. An "information service" is "the offering of a capability for generating, acquiring, storing, transforming, processing, retrieving, utilizing, or making available information via telecommunications."[70]

The FCC initially addressed the characterization of VoIP services for purposes of USF contributions in a Report to Congress in 1998.[71] The FCC tentatively drew a line between computer-to-computer IP telephony and phone-to-phone IP telephony (which, among other characteristics, was defined as interconnected with the PSTN). The FCC

67 47 U.S.C. § 254 (b)(3), h(1)(B) (2006). *See* W. Lavey, *Some Legal Puzzles in the 1996 Statutory Provisions for Universal Telecommunications Services*, Making Universal Service Policy 179 (B. Cherry et al. 1999); W. Lavey, *The Public Policies That Changed the Telephone Industry into Regulated Monopolies: Lesson from Around 1915*, 39 Fed. Com. L. J. 171 (1987).

68 47 U.S.C. §§ 254(d), 153(46) (2006)

69 47 U.S.C. §§ 254(d), 153(43) (2006).

70 47 U.S.C. § 153(20) (2006).

71 *Federal-State Joint Board on Universal Service*, Report to Congress, 13 FCC Rcd 11501, ¶¶ 87–90 (1998).

made the following observations (subject to the development of a complete record and without ordering any form of VoIP to contribute to the USF): (1) phone-to-phone IP telephony services "bear the characteristics of 'telecommunications services,'" and (2) "[w]ithout regard to whether 'telecommunications' is taking place in the transmission of computer-to-computer IP telephony, the Internet service provider does not appear to be 'provid[ing] telecommunications to its subscribers.'"

As described in section II.A above, the FCC adopted a series of orders starting in 2005 declaring Internet access services to be information services. Some Internet access services, especially DSL provided by local telephone companies, had been treated as a telecommunications service before such FCC order, and were making substantial USF contributions; these Internet access services were subsequently exempted from USF contributions.

In determining the categorization of VoIP services in 2006, the FCC distinguished interconnected VoIP services from other VoIP offerings. The FCC looked to four key features of interconnected VoIP services: "(1) enable real-time, two-way voice communications; (2) require a broadband connection from the user's location; (3) require IP-compatible customer premises equipment; and (4) permit users to receive calls from and terminate calls to the public switched telephone network."[72]

Without deciding whether to classify interconnected VoIP service as a telecommunications service or an information service, the FCC found that interconnected VoIP providers provide interstate telecommunications. The FCC found that a provider of an interconnected VoIP service is a "provider of telecommunications" because it supplies PSTN transmission to end users as a component of the VoIP service.[73] The FCC applied this characterization regardless of whether the interconnected VoIP provider owns or operates its own transmission facilities, or obtains transmissions from third parties.

This approach did not reach the issue of how to characterize VoIP providers that are not interconnected with the PSTN. As discussed below, this line-drawing fit with the FCC's policy analysis. Furthermore, the approach that depends on provision of PSTN transmissions as a component of a VoIP service is not exposed to the increasing convergence of transmission and application functions. Even for providers of VoIP services entailing extensive features of information services, they are "providers of telecommunications" as long as the services are interconnected with the PSTN.

C. Policy Reasons for Requiring Interconnected VoIP Services to Contribute to the USF

The FCC focused on three policy reasons that the public interest requires interconnected VoIP services to contribute to the USF. Two reasons are based on the substitutability of interconnected VoIP services for the telecommunications services that contribute to the USF, and the FCC's expectation that interconnected VoIP services will continue to

72 *USCM*, *supra* note 66, 21 FCC Rcd at 7526; 47 C.F.R. § 9.3 (2005).

73 *USCM*, *supra* note 66, 21 FCC Rcd at 7539–40.

grow dramatically and increasingly replace telecommunications services.[74] The first policy reason points to the stability of the revenue base for the USF.[75] The next policy reason looks to the principle of competitive neutrality (level playing field); USF support mechanisms should not unfairly advantage one provider over another or one technology over another.[76] Finally, without regard to substitutability, a third policy reason reflects that interconnected VoIP providers use the PSTN, which is supported by the USF, and benefit from the USF's programs to make services more widely available and affordable.[77]

While the third policy reason does not apply to noninterconnected VoIP services, the first two policy reasons do. Note that the FCC requires USF contributions from satellite and mobile-to-mobile interstate commercial wireless services, even for revenues derived without using the PSTN.[78] However, even if the FCC found the substitutability to noninterconnected VoIP services sufficiently compelling to support the first and second policy reasons, the FCC's definitional approach would have to change to make these services contributors to the USF; in light of the statutory provision limiting USF contributions to providers of interstate telecommunications, the FCC would have to find that these services provide telecommunications even though they do not include any use of the PSTN.

Among the highlights of the FCC's decision to make interconnected VoIP services contribute to the USF are

1. Much like the concerns of the Los Angeles Controller in pointing to substitution from traditional telephone services to VoIP as causing erosion of UUT revenues, the FCC expanded the scope of contributors to USF to promote stable funding.
2. Unlike the taxes in Pennsylvania, New York, Tennessee, and Virginia discussed above, the FCC did not categorize any VoIP services as telecommunications services, and instead distinguished among VoIP services based on whether they are interconnected with the PSTN.
3. Responding to the same concerns as the staff of the Joint Committee on Taxation regarding the convergence between communications and information services, the FCC distinguished some VoIP services based on their supply of PSTN transmission as a component of the service, a line-drawing that will likely survive the increasing integration of information services applications into these VoIP services.[79]

---

74 *Id.* at 7541.

75 "If we do not require interconnected VoIP providers to contribute, the revenue base that supports the Fund will continue to shrink. . . . We believe that this trend threatens the stability of the Fund. . . ." *Id.* at 7542.

76 *Id.* at 7541.

77 *Id.* at 7540.

78 FCC, Telecommunications Reporting Worksheet, FCC Revised Form 499-A (2006), Instructions at 25–26 (2006). By contrast, *see* section IV.A, *supra* (New York tax on telecommunications services applies to those mobile service that are interconnected to the PSTN, but not to other mobile services).

79 Even with additional information-services features (perhaps making the service predominately an offering of a capability for generating, acquiring, storing, transforming, processing, retrieving,

VI. LESSONS FOR TAXES ON TELECOMMUNICATIONS SERVICES

The telecommunications industry's dynamic growth of new technologies, offerings, and providers strongly benefits the economy and society. The greater capabilities, expanded availability, and lower prices of services contribute to efficiency and access to information and provide many other benefits. Internet-related services have been a major part of these developments.

On the other hand, this dynamism makes industry-specific and service-specific taxation difficult and unwise.[80] Definitions of taxable providers and offerings become outdated, leading to unstable tax revenues and distortions to competition and technology selection. Moreover, the convergence of heavily- taxed telecommunications services and less-taxed information services leads to uncertainties in how agencies and courts will draw lines. Again, Internet-related services have contributed to these problems. Yet, there continues to be general federal, state, and local political support for heavy telecommunications industry-specific and service-specific taxes.

As Internet telecommunications services developed, they spurred developments in many of these taxes. The federal communications excise tax was narrowed by the courts and then the IRS to exclude long-distance services and bundled services; VoIP technologies fostered flat-rate pricing without regard for traditional local versus long-distance geographic distinctions or elapsed transmission time. The federal Internet tax moratorium barred state and local taxation of Internet access services plus a growing list of ancillary offerings; Congress was also forced to address a growing list of excluded IP-based content offerings. Although several state and local governments have communications taxes that attempt to be competitively neutral and technology neutral, other jurisdictions draw lines around traditional utility services, and many state and local taxes face challenges from their exclusion of information services. Finally, the FCC (the federal agency with the greatest expertise in addressing Internet-related services) expanded the scope of USF contributors to include interconnected VoIP providers, but has not achieved competitive or technological neutrality relative to other VoIP services.

There are some suggestions that Internet telecommunications services are on the road to a level of tax burdens similar to products and services generally. Such evidence includes the 2007 legislation extending the federal tax moratorium on Internet access services; the exclusion of VoIP from the federal excise tax through the combination of court cases followed by the IRS Notice together with Congress's failure to revise the tax; and the FCC's exclusion of Internet access services from USF contributions. While these three federal actions are favorable to Internet telecommunications services providers and consumers, there are other developments cautioning against extrapolating these three actions. Many heavy state and local industry-specific taxes apply to VoIP and various other IP transmission services (some through legislative amendments or agency interpretations), and Congress was careful not to preempt such taxes. Additionally, the FCC expanded

---

utilizing, or making available information), interconnected VoIP calls will still supply PSTN transmission to end users as a component of the VoIP service.

80 *See* Lavey, *Pitfalls*, *supra* note 5.

USF contributions requirements to encompass interconnected VoIP services and has no inclination to exclude various other IP transmission services from this burden.

Conceptually, the long-term direction forward is contained in part of the Internet tax moratorium. The Internet Tax Freedom Act of 1998 and each of its three extensions bans state and local authorities "multiple or discriminatory taxes on electronic commerce."[81] Following this approach, Internet-based sales of products and services should not be subject to special taxes because of the e-commerce technology, but also should not be excluded from taxes applicable to other means of selling or providing such goods. The result is competitive and technology neutrality as well as more stable tax revenues. From a competitive fairness point of view, telecommunications providers and services should also not be subject to multiple or discriminatory taxes. Nor should they be excluded from general sales and business taxes. This approach yields greater certainty and stability of tax revenues as telecommunications providers and services continue to converge with information services and evolve in other ways.

It would be reckless to predict that Internet-related developments will bring about this change in federal, state, and local laws. A generation ago, before the Internet, telecommunications industry-specific and service-specific taxes encountered many challenging developments, including new technologies (cellular and other commercial radio services), new industrial organizations (AT&T's divestiture of the Bell Operating Companies, and new competitive providers of long-distance and local landline services), and new marketing approaches (unregulated sales of customer premises equipment and prepaid calling cards). The industry-specific and service-specific taxes did not fade away and yield to the general business taxes on sales. Instead, government authorities adapted these taxes through broader definitions of the covered offerings. The result has been billions of dollars annually of "excess tax" payments by the telecommunications industry and consumers of its services compared to general business taxes, as described in section I above.

The recent federal tax developments described in section III above suggest that the political will for neutrality in taxing the communications industries and services versus the information industry or businesses generally still has a long way to go and needs to be reinforced. On the one hand, VoIP services contributed to the considerations by Congress and the IRS following court cases on the 3 percent federal communications excise tax, resulting in exclusion of long-distance and bundled services from that tax. The telecommunications industry cheered the narrowing of this special tax burden. On the other hand, it was the Internet Tax Freedom Act and its extensions that granted special protection for Internet access services from general state and local sales taxes as well as from the much higher state and local taxes on the telecommunications industry and its services. Again, the telecommunications industry cheered the granting of this special tax moratorium.

While the Internet is overcoming geographic distances and offers the hope of decreasing income, cultural, and other disparities, it has shaken but not fundamentally unsettled the long-enduring political forces for telecommunications industry-specific and service-specific taxes and exemptions.

---

81 P.L. No. 105-277, § 1101(a)(2) (1998).

Chapter 28

United States: Sales Taxes in the Digital Environment

Arthur R. Rosen
McDermott Will & Emery LLP

I. GENERAL BACKGROUND

Sales taxes began to take root in the United States in the 1930s as state governments struggled to address the dramatic fiscal effects of the Great Depression.[1] Over the next several decades, states throughout the country adopted sales taxes; by 1990, 45 states and the District of Columbia had adopted such a tax. Largely spurred by the decision of the U.S. Supreme Court in *McLeod v. Dilworth*,[2] complementary use taxes were also enacted to guard against easy tax avoidance.

As a direct consequence of each state being sovereign (except to the extent certain sovereign rights were ceded to the federal government through the adoption of the U.S. Constitution in 1789),[3] each state's sales and use tax law is quite distinct from that of any other state.[4] Moreover, local jurisdictions commonly impose their own sales and use taxes, either independently of the state[5] or merely by adding an additional tax rate to the state rate.[6] Thousands upon thousands of jurisdictions now impose sales and use taxes.

State and local sales and use taxes have become a major source of revenue for those jurisdictions that impose them. For 2006, state sales and gross receipts tax collection

1 Richard D. Pomp & Oliver Oldman, State and Local Taxation 6-3 (5th Ed. 2005).

2 McLeod v. Dilworth, 322 U.S. 327 (1944).

3 U.S. Const. amend. X.

4 For example, New Jersey does not impose sales tax on purchases of clothing, whereas New York imposes sales tax on purchases of clothing over $110, and California imposes sales tax on all purchases of clothing.

5 *See, e.g.*, Ala. Code § 11-51-200.

6 *See, e.g.*, Ill. Comp. Stat. § 5/8-11-6.

totalled over US$330 billion, including special sales taxes on items such as motor fuels, tobacco products, and insurance premiums.[7]

So what are sales and use taxes? They are government exactions imposed on certain sales with the consideration paid by the purchaser being the tax base; they are thus consumption taxes as well as transaction taxes. In some states, the tax is technically imposed on the vendor for the privilege of engaging in business in that state,[8] while in other states the tax is imposed on the purchaser but collected by the vendor.[9] In the former category of states, the vendor has the right to (and, as a practical matter, always does) pass the tax explicitly through to the purchaser. In both situations, therefore, the tax is generally collected by the vendor from the customer and then remitted by the vendor to the taxing state.

With three pronounced exceptions,[10] sales and use taxes are generally imposed upon (1) all retail sales (i.e., those not for resale) of tangible personal property and (2) specifically identified services.[11] Exemptions are commonly provided for certain sellers and purchasers,[12] for certain products,[13] and for certain uses.[14]

Although it is standard for a sales and use tax to be imposed on the transfer of title *or* possession, the states—and most localities—follow the "destination rule," which provides that (1) for sales of tangible personal property, only the jurisdiction in which the purchaser receives the items will impose its tax and (2) for sales of services, only the jurisdiction where the service is performed will impose its tax.

The spectacular growth of e-commerce that began in the middle of the 1990s caused a great deal of concern among state and local tax officials. They feared that consumers' ability to purchase goods and certain services from remote vendors over whom the consumer's state lacks jurisdiction to require tax collection would reduce tax revenues significantly. Over time, that concern over lack of jurisdiction was matched or exceeded by the concern that many items that were previously sold in tangible form (e.g., music

---

7 U.S. Census Bureau, State Government Tax Collections: 2006, available at www.census.gov/govs/statetax/ 0600usstax.html. This information excludes local sales and use taxes.

8 Pomp & Oldman, *supra* note 1, at 7-1; *see also, e.g.*, Wis. Stat. Ann. § 77.52(1); Cal. Rev. & Tax. Code § 6051; Ark. Code Ann. § 42-1312(A).

9 *See, e.g.*, Utah Code Ann. §§ 59-12-103(1), 59-12-107(6); Ind. Code Ann. §§ 6-2.5-2-1, 6-2.5-2-1(b).

10 Haw. Rev. Stat. § 237-13; S. D. Codified Laws §§ 10-45-1.14, 10-46-2; N. M. Stat. 1978, § 7-9-3.5.

11 Hellerstein, *State Taxation*, ¶ 15.01 (WG&L 2008).

12 Purchases for resale (*see* N.Y. Tax Law § 1101(b)(4)(i)(A) (McKinney Interim Supp. 1900–2000), Cal. Rev. & Tax. Code § 6007 (West 1998); Pa. Stat. Ann. tit. 72, § 7201(k)(8) (West Supp. 1999); Va. Code Ann. § 58.1-602; N.J. Stat. Ann. § 54:32B-2(e); Ohio Rev. Code Ann. § 5739.01(E)(1)); some government bodies N.C.Gen. Stat. § 105-164.13(17) (federal government).

13 Ingredients or components in tangible personal property (*see* Ark. Code Ann. § 26-52-401(12)(B) (Michie Supp. 1999); Va. Code Ann. § 58.1-608(3)(b)(i)); and medications or food; J. Due & J. Mikesell, Sales Taxation: State and Local Structure and Administration 75–76 (2d ed. 1994) (25 states exempt food).

14 Products and machinery used in manufacturing (*see* Ohio Rev. Code § 5739.01(E)(9) (Banks-Baldwin Supp. 1999), Conn. Gen. Stat. § 12-408, Me. Rev. Stat. Ann. tit. 36, § 1760(74) (West 1990), Ohio Rev. Code Ann. § 5739.01(E)(8)).

on CDs) and thus taxable were now being sold in electronic form (e.g., downloadable music) and thus nontaxable. Several attempts have been made to address these concerns. First, the National Tax Association convened the Telecommunications and Electronic Commerce Project, a two-year process that brought together government officials and business representatives—agreement on major issues could not be achieved and so the effort was abandoned.[15] Next, Congress formed the Advisory Commission on Electronic Commerce[16] to deal with these concerns, but, once again, agreement between the states and the business community could not be reached.[17] Finally, a number of states established the Streamlined Sales Tax Project, which has evolved into the formal Streamlined Sales Tax Governing Board; approximately twenty states are fully participating and have tried to amend their sales tax laws to ease the tax collection burden for vendors with the ultimate goal of addressing the two major e-commerce concerns: jurisdiction over remote sellers and taxability of products that exist in electronic form without any tangible medium.[18] Some observers believe that the streamlined effort will ultimately fail to achieve its goals because states are unwilling to make the necessary major changes to their sales and use tax laws; others believe that, within a few years, many more states—including the larger states—will join the effort fully and will drive the effort to full success.

This article will explore how sales and use taxes are being imposed and administered in the digital environment (i.e., in the e-commerce world) in terms of (1) an out-of-state vendor being required to collect and remit a state's sales and use tax, (2) the taxability of electronically delivered items, and (3) compliance concerns.

II. REQUIREMENT TO COLLECT

A. Background

As noted above, a practical problem associated with sales and use taxes is that the state where a purchased item is received or where the use of a purchased item occurs may not have the legal jurisdiction to require an out-of-state vendor to collect and remit the tax. Although the individual consumers and businesses in the state are usually legally liable for paying the use tax as purchasers, the state has no feasible way to collect the

15 National Tax Association, *Communications and Electronic Commerce Tax Project, Final Report* 5 (Sept. 7, 1999), available at http://www.ntanet.org/ecommerce/final.pdf.

16 The Internet Tax Freedom Act, P.L. No. 105-277 (The Commission met six times during 1999 and 2000 and delivered its report to Congress on April 12, 2000, when its term ended).

17 Advisory Commission on Electronic Commerce, *Report to Congress* (April 12, 2000), available at http://www.law.gmu.edu/techcenter/programs/advisory_commission/acec_report.pdf.

18 *See*, Streamlined Sales and Use Tax Agreement, Appendix C, Part II (December 12, 2007); A. Rosen & S. Haffield, *Sales and Use Taxes: Streamlined Sales Tax System*, Tax Management Multistate Tax Portfolios, ¶ 1270.01.C.2 (BNA 2005); s*ee also*, S. 1586, 105th Cong. (1998), S. 545, 104th Cong. (1995), S. 1825, 103 Cong. (1994).

tax directly from the overwhelming majority of such purchasers. This has been a problem for the states since shortly after they first began imposing the tax.[19]

In 1967, the U.S. Supreme Court ruled that a state could not require a seller with any physical presence in that state to collect and remit that state's use taxes.[20] Subsequently, states enacted statues boldly disregarding that Supreme Court decision. One of those statutes was struck down by the Supreme Court in *Quill Corp. v. North Dakota*.[21]

Prior to the *Quill* decision, no clear distinction had been made between the nexus standard (i.e., the connection that must exist between a state and a person before an exercise of a state's jurisdiction to tax can be sustained) that is required by the U.S. Constitution's Due Process Clause and the nexus standard required under the Constitution's Commerce Clause. The *Quill* Court ruled that the Due Process Clause requires only that a person have "minimal contacts" with a state for the state to have jurisdiction over that person. According to the decision, Quill's purposeful direction of its economic activities into North Dakota (sending advertising material in the state and selling and shipping goods to North Dakota customers) was sufficient to satisfy due process concerns.

The Court further determined that to satisfy the Commerce Clause, however, the out-of-state person must have a "substantial nexus" with the taxing state. For the purposes of sales and use tax collection, the Court concluded that "substantial nexus" exists when the seller has physical presence in the taxing state. However, because the substantial nexus criterion is dormant or negative Commerce Clause jurisprudence (i.e., court-made law developed in the absence of specific congressional action that Congress can override by so acting), Congress has the right to decide whether to grant states the authority to require tax collection from remote sellers. While bills that would grant the states such power have been introduced,[22] Congress has declined to act on them.

The physical presence required by *Quill* may arise as a result of the activities of others acting on behalf of the taxpayer. A review of authority concerning attributing nexus from an instate person to an out-of-state company leads to the conclusion that the out-of-state company may be subject to the taxing jurisdiction of the state only where the instate person engages in "market enhancement" activities on behalf of the out-of-state company.

In *Scripto, Inc. v. Carson*,[23] the U.S. Supreme Court held that a Georgia corporation with no property or employees in the state of Florida had taxable nexus (for sales and use tax purposes) with Florida based solely on the use of independent third-party brokers to sell its products. The Court held that the solicitation of orders by independent jobbers satisfied the nexus requirements notwithstanding the fact that they were not employees because "such a fine distinction [as that between independent contractors

19 *See*, Nelson v. Sears, Roebuck & Co., 312 U.S. 359 (1941); Nelson v. Montgomery Ward & Co., 312 U.S. 373 (1941).

20 National Bellas Hess v. Illinois Dept. of Rev., 386 U.S. 753 (1967).

21 Quill Corp. v. North Dakota, 504 U.S. 298 (1992).

22 108th Congress: S. 1736: Streamlined Sales and Use Tax Act, S. 2152 [109th]: Sales Tax Fairness and Simplification Act; 109th Congress: S. 2153: Streamlined Sales Tax Simplification Act; 110th Congress: H.R. 3396 & S. 34.

23 Scripto, Inc. v. Carson, 362 U.S. 207 (1960).

and employees] is without constitutional significance."[24] The independent contractors were viewed by the Supreme Court as conducting the taxpayer's business in Florida because they were conducting "continuous local solicitation in Florida" on behalf of the taxpayer. According to the Court, the requisite inquiry in attributing the activities of another who is physically present in the state is "the nature and the extent of the activities" in the state.

In *Tyler Pipe Industries v. Washington State Department of Revenue*, the U.S. Supreme Court revisited the issue of agency-based attributional nexus in the context of a direct tax.[25] At issue was whether Washington could impose its business and occupation tax on an out-of-state wholesaler that had no office, property, or employees in Washington, based solely on the solicitation of business by an independent contractor who was in that state. In holding that Tyler Pipe had taxable nexus with Washington under *Scripto*, the Supreme Court affirmed the Washington Supreme Court's holding that the "crucial factor governing nexus" is whether the activities performed by the independent contractor on behalf of the out-of-state company are "significantly associated with the taxpayer's ability to establish and maintain a market in [the] state for the sales."[26] Accordingly, in applying the physical presence standard, an out-of-state vendor will be considered physically present instate, and thus may be subject to its sales and use tax laws, if the vendor's representatives are physically present in the state *and* those representatives engage in the following activities on the merchant's behalf: "continuous local solicitation" of orders for the merchant's goods; "exploitation of the consumer market;" "establish[ment] and maintain[enance of the merchant's] market;" and "calling on [the merchant's] customers and soliciting orders."[27] Case law from several states has consistently interpreted the Supreme Court's attributional nexus precedent, and there has been no major movement by state courts to extend the *Scripto* and *Tyler Pipe* nexus attribution rules any further than attribution from local solicitation activities.[28]

B. Application to the Digital Environment

What does all this mean for a business (vendo X) with all of its personnel, tangible property, and activities in state A that sells to customers located throughout the country? It is clear that under current law, no state other than state A can require vendor X to

---

24 *Id.*, at 211.

25 Tyler Pipe Industries v. Washington State Department of Revenue, 483 U.S. 232 (1987).

26 *Id.*, at 250.

27 *Scripto*, *supra* note 23, at 212; *Tyler Pipe*, supra note 25, at 249; *accord*, National Geographic Society v. California Board of Equalization, 430 U.S. 551 (1977).

28 House of Lloyd v. Commonwealth, 694 A.2d 375, 377 (Pa. Commw. 1997); In re Family of Eagles, Ltd., 66 P.3d 858, 865 (Kan. 2003); Department of Revenue v. Share International, Inc., No. 92-2918 (Fla. 2d Cir., Nov. 16, 1993), *aff'd*, 667 So.2d 226 (Fla. 2d Dist. 1995), *aff'd*, 676 So.2d 1362 (Fla. 1996), *cert. den.*, 519 U.S. 1056 (1997); JS&A Group, Inc. v. SBE, No. 1075021 (Cal Ct. App. 1997); J.C. Penney Nat'l Bank v. Johnson, 19 S.W.2d 831, 841 (Tenn. Ct. App. 1999); Baker & Taylor, Inc. v. Kawafuchi, 82 P.3d 804, 813 (Haw. 2004).

collect its sales and use tax (of course, if the customer's state imposes tax on the transaction, the purchaser is liable for the tax, but it is rare, outside the context of purchases made by large businesses, that the tax is ever actually paid). At what point, if any, does this situation change as vendor X begins activity that occurs or has an effect in other states?

Does vendor X become subject to state B's tax laws and need to start collecting and remitting that state's sales and use tax on vendor X's sales to the customer in state B if vendor X sends mass, unsolicited e-mails, or spam to potential customer in state B? What if vendor X negotiates and enters into a long-term contract with a customer in state B? What if vendor X ships goods into state B? In none of these situations has vendor X established a physical presence in state B, and so vendor X needs not collect and remit state B's sales and use tax.

Suppose vendor X has its Web site residing on a server (owned and operated by a third party) that is located in state B. Can the physical presence of the server or its owner/operator be attributed to vendor X, thereby making vendor X effectively physically present in state B? Current federal law prohibits such attribution,[29] but even in the absence of that specific law, such attribution would appear to be inappropriate for several reasons. Even though the Web site may fit into the *Scripto* and *Tyler Pipe* "establishing and maintaining the market" category, it would also seem to constitute pure advertising and thus not a predicate for taxation. The bulk of the law in this area provides that general, nontargeted advertising does not even constitute a minimal connection with a state as required for due process purposes,[30] let alone the substantial nexus required for Commerce Clause purposes, and thus for state taxation purposes. Second, the fortuitous presence of the server in state B has absolutely nothing to do with vendor X's establishment and maintenance of a market in state B—*Scripto*'s and *Tyler Pipe*'s focus on the benefit of instate activity helping the instate market (face-to-face marketing) seems to demonstrate that the attribution condoned in those cases would be inappropriate for vendor X with merely a Web site on a server in state B. Those visiting the Website have no idea as to the server's location—the location in state B has absolutely no special effect on customers or potential customers in state B. Finally, the physical presence required by *Quill* must be more than de minimis,[31] and the server's hosting the Web site and the presumably occasional servicing of the Website by the server owner's personnel seem quite minimal.

---

29 Internet Tax Freedom Act Amendments Act of 2007, Pub.L. No. 110-108, § 4 (amending § 1105 (5)(E)("Intenet Access includes a homepage . . .")).

30 Growden v. Ed Bowlin & Assoc., 733 F.2d 1149 (5th Cir. 1984); Montgomery Ward & Co. v. State Board of Equalization, 272 C.A.2d 728 (Cal. Ct. App. 1969); Digital Control Inc. v. Boretronic, Inc., 161 F. Supp.2d 1183 (W.D. Wash. 2001); *see also*, Cybersell Inc. v. Cybersell Inc., 130 F3d 414 (9th Cir. 1997); Core-Vent Corp. v. Nobel Indus. AB, 11 F.3d 1482, 1485 (9th Cir.1993); Bensusan Restaurant Corp. v. King, 937 F. Supp. 295, (S.D.N.Y. 1996); Electronic Broking Services, Limited v. E-Business Solutions & Services, No. JFM-03-1350, 2003 U.S. Dist. LEXIS 17897 (D. Mary. Sept. 30, 2003); Ragonese v. Rosenfeld, 722 A.2d 991 (N.J. Super Ct. 1998); Toys "R" Us Inc. v. Step Two SA, 3rd Cir. No. 01-3390 (Jan. 27, 2003).

31 *Quill, supra* note 21, at 316, n. 8; *see also*, *National Geographic Society*, *supra* note 27.

What if vendor X makes arrangements with another person that maintains a store in state B for that other person to accept returns from (and provide refunds to) vendor X's customers in state B? Are the store's activities sufficient to allow attribution to vendor X? California courts have split on the issue,[32] while a federal district court in Louisiana has answered "no."[33] The facts in these cases were quite similar. Corporations sold books and related items to customers throughout the country who ordered the merchandise from the vendors' Web sites; the purchased items were then mailed or shipped to the customer. The vendors had affiliates (i.e., different legal persons) operating physical brick-and-mortar stores in the taxing state. The state revenue agencies claimed that certain activities conducted by the instate affiliates were performed to assist the vendors in establishing and maintaining their instate markets (the technical statutory arguments in the California cases were a variation on this theme). These activities, which varied in each of the three cases, were engaging in joint advertising, running a common gift card program, giving cash refunds at the stores for returned items that had been purchased from the online vendor, and giving away coupons that advertised the online vendor. The California Board of Equalization ratified its auditors' attribution approaches (affirmed, in one case, by a trial-level court) while the federal district court found that such activities were insufficient to permit an extension of tax jurisdiction over the out-of-state vendors. Although the specific facts adduced in these cases are not identical to those in some slightly older cases,[34] the federal court's conclusion is consistent with all those older cases.

Several states have enacted statutes that specifically seek to impose collection responsibility on out-of-state vendors that have instate brick-and-mortar affiliates;[35] it would seem that such statutes are unconstitutional because they (1) fail to recognize that each legal person must generally be treated separately for jurisdictional purposes[36] and

---

32 *See*, Borders Online, LLC v. State Board of Equalization, 129 Cal. App. 4th 1179 (Cal. Ct. App. 2005); Barnesandnoble.com v. State Bd. of Equalization, No. CGC-06-456465 (Superior Court, San Francisco County, Sept. 7, 2007).

33 St. Tammany Parish Tax Collector v. BarnesandNoble.com, Dkt. No. 05-5695 (E.D. La. 2007).

34 Bloomingdale's By Mail, Ltd. v. Pennsylvania Dep't of Revenue, 130 Pa. Commw. 190, 198, 567 A.2d 773, 778 (1989) *aff'd*, 527 Pa. Commw. 347, 591 A.2d 1047 (1991); SFA Folio Collections, Inc. v. Comm'r, 73 Ohio St. 3d 119 (Ohio 1995); SFA Folio Collections, Inc. v. Bannon, 585 A.2d 666 (Conn. 1991).

35 *See, e.g.*, Washington Rev. Code §§ 82.08.050(7) (2003) and 82.12.040(5) (2005); Ala. Code § 40-23-190 (2003); Ky. Rev. Stat. § 139.340(2)(f) (2005); N.Y. Tax Law § 1101(b)(8)(i)(C)(I) (proposed effective 2008).

36 *See, e.g.*, SFA Folio Collections, Inc. v. Bannon, 217 Conn. 220, 229–31 & 233–34 (1991) (refusing to impute nexus from bricks-and-mortar retailer to mail-order retailer when the retailers were separate corporate entities owned by the same parent company, sharing some directors and officers, using the same trademarks and logos, selling similar merchandise, and sharing financial and market information); *Bloomingdale's By Mail, Ltd., supra* note 34, at 198 (1989) (holding that affiliation alone was insufficient to create nexus); *SFA Folio Collections, Inc., supra* note 34, at 122–23 (Ohio 1995) (rejecting unitary business entity argument that would impute nexus to affiliated, out-of-state seller); Current, Inc. v. State Board of Equalization, 24 Cal.App.4th 382, 391 (Cal. App. 1 Dist. 1994) (holding that nexus could not be imputed between companies that did not have integrated operations or management and were organized as separate and distinct entities); *see also*, The People of the State of New York v. American Bell

(2) go beyond the law as set forth in *Scripto* and *Tyler Pipe* (which cases, the U.S. Supreme Court has said, are the furthest extension of jurisdiction the Court has ever condoned).[37]

Consequently, unless there is a federal law change in connection with the streamlined effort, an out-of-state vendor (one with no physical presence in the state) needs not collect and remit a state's sales and use tax unless there is a physically present person in the state that is helping the vendor to establish and maintain the instate market.

III. TAXABILITY

A. Background

As discussed earlier, sales and use taxes are generally imposed on sales of tangible personal property. "Tangible" is commonly defined as something that can be seen, felt, or touched.[38] What was "tangible" was quite clear and caused little debate until the ownership and use of computers became common.

B. Application to the Digital Environment

As more and more products become digitized and capable of existing solely in electronic form, more and more transactions fall outside the scope of "sales of tangible personal property." Consequently, such transactions are not automatically subject to most states' sales and use taxes. States have taken different paths in responding to this.

For decades, states have treated canned, or prewritten, software as subject to tax as tangible personal property, asserting that once an item of intellectual property becomes commonly sold in tangible form (e.g., a record or a book or canned software), then the purchaser is really purchasing the tangible item. As a next step, many states are looking to the functionality of an item that exists solely in electronic form and, if that functionality is the same as an item that traditionally existed in tangible form, are seeking to tax sales of the item in the same manner as the tangible equivalent. Some states have done this statutorily,[39] some by regulation,[40] and some by audit and litigation.[41]

Telephone Company, 117 N.Y. 241; 22 N.E. 1057 (Ct. App. NY 1889); Procter & Gamble Co. v. Newton, 289 F. 1013 (S.D.N.Y. 1923); United States Rubber Co. v. Query, 19 F.Supp. 191 (E.D.S.C. 1937).

37 *Quill, supra* note 21, at 306.

38 Okla. Stat. § 1352(24) (2007); Utah Code Ann. § 59-12-102 (2008). *See also*, Dine Out Tonight Club, Inc. v. Department of Revenue Services, 210 Conn. 567 (1989); Citizen and Southern Systems, Inc. v. South Carolina Tax Commission, 280 S.C. 138 (1984).

39 N.Y. Tax Law § 1101(b)(6).

40 Idaho Admin. Rules 35.01.02.027(4); La. Admin. Code 61:I.4301 Tangible Personal Property (a)(iv).

41 Graham Packaging Company, LP v. Pennsylvania, 652 F.R. 2002 (Pa. Commw. Ct. 2005).

The streamlined sales tax effort, at its very start, defined tangible personal property to include prewritten software.[42] The Streamlined Governing Board has already adopted uniform definitions for certain types of digital products (digital audio-visual works, digital audio works, and digital books), and others will likely be adopted in the future.[43] There is a great debate, however, as to whether purchases of all items that exist solely in electronic form should be taxable unless specifically exempted by a state legislature or whether a state legislature should be required to impose tax affirmatively on specifically defined items.

Many observers believe that the sales tax bases in most—if not all—states will be expanding to cover more and more services. If this occurs explicitly, then the distinction between tangible items and electronically existing/electronically delivered items will fade in significance.

IV. COMPLIANCE

A. Background

In a traditional retail store setting, the sales tax compliance burden borne by the vendor is generally limited to knowing which items are taxable and which are not; this is often a substantial task. When a vendor has remote customers, the vendor must also know the details of the sales and use tax law in effect where each customer receives the purchased item. For each customer's jurisdiction, the vendor must know what is taxable, who is exempt, the applicable tax rate, return and remittance requirements, and other information relevant to taxation. This is an enormous burden that has been recognized by states,[44] businesses,[45] and even the U.S. Supreme Court.[46]

B. Application to the Digital Environment

The burden imposed on a vendor obviously becomes greater as the number of jurisdictions where customers are located increases. For a vendor that sells via the Internet, the burdens are virtually impossible to bear. Nevertheless, if a vendor has a physical presence in a customer's jurisdiction, either itself or through attribution (as discussed above), it must comply.

---

42 Streamlined Sales Tax Project, Tangible Personal Property Issue Paper, 2 (April 15, 2002), available at http://www.streamlinedsalestax.org/library/TPP%20issue%20paper%204-15-02.pdf.

43 Streamlined Sale and Use Tax Agreement § 332(A) (September 20, 2007).

44 Eighteen states have enacted legislation conforming to the streamlined sales tax, in recognition of and in an effort to ease the compliance burden for vendors.

45 Committee on the Judiciary, Oversight Hearing on the "Streamlined Sales and Use Tax Agreement: States' Efforts to Facilitate Sales Tax Collection from Remote Vendors," Testimony of George S. Isaacson, Esq., Tax Counsel for the Direct Marketing Association, October 1, 2003.

46 *Quill, supra* note 21, at 313, n. 6.

Fortunately, a number of companies offer systems and services to assist the vendor in meeting such burdens. The Streamlined States Tax Governing Board certifies certain service providers and certain software so that a vendor utilizing such a service or software has only limited exposure for errors in the collection and remittance activities related to states that are members of the governing board.

V. CONCLUSION

Sales and use tax laws were developed to tax sales of tangible personal property and locally delivered services. The dramatic growth of the digital environment has put a great strain on these tax systems. State and local governments, as well as businesses throughout the country, are working to address the many issues that have been raised. Only time will tell whether sales and use taxes—and those who administer them—are flexible enough to allow such taxes to survive as major revenue sources for state and local governments.

Chapter 29

United States: State Income and Franchise Taxes in the Digital Environment

Arthur R. Rosen
McDermott Will & Emery LLP

I. INTRODUCTION TO CYBERSPACE REALITY

It is difficult—if not impossible—to read the state and local tax press or attend state and local tax programs without being presented with various thoughts and analyses regarding the manner in which a business engaged in one of the various aspects of electronic commerce is being or should be taxed. Although it is safe to assume that the significance of e-commerce to our economy will only continue to increase, and while such significance will certainly cause even more dislocations in state taxing systems than we have already witnessed, numerous state tax issues are clearly "in play" today and require current reactions. It is in this context that this chapter discusses certain fundamental state income, franchise, and business activity tax principles and examines their application to e-commerce in the current legal environment.

A. Defining E-Commerce

To analyze the correct application of state and local tax principles to transactions in the digital environment, it is important first to understand what the digital environment is. The best approach is to view the area as being composed of four segments. First, and the most prevalent today, is the ordering of tangible personal property through electronic or digital channels, such as using a home computer to access, over the Internet, a company's Web site to order a shirt that is delivered by mail or common carrier. Second is the ordering and receipt of digitized products through electronic channels, such as using the Internet to download a music album or receiving, over the Internet, a service that affects your computer. The third area of concern in the digital environment is the receipt of tangible personal property through electronic channels.[1] Fourth, the mere use of electronic channels, irrespective of the object of the communication, is an integral part of the digital environment and, hence, telecommunications may itself need to be considered.

B. The Players

Most of today's unaddressed state tax issues in this chapter focus on Internet-related transactions, which can involve several different actors. Companies that provide access to the Internet are called Internet service providers (ISPs); they provide either a direct link from a user's computer to an Internet connection or from a telecommunications "point of presence" to an Internet connection. Companies that provide electronic access of their own proprietary databases to customers are called online service providers. Content Providers are companies that provide information and services over the Internet or over proprietary subscriber networks. Hardware and software companies provide the physical structure, the technology, and the programs for connecting to and for navigating the Internet. For example, a telephone company may maintain the telephone lines through which a customer may connect to an ISP and through which the ISP routes communications to and from the Internet. Software companies provide programs that, once installed on a computer, help search the Internet and provide for downloading capabilities. In the provision of these various services, companies can, and often do, provide more than one of the above-mentioned services.

C. The Role of Telecommunications

Accompanying the past few years' explosive growth in the provision of Internet services has been a great change in the methods used to provide telecommunication services. The most significant change in this area may be due to the growth of wireless telecommunications services and voice over Internet protocol (VoIP). One example of such telecommunications services is paging or text-messaging services—one-sided communication wherein either a telephone number or a message is relayed to an individual from a person who is trying to contact such individual. In the provision of such paging/text-messaging services, the paging company will receive the message and then relay it to all its sites to which the individual has subscribed, whether or not the individual is there.

Another example of such wireless telecommunications services is cellular telecommunications services. The provision of cellular services is the provision of telecommunication services wherein the individual can both place and receive transmissions from a cellular telephone. While radio transmissions are utilized for the

---

1 Technically speaking, this is currently available only through the use of fictional replicators, such as those onboard Starship Enterprise or Starship Voyager, but at present this issue may also come into play depending upon how a state chooses to define tangible personal property.

ultimate connection with the cellular telephone, landline and Public Switched Network (PSN) facilities are often used also.

Furthermore, another newer telecommunication service is the provision of digital services. By using digital technology instead of analog technology, it is possible to send more information, which results in clearer transmissions. With digital technology, information is converted into numbers and then can be sent anywhere and reconverted when it reaches its destination. (The Internet uses digitized information.) With the onset of digital technology, it is possible to send many different types of information at the same time, such as sound and pictures.

There has been a general agreement throughout the state tax community that in taxing telecommunications, there should be an effort to separate "conduit" activities from "content" activities or, in other words, to keep the "media" separate from the "message." However, this is getting increasingly difficult as the distinction between telecommunication providers, ISP, online service providers, and hardware and software companies becomes increasingly blurred and as bundled pricing schemes become more prevalent. Furthermore, telecommunications companies have their own issues—apart from those that arise from computer-related transactions—concerning the provision of pure telecommunications using new technologies, such as issues that arise in the provision of paging and cellular telecommunication services.

D. Today's Issues

While policy makers and economists might argue that "economically equivalent" transactions should bear identical tax consequences, statutes are usually not as vague as to mandate that "economically equivalent" transactions be subject to tax.

The most significant issue in the area of corporate income and franchise tax focuses on nexus. More specifically, the relevant issue is when an entity has nexus with a state such that it is subject to the state's corporate income/franchise or other "business activity" tax. In examining this issue, it will be necessary to look not only at constitutional principles but also at the provisions of Public Law 86-272.

Another important issue in the digital environment concerns the sourcing of electronic transactions for purposes of both apportioning a corporate income/franchise tax and for determining where a transaction has occurred for purposes of the sales and use tax. This area is of growing importance, especially as states are coming to rely more and more on the receipts factor of the apportionment formula. Generally, in sourcing receipts for purposes of the receipts factor, services are sourced according to the cost of performance, and sales of property are sourced to the destination of the property sold. Thus, if an electronic transaction is considered to be the provision of a service, it should be sourced to where the seller's employees are performing the relevant service. If an electronic transaction is considered to be the sale of intangible property, the sale should be sourced to where the intangible property is delivered, which could be either at the site where the vendor delivers the property to the Internet or the site where the customer receives it.[2] It is, of course, not always clear as to whether an electronic transaction is a sale of property or the provision of a service. This issue—situsing—will not be discussed in this chapter.

II. LEGAL BACKGROUND/FRAMEWORK[3]

A. Nexus/Taxability

Under fundamental constitutional principles, in order to impose a tax upon a taxpayer or impose a duty to collect tax upon such entity, the tax must satisfy the requirements of the Due Process Clause and the Commerce Clause. Furthermore, before a state can impose a tax upon an entity, the requirements of P.L. 86-272 must be satisfied.

1. Due Process Clause The Due Process Clause specifies that no "State [shall] deprive any person of life, liberty, or property, without due process of law."[4] In interpreting this provision, the U.S. Supreme Court stated that the Due Process Clause of the U.S. Constitution requires only that a corporation have "minimum contacts" with the taxing state.[5] The intent of the Due Process Clause is to ensure fairness and to give notice to those who could be subject to tax.[6] The presence in a state that is necessary to satisfy the Due Process Clause is "comparable to" that needed to support a state court's jurisdiction over a defendant in a civil matter.[7] This civil in personam standard is met if the entity purposefully directs its activity into a jurisdiction.[8] The Due Process Clause does not require physical presence in the taxing state.[9]

In *World-Wide Volkswagen Corp. v. Woodson*, the U.S. Supreme Court affirmed the principle that, in a civil matter, the minimum contacts with the forum state must come as a result of the defendant's own action and not as a result of unilateral actions by the plaintiff.[10] A corporation can be sued in a state, under the Due Process Clause, when the corporation "delivers its products into the stream of commerce with the expectation that they will be purchased by consumers in the forum state," because the defendant's conduct and connection with the forum state are such that it should "reasonably anticipate being hauled into court there."[11] However, in *Asahi Metal Industry Co., Ltd. v. Superior Court of California*, the Supreme Court's plurality decision specified that "the placement of a product into the stream of commerce, without more, is not an act

---

2 Sales of tangible personal property ordered over the Internet raise no new issues.

3 Cognoscenti may wish to skip this section and proceed to section III, "Internet Taxability Implications."

4 U.S. Const. amend. XIV, § 1.

5 Quill Corp. v. North Dakota, 504 U.S. 298, 307 (1992).

6 *Id.* at 312.

7 *Id.* at 307–8.

8 *Id.*; Burger King v. Rudzewicz, 471 U.S. 462, 476 (1985).

9 *Burger King, supra* note 9.

10 World-Wide Volkswagen Corp. v. Woodson, 444 U.S. 286 (1980).

11 *Id.* at 298.

of the defendant purposefully directed toward the forum State. . . . [A] defendant's awareness that the stream of commerce may, or will sweep the product into the forum State does not convert the mere act of placing the product into the stream into an act purposefully directed toward the forum State."[12]

2. Commerce Clause In addition to meeting the requirements of the Due Process Clause, a tax must meet the requirements of the Commerce Clause. The Commerce Clause specifies that "[t]he Congress shall have the power . . . [t]o regulate commerce . . . among the several States."[13] In *Quill Corp. v. North Dakota*, the U.S. Supreme Court specified that the Commerce Clause requires that a corporate taxpayer (or tax collector, in the case of use taxes) have "substantial nexus" with the taxing state.[14] Furthermore, the Court determined that a corporation "may have the 'minimum contacts' with a taxing State as required by the Due Process Clause, and yet lack the 'substantial nexus' with that State as required by the Commerce Clause."[15] Finally, the Court held that, in the area of use tax collection, the substantial nexus standard would be met by physical presence; in other words, a corporation must be physically present in a state for that state constitutionally to impose collection responsibilities upon the corporation.[16] The degree of presence in a state necessary to satisfy the Commerce Clause is uncertain with respect to the imposition of gross receipts, income, and franchise taxes, and state courts have split on whether the standard should be the same in the context of imposing a tax directly on a person—as compared to merely imposing a duty to collect a tax from others.[17] The Supreme Court has declined to resolve the issue.[18]

If physical presence is the standard, as the U.S. Supreme Court determined for sales tax purposes in *Quill*, then how much physical presence is enough to warrant taxation? Clearly, a de minimis presence, such as a very small amount of property in a state, is not enough.[19] There are no cases that provide de minimis guidelines in the income tax realm. However, if the same standard should apply to all types of taxes, then the state court opinions regarding what constitutes a de minimis presence for sales and use tax purposes provide some guidance as to how much activity a state considers to be enough to satisfy the U.S. Constitution.

---

12 Asahi Metal Industry Co., Ltd. v. Superior Court of California, 480 U.S. 102 (1987).

13 U.S. Const. art. I, § 8, Cl. 3.

14 *Quill, supra* note 5, at 311.

15 *Id.*, at 305–6.

16 *Id.*, at 317–18.

17 *See*, Geoffrey, Inc. v. South Carolina Tax Comm'n, 437 S.E.2d 13 (S.C. 1993), *cert. denied*, 510 U.S. 992 (1993), Lanco, Inc. v. Dir., Div. of Taxation, 980 A.2d 176 (N.J. 2006), *cert. denied*, 127 S. Ct. 2974 (June 18, 2007), Tax Comm'r of West Virginia v. FIA Card Services f/k/a MBNA America Bank, N.A., 2006 W. Va. LEXIS 132 (2006), *cert. denied*, 127 S.Ct. 2997 (June 18, 2007), J.C. Penney Nat'l Bank v. Johnson, 19 S.W.3d 831, 839 (Tenn. Ct. App. 1999); *see also*, National Geographic Society v. California Board of Equalization, 430 U.S. 551 (1977), regarding support for the argument that a greater nexus standard is appropriate when a tax is being imposed, rather than merely a tax collection responsibility.

18 510 U.S. 992 (1993); 127 S. Ct. 2974 (June 18, 2007); 127 S.Ct. 2997 (June 18, 2007).

19 *See, Quill, supra* note 5 (a few floppy diskettes were not enough to warrant tax collection obligations).

In *Goldberg v. Sweet*, the U.S. Supreme Court determined the constitutionality of a tax imposed by the state of Illinois on the provision of telecommunications services.[20] In this case, although the Court sustained Illinois' tax on interstate calls that were (1) originated or terminated in Illinois and (2) charged to an Illinois service address or billed or paid within Illinois, the Court further stated "[w]e doubt that States through which the telephone call's electronic signals merely pass have a sufficient nexus to tax that call. We also doubt that termination of an interstate telephone call, by itself, provides a substantial enough nexus for a State to tax a call."[21] In *Florida Department of Revenue v. Share International, Inc.*, the Florida Supreme Court determined that a corporation did not have substantial nexus with Florida for purposes of collecting sales tax on its mail-order sales into Florida.[22] The corporation manufactured and distributed chiropractic supplies and sold its products through direct mail. For three days every year, the corporation's president and vice president were speakers and coordinators at a national seminar in Florida, at which seminar the corporation's products were displayed and sold (sales tax was collected on these in-state sales). The Florida Supreme Court determined that the corporation did not have substantial nexus with Florida and, thus, could not be compelled to collect and remit use tax on mail-order sales to Florida residents.[23]

In *Care Computer Systems, Inc. v. Arizona Department of Revenue*, the Arizona Board of Tax Appeals determined that a company did not have nexus with Arizona sufficient for imposition of the transaction privilege tax.[24] In *Care*, the company sold and leased computer systems to nursing homes. The board determined that "[a] business whose contacts within Arizona are a one day salesperson visit per year, 21 days per year visits by non-resident training personnel and two personal computers subject to a short term lease purchase agreement, does not have a constitutionally sufficient nexus for the application of the transaction privilege tax."[25]

In addition to nexus that is caused by an entity's own activities, a commonly arising issue is that nexus will be caused by the activities of a related entity. The U.S. Supreme Court has also held that the same standard for attributing the instate activities of a related party applies with regard to both sales and use taxes and income and franchise taxes.[26]

In *Bloomingdale's by Mail, Ltd. v. Pennsylvania Dept. of Rev.*, the Pennsylvania Commonwealth Court determined that a corporation did not have nexus due to the activities of its affiliate and thus did not have an obligation to collect use tax on the

---

20 Goldberg v. Sweet, 488 U.S. 252 (1989).

21 *Id.* at 263.

22 Florida Department of Revenue v. Share International, Inc., 676 So.2d 1362 (Fla. 1996), *cert. denied*, 117 S.Ct. 685 (1997).

23 *Id.*

24 Care Computer Systems, Inc. v. Arizona Department of Revenue, 1995 Ariz. Tax LEXIS 24 (Apr. 4, 1995).

25 *Id.*

26 Scripto, Inc. v. Carson, 362 U.S. 207 (1960); *see also,* Tyler Pipe Indust. v. Washington, 483 U.S. 232 (1987) (applying same approach in the context of a direct tax liability).

shipment of goods into Pennsylvania.[27] In *Bloomingdale's By Mail*, the corporation's only connection with Pennsylvania was the solicitation of sales through catalogs mailed into Pennsylvania from outside of the state and the shipment of goods into Pennsylvania from outside of the state. Substantial nexus was not found through the presence of an affiliate that maintained retail stores in Pennsylvania because the stores "do not solicit orders on [the catalog company's] behalf nor act as its agents in any fashion and [the catalog company] does not solicit orders for [the in-state stores]."[28] The only connections between the catalog company and the stores were two documented instances where a catalog item was returned to a store in Pennsylvania—even though the catalog specified that items should be returned only by mail—and the fact that the catalogs and the stores used the same advertising themes.[29]

In a similar case, the Supreme Court of Ohio came to a similar conclusion.[30] In *SFA Folio*, the court determined that a corporation that sold goods to Ohio residents through catalogs that were shipped to customers from outside of Ohio did not have substantial nexus with Ohio, due to the presence in Ohio of an affiliate that maintained several stores in Ohio, and thus did not have an obligation to collect Ohio use tax. The court held that the catalog corporation did not maintain a place of business in Ohio merely because its affiliated corporation maintained retail stores in Ohio, since the affiliated corporation did not sell any merchandise for the catalog corporation. In addition, the fact that the affiliated corporation accepted some returns from products that had been purchased through the catalog and distributed the catalogs at its stores did not create the substantial nexus required under the Commerce Clause.

In *Current, Inc. v. California State Board of Equalization*, a California Court of Appeals determined that a corporation did not have sufficient nexus with California such that it was forced to collect California's use tax on sales of goods shipped into California merely because it was acquired by a corporation that did have nexus with California; there was no agency relationship between the two entities.[31]

Another issue that arises in determining whether an entity has nexus for tax purposes with a state is whether nexus can be created through the activities of unrelated parties. For example, in *Service Merchandise Company, Inc. v. Arizona Department of Revenue*, the Arizona Court of Appeals determined that Arizona could impose use tax on the taxpayer due to catalogs that were sent into Arizona by an out-of-state printer because the taxpayer had sufficient nexus with Arizona to satisfy Commerce Clause principles.[32] The taxpayer "determined that Arizona households would receive the catalogs and fliers and directed that they be sent into Arizona. The purpose of

---

27 Bloomingdale's By Mail, Ltd. v. Pennsylvania Dept. of Rev., 130 Pa. Commw. 190, 567 A.2d 773 (Pa. Commw. Ct. 1989).

28 *Id.* at 198.

29 *Id.*

30 SFA Folio Collections, Inc. v. Tracy, 73 Ohio St.3d 119, 1995 Ohio LEXIS 1757 (S. Ct. Ohio, 1995).

31 Current, Inc. v. California State Board of Equalization, 24 Cal. App. 4th 382, 1994 Cal. App. LEXIS 349 (Ct. App. Cal. 1994).

32 Service Merchandise Company, Inc. v. Arizona Department of Revenue, 937 P.2d 336, 1996 Ariz. App. LEXIS 215, (Ariz. Ct. App. 1996).

sending the catalogs into Arizona was to encourage Arizona residents either to shop in one of the [taxpayer's] two . . . stores in Arizona or to order goods by mail. Although it only has two stores in Arizona, its presence is not so minimal that the nexus between Arizona and [the taxpayer's] efforts to distribute catalogs and fliers in [Arizona] is insubstantial."[33] The court implicitly found that the U.S. Postal Service, when conducting its activities in Arizona, was the agent of the out-of-state shipper and thus attributed those instate activities to the out-of-state shipper. Although this was a finding that the out-of-state shipper conducted activities in the state for purposes of determining whether it used the property in the state, it is not dissimilar from attributing nexus.

In a similar case involving the attribution of activities (but not nexus), the Maryland Tax Court determined that a taxpayer was subject to the imposition of use tax in Maryland on advertising flyers that were sent into Maryland from out of state by the printer of the flyers, even though the flyers advertised the services and goods of the taxpayer's clients, not of the taxpayer.[34] The tax court specified that the taxpayer (1) was involved in the provision of advertising services, which were primarily carried out through the mailings; (2) determined the mailing zones for the advertisements; (3) provided the artwork for the advertisements; (4) ordered the printing; (5) directed the distribution and reserved the mail date for the advertisements; and (6) provided the out-of-state printer with the mailing labels for each envelope.

Finally, several courts in different states, when dealing with similar fact patterns concerning the activities of teachers in connection with the sales of books to students, have come up with differing conclusions regarding the attribution of nexus. In *Matter of Scholastic Book Clubs Inc.*, the Kansas Supreme Court determined that the taxpayer was required to collect Kansas sales tax on book orders due to the activities of teachers in Kansas on behalf of the taxpayer.[35] The taxpayer was a mail-order children's bookseller that sent catalogs to schoolteachers who then distributed the catalogs to their students and collected and submitted the orders to the taxpayer. In return for their activities on behalf of the taxpayer, the teachers received bonus merchandise for the student purchases. The Kansas Supreme Court determined that the teachers were the taxpayer's implied agents because the teachers acted under the taxpayer's authority in selling the books. Cases addressing the same issue with the same fact pattern (and coming to different conclusions) include *Scholastic Book Clubs v. State Bd. of Equalization,*[36] *Pledger v. Troll Book Clubs*,[37] and *Troll Book Clubs v. Tracy*.[38]

---

33 *Id.* at 341.

34 Val-Pak Direct Mail Promotions of Maryland, Inc. v. Comptroller of the Treasury, Sales Tax Nos. 859, 860, and 861, 1996 Md. Tax LEXIS 7 (Md. T.C. 1996).

35 Matter of Scholastic Book Clubs Inc., 1996 Kan. LEXIS 117 (Kansas Sup. Ct., July 12, 1996).

36 Scholastic Book Clubs v. State Bd. of Equalization, 207 Cal. App. 3d 734, 255 Cal. Rptr. 77 (1980) (once a publisher accepted an order submitted by a teacher, the publisher ratified the teacher's authority to act on its behalf and an agency relationship was created).

37 Pledger v. Troll Book Clubs, 316 Ark. 195, 871 S.W.2d 389 (1994) (no agency relationship existed—and thus no nexus was created—because there was a lack of the requisite control).

38 Troll Book Clubs v. Tracy, Ohio Bd. of Tax App., Case No. 92-Z-590 (Aug. 19, 1994) (the teachers were not controlled by the publishing company, and thus no nexus was created).

Those states that have limited the physical presence requirement to the sales and use tax arena tend to employ a variation of the "economic nexus" theme when it comes to income/franchise taxes. Under an economic nexus standard, an out-of-state company is deemed to have nexus with a jurisdiction merely by receiving income from within the state, usually from licensing fees relating to intangible assets or from the presence of customers in the state.[39]

The relatively recent New Jersey Supreme Court decision in *Lanco, Inc. v. Director, Division of Taxation*[40] is quite significant. The court in *Lanco* addressed the question of whether "New Jersey may constitutionally subject a foreign corporation to the corporation business tax when the corporation lacks physical presence in New Jersey but derives income through a licensing agreement with a company conducting retail operations in New Jersey," and the court answered in the affirmative. While all of the passive investment company cases relied upon by the court involved situations in which a foreign company was subjected to tax because its intangible property (marketing intangibles) was used in the state in such a way as to become an integral part of the licensee's business in the state, the actual holding of *Lanco* presents an even lower threshold: deriving income from licensing fees attributable to New Jersey is sufficient to justify tax imposition. Unlike previous intangibles cases, the court required no proof that the intangible property was integral to an instate business, no proof that the intangible property was used in New Jersey, and no proof that the licensor and licensee were related; rather, evidence that the income was derived from licensing fees attributable to the state was sufficient.[41]

The economic nexus doctrine first arose in situations involving "abusive" out-of-state passive investment companies,[42] but it is now being applied in many other situations,

---

Also, for a more comprehensive discussion on attributional issues, *see* Rosen, *Jurisdictional Limitations: Attributional Nexus*, 1430 Tax Management Portfolio.

39 *See, e.g.,* Geoffrey, Inc. v. Commissioner of Revenue, Mass. A.T.B. Dkt. No. C271816 (Mass. App. Tax. Bd. July 24, 2007); Praxair Technology, Inc. v. Division of Taxation, Letter Decision Tax Ct. Dkt. No. 007445-05 (June 18, 2007) (appeal pending); Lanco, Inc. v. Director, New Jersey Division of Revenue, 908 A.2d 176 (2006), *cert. denied*, 127 S. Ct. 2974 (June 18, 2007); Geoffrey, Inc. v. Oklahoma Tax Commission, 132 P.3d 632 (Okla. Ct. App. 2005); Department of Revenue v. Gap (Apparel), Inc., 886 So.2d 459 (La. Ct. App. 2004); Acme Royalty Company v. Director of Revenue, 96 S.W.3d 72 (Mo. 2002); Geoffrey, Inc. v. South Carolina Tax Commission, 437 S.E.2d 13, *cert. denied*, 510 U.S. 992 (1993); J.C. Penney Nat'l Bank v. Johnson, 19 S.W.3d 831 (Tenn. Ct. App. 1999); Tax Commissioner v. FIA Card Services, N.A. (f/k/a MBNA America Bank, N.A.), 640 S.E.2d 226 (W.V. Sup. Ct., 2006), *cert. denied*, 127 S.Ct. 2997 (June 18, 2007).

40 Lanco, Inc. v. Director, Division of Taxation, 908 A.2d 176 (N.J. 2006), *aff'g*, 879 A.2d 1234 (N.J. Super. App. Div. 2005), *rev'g*, 21 N.J. Tax Ct. 200 (N.J. Tax Ct. 2003), *cert. denied*, 127 S. Ct. 2974 (June 18, 2007).

41 *See also* Praxair Technology, Inc. v. Division of Taxation, Letter Decision, N.J. Tax Dkt. No. 007445-05 (June 18, 2007) (appeal pending) (allowing imposition of tax on out-of-state company who licensed patents for use in New Jersey).

42 *See, e.g.* Bridges v. Geoffrey, Inc., La. Ct. App. (1st Cir.) Dkt. No. 2007 CA 1063 (Feb. 8, 2008), A & F Trademark, Inc. v. Tolson, 605 S.E.2d 187 (N.C. Ct. App. 2004), *cert. denied*, 126 S. Ct. 353 (2005), Dep't of Revenue v. Gap (Apparel), Inc., 886 So. 2d 459 (La. Ct. App.

including ordinary third-party licensing arrangements and the provision of intangible property or services to customers.[43]

3. P.L. 86-272 In addition to the constitutional provisions that determine when a state can impose tax upon an entity, states are prohibited from imposing income tax (or a tax measured by income) upon an entity—due to a federal statute—unless certain requirements are met. Under this provision,

> no State, or political subdivision thereof, shall have power to impose, for any taxable year . . . , a net income tax on the income derived from within such State by any person from interstate commerce if the only business activities within such State by or on behalf of such person during such taxable year are either, or both, of the following:
> (1) the solicitation of orders by such person, or his representative, in such State for sales of tangible personal property, which orders are sent outside the State for approval or rejection, and, if approved, are filled by shipment or delivery from a point outside the State; and
> (2) the solicitation of orders by such person, or his representative, in such State in the name of or for the benefit of a prospective customer of such person, if orders by such customer to such person to enable such customer to fill orders resulting from such solicitation are orders described in paragraph (1).[44]

This statute only works to grant protection in very certain circumstances and only against the imposition of taxes on or measured by income; relief from the imposition of a sales and use tax or a non-income-based franchise tax or a duty to collect sales or use tax can only arise from constitutional principles (or, of course, state constitutional, statutory, regulatory, or case law authority). Public Law 86-272 protection applies only to interstate commerce. Under this statute, (1) the only permissible business activity in a state is solicitation of orders of tangible personal property, (2) approval or rejection of such orders must occur outside of the state, and (3) the property to fulfill such orders must be shipped or delivered from outside of the state. In making the determination whether an entity's activities fall under such protection, the activities of independent contractors are distinguished from the activities of employees. "Even if engaged in exclusively to facilitate requests for purchases, [however,] the maintenance of

---

2004), and Geoffrey Inc. v. South Carolina Tax Comm'n, 437 S.E.2d 13 (S.C. Sup. 1993), *cert. denied*, 510 U.S. 992 (1993).

43 In *Tax Comm'r of West Virginia v. MBNA America Bank, N.A.*, 640 S.E.2d 226 (W. Va. 2006), *cert. denied*, 127 S.Ct. 2997 (June 18, 2007) the court established a new "significant economic presence" standard. This newly crafted standard looks to the due process requirement of purposeful direction and measures the degree of those contacts. The degree is measured by the frequency, quantity, and systematic nature of the taxpayer's economic contacts in the state. While the court pointed toward the systematic and continuous nature of MBNA's direct-mail and telephone solicitation in the state, it also noted the company's gross receipts of US$8–10 million, thus satisfying its own economic presence standard.

44 P.L. 86-272, 15 U.S.C. § 381 (1959).

an office within the State, by the company or on its behalf, would go beyond the 'solicitation of orders.'"[45]

In *Wisconsin Dep't of Revenue v. William Wrigley, Jr., Co.*, the U.S. Supreme Court determined whether a company had engaged in more than solicitation in Wisconsin, thus forfeiting its protection from the imposition of income tax in the state.[46] The Court held that the demarcation between protected solicitation and other activities is the "clear line . . . between those activities that are entirely ancillary to requests for purchases—those that serve no independent business function apart from their connection to the soliciting of orders—and those activities that the company would have reason to engage in any way but chooses to allocate to its in-state sales force."[47] The Court further held that even though the provision of a car and free samples to local salespeople is protected "because the only reason to do it is to facilitate requests for purchases," the servicing of goods in the state by salespeople would not be protected solicitation "since there is good reason to get that done whether or not the company has a sales force."[48]

In *Wrigley*, the U.S. Supreme Court did note that there was a de minimis exception to the rule that any activities in the state beyond solicitation would forfeit Public Law 86-272 protection.[49] The Court refused to accept Wisconsin's claim that the use of the term "only" in Public Law 86-272 means that *any* activities beyond solicitation may result in taxation.[50] Instead, the Court applied the de minimis principle and found that "whether in-state activity other than 'solicitation of orders,' is sufficiently *de minimis* to avoid loss of the tax immunity conferred by Section 381 depends upon whether that activity establishes a nontrivial additional connection with the taxing State."[51]

B. Sourcing

In addition to the question of whether a state can impose a tax or a duty to collect tax on an entity, another issue that must be considered is the sourcing of the income or activities on which the tax is being imposed. Under the Due Process Clause, a state can tax *only* that portion of the corporation's income that is fairly apportioned to the state.[52] Furthermore, under the Commerce Clause, four requirements must be met before a state tax will be said to meet the Commerce Clause requirements: (1) the activity being taxed must have substantial nexus with the taxing state, (2) the tax must be fairly apportioned, (3) the tax must not discriminate against interstate commerce, and (4) the tax must be fairly related to the services provided by the state.[53] The first requirement—the nexus requirement—was discussed above. The second requirement makes

45 P.L. 86-272 § 381(c).

46 Wisconsin Dep't of Revenue v. William Wrigley, Jr., Co., 505 U.S. 214 (1992).

47 *Id.* at 228.

48 *Id.* at 229.

49 *Id.* at 231.

50 *Id.*

51 *Id.* at 232.

52 Allied Signal, Inc. v. Director, 504 U.S. 768, 778; 112 S.Ct. 2251 (1992).

53 Complete Auto Transit, Inc. v. Brady, 430 U.S. 274 (1977).

it clear that a tax must be fairly apportioned before it can be said to satisfy the Commerce Clause. In determining whether a tax is fairly apportioned, two tests are used: (1) the internal consistency test and (2) the external consistency test.[54] A tax (1) will pass the internal consistency test when no multiple taxation would result if every state imposed an identical tax to the tax being evaluated and (2) will pass the external consistency test when a state taxes only that portion of the revenues from interstate activities that reasonably reflects the instate component of such activities.[55]

In *Standard Oil Co. v. Peck*, the U.S. Supreme Court held that Ohio, the state of domicile of the taxpayer, could not impose a personal property tax on the full value of several boats and barges owned by the taxpayer because the vessels were operating in waters of other states and thus could be subject to tax in such other states.[56] "The rule which permits taxation by two or more states on an apportionment basis precludes taxation of all of the property by the state of domicile. Otherwise, there would be multiple taxation of interstate operations and the tax would have no relation to the opportunities, benefits, or protection which the taxing state gives those operations."[57]

The U.S. Supreme Court has also held that, once it has been determined that income may be apportioned to one or more states, no state should be able to impose a tax on all of the taxpayer's income.[58] "In order to prevent multiple taxation of interstate commerce, this Court has required that taxes be apportioned among taxing jurisdictions, so that no instrumentality of commerce is subjected to more than one tax on its full value. The corollary of the apportionment principle, of course, is that no jurisdiction may tax the instrumentality in full."[59] Furthermore, the state of a corporation's domicile does not have the exclusive right to tax intangible property owned by the corporation.[60] "'The reason for a single place of taxation no longer obtains' when the taxpayer's activities with respect to the intangible property involve relations with more than one jurisdiction."[61]

In *Goldberg*, in addition to approving the specific taxing structure at issue, the U.S. Supreme Court acknowledged that the structure of taxation must be adapted for changes in technology.[62] More specifically, the Supreme Court, in upholding Illinois' scheme for taxation of telephone services in *Goldberg*, stated that "it [is] significant that Illinois' method of taxation is a realistic legislative solution to the technology of the

---

54 Goldberg v. Sweet, 488 U.S. 252 (1988).

55 *Id.* at 261–65.

56 Standard Oil Co. v. Peck, 342 U.S. 382; 72 S.Ct. 309 (1952).

57 The Supreme Court decided *Standard Oil* under the Due Process Clause of the Constitution even though the Court's opinion clearly addresses Commerce Clause concerns. *See,* Walter Hellerstein, *State Taxation of Corporate Income from Intangibles: Allied-Signal and Beyond*, 48 Tax L. Rev. 739, 805 n.355 (1993).

58 Japan Line, Ltd. v. County of Los Angeles, 441 U.S. 434, 447 (1979).

59 *Id.*

60 Mobil Oil Corp. v. Commissioner of Taxes of Vermont, 445 U.S. 425; 100 S.Ct. 1223 (1980).

61 *Id.* at 445 (citing, Curry v. McCanless, 307 U.S. 357, 367 (1939)).

62 *Goldberg*, 488 U.S. 252.

present-day telecommunications industry."[63] By virtue of the Court's language in *Goldberg*, it is clear that the Court supports the evolution of the taxing system to accommodate new technology.

III. INTERNET TAXABILITY IMPLICATIONS

A. Due Process Issues

In determining whether a state can impose tax or a duty to collect tax upon an entity under the Due Process Clause, nontax civil cases in which the Due Process Clause has been applied to situations involving the Internet are helpful because, as noted above, the Due Process nexus standard for state tax purposes is "comparable" to the standard for nontax civil cases. In *CompuServe, Inc. v. Patterson*, the Sixth Circuit Court of Appeals determined that Ohio had personal jurisdiction over the defendant because the defendant "knowingly made an effort—and, in fact, purposefully contracted—to market a product in other states, with [the] Ohio-based [plaintiff] operating, in effect, as his distribution center.[64] Thus, it is reasonable to subject [the defendant] to suit in Ohio, the state which is home to the computer network service he chose to employ."[65] In coming to this conclusion, the court noted that the defendant purposefully availed himself of the privilege of doing business in Ohio. He "took actions that created a connection with Ohio. . . . He subscribed to [the plaintiff's network] service, and then he entered into the Shareware Registration Agreement [with the plaintiff] when he loaded his software onto the [plaintiff's] system for others to use and, perhaps, purchase. Once [the defendant] had done those two things, he was on notice that he had made contracts, to be governed by Ohio law, with an Ohio-based company. Then, he repeatedly sent his computer software, via electronic links, to the [defendant's] system in Ohio, and he advertised that software on the [defendant's] system. Moreover, he initiated the events that led to the filing of this suit by making demands of [the defendant] via electronic and regular mail messages."[66]

The court in *Compuserve* specifically stated that it was not opining on other factual situations. For instance, the court explicitly did not hold that the defendant "would be subject to suit in any state where his software was purchased or used," or that he would be subject to suit "by another party from a third state to sue [the defendant] in Ohio for, say, a 'computer virus' caused by his software," or that the plaintiff could "sue any regular subscriber to its service for nonpayment in Ohio."[67]

In *The Hearst Corporation v. Goldberger*, a district court in the Southern District of New York determined that New York did not have personal jurisdiction over the defendant when the defendant's only contact with New York, prior to the litigation, was

---

63 *Id.* at 265.

64 CompuServe, Inc. v. Patterson, 89 F.3d 1257, 1996 U.S. App. LEXIS 17837 (6th Cir. 1996).

65 *Id.* at 1263.

66 *Id.*at 1264.

67 *Id.* at 1268.

the establishment of a Web site that could be accessed by people all over the world, including New York, because the defendant was not transacting business in New York.[68] The defendant had established his Web site *but did not yet have any services or products to sell* and thus *had not yet sold any services or products to individuals in New York,* although the defendant's Web site *had been accessed by people from New York*, in addition to people from other states and other countries. Defendant's "Internet web site thus is most analogous to an advertisement in a national magazine. Like such an ad, [defendant's] Internet web site may be viewed by people in all fifty states (and all over the world too for that matter), but it is not targeted at the residents of New York or any other particular state. . . . New York law is clear, however, that advertisements in national publications are not sufficient to provide personal jurisdiction. . . . Even advertisements targeted at the New York market have been found to be insufficient."[69] After the litigation had commenced, the defendant sent e-mails to and received e-mails from New York. Since these were sent and received after the commencement of litigation, they were not relevant in determining whether New York had personal jurisdiction over the defendant. In any event, the court noted that the e-mails were the equivalent of letters or telephone calls and were insufficient to provide New York with personal jurisdiction over the defendant.

In another case, a district court in the Southern District of New York determined that New York did not have personal jurisdiction over a defendant, for purposes of the Due Process Clause, when the defendant's only connection with New York was the establishment of a Web site that could be accessed from anywhere, including from New York.[70] In this case, the defendant's Web site listed a number that could be called to order tickets at the defendant's club, but the tickets could not be ordered through the Web site. In addition, any tickets ordered would have to be picked up at the defendant's club in Missouri because the defendant would not mail the tickets to purchasers. The defendant "simply created a Web site and permitted anyone who could find it to access it. Creating a site, like placing a product into the stream of commerce, may be felt nationwide—or even worldwide—but, without more, it is not an act purposefully directed toward the forum state. There are no allegations that [the defendant] actively sought to encourage New Yorkers to access his site, or that he conducted any business—let alone a continuous and systematic part of its business—in New York."[71] While this decision was affirmed by the Court of Appeals, the Court of Appeals did not reach this Due Process argument because it decided that New York did not have jurisdiction over the defendant under New York's long-arm statute.[72]

In Connecticut, a District Court came to a different conclusion when it determined that Connecticut had personal jurisdiction over the defendant because the defendant

---

68 The Hearst Corporation v. Goldberger, 1997 U.S. Dist. LEXIS 2065 (S.D.N.Y. 1997).

69 *Id.* at 31–33 (citations omitted).

70 Bensusan Restaurant Corporation v. King, 937 F.Supp. 295, 1996 U.S. Dist. LEXIS 13035 (S.D.N.Y. 1996).

71 Citations omitted.

72 Bensusan Restaurant v. King, 1997 U.S. App. LEXIS 23742 (2nd Cir. 1997).

purposefully availed itself of the privilege of doing business in Connecticut.[73] The defendant "directed its advertising activities via the Internet and its toll-free telephone number toward not only the state of Connecticut, but to all states. The Internet as well as toll-free numbers is designed to communicate with people and their businesses in every state. Advertisement on the Internet can reach as many as 10,000 Internet users within Connecticut alone. Further, once posted on the Internet, unlike television and radio advertising, the advertisement is available continuously to any Internet user."[74]

In *Heroes, Inc. v. Heroes Foundation*, a district court determined that the District of Columbia had personal jurisdiction over a defendant that had an advertisement placed in the Washington Post and that had a Web site that could be accessed from the District of Columbia.[75] Because the defendant had the other contact to the District of Columbia in addition to the fact that its Web site could be accessed there, "the Court [did] not [need to] decide whether the defendant's home page by itself subjects the defendant to personal jurisdiction in the District. In weighing the importance of this particular contact, however, the Court note[d] that the defendant's home page explicitly solicits contributions, and provides a toll-free telephone number for that purpose. The home page also contains the defendant's allegedly infringing trademark and logo, the subject of the plaintiff's underlying claims. And the home page is certainly a sustained contact with the District; it has been possible for a District resident to gain access to it at any time since it was first posted."[76]

A district court in the Western District of Pennsylvania determined that Pennsylvania had personal jurisdiction over the defendant where Pennsylvania individuals subscribed to the defendant's information service, which was provided through the Internet.[77] The subscribers signed up by filling out applications while visiting defendant's Web site. Of the defendant's 140,000 paying subscribers, 3000 were located in Pennsylvania, and the defendant had also entered into agreements with seven Internet access providers in Pennsylvania to have access to the providers' subscribers. The court stated that "[w]e are being asked to determine whether [the defendant's] conducting of electronic commerce with Pennsylvania residents constitutes the purposeful availment of doing business in Pennsylvania. We conclude that it does. [The defendant] has contracted with approximately 3,000 individuals and seven Internet access providers in Pennsylvania. The intended object of these transactions has been the downloading of the electronic messages that form the basis of this suit in Pennsylvania."[78] In addition, the defendant "repeatedly and consciously chose to process Pennsylvania residents' applications and to assign them passwords. [The defendant] knew that the result of these contracts would be the transmission of electronic messages into Pennsylvania. The transmission of these files was entirely within its control. . . . [The defendant] was

73 Inset Systems, Inc. v. Instruction Set, Inc., 937 F.Supp. 161; 1996 U.S. Dist. LEXIS 7160 (D. Conn. 1996).

74 *Id.*

75 Heroes, Inc. v. Heroes Foundation, 958 F.Supp. 1 (D.D.C. 1996).

76 *Id.* at 5.

77 Zippo Manufacturing Company v. Zippo Dot Com, Inc., 952 F.Supp. 1119 (W.D. Pa. 1997).

78 *Id.* at 1125–26.

under no obligation to sell its services to Pennsylvania residents. It freely chose to do so, presumably in order to profit from those transactions. If a corporation determines that the risk of being subject to personal jurisdiction in a particular forum is too great, it can choose to sever its connection to the state. If [the defendant] had not wanted to be amenable to jurisdiction in Pennsylvania, the solution would have been simple—it could have chosen not to sell its services to Pennsylvania residents."[79]

The majority of these cases indicate a trend toward establishing nexus through the accessibility of a Web site by a state's residents (irrespective of the location of the site) *plus* some other presence in the state. The conclusion in some of these cases that Web site alone is enough seems contrary to the principle—addressed in *World-Wide Volkswagen*, *Asahi Metal*, and *Bensusan*—that a third party's actions (even if foreseeable by a defendant) cannot cause a defendant to have nexus with a state. Moreover, even if the accessibility of an out-of-state Web site by a state's residents can make the owner of that Web site subject to the civil jurisdiction of the residents' state, the state tax jurisdictional standard under the Due Process Clause may be greater than that required for in personam jurisdiction. This is supported by the Supreme Court, in *Quill*, noting that the two jurisdictional standards are merely "comparable."[80]

B. Commerce Clause

As for the Commerce Clause, unlike with the Due Process Clause, there is little authority in which to determine when the Commerce Clause will be satisfied in the context of e-commerce.[81] More specifically, there is a question as to whether the Commerce Clause bright-line standard of physical presence (or safe-harbor of no physical presence) that was set forth in *Quill* is applicable to state tax liabilities other than the obligation to collect use tax in a state, although much of the U.S. Supreme Court's language in *Quill* surely appears to apply to sales tax impositions as well. As discussed in section II of this chapter, it is not clear whether a different standard or standards will apply for the imposition of gross receipts, franchise, or income tax by a state; many states hold that a physical presence requirement only applies to sales and use taxes.[82] The correct answer is that the same standard—or even a more stringent standard—should apply in determining whether an individual or entity is subject to the imposition of gross receipts, franchise, or income tax by a state, because the reasoning set forth in *Quill* is even more appropriate when tax is actually borne by the

---

79 *Id.* at 1126–27.

80 *See, supra* note 7.

81 In *Quill*, the Supreme Court enunciated the physical presence nexus standard only in the context of a state's authority to impose a duty to collect use tax upon a mail-order company. (It is important to keep in mind when discussing Commerce Clause issues and the Internet that the Commerce Clause cases discussed above were decided under "negative" or "dormant" Commerce Clause principles. Thus, all of the principles set forth above can be changed by congressional action.)

82 *See, supra* notes 40–44.

out-of-state individual or entity as opposed to merely placing a duty to collect tax on such person.[83]

Applying these Commerce Clause cases in the context of e-commerce answers the question of whether the appearance of a logo on a screen is the equivalent of having property in a state for purposes of the *Quill* physical presence standard. This appearance of a logo on a screen should not be considered physical presence in a state because (1) there is no convincing authority (with all due respect to New Mexico and South Carolina) that "property" to which *Quill* referred can include intangible property; (2) the temporary showing of a transitory image is surely de minimis (even compared to the floppy disks that were present in North Dakota but found to be inconsequential in *Quill*); and (3) the broadcaster owns the rights to the logo but doesn't own the projection of the logo on the screen.

Another issue that arises is whether the presence of a telecommunications service provider's equipment in a state should be attributable to an out-of-state vendor when the equipment is used by an instate resident to order from the vendor. The proper answer is that the presence of the telecommunications provider cannot be attributed to the vendor because there is no agency relationship[84] since (1) the vendor does not control the telecommunications provider, (2) the telecommunications provider does not hold itself out as being the vendor, (3) the telecommunications provider cannot bind the vendor, (4) there is no fiduciary relationship between the telecommunications provider and the vendor, and (5) the telecommunications provider is pursuing its own business, not that of the vendor.

A similar issue concerns the presence of an ISP's equipment or an online service provider's equipment in a state: should such equipment be attributable to an out-of-state vendor? Again, the equipment should not be attributed to the out-of-state-vendor because there is no agency relationship between the vendor and either the ISP or the online service provider. New York's Department of Taxation and Finance has taken this position as it has issued a notice in which it provides that nexus is not created through a New York ISP.[85]

Does the fact that the equipment that hosts the vendor's Web site is in a particular state mean that the out-of-state vendor has a taxable physical presence in the state of the host computer? Despite Texas's position on this subject,[86] the proper answer is no. Even if the presence of intangible property were a basis for establishing taxable nexus, the Web site is certainly de minimis. New York's Department of Taxation and Finance has issued a notice in which it has taken a position consistent with this viewpoint. The notice provides that nexus is not created merely by the appearance of advertising on a New York server.[87] Illinois, however, has indicated that the presence of an Internet

83 *See* National Geographic Society v. California Board of Equalization, 430 U.S. 551 (1977).

84 *See,* Current, Inc. v. California State Board of Equalization, 24 Cal. App. 4th 382, 1994 Cal. App. LEXIS 349 (Ct. App. 1994); Rosen, *Jurisdictional Limitations: Attributional Nexus*, 1430 Tax Management Portfolio.

85 Important notice, 1997 N.Y. Tax LEXIS 43 (Jan. 24, 1997).

86 *See*, Texas Comptroller's Tax Policy Director Addresses Taxation of Internet, 97 STN 75-61 (Apr. 18, 1997).

87 Important notice, 1997 N.Y. Tax LEXIS 43 (Jan. 24, 1997).

access provider in Illinois could provide nexus on behalf of an out-of-state retailer so as to force such retailer to collect use tax on sales into Illinois if the Internet access provider performs sufficient activities on behalf of the out-of-state retailer's Internet selling operation.[88]

C. P.L. 86-272

In addition to the Due Process and the Commerce Clause issues, e-commerce raises unique problems in the context of determining whether protection from the imposition of income tax is available under P.L. 86-272. For example, is there any legitimate distinction between solicitation (the protected activity under the federal law) performed through traditional means and solicitation performed electronically? The correct interpretation is that there should be absolutely no difference between solicitation performed through traditional means and solicitation performed electronically, because there is absolutely no authority—in the statute, obvious legislative intent, the congressional record, or in common sense—to make any distinction. Thus, the presence in a state of a kiosk and a computer terminal by which a customer can order items from a company should not cause the company to have nexus with the state because there is no real difference between the presence of the kiosk and terminal and the presence of a sales person in the state who is soliciting orders. Since the presence of the sales person would be protected by P.L. 86-272, so should the presence of the kiosk and terminal.

Additionally, questions arise as to what the term "ancillary" means in the context of the Internet?[89] For example, will a relationship with a telecommunications service provider or with an ISP that has substantial property in a state and therefore nexus with the state prove to be ancillary? The correct position is that such relationships should prove to be ancillary since a salesperson's bringing an automobile into a state and a company's owning an in-store display rack are considered to be protected instate solicitation; the modern tools of accomplishing the same tasks should clearly be granted equal protection, especially in light of the fact that the traditional automobile and display rack were owned by the vendor and the solicitation was performed solely by the vendor's employees or agents (in contrast to using a third party, as is the usual case with e-commerce).

Another P.L. 86-272 issue that warrants attention is whether the establishment of an Internet Web-site that can be accessed by users in a state should be deemed akin to the opening of an office in that state such as would cause a corporation to lose its protected status under P.L. 86-272. The proper analysis results in a determination that establishment of a Web site should not result in the loss of P.L. 86-272 status, since the establishment of a Web site does not raise the same issues that maintenance of an instate office does. The maintenance of an office "exception" in P.L.86-272 is based on traditional concepts of presence: having an interest in real property in the jurisdiction

---

88 PLR No. ST-97-0070-GIL (Feb. 5, 1997).

89 Activities ancillary to solicitation are, pursuant to *Wrigley*, protected under the federal law.

and the presence being regular and systematic.[90] Moreover, if the purpose of P.L. 86-272 is to make pursuing interstate commerce feasible by prohibiting taxation when there is perhaps intermittent, difficult-to-track presence[91], the maintenance of an office instate will not raise such problems, while the maintenance of a Web site that allows instate consumers access will.

Furthermore, another interesting albeit futuristic issue that arises in the context of P.L. 86-272 is whether the downloading of a tangible item from a seller's Web site by a customer is deemed to be the delivery of such item from inside the state such that the seller's P.L. 86-272 protection is lost. While the technology that would enable delivery of tangible property electronically has not yet been refined (it may be worthwhile to note that the delivery of the contents of a compact disc is the delivery of intangible *music*, not the delivery of a tangible compact disc), such property should be considered to have been delivered from outside the state because (1) the vendor loses control over the property outside the state, and (2) this is clearly "less than" using one's own trucks to deliver property, which is clearly protected by the federal statute itself.

IV. TELECOMMUNICATION TAXABILITY IMPLICATIONS

In addition to the issues that arise in the context of attempting to apply Due Process Clause and Commerce Clause concepts to the digital environment, issues concerning these matters also arise in attempting to apply these concepts to telecommunications and the technology that exists today.

A. Due Process Issues

Some Due Process Clause issues that arise in the context of telecommunications are

1. Whether wireless telecommunication service providers are considered to be purposefully directing their economic activity into those states with which their only connection is the entering into of a contract with another wireless service provider so as to satisfy the requirements of the Due Process Clause.
2. Whether the permitting of residents in a state to receive a satellite transmission is considered to be purposeful direction of economic activities into that state.
3. Whether the permitting of a nonresident who is "roaming" in a state to receive a satellite transmission is purposeful direction of economic activities into that state.

---

90 *See*, Rosen, *Technical and Policy Aspects of Crossing the Presence Threshold*, 1997 State Tax Notes, 97 STN 158-33.

91 *See,* Matter of Orvis Company, Inc. v. Tax Appeals Tribunal, 86 N.Y.2d 165, 654 N.E.2d 954 (Ct. App. 1995) (Bellacosa, J., dissenting).

While there is no clear cut answer, under the principles set forth by the U.S. Supreme Court in *Asahi*, it seems that these activities should not create nexus as these activities merely constitute "placement of a product into the stream of commerce."

B. Commerce Clause Issues

The characteristics of wireless telecommunications often make it difficult under traditional sales and use taxation statutes, when considering Commerce Clause implications, to determine which state and/or local jurisdiction has the right to tax a specific wireless transmission, which charges or what portions of a bill are attributable to a specific jurisdiction, and who is the vendor and who is the customer. These problems can arise when (1) the originator and/or the recipient of a wireless transmission has no fixed service address (2) telecommunications providers cannot determine from which taxing jurisdiction a transmission has been placed or within which taxing jurisdiction a wireless transmission has been received; or (3) either the originator or the recipient of a wireless transmission moves through more than one taxing jurisdiction during the course of one telephone call. Additional problems arise because the wireless industry currently utilizes different billing arrangements.

Moreover, the states have established, and will likely continue to establish, disparate taxing methods to tax wireless transmissions. Such different methods of taxation cause an impossible administrative burden for the states, a bookkeeping and compliance nightmare for the service providers, and unfair multiple levels of taxation of wireless telecommunication transmissions for the customers.

Since this issue is so multijurisdictional, this is one area that might have to be regulated by Congress so as to prevent states from inflicting different taxing schemes on telecommunications services. Congress clearly has the power to act; as a matter of fact, Congress enacted the 1996 Telecommunications Act, which restricts taxation of direct broadcast satellite gross receipts by local jurisdictions.[92] The enactment of this legislation is a crystal-clear indication of Congress's ability to regulate the provision of wireless telecommunication services.[93]

---

92 1996 Telecommunications Act, § 602.

93 *See also*, Communications Act of 1934, § 332(c)(3) (legislation preempting the regulation by the states of cellular telecommunication services rates).

PART VIII

International Business Companies

Chapter 30

Cyprus: E-Commerce Taxation in Cyprus

George N. Apostolou
Apostolou & Co. LLC

I. E-COMMERCE IN CYPRUS: OVERVIEW

It must be noted from the outset that the present chapter aspires to merely provide readers, be they businessmen or legal professionals, with an initial overview of the main issues that an e-commerce enterprise is required to address within the present Cypriot business and tax environment. An in-depth analysis of the subject cannot and was never intended to be provided herein.

The Republic of Cyprus is well-known amongst taxation and tax-planning experts around the world for its favorable tax regime. It is not known for its incentives to e-commerce businesses. In fact, e-commerce is still very limited in Cyprus itself, despite an increase in Internet usage both in households and in microbusinesses on the island.[1] Despite the efforts and progress recorded in both the private and public sector, there seem to be still considerable untapped opportunities for e-commerce and e-business in Cyprus,[2] and the latter is a, mostly, "virgin" market in this respect.

It seems to be merely a matter of time before Cyprus develops into one of the most important hubs for e-commerce activities around the globe. This chapter attempts to shed what little light it can on the reasons behind this slow start and Cyprus's future in e-commerce and e-business, but most importantly the effect of the pertinent Cyprus and European Union (EU) taxation legislation and principles thereon.

---

1 Bouli Chadjioannou, *E-Commerce Not Making Headway in Cyprus*, The Cyprus Weekly (Dec. 7–13, 2007).

2 Lina Nearchou-Ellinas, The Use of the Internet in Small Firms in Cyprus: The Gender Prospective (2004) UNECE programme on Women's Entrepreneurship. http://www.unece.org/ie/enterp/women/documents/elli.pdf (accessed February 15, 2007).

A. The Boring World of Statistics

Even though statistics constitute a, perhaps, crude snapshot of the present and are admittedly tediously boring to study, they do, sometimes, assist in pin-pointing the proclivity of the surveyed population at certain time. In Cyprus, a series of annual surveys provide this snapshot.

According to the Statistical Service of the Republic of Cyprus, the percentage of enterprises that used a computer during January 2007 is 94.5 percent, unchanged from 2006. All large (250 employees or more) and almost all medium-size enterprises (50–249 employees) used computers and the Internet. In small enterprises (10–49 employees) there was an increase in Internet usage (from 82.0% in 2004 to 83.7% in 2006 and now to 85.9% in 2007).[3]

For 2007, the percentage of households on the island that have a computer is 52.9 percent (51.9% in 2006). The percentage of households with Internet access from home increased from 36.7 percent in 2006 to 38.9 percent in 2007. There was a significant increase in Internet connections via broadband, where the percentage increased from 33.0 percent (of households with Internet access) in 2006 to 51.2 percent in 2007.

The percentage of individuals of age 16–74 years who have used a computer during the first quarter of 2007 was 47.0 percent, while for 2006 it was 44.1 percent. The percentage of individuals who have used the Internet increased as well, from 33.8 percent in 2006 to 38.1 percent in 2007. As far as Internet usage is concerned, there was a significant increase (from 12.7% in 2006 to 19.9% in 2007) in the interaction with the public sector, as well as in Internet banking (from 6.1% in 2006 to 11.9% in 2007).

Importantly, the percentage of individuals ordering products and services via Internet kept increasing (from 5.1% in 2005 to 6.7% in 2006 to 7.8% in 2007). These orders were mainly tickets for travel and holiday accommodation.

It must be noted that only 7.3 percent of local companies, with access to the Internet, have received orders online in 2006. As with online purchases, in most Cypriot companies, sales on line represent only a small percentage of total sales.

And then there are the households and the individuals. The latter, specifically, seem to be even less enthusiastic about e-commerce than local companies, with only 7.8 percent of them having bought goods or services for their personal use online (5.0% in 2006 and 2.7% in 2004). A very recent EU survey indicates that up to 20.0 percent of locals, ages 16–74, avoided using the Internet in 2006 because of security concerns, whilst only 10.0 (against an EU average of 30.0%) used it for shopping during 2007.[4] Ticket and hotel bookings are the most popular choices to date, with one in three Cypriots who purchased goods or services online in 2007. The second most popular were books, magazines, and newspapers (33.6%), followed by clothing and sporting goods (29.1%), and films and music (23.6%). Although there seems to

---

3 *Annual Survey on Information and Communication Technologies Usage and E-Commerce in Enterprises & Annual Survey Information and Communication Technologies Usage and E-Commerce in Households and by Individuals*, The Statistical Service of the Republic of Cyprus (Apr. 4, 2007).

4 News Release, Eurostat, 18/2008 (Aug. 2, 2008).

be a clear propensity toward increasing Internet usage on the island, local companies and individuals are slow to adopt it and still remain seemingly lukewarm about e-commerce.

On a small island in the far reaches of the eastern Mediterranean Sea, with a market of less than a million people and a volume index of Gross Domestic Product per Capita at PPS[5] 94 percent of the EU27 average[6] this was, perhaps, to be expected. Furthermore, having survived—century upon century—numerous conquerors, including the Lusignans, the Venetians, the Ottomans and, most recently, the English, Cypriots are a conservative people by nature.

Cyprus's e-commerce activities have recently grown to include, amongst others, an extensive range of e-banking services offered by all major banking institutions on the island, the payment and issuance of certain licenses and utility bills, as well as the submission of documents to certain public authorities[7] and certain types of online securities dealing.

B. Cyprus as an E-Commerce Hub

Cyprus's weakness to effectively promote e-commerce locally until now turns to strength when viewed from the outside. Since the July 1974 illegal invasion and occupation of 36.2 percent of the island by Turkey, the Republic of Cyprus has focused its revenue-generating efforts, mainly, on tourism and the redevelopment of the island as a service-providing center first and foremost. Today, the Republic of Cyprus enjoys a unique place as the member state with the lowest corporate tax rate in the European Union, which is the choice of preference for thousands of investors the world over.

Cyprus' modern and efficient legal, accounting and banking sectors are all based on English practices and traditions, which faithfully adhere, at the same time, to the most modern international standards. Its liberal foreign direct investment regime allows up to 100 percent foreign participation in most sectors of the economy, there is no exchange control, and the freedom of movement of foreign currency has now been long established.

In addition to this, the Republic of Cyprus is a signatory of double-taxation avoidance treaties with over forty countries, providing thus a low tax jurisdiction with low setup and operating costs for companies and holding companies (no taxation on dividends to corporate bodies) whilst maintaining excellent, state-of-the-art telecommunications, a sophisticated business infrastructure, and easy access by air and sea. Finally, it is one of the few markets where investors can find highly qualified and trained managerial, clerical, and technical staff available at a reasonable wage.

The island is renowned mostly for its international business companies, which are frequently used as holding companies, and as one of the world's leaders in the

---

5 Purchase power standards.

6 News Release, Eurostat, 90/2007 (June 28, 2007).

7 E.g., the electronic payment and issuance of one's road tax license by the Department of Road Transport, Ministry of Communications and Works, and the online application for the approval of a company or trade name by the Department of the Registrar of Companies and Official Receiver, Ministry of Commerce.

establishment of ship-management and shipping entities. Moreover, its central and strategic geographical location at the crossroads of Europe, Asia, and Africa make Cyprus ideal for the establishment of e-commerce on the island. Additional benefits include competitive labor and overhead costs for setting up a business in Cyprus.

All of the above constitute distinct incentives for establishing an e-commerce business presence, or a company holding shares in such an entity, in the republic. This chapter shall examine the advantages and disadvantages of the island in this respect later on.

II. NATIONAL AND EU LEGISLATION AFFECTING E-COMMERCE IN CYPRUS

Before giving an overview of the Cypriot e-commerce market's different sectors, it must be noted from the outset that two of the most important pieces of EU legislation on e-commerce have all been adopted in national legislation[8] and applied in Cyprus since 2004, although little has been done in practical terms on the side of administrative implementation: These pieces of legislation are

- Directive 2000/31/EC of the European Parliament and of the Council of June 8, 2000, on certain legal aspects of information society services (in particular e-commerce) in the internal market, which provides, inter alia, for the basic establishment and information requirements for e-commerce service providers as well as the framework of commercial communications and procedures during an e-commerce order, but does not have any application for taxation purposes; and
- Directive 1999/93/EC of the European Parliament and of the Council of December 13, 1999, on a community framework for electronic signatures as well as Decision 2000/709/EC of the European Commission of November 6, 2000, on the minimum criteria to be taken into account by member states when designating bodies in accordance with Article 3 (no. 4) of Directive 1999/93/EC of the European Parliament and of the Council on a community framework for electronic signatures.

Moreover, Directive 97/7/EC of the European Parliament and of the Council of May 20, 1997, on the protection of consumers in respect of distance contracts has been adopted in Cypriot national law through Law 14(I)/2000.

A. Banking and Investment Services Sectors

Cyprus has been a fully fledged member of the European Union since May 1, 2004; therefore, its national primary and secondary legislation follows and adheres to EU

8 Certain Legal Aspects of Information Society Services, in particular Electronic Commerce and Pertinent Issues Law, 156(I) (2004, as amended and corrected by Law 97(I) (2007)); *See also*, The Legal Framework for Electronic Signatures, L. 188(I)/2004.

legislation. However, although EU law applies in Cyprus just as it applies to the other 26 member states in the European Union, Cyprus is just waking up to expanding its secondary legislation concerning e-commerce.

Although, e-commerce is basically defined as the provision or purchase of services or goods by electronic means, especially including the Internet, local and international e-commerce activities within Cyprus have, until now, been of limited breadth and are still at an embryonic stage. The recent developments are almost certainly set to lead both lawmakers and regulators to expand and develop the legislative "neurons" necessary for e-commerce to evolve further in Cyprus and to become an inseparable part of the Cypriot economy on a scale grander than what has been experienced until today.

The issuance by the Central Bank of Cyprus of its Directive on Transactions Effected by Electronic Payment Instruments in April 2004, which effectively implemented Recommendation 97/489/EC of July 30, 1997, of the Commission of the European Communities and at same time complemented the national consumer credit laws,[9] allowed the Cypriot banking and financial industries to develop the provision of their online services within a better, more certain, and highly regulated legal framework.

This has led to even traditionally conservative institutions, such as the Cooperative Central Bank, Ltd. and the Cypriot cooperative credit institutions, to roll up their sleeves and prepare to enter the Internet banking sector so as to offer e-banking to their customers as early as 2008.

Along with electronic banks, stock exchange transactions and the provision of current online stock and price information from the Cyprus Stock Exchange have also been made possible and available to investors since late 2000, first by the commercial banks and then by several high-profile brokerage firms. The provision of investment services, including the provision of these services electronically, is regulated by the recently enacted Investment Services and Activities and Regulated Markets Law.[10]

Finally, becoming an EU member state has helped give Cyprus significant headway in cross-border provision of banking and investment services. A credit, cooperative, or electronic money institution established within the European Union may now either establish itself within the republic or directly provide its services, across EU borders, to Cypriot consumers.

According to the pertinent provisions of the banking laws[11] and cooperative societies laws,[12] a credit, cooperative society, or electronic money institution authorized and supervised by the competent authorities of another member state of the European Union may provide in Cyprus banking services and offer investment services as well as non-core investment services, without needing a license from the Central Bank of

9 Consumer Credit Law, 39(I) (2001, as amended by Laws 116(I) (2001); 34(I) (2002); 77(I) (2002); 33(I) (2004); and 92(I) (2007)).

10 Law 144(I) (2007).

11 Banking Law, 66(I) (1997, as amended by Laws 94(I) (2000); 119(I) (2003); 4(I) (2004); 151(I) (2004); 231(I) (2004); 235(I) (2004); and 20(I) (2005)).

12 Cooperative Societies Law, 22 (1985, as amended by Laws 68 (1987); 190 (1989); 8 (1992); 22(I) (1992); 140(I) (1999); 140(I) (2000); 171(I) (2000); 8(I) (2001); 123(I) (2003); 124(I) (2003); 144(I) (2003); 5(I) (2004); 170(I) (2004); 230(I) (2004); 23(I) (2005); 49(I) (2005); 76(I) (2005); 29(I) (2007); 37(I) (2007); and 177(I) (2007)).

Cyprus. Such a credit, cooperative, or electronic money institution may operate in Cyprus by either establishing a branch or by offering services on a cross-border basis for which it has received an authorization by the competent authorities of its home member state.

The legal framework for the establishment and operation of electronic money institutions on the island is regulated by the Electronic Money Institutions Law,[13] which adopted into national law the provisions of Directive 2000/28/EC of the European Parliament and of the Council of September 18, 2000, amending Directive 2000/12/EC (related to the taking up and pursuit of the business of credit institutions) and of Directive 2000/46/EC of the European Parliament and of the Council of September 18, 2000, (on the taking up, pursuit of, and prudential supervision of the business of electronic money institutions).

The banking and investments sector is by far the most developed e-commerce sector in Cyprus with major banks—from member states such as England, France, Greece, Romania and Bulgaria, to name a few—as well as important financial institutions setting up shop on the island both physically as well as electronically.

B. Commercial Sector

The most recent and exciting development in the underdeveloped Cypriot commercial e-commerce sector has been the emergence of the first online, fully electronic shopping mall, set up with the purpose of promoting local e-business. Theis e-mall allows e-shop owners to control their online stores' products, manage electronic orders and delivery of products, and secure credit card payments.

The main legislation allowing for the establishment of any Cypriot company, including an international business company and a holding company with a registered office or a place of business in Cyprus, are the Companies Law.[14]

C. Telecommunications and Postal Services Sectors

Telecommunications and postal services, and their provision within the Republic of Cyprus, are mainly governed by the regulation of electronic communications and postal regulation laws,[15] which have transposed EU legislation into Cypriot national law and provide, amongst other things, for the appointment of a commissioner for electronic communications and postal regulation as well as for the establishment and operation of the commissioner's office. Several pieces of secondary legislation

---

13 Electronic Money Institutions Law, 86(I) (2004).

14 Companies Law, § 113, (as amended by Laws 19 (1963); 21 (1967); 27 (1967); 9 (1968); 76 (1977); 17 (1979); 105 (1985); 198 (1986); 19 (1990); 46(I) (1992); 96(I) (1992); 41(I) (1994); 15(I) (1995); 21(I) (1997); 82(I) (1999); 149(I) (1999); 2(I) (2000); 2(I) (2000); 135(I) (2000); 151(I) (2000); 76(I) (2001); 70(I) (2003); 167(I) (2003); 92(I) (2004); 24(I) (2005); 129(I) (2005); 130(I) (2005); 98(I) (2006); 124(I) (2006); 70(I) (2007); 71(I) (2007); 131(I) (2007); and 186(I) (2007).

15 Electronic Communications and Posts Law 112(I)/2004 as amended by Laws 84(I)/2005, 149(I)/2005, 67(I)/2006, 113(I)/2007 and 134(I)/2007.

have also been passed in this sector, although there is significant room for development and regulation of the sector's legal framework. It must be noted also that recent developments have seen the slow but growing liberalization of parts of this sector. For instance, new companies have started to challenge the Cyprus Telecommunications Authority's monopoly, especially in the Internet service provider (ISP), hosting services, and telephony services subsectors of the market, and have recently begun to make significant headway by offering competitive pricing, upgraded services, and a rich variety of alternative products.

The postal sector, by contrast, has been much slower to develop even though the appropriate national legislation regulating it to EU standards has been in place since 2004. The main reason behind this is thought to be that the small size, and therefore small profit margins, of the Cypriot postal market has deterred large companies from entering it. Despite this, however, the number of national courier services has increased, with some courier service providers offering their customers the ability to monitor dispatched mail or packages electronically.

D. Taxation

Taxation presents the main benefit as well as the major obstacle for the establishment of e-commerce companies in Cyprus and, indeed, in the entire European Union. Offshore establishment can significantly benefit e-businesses via e-commerce taxation, whether these deal in digital or physical products and/or services. Cyprus offers one of the most attractive direct tax-planning solutions, both in the European Union and—indeed—the world, for any company that is permanently established on the island and exercises its management and control in Cyprus, including e-commerce businesses. Direct taxation of corporate bodies and individuals is regulated by the Cypriot income tax laws.[16]

Where problems arise, however, or rather where Cyprus's advantages wither in comparison to other offshore non-EU jurisdictions, is when it comes to the indirect taxation applied to the distance selling of goods and/or services provided via electronic means. An example of indirect taxation applies in Cyprus is the value-added tax (VAT), which currently stands only at 15 percent, one of the lowest rates in Cyprus.[17]

However, Cyprus is obliged to follow and apply EU legislation, and therefore the EU's VAT strategy and philosophy in e-commerce transactions. This strategy and philosophy distinguish between the normal supply of services or goods, in which case the charging of VAT is at the rate of the country in which the supplier is located, and the situation where the supply of services or goods is effected over an electronic network.[18]

---

16 Income Tax Law, 118(I) (2002, as amended by Laws 230(I) (2002); 162(I) (2003); 195(I) (2004); 92(I) (2005); 113(I) (2006); 80(I) (2007); and 138(I) (2007)).

17 Value-Added Tax Law, 95(I) (2000, as amended by Laws 93(I) (2002); 27(I) (2003); 172(I) (2003); 95(I) (2004); 88(I) (2005); 100(I) (2005); 131(I) (2005); 148(I) (2005); 64(I) (2006); 86(I) (2006); 87(I) (2006); 48(I) (2007); 129(I) (2007); 141(I) (2007); 142(I) (2007); and amended and corrected by Law 143(I) (2007).

18 Council Directive 2002/38/EC, (May 7, 2002, amending temporarily Directive 77/388/EEC as regards the VAT arrangements applicable to radio and television broadcasting services and certain electronically supplied services).

Taxation issues are discussed below, in greater detail and scrutiny, under the light of modern e-commerce business requirements.

E. Personal Data Protection

Cyprus has adopted the requisite EU data protection legislation by enacting the Processing of Personal Data Law, 138(I)/2001.[19]

III. DIRECT TAXATION OF A CYPRIOT E-COMMERCE COMPANY

Under the Cypriot income tax laws,[20] a company, including an e-commerce entity, which is established in the Republic of Cyprus, is taxed on its worldwide trading profits.[21] This means that the company must be permanently established on the island.[22] Cypriot tax law is based on the current EU directives as well as the principles and guidelines of the Organization for Economic Cooperation and Development (OECD).[23]

The basic type of direct taxation concerning all corporate bodies in Cyprus is the homogenous corporate taxation rate of 10 percent, which also applies to an e-commerce company permanently established on the island. For an e-commerce company to be allowed to enjoy the aforementioned favorable corporate tax rate, it must be either permanently established within the Republic of Cyprus or maintain its management and control on the island. Specifically, the Cypriot income tax laws define "permanent establishment" as a fixed place of business through which the business of an enterprise is wholly or partly carried on.[24] It must be particularly noted that the term "permanent establishment" does not include

1. The use of facilities solely for the purpose of storage, display, or delivery of goods or merchandise belonging to the enterprise;
2. The maintenance of a stock of goods or merchandise belonging to the enterprise solely for the purpose of storage, display, or delivery;
3. The maintenance of a stock of goods or merchandise belonging to the enterprise solely for the purpose of proceeding with another enterprise;

---

19 As amended by Law 37(I) (2003).

20 Income Tax Law § 5.

21 Provided the existence of bilateral avoidance of double-taxation treaties/agreements between the Republic of Cyprus and third countries allows and favors this.

22 If a company has its majority of board directors, statutory seat, and board meetings in Cyprus, it is considered as managed and controlled in Cyprus by the Cypriot tax authorities.

23 OECD Model Tax Convention on Income and Capital, art. 5 (July 2005); *See also*, Commentary on the OECD Model Tax Convention concerning the issue of an application of the current definition of permanent establishment in the context of e-commerce, Committee on Fiscal Affairs (Dec. 22, 2000).

24 The term especially includes, inter alia, (1) a place of management, (2) a branch, (3) an office, (4) a factory, and (5) a workshop.

4. The maintenance of a fixed place of business solely for the purpose of carrying on, for the enterprise, any other activity of a preparatory or auxiliary character; and
5. The maintenance of a fixed place of business solely for any combination of activities such as the keeping of a place of management, a branch, an office, a factory, and/or a workshop, provided that the overall activity of the fixed place of business resulting from this combination has a preparatory or auxiliary character.

It must be added that where a person, other than an agent of independent status, is acting on behalf of an enterprise and has and perhaps habitually exercises in the Republic of Cyprus an authority to conclude contracts in the enterprise's name, the enterprise shall be deemed to have a permanent establishment in Cyprus in respect of any activities which that person undertakes on its behalf, unless these activities are limited to the ones mentioned in items (1) to (5) above.

An agent of independent status, such as a broker, a general commission agent, or an ISP on whose server the enterprise's Web site is hosted, who is acting in his or her ordinary course of business, merely assists an enterprise to conduct business in Cyprus through himself or herself. As such, this assistance would not be a basis on which the enterprise would be afforded permanent establishment status.

Unlike the tax practices in other countries, such as Portugal and Spain, it is abundantly clear from the wording of the Cypriot legislation that some sort of physical presence is a requirement for an enterprise to be deemed as "permanently established" in the republic. A Web site, in itself, will not constitute permanent establishment. A Website-hosting arrangement will also not result in permanent establishment for the enterprise that carries on business through that Web site, and an ISP will not, except in highly unusual circumstances, constitute a dependent agent of another enterprise so as to constitute a permanent establishment of that enterprise in Cyprus. On the other hand, it must also be made clear that human intervention is not a prerequisite for permanent establishment to exist.

The issue as to whether computer equipment or hardware, such as a server or a server in conjunction with other computer hardware or software, such as a Web site, that are present at a certain location constitute a permanent establishment will depend on whether the functions performed by or through these exceed the preparatory or auxiliary threshold set both by Cypriot tax legislation and the OECD Model Tax Convention provisions. It is certain, however, that the existence of a server for advertising distance selling or of a warehouse on the island solely for storage or delivery purposes would not—in themselves—be sufficient.[25] On the other hand, if an enterprise conducts its business through a specific Web site and owns or leases and operates the server on which its Web site is hosted, and the enterprise owns or leases the premises where the server is located, these circumstances could very well constitute a permanent establishment, provided that the rest of the legal requirements of Cypriot taxation

25 However, if the server functions so as, for example, to conclude the contract for sale with the customer, to process the payment, and to arrange for the automatic dispatch and delivery of the goods or the services through the computer equipment located in the fixed place of business, then this would probably constitute a permanent establishment.

legislation are fulfilled (i.e., a fixed place of business through which the enterprises' business is carried on either partly or wholly; that is, the equipment, for instance, located at the specific location for a sufficient period of time provides the enterprise with the facilities in order to perform its business functions).

It must be noted that the presence of personnel is unnecessary for an enterprise to be deemed as wholly or partly carrying on business at a location when no personnel are required because of the character of the business activities. For example, a fully automated warehouse, used for more than auxiliary or preparatory activities or functions, along with the presence of a server and a Web site, all located at a fixed place of business in Cyprus, could also constitute a permanent establishment.

Examples of auxiliary or preparatory activities/functions include the provision of a communications link between suppliers and customers, the advertising of goods or services, the relaying of information through a mirror server for security and efficiency purposes, and the gathering or supplying of market or other data, or information. However, in circumstances where these activities or functions form an essential and significant part of the business activities of an enterprise or where other core functions[26] of this enterprise are carried on through the computer equipment, a permanent establishment could be found provided the equipment constitutes a fixed place of business for the enterprise.

IV. INDIRECT TAXATION OF A CYPRIOT E-COMMERCE COMPANY AND OF AN E-COMMERCE COMPANY SUPPLYING GOODS AND/OR SERVICES IN CYPRUS

A. General

Indirect taxation on the operation of a Cypriot e-commerce company includes excise duties and VAT, depending on the goods or services offered by such a company and whether these are delivered within the member states of the European Union. Indirect taxation, as mentioned above, is also imposed on goods and/or services that an e-commerce company based in another member state of the European Union, or outside the European Union, supplies in Cyprus.

The sixth Directive 77/388/EEC as regards the VAT arrangements applicable to certain electronically supplied services and radio and television broadcasting services, as amended by Council Directive 2006/112/EC of November 28, 2006 on the common system of VAT, has been implemented by the national Value-Added Tax Law, 95(I)/2000, as amended. Council Directive 2002/38/EC of May 7, 2002, amending and amending temporarily the aforementioned Directive 77/388/EEC, came into force on July 1, 2003, to ensure a level playing field between non-EU businesses and EU businesses regarding electronically supplied services provided within member states. The aforementioned

26 These depend on the nature of the business carried on by the specific enterprise. The general test here would be to examine the nature of the activities performed by the enterprise at the specific location in the light of the business carried on by that enterprise.

directive had its period of application extended to December 31, 2006, by Directive 2006/58/EC, and the European Commission has extended the aforementioned period of application to December 31, 2008. Under this current legal regime, electronic services supplied digitally for consumption outside the European Union are exempt from VAT, although they are subject to VAT when supplied to a member state.

B. Cypriot VAT Rates

VAT is charged on every supply of goods or services, within the Republic of Cyprus, at the standard rate of 15 percent. The reduced rate of 5 percent is imposed, amongst others, on the supply of coffins; on services of writers or artists; on the supply of fertilizers, animal food, live animals, seeds, newspapers, books, and periodicals; on certain products for persons with special needs; on ice cream and certain types of nuts; transport of passengers and their accompanying luggage by urban and rural buses; and the renting of camping sites and caravan parks. As of October 19, 2007, the following, amongst others, are taxable at the reduced rate of 5 percent: animal feed, confectionary products, bottled water, juices, and pharmaceutical products that were previously taxed at the standard rate of 15 percent.

As of August 1, 2005, the following are taxable at the reduced VAT rate of 8 percent: transport of passengers and their accompanying luggage within Cyprus, by urban, suburban, and rural taxis as well as tour and suburban buses. The VAT reduced rate of 8 percent is also imposed as of January 1, 2006, on restaurant services and the supply of food in the course of catering (except the supply of alcoholic beverages, wine, and beer, which is chargeable at 15%), as well as on the provision of accommodation by the hospitality sector. As of January 1, 2006, the transport of passengers and their accompanying luggage by sea within Cyprus is taxable at the VAT rate of 8 percent. Certain supplies of goods or services are zero-rated: the supply, hiring, and repair of seagoing vessels and aircrafts; the supply of services to meet the direct needs of seagoing vessels; the supply of goods entered into customs regime; and the supply of medicines and food (except the supply of food for catering). In addition, a supply of goods is zero-rated if the VAT commissioner is satisfied that the goods have been exported or supplied to a registered person in another member state. No VAT is charged on supplies of goods or services that are exempted under the VAT legislation; leasing or letting of immovable property; the supply of immovable property with the exception of buildings or parts of buildings and the land on which they stand, if the application for a building permit was submitted after May 1, 2004; financial services; lotteries; medical care; social welfare; education; sports; cultural services; and insurance transactions.

C. Duty of a Cypriot E-Commerce Company to Register with the Cypriot VAT Authorities

When an e-commerce company permanently establishes itself in the republic and trades as a distant seller of services and/or goods from Cyprus to consumers in another member state, that company has a duty under Cypriot VAT legislation to register with the Cypriot VAT register provided

1. That at the end any given month, the value of that company's taxable annual transactions expiring then has exceeded the sum of €15,600; or
2. That at any given point in time, there are valid reasons to believe that the value of that company's taxable transactions during a thirty-day period, commencing from that point in time, will exceed €15,600.

In both cases, the company will be required to report to the competent district VAT office as its duty to register if under (1) within thirty days from the end of the pertinent month and if under (2) before the end of the thirty-day period within which the obligation for registration arises.

D. Duty to Maintain Books and Records

In accordance with section 43 and the Tenth Schedule of the Cypriot VAT Law, every taxable person must keep books and records and maintain them for at least seven years after the completion of the entries or deeds written therein, unless the Cypriot VAT commissioner, by relevant notification to the person concerned, fixes otherwise. Every taxable person has to keep books and records of all the taxable supplies of goods or services it makes or receives in the course of business and for intracommunity transactions it makes. Books and records must be kept up-to-date, with adequate information and in a manner that enables taxable persons to use them to calculate the payable or claimable amount of tax and fill in tax declarations. Books and records must also be kept in a manner that Cypriot VAT officers can easily examine in order to verify VAT declarations, but this manner should not be contrary to business practices. In addition, Cypriot VAT legislation provides for special arrangements concerning keeping books and records in connection with special regimes, such as retail schemes, profit margin schemes, and others. Taxable persons must keep and preserve the required books and records on the business' premises.

E. Duty of an E-Commerce Company Based Abroad and Trading in Cyprus to Register with the Cypriot VAT Authorities

Foreign traders who carry out taxable transactions in Cyprus need to be registered in the following circumstances:

1. If at any time during the previous 12 months, the total value of their taxable transactions exceeded the threshold for registration in Cyprus, which is €15,600, and
2. If it is believed that the total value of their taxable transactions will exceed €15,600 at any time during the next thirty days; or

3. If they are established in another EU member state and carry out distance selling to nontaxable persons in Cyprus, the value of which sales exceeds €35,000 at any time during a calendar year; or
4. If they acquire goods in Cyprus during any calendar year from a trader registered in another member state, the value of which sales exceeds or is expected to exceed €10,266.

More specifically, if an e-commerce company based in another EU member state provides services or goods through distance selling to nontaxable persons/consumers in the Republic of Cyprus, that company has the duty to register itself with the Cypriot VAT registry and to pay the VAT in the republic, if at any time during a calendar year the total value from its distance selling activities exceeds €35,000.

If an e-commerce trader is not resident in the republic but is based outside the European Union, transacts business in Cyprus, and is liable or entitled to registration in the VAT registry, the competent VAT authorities may appoint a person who is resident in the republic and is recommended by the trader to act on its behalf for VAT matters (a VAT representative), or require security for the protection of public revenue. Persons resident in another EU member state or legal persons incorporated in another member state, however, are not obliged to appoint a VAT representative.

Foreign traders do not have to register for VAT in respect of acquisitions for which the Cypriot purchaser is liable for the VAT or in respect of services for which the chargeback procedure is applied.

F. Distance Selling

When a VAT-registered person in an EU member state sells and delivers goods to a nonregistered and nontaxable person in another EU member state, then the former person performs what is known as "distance selling." Most e-commerce activities concerning goods would fall within the scope and the definition of this term.

G. VAT Reverse Charge for Distance-Selling Transactions

A trader that is VAT-registered in a member state (the source member state) and performs deliveries in another member state (the destination member state) has a duty to pay VAT in the source member state up to where the value of that trader's distance-selling activities exceeds the registration threshold in the destination member state. Once this occurs, the trader will have a duty to become registered with the VAT authorities of the destination member state and pay VAT there.

If the purchaser in a distance-selling transaction is located outside the European Union or is a person resident in an EU member state but in a country other than the one where the supplier of electronic services is situated, and he or she receives electronic services for the purposes of a business or a profession he or she performs, then the electronic services are deemed to be taking place and thus subject to VAT where the receiver of the electronic services is situated and not where the services' supplier is resident or established. Therefore, an e-commerce company established in Cyprus that performs such services to a person situated either in another member state or a third country, who is a taxable person (if within the EU) and who receives electronic services for the purposes of the business he or she performs (if within the EU), then the place of provision of services is deemed to be the country where the person receiving the services is situated. The chargeable VAT, therefore, will not be the Cypriot rate but the rate of the country where the person receiving the services is situated.

When the aforementioned services are provided either to a person situated in another EU member state who *does not* use them for business purposes within the republic, or to a taxable or nontaxable person situated within the republic, then there is no reverse charge of VAT, or the chargeable VAT will be the applicable Cypriot rate.

V. CONCLUSION

The Republic of Cyprus is an excellent jurisdiction in which to establish an e-commerce company due to one of the most favorable tax regimes in the European Union, with the lowest direct and indirect taxation rates in the European Union, its excellent geographic position, and its safe, secure, and reliable professional services infrastructures. Even where a foreign investor wishes not to incorporate a Cypriot e-commerce company, there are other favorable paths that the investor may use to enjoy the republic' favorable e-commerce taxation benefits, such as a Cypriot holding company with all the benefits that this can bestow a foreign investor,[27] the re-domicile of a foreign e-commerce company's registered office, or the registration of an e-commerce company as a European Company (Societas Europea), which will operate from the Republic of Cyprus.

---

27 In summary, these benefits include lowest corporate tax rate in the European Union at 10%; one of the lowest top statutory personal income tax rate at 30%; extensive double-taxation treaties network with over forty countries, enabling lower withholding tax rates on dividend or other income received from the subsidiaries abroad; no withholding tax on dividend income received from subsidiary companies abroad under certain conditions; no withholding tax on dividends received from EU subsidiaries; no withholding tax on capital gains and income on the disposal of neither the shares of the subsidiary's share capital nor the shares of the Cyprus holding company; no tax on capital gains or income on the liquidation of the Cyprus holding company; no withholding tax on distribution of profits; outward dividends by the Cyprus Holding Company to its nonresident shareholders are exempt from any withholding taxes; profits earned from a permanent establishment abroad are fully exempt from Cypriot tax, subject to certain conditions; a diversified group of Cyprus companies belonging to a Cyprus holding company can set off group relief for the utilization of tax losses, no minimum holding period.

Chapter 31

Netherlands Antilles: Possibilities for E-Commerce Activities

Anjli Finessi
Loyens & Loeff

I. INTRODUCTION

The ever-expanding use of electronic means to provide financial services, conduct trade, and pursue other commercial endeavors—referred to hereinafter as e-commerce—has led to the introduction of several laws in the Netherlands Antilles in recent years. These laws were aimed at promoting transparency and access to the marketplace, as well as guaranteeing electronic traffic trustworthiness and the removal of obstacles in the existing legislation. This chapter provides an overview of existing legislation relevant to e-commerce activities.

Section II will examine fiscal legislation as it applies to traditional Netherlands Antilles trading companies operating through a permanent establishment located outside the Netherlands Antilles (*see* section II.A.1), as well as permanent establishments of foreign corporations operating in the Netherlands Antilles according to the Profit Tax Ordinance of 1940 (*see* section II.A.2). The sales c.q. turnover tax implications of the provision of goods and services by the above-mentioned entities will also be examined in this chapter, specifically in sections II.A and II.B.

Subsequently, the Economic Zones Ordinance 2000 will be scrutinized. To stimulate foreign investment, the Netherlands Antilles introduced the National Ordinance on Economic Zones, effective January 1, 2001. The Economic Zone (referred to hereinafter as E-Zone) legislation replaced the former Free Zone legislation, transforming "Free Zones" into "E-Zones." However, the E-Zone legislation aim is broader in scope because it also intends to attract e-commerce activities to the Netherlands Antilles, whereas the former Free Zone legislation only provided tax facilities for import and distribution of tangible goods. Based on the provisions of the National Ordinance on Economic Zones, an E-Zone is described as an area where goods can be stored, repackaged, processed, assembled, and so forth, and services can be provided. However, there are restrictions for companies that want to operate from an E-Zone. These restrictions, conditions for establishment, and the specific tax incentives offered as well as the practical consequences for e-commerce will be discussed in detail in paragraph II.D.

Section II will close with an overview of the recently introduced General Ordinance on Tax Laws, which regulates everything from the obligations of taxpayers to file tax returns on a timely basis and pay taxes, to taxpayers' legal recourse, auditing and reporting requirements, and mutual assistance provisions.

Section III will cover a variety of legislation of interest to a person considering whether to establish an e-commerce activity in the Netherlands Antilles. Among other issues, section III will examine in detail the National Ordinance Agreements via Electronic Means, because this piece of legislation aims to remove uncertainties and to facilitate electronic traffic and guarantees fundamental values and standards in the electronic environment. For example, this ordinance attaches the same legal consequences to both electronic and written signatures, and confirms the validity of legal acts performed by electronic means. It also regulates the evidentiary value of electronic documents. The national ordinance, furthermore, contains territorial restrictions and choice-of-law stipulations, given the cross-border aspects inherent in e-commerce activities.

Section III discusses the National Ordinance Offshore Games of Hazard, which was introduced to stimulate the establishment of online gaming sites in the Netherlands Antilles while maintaining the high regulatory standards and good reputation of this jurisdiction. Finally, regulations regarding bankruptcy, director's liability, and penal sanctions will be discussed.

Section IV discusses the Tax Arrangement for the Kingdom of the Netherlands, comparable to a tax treaty for avoidance of double taxation between the member countries of the Kingdom of the Netherlands, as well as several tax information exchange agreements of interest to persons considering inbound investment in the Netherlands Antilles. In addition, this chapter addresses the question of whether the Netherlands Antilles can be qualified as a tax haven according to the standards set by the Organization for Economic Cooperation and Development (OECD) and the Council of Ministers of the European Union (Ecofin).

Section V will provide some conclusions drawn from the preceding chapters and offer recommendations on future directions of the Netherlands Antilles tax and other laws, if it is to remain competitive in attracting e-commerce activities to the islands.

II. NETHERLANDS ANTILLES: TAX LAWS

A. National Ordinance on Profit Tax 1940

In the Netherlands Antilles, consisting of Curaçao, Bonaire, St. Martin, Saba, and St. Eustatius, the corporate income tax is called "profit tax." Taxation of corporate and other legal entities in the Netherlands Antilles is governed by the Profit Tax Ordinance 1940 (*Landsverordening op de Winstbelasting 1940*), as amended, hereinafter referred to as PTO.

1. Taxation ozorporation Profit

A. OVERVIEW OF THE CORPORATE TAXATION SYSTEM

i. Profit Tax From January 1, 2001, Netherlands Antilles resident corporations are subject to profit tax on the aggregate of net profit at a rate of 30 percent; including the island surcharge, which is 15 percent of the profit tax rate for all islands, the rate becomes 34.5 percent. Profit tax is levied from the profits of qualifying entities, which are divided into three categories:

1. *Resident entities*—Entities resident in the Netherlands Antilles such as public limited liability companies (*naamloze vennootschap*; hereinafter NV); private limited liability companies (*besloten vennootschap*; hereinafter BV); joint stock limited partnerships (*commanditaire vennootschap op aandelen*); other corporations or associations whose capital is divided into shares, be this in whole or in part; cooperative associations (*coöperatie*); and mutual insurance companies (*onderlinge waarborgmaatschappij*)
2. *Certain resident associations and foundations*—Resident associations whose capital is not divided into shares, and resident foundations from businesses other than exclusive promotion of a general social interest
3. *Certain nonresident entities*—Entities not resident in the Netherlands Antilles conducting business operations (a) by means of a permanent establishment within the Netherlands Antilles; (b) from immovable property situated within the Netherlands Antilles or from any rights concerning such property; (c) as well as from debt-claims, including noncommercial claims, which, as far as the principal sum is concerned, are secured by a mortgage established on such property

The PTO mandates that if an entity is incorporated or set up under the laws of the Netherlands Antilles, the Netherlands Antilles shall be considered the country of residence of that entity. Only in the case of a treaty (*see* section IV), is it possible for a legal entity organized in the Netherlands Antilles to be considered a nonresident because of its effective management being carried out outside of the Netherlands Antilles. If no treaty is applicable, the entity will always be subject to profit tax in the Netherlands Antilles.

The PTO contains general rules regarding determination of the taxable profit. The PTO follows the principle of "sound business practice" (*goed koopmansgebruik*)[1] and the at arm's-length principle. In general, and for tax purposes, profit is defined as the net sum of the benefits acquired, under any name and in any form whatsoever, by any of the legal entities mentioned above, from business operations and from capital, even if not used as business capital by that person. These benefits shall include the profit obtained from the alienation of property that was not intended to be sold and, in general, any benefit obtained with such property even if obtained after operations were ceased. As per the PTO, a taxable entity shall be deemed to conduct a business with the aid of its entire equity.

---

1 It is beyond the scope of this chapter to further outline the principle of sound business practice. In general, this principle is a "dynamic" principle that has developed and continues its development; indeed, this topic is addressed by jurisprudence and literature.

ii. Withholding Taxes The Netherlands Antilles do not levy a withholding tax on outgoing interest and royalty payments or on dividends. Although a dividend withholding tax has been introduced in connection with the tax system overhaul in 2001, the enacted ordinance will only enter into force on a date yet to be determined by national decree. Up to December 2008, such decree had not yet been issued.

iii. Capital Tax The Netherlands Antilles do not levy a capital tax.

B. ALLOCATION OF BUSINESS PROFIT TO FOREIGN PERMANENT ESTABLISHMENTS The Netherlands Antilles method of calculating a foreign permanent establishment's profit is to consider that permanent establishment as an independent part of the company to which it belongs. Although the permanent establishment is considered to be independent from the company as a whole, transactions, for example, interest and royalty payments between the permanent establishment and the head office, will normally be disregarded, unless such payments are internally administered as being remunerations by the payor for the use of assets that are not attributed to its own business activities. Likewise, the PTO contains a provision that aims to avoid double taxation with regard to income resulting from foreign permanent establishments of domestic entities. This provision is mainly based on the participation exemption and the principle that the taxation of foreign permanent establishments should not differ substantially from the taxation of foreign subsidiaries. Therefore, similar to the treatment of income received from foreign subsidiaries, a 95 percent exemption applies with regard to income from foreign permanent establishments, in case of positive as well as negative financial results therefrom. Foreign real estate may also be part of a foreign permanent establishment for Netherlands Antilles profit tax purposes.

In determining the taxable profit and the exemption, the foreign profit tax to which the permanent establishment is subject is deductible. No further credit is granted with regard to this foreign profit tax. To benefit from the 95 percent exemption in the Netherlands Antilles, it is not a condition that the Netherlands Antilles company actually pays tax in the country in which the permanent establishment is located with regard to this income. If tax is paid, it may be deducted, and the 95 percent exclusion will be calculated on the balance remaining thereafter.

C. EXAMPLE CALCULATION AND TAXATION OF PERMANENT-ESTABLISHMENT PROFIT

Netherlands Antilles Company (NA) with a Foreign Permanent Establishment (PE)	
Assumptions	
Gross result NA company including income from PE	1500
Gross result from PE	1000
Foreign profit tax on PE result	300
Result	
Taxable profit in the Netherlands Antilles (1500–300)	1200
Exemption result PE (95% × (1000–300))	665
Taxable result in the Netherlands Antilles (1500–665–300)	535
Tax in the Netherlands Antilles (at 34.5%)	185

The effective tax rate in the Netherlands Antilles on the income from the PE in this example comes to 1.2 percent ((535–500) × 34.5%). The maximum effective Netherlands Antilles tax rate on foreign PE income is 1.725 percent, in the case no foreign profit tax has been paid on the income of the PE.

2. Taxation of Profit of a Netherlands Antilles Permanent Establishment of a Foreign Company Business profits of foreign companies acquired through a permanent establishment in the Netherlands Antilles will be subject to Netherlands Antilles profit tax at the rate of 34.5 percent. In determining this permanent establishment income, the provisions of the PTO are applicable in accordance with the taxation of domestic entities, which implies that a permanent establishment can, for instance, benefit from the participation exemption. Note that Netherlands Antilles real estate or rights related thereto, belonging to the business capital of a foreign company, are deemed to form part of a Netherlands Antilles permanent establishment of that foreign company. Profits and capital gains resulting from such real estate will therefore be taxable for Netherlands Antilles profit tax purposes.

A. RELEVANCE AND APPLICATION OF THE OECD MODEL TAX CONVENTION The PTO defines a permanent establishment along the guidelines of the OECD Model Tax Convention on Income and Capital. In general, a permanent establishment is described as a permanent place or construction through which or with the use of which the activities of a company are partly or wholly exercised. More specifically, like the OECD definition, the PTO contains a non-limitative enumeration regarding the existence of a permanent establishment, which includes:

- a place of management;
- a branch;
- an office;
- a workshop, and
- a place of extraction of natural resources.

Furthermore, a permanent representative is also considered to constitute a permanent establishment. A permanent establishment does not include the maintaining of (1) a stock of goods solely for the purpose of storage or display; (2) a fixed location solely for purchasing of goods for the entity; or (3) a fixed location solely for advertising purposes, for furnishing and gathering information, scientific research, and similar activities, if said activities are of a preparatory nature or are considered ancillary activities for the entity.

In accordance with the OECD Model Tax Convention on Income and Capital, the Netherlands Antilles PTO does not contain a so-called force-of-attraction mechanism once the existence of a permanent establishment is ascertained. To become liable to Netherlands Antilles profit tax, profits derived in the Netherlands Antilles have to be acquired through or with the use of the permanent establishment. At this time, neither the local government nor the tax authorities have made any statements concerning the definition of a permanent establishment as it relates to e-commerce activities, for example, whether the location of a server constitutes such a permanent establishment.

In general, the Netherlands Antilles follow the guidelines set by the OECD when it comes to the interpretation of terminology. In addition, jurisprudence of the Dutch Supreme Court is relied upon to clarify legal concepts.

Michael Lambooij posits, in his article published subsequent to the publication of the OECD's clarification on the application of the permanent establishment definition in e-commerce—Changes to the Commentary on the Model Tax Convention on Article 5[2]—that in situations where an enterprise conducts business in a country, other than the country in which it is established, solely through a "virtual" presence (i.e., a Web site), or the enterprise solely has a technical presence (i.e., a server), this activity will not usually lead to the conclusion that there is a permanent establishment.[3] The presence of personnel is not a requirement for having a permanent establishment according to the OECD commentary. The sole presence of automated equipment somewhere, such as coin-operated vending machines and slot machines, may, on the other hand, be considered as having business assets enabling an entrepreneur to operate his business there, and therefore potentially qualify it as a permanent establishment. The requirements for ascertaining the presence of a permanent establishment can be summarized as follows: there must be a distinct and separate enterprise run with the aid of permanent business premises available to enterprise X at all times. According to Lambooij, application of these requirements will rarely lead to the conclusion that there is a permanent establishment in the case of e-commerce.[4]

B. National Ordinance on Sales Tax 1999

The Netherlands Antilles has two systems of turnover tax. One that is applicable in the Leeward islands of Curaçao and Bonaire ("applicable territory") and will be discussed in this paragraph; the other system is applicable in the Windward islands composed of St. Martin, Saba, and St. Eustatius (see section II.C).

1. Curaçao and Bonaire The turnover tax in Curaçao and Bonaire is called *Omzetbelasting* (OB), generally translated as "sales tax," and is levied at the rate of 5 percent on invoices for goods sold and services rendered by an entrepreneur acting as such within the applicable territory.

According to the National Ordinance on Sales Tax 1999 (*Landsverordening omzetbelasting 1999*; hereinafter LOB), sales tax is levied on the following, (1) deliveries of goods within the applicable territory by entrepreneurs within the scope of their business; and (2) services provided within the applicable territory by entrepreneurs within the scope of their business. According to the LOB, deliveries of goods include:

1. the transfer of ownership of goods on the basis of an agreement;
2. the supply of goods on the basis of hire purchase or financial leasing;

---

2 OECD Committee on Fiscal Affairs 2000.

3 Lambooij 2001, 145.

4 Lambooij *supra* note 3, at 151.

3. the transfer of ownership of goods that form part of an agreement to affix those goods to another good;
4. use of goods for purposes other than for business activities, as a result of which the goods will leave the manufacturer's business capital;
5. the transfer of ownership of goods under a claim by or on behalf of the government; and
6. use of goods produced by the enterprise for business activities in cases where, if the goods had been obtained from a nonaffiliated entrepreneur, sales tax would have been charged.

For sales tax purposes, in principle, the place of delivery of goods and performance of services has been determined to be the place where the entrepreneur or the permanent establishment is located and from which he or she provides deliveries of goods or services within the scope of his or her business. Services are defined as all performances other than deliveries of goods, provided for consideration. The following services, among others, do not qualify as services for sales tax purposes: (1) services provided to qualifying offshore companies and offshore banks, performed by lawyers, legal and tax advisors, administrative and trust offices, accountants, and notaries in that capacity; and (2) services performed by entrepreneurs established within the applicable territory to entrepreneurs established in an E-Zone (see section II.D). The determination of the place where a service is provided, however, is more complicated than that with respect to the delivery of goods, because there are several exceptions to the general rule. As mentioned, the basic rule is that a service has been provided within the applicable territory if the entrepreneur who renders the service is a resident of, or is established within, the applicable territory or has a permanent establishment from which he or she provides services within the scope of his or her business. Some of the exceptions relevant to this chapter include:

1. Certain services stipulated by ministerial decree,[5] where the place of performance is determined to be the customer's place of residence or the place where the customer has a permanent establishment to which the service is provided;
2. The place of service provided by nonresident entrepreneurs is the place where the service has been provided;
3. The place of service provided in connection with real estate will be the place where the real estate is situated. Also in connection with the rental of goods, the place of the performance is determined as the place where the goods are at one's disposal.

C. National Ordinance on Turnover Tax 1997

1. St. Martin, St. Eustatius, and Saba In St. Martin, St. Eustatius, and Saba, the tax is called *Belasting op Bedrijfsomzetten* (BBO) and is levied at the rate of 3 percent of total turnover. Other than the difference in taxable base (invoiced amount versus total

---

5 P.B. 1999, no. 98.

turnover), the differences between the LOB and the Turnover Tax Ordinance are minimal and fall outside the scope of this chapter.

D. National Economic Zones Ordinance 2000

The Netherlands Antilles introduced various laws to encourage and facilitate e-commerce. The National Ordinance on Economic Zones (*Landsverordening economische zones 2000*; hereinafter EZO) was introduced on February 12, 2001, to include new ways of doing business by electronic means, both in physically traded goods and in the provision of services. EZO replaces the National Ordinance on Free Zones 1975, which regulated the establishment of trading companies with a focus on physical import and export of goods. EZO regulates the establishment of physically demarcated economic zones that provide operational and other benefits to qualifying corporate entities acting as international distribution centers trading goods primarily into foreign countries or international service providers offering qualifying services primarily to organizations abroad or to companies located in an economic zone. In practice, and due to the limited space required for the provision of e-commerce services, several existing trust companies also applied and obtained permission to be designated as economic zones; and many E-Zone companies can be and are hosted at their premises.

1. Qualifying E-Zone Activities Based on the provisions of the EZO, an E-Zone can be described as an area where movable tangible goods can be stored, repackaged, processed, machined, assembled, packaged, displayed, and released, or handled in any other way and from where services can be provided. Qualifying services include maintenance and repair services of goods belonging to companies that operate their business outside the Netherlands Antilles; maintenance and repairs of machines and other equipment located abroad, using goods stored in an E-Zone; and other forms of services aimed at supporting foreign business, including warehousing, new internationally oriented trade, and trade-supporting activities, or other service-providing activities, that can be performed by means of, or for, electronic communication and information facilities. In practice, the latter-permitted activity includes all kinds of business enterprises, provided that the business can be done electronically, commonly referred to as e-commerce, including online gaming.

There are, however, some restrictions for companies who want to operate from an E-Zone. For example, E-Zone companies may not be financial service providers, cannot be insurance or re-insurance companies, and cannot provide certain services, such as management services for companies whose statutory seat or actual management is located in the Netherlands Antilles, services performed by trust operations, services rendered by civil law notaries, lawyers, public accountants, and tax advisers, and related services.

2. Conditions for Establishment of an E-Zone Business In principle, only legal entities with a capital divided into shares, such as the NV or the BV, or a similar foreign legal entity, are allowed to operate from an E-Zone. To obtain the necessary license from the island government, a company must show that it will contribute to the economic growth of the Netherlands Antilles by generating employment and/or foreign currency. E-Zone companies must prove that their business activities are primarily focused on foreign trade and/or offering services to customers located outside the Netherlands Antilles. However, an E-Zone company may be allowed to trade with customers in the Netherlands Antilles, provided it is granted explicit permission to do so by the island government. Turnover generated by domestic trade may not exceed 25 percent of the total turnover. Trading between companies within the E-Zone is also allowed and is not considered to be domestic trade.

3. Tax Incentives Companies qualifying for E-Zone status by law are guaranteed a profit tax rate of 2 percent, including island surcharges, up to and including December 31, 2025. The aforementioned rate shall not apply to the extent that such profit is obtained from the domestic delivery of goods, or from the domestic provision of services, or in the case of services rendered to a domestic company with which it is affiliated in any form. The rate applicable to turnover from transactions with domestic counterparts is the regular profit tax rate of 34.5%, including island surcharges. As mentioned, the E-Zone company is in principle only allowed to deliver goods and render services to customers who are not resident in the Netherlands Antilles (>75% of the total turnover).

In addition, E-Zone companies enjoy exemptions for various other duties and taxes if certain conditions are met. Exemptions can be obtained for:

- Both import duties and taxes pursuant to the LOB on the stocking of goods destined for an economic zone and on the qualifying release of goods (*invoerrecht en omzetbelasting*);
- Sales tax on services pursuant to the LOB as meant in the Ministerial Decree of 1999 (see section II.B.1.), Article 1, paragraph 1, subparagraph h;
- Excise duty on goods destined for an economic zone (*accijns*);
- Economic levies pursuant to the National Ordinance on Import and Export on goods destined for an economic zone (*economische heffing*); and
- Property taxes (*grondbelasting*).

E. General Ordinance on Tax Laws

The General Ordinance on Tax Laws 2001 (*Algemene landsverordening Landsbelas tingen*; hereinafter ALL) stipulates the obligations of taxpayers regarding filing of tax returns and payment of tax, and provides for sanctions in case of late filings or payment omissions. The ALL requires taxpayers to draw up clear and comprehensive accounts of all business transactions, keep these documents for ten years, and provide information to the tax authorities when requested. The obligation to provide information is extended to shareholders of corporate entities and other third parties, such as accountants, and the tax authorities may carry out searches and inspections to find information regarding tax matters at the business location of the corporate entity and with the third parties mentioned in the ALL.

The ALL also contains a chapter on mutual assistance on tax matters in international relations. The Netherlands Antilles is obliged to provide information to other countries' competent tax authorities when there is a convention for the avoidance of double taxation, or a convention for the exchange of tax information with these countries, or if this obligation is a consequence of an international treaty to which the Netherlands Antilles is a party. The information to be exchanged is similar to the information that the Netherlands Antilles authorities would request.

In 2006, the ALL was amended at the request of the United States of America, expanding the possibilities to exchange tax information in the local legislation. The Tax Information Exchange Agreement between the United States and the Netherlands Antilles, which had been signed in 2002, required this amendment so it could enter into force. Since 2006, it is also possible for the Minister of Finance, who is the competent authority in the Netherlands Antilles, to authorize that officers of the requesting foreign competent authority carry out inspections in the Netherlands Antilles together with officers of the Netherlands Antilles tax department, at the location of the taxpayer being examined. These inspections are subject to reciprocity rights. It is also since 2006 that the Minister of Finance has the authority to provide tax information spontaneously to a foreign country if he or she believes that without the information the other country would not levy tax, which is owed to it, or would reimburse sums that are not due to the taxpayer, or if the Netherlands Antilles grants a reimbursement that may influence the tax level in the other country, or if the minister becomes aware of transactions that would lead to the foreign country not being able to levy tax, and, in general, when the minister feels that exchange of tax information is necessary.

1. Auditing and Reporting Requirements Every legal entity is required to draw up clear and comprehensive accounts of all business transactions and keep these documents for ten years. Unless the articles of association determine a shorter period, the board of directors of an entity, as per the stipulations of the Netherlands Antilles Civil Code, should submit the annual accounts, consisting of at least a balance sheet and a profit and loss account with explanatory notes, to the general meeting of shareholders for approval within eight months after the end of the relevant fiscal year. The board of directors has the obligation to file the annual accounts with the trade register within eight days after adoption by the general meeting of shareholders, only if all of the following conditions are met:

1. The company in question is a Netherlands Antilles private limited liability company (NV).
2. The company together with its subsidiaries, if any, employs, at any time in the period between one month before and one month after the date of the balance sheet, at least twenty employees, collectively working at least twenty man-days, engaged pursuant to an employment contract with the company, an affiliated company, an employment agency, or a similar institution.
3. The value of the company's assets, according to a balance sheet drawn up in accordance with standards laid down up by the International Accounting Standards Board

(IASB), amounts to more than NAfl. 5 million (or its equivalent in another currency).

4. The net turnover during the financial year, calculated with due observance of IASB standards, amounts to more than NAfl. 10 million (or its equivalent in another currency).

III. NETHERLANDS ANTILLES: ANCILLARY LAWS

A. National Ordinance on Agreements via Electronic Channels

The National Ordinance on Agreements via Electronic Channels (*Landsverordening overeenkomsten langs electronische weg*; hereinafter LOLE) of December 29, 2000, aims to remove uncertainties and facilitate electronic traffic, on the one hand, while guaranteeing a number of fundamental values and standards in an electronic environment on the other. This national ordinance attaches the same legal consequences to both electronic and written signatures, and confirms the validity of legal acts performed by electronic means. It also regulates the evidentiary value of electronic documents. LOLE contains territorial restrictions and choice-of-law stipulations given the cross-border aspects inherent in e-commerce activities. The provider's nationality, place of residence, or domicile is not relevant in this context.

To begin with, the LOLE stipulates that all commercial communication directly or indirectly aimed at bringing about an agreement should be recognizable as such. Commercial communication includes all forms of offering and recommending goods and services, businesses and persons, including advertising and direct marketing by electronic means, aimed at recipients in the Netherlands Antilles. Transmittal by electronic means includes the transmission or storage of data that is converted for this purpose into a series of electronic, radio-electric, electromagnetic, or optic signals. In addition, the person on behalf of whom the commercial communication takes place must be clearly identifiable. Finally, the LOLE stipulates that state decrees containing general administrative orders (*ministeriële beschikking met algemene werking*; hereinafter state decree) can (1) outlaw certain categories of communications; (2) establish categories of persons to whom it is prohibited to direct commercial communication; and (3) list the agreements that may not be concluded by electronic means or must remain accessible by non-electronic means as well. In general, the state decree aims to regulate the content and nature of commercial communication, the nature or magnitude of electronic trade, and the target group.

1. Electronic Agreements Regarding electronic agreements, the LOLE stipulates that the provider of commercial communications must make the terms and conditions governing the agreements to be concluded by electronic means, including any possible general terms and conditions, available to the other party in such a way that the other party is able to save and reproduce the same at a later date, or shall provide a written copy of the general terms and conditions. In addition, the provider must supply the agreement to the other party, either before or at the time of signing of the electronic agreement, in such a way that the other party can effectively and easily review it and correct possible errors before signing.

2. Electronic Signatures In a paperless environment, it is simpler to manipulate information, because electronic information, including all forms of data, text, images, sound, codes, computer programs, software, and data files, does not form an integral part of the information delivery method. It is therefore imperative to ascertain the identity of the sender of the information and assure that the information has not been altered during the transmission thereof.[6] The LOLE confirms that an electronic signature, including scanned signatures and biometric identification methods, shall have the same legal effect as a handwritten signature and that it shall have the same evidentiary value. In other words, electronic signatures may be admitted as evidence in legal proceedings.

Furthermore, a certification provider (a so-called trusted third party) may issue a certificate, which is essentially a confirmation from a third party addressed to the receiver of a commercial communication that confirms this information is coming from a certain individual or legal entity. The position and appointment of a certification provider is regulated separately from the LOLE. Anyone who fulfills certain conditions regarding trustworthiness (such as a bank, public notary, telecommunications provider, even an entity established specifically for this purpose) may be designated as a certification provider.[7] Certificates also serve to provide legal evidence on the condition that the certification provider, being either an individual or legal entity, meets the regulations as laid down in the above-mentioned regulations or, alternatively, the certification provider guarantees the accuracy of the certificate.

To safeguard the trustworthiness of certification providers, the LOLE stipulates that these providers can be held liable for losses suffered by a third party who, within reason, relies on a certificate in connection with:

- The correctness, at the time of issue, of all data recorded in the certificate and the recording in a certificate of all data prescribed for such a certificate;
- The guarantee that the signatory identified in the certificate was the holder, at the time the certificate was issued, of the data used to produced the signature, which corresponds with the data given or identified in the certificate for the verification of the signature; and
- The guarantee that the data used for the production and verification of the signature—in case they are both generated by the certification provider—can be used complementarily.

A certification provider can also be held liable for losses suffered by a third party who reasonably relied on a certificate issued by a certification provider who did not register the cancellation of said certificate, unless that certification provider can prove that he or she did not act negligently. Finally, a certification provider cannot be held liable for

---

6 Frielink 2000, 6.

7 *Id.* at 9.

losses suffered as a consequence of the use of a certificate exceeding the certification provider's restrictions indicated on the certificate, provided these restrictions are known to third parties.

Lastly, the state decree stipulates further rules concerning electronic signatures; their recognition thereof for other than civil law purposes; the certification process and certification providers; the supervision of certification providers; the recognition of certificates and certification providers; and the method for providing certain guarantees.

3. Service Provider's Liability A service provider is an individual or legal entity whose services facilitate the transmittal of information by electronic means. The LOLE stipulates that under the following conditions, a service provider cannot be held liable for the content of commercial communication, or other information dispatched by electronic means through or stored on its servers, provided that

- The information does not originate from the service provider.
- The service provider did not select the recipient of the information.
- The service provider did not select or alter the information transmitted.
- The service provider is not aware that the information is unlawful or concerns illegal activities.
- The service provider does not infringe upon any prohibitions by offering his or her services.

A service provider is obligated to remove or block access to information, when ordered by or on behalf of the Netherlands Antilles Minister of Justice, and when the service provider discovers that certain information is unlawful or concerns illegal activities. The minister may only order the removal of information or prohibit access thereto if the information is unlawful or concerns illegal activities, is in contravention of public order or public decency, or if the public interest or the safety of the Netherlands Antilles requires this action.

4. Privacy The transmission of information by electronic means, especially personal data, is particularly sensitive to unauthorized viewing and retransmission. Therefore, it is necessary to establish clear rules to protect the confidentiality of information and the privacy of users, including originators and recipients of electronic communications. The LOLE contains a number of articles dealing specifically with this issue. These include rules in connection with the processing of received information, the retransmission of information to third parties, the destruction of unnecessary information, confidentiality of information, and the use of cryptographic techniques to disguise and protect information.

5. Supervision of, Investigation of, and Sanctions against Criminal Offenses None of the above-mentioned rules have much effect if the breaking thereof is not punishable by law. To combat contravention of the rules, the LOLE contains stipulations regarding supervision and compliance. The supervising officials designated for this purpose by state decree are exclusively authorized, insofar as reasonably required for the performance of their duties, to do the following:

- Request all information;
- Demand to inspect all books, documents, and other data carriers, and to make copies thereof, or to remove them temporarily from the premises for this purpose;
- To subject goods to inspection and examination, to remove them temporarily from the premises for this purpose, and to take samples thereof;
- To enter all places with the exception of private residences, whether or not with the aid of the strong arm of the law, without the express consent of the occupant and, if necessary, accompanied by persons designated by them; and
- To enter private residences or parts of vessels used as a private residence without the explicit permission of the occupant only with a court order.

Only persons required by their office, profession, or statutory provisions to maintain secrecy (confidentiality) may refuse to cooperate with the supervising officials insofar as this refusal ensues from their legal obligation. Investigation of criminal offenses shall be performed by persons so designated by state decree or mentioned in the Code of Criminal Procedure. The imposition of administrative sanctions, penalties, and jail sentences is also extensively covered in the LOLE but will not be discussed because those matters are outside the scope of this chapter.

B. National Ordinance on Offshore Games of Hazard

The National Ordinance on Offshore Games of Hazard entered into law in 1993 (*Landsverordening buitengaatse hazardspelen,* P.B. 1993, no. 63). Pursuant to this law, legal entities established in the Netherlands Antilles can obtain a master license from the governor of the Netherlands Antilles to provide gaming activities from this territory by means of utility services, including via telecommunication facilities and the Internet. Holders of a gaming license should also be in possession of an establishment permit (*vestigingsvergunning*), management license (*directievergunning*), and residence permit (*verblijfsvergunning*), if applicable. The applicant should be able to produce contracts with the utility service provider for the use of said services. It is possible to operate on the basis of a sublicense under the umbrella of a master license, however, only for the games for which the master license has been granted. The usual conditions regarding business permits and related documentation remain applicable.

1. Conditions to Obtain a License According to policy guidelines published by the Curaçao Internet Gaming Association,[8] to obtain a gaming license, the following conditions must be met. A written application must be submitted to the governor on duly stamped paper (*gezegeld papier*), stating among other information, from which

8 *See* http://www.ciga.an/policy.htm.

island territory the applicant wishes to operate and should be accompanied by the following documentation:

1. A certificate of registration from the Chamber of Commerce showing that the entity was organized under the laws of the Netherlands Antilles and including the company's statutory purpose;
2. Full name and address of all parties involved in the enterprise, including the ultimate beneficial owner(s), place of residence, nationality, passport number and, if possible, social security number as well as any other information that may be deemed relevant for the purpose of identifying and screening of mentioned parties;
3. A business plan as well as a feasibility study covering the first five years of operations, which includes information on the location where and the manner in which the games of hazard will be offered and operated; the number of expected employees (both hired locally and brought in from abroad); and the manner in which the business is going to contribute to the development of the Netherlands Antilles; and
4. Two legal opinions: the first from a locally registered attorney or civil law notary containing a reasoned declaration that the proposed activities of the company are not in contravention of local anti-money-laundering legislation (*Landsverordening strafbaarstelling witwassen van geld,* P.B. 1993, no. 52); in the case of a United States operator or services to be provided in the United States, the second opinion must be provided by an attorney admitted to the Federal Bar of the United States, containing a reasoned declaration that the proposed activities of the company are not in contravention of U.S. federal legislation regarding games of hazard.

In general, upon submission of a completed application, the department has six weeks to conduct an investigation. If after that time no objection has been raised, a five-year license may be granted to the applicant. If the investigation has not yet been completed at the end of the six-week period, a temporary license may be granted for six months pending the outcome of the investigation.

C. Civil Code of the Netherlands Antilles

In 2004, the new Book 2 of the Netherlands Antilles Civil Code (hereinafter NACC) was introduced and replaced the old Commercial Code dating from 1935. Book 2 of the NACC regulates the corporate obligations of all legal entities and addresses issues such as buyouts, mergers, divisions, statutory seat conversions, forced transfers, capital reductions, statutory audit, and disclosure. For the purposes of this article, only the stipulations regarding a director's liability in the case of bankruptcy will be closely examined.

As mentioned in section II.E, the NACC prescribes that the board of directors of a legal entity is required to keep records of its financial position and activities, in such a manner that the entity's rights and obligations are known at all times. This includes keeping books, records, and other data for a period of ten years. The board of directors must draw up the entity's annual accounts within eight months from the end of the financial year, and these accounts must be approved in an annual general meeting of shareholders.

1. Director's Liability in the Case of Bankruptcy In case of bankruptcy of a private limited liability company or a public limited liability company, each managing director shall be personally and severally liable for the deficit—amount of the debts that cannot be offset with other assets—if an issue about improper management arises and it is probable that this improper management was a significant cause for the bankruptcy. If the obligations mentioned in the previous paragraph were not complied with, for example, no annual accounts are available or the annual accounts were not drawn up within the prescribed time frame, there will be a presumption of improper management on the part of the director(s) and that this improper management is a significant cause of the bankruptcy. A director can only exculpate from liability if he can prove, considering the scope of his duties and the period during which he held office, that he cannot be blamed for the improper management and that he was not negligent in taking measures to avert the improper management consequences. Only improper management taking place during the three years preceding the bankruptcy will be considered. For the purposes of determining liability, any person who within the three years preceding bankruptcy set the policies of the legal entity or contributed to such policy setting as if he were a managing director, shall be deemed to be on par with a managing director.

The foregoing shall also apply, or apply analogously, in respect of the liability of a managing director of a legal entity governed by foreign laws, if such entity is declared bankrupt in the Netherlands Antilles. Those persons charged with the management of the foreign entity in the Netherlands Antilles shall also be liable. The liability of a legal entity that acts as managing director (manager-entity) of another legal entity (managed-entity) shall extend to any individual acting as managing director of the manager-entity at the time the liability arose. Such liability is personal and several as described above.

D. Penal Code of the Netherlands Antilles

The introduction of the LOLE and the Ordinance on Offshore Games of Hazard required the amendment of the Netherlands Antilles Penal Code to make the criminal sanctions and penalties stipulated in the former enforceable under the Netherlands Antilles legal system. These amendments have all entered into force.

IV. TREATIES FOR THE AVOIDANCE OF DOUBLE TAXATION

A. Are the Netherlands Antilles a Tax Haven?

In December 2001, the so-called New Fiscal Regime (NFR) for the Netherlands Antilles became effective retroactively from January 1, 2001. The NFR was meant to dispel the image of the Netherlands Antilles as a tax haven, modernize its fiscal legislation in line with generally accepted OECD standards, and position it to conclude treaties for the avoidance of double taxation. Also, the Tax Arrangement for the Kingdom of the Netherlands was amended with effect from January 1, 2002 (see section IV.B below).

One of the salient features of the new tax regime was the abolition of the "offshore regime" regulated by the Netherlands Antilles Profit Tax Ordinance of 1940. For existing qualifying offshore companies, stipulations were made to secure their fiscal treatment—the "grandfathering rules." This so-called grandfathering period will expire at the end of the 2019 financial year.

In addition to the reporting and exchange of tax information requirements prescribed by the ALL (previously discussed in section II.E), the Netherlands Antilles is also compliant with regulations issued by the entities supervising financial transactions, and is therefore in good standing with the Financial Action Task Force (FATF) and its Caribbean counterpart, the CFATF. Regarding anti-money-laundering legislation, various laws are in force since 1993, such as the National Ordinance imposing a sanction in the case of money laundering (1993) and the National Ordinance requiring reporting of unusual transactions (1996), which requires banks to report certain financial transactions. Before a bank account can be opened, prospective clients must supply their personal information and, in the case of a foreign client, a letter of reference from their bank and another bank in their home country (National Ordinance of 1996). The reporting obligations were extended to trust companies in the Netherlands Antilles in 1996, and these trust companies also became subject to the supervision of the Central Bank since 2001. Further measures to combat money laundering will be introduced by extending the reporting requirements to accountants, lawyers, tax advisers, real estate agents, and jewelers.

As a result of the introduction of all of the above-mentioned legislation, the Netherlands Antilles has been removed from the OECD's list of jurisdictions practicing harmful tax competition. In addition, considering that the Netherlands Antilles tax system is in compliance with the highest standards prescribed by the OECD and in accordance with the tax systems of the member states of the European Union and, in particular, with that of the Netherlands, the Netherlands Antilles cannot be considered a tax haven.

At this time, the Netherlands Antilles has only one treaty for the avoidance of double taxation—that with Norway. This treaty has been in force since December 17, 1990. According to the Web site of the Secretary of Fiscal Affairs of the Netherlands Antilles[9] Alex Rosaria, the governments of the Netherlands and the Netherlands Antilles are currently or will soon be in negotiations with various jurisdictions for the conclusion of treaties for the avoidance of double taxation, among them Australia, Colombia, Ecuador, Jamaica, Mexico, Spain, United Arab Emirates, and Venezuela.

---

9 *See* http://www.gov.an/Website/wsarosaria.nsf/dx/status-of-tax-treaties-negotiations-netherlands-antilles.htm.

B. The Tax Arrangement for the Kingdom of the Netherlands

The Netherlands Antilles are party to the Tax Arrangement for the Kingdom of the Netherlands (hereinafter TAK), which is an arrangement between the various territories of the Kingdom of the Netherlands with the characteristics of a treaty for the avoidance of double taxation. As part of the complete package of legislative changes that took place to dispel the image of the Netherlands Antilles as a tax haven, the TAK was also amended effective 2002. The major changes include:

- Dividends paid by a Netherlands subsidiary to a Netherlands Antilles parent corporation that has a shareholding of at least 25 percent of the nominal paid-up capital of the subsidiary will, in principle, be subject to Netherlands dividend withholding tax at a rate of 8.3 percent. For Netherlands Antilles profit tax purposes, a 100 percent participation exemption applies to said dividends and related capital gains.
- Dividends paid to a Netherlands Antilles company that holds less than 25 percent of the nominal paid-up capital of the Netherlands subsidiary will, in principle, be subject to Netherlands dividend withholding tax at a rate of 15 percent pursuant to the TAK. This type of dividend income and related capital gains qualify for a 95 percent participation exemption for Netherlands Antilles profit tax purposes.

C. Tax Information Exchange Agreements

Although agreements for the exchange of tax information (hereinafter TIEA) do not contain provisions for the avoidance of double taxation, they are bilateral agreements under which territories agree to cooperate in tax matters through exchange of information. Specifically, the TIEA's object and scope targets each country's assistance to assure the accurate assessment and collection of taxes, to prevent fiscal fraud and evasion, and to develop improved information sources for tax matters. The model agreement was developed by the OECD as a result of its work undertaken to curb harmful tax practices as meant in the 1998 OECD Report "Harmful Tax Competition: An Emerging Global Issue." The agreement thus represents the standard of effective exchange of information for purposes of the OECD's initiative on harmful tax practices. By negotiating and eventually signing such a TIEA, jurisdictions implicitly acknowledge that the Netherlands Antilles is not a tax haven and that its citizens may feel free to conduct business in, with, and from the Netherlands Antilles.

A TIEA was signed between the Netherlands Antilles and the United States of America on April 17, 2002, and entered into force on March 21, 2007. The taxes covered by this TIEA include all U.S. federal taxes as well as Netherlands Antilles income tax, wage withholding tax, profit tax, and island surcharges on both income and profit taxes. From March 21, 2007, this agreement also allows U.S. taxpayers to claim a tax deduction for expenses associated with a convention held in the Netherlands Antilles to the same extent as these expenses would have been deductible if the convention had been held in the United States (see also Revenue Ruling 2007-28 of the Internal Revenue Service of the United States Department of the Treasury). A TIEA was signed between the Netherlands Antilles and Spain on June 10, 2008. This agreement will enter into force once the Netherlands Antilles and Spain have completed all steps required by their respective national legislation. According to Mr. Rosaria's Web site, TIEAs have been signed or are being negotiated between the Netherlands Antilles and Australia (entered into force on April 19, 2008); Canada (initiated on June 18, 2008); Denmark (in negotiation); Faroe Islands (in negotiation); Finland (in negotiation); Greenland (in negotiation); Iceland (in negotiation); Mexico (initiated on November 28, 2007); New Zealand (signed on March 1, 2007); and Sweden (in negotiation).

V. OUTLOOK, SUMMARY, AND CONCLUSIONS

A. Outlook

After years of introducing fiscal legislation to promote the establishment of e-commerce businesses in the Netherlands Antilles, finally the department in charge of business license regulation and other government authorities seem to have caught up and understood the positive impact and expansion that this field could bring to the local economy. In recent months, licenses have been granted to nongovernmental telecommunication providers and private Internet service providers, thereby ending the government monopoly on telecommunications and opening the door for increased competition and, subsequently, decreased costs for the consumer. The opening of the telecommunications market brought an increased level of public and private investment in fiber-optic cabling and other infrastructure. This has led to a favorable environment for e-commerce. In addition, the government has committed itself to reducing the red tape experienced by foreign entrepreneurs wishing to establish a business in the Netherlands Antilles, and measures to simplify establishment in the E-Zone are being discussed. All these developments, in combination with the Netherlands Antilles' strategic geographic location between North, South, and Central America and its multilingual workforce, [10] uniquely position the Netherlands Antilles as a hub location for e-commerce business aimed at the Americas, the establishment of call-centers/outsourced customer service activities, and any other businesses that can benefit from its location, tax regime, and highly developed infrastructure.

B. Summary and Conclusions

It is clear that great strides have been made in the past ten years to create a fiscal and legislative framework beneficial to conducting e-commerce activities in the Netherlands Antilles. Among them, the E-Zone legislation introduces a favorable tax regime for qualifying businesses; the General Ordinance on Tax Laws establishes a uniform set of rules benefiting fiscal transparency; the expanded possibilities to exchange tax

---

10 The majority of the educated work force is proficient in at least Dutch, English, and Spanish. Other commonly spoken languages are French, Portuguese, and German.

information greatly increase the appeal of the Netherlands Antilles for the establishment of foreign corporations; and the regulation of electronic agreements and commercial communication guarantees a high level of security and reliability and provides clarity on legal issues inherent in cross-border transactions. Finally, as evidenced by the concluded, ongoing, or soon-to-be-initiated negotiations for the conclusion of treaties for the avoidance of double taxation and agreements for the exchange of tax information with many of the major industrialized nations of the world, the Netherlands Antilles have successfully shed their image as a tax haven and are poised to reclaim their position as a leading financial and commercial center in the Caribbean region, if not the world.

Chapter 32

St. Kitts & Nevis: E-Commerce Taxation in Saint Kitts & Nevis

K. Alex Woodley
Permanent Mission of St. Kitts & Nevis to the United Nations

I. INTRODUCTION

The islands of St. Kitts and Nevis, with a total population of about 40,000, are located in the northern part of the Leeward islands in the Eastern Caribbean. Tourism, investment, and financial services have fast emerged as the islands' primary business attractions. Information technology and telecommunications also play a very important role in the economic development of the islands. The government of St. Kitts and Nevis is aware of the need to expand its infrastructure to deliver information and communication technology (ICT) services, and recognizes the high prices users pay for international calling, Internet use, and leased lines.[1] These costs impact traditional industries, which depend on communications to market and sell their services and goods, but the cost is highest for new information-based sectors, hindering their ability to compete effectively in the global market.[2]

II. E-COMMERCE LEGISLATION IN ST. KITTS AND NEVIS

A. Introduction

E-Commerce is not overlooked by the taxation authorities in St. Kitts and Nevis, but the government recognizes that tracking all goods and services purchased over the Internet is a challenging task. Moreover, the borderless nature of e-commerce makes it

1 Gov't of St. Kitts & Nevis, *National Information and Communication Technology (ICT) Strategic Plan* [NISP], http://unpan1.un.org/intradoc/groups/public/documents/tasf/unpan024901.pdf (last visited Aug. 27, 2008).

2 *Id.*

difficult to define where income is earned, product is produced, or value is added, thus making it difficult to determine which countries have jurisdiction to tax e-commerce transactions.[3]

The government highlighted electronic transactions, ICT crimes, data protection, and intellectual property rights as areas where revisions to current legislation and creation of new legislation are needed (*see* "St. Kitts & Nevis National Information and Communications Technology (ICT) Strategic Plan," *infra*).[4] To further the federation's visibility and activity in e-commerce, the government also intends to draft regulations that will allot each citizen a free e-mail addresses and each corporation a reasonably priced domain name.[5]

The Ministry of Finance, Sustainable Development, Information and Technology has stated that as of 2008, three pieces of ICT legislation are being reviewed to enhance the regulatory environment for the conduct of electronic transactions, including the protection of information and computer systems used in electronic transactions.[6] In addition, the federation, recognizing the need for anticybercrime legislation, has proposed to review and revise the Computer Crimes Bill to create a Computer Crimes Forensic Unit to regulate e-surveillance and spamming issues, as well as the handling of electronic evidence.[7]

Current legislation is being revised to make electronic records and electronic evidence legally valid. In addition, the federation is drafting new legislation implementing e-signature verification by an authentication agency and defining terms and standards for e-contracts. This legislation is expected to be in force in the next five years.[8]

B. St. Kitts and Nevis National ICT Strategic Plan

1. Introduction With the close of St. Kitts and Nevis' sugar industry in 2005, the government recognized the need to re-engineer the islands' economy, and focused their efforts on the development of e-commerce on the islands.[9]

While the St. Kitts and Nevis National Assembly has not yet passed e-commerce legislation, the government recognized the need for such legislation and released a substantial report (the ICT Report) outlining the island nation's plan to modernize its legal system to accommodate the emergence of e-commerce as an booster shot for the islands' economy.[10]

---

3 IBLS, Inc., *Offshore E-Commerce Taxation*, available at http://www.ibls.com/ebooks.aspx?s=view&id=107 (last visited Aug. 27, 2008).

4 *See* Gov't of St. Kitts & Nevis, *supra* note 1, at 3.

5 *Id.* at 40.

6 Ministry of Finance, Sustainable Development, Information & Technology, St. Kitts & Nevis, *ICT Legislation (2008)*, available at http://gip.gov.kn/ct.asp?xItem=553&ctNode=239&mp=7 (last visited Aug. 27, 2008).

7 *See* Gov't of St. Kitts & Nevis, *supra* note 1, at 33.

8 *Id.* at 45, 48.

9 *Id.* at 6.

10 *Id.*

2. *The Development of ICT Legislation in St. Kitts Nevis*

A. IN GENERAL The ICT Report explores the nation's need for the development of e-commerce legislation to foster development on the islands. The report charges the National Assembly with the task of drafting e-commerce legislation in four primary areas:[11]

1. Electronic transactions
2. ICT crimes
3. Data protection
4. Intellectual property rights

E-Commerce legislation in St. Kitts and Nevis is at an early stage of development, but the modernization of the islands is sure to occur if the government follows through on the recommendations laid out in the ICT Report.

B. ELECTRONIC TRANSACTIONS LEGISLATION The development of electronic-transactions legislation is slated to include recognition of electronic contracts (e-contracts), creation of e-signature infrastructure, and the institution of e-government services. E-Signature infrastructure will include creation of a certification authority (CA) and facilities for accreditation of certification service providers (CSP).[12]

C. CREATION OF AN ICT CRIMES UNIT The ICT Report also calls for the formation of an ICT Crimes Unit (ICTCU) to[13] (1) facilitate a review of the Computer Crimes Bill; (2) analyze policy with respect to spamming and e-surveillance; (3) establish "a specialized Digital Forensic Lab in the Police Department for the enforcement of" computer crimes laws; (4) develop a framework for analysis of electronic forensic evidence; and (5) establish relationships with international e-crimes enforcement agencies.

D. DATA PROTECTION LEGISLATION St. Kitts and Nevis' goal with respect to data protection is full compliance with the European Union Directive on Data Protection[14] and "international legal standards for the development of the IT enabled services sector and the business process outsourcing sector." The government will also encourage "institutional development to facilitate data protection and privacy issues."[15]

E. INTELLECTUAL PROPERTY LEGISLATION The development of legal standards with respect to intellectual property rights on the islands will take place "in conjunction with the United Nations Commission on International Trade Law (UNCITRAL) Secretariat."

---

11 *Id. at 10.*

12 *Id.* at 11.

13 *Id.*

14 *See* European Parliament, *Directive 95/46/EC on the Protection of Individuals with Regard to the Processing of Personal Data and on the Free Movement of Such Data*, available at http://ec.europa.eu/justice_home/fsj/privacy/docs/95-46-ce/dir1995-46_part1_en.pdf.

15 *See* Gov't of St. Kitts & Nevis, *supra* note 1, at 10.

The government will also formulate regulations to ensure that intellectual property rights are protected in St. Kitts & Nevis in compliance with international standards.[16]

III. TAXATION

A. Introduction

The Customs (Control & Management) Act No. 4 of 1992, Tariff, Income Tax Ordinance, Hotel Aids Ordinance, and the Betting and Gaming Act of 1999 are the Federation of St. Kitts and Nevis' domestic laws governing taxation of all goods and services. There is no separate law governing taxation of e-commerce transactions. Therefore, for taxation purposes, e-commerce transactions are treated the same as transactions in other channels of commerce.

B. Domestic Tax Law

1. Introduction The Federation of St. Kitts and Nevis has no personal income tax, net worth tax, gift tax, sales tax, turnover tax, or estate duty tax.[17] Domestic companies are subject to corporate and withholding taxes; however, companies conducting business solely with nonresidents of the federation are not subject to these taxes.[18] There is an import tax, customs duty tax, service tax, excise tax, consumption tax, and a capital gains tax on assets disposed within one year of purchase.

Many businesses qualify for development and tax concessions under the fiscal incentives act.[19]

2. Income Tax

A. IN GENERAL There is no personal income tax in St. Kitts and Nevis. Foreign nationals working in the federation are required to obtain a work permit at an annual charge of US$635.[20] Only domestic companies are required to pay the income tax. Taxation is based on financial statements adjusted for inflation.[21] A capital gains tax is charged on profits or gains derived from transactions involving assets located in the federation that are disposed of within one year of the date of acquisition.[22] This tax does not apply to trusts, limited partnerships, and exempt companies or enterprises, which have been granted a tax concession.[23]

---

16 *Id.* at 12.

17 St. Kitt's Marketing & Development Dept., *Taxation*, available at http://www.skbfinancialservices.com/taxation.php (last visited Aug. 27, 2008).

18 Companies Act, no. 22 (1996) (St. Kitts & Nevis).

19 Fiscal Incentives Act, no. 17 (1974) (St. Kitts & Nevis).

20 St. Kitts & Nevis, *Information Regarding Employment and/or Residency, Saint Kitts and Nevis*, http://www.stkittsnevis.org/visainfo.html (last visited Aug. 27, 2008).

21 *Id.*

22 *See* St. Kitts' Marketing & Development Dept., *supra* note 17.

23 *See id.*

Companies registered with the Federation of St. Kitts and Nevis can repatriate all profits, dividends, and imported capital.[24]

B. TAX INCENTIVES Incentives are available under the Fiscal Incentives Act for the setting up of manufacturing and other types of businesses in the federation.[25] The incentives include a tax holiday, waiver of customs duties, export allowances, and other incentives, depending on the nature of the business to be established.[26] The length of the tax holiday granted by the Fiscal Incentives Act depends on the amount of value added in St. Kitts and Nevis and whether the business exports exclusively outside the CARICOM (Caribbean Community and Common Market) region.[27]

3. Customs Duty and Tariff The customs regulations provide basic principles for the transfer of goods and vehicles across the customs border of St. Kitts and Nevis; establish the customs regimes; and set fees for duty, excise, and dues for storage of goods.[28] They also regulate the procedure for the customs registration of goods.[29] The Customs Act and the Tariff Act do not specifically provide for the taxation of transactions in e-commerce.[30]

A customs duty is charged on all goods imported in St. Kitts and Nevis. The consumer is charged a tax upon ownership of goods. Customs duties and taxes are collected based on the value stated on the invoice, receipt, or other proof of purchase.[31] Imported goods may be delivered or removed on importation until the importer has paid to the customs officer any duty chargeable thereon.[32] St. Kitts and Nevis has adopted the Common External Tariff (CET) of CARICOM, which ranges from 5 percent to 20 percent. In March 2008, the CARICOM heads of government discussed a temporary suspension of the CET for a period of two years so that member governments could drop duties as needed to counteract rising food prices and the cost of living.[33] The government also imposed a stamp tax of 2 percent on imports, a 15 percent consumption tax on numerous products, and a 3 percent customs service charge on all goods. Customs administration places a value on the goods by determining the price which goods would fetch a sale, as mentioned in paragraph (b) of subsection (3) of Section 3 of the Customs Control Act and according to the Customs Control Act.[34]

---

24 St. Kitts & Nevis, *Facts and Information about Saint Kitts & Nevis*, http://www.stkittsnevis.org/facts.html (last visited Aug. 27, 2008).

25 Fiscal Incentives Act, *supra* note 19.

26 *Id.*

27 *Id.* CARICOM stands for Caribbean Community and Common Market. "In 1972, Commonwealth Caribbean leaders at the Seventh Heads of Government Conference decided to transform the Caribbean Free Trade Association (CARIFTA) into a Common Market and establish the Caribbean Community, of which the Common Market would be an integral part." Caribbean Community (CARICOM) Secretariat, *The Caribbean Community*, http://www.caricom.org/jsp/community/community_index.jsp?menu=community (last visited Aug. 27, 2008).

28 *Id.*

29 *Id.*

30 Customs (Control & Management) Act, no.4 (1992) (St. Kitts & Nevis).

31 *Id.*

32 *Id.*

33 Gov't of St. Kitts and Nevis, *supra* note 1, at 1.

34 Customs (Control & Management) Act, *supra* note 30, at 4.

C. Withholding Tax

In St. Kitts & Nevis, individuals and ordinary companies remitting payments to persons outside the federation must deduct a 10 percent withholding tax from profits, administration, management or head-office expenses, technical service fees, accounting and audit expenses, royalties, non-life insurance premiums, and rent.[35] Withholding tax does not apply to the profits of an approved enterprise enjoying benefits under the Fiscal Incentives Act.[36] It also does not apply to exempt trusts, limited partnerships, companies, or foundations.[37]

D. Treaty Law

1. Introduction St. Kitts and Nevis participate in the OECD's Initiative on Harmful Tax Practices by committing to the principles of transparency and effective exchange of information.[38] In addition, the federation has made amendments to the Companies Act as a measure to ensure further transparency.[39] The federation will ensure that information on beneficial ownership is available to its tax or regulatory authorities and remains committed to protecting its economic interests and fiscal autonomy in any negotiation with the OECD.[40]

St. Kitts and Nevis adopted the Multilateral 1994 CARICOM Income Tax Agreement for the avoidance of double taxation and the prevention of fiscal evasion with respect to taxes on income, profits or gains, and capital gains to encourage regional trade and investment. The agreement applies to any person who is a resident of one of the member states. St. Kitts and Nevis agreements are based on the United Nations Model Tax Convention.

2. Source Rules

A. FEES FOR ROYALTIES Royalties are taxed at the rate of 15 percent of the gross amount and are taxed only in the state in which the royalty payments arise.[41] Royalties are deemed to arise in the member state in which the copyright, patent, trademarks; design, model, plan, secret formula, process or nonpatented technical knowledge, or other similar intangible property is used.[42] The term "royalty" means any payment received as consideration for[43]

---

35 *See* St. Kitt's Marketing & Development Dept., *supra* note 17.

36 *Id.*

37 *Id.*

38 Statement on the OECD Harmful Tax Initiative by Dr. Denzil L. Douglas, Prime Minister and Minister of Finance, Development, Planning and National Security of the Federation of St. Kitts and Nevis, available at http://www.oecd.org/dataoecd/38/59/2071109.pdf (last visited Aug. 27, 2008).

39 *Id.*

40 *Id.*

41 *Id.* at Art.13 (1).

42 *Id.* at Art. 13(2).

43 *Id.* at Art. 13(3).

- The use of or the right to use any literary, artistic, or scientific copyrighted work including cinematograph films and films or tapes of radio or television broadcasting, any patent, trademark, design or model, plan, secret formula or process, or other like property or rights;
- The use of or the right to use industrial, commercial, or scientific plant or equipment; and
- Information concerning industrial, commercial, or scientific experience.

B. BUSINESS CONNECTION In general, tax conventions allow a country to levy corporate income tax on income attributed to companies that have certain level of economic activity in that jurisdiction. Having a permanent establishment in a jurisdiction is an example of activity sufficient to subject a business to tax in that jurisdiction. This minimum level of activity that will result in a permanent establishment includes the presence of an office or factory. Moreover, the presence of dependent agents and employees of the company, or managing or controlling the company from a jurisdiction may result in a permanent establishment. Electronic commerce normally avoids any physical presence of a company where it is doing business, and thus does not constitute a permanent establishment under current principles.

IV. INTERNET GAMING

The Betting and Gaming (Control) Act 1999 was passed to legalize and regulate physical gaming, computer Internet gaming, horse or greyhound betting, and sports-book betting. It also provides for the establishment of a Gaming Board, which is responsible for controlling and regulating gaming, the granting or revoking of licenses issued under the act, and fostering the development of e-commerce.

In order to operate an Internet or online gaming enterprise, a company must be registered in the federation and granted approval. A processing fee per individual, registration fee, and an annual fee are payable to obtain and maintain the license. For a physical gaming license, the applicant must be the owner or manager of a hotel of not less than 200 rooms, have a good reputation, and the means and the organization to establish a gaming room or rooms suitable for gaming activities.[44]

V. CONCLUSION

The location of St. Kitts and Nevis and its telecommunication infrastructure make it a suitable e-commerce center. The economic policy of the government supports information technology, but St. Kitts and Nevis must update its laws. For e-commerce to flourish and become a significant economic factor, market participants must have confidence that transactions will follow guidelines, and that the rule of law will protect stakeholders.[45]

---

44 Betting and Gaming (Control) Act (1999) (St. Kitts & Nevis).

45 Gov't of St. Kitts and Nevis, *supra* note 1, at 1.

A basic legal framework must cover an extensive list of issues and policies for electronic transactions, digital signatures, privacy, data protection, cybercrime, consumer rights, dispute resolution, and jurisdiction of courts.[46] The absence of a regulatory framework does not preclude online commerce, but it will limit the value and growth potential of electronic markets.[47] The government should also examine issues of compliance with regard to voluntary reporting by the taxpayer who operate e-commerce businesses.

---

46 *Id.*
47 *Id.*

Biographies

George N. Apostolou received his LL.B. (Hons) in 1999 after graduating second in his class from City University London. In 1999, he went through the bar vocational course at Inns of Court School of Law, and in 2000 he was called to the Utter Bar of England and Wales by Middle Temple. In 2001, George accepted an offer from City University's Law Department to become a visiting lecturer to the University's Cass Business School students, teaching contract law, tort law, and company law. At the same time, George read law at King's College, London, from which he received an LL.M. with merit, in corporate and commercial matters, in September 2001. George returned to Cyprus in 2001 where he worked as a pupil advocate and later as a lawyer in the most prominent shipping law firm in Cyprus. In 2003, he accepted a position in the legal department of the Cyprus' Cooperative Central Bank, Ltd. and was promoted to head of the department in January 2007. In September 2007, George established his own practice and joined another fellow professional to set up Christoforou & Apostolou Law Firm. George is currently the head partner of the Corporate and Commercial Department of Apostolou & Co. LLC Law Firm, and his areas of expertise include corporate and commercial law, shipping law, tax law, tax planning, banking and finance laws, securities law, and insurance law matters.

Ignacio Arráez Bertolín is a member of Castro, Suerio & Varela. He graduated in law from the *Universidad Autónoma de Madrid* and holds a master's degree in tax law from the *Universidad San Pablo CEU*. Mr. Arráez began his legal career in the Department of Legal Finance at Telefonica de España, S.A. In 1998 he founded his own law firm, Arráez & Asociados, S.A., which in January of 2005 was integrated into Cremades & Calvo-Sotelo, where he became director of the Tax Law Department. His practice focuses on tax advice for M&A and corporate reorganizations, real estate, tax planning, and tax controversy and litigation. He is also a professor at *Universidad San Pablo CEU* on the master's program on fiscal advice. He has published numerous articles about tax and is often queried about current economic matters by the media.

Gwenaëlle Bernier is the partner (*Avocate Associée*) in charge of the value-added tax (VAT) practice in the international office of the tax firm Fidal. She is also a member of the VAT Steering Group of the VAT network of KPMG, of which Fidal is the tax correspondent for France. She is highly experienced in cross-border VAT issues, VAT planning, and supply-chain transactions. Ms. Bernier and her team specialize in consulting on indirect taxes to multinational enterprises looking to improve their operational performance, manage their indirect tax risk, transform their existing trading models, or utilize new technologies (e.g., e-commerce, development of electronic invoicing systems, ERPs, and tax engines).

Rossana Neaime Bonaldo is an attorney based in São Paulo, Brazil, with the boutique business consultancy of Optimizers Consultores, where she represents large companies on operational compliance and business security. She previously worked for Deloitte & Touche's corporate business investigation and tax division. She graduated from Universidade Paulista, with her civil court specialization having been earned via Escola Superior de Advocacia.

Professor William H. Byrnes, IV is the assistant dean of Thomas Jefferson School of Law, where he has pioneered distributive legal education in the United States and abroad. Before joining Thomas Jefferson, Professor Byrnes received tenure and full professor status from St. Thomas University School of Law (Miami) in 2005. Prior to his tenured academic career, Professor Byrnes was a senior manager, then an associate director for international tax at Coopers and Lybrand, which subsequently merged into Price Waterhouse. Professor Byrnes has consulted for a number of governments on their fiscal policy, including South Africa, Botswana, the United Kingdom, the British Virgin Islands, Turks and Caicos, Anguilla, and Montserrat. He is the primary author and team leader of the 900-page, UK-commissioned *Report on the Economic, Socio-Economic, and Regulatory Impact of the Tax Savings Directive* and the *EU Code of Conduct on Business Taxation upon Selected Offshore Financial Centers*, as well as the *Competitiveness Report for Selected Offshore Financial Centers*. He is a co-author for International Trust Laws & Analysis (Kluwer Law International) and a forthcoming treatise, Money Laundering, Financial Crimes, Compliance & Asset Forfeiture. For Thomson-West, he is the revisions author of *Nonresident Aliens & Foreign Corps* (Mertens, no. 45), and a co-author for *Claims for Refund* (Mertens, no. 58), *Income Tax Returns and Disclosure* (Mertens, no. 47), and *Alimony and Divorce* (Mertens, no. 31A). He served as an editor to Walter Diamond of the Diamond loose-leaf series and is now the revising author of Tax and Trade Briefs, Tax Havens of the World, and Treaty Withholding Guide, Matthew Bender (New York). Moreover, he co-authored the book Tax Reform for South Africa and served as managing editor of the Exchange Control Encyclopedia, which was amalgamated into Butterworths' Exchange Control Encyclopedia. For Thomson Tax, he is the author for the U.S. chapter for International Tax Systems and Planning Techniques.

Raymond P. Carpenter, Sr. is a partner in the Atlanta office of Holland & Knight, where he engages in the general practice of law with an emphasis on state and local taxation law and tax-exempt organizations. Mr. Carpenter consults with large multistate corporations to limit the state tax impact of corporate decisions and activities. He has successfully litigated key issues involving the ad valorem taxation of leased equipment, the definition and valuation of computer software, and the taxation of promotional advertising materials. In addition, he negotiates with various governmental authorities to secure exemptions for purchases of manufacturing machinery and equipment, and to qualify for tax incentives and tax credits. He is the author of the Georgia chapter of the *American Bar Association Property Tax Practice Manual*, the author of the Georgia chapter of the *RIA Manual on Sales and Use Taxation*, and a regular contributor to various journals, including the SOUTHEASTERN TAX ALERT. In the JOURNAL OF STATE AND LOCAL TAXATION, he published an article entitled, *Sales and Use Taxation of Service Transactions: The Florida Experiment*. He is admitted to practice before the Georgia Supreme Court, the Court of Appeals, and Superior Courts of the state of Georgia, as well as the Federal District Court for the Northern District of Georgia, the Fifth and Eleventh Circuit Courts of Appeal, and the U.S. Tax Court. Mr. Carpenter earned his B.A. in economics and accounting from the University of Arkansas, Fayetteville Campus where he performed honors studies in economics. He earned his J.D. from Emory University School of Law.

David W. Chodikoff, B.A. (Spec. Hons.), M.A., LL.B., is a partner of Heenan Blaikie LLP, a Canadian national law firm. David was a former Crown counsel and criminal prosecutor. He represented the Minister of National Revenue (Canada) in hundreds of tax cases. David's areas of practice include tax litigation and international tax dispute resolution. David has published widely on the subjects of advocacy and taxation. David was the conceptualizer, co-editor and contributor to ADVOCACY & TAXATION IN CANADA (Irwin Law 2004), the first book of its kind in Canada. David is also the co-editor and a contributor to TAXATION & VALUATION OF TECHNOLOGY (Irwin Law 2008). David is currently working on four books. He is the Senior Canadian editor of THE TAX ADVISORS' GUIDE TO THE CANADA-U.S. TAX TREATY (Thomson Carswell, expected Fall 2008); author of HOT SPOTS IN TAX LITIGATION (LexisNexis Butterworths, expected 2009); co-editor and contributor of TAXATION AND VALUATION OF CONSUMER BUSINESSES (Irwin Law, expected 2009); and co-editor and contributor of TAXATION AND VALUATION OF MANUFACTURING BUSINESSES (Irwin Law, expected 2010).

Jacques Bernard de Servigny is the managing partner of the Belgrade, Budapest, and Kyev offices of Gide Loyrette Nouel. After years in Paris where he developed expertise in taxation, cross-border transactions, and mergers and acquisitions, Mr. de Servigny has been a driving force behind the development of Gide Loyrette Nouel's activities in Central and Eastern Europe. He opened GLN's Budapest office in 1993, GLN's Bucharest office in 1998, GLN's Belgrade office in 2004, and then GLN's Kyev office in 2006. He has acquired considerable experience throughout the CEE region in all aspects of corporate law, including corporate finance, banking and securities, large projects and privatizations, mergers and acquisitions, competition law, real estate, construction, and international taxation.

Graciela M. Diedrich is an attorney in the Ciudad Juarez office of Baker & McKenzie. She received her law degree form Escuela Libre de Derecho (appraised as the best law student, class of 1980). Her legal experience relates to general corporate, transactional work, foreign investments, strategic alliances, mergers and acquisitions, banking and finance, corporate financing, real estate, tax planning in general, permanent establishments, international tax planning, cross-border transactions, taxation of nonresidents, and corporate taxation. Ms. Diedrich has written and lectured on these subjects.

J. Richard Duke is a principal of the Duke Law Firm, P.C., in Birmingham, Alabama. He was named to the list of "Top 100 Attorneys" in the United States by WORTH magazine in 2005, 2006, and 2007. He received his LL.M. in taxation from the University of Miami School of Law and received his J.D. from the Cumberland School of Law of Samford University. He is an adjunct professor of law in the Walter H. Diamond and Dorothy B. Diamond Graduate Law Program in International Tax and Financial Services at Thomas Jefferson School of Law. Mr. Duke has also taught at the Diamond & Diamond Program in International Taxation at St. Thomas University School of Law, served as a professor of law at Aristotle University College of Law, and adjunct professor of law at the Cumberland School of Law of Samford University (international tax and asset protection planning). He is a member and distinguished fellow of the Royal Society of Fellows (RSOF) and a member of the International Tax Planning Association; Society of Trust and Estate Practitioners (STEP); International Bar Association (section on business law, committee on taxes); Inter-American Bar Association; Tax Section of the American Bar Association; Real Property, Probate & Trust Law Section of the American Bar Association (committee on asset protection planning); International Law and Practice Section of the American Bar Association (committees on international taxation and international property, estate and trust law, international private client group); the Florida Bar (real property, probate and trust law section, tax section, and international law section); and Alabama State Bar (tax section). Mr. Duke is the author of various chapters, including *Tax Compliance and Reporting For Offshore Trusts* and *Uses of Foreign Life Insurance in International Estate Planning*, ASSET PROTECTION STRATEGIES: PLANNING WITH DOMESTIC AND OFFSHORE ENTITIES (American Bar Association); *Use of Trusts by U.S. Citizens in International Tax Planning*, TRUSTS IN PRIME JURISDICTIONS (Kluwer Law International; co-author of CONTROLLED FOREIGN CORPORATION GUIDE; and co-author of LEGAL WAYS TO SAVE TAXES, OFFSHORE TAX STRATEGIES, and OFFSHORE TAX BOOT CAMP MANUAL (2nd ed., Prairie Village, KS: Research Press).

Szabolcs Erdős is an economist and a registered tax advisor (certified by the Ministry of Finance). Having been a tax specialist in the tax department of Ernst & Young for five years, he joined the tax team of Gide Budapest in October 2007. Szabolcs has gained significant tax advisory expertise in the field of Hungarian and international corporate income tax, value-added tax, and related corporate taxation matters, including tax planning, tax due diligence, and tax authority procedures. He has additional experience in expatriate taxation and accounting.

Rudolf Ezeani (LL.B., BL, LL.M., MBA, ACITN), barrister and solicitor of the Supreme Court of Nigeria, is a partner in the Lagos law firm Adejumo Ekisola and Ezeani, with expertise in tax and commercial law. Mr. Ezeani has advised and represented clients on these matters, amongst others, for over 16 years. He is the author of several articles on topics such as the establishment of businesses in Nigeria, money laundering, privatization, and land use.

Enrico Fadani was educated at the University of Heidelberg (J.D., 1994) and the University of Bologna (International Law Programme, 1990). He was admitted to the Italian Bar Association in 1998 and to the German Bar Association in 1995, and qualified as a German tax attorney in 2003. He is a partner of the Italian law firm NCTM and head of the German Desk. His practice includes corporate and commercial law, international tax, and customs duties litigation. He is known through several publications, conferences, and speeches on international law and tax issues.

Anjli Finessi is a senior tax attorney based in the Netherlands Antilles office of Loyens & Loeff. Upon completion of her bachelor of arts degree in the United States at Dartmouth College in 1990, Ms. Finessi worked for several years in the International Tax Department of a Big Four company in Tokyo, Japan, after having spent a year as a paralegal in the International Finance Department of Coudert Brothers in New York City. She joined Loyens & Loeff in 1999 as a student-trainee while completing a master's degree in fiscal law at the University of Amsterdam. At Loyens & Loeff Ms. Finesse specializes in international corporate tax advice and is also active in the national tax practice of its Netherlands Antilles and Aruba offices.

Erika Jupe is a partner in the corporate tax unit of Osborne Clarke and has wide experience advising both UK and multinational groups on a broad range of corporate tax issues. She advises on all aspects of corporate tax issues, including value-added tax, stamp duties, and SDRT and cross-border tax issues, with a particular emphasis on mergers and acquisitions and joint ventures. She has a particular interest in e-commerce and the tax issues that flow from it. Erika qualified as a solicitor in 1990 and worked in the corporate tax department of Slaughter and May for 6½ years before joining Osborne Clarke in 1997. She became a partner in 1998.

Stanley R. Kaminski is a partner in the Chicago office of Duane Morris LLP. He concentrates his practice in the areas of multistate and local tax law, including sales/use tax, franchise tax, and income tax issues. His practice also encompasses unclaimed or abandoned property/escheat issues. Mr. Kaminski provides planning advice and handles audits and litigation matters for both companies and individuals. Previously, he served as the City of Chicago's first chief assistant corporation counsel for taxation. He has been involved in hundreds of cases in the state and local tax area. A popular lecturer and teacher, Mr. Kaminski has presented seminars and taught classes on a variety of state and local tax and unclaimed property topics, including those involving nexus, apportionment, and audit issues. He is a regular lecturer at the Council on State Taxation's "Advanced Sales Tax School" as well as a frequent speaker for other organizations. Mr. Kaminski has also written numerous articles and chapters on state and local taxes and unclaimed property, such as for the Research Institute of America, State Tax Notes, Tax Management, Inc., and Matthew Bender. Mr. Kaminski is a past chairman and present member of the Chicago Bar Association's State and Local Tax

Committee and the Illinois State Bar Association's State and Local Tax Section Council, as well as a member of the ABA's State and Local Tax Committee and chairman of the Chicago Department of Revenue's Director's Advisory Committee. He is also a certified public accountant and received his B.S.C. degree in Accounting (with highest honors) and his J.D. degree from De Paul University.

Horace King (Chaowu Jin) is an associate professor of law at the Central University of Finance & Economics School of Law in Beijing and adjunct professor of law at the Thomas Jefferson School of Law in San Diego, CA. His publications include CHINESE TAX LAW (Beijing: Law Press 2004); THE REGULATORY ENVIRONMENT OF CHINESE TAXATION (Buffalo: William S. Hein 2006); and COMPETITION LAW IN CHINA (Buffalo: William S. Hein 2002). He holds a Ph.D. in economic law (Peking University) and an LL.M. in taxation (University of Florida).

Machiel Lambooij is a tax lawyer (advocaat) and heads the tax department of the Amsterdam office of Freshfields Bruckhaus Deringer. He specializes in international tax matters and has been involved in many matters focusing on TMT-related tax issues. He is the author of several international publications on the tax consequences of e-commerce and has spoken at various conferences on the subject. He was a member of a committee that contributed to the Netherlands Ministry of Finance report *Taxes in a World without Distance*, in which the Netherlands government's position toward e-commerce taxation was developed.

Warren G. Lavey is a partner in the Chicago office of Skadden, Arps, Slate, Meagher & Flom LLP. He advises on regulatory strategies and proceedings before federal, state, and municipal regulatory commissions as well as foreign governments; on corporate deals involving U.S. and non-U.S. telecommunications ventures and suppliers to telecommunications companies; on antitrust issues relating to telecommunications; and on technology aspects of Internet, software, and computer services transactions. Mr. Lavey is the former special assistant to the chief of the Common Carrier Bureau of the Federal Communications Commission, and has served as an adjunct professor at Northwestern University and Washington University. He received his J.D., magna cum laude, from Harvard Law School in 1979; a diploma in economics, first-class honors, from Cambridge University in 1976; and his M.S. and A.B., summa cum laude in applied mathematics from Harvard University in 1975.

Olena V. Losevska is a partner with International Law Offices, which has offices in Odessa, Kiev and Nikolaev. She has 15 years of experience working mostly for foreign clients. Her practice focuses on commercial and corporate law issues, project finance, real estate, and construction.

Kyle Eric Mandy is a Director of Werksmans Tax & Advisory Services (Pty) Ltd. and has been a member of the South African Institute of Chartered Accountants since 1998. He joined the Werksmans tax division in July 2007 after having spent seven years in the Johannesburg office of PricewaterhouseCoopers Tax Services. He has extensive experience in all aspects of corporate tax, including mergers and acquisitions, capital gains tax, international tax, share incentive schemes, dispute resolution, and tax-effective structuring, as well as providing advice in respect of value-added tax, employees tax, estate planning, and transfer taxes.

Orhan Yavuz Mavioğlu, LL.M., incorporated and serves as the managing partner of ADMD Law Offices. He has been a member of the Istanbul Bar since 2000, and passed the New York bar exam in 2003 as an attorney at law. He was educated at Columbia University Law School (LL.M. in U.S. law, 2004), Istanbul University Law School (LL.M. in financial law and taxation in 2003), Marmara University European Union Institute (LL.M. in European Union law in2003), and Marmara University Law School (LL.B. 1999). He has also been registered as a patent and trademark representative on behalf of the Turkish Patent Institute and European Patent Organization since 2001. Mr. Mavioglu worked previously in the Istanbul office of Altheim (2002–2003). Mr. Mavioglu's practice focuses on corporate transactions, project finance, taxation, and arbitration. He speaks English and Turkish.

Peter Norman is a partner in the Sydney office of the law firm Deacons, where he has worked since 2005 and is head of the Tax Group. He was previously a partner of the international law firm Coudert Brothers, where he had worked since 1986. Mr. Norman was a lecturer at the Law School of the Australian National University and has been a part-time lecturer in postgraduate studies in international taxation at the University of Sydney Law School. He holds a B.A. and LL.B. (first-class honors) from Macquarie University, Sydney, and an LL.M. from the University of Virginia, where he was a Fulbright Scholar. He is admitted to practice in New South Wales, Victoria, the Australian Capital Territory, and in England and Wales.

Maji Christine Rhee is Professor of Korean and Japanese Language and Literature at Portland State University and currently an LL.M. candidate in international taxation at Thomas Jefferson School of Law's International Tax and Financial Services Graduate Program. Rhee is legal translator in Korean and Japanese. Her major publications include a dictionary of English-Korean criminal law and criminal procedures and articles on the notion of invalidity. She contributed to the Thomas Jefferson School of Law's LL.M. program with the research and writing for the article on Japan included in this publication.

Arthur R. Rosen is a partner in the New York office of McDermott Will & Emery LLP, from where he chairs the firm's nationwide state and local tax practice. His practice focuses on tax planning and litigation relating to state and local tax matters for corporations, partnerships, and individuals. Formerly the deputy counsel of the New York State Department of Taxation and Finance as well as counsel to the governor's Temporary Sales Tax Commission and tax counsel to the New York State Senate Tax Committee, Mr. Rosen has held executive tax management positions at Xerox Corporation and AT&T. In addition, he has worked in accounting and law firms in New York City. Mr. Rosen is a fellow of the American College of Tax Counsel and is listed in the *Best Lawyers in America* and in the *Best Lawyers in New York*. Mr. Rosen is a past chair of the State and Local Tax Committee of the American Bar Association's Tax Section and a past chair of the National Association of State Bar Tax Sections. He is a member of the Executive Committee of the New York State Bar Association's Tax Section, and has served as co-chair of its Committees on New York State Tax Matters, New York City Tax Matters, and State and Local Tax Matters. He also served as president and chairman of the NYU Tax Society and is an active member of the Institute for Professionals in Taxation. Mr. Rosen serves as a member of the New York State Commissioner of Taxation and Finance's advisory council, the New York City Commissioner of Finance's advisory council, and the New York City Tax Appeals Tribunal's advisory council. He is the editor of the monthly newsletter *Inside New York Taxes*; co-editor of the semi-monthly newsletters *New York Tax Highlights* and *New York Tax Cases*; the original editor-in-chief of CCH's *E-Commerce Tax Alert*; and was the monthly tax columnist for the E-Commerce Law Journal. He has written numerous articles that have appeared in publications such as the Journal of Taxation, the Journal of State Taxation, the Journal of Bank Taxation, the State and Local Tax Lawyer, Multistate Tax Analyst, Inc. Magazine, the Assessment Digest, the Journal of New York Taxation, and The Tax Executive. In addition, he has spoken extensively throughout the country on state and local tax matters.

George Rosenberg is an advocate, was admitted to the Israel Bar in 1969, and is currently a senior partner at Rosenberg, Keren-Polak & Co. He was previously admitted to the Quebec, Canada Bar in 1962. He was educated at McGill University in Montreal (B.A., 1957; B.C.L., 1960) and the University of Paris (Faculté de Droit, 1960–61). He practiced in Montreal until 1968 when he emigrated to Israel, where he has been in private practice since 1969. He also practices as a foreign lawyer in Zurich, Switzerland, where his firm has had a branch office since 1998. Mr. Rosenberg has developed a broad range of experience in commercial law with particular emphasis on international tax planning, trusts, corporate law, and international transactions. He has also published widely, for example, "Legal Aspects of Doing Business in the Middle East—Israel" (International Business Series, Kluwer Law and Taxation Publishers), "International Joint Ventures in Israel" (International Joint Ventures, Matthew Bender & Company, Inc.), and various taxation journals. He is a member of the International Bar Association (past national reporter for Israel on the tax committee), American Bar Association, Union International des Avocats, International Tax Planning Association, and Society of Trust and Estate Practitioners.

Carmen Sanabria Gomez is a senior lawyer with Cárdenas & Cárdenas Abogados Ltda. in Bogotá She received an LL.M. from the London School of Economics and Political Science in 1999 and was awarded a scholarship from the British government (Chevening Scholarship). She received a J.D. and degree in tax law from the University del Rosario in 1995. She served as a panelist in the tax debate of the Tax Symposium of the Colombian Institute for Tax Law in Cartagena in 2006. She was previously a senior lawyer of the Legal and Tax Division of Arthur Andersen & Cía in Colombia from 1995–1997.

Dr. Patrick Sinewe is a senior European consultant at Bird & Bird, having joined the firm in 2007 to build up its German tax group. Dr. Sinewe advises in all areas of international and corporate tax law and specializes in restructuring and group tax law as well as in M&A, LBO, and private-equity-related tax issues. He has broad experience in restructuring processes and related value-added tax (VAT) issues. He was admitted to the bar in Frankfurt in 2001 and obtained a degree as tax consultant (*Steuerberater*) as well as certified tax law expert (*Fachanwalt für Steuerrecht*) in 2004. Before joining Bird & Bird, Dr. Sinewe worked in the tax department of Mayer Brown for six years. He has broad expertise in respect of domestic and cross-border tax restructuring, financing and joint venture structures, cross-border real estate transactions, and VAT implications

Theodoros Skouzos is a practicing advocate with Iason Skouzos & Partners, a family firm. He received an LL.B. exempting in French law and a "License en droit" from the University of Northumbria at Newcastle, serving the third year of program at the University of Orleans, where he was honored with the title of best foreign student enrolled that year. Mr. Skouzos received his LL.M in European Union business law from the University of Amsterdam. He then returned to Greece to complete his military service, qualifying for and attaining the rank of sergeant of the intelligence unit. In 2002, he was licensed as an advocate by the Athens Bar Association. Since then he has been practicing commercial and tax law at the family practice founded by his father Iason, who is also an advocate specializing in tax law. From 2003–2007 Mr. Skouzos was legal counsel for Halyvourgiki S.A., the oldest steel company in Greece. He is also a founding member of the Association of International Tax Consultants and author of the chapter on Greece in the series GETTING THE DEAL THROUGH: TAX ON INBOUND INVESTMENT 2008.

Christopher M. Sove, J.D., is senior publications editor for the Thomas Jefferson School of Law International Tax and Financial Services Program. He is presently editor for a number of major publications, including a forthcoming treatise, MONEY LAUNDERING, FINANCIAL CRIMES, COMPLIANCE & ASSET FORFEITURE, and the Walter H. & Dorothy B. Diamond publications, FOREIGN TAX AND TRADE BRIEFS, TAX HAVENS OF THE WORLD, and TREATY WITHHOLDING GUIDE. He also served as editor for four chapters of Mertens, LAW OF FEDERAL INCOME TAXATION. Christopher Received his B.A./B.S. in mathematics and computer science from Eastern Michigan University and his J.D. from Thomas Jefferson School of Law.

Onur Ulusakarya is an associate at ADMD Law Office, Istanbul Turkey. He received his LL.B. from Yeditepe University Law School. Mr. Ulusakarya previously worked for the Legal Department of Kocfinans A.S. from 2004–2005. He was a founding member of the International Law Students Association (ILSA) at Yeditepe University and a member of the Yeditepe University Law and Debate Association. His practices involve project finance, tax and arbitration, competition law, corporate transactions, labor law, and commercial litigation. He speaks English, German, and Turkish.

K. Alex Woodley was born in St. Kitts and Nevis. Ms. Woodley earned her bachelor's of business administration (BBA) from Pace University in New York in 1996 and completed the examination of certified public accountants (CPA) in 2001. She earned her LL.M. in international taxation and offshore money centers from St. Thomas University School of Law in 2004. Ms Woodley joined the Permanent Mission of St. Kitts and Nevis to the United Nations and has been a member of its delegation to the United Nations General Assembly since 1996. Ms Woodley represents St. Kitts and Nevis in meetings at the United Nations in the capacity of diplomatic counselor and assumes responsibility as officer-in-charge in the absence of the ambassador. Ms Woodley also provides investment information to potential investors interested in St. Kitts and Nevis and participates in meetings on tax planning and money laundering. Ms Woodley participated in the International Tax and Anti-Money Laundering Conference in Grand Cayman and the United Nations Committee of Experts on International Cooperation in Tax Matters in Geneva. Ms Woodley is a member of the Association of International Certified Public Accountants (AICPA) and the American Bar Association (ABA).

About the Editors

Editor-in-Chief **Ana D. Penn** is the founder and CEO of IBLS. IBLS, a global online publisher, was created to empower professionals to design successful business strategies in the online economy. As part of a multicontent strategy plan, IBLS has partnered with top-tier global law firms and created a strategic knowledge database. In addition, IBLS has fostered professional partnerships with many international businesses and government organizations and institutions, such as the Federal Trade Commission in the United States, and the EU Information Society. Ms. Penn is also the founder and director of E-Commerce University. E-Commerce University delivers Internet and e-business knowledge through innovative learning programs. Finally, Ms. Penn is the Creator and Executive Director of the Global E-Commerce Council (GECC), a central platform for global coordination and networking for participants in the new online economy. Ms. Penn holds an LL.M. in international banking and finance law from Boston University School of Law; an LL.M. in taxation from Golden Gate University School of Law; and a J.D. from Western State University College of Law. She also studied European Community law at Cambridge University, Gonville, and Caius College.

Martha L. Arias, IBLS director and senior editor, is an attorney practicing e-commerce/Internet and immigration law in Miami, Florida. Mrs. Arias holds a J.D., an LL.M., and a LL.B. (Abogado) degree. Ms. Arias possesses in-depth knowledge of e-commerce and Internet law legislation. She has participated as a speaker in conferences on e-commerce law and has published more than 800 articles on e-commerce-related issues in the IBLS database. Her articles have been quoted by popular Internet outlets, including Wikipedia.org and E-Commerce Times News. Ms. Arias prepares IBLS's e-books (available at www.ibls.com) and is currently an online e-commerce law professor for IBLS.

Index

Printed in the USA/Agawam, MA
January 23, 2014
584461.175